A GUIDE TO THE NAVAL RECORDS IN THE NATIONAL ARCHIVES OF THE UK

A GUIDE TO THE
NAVAL RECORDS IN
THE NATIONAL ARCHIVES
OF THE UK

Edited by

Randolph Cock and N A M Rodger

LONDON
INSTITUTE OF HISTORICAL RESEARCH
THE NATIONAL ARCHIVES OF THE UK

Published by
UNIVERSITY OF LONDON
SCHOOL OF ADVANCED STUDY
INSTITUTE OF HISTORICAL RESEARCH
Senate House, London WC1E 7HU

in conjunction with

THE NATIONAL ARCHIVES OF THE UK
London

© Crown copyright 2006

ISBN 978 1 905165 16 2

Cover illustrations:
TNA, ADM 1/8331, Navy recruitment poster, Stokers required (1913)
Extracts from TNA, ADM 1/8331, Royal Navy recruitment poster, RVNVR Signal Branch (1917)

Contents

Introduction — 13
  1 Editorial Conventions — 14
  2 Layout — 15
  3 Abbreviations — 16
  4 Acknowledgements — 19
  5 Works Cited — 19

Administrative History — 23
  1 Medieval Government — 23
  2 Tudor, Early Stuart and Interregnum Government — 23
  3 Naval Administration, 1660–1832 — 25
  4 Naval Administration from 1832 — 29
  5 Colonial and Commercial Departments from 1660 — 30
  6 Home and Foreign Departments from 1660 — 31
  7 Military and Air Departments from 1660 — 31
  8 Financial Departments from 1660 — 33
  9 Cabinet and Ministry of Defence — 33

Document Lists — 35
  1 The Medieval Chancery — 35
  2 The Medieval Exchequer — 37
  3 The Wardrobe and Chamber — 38
  4 Parliament — 39
  5 Secretaries of State, 1509–1640 — 39
  6 Exchequer Accounts, 1544–1642 — 40
  7 Lord Admiral, Admiralty Board and Admiralty Commission, 1532–1660 — 42
  8 High Court of Admiralty — 43
  9 Vice-Admiralty Courts — 45
  10 Prize Goods, Prize Office and Prize Commissioners — 46
  11 Parliamentary Naval Administration, 1642–60 — 47
  12 Privy Council Minutes and Orders, 1540–1978 — 48
  13 Privy Council Correspondence and Papers, 1481–1974 — 48
  14 Prize Appeals Commissioners — 52
  15 Secretaries of State, 1660–1782 — 52
  16 Home Secretary and Home Office, 1782–1979 — 54
  17 Other Home Departments — 55

18	General Register Office	57
19	Ministry of Home Security, 1939–46	58
20	Foreign Secretary and Foreign Office, 1782–1979, Departmental Correspondence	59
21	Foreign Office, General Correspondence by Country, to 1906	60
22	Foreign Office, General Correspondence not Arranged by Country, to 1906	61
23	Foreign Office Confidential Print	62
24	Foreign Office Registered Files, 1906–66	63
25	Foreign Office Registered Files, 1966–75	65
26	Foreign Secretary, Private Office	68
27	Government Code and Cypher School	69
28	Allied Control Commission for Germany and Austria	70
29	Other Foreign Departments	71
30	British Ambassadors, Ministers and Consuls	72
31	Other Ministers and Representatives Abroad	78
32	Treaties	79
33	Secretary at War and War Office, 1661–1855	80
34	Secretary of State for War and the Colonies, 1794–1855	81
35	Secretary of State for War and War Office, 1855–1964	81
36	War Office Registered Files	82
37	War Office Reports and Memoranda	86
38	Chief of the Imperial General Staff	89
39	Directorate of Military Operations and Intelligence	89
40	Other General Staff Directorates	91
41	War Office, Medal Rolls	92
42	Military Headquarters	92
43	War Diaries	96
44	Ordnance Bodies, 1855–1950	96
45	Other War Office Establishments	97
46	Other Supply Departments	98
47	Colonial Departments etc.	99
48	Dominions Office, later Commonwealth Relations Office, 1925–68	100
49	Treasury, Correspondence	102
50	Treasury, Departmental Accounts	103
51	Treasury, Chancellor of the Exchequer's Office	104
52	Treasury, Finance Department	104
53	Treasury, Supply Department	105
54	Treasury, Establishments Department	106
55	Treasury, Defence Personnel Division	107
56	Treasury, Defence Policy and Material Division	108
57	Treasury, other Divisions and Departments	109
58	Treasury, Committees	111
59	Treasury, Miscellaneous	112
60	Paymaster-General of the Forces	113

61	Paymaster of Marines and Marine Pay Office	113
62	Boards of Customs and Excise	114
63	Board of Stamps and Taxes, later Inland Revenue	116
64	Audit Office	117
65	Other Financial Departments	117
66	Civil Service Departments	118
67	Exchequer, 1660–1871	119
68	Surveyors-General, later Commissioners of Woods and Forests, later Crown Estates Commissioners	121
69	Board of Trade and Plantations, 1696–1782	122
70	Committee on Trade and Plantations, 1784–6; Board of Trade, 1786–1964	122
71	Board of Trade Marine Department	124
72	Admiralty Harbour and Railways Departments, 1848–62, later Board of Trade and Ministry of Transport Harbour and Railways Departments, 1862–1964	126
73	Registrar-General of Shipping and Seamen	126
74	Law Officers of the Crown (Attorney-General and Solicitor-General)	127
75	Treasury Solicitor	128
76	General Post Office	129
77	Court of Chancery	130
78	Court of Exchequer	133
79	Prerogative Court of Canterbury	135
80	Other Courts	136
81	Admiralty: Warrants and Patents, 1660–1964	137
82	Lord High Admiral, 1660–73 and 1702–8	137
83	Admiralty Board	138
84	First Lord of the Admiralty and Private Office	140
85	Admiralty Secretariat: Reports from Flag Officers, 1693–1839	140
86	Admiralty Secretariat: Letters from Officers, 1698–1839	142
87	Admiralty Secretariat: Letters from other Naval Boards, 1673–1832	142
88	Admiralty Secretariat: Letters from Naval Yards, 1701–1839	143
89	Admiralty Secretariat: Letters from Marine Establishments	144
90	Admiralty Secretariat: Letters from other Naval Officials and Establishments	144
91	Admiralty Secretariat: Letters from other Officials and Departments	145
92	Admiralty Secretariat: other In-letters	146
93	Admiralty Secretariat: Out-letters	147
94	Admiralty Secretariat, General Correspondence	149
95	Admiralty Secretariat, Military Branch	150
96	Admiralty Secretariat, other Branches	151
97	Admiralty and Navy Board, Admirals' Journals and Ships' Logs	153
98	Admiralty Secretariat: Foreign Intelligence and Geographical Information	153
99	Admiralty Secretariat etc.: Captured Enemy Documents	154
100	Admiralty Office Papers	155
101	Admiralty Secretariat: Miscellanea	156

102	Admiralty Secretariat: Record Office	158
103	Admiralty Secretariat: 'Cases' and Particular Subjects	159
104	Admiralty, Surveyor, later Controller of the Navy	160
105	Admiralty, Director of Naval Construction	161
106	Controller of Steam Machinery, later Engineer-in-Chief of the Navy, 1837–1964	162
107	Naval Ordnance Department, later Naval Staff Gunnery Division	163
108	Admiralty, Dockyards and Works Departments	163
109	Admiralty Transport Department	164
110	Physician-General, later Medical Director-General of the Navy	165
111	Admiralty, Controller of Victualling	166
112	Accountant-General of the Navy	167
113	Solicitor of the Admiralty	168
114	Marine Office	168
115	Royal Marine Divisions	169
116	Naval Staff and Divisions	172
117	Naval Staff, Naval Intelligence Division	173
118	Royal Naval Scientific Service	174
119	Admiralty Research and Technical Establishments	175
120	Greenwich Hospital	177
121	Greenwich Hospital: Pensions Office	180
122	Greenwich Hospital Schools	181
123	Royal Observatory and Board of Longitude	182
124	Naval Funds and Charities	183
125	Naval Shore Organisations	184
126	Naval Colleges	185
127	Other Admiralty Officials and Departments	185
128	Admiralty Publications	187
129	Navy Board, 1546–1642, and Navy Commission, 1642–60	189
130	Navy Board, 1660–1832	190
131	Navy Board: Out-letters and Orders	192
132	Navy Board, In-letters	194
133	Navy Board, Particular Subjects	196
134	Controller of the Navy, 1660–1832	197
135	Surveyor of the Navy, 1660–1832	197
136	Navy Board Accounts Department	198
137	Controller of Storekeepers' Accounts, 1671–1796; Navy Board Stores Department, 1796–1832	199
138	Navy Board Transport Service	199
139	Navy Office Papers	200
140	Bill Office	200
141	Ticket Office	201
142	Dockyards and other Naval Yards	201
143	Chatham Dockyard	202

144	Deptford Dockyard	203
145	Plymouth, later Devonport Dockyard	204
146	Portsmouth Dockyard	206
147	Sheerness Dockyard	207
148	Woolwich Dockyard	207
149	Other Home Yards	208
150	Mediterranean Yards	209
151	West Indies Yards	210
152	Atlantic Yards	211
153	Eastern Yards	213
154	Other Overseas Yards	214
155	Chatham Chest, later Greenwich Chest	215
156	Treasurer of the Navy	215
157	Navy Pay Office	217
158	Ships' Muster and Pay Books	219
159	Sick and Hurt Board, 1653–1806	220
160	Transport Board Medical Department, 1806–16	221
161	Victualling Board Medical Department, 1817–32	221
162	Naval Hospitals and Hospital Ships	222
163	Royal Naval Hospital, Haslar	222
164	Other Royal Naval Hospitals at Home	224
165	Other Royal Naval Hospitals Overseas	225
166	Sick and Hurt Board Prisoner of War Department, 1653–1796	227
167	Transport Board Prisoner of War Department, 1796–1822	228
168	Victuallers of the Navy and Victualling Board, 1543–1832	229
169	Deptford, later Royal Victoria Victualling Yard	232
170	Portsmouth, later Royal Clarence Victualling Yard	232
171	Plymouth, later Royal William Victualling Yard	233
172	Other Home Victualling Yards and Depots	234
173	Other Overseas Victualling Yards and Depots	235
174	Transport Board, 1689–1717	237
175	Transport Board, 1796–1816	237
176	Victualling Board Transport Committee, 1816–32	238
177	Board of Revision	239
178	Royal Navy, Records of Home Stations	239
179	Royal Navy, Records of Foreign Stations	241
180	Royal Navy, other Squadrons, Ships and Units	245
181	Royal Naval Air Service and Fleet Air Arm	245
182	Ordnance Board, 1546–1660	246
183	Ordnance Board, 1660–1855	247
184	Ordnance Board Members and Officials	249
185	Ordnance Establishments	250
186	The Cabinet, to 1916	251

187	The War Cabinet, 1916–19	252
188	The Cabinet, 1919–39	253
189	The War Cabinet, 1939–45	254
190	Committee of Imperial Defence	255
191	Chiefs of Staff Committee, 1923–45	257
192	Committee of Imperial Defence, later Cabinet Office, Historical Section	258
193	The Cabinet, 1945–74	259
194	Prime Minister and Minister of Defence	259
195	Central Statistical Office	261
196	Office, later Ministry of Works	262
197	Ministry of Works, Maps, Plans and Photographs	263
198	Property Services Agency	264
199	Board, later Ministry of Agriculture	265
200	Department of the Environment and Predecessors	265
201	Board, later Ministry of Education, later Department of Education and Science, 1899–	266
202	Ministry of Labour, later Department of Employment, 1916–	268
203	Ministry of Pensions, later Pensions and National Insurance, 1917–66	270
204	Air Ministry, 1918–64	270
205	Secretary of State for Air, Private Office	273
206	Air Staff	274
207	Air Staff Directorates	276
208	Air Ministry Research Establishments etc.	277
209	Royal Air Force Commands	278
210	Royal Air Force, Operations Record Books	279
211	Ministry of Health, 1919–	281
212	Medical Research Council	281
213	Ministry of Transport, 1919–	282
214	Ministry of War Transport, Ministry of Transport, Board of Trade etc., Control of Shipping Departments	283
215	Ministry, later Central Office of Information, 1939–	284
216	Ministry of Fuel and Power, later Department of Energy, 1942–	284
217	Ministry of Defence, 1947–	285
218	Ministry of Defence, Registered Files	286
219	Ministry of Defence, Committees, Departments and Directorates	287
220	Chief of Defence Staff, Registered Files	289
221	Ministry of Defence Research Establishments	290
222	Ministry of Aviation, 1959–66	291
223	Atomic Energy Agency	292
224	Other Ministers and Departments	292
225	Quasi-Official and other Bodies	294
226	Chartered and other Companies	295
227	Railway Companies	297

228	Learned Societies, Professional Bodies etc.	298
229	International and Inter-Governmental Bodies	298
230	Miscellanea	299
231	Appendix I: Officers' Service Records	300
232	Appendix II: Ratings' Service Records	313
233	Appendix III: Civilian Employees' Service Records	315
234	Appendix IV: Royal Marine Service Records	315
235	Appendix V: Committees and Commissions	316
236	Appendix VI: Personal Collections	321

Index 331

Introduction
N A M Rodger

This is a guide to records in The National Archives of the UK (TNA) about preparing, supporting and conducting naval warfare and naval activities. It includes, but is not limited to, records created by the Royal Navy and the government departments which directed and supported it. Its object is to lead researchers to all records which are substantially concerned with naval affairs. Particularly in the twentieth century World Wars, when the machinery of central government reached into most areas of national life and was mostly directed towards the war effort, there are few public records which have no possible naval connections, but this guide limits itself to those which bear directly on the Royal Navy or naval activity. Even so the quantity of records which it covers is very large, and the information has had to be severely compressed.

Naval warfare is one of the most popular subjects of research in TNA, but readers are frequently frustrated in their search for information, and a high proportion of the relevant records are seldom consulted – partly because of the widespread misapprehension that the record group ADM (for 'Admiralty') contains all the naval records. The public records are in principle arranged according to natural archival conventions, that is to say with the division of the records into groups and series exactly reflecting the organisation of the administrations which created them. In this way the arrangement as well as the content of the archives provides the historian with essential evidence. This is unquestionably the proper and natural way to organise any archive, but in practice it leaves two serious obstacles in the way of very many researchers. First, it is inherent in the archival approach that the researcher needs to be familiar with the administration which created the records which bear on his or her subject. It would be an excellent thing, no doubt, if historians amateur and professional did prepare themselves to use the national archives by immersing themselves in the history of bureaucracy, but in practice not many do. Even academic historians often know little administrative history, are not persuaded that they need to learn any, and are more accustomed to thinking of documents in terms of the subjects that they deal with than the manner in which they were created. What is worse, those who do understand the administrative history more often than not find that the vicissitudes of time, archival mismanagement and governmental reorganisation have so severely disrupted the natural archival structure of the public records that their knowledge is of limited use. It is a commonplace of research in the naval records to find a single archival series accidentally divided between several widely scattered locations, or a single function of government passing through the hands of five or six successive ministries in the course of the twentieth century.

The intention of this guide is to help all researchers to understand the naval records and to find what they want, regardless of how much or little administrative history they know, or want to know. The method has been to re-assemble the records, on paper, as nearly as possible into an ideal structure in which the records of each administrative unit are gathered together in a list or lists. These lists combine records drawn from many TNA groups and series, and they have been indexed in detail. A short administrative history provides background information for those who desire to understand how the administration grew up, and what responsibilities of government gave rise to which records. Throughout this guide, numbers in square brackets refer to the numbered lists.

The guide includes public records deposited outside The National Archives in the National Maritime Museum and the Post Office Archives. It also refers to some documents which have strayed from official custody and are now in the British Library, Cambridge University Library or the Bodleian Library, Oxford, and which are known to fill gaps in the records. These references are not in the least comprehensive, but what relevant knowledge is to hand has been incorporated.

1 Editorial Conventions

Archivists and administrative historians will be familiar with the fact that administrative organisations almost invariably work in a relationship with others, and that these working relationships generate records in each organisation concerned. If Ministry A writes to Office B, at least two copies of the correspondence ought to be preserved: the original in-letters as received in Office B, the copy out-letters in Ministry A. Before the invention of mechanical copying, these out-letters were usually copied into books, either as complete texts (letter books) or in abstract (entry books), and sometimes in-letters were as well. For many archival and historical purposes the distinction between in- and out-letters is important, and it is usually indicated in TNA series lists, but in practice it generates difficulties for readers. Many users of the public records are unfamiliar with the principle that a correspondence will necessarily be between two or more parties, and ought in principle to be recorded in two or more places. Even those who are aware of the principle often do not know enough administrative history to locate the copies in practice. For this reason, the decision has been taken to ignore the distinction between in- and out-letters in this highly compressed guide, and to treat them simply as two copies of a single correspondence, listed in full under both sender and recipient. This editorial method involves a considerable degree both of simplification and duplication, but it is intended to provide enquirers with a view of the entire relevant archive, regardless of the direction from which they approach it. It will then be straightforward to advance from this guide to the more detailed information in the series lists, most of which are now available online (www.nationalarchives.gov.uk). Similar principles have been applied to all administrative processes which generated multiple copies. For example, where an official submitted his accounts to one or more auditing bodies, the accounts have been listed under both the accountant's name and the auditor's. It is common for record series to have suffered losses over time, but this approach makes it as easy as possible to identify parallel copies from which to fill the gaps.

Introduction

The development of mechanical copying during the nineteenth century brought a progressive change to a new administrative structure throughout government, in which all papers and correspondence, incoming, outgoing and internal, were gathered into subject files. These in turn were usually indexed in central departmental registries which tracked their movements and contents. Such records have in some cases been transferred to TNA complete with their original registries. More often, however, the size of the original registries (usually in card-index form), and the weeding of the original records, made this impracticable. The means of reference to most series of registered files in TNA are lists of file titles. Many of these lists are extremely long and cover a very wide range of subjects, in random order. This guide attempts to give an idea of the nature and range of the naval records in such series by providing illustrative lists. In most cases the series lists are too long to provide comprehensive coverage within the scope of this guide, but since they can be searched online for any particular word or name, it is not necessary. So long as the file titles in the series list adequately sum up the contents (which however is not invariably the case), such online searches ought to lead the enquirer to the subject. With older records arranged by administrative function rather than by subject such detailed searches can usually only be done by hand, but this guide ought at least to indicate the most likely places to look.

Although the lists are arranged by archival provenance, as far as it can be determined, some records are classified in other ways in the Appendices [231–6]. Appendices I–IV [231–4] are a collection of records in the nature of service records of individuals, which have been arranged in a subject classification derived from *Naval Records for Genealogists*, in which they are described in more detail. Appendix V [235] is a chronological list of *ad hoc* committees, commissions and the like, whose records are scattered in unlikely places. Appendix VI [236] is an alphabetical list of private papers, personal collections and other assemblages of records relating to named individuals.

2   Layout

The lists are arranged in chronological order, but entries relating to identical or closely related records have been grouped together under their earliest date. In the lists a colon has been used to introduce a series of items under the same description (that is, to eliminate the need for ditto marks), and words following the colon, or inset in brackets, modify the main descriptor. Thus among the records of the Treasurer of the Ordnance [184], we find the following four entries:

Bill books:	1661–1783	WO 51/3–313
	1783–1859	WO 52/1–782
(Sea Service)	1678–99	WO 50/13–14
(quarterly bills)	1694–1752	WO 50/2–11

The first two entries are bill books, the third bill books for the Sea Service, the fourth books of quarterly bills. In the records of the Victualling Board [168] is the following:

Out-letters:		1683–9	ADM 110/1
		1702–1822	ADM 110/2–81
(register)		1814–31	ADM 110/82–5
(to Secretaries of State)		1689–99	SP 42/1–5
(to the Admiralty):		1704–1809	NMM: ADM/D/1–52
		1765–6	NMM: ADM/DP/101
		1770–80	NMM: ADM/DP/102–12
		1781–1822	NMM: ADM/DP/1–42
		1821	NMM: ADM/DP/201A–201B
		1822–32	ADM 1/3775–801
(to Agent-Victualler Plymouth):		1762–5	ADM 174/294–7
		1780–91	ADM 174/298
(to Agent-Victualler Portsmouth):		1809–11	ADM 114/68–9
		1831–4	ADM 224/13–14
(on surgeons' pay and promotion)		1817–32	ADM 105/1–9
(enquiries about prisoners of war)		1818–22	ADM 98/314

This indicates two entries of general out-letters followed by a register of them, then letters to the Secretaries of State, the Admiralty (six entries), the Agent-Victuallers at Plymouth and Portsmouth (two entries each), letters about surgeons, and letters responding to enquiries about prisoners of war.

Where no date or piece numbers are specified, the documents concerned have not yet reached The National Archives.

3 Abbreviations

AA	Anti-aircraft
AEA	Atomic Energy Agency
AEF	Allied Expeditionary Force
AOC	Air Officer Commanding
AOC-in-C	Air Officer Commanding-in-Chief
ARE	Admiralty Research Establishment
A/S	Anti-submarine
ASWE	Admiralty Surface Weapons Establishment
ATS	Auxiliary Territorial Service
AUWE	Admiralty Underwater Weapons Establishment
BL	British Library
BS	British standard
CAM	Catapult-armed merchant ships
CCMS	Control commission mine-sweeping
CG	Coastguard

CID	Committee of Imperial Defence
C-in-C	Commander-in-Chief
CUL	Cambridge University Library
DD	Discharged dead
D/F	Direction-finding
DNC	Director of Naval Construction
DNI	Director of Naval Intelligence
DNO	Director of Naval Ordnance
DSO	Distinguished Service Order
ERA	Engine-Room Artificer
FAA	Fleet Air Arm
FO	Flag Officer
GCCS	Government Code and Cypher School
GCHQ	Government Communications Headquarters
GH	Greenwich Hospital
GOC	General Officer Commanding
HCA	High Court of Admiralty
HEIC	Honourable East India Company
HM	Her/His Majesty's
HM s/m	Her/His Majesty's Submarine
HMB	His Majesty's Bark
HMC	Historical Manuscripts Commission
HMS	Her/His Majesty's Ship
HMSO	Her/His Majesty's Stationery Office
HMY	Her/His Majesty's Yacht
HQ	Headquarters
HRH	Her/His Royal Highness
HS	Hospital Ship
IoM	Isle of Man
IoW	Isle of Wight
LSL	Landing ship logistics
MoD	Ministry of Defence
MoD(N)	Ministry of Defence, Navy Department
MV	Motor vessel
NATO	North Atlantic Treaty Organisation
NCO	Non-commissioned officer
NID	Naval Intelligence Department/Division
NMM	National Maritime Museum
NRS	Navy Records Society
NS	New series/style
NSW	New South Wales
PLA	Port of London Authority
PO	Post Office

POW	Prisoner of war
PRO	Public Record Office
PRS	Pipe Roll Society
QARNNS	Queen Alexandra's Royal Naval Nursing Service
RAF	Royal Air Force
RAN	Royal Australian Navy
RCN	Royal Canadian Navy
RDF	Radio direction-finding [i.e., radar]
RE	Royal Engineers
RFA	Royal Fleet Auxiliary
RFC	Royal Flying Corps
RFR	Royal Fleet Reserve
RIN	Royal Indian Navy
RM	Royal Marines
RMA	Royal Marine Artillery
RMLI	Royal Marine Light Infantry
RN	Royal Navy/Naval
RNA	Royal Naval Academy
RNAD	Royal Naval Armament Depot
RNAS	Royal Naval Air Service/Station
RNAY	Royal Naval Air Yard
RNC	Royal Naval College
RNEC	Royal Naval Engineering College
RNH	Royal Naval Hospital
RNorN	Royal Norwegian Navy
RNR	Royal Naval Reserve
RNVR	Royal Naval Volunteer Reserve
RRS	Royal Research Ship
SAAF	South African Air Force
SBNO	Senior British Naval Officer
SEAC	South-East Asia Command
SHAEF	Supreme Headquarters Allied Expeditionary Force
SNO	Senior Naval Officer
SOE	Special Operations Executive
SS	Steam ship
TB	Torpedo-boat
TS	Training ship
UK	United Kingdom
US	United States [of America]
USAF	United States Air Force
USN	United States Navy
USSR	Union of Soviet Socialist Republics
VC	Victoria Cross

WAAF	Women's Auxiliary Air Force
WO	War Office
WRNS	Women's Royal Naval Service
W/T	Wireless telegraphy

4 Acknowledgements

The editors are grateful for the help of Rose Mitchell, Geraldine Beech, Eunice Gill, Bruno Pappalardo, Aidan Lawes, Ed Hampshire, Simon Kitching, Helen Watt, Dr. Jonathan Mackman, Dr. Paul Dryburgh, Dr. Pamela Nightingale, Brian Oldham, Adrian Webb, Sue Lumas, John Hailey, Dr. Mike Duffy, Dr. Peter Le Fevre and Roelof Van Gelder.

5 Works Cited

Printed primary sources

Barbot on Guinea: the Writings of Jean Barbot on West Africa, 1678–1712, ed. P E Hair, A Jones and R Law (2 vols., Hakluyt Society, 2nd ser., 175–6, 1992)
The Black Book of the Admiralty, ed. Sir T Twiss (4 vols., 1871–6)
Book of Prests of the King's Wardrobe for 1294–5, ed. E B Fryde (Oxford, 1962)
Calendar of Chancery Warrants Preserved in the Public Record Office (1927)
Calendar of Close Rolls (47 vols., 1892–1963)
Calendar of Documents Relating to Scotland Preserved in Her Majesty's Public Record Office, ed. J Bain (4 vols., Edinburgh, 1881–8)
Calendar of Documents Relating to Scotland Preserved in the Public Record Office and the British Library, vol. 5: *Supplement*, ed. G G Simpson and J D Galbraith (Edinburgh, 1986)
Calendar of Inquisitions Miscellaneous, Chancery, Preserved in the Public Record Office (8 vols., 1916–2005)
Calendar of Liberate Rolls (5 vols., 1917–64)
Calendar of Memoranda Rolls (Exchequer) Preserved in the Public Record Office: Michaelmas 1326–Michaelmas 1327, ed. R E Latham (1968)
Calendar of Patent Rolls (52 vols., 1891–1916; 19 vols., 1924–)
Calendar of Patent Rolls Edward VI, 5 (1929)
Calendar of Signet Letters of Henry IV and Henry V, ed. J L Kirby (1978)
Calendar of State Papers, Colonial ... America and West Indies (38 vols., 1860–1994)
Calendar of State Papers, Domestic ... Charles I, 1625–1649 (23 vols., 1858–97)
Calendar of State Papers, Domestic ... Commonwealth, 1649–1660, ed. M A E Green (13 vols., 1875–86)
Calendar of State Papers, Domestic ... Edward VI, 1547–1553, ed. C S Knighton (1992)
Calendar of State Papers, Domestic ... James I, ed. M A E Green (4 vols., 1857–9)
Calendar of State Papers, Domestic ... Edward VI, Mary, Elizabeth I and James I, ed. R Lemon and M A E Green (12 vols., 1856–72)

Calendar of State Papers, Domestic … Mary I, 1553–1558, ed. C S Knighton (1998)
Calendar of Treasury Books and Papers, 1729–1745, ed. W A Shaw (5 vols., 1897–1903)
Calendar of Treasury Papers, 1556–1728, ed. J Redington (6 vols., 1868–1889)
Calendar of Various Chancery Rolls … 1277–1326 (1912)
Catalogue des Rôles Gascons, Normands et Français Conservés dans les Archives de la Tour de Londres, comp. T Carte (2 vols., 1743)
Close Rolls of the Reign of Henry III (14 vols., 1902–38)
A Collection of the State Papers of John Thurloe, ed. T Birch (7 vols., 1742)
Excerpta e Rotulis Finium in Turri Londinensi Asservatis … AD 1216–1272 (2 vols., 1835–6)
Forty-first Annual Report of the Deputy Keeper of the Public Records (1880)
Forty-second Annual Report of the Deputy Keeper of the Public Records (1881)
Forty-fourth Annual Report of the Deputy Keeper of the Public Records (1883)
Forty-eighth Annual Report of the Deputy Keeper of the Public Records (1887)
Gascon Rolls Preserved in the Public Record Office, 1307–1317, ed. Y Renouard (1962)
Gifts and Deposits (List and Index Society, 11, 1966)
The Jacobean Commissions of Enquiry, 1608 and 1618, ed. A P McGowan (NRS, 116, 1971)
Journal of the Commissioners for Trade and Plantations (14 vols., 1920–38)
Letters and Papers, Foreign and Domestic, of the Reign of Henry VIII, ed. J S Brewer (22 vols. in 38, 1862–1932)
List of Documents of the Household and Wardrobe, John to Edward I, [ed. P M Barnes] (1964)
The Manuscripts of the House of Lords (4 vols., Historical Manuscripts Commission, 17, 1887–94)
The Manuscripts of the House of Lords (16 vols. in 12, NS, 1900–77)
The Memoranda Roll for the Michaelmas Term of the First year of the Reign of King John (1199–1200): Together with Fragments of the Originalia Roll of the Seventh Year of King Richard I (1195–6), the Liberate Roll of the Second Year of King John (1200–1) and the Norman Roll of the Fifth Year of King John (1203) (Pipe Roll Society, NS, 21, 1943)
The Memoranda Roll of the King's Remembrancer for Michaelmas 1230–Trinity 1231, ed. C Robinson (Pipe Roll Society, NS, 11, 1933)
Memoranda Rolls 16–17 Henry III Preserved in the Public Record Office, ed. R Allen Brown (1991)
Naval Accounts and Inventories in the Reign of Henry VII, 1485–8, 1494–7, ed. M Oppenheim (NRS, 8, 1896)
The Parliament Rolls of Medieval England, 1275–1504, ed. C Given-Wilson (CD-ROM, 2005)
Patent Rolls of the Reign of Henry III … 1216–1225 (1901)
Patent Rolls of the Reign of Henry III … 1225–1232 (1903)
Proceedings and Ordinances of the Privy Council of England, ed. Sir N Harris Nicolas (7 vols., 1834–7)
Rôles Gascons, ed. F Michel and C Bémont (4 vols. in 5, Paris, 1885–1906)
Rotuli de Liberate ac de Misis et Praestitis, ed. T D Hardy (1844)
Rotuli de Oblatis et Finibus in Turri Londinensi Asservati, ed. T D Hardy (1835)
Rotuli Litterarum Clausarum in Turri Londinensi Asservati, ed. T D Hardy (2 vols., 1833–44)
Rotuli Litterarum Patentium in Turri Londinensi Asservati, ed. T D Hardy (1835)

Rotuli Normanniae in Turri Londinensi Asservati (1835)

Rotuli Parliamentorum (6 vols., 1767–77)

Rotuli Scotiae in Turri Londinensi et in Domo Capitulari Westmonasteriensi Asservati (2 vols., 1814–19)

Royal Navy Lieutenants' Passing Certificates, 1691–1902, ed. B Pappalardo (2 vols., List and Index Society, 289–90, 2001)

State Papers Supplementary, 1: General Papers to 1603 (List and Index Society, 9, 1966)

Statutes of the Realm (11 vols., 1810–28)

Treaty Rolls Preserved in the Public Record Office, ed. P Chaplais and J Ferguson (2 vols., 1955–72)

Secondary sources

Horwitz, H, *Exchequer Equity Records and Proceedings, 1649–1841* (Public Record Office Handbook, 32, Kew, 2001)

Pappalardo, B, *Tracing your Naval Ancestors* (Kew, 2003)

Rodger, N A M, *Naval Records for Genealogists* (Public Record Office Handbook, 22, 1988)

Administrative History

1   Medieval Government

All government in medieval England grew out of the royal court, and its principal departments the **Chancery** [1] and **Exchequer** [2] were courts in a double sense, exercising both judicial and administrative functions. Each department dealt with the full range of business which fell under royal authority, including all forms of warfare. The Chancery was chiefly concerned with correspondence, the issuing of writs (orders) and other written business. The Exchequer was the central financial and auditing department. By the fourteenth century both departments had acquired permanent accommodation in or near Whitehall, but the king and his court were still peripatetic, and often far away. Especially in wartime, English kings needed more informal and mobile administrations able to accompany them on campaign. These were the **Wardrobe and Chamber** [3], which at various periods dealt with large responsibilities; both issued and audited considerable sums, but never assumed a permanent administrative structure. Among the Wardrobe and Chamber clerks of the fourteenth and fifteenth centuries were some named as Clerks of the King's Ships, but they were only one of several channels for orders and money for ships and fleets, and not in any sense an embryonic naval administration. Moreover, these informal, 'private' administrations were expressions of royal independence as well as practical need, often associated with misgovernment, and particularly with the misappropriation of money voted by **Parliament** [4] for such national purposes as the defence of shipping and the seacoasts. They were therefore unpopular, and when royal authority was weak, Wardrobe and Chamber finance tended to decline or disappear. The **Lord Admiral** [7] of England was a great officer of state, who might on occasion exercise actual command of fleets at sea, but who had no administrative functions. His principal responsibility was the **High Court of Admiralty** [8], which tried maritime causes according to Roman law, and incidentally provided him with a substantial income. The early records of this court include most of what documents survive of the Lord Admiral's naval functions. His deputies, the Vice-Admirals of Counties (usually the Lords Lieutenant in another capacity), had local **Vice-Admiralty Courts** [9], and so in later centuries did the Governors of many British colonies.

2   Tudor, Early Stuart and Interregnum Government

New forms of government developed in the sixteenth century. The sovereign's leading advisers were gathered in the body known as the **Privy Council** [12–13], the all-purpose central authority of Tudor government. Originally this was a select group of the full royal council, but in time it became too large for effective government. By the eighteenth century executive authority had migrated to a new select group, the Cabinet, although the 'King in Council' continued to be the formal origin of orders carrying royal authority. Petitions and appeals against the judgements of royal courts came before the Privy Council, whose judicial committee, in its capacity as the court of appeals from the High Court of Admiralty, was known as the **Prize Appeals Commissioners** [14].

The king's private secretary, now named the **Secretary of State** [5], developed in the sixteenth century into a chief minister (subsequently two) who handled the full range of Crown business. The Lord Treasurer was now the chief financial officer of the Crown, and under new procedures the **Exchequer** acted as a court of audit, before which Crown officials 'declared' their accounts [6]. In 1546 a number of officials concerned with the growing English Royal Navy were gathered into a body known as the 'Council of the Marine', later called the **Navy Board** [129]. These officials still had individual responsibilities (and many private activities), but they met collectively to consider naval administration, and to act as an advisory committee to the Lord Admiral. The Navy Board provided the core of the first stable and permanent English naval administration, responsible for everything to do with building and maintaining ships, and for running the new **dockyards** [142–6]. The Navy Board's connection with the Lord Admiral helped to push his office in the direction of a professional interest in naval administration and warfare. The **Treasurer of the Navy** [156] was originally one of the members of the Navy Board, but the office evolved into an independent one, in effect the Navy's banker, responsible to the Lord Treasurer and declaring the Navy's accounts at the Exchequer, although leaving both expenditure and detailed financial administration to the Navy Board. From 1550 another permanent Crown organisation was responsible for victualling the king's ships, and from 1565 it was run by a single **Victualler of the Navy** [168] (subsequently a syndicate) who accepted a standing contract to provide all food and drink. The Navy Board followed the very similar **Ordnance Board** [182], incorporating the older office of Master of the Ordnance, which was responsible for keeping and issuing all sorts of weapons and warlike stores to ships and armies. Originally one person, the Master of Naval Ordnance, was a member of both boards and acted as a link between them, but this office lapsed on the death of Sir William Winter in 1589. The **Chatham Chest** [155] was a charitable fund, established in 1590, and supported by compulsory deductions from seamen's wages. It paid pensions or lump sums to wounded or disabled men and to the widows of men killed in action or on service.

Naval administration was not significantly changed in structure under the early Stuarts, but it suffered a good deal from corruption and shortage of money. Between 1618 and 1628 the Navy Board, exposed by a commission of enquiry as incompetent and dishonest, was replaced by a special **Navy Commission** [129]. Soon after the Board was restored the Lord Admiral the Duke of Buckingham was murdered. His office was then put into commission, the new **Admiralty Board** [7] being in effect a committee of the Privy Council. At the same time the High Court of Admiralty was removed from Admiralty authority and placed directly under the Crown, where it remained. In 1638 the office of Lord Admiral was revived for the king's infant son James, Duke of York, with the Earl of Northumberland acting in his place. In the constitutional crisis of 1642 which marked the start of the first Civil War, Parliament secured control of the Navy, appointed an **Admiralty Commission** [7] to replace Northumberland, and named the Earl of Warwick initially as its Commander-in-Chief, then from 1643 to 1645 as Lord Admiral [7]. In that year the Admiralty was again placed in commission, but Warwick continued to act as the leading member of the new Admiralty Commission, which in turn answered to the **Admiralty and Cinque Ports Committee** of Parliament [11]. The **Navy and Customs Committee** [11] of Parliament controlled naval revenue, while the functions of the Navy Board were continued by a mixed **Navy Commission** [129], combining professional and Parliamentary members. The active members of the Navy and Customs Committee, the distinct Customs Commission of 1643, the 1642 and 1645 Admiralty Commissions, the **Prize Commission** [10] of 1644, and the Parliamentary representatives on the Navy Commission were virtually the same, and these bodies shared premises and staff. Their records were intermingled then, and have been further confused by subsequent archivists.

Parliamentary victory in the first Civil War was immediately followed by political crisis and the military coup of 1647, which in turn, in the summer of 1648, provoked a mutiny in the fleet, half of which deserted to the exiled royalists. Warwick was restored as Lord Admiral, in the vain hope that he might be able to win back the deserters, but the expulsion of all remaining opponents of military rule from Parliament in December 1648 made his position impossible. In February 1649 he was dismissed and the powers of Admiralty transferred to the new **Council of State** [11], which combined the senior officers of the Army and their Parliamentary allies. The Council in turn appointed an Admiralty Committee the following month. This complex and overlapping structure reflected the political rivalries of the new regime. The outbreak of the first Dutch War in 1652 rapidly exposed its inefficiencies, and the defeat of Dungeness in November brought a return to a simpler and more traditional structure. The Parliamentary Navy Committee was eliminated, Admiralty authority was given to a new (and smaller) **Admiralty Commission** [7], and administration remained in the hands of the **Navy Commission** [129]. When Cromwell seized power in 1653 the members of the Admiralty Commission were replaced by soldiers loyal to him, but the administrative structure remained largely unchanged until the restoration of the monarchy in 1660. Another innovation prompted by the requirements of the Dutch War was the creation in 1653 of the first **Sick and Hurt Board** [166], responsible for the care of ill or wounded men ashore, for paying pensions to the wounded or widowed, and for prisoners of war. Although not formally dissolved, the Board ceased to exist in the late 1650s as the war effort against Spain collapsed for want of funds. Throughout the Interregnum the victualling organisation continued to function in the same form as before, but in 1657 the impossibility of persuading any contractors to accept the office led to the establishment of a salaried **Victualling Board** [168]. The **Ordnance Board** [182] likewise continued to operate from 1642 to 1660, although in 1653 it was made formally subject to Admiralty authority.

3   Naval Administration, 1660–1832

At the restoration of Charles II in 1660, the pre-war forms of naval administration were reinstated, but incorporating some of the innovations, and many of the personnel, of the Interregnum. James, Duke of York assumed his office as **Lord Admiral** [82], although much naval policy and administration was transacted at the **Privy Council** [12–13] or one of its committees, often in the presence of Charles II who was keenly interested in his Navy. The **Secretaries of State** [15] continued to act as all-purpose chief ministers, and among the State Papers are many of the records of naval administration (including all those of the Navy Board up to 1673). The **Navy Board** [130–3] was restored in an extended and strengthened form. The **Sick and Hurt Board** [159] was revived at the outbreak of war in 1664, but dissolved at the peace of 1674. Victualling was once more entrusted to a series of contractors, but in 1683 it reverted to a salaried board on the 1653 model. The 1673 political crisis which flowed from the unsuccessful third Dutch War obliged Charles II to accept his brother's resignation as Lord Admiral of England. Once more the office was placed in commission, the new **Admiralty Board** [83] being formed from the existing Privy Council Admiralty Committee. Much naval business continued to be transacted by the Privy Council in the presence of the king and his brother (still Lord Admiral of Scotland). The exclusion crisis of 1679 forced Charles II to retreat further, sending his brother into exile and establishing a new Admiralty Board dominated by Parliamentarians. Only in 1684 did the king feel strong enough to regain control over his Navy, dismissing the Admiralty Board and taking personal control of the Admiralty. When James II succeeded his brother the following year he continued this arrangement. Samuel Pepys, Admiralty Secretary to both monarchs, was in effect, though not in name, a naval minister. At Pepys's suggestion the Navy Board was replaced for two years, 1686–8, by another special **Navy Commission** [130] with a mandate for reform.

The revolution of 1688–9 drove James II into exile, and destroyed the Admiralty structure that he had created. The existing administrative bodies (the **Navy Board** [130–141], **Victualling Board** [168] and **Ordnance Board** [183–4]) continued to function as before. The **Sick and Hurt Board** [161 and 166] was revived for another war from 1689 to 1698 and again from 1702 to 1715. A new **Admiralty Board** [83] of Parliamentarians was established, but inherited little real power. Admiralty decisions were now often taken by William III in person, and executed by his **Secretary of State** [15], the Earl of Nottingham, sometimes without the knowledge of the Admiralty Board. Under the Secretary of State's authority a new **Transport Board** [174] handled the movement of troops and their supplies to Ireland and later the continent. During William III's reign (especially after the dismissal of Nottingham in 1693) the status of the Admiralty Board tended to rise, partly because the House of Commons used it as an instrument to increase its control over money bills, but the king was disgusted by its aggressively partisan politics, and just before his death in 1702 he replaced it with another **Lord Admiral** [82], the Earl of Pembroke. Queen Anne then installed her husband Prince George of Denmark as Lord Admiral, with a **Council** [82] which functioned much in the manner of an Admiralty Board. On Prince George's death in 1708 Pembroke was re-appointed, but the following year the incoming Whig administration reverted to an **Admiralty Board** [83]. This remained the form of Admiralty administration until 1964, with the exception of the two years 1827–8, when the office of Lord Admiral (with a Council) was revived for the Duke of Clarence. During this period, however, the existing records were continued unaltered, so that for the purposes of this guide Clarence's service can be ignored.

The Admiralty Board of the eighteenth and early nineteenth centuries was in principle made up of equals, but in practice the **First Lord of the Admiralty** [84], who usually sat in Cabinet, was the responsible minister, and his colleagues little more than placemen. Most boards included one or more officers, and some of them were of professional or political standing, but there was no office equivalent to the modern First Sea Lord as professional head of the Navy. Often described as the 'head' of the naval administrative system, the Admiralty might more accurately be described as its centre. Ultimate authority still resided with the king, in practice with the **Cabinet** [186], and major operations were set in motion by orders to the Admiralty from one of the **Secretaries of State** [15]. Combined operations were directly controlled by a Secretary of State, who alone could give orders to both admirals and generals, and in such cases the Admiralty formally relinquished control of the squadron concerned for the duration of the operation. Although admirals commanding such expeditions did not cease to correspond with the Admiralty, they rendered their formal reports to the Secretary of State. The **Admiralty Secretariat** [85–93] represented the communications centre of the Navy. It received orders from the Secretaries of State, it corresponded on a footing of equality with the **Ordnance Board** [183] and other departments, while it issued orders to, and received reports from, the subordinate naval boards and officers of the Navy. Important Admiralty orders and letters were issued in the form of 'Lords' Letters', signed by three or more members of the Board, but the bulk of Admiralty correspondence was conducted by the Secretary of the Admiralty in the Board's name. The Admiralty's legal business was handled by the **Solicitor of the Admiralty** [113]. The formation in 1755 of a Corps of Marines as part of the Navy, replacing the former Marine Regiments of the Army, entailed the establishment of a **Marine Office** [114] in the Admiralty. Originally this was a civilian body, but from 1802 it provided the Secretariat of the Senior Marine Officer, the **Colonel-Commandant in London** (later **Adjutant-General**) [114], who corresponded with the **Marine Divisions** [115] and Marine officers at sea. Also a department of the Admiralty, established in 1732, was the **Charity for Sea Officers' Widows** [124], an official pension fund supported by compulsory deductions from officers' pay, which paid means-tested widows' pensions. The Admiralty also administered the **Poor Knights of Windsor** [124], a resident charity for meritorious former officers established in 1798, and the **Compassionate Fund**, later **Compassionate List** [124], established in 1809, which paid pensions to the orphans or other dependants of officers killed in action.

Other organisations belonging to or dependent on the Admiralty included **Greenwich Hospital** [120–1], the principal source of long-service pensions for warrant officers and ratings, which admitted resident in-pensioners, and paid out-pensions to non-residents, besides administering **Schools** [122] for the children of naval men. The Hospital was supported in part by a compulsory levy on seamen's wages collected by the **Sixpenny Office** [127], which also inherited the residual functions of the **Register Office** [127], set up in 1696 as part of an unsuccessful attempt to establish a volunteer reserve of seamen for naval service. The Admiralty had partial oversight of the **Royal Observatory** [123], established in 1675 under the direction of the **Astronomer-Royal** [123], and nominated its **Board of Visitors** [123]. It also had responsibility for the **Board of Longitude** [123], established under the 1713 Longitude Act to administer a prize offered for improvements in navigation, and for the **Nautical Almanac Office** [123], which from 1767 compiled and published the astronomical tables which made it possible to determine longitude by the method of lunar traverses. The **Royal Naval Academy** [126], established at Portsmouth in 1737 and renamed Royal Naval College in 1812, educated a small proportion of the Navy's future commissioned officers. The **Impress Service** [125], first formed in 1743, was a wartime, shore-based recruiting organisation manned by officers and men of the Navy. The **Sea Fencibles** [125], in existence between 1793 and 1815, were a sort of naval coastal militia. Other naval shore organisations included (1803–15) the chain of **Signal Stations** [125], while from 1816 to 1831 a joint naval and Treasury organisation, the **Coast Blockade** [125], attempted to suppress smuggling. Other Admiralty officials included the **Hydrographer of the Navy** [127], first appointed in 1795, and the **Chaplain-General**, later **Chaplain of the Fleet** [127], created in 1812.

The **Navy Board** [130–41] continued during the eighteenth century to have responsibility for the dockyards, shipbuilding and repair. In principle its members acted collectively, and its records cover the whole range of its activities, but it is possible to distinguish some of the activities of the principal officers of the Navy. The **Controller** [134], always a Captain RN on half-pay, acted as the chairman and leading member of the Board. The **Surveyor** [135], always a former dockyard Master Shipwright, was the Navy's principal warship designer. By the end of the eighteenth century there were three joint Surveyors with a small drawing office. Within the **Navy Office** [139] there were several distinct departments. The **Bill Office** [140] issued Navy Bills in payment for all sorts of goods and services, while the **Ticket Office** [141] handled the payment of officers' and men's pay. (Its counterpart the **Navy Pay Office** [157] was part of the **Treasurer of the Navy's** [156] Department.) The Bill and Ticket Offices covered most of the Board's financial and accounting responsibilities, and in 1796 they were combined into the new **Accounts Department** [136]. At the same time a new **Stores Department** [137] was created from the responsibilities of the former **Controller of Storekeepers' Accounts**. The Navy Board also operated its own **Transport Service** [138].

Like the Navy Board, the **Victualling Board** [168] grew in size and importance during the eighteenth century. Its major home **Victualling Yards** at Deptford, Portsmouth and Plymouth [169–71] were very large manufacturing and packing establishments, while other **Victualling Yards and Depots** [172–3] were maintained throughout the world. The Victualling Board, the Navy Board, the Ordnance Board and the Treasury (for Army victuallers) all maintained independent transport services. Competition between them during the American War of Independence generated much waste and inefficiency, so in 1796 they were amalgamated into a new **Transport Board** [175]. As the servant of three masters (the Admiralty, the Treasury and the Ordnance Board) the new Board created some constitutional anomalies, but it was efficient in carrying out its responsibilities.

The **Sick and Hurt Board**, once more revived in 1740 and then retained permanently, was as before responsible for the **Naval Hospitals** [164–5] ashore (including the new hospitals of **Haslar** [163] near Portsmouth and Stonehouse near Plymouth which were the largest in the country), and in wartime for prisoners of war [166], but had only limited responsibilities for physicians and surgeons afloat. Towards the end of the eighteenth century there was a tendency for the Board to become more medical in its composition and interests, while at the same time its administration and accounting sank into disorder. For this reason the **Prisoner of War Department** [167] was in 1796 transferred to the new Transport Board. Ten years later the Sick and Hurt Board was abolished altogether and its responsibilities also transferred to the more efficient **Transport Board** [160], of which the medical members of the former Sick and Hurt Board became the Medical Committee. When the Transport Board in turn was abolished in 1816, all three services became part of the Victualling Board, which now had both a **Transport Committee** [176] and a **Medical Department** [161].

4   Naval Administration from 1832

In 1832 the incoming Whig 'Reform Ministry', inspired by Benthamite ideas of individual responsibility, abolished the Navy and Victualling Boards, placing the whole naval administration directly under the Admiralty. In the new system each branch was headed by a senior official who reported to a member of the Admiralty Board. The offices of the former naval boards, however, continued until 1860 to be housed in Somerset House, a mile away from the Admiralty in Whitehall, and the records continue to reflect a distinction between the central correspondence, conducted by the Secretary of the Admiralty in the name of the Admiralty Board, and the administrative branches in Somerset House which conducted their own correspondence (including that with the Admiralty). The business of the Admiralty Secretariat was now divided into branches for each member of the Board. Thus, the **Military Branch** ('M Branch') [95] was the First Naval Lord's, and dealt with the movements of the fleet; the **Naval Branch** ('N Branch') [96] was the Second Naval Lord's, and dealt with personnel, and so on. The Ships Branch of the **Surveyor**, later **Controller of the Navy** [104], inherited a major part of the Navy Board's duties, and stayed in Somerset House until 1860. Other technical officers and departments under the Controller included the **Controller of Steam Machinery** [106], the Chief Constructor, later **Director of Naval Construction** [105], and the **Naval Ordnance** [107], **Dockyards** and **Works Departments** [108]. Also among the Somerset House departments were the **Transport Department** [109], the **Physician-General** (later **Medical Director-General**) [110], the **Controller of Victualling** [111] and the **Accountant-General** [112], who inherited the work of the former Navy Board Accounts Department.

The correspondence of the Admiralty Secretariat was organised according to a scheme devised in 1806–7 and then applied retrospectively from 1793, in which all in-letters were filed or bound according to correspondent and date, and the whole correspondence, in- and out-letters together, was both indexed and abstracted in the massive volumes of the 'Admiralty Index and Digest'. Until 1860 most of the Somerset House departments retained separate records, but thereafter the bulk of Admiralty record-keeping was centralised in the **Admiralty Record Office** [102], and later in the nineteenth century these records were heavily 'weeded' under the provisions of the first Public Record Acts. From the mid 1880s the Index and Digest was no longer kept up to date, as a complete record of all correspondence, but was written up retrospectively after routine correspondence had already been discarded. By then Admiralty record practice was changing in other ways. From the 1840s draft out-letters were often put together with the in-letters, forming embryonic correspondence files, and this in turn encouraged the development of 'subject files'. The bulkier subject files, known in the Admiralty Record Office as **Cases** [103], were bound up into books.

The establishment of the **Naval Staff** in 1912 (with its civilian Secretariat provided by M Branch) greatly strengthened the Admiralty's operational and planning capacity, as well as installing large numbers of naval officers in what had been a largely civilian office. The Naval Staff absorbed the existing 'Service' departments of **Naval Intelligence** [117] and **Naval Ordnance** [107]. The bulk of records generated by ships and commands of the Royal Navy itself are preserved in the form of correspondence and papers received by the Admiralty. Ships' reports of proceedings are thickly scattered among the records used by the official historians of the First and Second World Wars [180]. **Admirals' Journals** [97], **Ships' Logs** [97], **Musters** and **Pay Books** [158] were returned to various departments of the Admiralty and Navy Board. The domestic archives of **Squadrons** and **Stations** [178–9] were not regularly preserved until the mid nineteenth century, although earlier station records survive in a variety of places. Some squadron and air station records of the **Royal Naval Air Service** and **Fleet Air Arm** [181] have been preserved.

Many naval **Research and Development Establishments** [119] were overseen by divisions of the Naval Staff, while others, particularly those engaged in fundamental research, were the responsibility of the **Director of Scientific Research** [118].

5   Colonial and Commercial Departments from 1660

In 1696 a new body, the **Board of Trade and Plantations** [69], was established to represent colonial and shipping interests in the government. Its functions were partly advisory and partly executive. Although it had no minister of Cabinet rank, it was involved in the planning of military and naval operations in the colonies. In 1768 a third 'American' or 'Colonial' Secretary of State was created, and the Board of Trade was placed under his authority, in effect becoming his department. Both the Colonial Secretary and the Board were abolished in 1782, when colonial affairs briefly passed to the Home Secretary, but the want of specialist advice was speedily felt. In 1784 a Privy Council **Committee on Trade and Plantations** [70] was created, which in 1786 became a new **Board of Trade** [70]. In 1801 colonial responsibilities were transferred to the **Secretary of State for War** [34], leaving the Board to handle commercial matters. The War and Colonial Departments remained linked until 1855 when a new **Colonial Office** [47] with its own Secretary of State was created. This department was responsible for all British Crown Colonies (and certain other territories) until 1968. Relations with the self-governing Dominions passed in 1925 to a new **Dominions Office**, later **Commonwealth Relations Office** [48], likewise abolished in 1968, when the residual responsibilities of both were amalgamated with those of the Foreign Office. All these departments were involved to varying degrees with the planning and execution of military and naval operations which took place in the colonies or involved colonial forces.

The **Board of Trade** [70] took on wider responsibilities in the nineteenth century, including a **Marine Department** [71] to administer the Merchant Shipping Acts, and a **Harbour and Railways Department** [72] transferred from the Admiralty in 1862. The Marine Department became the **Ministry of Shipping** 1917–21 [71], with the addition of the **Admiralty Transport Department** [109], and both later formed the **Ministry of War Transport** 1941–6 [71]. In 1919 the Marine Department reverted to the Board of Trade, but responsibility for harbours and railways passed to the new **Ministry of Transport** [213]. The Marine Department was also in charge of the **Registrar-General of Shipping and Seamen** [73], who had important functions in relation to the

Royal Naval Reserve, and in 1921 took over peacetime responsibility for the **Coastguard Service** [71] from the Admiralty. Naval control of merchant shipping in wartime [214] was exercised by a unit manned by Royal Navy officers, but at various times within the Board of Trade, the Ministry of War Transport, the Ministry of Transport and the Ministry of Shipping.

6   Home and Foreign Departments from 1660

Before the mid nineteenth century, British central government had very little to do with home affairs, which were the responsibility of magistrates and other local officials acting under the guidance of the **Lords Lieutenant of the Counties** [225]. Those (mainly judicial) duties which did belong to central government were discharged by either of the two Secretaries of State. In 1782 their responsibilities were redistributed into home and foreign departments. The **Home Secretary** [16] inherited the oversight of military and naval operations, but only until 1794, when they were transferred to the new War and Colonial Department. Thereafter the Home Office's responsibilities touched on naval affairs chiefly in relation to naval establishments in Britain. The **General Post Office** [76] administered the overseas Packet Service, except from 1836 to 1860 when it was transferred to the Admiralty [106].

During the twentieth century the general growth of government regulation of many aspects of daily life generated further points of contact. The **Ministry of National Service** [17] and **Ministry of Home Security** [19] were involved with naval manpower, the **Factory Inspectorate** [17] had some oversight over dockyards and naval industrial establishments. The **Aliens Office** [17] and the **Security Service** [17] were concerned with foreigners and spies in Britain. The **General Register Office** [18] conducted the national censuses which included naval personnel. The **Office**, later **Ministry of Works** and its successors [196–8] were responsible for government buildings, eventually including dockyards and naval establishments. Other aspects of domestic government, all having connections with the Navy and naval warfare, belonged to the **Ministry of Agriculture** [199], the **Department of the Environment** [200] and its predecessors, the **Ministry of Education** [201], the **Ministry of Labour** [202], the **Ministry of Pensions** [203], the **Ministry of Health** [211] and the **Department of Energy** [216].

In 1782 foreign affairs became the responsibility of the new **Foreign Secretary** and **Foreign Office** [20–6]. Diplomacy and strategy provided numerous points of contact with naval affairs, while officers abroad often corresponded with British **Ambassadors, Ministers and Consuls** [30–1]. The Foreign Office's modern responsibilities included the **Government Code and Cypher School** [27], which served all the Services with signals intelligence.

7   Military and Air Departments from 1660

The principal military department of the Crown at the restoration of Charles II was the **Ordnance Board** [183–4], which continued to be responsible for the issue of arms, ammunition and warlike stores to all services. Its heavy guns and small arms were largely manufactured by contractors, but from 1759 it began to manufacture its own powder. Ordnance establishments known as **Gunwharves** [185] were maintained at home and overseas naval yards, together with powder magazines. The rise of the Royal Artillery and Royal Engineers in the eighteenth century added large permanent military corps to its responsibilities. The Board was made the scapegoat for military disappointments during the Crimean War and abolished in 1855, when its responsibilities, including the supply of naval guns, passed to the War Office.

The horse and foot regiments of the regular Army (very few in 1660) were largely the responsibility of their colonels, who managed and in some senses owned them. In wartime they took the field under the authority of commanders-in-chief appointed by the Crown, and at some periods in the eighteenth century the Army had a permanent Commander-in-Chief, but the only Crown administrative oversight of them was provided by the **Secretary at War**, a sub-ministerial office created in 1661 with a small department known as the **War Office** [33], and abolished with the Ordnance Board in 1855. The **Paymaster-General of the Forces** [60] was responsible for the Crown's financial dealings with the regular army, and his subordinate the **Paymaster of Marines** [61] handled the Marine Regiments. When the Corps of Marines under Admiralty authority was created in 1755, he and his department, the **Marine Pay Office** [61], were transferred to the Treasurer of the Navy. In 1794 a third Secretaryship of State was created, the **Secretary of State for War** (from 1801 **War and the Colonies**) [34], which took over the military and naval responsibilities of all three Secretaries. It was now to this new Secretary of State that naval commanders-in-chief on combined operations, or those on stations (such as the Mediterranean) with important diplomatic responsibilities, reported. The new Secretary for War and his department (often called the War Office) should not be confused with the older, but subordinate office of Secretary at War and his War Office.

In 1854–5 the responsibility for the colonies was transferred to the new **Colonial Office** [47], and the abolition of both the Ordnance Board and the Secretary at War left the (new) **War Office** [36–7] solely responsible for the Army. There remained, however, a substantial anomaly. The War Office, like the Ordnance Board but unlike the Admiralty, was an administrative organisation with no operational authority: all Army units served and fought under the authority of a Commander-in-Chief appointed, in principle, by the Crown. Although the War Office inherited some of the records of these **Headquarters** [42], it had no formal command over them. However, the creation of the **Imperial General Staff** [38–40] provided the Army with central professional planning and leadership. Unlike both the Admiralty and the Ordnance Board, the War Office had no responsibilities for manufacture or production. After 1855 the War Office was responsible for production only on the former ordnance side, where a series of successor bodies (with naval representation) [44] controlled the Royal Arsenal, Powder Mills and Gun Factory [185] which the War Office had inherited. Non-ordnance supplies came entirely from outside contractors, and the War Office deployed almost no technical or managerial expertise to regulate them. To remedy this deficiency a series of supply departments were created for the Army, and later the RAF. These were the **Ministry of Munitions** (1915–21), the **Ministry of Supply** (1939–59), the **Ministry of Aircraft Production** (1939–46), the **Ministry of Production** (1942–5) [46] and the

Ministry of Aviation (1959–66) [222], each of which had some responsibilities (particularly for aircraft) to the Admiralty and the Navy.

The Royal Air Force, created in 1918 by the fusion of the Royal Naval Air Service and Royal Flying Corps, came under the authority of the **Air Ministry** [204], which inherited the records of the two services. It was Air Ministry policy to fuse and reclassify these records in such a way as to extinguish the archival traces of its predecessors, so that the bulk of the records of the RNAS can no longer be identified as such without going to the level of the individual file or item. The Air Ministry incorporated the **Air Staff** [206–7] and maintained various research establishments [208], but it was structured on the model of the War Office rather than the Admiralty; that is to say it had no operational command responsibility, which belonged to various **RAF Commands** [209], and no manufacturing or supply functions. The Air Ministry preserved numerous reports of all sorts of air operations, and the **Operations Record Books** [210] of individual squadrons, including those of Coastal Command and other units engaged in maritime warfare.

8   Financial Departments from 1660

Although the **Exchequer** [67] continued to function as a court of audit until the nineteenth century, when it was succeeded by the **Audit Office** [64], the Crown's central financial department was now the **Treasury** [49–59]. It took a close and growing interest in all Crown expenditure, including every aspect of the Navy. The Treasury also supervised the revenue boards (the **Boards of Customs and Excise** [62] and the **Board of Stamps and Taxes**, later **Inland Revenue** [63]) and the **Commissioners of Woods and Forests** [68]. In 1835 the new office of **Paymaster-General** [65] amalgamated the former offices of Paymaster-General of the Forces, Treasurer of the Navy and Treasurer of the Ordnance, from which it inherited many records of naval and Marine half-pay and pensions. With the creation of a unified **Civil Service** in 1855 the Treasury became responsible for this as well [66].

9   Cabinet and Ministry of Defence

Although the group of senior ministers known as the **Cabinet** [186] had existed from the seventeenth century, it had no permanent secretariat until 1916. At that point various records of Cabinet proceedings going back to the mid nineteenth century were assembled. The new Cabinet Office was based on the staff of the existing inter-departmental **Committee of Imperial Defence** [192], which itself succeeded various Cabinet and inter-departmental committees going back to the 1870s. The **War Cabinet** 1916–19 [187] combined both, but on the coming of peace the Committee of Imperial Defence resumed its separate existence. From 1936 it had its own Minister for the Co-ordination of Defence, although he had no formal responsibility to Parliament. On the outbreak of war in 1939 the Committee was again absorbed into the **War Cabinet** [189] machinery. When Winston Churchill became **Prime Minister and Minister of Defence** [194] in 1940, a 'Ministry of Defence' was created within the Cabinet Secretariat, and in 1947 this became a separate **Ministry of Defence** [217] with its own minister – in effect a strengthened form of the old Committee of Imperial Defence. This in turn formed the basis of a new unified **Ministry of Defence** in 1964 when it absorbed the former Service departments. The Cabinet Office, Committee of Imperial Defence and Ministries of Defence incorporated numerous inter-departmental committees of varying levels, including the **Chiefs of Staff Committee** [191] and its sub-committees. The Committee of Imperial Defence, later the Cabinet Office, also maintained a **Historical Section** [192] responsible for the Official Histories of the two World Wars.

Document Lists

1   The Medieval Chancery

The Patent Rolls contain the official copies of royal letters patent under the Great Seal, that is, public grants of all sorts of offices and privileges. They include appointments of military and naval commanders. During the fourteenth century they came to be used largely for the enrolment of grants of Crown lands, denization and the more important public offices; for proclamations and commissions; and, until 1853, for patents of invention.

The Close Rolls record private royal orders addressed to named individuals. Early rolls cover every aspect of government, including much military and naval business, but during the fourteenth century they become increasingly formal, and by Tudor times actual correspondence has been replaced by the enrolment of private deeds, mostly of conveyance. Letters patent and close issued in or relating to Gascony are recorded on the Gascon Rolls, and those issued in or relating to Normandy on the Norman Rolls. Chancery documents relating to Scotland, and particularly to war against Scotland by sea and land, are recorded on the Scots Rolls; those relating to Wales before incorporation on the Welsh Rolls. The Treaty Rolls record not only treaties and diplomatic documents but the administration of the Channel Isles, Calais and other English territories in France (excepting Gascony), with much military and naval matter.

Chancery warrants are royal orders, chiefly under the Signet or Privy Seal, to issue letters patent or close under the Great Seal. They cover the whole range of business represented by the Patent and Close Rolls, and each ought to have a corresponding enrolment, although not all do, and the warrants often give more detail than the enrolment. C 81/1656 are naval orders, and C 81/1757–9 military and naval, undated (but mostly fourteenth-century).

The Liberate Rolls record writs (royal orders) ordering expenditure from the Exchequer, or allowing sums already expended against accounts to be audited there. They initially cover the whole range of royal business involving any expenditure, but by the mid fourteenth century consist only of annual payments of fees. The same writs were recorded on receipt by the Exchequer in E 403/1200A–1288.

The Fine Rolls record payments in money or kind for all sorts of grants and privileges, including some relating to naval affairs.

Inquisitions were judicial enquiries into disputes, lawsuits, alleged crimes and the like. A number have to do with shipping and naval affairs.

The Chancery Miscellanea, Ancient Correspondence and Ancient Petitions are artificial classes, made up in the nineteenth century from Chancery and other documents. They include much to do with war and trade at sea.

Patent Rolls   1201–1952   C 66/1–5490   continuing
[Text 1201–16 printed in *Rotuli Litterarum Patentium in Turri Londinensi Asservati*, ed. T D Hardy (1835); 1216–32 printed in *Patent Rolls 1–16 Henry III* (2 vols., 1901–3); calendared 1232–1509 and 1547–82 in *Calendar of Patent Rolls* (52 vols., 1891–1916; 19 vols., 1924–); calendared 1509–47 in *Letters and Papers, Foreign and Domestic, Henry VIII*, ed. J S Brewer, J Gairdner and R H Brodie (21 vols., with 2 vols. addenda, 1862–1932).]

Close Rolls   1200–1   C 64/1
                1200–4 and 1225–6   C 62/1–4
                1204–1509   C 54/1–376
[Text 1200–1 printed by Pipe Roll Society, NS, 21 (1943), pp. 91–7 and in *Rotuli Normanniae* (1835); 1200–4 printed in *Rotuli de Liberate ac de Misis et Praestitis* (1844); 1204–27 printed in *Rotuli Litterarum Clausarum in Turri Londinensi Asservati*, ed. T D Hardy (2 vols., 1833–44); 1227–72 printed in *Close Rolls Henry III* (14 vols., 1902–38); calendared 1272–1509 in *Calendar of Close Rolls* (47 vols., 1892–1963); calendared 1509–47 in *Letters and Papers ... of Henry VIII*.]

Chancery Warrants   1230–1485   C 81/1–1796
[Calendared 1230–1326 in *Calendar of Chancery Warrants* (1927); calendared 1399–1422 in *Calendar of Signet Letters of Henry IV and Henry V*, ed. J L Kirby (1978).]

Gascon Rolls   1254–1468   C 61/1–144
[Text 1242–1307 printed in *Rôles Gascons*, ed. F Michel and C Bémont (4 vols. in 5, Paris, 1885–1906); 1307–17 printed in *Gascon Rolls, 4*, ed. Y Renouard (1962).]

Norman Rolls   1201–4 and 1417–22   C 64/2–17
[Text 1200–4 and 1417–18 printed in *Rotuli Normanniae* (1835); calendared 1418–22 in 41st and 42nd *Deputy Keeper's Reports*.]

Scots Rolls   1290–1516   C 71/1–113
[Text printed in *Rotuli Scotiae* (2 vols., 1814–19), with the omission of certain types of documents. Not included in *Calendar of Documents Relating to Scotland 1108–1509*, ed. J Bain (4 vols., Edinburgh, 1881–8) but omissions are noted in vol. 5 *Supplement*, ed. G G Simpson and J D Galbraith (Edinburgh, 1986), which can be used as a means of reference to the *Rotuli Scotiae*.]

Welsh Rolls   1276–95   C 77/1–7
[Calendared in *Calendar of Various Chancery Rolls, 1277–1326* (1912).]

Treaty Rolls   1234–1674   C 76/1–223
[Texts 1234–1325 and 1337–9 printed or calendared in *Treaty Rolls Preserved in the Public Record Office*, ed. P Chaplais and J Ferguson (2 vols., 1955–72); calendared 1327–1460 in *Catalogue des Rôles Gascons, Normands et Français Conservés dans les Archives de la Tour de Londres*, comp. T Carte (2 vols., 1743); calendared 1413–22 and 1422–60 in 44th and 48th *Deputy Keeper's Reports*.]

Liberate Rolls	1226–1377	C 62/5–144

[Text 1200–4 printed in *Rotuli de Liberate ac de Misis et Praestitis*, ed. T D Hardy (1844); calendared 1226–72 in *Calendar of Liberate Rolls* (5 vols., 1917–64).]

Fine Rolls	1199–1648	C 60/1–553

[Text 1199–1216 printed in *Rotuli de Oblatis et Finibus* (1835); selections 1216–72 printed in *Excerpta e Rotulis Finium* (2 vols., 1835–6); calendared 1272–1471 (20 vols., 1911–49) and 1547–53 in *Calendar of Patent Rolls Edward VI*, 5 (1929).]

Inquisitions Miscellaneous	1219–1485	C 145/1–330

[Calendared 1219–1485 in *Calendar of Inquisitions Miscellaneous* (8 vols., 1916–2005).]

Chancery Miscellanea	1220–1476	C 47/2/1–63

[Some of these documents are listed in *List of Documents of the Household and Wardrobe, John to Edward I*, [ed. P M Barnes] (1964).]

Ancient Correspondence	1175–1509	SC 1/1–64
Ancient Petitions	1216–1625	SC 8/1–364

[Many parliamentary petitions are printed in *Rotuli Parliamentorum*.]

2   The Medieval Exchequer

The Pipe Rolls (partly duplicated by the Chancellor's Rolls) are the formal annual accounts of the realm, including much miscellaneous military and naval expenditure, especially that incurred by sheriffs as the principal royal accounting officials in the shires. They include the accounts of William of Wrotham as Keeper of Ports and Galleys 1206–14. E 372/136 deals with the 1290 Welsh campaign. 'Foreign' accounts (that is, those extraneous to usual Exchequer business) include Wardrobe, Works, military and naval accounts up to 1368, and in some cases later. From 1369 these foreign accounts were recorded separately; they include naval expenses, wages, repairs, arresting and surveying shipping, and some shipbuilding. Among them (and in E 315/316–17) are some of the accounts of the Clerks of the King's Ships.

Warrants for issue are orders to make payments from the Exchequer, in many cases for wages or other naval expenses, of which there is full and useful detail up to 1485. The same payments are recorded in less detail on the Issue and Tellers' Rolls.

Exchequer Liberate Rolls record the receipt in the Exchequer of the writs of Liberate issued by Chancery, together with other payments made without writ. There are numerous payments for all sorts of naval services, not all entered in the Chancery Liberate Rolls, C 61.

The Memoranda Rolls contain notes of all sorts of Exchequer business, including much military and naval expenditure. Up to the 1330s the two series are substantially identical, but thereafter they diverge progressively.

Pipe Rolls	1129–30 and 1155–1368	E 372/1–212 contd. to 1832

Chancellor's Rolls	1233–1339	E 352/1–32

[Text to 1221 printed in Pipe Roll Society. List and Index Society, 11 lists naval accounts on the Pipe and Chancellor's Rolls 1232–1457.]

Chamber and other foreign accounts	1219–34	E 364/1
Foreign accounts	1369–1458	E 364/2–92
Warrants for issues	1399–1485	E 404/15–78 contd. to 1837

[Indexed in List and Index Society, 9, pt. 2.]

Issue Rolls	1240–1480 and 1567–1797	E 403/1–1692
Tellers' Rolls	1462–85	E 405/3–74 contd. to 1640
Liberate Rolls	1219–1306	E 403/1200A–1288
King's Remembrancer's Memoranda Rolls	1217–1926	E 159/1–789

[Text 1230–1 printed in Pipe Roll Society, NS, 11 (1933); 1231–3 printed in *Memoranda Rolls 16–17 Henry III*, ed. R Allen Brown (1991); calendared 1326–7 in *Calendar of Memoranda Rolls (Exchequer) ... 1326–1327*, ed. R E Latham (1968).]

Lord Treasurer's Remembrancer's Memoranda Rolls	1217–1835	E 368/1–804
Enrolled accounts, Purveyors (of Victualling)	1324–78	E 358/1–5
Enrolled accounts, Clerks of King's Ships	1344–64	E 372/203–209
Declared accounts, Sir E Howard, Lord Admiral	1511–12	E 351/210
Roll of Yarmouth grievances against Cinque Ports	1297	E 163/2/8

3   The Wardrobe and Chamber

The 'Accounts various' consist of vouchers delivered by accountants passing their accounts. Although listed under the Exchequer, many of them are actually Wardrobe or Chamber accounts never audited at the Exchequer. They were created by officials such as the Clerks of the King's Ships, and cover all sorts of naval and military expenditure. E 101/68–74 are indentures of retinue, listed in detail in List and Index Society, 11, pt. 2 with references to the associated warrants in E 404. Tudor and later documents in E 101 include a wide variety of accounts and financial documents relating to naval, military and ordnance expenditure. The 'Exchequer Books' include bound volumes of Chamber accounts. Other Wardrobe or Chamber accounts which were audited by the Exchequer, including some of those kept by Clerks of the King's Ships, are listed there [2] under 'Enrolled and foreign accounts'.

Accounts various	1211–1760	E 101/3–683
Accounts for Welsh War	1294–5	E 36/202

[Printed in *Book of Prests of the King's Wardrobe for 1294–5*, ed. E B Fryde (Oxford, 1962).]

Accounts of T Rogers, Clerk of King's Ships	1485–8	E 36/7
Accounts, expedition to France	1492	E 36/208 and 285
Accounts of R Brigandine, Clerk of King's Ships	1494–1502	E 315/316

[Printed in *Naval Accounts and Inventories in the Reign of Henry VII*, ed. M Oppenheim (NRS, 8, 1896).]

Accounts, Clerk of King's Ships	1523–30	E 315/317
Ordnance indentures	1496	E 36/8
Accounts of R Brigandine, Clerk of King's Ships	1498–1500	E 36/6
Accounts of J Hopton, Clerk of King's Ships	1510–21	E 36/10–13
Naval and ordnance accounts	1512–14	E 36/2
Building *Henry Grace à Dieu*	1512–14	E 36/5

4 Parliament

Statutes 1277–1469 are incompletely recorded on the Statute Rolls, and from 1483 fully recorded on the Parliament Rolls. They also record petitions and answers, many of them bearing on commerce and naval affairs, but these gradually disappear 1483–1628. For Interregnum Parliamentary naval administration see Lists 7 and 11. Later Parliamentary records are preserved in the House of Lords Record Office.

>[Calendared 1678–93 in *The Manuscripts of the House of Lords* (4 vols., Historical Manuscripts Commission, 17, 1887–94), continued to 1718 by *The Manuscripts of the House of Lords* (12 vols., NS, 1900–77).]

Statute Rolls	1277–1469	C 74/1–8
Parliament Rolls	1289–1322	SC 9/1–27
Parliament Rolls	1327–1628	C 65/1–190

>[Printed, 1277–1504, in *Rotuli Parliamentorum* (6 vols., 1767–77), and now re-edited by C Given-Wilson, *Parliament Rolls of Medieval England* (CD-ROM, 2005); statutes printed in *Statutes of the Realm* (11 vols., Record Commission, 1810–28).]

5 Secretaries of State, 1509–1640

From the reign of Henry VIII the records of the Secretary (from 1540 the two Secretaries) of State (the 'State Papers') are the principal record of the formation and execution of policy by the king in Council. The State Papers cover all aspects of government, and frequently incorporate reports and papers made by all sorts of ministers and officials. The papers from 1547 were later bound up in four series: Domestic, Foreign, Scotland and Ireland, and from 1577 the State Papers Foreign begin to be divided by country. Although the State Papers Foreign naturally deal with foreign policy, grand strategy and foreign intelligence, specifically English naval business is usually recorded in the State Papers Domestic. Only those State Papers most useful to the naval historian are mentioned here. Others are listed under the departments from which they emanated: Admiralty Board, Navy Board, Ordnance Board, and so on.

State Papers Henry VIII	1509–47	SP 1/1–246

>[Calendared (with many other documents) in *Letters and Papers ... of Henry VIII*.]

State Papers Domestic Edward VI	1547–53	SP 10/1–19

[Calendared in *Calendar of State Papers, Domestic ... Edward VI, 1547–1553*, ed. C S Knighton (1992).]

State Papers Domestic Mary I	1553–8	SP 11/1–14

[Calendared in *Calendar of State Papers, Domestic ... Mary I, 1553–1558*, ed. C S Knighton (1998).]

State Papers Domestic Elizabeth I	1558–1603	SP 12/1–289
	1558–1603	SP 13/A–H

[Partly calendared in *Calendar of State Papers, Domestic ... Edward VI, Mary, Elizabeth I and James I*, ed. R Lemon and M A E Green (12 vols., 1856–72).]

'Book for Sea Causes'	1559	SP 12/2–3
Spanish attack on Sir J Hawkins	1569	SP 12/53
Survey of merchant fleet	1582	SP 12/156
Survey of queen's ships, rigging and tackle	1588	SP 12/220
Office and powers of Lord Admiral	c.1590	SP 12/237
Warrants for money for naval services	1596–8	SP 12/258
State Papers Domestic James I	1603–25	SP 14/1–216
State Papers Domestic, Addenda	1547–1625	SP 15/1–43

[Calendared in *Calendar of State Papers, Domestic ... James I*, ed. M A E Green (4 vols., 1857–9).]

Commission of Naval Enquiry	1608	SP 14/41
Commission of Naval Enquiry	1618	SP 14/100–1
State Papers Domestic Charles I	1625–49	SP 16/1–542

[Calendared in *Calendar of State Papers, Domestic ... Charles I* (23 vols., 1858–97).]

Trinity House ordnance certificates	1628–38	SP 16/16–17
Ships' musters	1626	SP 16/22–3
Commission of Naval Enquiry	1626–7	SP 16/45
Register of letters of reprisal	1628–37	SP 16/130
Survey of seamen	1628	SP 16/135
Survey of ships in London	1629	SP 16/137
Survey of HM Ships with manning schemes	1633	SP 16/220
Northumberland enquiry into naval administration	1636	SP 16/336–8
Summer Fleet proceedings	1637	SP 16/372

6 Exchequer Accounts, 1544–1642

Under procedures developed from the fifteenth century and fully established in 1560, Crown officials accounted for public money by 'declaring' accounts annually in the Exchequer. These accounts represent their formal accounting relationship with the Crown rather than the current expenditure of their departments – especially in the many cases in which a department's income came from more than one source, or did not all pass through the hands of the accounting officer nominally responsible. Several copies of declared accounts in slightly different forms were kept in different departments of the Exchequer. The 1599 London Ship Money account, listed here for convenience, is a Subsidy Roll (that is, a record of tax revenue received) rather than a declared account.

Treasurer of the Navy:	1544–1715	E 351/2193–352 and 2587–97
	1558–1642	AO 1/1682/1–1706/89
	1558–60	AO 1/1784/297
(West Indies expedition)	1585	AO 1/1685/20A
(West Indies expedition)	1595–6	AO 1/1688/30–1
(Cadiz expedition)	1597	AO 1/1830/546
Prize goods:	1544–1715	E 351/2502–47
	1593–1632	AO 1/1811/437–43
Naval Victuallers:	1547–1642	E 351/2353–447
	1558–1642	AO 1/1784/298–1802/394
(Rhé expedition)	1626–31	AO 1/1798/372–3
(miscellaneous)	1543–97	E 351/2471–500
Master of Naval Ordnance:	1546–89	E 351/2599–607
	1557–60	AO 1/1832/1
Master and Surveyor of Ordnance:	1546–61	E 351/2614–16
	1561–1604	AO 1/1832/1A–1833/12
	1561–6	E 351/2602
	1563–87	E 351/2617–29
	1588–92	E 351/2609
	1592–1603	E 351/2630–9
	1596–7	E 351/2612
	1625–32	AO 1/1833/13
Lieutenant of Ordnance	1561–1640	AO 1/1834/14–1844/65
Roperies	1573–6	AO 1/2477/256
Earl of Bedford, Spanish voyage	1574	AO 1/292/1095
Treasurer of Ordnance	1587–8	AO 1/1846/68–70
Storekeeper of Ordnance	1589–92	AO 1/1906/242
Transport Service	1589–1610	AO 1/2304/1–7
Earl of Essex, Islands voyage:	1596–7	E 351/2611–12
	1597	AO 1/1830/546
Subsidy Roll, London Ship Money	1599	E 179/314
'Benevolence' for RN	1614–17	AO 1/1532/1
Commission of Naval Enquiry	1618	AO 1/1830/547 8
Commission of Naval Enquiry	1626–8	AO 1/861/1
Squadron for the North	1627–9	AO 1/1830/549–50
Spaniards shipwrecked on Dorset coast	1628–9	AO 1/2132/1

7   Lord Admiral, Admiralty Board and Admiralty Commission, 1532–1660

No discrete collection of Admiralty records (other than those of the High Court of Admiralty [8]) exists before 1642, but some items can be identified among the State Papers and elsewhere. Most Admiralty records among the State Papers are included in the various series of the *Calendars of State Papers, Domestic*, but in the *Calendar of State Papers, Domestic ... Commonwealth*, ed. M A E Green (13 vols., 1875–86), covering 1649–60, the different committees and commissions are inextricably confused.

Letters patent:	1532–1810	ADM 7/723–6
(Lord Howard of Effingham)	1585	CRES 40/18
Standing orders	c.1620	ADM 7/729
Secretary's out-letters	1624–60	SP 14/215
Orders to FO, Captains etc.	1625–37	SP 16/157
Warrants to Vice-Admirals of Counties, judges and officials of Admiralty Courts etc.	1628–37	HCA 50/2
Calendar of Admiralty orders	1629–32	SP 16/156
Board orders and minutes:	1632	SP 16/228
	1634–5	SP 16/264
	1637–8	SP 16/353
Out-letters and orders:	1642–3	SP 16/494
	1644	SP 16/504
	1645	SP 16/509
	1646–7	SP 16/512
	1648–9	SP 16/518
	1649–53	SP 46/114–15
	1653–6	ADM 7/674
	1656–60	ADM 2/1729–31
(to Navy Commission):	1653	SP 18/43–4
	1654	SP 18/93
	1655	SP 18/120–1
	1656	SP 18/152
	1657	SP 18/178
	1658	SP 18/199
	1659	SP 18/218
	1660	SP 18/225
Commission minutes:	1645	Bodleian Library, MS. Rawlinson C.416
	1646–8	ADM 7/6731
	1648	BL, Additional MS. 9305
	1657–60	ADM 3/273–4
In-letters:	1653	SP 18/45–62
	1654	SP 18/78–92
	1655	SP 18/103–18

	1656	SP 18/132–50
	1657	SP 18/161–76
	1658	SP 18/187–97
	1659	SP 18/207–17
	1660	SP 18/222–5
	1653–8	SP 46/116–18
(petitions etc.):	1653	SP 18/64
	1655	SP 18/122
Miscellaneous correspondence	1651–7	SP 46/96–9

8 High Court of Admiralty

These are records (many of them calendared in List and Index Society, 27) of the Instance and Prize jurisdictions of the court. As an instance court it handled all sorts of suits, both national and international, by mariners, merchants and shipowners. As a wartime prize court it adjudged captured ships and cargoes as enemy property, and therefore lawful prize, or otherwise ordered their release. The ship's papers of prizes (often including private correspondence and other writings found aboard) were put into court as evidence, and in many cases remain among the court records. In wartime the court also received documents from shipowners seeking authorisation by 'letters of marque' to cruise as privateers against enemy shipping. The High Court of Admiralty heard appeals from Vice-Admiralty Courts [9] in the counties and colonies.

Black Book of the Admiralty	c.1450	HCA 12/1
[Printed as *The Black Book of the Admiralty*, ed. Sir T Twiss (4 vols., 1871–6).]		
Warrants, monitions and decrees	1515–1761	HCA 39/1–55
Act books, minutes of acts	1524–1786	HCA 3/1–290
Libels, allegations, decrees, sentences	1526–1814	HCA 24/1–176
Exemplars	1531–1768	HCA 14/1–79
Examinations and answers	1536–1826	HCA 13/1–272
Interrogatories	1541–1733	HCA 23/1–30
Marshal, warrant books:	1541–1859	HCA 38/1–80
	1802–56	HCA 55/1 3
	1925–63	HCA 62/1–3
	1963–90	HCA 63/1–7
Letters of marque: warrants, bonds and bails	1549–1815	HCA 25/1–229
(declarations)	1689–1809	HCA 26/1–111
Documents etc. extracted from prize papers	1578–c.1852	HCA 65/1–57
Early case papers	1586–1778	HCA 15/1–58
Ships' books and papers	1624–1818	HCA 30/634–773
Documents presented in evidence	1625–1776	HCA 30/545–59
Warrants to judges and officials:	1628–37	HCA 50/2
	1660–1973	HCA 50/3–25

	1663–84	ADM 2/1755
	1673–88	ADM 6/404
	1689–1815	ADM 2/1045–78
Prize claims	1643–64	HCA 30/494–507
Sentences and interlocutories	1643–1854	HCA 34/65
Journal, Prize Court	1650–64	HCA 2/280
Prize distributions	1650–70	HCA 2/392
Intercepted mails	1652–1811	HCA 30/223–411
Miscellaneous accounts	1653–73	HCA 2/75–6
Fees:	1656–1750	HCA 2/157–77
	1666–79	HCA 2/244–6
	1673–1759	HCA 2/80–95
Cash books	1661–1759	HCA 2/438–45
Declared accounts: Receiver of Prizes	1664–1825	AO 3/3–18
(Registrar of Prizes):	1806–14	AO 3/17
	1831–2	AO 2/16 and 18
	1832–3	AO 2/24
(Receiver of Droits):	1830–5	AO 2/18, 22, 28 and 30
	1848–54	AO 20/42/1
Prize papers:	1664–74	HCA 32/6–12
	1689–1700	HCA 32/13–34
	1702–27	HCA 32/46–93
	1739–48	HCA 32/94–160
	1756–63	HCA 32/161–259
	1777–84	HCA 32/260–493
	1793–1817	HCA 32/494–1820
(indexes):	1793–1817	IND 1/10324–5
	1803–15	HCA 32/1848–9
Monitions	1664–1815	HCA 31/1–92
Lists of prizes	1680–1812	HCA 30/774–9
Receipt books	1698–1853	HCA 2/460–523
Letters of attorney (prize)	1700–1858	HCA 30/15–63
Condemnations of men-of-war for Head Money vouchers	1710–1833	ADM 43/1–80
Assignation books:	1718–1840	HCA 8/1–161
	1796–1802	HCA 9/1–40
	1803–10	HCA 10/1–38
	1803–10	HCA 11/1–89
Marshal, Judge etc., letters to Admiralty	1740–1839	ADM 1/3878–910
Accounts, Navy Agents etc.	c.1740–1860	HCA 2/1–571
Prize reports	1745–95	FO 83/1
Royal warrants for grants to RN out of prize droits:	1760–1857	HCA 40
(register)	1760–1857	HCA 40/28

Minute books:	1777–1842	HCA 28/1–50
(prize):	1779–1827	HCA 30/114–57
	1802–10	HCA 29/1–43
Decisions in prize cases	1780–82	SP 41/144
Interlocutory decree books	1793–1824	HCA 22/1–83
Proctor's accounts, neutral ships etc.	1794–1820	ADM 17/54–6
Register of appeals from Vice-Admiralty Courts	1800–17	AO 16/1
Bail bonds (Prize Agents)	1803–27	HCA 30/74–6
Ships detained under embargoes	1806–40	HCA 30/977–85
Prize case, US Schooners *Tigress* and *Scorpion*, Lake Huron	1814–20	ADM 49/10
Letter books	1842–58	HCA 58/8–9
Admiralty correspondence concerning prizes	1844–7 and 1855	TS 18/355
Records of the Russian War:	1854–60	HCA 33
(register)	1854–60	HCA 40/28
(prize papers)	1854–6	HCA 30/1027–8
(prize papers, register)	1854–6	HCA 30/987–90
Naval prize account registers:	1855–85	HCA 30/525 and 987–90
	1885–1916	HCA 30/1004–5
Ships' logs	1862–6	HCA 30/780–6
Calendar of prisoners	1868–1971	HO 140/1–921
Naval Prize Tribunal	1918–21	CO 839/1
Prize Courts, original correspondence:	1939–51	CO 969/1–314
(registers)	1941–51	CO 988/1–12

9 Vice-Admiralty Courts

The majority of colonial Vice-Admiralty Court records survive, if at all, in the archives of the former colonies concerned. With the Vice-Admiralty Courts it is convenient to include the Mixed Commissions (that is, *ad hoc* international courts) established under the terms of various treaties for the suppression of the slave trade, to adjudicate captured slavers.

Proceedings:	1593–1875	HCA 49/1–106
	1805–25	HCA 30/790–6
Letters to Admiralty	1740–1839	ADM 1/3878–910
Patents of appointment	1746–1890	ADM 5/38–75
Registrars' accounts and returns	1793–1825	AO 3/16
Register of appeals against Vice-Admiralty Court decrees	1800–17	AO 16/1
Slave Trade Mixed Commissions:	1822–7	HCA 30/787–9
(Sierra Leone)	1819–68	FO 315/1–96
(Havana)	1819–69	FO 312/1–67

(Jamaica)	1843–51	FO 314/1–3
(Cape Town)	1843–70	FO 312/1–43
Reports, St. Helena	1846–58	FO 84/651, 696, 738, 776, 817, 859, 887, 921, 951, 977, 1003 and 1056

10   Prize Goods, Prize Office and Prize Commissioners

Records of naval authorities accounting for prizes and prize goods, of which one tenth was due to the Lord Admiral until 1629, and thereafter the Crown until 1708. They include the Prize Commissions 1694–8 and 1702–8, and several special commissions established to handle vessels seized without declaration of war or in other legally doubtful circumstances.

Declared accounts:	1544–1715	E 351/2502–47
	1593–1632	AO 1/1811/437–43
	1643–9	AO 1/1812/443A–B
	1664–1715	AO 1/1812/444–1820/481
(French ships taken before declaration of war)	1756	AO 1/1820/482
(Dutch prizes)	1795–1813	AO 1/1820/482A
Prize tenths	1628–37	HCA 2/62
Receipt book	1628–53	HCA 2/459
Fees:	1647–9	HCA 2/243
	1656–1750	HCA 2/157–77
Journal	1650–64	HCA 2/280
Prize distributions	1650–70	HCA 2/392
Miscellaneous accounts	1653–73	HCA 2/75–6
Prize accounts:	1664–1706	AO 3/3/1–3
	1702–10	T 38/616–37
	1793–1825	AO 3/10–18
London Prize Commission, minutes	1672–4	PRO 30/32/4
Reports to the Admiralty	1694–1706	ADM 1/3661–2
Correspondence with Treasury	1702	T 64/195–6
Commission for Prizes taken as Reprisals	1744–5	SP 104/143
Prize cases	c.1755–62	PRO 30/8/80
Prize Office miscellanea	1785–1815	ADM 49/91
Danish etc. Prizes Commissions	1808–14	T 84/1
Portuguese Prizes Commission	1808–19	HCA 30/508–16
American Prizes Commission	1812–17	T 88/1

11 Parliamentary Naval Administration, 1642–60

From the outbreak of the first Civil War in 1642 to the military coup of December 1648, English central government was conducted under the authority of various Parliamentary committees. Thereafter real power was held by the Council of State, made up of the senior officers of the Army and selected Parliamentarians of their mind, until Cromwell in turn seized power in 1653 and made himself Lord Protector. The State Papers Domestic Interregnum, SP 18 and 25, are calendared in *Calendar of State Papers, Domestic ... Commonwealth*, ed. M A E Green (13 vols., 1875–86) – in which, however, the different committees and commissions are confused. An important printed collection, mainly of State Papers Foreign, is *A Collection of the State Papers of John Thurloe*, ed. T Birch (7 vols., 1742).

Admiralty and Cinque Ports Committee
Instructions   1647   ADM 7/729

Navy and Customs Committee
Minutes and orders   1642–4   Bodleian Library, MS. Rawlinson A.220–2
Miscellaneous papers   1644–53   SP 46/122B
Out-letters and orders: 1642–3   SP 16/494
                                             1644   SP 16/504
                                             1645   SP 16/509
                                             1646–7   SP 16/512
                                             1648–9   SP 16/518
                                             1649   SP 18/5 and 30
                                             1649–53   SP 46/114–15
Minutes   1649   Bodleian Library, MS. Rawlinson A.224
Financial orders: 1650–2   SP 46/102
                                             1651–3   SP 46/114
Miscellaneous correspondence   1651–7   SP 46/96–9

Council of State
Records   1649–60   SP 25/1–138
Admiralty Committee minutes: 1649–50   SP 25/123
                                             1650–3   Bodleian Library, MS. Rawlinson A.225–7
Council and Generals at Sea, orders to
    Navy Commission: 1649–50   SP 18/6 and 13
                                             1651–2   SP 18/18

12   Privy Council Minutes and Orders, 1540–1978

The registers contain full information about the business of the Privy Council, including (seventeenth–eighteenth centuries) much naval business. Some are printed in *Proceedings and Ordinances of the Privy Council of England*, ed. Sir N Harris Nicolas (7 vols., 1834–7).

Registers:		1540–1978	PC 2/1–872
		1660–74	PC 6/1
Naval minutes:		1660–1731	ADM 1/5246–7 and 5249–51
	(extracts)	1692–7	ADM 7/693
Foreign Affairs Committee, minutes		1667–76	SP 104/176–7
Minutes, including naval		1670–1928	PC 4/1–27
Naval Orders in Council:		1672–3	SP 44/39
		1673–9	ADM 2/1
		1674–9	ADM 2/1737–9
		1684–8	ADM 2/1727
		1684–8	ADM 2/1741–2
		1688–9	ADM 2/1743
		1708	ADM 2/1744
		1708–82	SP 42/139–40
	(digest)	1673–88	ADM 12/36D
	(pensions etc.):	1693–1710	ADM 49/174
		1830	ADM 49/175
	(additional regulations and instructions)	1805	ADM 1/5252
Committee on Trade and Plantations		1678–1806	PC 5/1–16
Joint meetings of Lords Justices and Admiralty Board	1692–8		ADM 1/5248

13   Privy Council Correspondence and Papers, 1481–1974

The miscellaneous series of papers covers the full range of the Privy Council's activities, arranged chronologically. Many of them are concerned with the Admiralty or Navy, and the following list includes only a sample. There is a very full index to persons and subjects incorporated in the series list. The 'Domestic, Military, and Naval Papers' are fully listed but not indexed. The 'Colonial Papers' include a few of naval interest. The final 'General Papers' series, which is fully indexed, includes some of naval interest. The four series overlap chronologically.

Correspondence		
Letters to Admiralty	1673–1839	ADM 1/5138–245
Irish Committee, correspondence with Admiralty	1689–90	ADM 2/1756
Memorials and reports from Admiralty	1695–1815	ADM 7/333–47
Correspondence:	1860–1956	PC 8/1–1827
(registers):	1839–1900	PC 6/4–9

	1860–1964	PC 9/1–101

Papers

Miscellaneous papers	1481–1809	PC 1/1–13
General papers	1671–1946	PC 1/142–4574
Colonial papers	1676–1822	PC 1/46–66
Domestic, military, naval etc. papers	1695–1799	PC 1/14–45
Instructions for Lord High Admiral	1673	PC 1/1/7
Navy clerks' fees for Mediterranean passes	1677	PC 1/1/8
Voiding of patent for making salt water fresh	1683	PC 1/11/150
Voiding of patent for making pitch and tar	1687	PC 1/11/150
Sick and Hurt Board, precedents	1689–1702	PC 1/13/97
Exchange of prisoners, precedents	1689–1702	PC 1/13/97
Impressment of seamen, precedents	1689–1711	PC 1/13/98
Pay and allowances of sea officers	1694	PC 1/13/94
Admiralty proposals for manning:	1695	PC 1/14/1
	1701	PC 1/14/4
	1702	PC 1/1/116
Petition: Capt. Waters for employment	1699	PC 1/14/2
(naval wives and widows)	1700	PC 1/1/57
(wives etc. of seamen imprisoned in France)	1702	PC 1/1/202
(ships to be freed from embargo):	1703	PC 1/1/231
	1779	PC 1/11/180
Navy Estimate for 10,000 men	1701	PC 1/1/74
Admiralty memorial to impress watermen	1701	PC 1/1/75
Proposed impress instructions	1701	PC 1/1/78
Admiralty request to impress coopers	1701	PC 1/1/89
Hoys etc. for victualling service	1701	PC 1/1/89
Admiralty memorial, sale of old boats	1701	PC 1/1/101
Sea-victuals for an additional 10,000 men	1702	PC 1/1/117
Sea-victuals for an additional 20,000 men	1702	PC 1/1/119
Orders for the speedy manning of the Fleet	1702	PC 1/1/142
Numbers of seafaring men in Anglesey	1702	PC 1/14/7
Seamen's wages paid out of surplus officers' half-pay	1702	PC 1/1/147
Rescue of impressed seamen:	1702	PC 1/1/154
	1704	PC 1/2/2
Appointment of GH Board	1702	PC 1/1/155
Lifting the press 'this side of Tilbury'	1702	PC 1/1/156
Winter reduction of the Fleet	1702	PC 1/1/169
HMS *Tartar* to be armed with three-pounder guns	1702	PC 1/1/169
Report on the preservation of the New Forest	1702	PC 1/1/172
Invention for preserving ships' bottoms	1702	PC 1/1/144

Accounts of Sir Henry Shere as Commissioner at Tangier	1702	PC 1/1/183
HMS *Resolution* to be armed with 24-pounder guns	1703	PC 1/1/212
Proposed establishment of men and guns for RN	1703	PC 1/1/213
Mayor of Whitby ordered to aid impressment	1703	PC 1/1/230
Magistrates ordered to aid impressment	1703	PC 1/1/232
Embargo to man the Fleet	1703	PC 1/1/233
Admiralty report: captains' petition for half-pay	1704	PC 1/2/8
(lieutenants')	1705	PC 1/2/11
(petition for convoys)	1704	PC 1/2/9
Pension for widow of Capt. F Emes	1705	PC 1/2/10
Grant of one-eighth of prizes to commodores	1706	PC 1/2/38
Rival claims to a prize	1707	PC 1/2/51
Ensigns to be worn by British ships	1707	PC 1/2/74
Navy Estimate for 40,000 men	1707	PC 1/2/75
Speeding repair of ships in dockyards	1708	PC 1/2/76
Pension for widow of Thomas Tuttel, hydrographer	1709	PC 1/2/161
Admiralty report, embargo of ships in plantations	1710	PC 1/14/21
Petition for payment of wages to third party	1712	PC 1/14/32
Murder of customs officer by crew of Dutch man-of-war	1712	PC 1/14/37
Petition of seamen and widows of the *Defiance*	1715	PC 1/14/96
Admiralty report in favour of Peter Cock, Pilot Extraordinary in the Navy	1717	PC 1/14/113
Precedents of dismissed sea officers restored to RN	c.1718	PC 1/13/95
Proposals for regulating naval affairs in Minorca	1718	PC 1/14/119
Petitions for shares of prizes	1722	PC 1/14/121–2
Pensions granted to the children of RN officers	1727–83	PC 1/13/96
Mayor of Liverpool obstructing press officers	1762	PC 1/7/28
Order to clear imprest on victualling agent	1763	PC 1/7/69
Navy Estimate for 16,000 men	1764	PC 1/7/121
Admiralty recommend purchase of prizes	1764	PC 1/3059A
Alterations to Portsmouth and Plymouth Dockyards:	1764	PC 1/7/125
(order approving plans)	1765	PC 1/7/166
Salaries of Board of Longitude	1765	PC 1/7/164
Abstract of unserviceable naval stores sold 1753–64	1765	PC 1/7/167
Petitions, for naval pensions	1766–72	PC 1/3060–76
HMS *Thames* to be discharged from quarantine	1771	PC 1/9/78
Customs duty on candles from HMS *Alarm*	1771	PC 1/15/85
Admiralty propose a lieutenant be restored to his rank	1771	PC 1/15/86
Pension for gunner of HMS *Enterprize*	1772	PC 1/15/91
Pension for Master Shipwright Chatham Yard	1773	PC 1/9/129
RNA Portsmouth, revised establishment	1773	PC 1/9/143
Navy Estimate for 28,000 men	1775	PC 1/10/95
Appointment of third Commissioner for Sick and Wounded	1777	PC 1/15/101

Navy Board report on pay and training of carpenters	1779	PC 1/11/139
Voiding of Wilkinson's patent for boring guns	1779	PC 1/11/150
Purchase of land for Marine barracks, Plymouth	1779	PC 1/11/151
Bounties and rewards for seamen	1779	PC 1/11/174
Admiralty report on murder in HMS *Quebec*	1779	PC 1/11/177
Admiralty memorial, issue of press warrants	1782	PC 1/12/156
Navy Estimate for 110,000 men	1783	PC 1/13/2
Marine Society to use some old ships	1783	PC 1/13/7
Admiralty papers: establishments etc.	1790	PC 1/18/20
(pensions, establishments, etc.)	1794	PC 1/21/33
Terms of hire of luggers by the Navy	1794	PC 1/23/39
Admiralty authorised to issue press warrants	1794	PC 1/23/39
Lignum vitae as a naval store	1794	PC 1/23/39
Admiralty papers on the scarcity of corn	1795	PC 1/29/64–73
Order authorising Admiralty to deal with mutiny	1797	PC 1/38/121
Anti-invasion measures, removal of buoys and lights	1797	PC 1/38/121
Mutiny at the Nore, execution of R Parker	1797	PC 1/38/123
Petitions from Admiralty, RN officers and men	1797	PC 1/40/129
Certificate from Lord Hood praising Lt. Gibson, killed at Tenerife	1798	PC 1/43/148
Pay of surgeons' mates in prison ships and gun boats	1798	PC 1/43/148
Prize money:	1799	PC 1/4519
	1806–7	PC 1/4560
Establishment of Navy Pay Office	1800	PC 1/3489
RNA Portsmouth	1800	PC 1/3510
Petitions for re-instatement of RN officers	1800–1 etc.	PC 1/3491, 3504B, 3520 etc.
Naval victualling	1803	PC 1/3578
Quarantine of HMS *Eagle*	c.1804	PC 1/4470
Board of Revision, reports	1805–9	PC 1/13/93
Admiralty report, purser's petition:	1833	PC 1/4424
(lieutenant's petition)	1834	PC 1/4439
Admiralty charts of Guernsey, Herm and Sark	1863–5	PC 1/2257
Admiralty report on venereal disease	1865	PC 8/59 and 63
Oath of First Lord of Admiralty	1906	PC 8/635
Charter of the RN Benevolent Fund:	1922	PC 8/951
	1969–74	PC 15/620–1
RN reservists serving as sheriff	1923	PC 8/998
Term of service of seamen and Marines	1938	PC 8/1358
Naval and Marine Pay and Pensions Act, 1865	1949	PC 8/1666
Committee on Naval Prize Law: minutes etc.	1900–4	PC 10/17–20
Charters of WRNS Benevolent Trust	1948–60	PC 15/1343–5
Charters of RN Association	1952–73	PC 15/617–19
Charter of RN Benevolent Trust	1969–74	PC 15/620–1

14 Prize Appeals Commissioners

These are appeals from decisions of the High Court of Admiralty.

Law Officer's opinions	1665–7	SP 9/240
Sentences	1672–1772	HCA 48/1–8
Act books and minutes	1689–1814	HCA 41/1–18
Papers:	1689–1833	HCA 42/1–574
	c.1755–62	PRO 30/8/257
	1780–4	HO 28/57–9
	1811	HCA 2/241
	1853–1902	HCA 53/1–2
Miscellanea	1689–1845	HCA 47/1–44
Assignation books:	1689–1802	HCA 43/1–38
	1793–1832	HCA 44/1–89
(index)	1793–1819	IND 1/8987
Case books:	1750–1818	HCA 45/1–71
	c.1745–52	PRO 31/17/36
Interlocutories	1794–1822	HCA 46/1–11
Letter books	1795–1864	HCA 58/1–12
Bill books	1833–65	PCAP 5
Printed appeal cases	1834–70	PCAP 3/1–35
Processes	1834–70	PCAP 1/1–35
Minutes	1866–1948	HCA 60/1–7
Appeals: United Kingdom	1914–21	CO 838/1–13
(overseas)	1914–19	CO 837/1–2
(naval)	1916–21	CO 836/1–2

15 Secretaries of State, 1660–1782

These are records of the Secretaries for the Northern and Southern Departments, together with those of the Colonial or American Secretary, 1768–82, which can now be identified. Colonial correspondence (including many dispatches from overseas expeditions and other combined operations) was mingled with the papers of the Board of Trade in the nineteenth century and reorganised on a geographical basis, but the bulk of that up to 1688 is in CO 1, and from 1688 to 1784 in CO 5. Correspondence in SP 44 up to 1704 is included in the *Calendar of State Papers, Domestic*.

Correspondence and papers, America and West Indies:	1574–1688	CO 1/1–69
	1606–1822	CO 5/1–1450

[Calendared in *Calendar of State Papers, Colonial ... America and West Indies* (38 vols., 1860–1994) to 1739.]

Out-letters: including naval:	1664–9	SP 44/17
	1668–74	SP 44/31
(colonial and naval)	1666–72	SP 44/24
Letters to naval boards, C-in-Cs:	1672–3	SP 44/39
	1679–84	SP 44/63
	1689–1706	SP 44/204
	1693–6	SP 44/205
	1701–84	SP 44/206–32
Naval warrants, including licences to enter foreign service	1674–1782	SP 44/334–85
Register of safe-conducts	1676–9	SP 44/49
Letters and orders to Admiralty:	1689–1839	ADM 1/4080–277
(covering foreign ambassadors)	1697–1708	ADM 1/4278
(index)	1698–1792	ADM 12/17–20
Letters from naval boards, C-in-Cs etc.	1689–99	SP 42/1–5
Admiralty and Navy Office lists of HM Ships, showing disposition, condition etc.	1693–1748	SP 42/111–16
Letters from Admiralty Board:	1695–1804	ADM 2/363–76
	1700–82	SP 42/6–66
Letters from other naval boards and miscellaneous	1700–21	SP 42/117–23
Letters from C-in-Cs and captains:	1700–72	SP 42/67–104
	1727–45	SP 42/105–10
Intelligence forwarded to Admiralty	1697–1748	ADM 1/3930–4
Law Officers' opinions	1704–82	SP 42/138
Orders in Council on Admiralty or naval affairs	1708–82	SP 42/139–40
Correspondence, Canada expedition	1710–13	CO 5/9
Correspondence of Sir J Wishart as Naval Envoy to the Netherlands	1711–12	SP 84/237
Miscellaneous naval papers	1722–82	SP 42/125–37
Correspondence copied for Parliament	1739–42	SP 42/141–3
Correspondence, Carthagena and Portobello expeditions	1740–3	CO 5/41–2
Passes to export tobacco to enemy ports	1745–9	C 67/86–92
Correspondence, Canada expeditions	1746–50	CO 5/44–5
Letters from naval and military C-in-Cs	1755–63	CO 5/46 and 53–63
Correspondence, Manila expedition	1762–3	CO 77/20
Colonial Secretary: letters from Admiralty:	1771–81	CO 5/119–32
	1776–82	CO 5/259–60
(letters to Admiralty)	1775–82	CO 5/254–5
Decisions in prize cases	1780–2	SP 41/144
Prize appeals	1780–4	HO 28/57–9

16   Home Secretary and Home Office, 1782–1979

The Home Secretary inherited most of the formal responsibility for naval and military business formerly dealt with by the Northern and Southern Secretaries, including supervision of Joint-Service operations. In 1794 these passed to the new Secretary of State for War, followed in 1801 by oversight of the colonies, but the Home Office continued to be involved in much other business relating to the presence of the Navy and its personnel in Britain. Judges' reports include many on criminals offering or pleading naval service in mitigation, and others relating to crimes committed in the dockyards or by naval personnel ashore.

The Home Office's nineteenth- and twentieth-century registered files are organised under subjects, including 'Naval', 'Ships', 'Military and Naval', and so on. Many other headings cover matters of naval interest, including 'Aliens' (for example German Navy deserters and Russian seamen), 'Children' (for example policy on enlisting boys in the Navy), 'Criminal', 'Prisons', 'Prisoners' and 'Lunacy' (for example of naval personnel), 'Dangerous Substances' (for example the explosion at the RN Cordite Factory in 1931), 'Deserters' (for example Admiralty proposals) and 'Disturbances' (for example use of naval forces to assist civil power).

Special commission to HEIC ships to seize pirates	1768–1827	HO 118/1
(requested)	1786	HO 44/41
Marshalsea Prison, Admiralty prisoners	1773–1842	PRIS 11/15–18
Admiralty warrant book	1779–1815	HO 29/1
Naval dispatches:	1782–4	CO 5/186
(Capt. George Vancouver)	1791–3	CO 5/187
(Toulon expedition):	1793–4	HO 28/14–15
	1793–4	HO 50/454
(Toulon and Corsica)	1793–6	FO 20/1–4
Letters from Admiralty:	1782–93	HO 28/1–13
(and naval boards etc.)	1794–1840	HO 28/16–56
Naval warrants, including licences to enter foreign service	1782–1969	HO 38/1–93
Letters from Ordnance Board	1783–1837	HO 50/364–76
Letters to Admiralty:	1784–1836	HO 29/2–7
	1808–9	ADM 1/4279
	1836–98	HO 34/1–88
Prize appeals	1780–4	HO 28/57–9
Miscellaneous Admiralty correspondence (transports etc.)	1783–1811	HO 28/60–3
Domestic correspondence, including naval:	1773–1861	HO 44/1–58
	1782–1820	HO 42/1–218
Judges' reports on criminals	1784–1829	HO 47/1–75
Entry books, Toulon and Corsica	1793	CO 173/3–4
Letters from other naval boards	1801–40	HO 28/27–56

Letters to Ordnance Board	1803–32	HO 51/137–9
Defence of dockyards, papers	1803–11	HO 50/66, 102, 131, 166, 189, 215, 240 and 260
Newgate Prison calendar, including Admiralty calendar	1815–21	HO 77/23–8
Naval Knights of Windsor	1841–62	HO 45/8730
Letters from Admiralty	1854–7	ADM 2/1698–701
Commission to Admiralty for determining prizes	1854–63	HO 118/1
Registered papers:	1839–1979	HO 45/1–26028
(registers)	1841–1957	HO 46/1–389
(supplementary)	1868–1959	HO 144/1–23516
Official Press Bureau, including Naval Censor's staff	1914–19	HO 139/1–55

Miscellaneous

Naval assistance for operations in Ireland	1921	HO 317/61
Billeting of naval personnel on state-managed pubs	1940–5	HO 185/166
Report of US Naval Technical Mission to Japan	1948	HO 228/2
Admiralty gamma ray measurements of British atomic bomb trials	1954	HO 228/17
Annexation of Rockall by HMS *Vidal*	1955	HO 342/84
Admission of Commonwealth citizens to UK to join RN	1963–9	HO 344/260

17 Other Home Departments

The Metropolitan Police was the only police force under central government supervision, and was responsible for the Dockyard Police. The Ministry of National Service was responsible for manpower planning. The Factory and Explosives Inspectorates had statutory duties in respect of naval establishments. The Home Office Aliens Office had oversight of foreigners in Britain, and the Security Service countered foreign espionage and subversion. The Irish and Welsh Offices represent central government's liaison with the devolved local government of those countries; relations with the Irish Republic passed to the Dominions Office soon after independence.

Metropolitan Police

Dockyard Police, letter books	1860–7	MEPO 1/48
Correspondence and papers, including Dockyard Police:	1816–1994	MEPO 2/1–11540
(special series, including naval matters, apprehension of deserters etc.)	1830–1974	MEPO 3/1–3157
Instructions for Dockyard Police	1860	SUPP 5/1020
	1864	MEPO 4/163

Ministry of National Service, 1916–20

Records, including RN and dockyard manpower	1914–20	NATS 1/1–1333

Fire Brigades Division, later Fire Services Department

Protection of Admiralty establishments from fire	1941–7	HO 187/1141
Admiralty *Ship Fire-Fighting Manual*	1942–9	HO 187/1543
Use of naval auxiliary boats	1943–5	HO 187/876–879 and 891
Naval fire boats to protect invasion vessels	1944–5	HO 209/6
National Fire Service Officers, transfer to Admiralty	1947–9	HO 187/1521
Wartime naval fire-fighting	1951	HO 346/33

Factory Inspectorate, later Health and Safety Executive

Inspections of Admiralty factories:	1914–18	LAB 15/1–151
	1914–18	HO 87/1–53
Explosives Inspectorate, Safety in Naval Laboratories Committee	1943–55	EF 4/16
Inspection of naval establishments	1969–76	LAB 14/2264
Radiation doses at Chatham Dockyard	1970–1	LAB 14/2513
Survey of asbestos workers, Devonport Dockyard	1972	LAB 105/11
Diving safety, RN Training School	1972–7	LAB 104/102
Transfer of health physicists from RN	1975–7	LAB 104/660
Investigation into fire in HMS *Glasgow*	1976–80	EF 7/477 and 16/26
Chairman's visit to Portsmouth Dockyard	1988	EF 7/2583 and 2620

Aliens Office, later Department

Yugoslav naval personnel serving in RN	1939–45	HO 213/1202
Admiralty and WO, prohibition of employment of aliens	1940	HO 213/2005
Naval ports to be protected areas	1940	HO 213/2012
Accommodation for Norwegian naval personnel	1943–5	HO 213/1828

Security Service (MI5)

Policy files, including naval security	1909–63	KV 4/1–313
Personal files, including enemy agents	1913–79	KV 2/1–2098

Marshalsea Prison

Account of Admiralty prisoners	1815	PALA 9/8
List of prisoners, including Admiralty	1842–3	PALA 9/7/5

Irish Office

RN W/T station in Irish Free State	1921–2	HO 351/117
Admiralty claim for loading War Department vessels	1922–3	HO 351/152
Admiralty contracts	1923	HO 267/325
Admiralty chocolate supplied to Northern Ireland prisons	1923	HO 348/14
Withdrawal of RN launches in Northern Ireland waters:	1923	HO 267/364
	1923	HO 348/4 and 17
RFR annual training:	1923	HO 267/339

	1923	HO 348/73
RNVR Division in Northern Ireland:	1923	HO 348/49
	1923–4	HO 267/382
Transfer of charts to Irish Free State	1923–6	HO 267/390 and 534
Visits of USN and RN vessels to Northern Ireland	1923–5	HO 267/338 and 340
Legal assistance for RN officers in criminal cases	1924	HO 267/473
Registration of the British Legion RN Club	1924	HO 267/491
Importation of Category C explosives by the Admiralty	1950–1	HO 401/22

Welsh Office

Naval base, proposed conversion to holiday camp	1940–6	BD 28/414–15
Admiralty water works for Llanegryn	1941–60	BD 11/770 and 821–2
Admiralty land requirements in Wales	1946–55	BD 28/261–2
RNAD Bridgend	1946–61	BD 41/174–6
Admiralty correspondence	1956	BD 23/24
Commercial development of Pembroke Dockyard	1957–66	BD 41/231
Use of Welsh language in Admiralty	1960	BD 23/204
Planning Division, dealings with Admiralty	1961–7	BD 28/747–8
RN Propellant Factory, Caerwent:	1964–7	BD 4/122
	1964–7	BD 40/57
HM Inspectorate of Schools, HMS *Conway*, HMS *Indefatigable*	1964–73	BD 50/1042
RNAD Milford Haven, maps	1967	BD 55/17–18
RNAS Brawdy	1968–75	BD 40/116–17
Disposal of RN sub-depot Dale Castle	1972	BD 32/28

18 General Register Office

This department was responsible for the central registration of births, marriages and deaths, and for conducting the national censuses.

Foreign registers and returns, including births, deaths and marriages at sea:	1627–1960	RG 33/1–163
(index)	1627–1925	RG 43/7
Marriages aboard HM Ships:	1842–89	RG 33/156
(index)	1842–89	RG 43/7
Correspondence, including RN births, deaths and marriages:	1874–1990	RG 48/1–3319
(Census enumeration of RN):	1900–1	RG 19/20
	1920–2	RG 19/58
	1959–61	RG 19/282
Census Returns: including HM Ships at home	1841 and 1851	HO 107/1–2531
(including HM Ships at sea and abroad):	1861	RG 9/4433–41
	1871	RG 10/5779–85

(Royal Navy):		1881	RG 11/5633–42
		1891	RG 12
(HM Ships):		1901	RG 13/5325–35
		1911	RG 14
		1921	RG 15
		1951	RG 16
		1961	RG 17
Circulars: Naval Marriages Act (1908)		1909	RG 41/2
(Naval Marriages Act 1915)		1915	RG 41/8
(RN marriages and deaths etc.)		1916–83	RG 41/9–13, 25, 37 and 78
Electoral registration: Portsmouth election and RN voters		1922–4	RG 50/5
National registration, recruitment under Military Training Act		1939	RG 28/207
Register of deaths from enemy action, Far East		1941–5	RG 33/11 and 132
Royal Commission on Population 1944–9, marriage allowance sample analysis of naval personnel		1946	RG 24/17

19 Ministry of Home Security, 1939–46

This wartime department was responsible for civil defence, particularly against air attacks.

O Division, air-raid shelters for naval establishments	1939–46	HO 205/15, 108 and 258
Key Points Intelligence Directorate: effect of air raids on naval supply and production	1940	HO 201/25
(war-production bottlenecks, Admiralty factories)	1945	HO 201/36
Intelligence Branch, naval intelligence reports etc.	1940–3	HO 199/128, 133, 137, 141–2, 150, 209, 424 and 442
Operation OVERLORD, Joint Planning Committee minutes	1943–4	HO 186/1699 and 1702
Research and Experiments Department		
War damage to private shipyards	1939–45	HO 192/1306–58
Ship damage reports (effect of bombs)	1940–3	HO 191/66
Camouflage Committee minutes	1940–3	HO 217/1–9
Bomb census: attacks on naval stations	1941–4	HO 198/131–2
(damage to surface ships)	1940–65	HO 198/201
Bomb-proof structures (USN Department)	1942	HO 195/13/332
Admiralty Fuel Experimental Station, trials	1942	HO 195/31/45
Damage to docks, harbours etc.	1942–3	HO 191/145
Naval mines	1942 and 1945	HO 196/12 and 30
Admiralty interest in line charges (snakes)	1943–4	HO 192/55
Naval decoy sites (Q Sites)	1944–5	HO 192/20
Visibility of targets in a naval searchlight beam	1944–5	HO 195/57/29 and 59/57–63

20 Foreign Secretary and Foreign Office, 1782–1979, Departmental Correspondence

The Foreign Secretary assumed the foreign responsibilities (the major part) of the former Northern and Southern Secretaries. This included many aspects of strategic and defence planning, and the collection of intelligence.

Correspondence with Admiralty:	1761–1822	FO 95/355–69
	1839	FO 84/301–3
	1840	FO 84/338 and 340
	1841	FO 84/383–5
	1842	FO 84/436–43
	1843	FO 84/492–8
	1844	FO 84/547–51
	1845	FO 84/606–12
	1846	FO 84/655–60
	1847	FO 84/701–6
	1848	FO 84/744–9
	1849	FO 84/781–5
	1850	FO 84/823–9
	1851	FO 84/863–6
	1852	FO 84/891–5
	1853	FO 84/924–6
	1854	FO 84/953–5
	1855	FO 84/980–1
	1856	FO 84/1008–9
	1857	FO 84/1037–8
	1858	FO 84/1067–70
	1859	FO 84/1096–100
	1860	FO 84/1122–4
	1861	FO 84/1148–50
	1862	FO 84/1182 6
	1863	FO 84/1206–9
	1864	FO 84/1226 9
	1865	FO 84/1251–3
	1866	FO 84/1266–8
	1867	FO 84/1280–2
	1868	FO 84/1293–5
	1869	FO 84/1309–11
	1870	FO 84/1327–9
	1871	FO 84/1345–6
	1872	FO 84/1358–9
	1873	FO 84/1380–1

	1874	FO 84/1403–4
	1875	FO 84/1419–20
	1876	FO 84/1456–8
	1877	FO 84/1488–90
	1878	FO 84/1520–2
	1879	FO 84/1549–50
	1880	FO 84/1576–9
	1881	FO 84/1604–7
	1882	FO 84/1624–5
	1883	FO 84/1647–8
(registers)	1808–90	FO 605/1–256
(register and index)	1822–90	FO 802/235
(Chief Clerk's department)	1854–1905	FO 366/400–1, 659, 688–92 and 745–6
Letters from Admiralty:	1777–1805	FO 83/2
	1801 and 1805	FO 95/9/3
	1805	FO 95/1/1
	1807	FO 95/1/6
	1808	FO 95/1/2
	1813	FO 95/7/7
	1815	FO 95/1/2
	1854–7	ADM 2/1698–701
(register and index)	1822–90	FO 802/235
(FOs etc.):	1812–13	FO 65/88
	1829–30	FO 78/182
(First Naval Lord)	1830	FO 95/9/5
Nootka Sound and Spanish Fleet, intelligence	1790	FO 95/7/4
Letters to Admiralty	1808–9	ADM 1/4279
Correspondence, slave trade	1816–92	FO 84/1–2276
Letters to public offices (including Admiralty)	1822–44	FO 91/1–11
Correspondence, Ottoman empire:	1827–8	FO 78/161–2 and 172–4
(blockade of Tangier)	1828	FO 52/30

21 Foreign Office, General Correspondence by Country, to 1906

The bulk of the Foreign Office's correspondence up to 1906 was organised by country rather than subject, but it includes much naval matter, for example:

Africa: Baikie's Niger expeditions	1853–60	FO 2/18, 23, 27, 31–2 and 34
(correspondence, including Admiralty):	1893	FO 83/1237–44
	1894	FO 83/1309–19
	1895	FO 83/1374–87

America (USA): Arctic expedition and HMS *Resolute*:	1855–7	FO 5/687
(Civil War)	1855–72	FO 5/933–1426
(Washington Conference)	1870–1	FO 5/1296–312
(register of correspondence)	1871	FO 317/2
(Geneva Arbitration):	1871–2	FO 5/1390–426
	1872	FO 97/439–40
(crimping in US ports)	1903	FO 5/2545
Brazil, naval reports on revolution	1894	FO 13/738
China: proceedings of HM naval forces at Canton	1856	FO 17/260
(reorganisation of Chinese Navy)	1885–99	FO 17/1170 and 1409
(status of Wei-Hai-Wei)	1902–5	FO 17/1767
Japan, Russian Fleet in Russo-Japanese War	1904–5	FO 46/660–2 and 668
Mexico, RN deserters, Mexico and British Honduras	1900–2	FO 50/530
Persia, proposed naval base in Persian Gulf	1900–5	FO 60/733–4
Russia, Baltic Fleet attack on British fishing boats	1904–5	FO 65/1729–35
Turkey: naval cemeteries	1855–99	FO 78/2012–13, 3196 and 5055
(Nile expedition, including naval operations)	1896–9	FO 78/4775, 4892–5 and 5049–52

22 Foreign Office, General Correspondence not Arranged by Country, to 1906

Other Foreign Office papers, not arranged by country, also cover naval affairs.

Naval intelligence:	1779–90	FO 95/7–8
	1781–1803	FO 95/2/1–3, 3/1–3 and 4/3
	1785	FO 95/4/6
	1790	FO 95/7/4
	[1793]	FO 95/4/6
Proposed expedition to River Plate	1790?	FO 95/7/4
Slave trade: including Admiralty	1816–92	FO 84/1–2276
(correspondence with Admiralty)	1838–67	FO 96/28–33
(RN officers' reports)	1857	FO 84/1040
Fugitive Slaves Commission, instructions to RN officers	1819–71	FO 84/1434 and 1441
Count Rosen, pension for intelligence to Baltic Fleet in 1810	1834	HD 3/6
Belligerent cruisers and prizes, Prusso-Danish War	1864	FO 83/248
Naval attachés, instructions etc.	1865–1908	FO 83/1648 and 2096
Foreign naval secrets	1874–86	FO 83/929
Naval salutes and exchange visits	1874–1905	FO 83/519, 796–7, 1766 and 2066–7
Blockades, general	1884–94	FO 97/570
Instructions to RN on outbreak of war	1887–1905	FO 83/1340–3, 1782 and 2093

Attack on British Schooner *Nemo*	1888–9	FO 97/515
Permissions to visit naval establishments	1889–91	FO 83/1072, 1127 and 1160
Hydrographic Conferences	1899–1905	FO 83/1722, 1845 and 2112
RNR	1902–3	FO 83/2202
Hospital Ships Conference, The Hague	1904–5	FO 83/2148

23 Foreign Office Confidential Print

The Foreign Office (and other departments) circulated for internal information printed copies of correspondence and papers on the issues of the day, often providing a convenient summary of the evidence scattered across many country- or subject-based record series.

French Fleet and dockyards	1811	FO 881/10185X
Niger expedition:	1840	FO 881/45
	1855	FO 881/671
	1862	FO 881/1110
Admiralty instructions to British Consuls	1845	FO 881/437
Admiralty rules on lights for steamers	1847	FO 881/98
Letters of marque and privateers:	1854	FO 881/334
	1856–7	FO 412/5
Naval operations at Canton	1856–60	FO 881/594–594A, 846 etc.
Slave trade, reports from RN officers	1858–86	FO 541/1–12, 20–6 and 47–50
Blockade of the Confederate States:	1861–3	FO 414/20–1
	1861–5	FO 881/1049–362
French ironclads and other naval intelligence	1862 etc.	FO 881/4150–1 etc.
Building of ironclads for Confederate States	1863	FO 412/11–13
Naval forces in the North American lakes	1864–5	FO 414/27
Draft law reports	1867	FO 96/258–345
Russian renunciation of 1856 treaty limits	1870	FO 881/1821
Regulations for admission of foreigners to dockyards	1873	FO 881/2769
Capture of Mombasa Fort by RN	1875	FO 881/2589
Suppression of slave trade:	1875	FO 881/2709
	1877 etc.	FO 881/3312, 3342, 3369, 3425 etc.
Movement of Mediterranean Fleet to Dardanelles	1878	FO 881/3432 and 3492
Privileges of mail steamers	1880–9	FO 412/20–1 and 31
Lists of British and foreign warships in commission	1881, 1886 etc.	FO 881/4423, 5260X etc.
Protection of submarine cables	1882–8	FO 412/19 and 22–5
Report on Spanish Fleet and dockyards	1884	FO 881/4916X and 5202X
Naval Estimates of foreign countries:	1884–5	FO 881/4964X
	1891	FO 881/6097X
	1894	FO 881/6461X

	1896	FO 881/6795X and 6970X
	1899	FO 881/7166X
Blockade of Greece by International Squadron	1886	FO 881/5471X
Anglo-French Naval Commission, New Hebrides:	1886–8	FO 881/5648 and 5687
	1886–8	FO 534/20–1
Colonial defence	1887–92	FO 412/33 and 51
French and Italian naval forces	1888	FO 881/5869X
Gilbert Islands Protectorate	1892	FO 534/58
Committee on Revision of Slave Trade Instructions	1892	FO 881/6543X
Naval prize regulations and procedure	1895	FO 881/8106
French naval policy and estimates	1899	FO 881/7108X
Report on foreign naval ordnance	1900	FO 881/7499X
Passage of the Dardanelles by Russian Fleet	1904–6	FO 418/20 and 37
Naval Prize Manual	1904–9	FO 881/8194X
Coaling of belligerent ships in international waters	1904–5	FO 412/77
Russian Baltic Fleet attack on British fishing boats	1905	FO 418/29
London Naval Conference	1906–8	FO 881/9328X, 9422X and 9750X
Collisions by HM Ships (compensation)	1907	FO 881/8858
Washington Naval Conference	1921–2	FO 412/116–18
Geneva Naval Conference	1927	FO 412/115

24 Foreign Office Registered Files, 1906–66

In 1906 the Foreign Office adopted a registered file system in which all its correspondence and papers were classified under a series of broad headings of which the most important was 'Political' (now FO 371/1–190967), including the War Department 1914–20, the Political Intelligence Department 1918–20 etc. These files were fully indexed, initially by a card index, subsequently in printed annual volumes. Naval affairs are to be found everywhere in these files and under many headings, some of the most important ones including 'Naval', 'Defence', 'General Defence', 'General Blockade', 'Political General Blockade', 'Planning Staff' and 'United Nations'. References to foreign navies are usually under the countries concerned. The following are a few examples:

Proposed naval conference	1908	FO 366/1144
Versailles Peace Conference: naval matters	1919	FO 608/248/14–35
(naval matters Russia)	1919	FO 608/200/15–19
Eastern Conference, Lausanne, naval terms	1922–3	FO 839/20, 39
Naval attachés: accommodation	1925	FO 366/824
(appointment)	1946	FO 366/1782
Admiralty procedure for dispatch of documents	1933	FO 366/918
Passport facilities for RN and RM officers	1933	FO 612/157
Chinese visas for naval officers	1933–8	FO 612/167
British subjects in Colombian Navy	1934	FO 612/173

Argentine Naval Commission	1938	FO 372/3281
Admission of Greek officer to RNC Greenwich	1938	FO 370/542
Admiralty Handbook on Abyssinia	1938	FO 370/566
Anglo-Scandinavian Naval Agreement	1939	FO 372/3352
Naval and war trade reporting officers	1939	FO 369/2530–2
Altmark incident	1940	FO 952/2
Political Warfare Executive, liaison with Admiralty	1941–4	FO 898/18
Naval operations in West Indies in 1803	1943	FO 370/827
Admiralty couriers for King's Messenger Service	1943	FO 850/13
Statue of a naval officer in Foreign Office	1944	FO 370/1048
British awards (medals etc.) to foreign naval personnel, and foreign awards to British naval personnel	1944–55	FO 372/3823, 3825, 4111, 4504, 6959, 7236, 7342 and 7352
Potsdam Conference, future of German Navy	1945	FO 934/4
Awards for rescuing crews of British ships	1946	FO 369/3590
Claims department, claims involving HM Ships	1946–7	FO 950/80, 138, 241
British naval cemeteries and war graves abroad	1946–51	FO 369/2502, 3745, 4024, 4056, 4088, 4090, 4115, 4135 and 4775
Publicity for Battle of River Plate	1947	FO 953/17
Publication of British Naval History of the Second World War	1948	FO 370/1711
Research Department, naval intelligence reports	1949	FO 370/1917
Corporal punishment in RN	1949	FO 370/1843
Sub-Lt. T Holland RNVR, allegedly held in Russia	1949	FO 369/4277
Duke of Edinburgh's engagements as RN officer	1950	FO 372/7061
Portrait of Admiral Cochrane for Rio Embassy	1950	FO 366/2863
Official History of the Second World War; draft of *The Economic Blockade*	1950–7	FO 370/2099, 2162, 2278 and 2513–18
Strategic importance of Formosa	1951	FO 371/92077
Duty-free privileges for Venezuelan Naval Mission at Barrow-in-Furness	1952	FO 370/2213
US request for naval stations in Bahamas	1953	FO 371/103553
Exchange of Christmas cards between hydrographers	1954	FO 371/108772
Maltese youths in Corfu seeking to join RN	1955	FO 369/5166
Naval victims of bomb at Bone, Algeria	1960	FO 369/5502
MoD's objections to vacating Admiralty Building	1964	FO 366/3336 and 3338
Visit to Portugal by Hydrographer	1965	FO 371/179949

25 Foreign Office Registered Files, 1966–75

In 1966 the Foreign Office adopted a new system of registered files grouped according to its geographical departments or 'desks'.

American and Latin American

Naval visits	1960 and 1970	FCO 7/1142 and 1470
Sales of ships etc.	1967–74	FCO 7/90, 173, 178, 241, 403, 1097–9, 1335, 1493, 1511, 1572, 1632, 1708, 1954–5, 2234, 2432 and 2615–16
Cuban warship requesting asylum	1968	FCO 7/557–8
Chilean independence celebrations	1970	FCO 7/1536
Passage for Mexican naval vessels	1970	FCO 7/1580–1
Naval visits to and from USA and Canada	1972–4	FCO 82/154, 461 and 464

Arabian and Middle East

Naval visits to Egypt	1974	FCO 93/410
Visits by Israeli Navy to Gibraltar	1974	FCO 93/454
Libyan naval training in UK	1974	FCO 93/375

Southern European

Malta Dockyard	1968–74	FCO 9/951, 1255, 1575–6 and 2040–1
Gibraltar, naval rules of engagement	1969–70	FCO 9/1078 and 1135
HMS *Ark Royal*, Spanish salvage attempt	1970–1	FCO 9/1303 and 1464
UK naval limitations in Mediterranean	1972	FCO 9/1476
RN training of HRH Prince of Wales	1972–3	FCO 9/1477 and 1636

South-East Asian

Singapore Naval Base	1967	FCO 11/91–2

Eastern

Sale of warships to Israel, Iran etc.	1966–73	FCO 17/1 1798

Far East and Pacific

US naval facilities on Diego Garcia:	1967–8	FCO 32/110–12
	1970–1	FCO 83/13–15
French naval visits	1972–4	FCO 32/935 and 1037

West and Central African

Warships and training for Nigeria:	1967–8	FCO 38/280–1 and 322
	1968–9	FCO 65/325–6
Naval facilities in Nigeria	1969	FCO 65/329

South African
Simonstown Agreement	1971, 1974	FCO 45/980 and 1613–16
Visits of HM Ships to Madagascar	1971	FCO 45/853
Diego Suarez Naval Base and French interests in Indian Ocean	1971	FCO 45/854
South African naval visit, political implications	1971	FCO 83/129

Western and United Nations
Western Fleet assembly	1967	FCO 27/380

Mediterranean
Malta Dockyard	1967–8	FCO 27/255 and 328–76

Northern
Warship visits etc.	1967–75	FCO 28/1–2434

East European and Soviet
Incidents involving HM and Soviet Ships	1968–72	FCO 28/831, 1153 and 2074
Romanian proposal for naval co-operation	1972	FCO 28/1997

North and East Africa
Defence aid to Kenya Navy	1967–8	FCO 31/239 and 241
Soviet warships in Casablanca	1968	FCO 39/468
Naval visits, naval mission etc. to Libya	1968–72	FCO 39/374–669 and 1267
RN participation in Beira patrol	1968–74	FCO 36/522–3, 668, 1487 and 1648
British participation in Ethiopian Navy Day	1971	FCO 31/792
Transfer of base to Mauritius	1971–2	FCO 31/902, 914 and 1244

Western European
Berlin defence planning	1967–8	FCO 33/281
Malta Dockyard	1967–8	FCO 33/374–5
Free French war memorial, Greenock	1971	FCO 33/1401
Naval protection of UK trawlers off Iceland ('Cod War')	1971–3	FCO 33/1313 and 2026–30
Anglo-French naval visits	1974	FCO 33/2442

Western Organisations
Restrictions on German naval forces	1967–71	FCO 41/271 and 879
Naval review	1968–9	FCO 41/368–9
Planning, strategy and NATO naval forces	1968–73	FCO 41/241–2, 656 and 1194
Soviet proposals for limitation of deployment of naval forces	1971	FCO 41/842

Naval visits	1971–3	FCO 41/816, 1081 and 1359
Symposium on Seapower, US Naval Academy, Annapolis	1973	FCO 41/1159
Naval on Call Force in Mediterranean	1973	FCO 41/1164

Gibraltar and South Atlantic

USN survey of Ascension Island for bunkering	1967–8	FCO 42/29
Sale of warships to Spain	1967–8	FCO 42/213
Gibraltar Dockyard:	1967–8	FCO 42/256
	1971	FCO 83/83

West Indian

USN jurisdiction	1967	FCO 44/97
Future of US naval base in Bermuda	1971–2	FCO 44/539
US naval firing range	1974	FCO 44/1005

Defence

Aden Naval Task Force	1967	FCO 46/64
Refit of HMS *Ark Royal*	1967–8	FCO 16/195
RN presence in Mediterranean	1967–8	FCO 46/2
Overseas visits of nuclear-powered submarines and warships	1967–74	FCO 46/111–12, 996–7 and 1152–6
Policy on supply of warships to foreign countries	1967–74	FCO 46/187 and 1241
Naval control of shipping	1967–70	FCO 46/103, 369 and 660
Anglo-Dutch naval collaboration	1968–73	FCO 46/441, 513–15 and 1086
USN facilities at Diego Garcia	1968–71	FCO 46/342–6 and 638–47
Training for Nigerian Navy	1969–70	FCO 46/467–9 and 544
Carrier force, HMS *Ark Royal*	1970	FCO 46/560
Planned closure of Far East Command	1970	FCO 46/618
Loan of RN personnel to Malaysia	1970	FCO 46/548–9
British involvement with Australian naval base at Cockburn Sound	1970	FCO 46/648
Joint NATO naval exercises	1970	FCO 46/666
Naval limitations in Indian Ocean; Soviet naval activity	1971–4	FCO 46/747–50, 870–1 and 1207
Anglo-French collaboration on naval gas turbines	1973	FCO 46/1085
Deployment of naval forces: flexibility of seapower	1973	FCO 46/951–2
Availability of RN vessels to meet overseas commitments	1974	FCO 46/1219
Disarmament, Soviet interest in naval limitations	1971	FCO 66/288

Consular

British naval cemeteries	1969–72	FCO 47/212, 385, 537, 544 and 592

Scientific Relations and Science and Technology

UK involvement in USN OMEGA Navigation System Project	1970	FCO 55/611
Overseas visits by nuclear-powered ships of RN	1970–1	FCO 55/537 and 736

Protocol and Conference

Implications of Prince of Wales serving in RN	1971–3	FCO 57/325, 421–2 and 553–6
Award for Rear-Adm. Templeton-Cotill	1973	FCO 57/489

Marine and Transport

Wreck of RFA *Ennerdale*	1970	FCO 76/50
Protection for UK trawlers, Cod War	1972	FCO 76/537–43

Personnel

Naval intelligence Singapore	1971	FCO 79/219

26 Foreign Secretary, Private Office

The Foreign Secretary's Private Office dealt particularly with matters of political sensitivity.

Sir Edward Grey, Admiralty correspondence	1905–16	FO 800/87–8
Sir William Malkin, legal opinions, German naval prize regulations, freedom of the seas etc.	1915–28	FO 800/920
American Civil War, seizure of British vessels	1915	FO 800/924
Removal of noxious persons from neutral vessels	1916–17	FO 800/942
C Harmsworth (Under-Secretary of State), 'The Blockade'	1919	FO 800/250
A Chamberlain, naval disarmament conferences etc.	1924–9	FO 800/256–63
Sir J Simon, naval disarmament conferences etc.	1931–5	FO 800/285–91
Sir Anthony Eden	1935–46	FO 954/1–34
Lord Halifax, including blockade and war aims	1938–40	FO 800/309–28
Blockade, Legal Sub-Committee, German exports	1938	FO 800/943
Lord Butler: Admiralty correspondence	1956	FO 1109/189
(pay of Naval Reserves)	1956–7	FO 1109/64
(secret minute by First Lord of Admiralty to Minister of Defence)	1957	FO 1109/65
G Brown, disarmament policy	1966	FO 800/959
Sir Alec Douglas-Home, Soviet naval activities in Cuba	1970–1	FCO 73/144

27 Government Code and Cypher School

The GCCS was established in 1918 to carry on the wartime work of wireless intelligence and cryptography which had been conducted by the Admiralty. It provided all the services and branches of government with cryptographic intelligence. 'Wireless News' was a bulletin summarising recent intercepts, mainly from eastern Europe.

'Wireless News'	1918–21	ADM 233/1–35
Histories of British signals intelligence	1914–45	HW 43/1–94
Naval Section: reports and correspondence	1914–46	HW 8/1–138
Room 40, GCCS Naval Section etc., papers	1914–51	HW 3/1–186
Reports of intercepted naval signals	1914–77	HW 41/1–432
Official Histories, First World War: History of German Naval Warfare	1914–18	HW 7/1–4
(W F Clarke, correspondence with Admiralty)	1915–17 and 1924	HW 7/24–5
Official Histories, Second World War:	1914–54	HW 50/1–95
	1938–45	HW 11/1–38
Cheadle Station, war diaries etc.	1917–45	HW 2/1–102
Security of naval cyphers	1917–50	HW 40/1–273
Diplomatic Section decrypts: (including Doenitz)	1919–45	HW 12/1–338
(International Naval Conference)	1930–6	HW 12/126–210
History of Work on Naval ENIGMA	1920–78	HW 25/1–34
Reports on Japanese naval communications	1928–39	HW 67/1
Co-operation with Russia on intelligence on German Navy	1931–45	HW 61/26–31 and 38–40
Policy papers, including NID papers etc.	1933–49	HW 14/1–164
Air Section reports, including naval air forces	1936–44	HW 21/1–92
Reports of Spanish activity	1936–45	HW 22/1–27
Naval war planning, expansion of naval signals intelligence	1937	HW 62/20/6
Naval Section, reports of naval decrypts	1938–45	HW 18/1–450
Naval accommodation and staffing at Bletchley Park	1939 45	HW 64/22
Intelligence summaries based on sigint	1939–45	HW 13/1–232
Combined Bureau Middle East, decrypts of Russian naval cypher messages	1940	HW 51/31
Liaison with naval intercept stations	1941–4	HW 51/16–18
Decrypts of German police communications, for naval section	1940–2	HW 16/6
Signals intelligence, including naval	1940–5	HW 1/1–3785
Sigint Centre Far East	1940–5	HW 4/1–31
German Section, including naval	1940–5	HW 5/1–767
Venona Project	1940–9	HW 15/1–62
German sigint reporting, mainly naval	1941–3	HW 73/2

German reading of British naval cyphers	1941–4	HW 73/1
Naval Section, Japanese naval decrypts	1941–5	HW 23/1–851
Reports to Admiralty and NID	1941–5	HW 19/278–86
Naval Section, Establishment Branch	1941–6	HW 64/1–4
Naval and Air Sections, reports based on Japanese Naval Air Force decrypts	1943–5	HW 27/1–64
Organisational charts for Naval, Military and Air Sections for Operation OVERLORD	1944	HW 20/545
Reports on Japanese Army and naval units	1944	HW 46/1
ISNAV, decrypts passed on naval ENIGMA links	1944–5	HW 19/261
Military Section, reports of Croatian naval traffic	1944–5	HW 26/1–5
Summary reports, Far East naval	1944–5	HW 44/1–9
Bulgarian naval activities	1944–5	HW 70
Weekly intelligence notes, Japanese Naval Air Force	1945–6	HW 28/137 and 139
Naval Section historical memoranda	1945–6	HW 3/134–49

28 Allied Control Commission for Germany and Austria

The British sectors of Germany and Austria, placed under military government on occupation in 1945, were in 1947 transferred to civilian administration under the Foreign Office. Its main series of registered files (FO 936/1–1430) includes, for example, naval control of shipping; the transfer of ex-German R-boats to the US Navy; Royal Navy seizure of German vessels under construction etc. Other files of naval interest include:

Allied Naval C-in-C Expeditionary Force	1943–4	FO 1038/146–7
Disposal of warships	1944	FO 945/863
Disposition of German warships	1944	FO 945/882
Naval Division, CCMS Naval Forces Section	1944–5	FO 1038/122–31
British naval forces Germany, progress reports	1944–7	FO 1005/1815–18
Naval Division, Austria, naval plans etc.	1944–8	FO 1020/366, 753–63 and 796
Permanent Committee on Naval Demilitarisation, minutes	1945	FO 1005/798
Commission for Naval Information	1945	FO 1038/145
Interrogation and intelligence reports, submarine blockade running	1945	FO 1078/37
Allied Control Authority, Naval Directorate: minutes	1945–6	FO 1005/794–7
(monthly reports)	1945–6	FO 1038/144
War Crimes Executive, Doenitz	1945–6	FO 1019/2 and 26
Tripartite Naval Committee/Commission, minutes etc.:	1945–7	FO 1038/132 and 156–8
	1946	FO 1036/698
	1950–5	FO 944/1130–1

	1953	FO 1005/1914
Wilhelmshaven: future	1945–8	FO 1051/617
(destruction of naval base)	1946–7	FO 943/75–6
RN organisation	1945–52	FO 1035/101
Destruction of Kiel Dockyard	1946	FO 938/72
Printing machine for RN armament depot	1946	FO 1031/44
Naval Division: work	1946–7	FO 945/8
(letters)	1946–8	FO 1007/430
(responsibility for disarmament)	1948	FO 1039/38
Future of Trappenkamp ex-naval depot	1946–7	FO 1006/418
War crimes, alleged murder of RN personnel	1946–7	FO 1012/734
Employment of ex-naval personnel:	1946	FO 1030/150 and 327
	1946–7	FO 1051/605
Redundant RN fuel installations, Cuxhaven	1946–7	FO 1062/422
German 'frozen' personnel (Dienstgruppen etc.), naval aspect	1946–8	FO 1038/181
Financial control of German naval services	1946–8	FO 1046/331
CSD transport organisation (naval aspect)	1946–9	FO 1038/191
Nuremberg Trial: Admirals Raeder, Doenitz and Schniewind	1946–55	FO 1060/489, 519, 1377 and 1388
Naval Committee (NAV), minutes	1947–8	FO 1005/815–18
Naval Document Centre (personnel records of German Navy)	1947–8	FO 1014/60 and 1011B
Control of ports, transfer from RN to CCG	1947–8	FO 1058/254 and 598
German naval facilities:	1948–9	FO 1032/1540 and 1575
(TVA Eckernforde)	1946–50	FO 1062/84–5, 430–1 and 501
(torpedo warhead depot, Tostedt)	1949–50	FO 1062/445
Transfer of craft from RN	1948–50	FO 1026/45–6 and 65
Four Power Naval Commission	1946–7	FO 1086/83 and 92–3

29 Other Foreign Departments

The Ministry of Blockade was in effect a Foreign Office department particularly concerned with the legal, commercial and diplomatic aspects of the allied naval blockade of Germany. The Ministry of Economic Warfare dealt with much the same business during the Second World War, including such subjects as the Blockade Committee, naval organisation, naval patrols in the Mediterranean and other places, oil for the Swedish Navy, sightings and attacks on enemy shipping, intelligence on movements of enemy shipping etc.

Ministry of Blockade, 1916–19

Foreign Trade Department, papers	1916–19	FO 833/1–18
Restriction of Enemy Supplies Department	1916–19	FO 845/1–11

Ministry of Economic Warfare, 1939–45
Papers   1939–45   FO 837/1–1338

30 British Ambassadors, Ministers and Consuls

These are examples of the very extensive domestic archives of British diplomatic representatives abroad, including much correspondence with the Admiralty and with Royal Navy officers on naval matters. From the nineteenth century the records are arranged geographically.

Consuls, letters to Admiralty (Mediterranean passes and intelligence):	1700–25	ADM 1/5114/13
	1719–1839	ADM 1/3825–48
	1738–42	ADM 1/5115/3–8
	1777–8	ADM 1/5117/8
	1786–90	ADM 1/5118/8
	1791	ADM 1/5119/11
	1792	ADM 1/5120/8
Consuls, letters from Admiralty (Mediterranean passes)	1730–1815	ADM 2/1319–25
Argentina: letters from officers of River Plate Survey	1871	FO 118/142
(Falkland Islands Naval Base)	1934	FO 118/654
(naval intelligence organisation, South America)	1938	FO 118/688
(visits of HM Ships)	1947	FO 118/758
(visit by Lord Mountbatten)	1963	FO 118/875
Brazil, Consul Bahia: from Admiralty	1815–87	FO 268/5
(from RN officers)	1821–90	FO 268/7 and 15
Brazil, Consul Pernambuco: from RN squadron at Rio de Janeiro	1865–80	FO 843/4, 7–8
(from Admiralty)	1877–80	FO 843/8
Brazil, Consul São Paulo, RN decorations	1947	FO 863/6
Brazil, Consul Rio de Janeiro, from SNO	1893–4	FO 128/197–9
Beirut, to and from RN officers	1840–3	FO 226/28 and 70
Belgium, to and from Admiralty	1815–84	FO 606/1–4, 10
Burma: naval affairs	1942–8	FO 643/8, 11, 68–9 and 89
(prize money in Burmese Navy)	1948	FO 643/89
Chile: to Admiralty and RN officers	1899–1916	FO 594/2
(from Admiralty and RN officers)	1881–92	FO 596/10, 17
(naval graves in Chile)	1932–6	FO 596/97
(HMS *Exeter*, assistance to earthquake victims)	1939	FO 596/98
(sale of British warships)	1949	FO 132/595
China: from RN officers:	1841–2	FO 677/21
	1902–4	FO 678/469–70

(naval affairs, in Chinese)	1837–60	FO 682/1974–93 and 2462–3
(naval affairs)	1848–1900	FO 1080/1–393
(naval operations, Canton)	1857	FO 228/234
(HM Ships, Wei-Hai-Wei)	1859–1917	FO 228/276–1997
(foreign officers in Chinese Fleet)	1895	FO 233/120/1
(German Navy in China)	1898	FO 233/122/8
(re-organisation of Chinese Navy)	1899	FO 233/123/16
(naval correspondence)	1905–10	FO 228/2407–8
(Wei-Hai-Wei, register of deaths, RN personnel)	1909–27	FO 681/69
(Naval Mission)	1914–17	FO 228/2644
(Kiangnan Dockyard)	1916–17	FO 228/2708
(use of Wei-Hai-Wei by USN)	1940	FO 676/438
(Chinese Naval Academy)	1948	FO 678/1314
Congo Brazzaville, rescue of *Empire Windrush* survivors	1954	FO 859/26
Danzig: Danish blockade	1849	FO 634/2
(blockade, prizes taken by HM Ships)	1854–5	FO 634/3–4
Denmark: including correspondence with Admiralty and RN officers	1781–1957	FO 211/1–847
(Anglo-Scandinavian Naval Agreement)	1939	FO 211/638
(visits of HM Ships)	1947	FO 211/708
Denmark, Consul Faroe Islands, naval matters	1941	FO 649/14–15
Ecuador, letters from RN officers	1830–61	FO 144/3, 8, 11, 16, 22 and 24
Egypt: letters to admirals	1833–9	FO 142/7
(duty on oil fuel for RN)	1915–25	FO 141/466/4
(enemy intelligence)	1917–18	FO 141/731/14
(salutes in Egyptian ports)	1917–29	FO 141/450/2
(HMS *Mallow* commended)	1918	FO 141/786/7
(Middle East situation)	1918	FO 141/790/9
(ship repair in Egypt)	1918–21	FO 141/456/2
(fraud of Navy Agent at Suez)	1921–3	FO 141/783/5
(Egyptian naval ranks)	1921–8	FO 141/480/24
(naval operations against Sudan disturbances)	1924	FO 141/805/2
(training of Egyptian officers)	1925–30	FO 141/485/1
(British Naval Mission to Greece)	1928–9	FO 141/507/1
(naval war graves in Egypt)	1930	FO 141/501/11
(small craft for service in Egypt)	1930	FO 141/619/5
(naval operations against Hejaz rebels)	1932	FO 141/724/5
(HM Ships and Egyptian customs)	1933	FO 141/760/10
(British naval stations in Persian Gulf)	1935	FO 141/533/22
(British fleet and war with Italy)	1935	FO 141/574/12
(compensation to Claridges Hotel, Cairo)	1937	FO 141/662/3
(Mutevellian's invention)	1937–8	FO 141/630/21
(French Fleet at Alexandria)	1942–3	FO 141/846 and 859

(Admiral Cunningham, audience with King Farouk)	1945	FO 141/1075
(Admiralty correspondence)	1946	FO 891/187
(British technicians in Egyptian Navy)	1951	FO 141/1445
Finland: naval affairs	1919–32	FO 511/1–87
(British naval war grave)	1925	FO 753/21
France, Consul La Rochelle, from Admiralty	1818–68	FO 623/5
French Indo-China: Naval Attaché's reports	1950	FO 959/52
(report of Naval Liaison Officer)	1950	FO 959/58
Genoa, accounts for supplying RN at Toulon	1793	AO 1/578/505
Greece: from FOs	1828–61	FO 286/6, 23, 37, 78, 105, 123 and 169
(to RN officers)	1828–59	FO 286/12, 97
(enemy submarine activities)	1917–18	FO 286/664
(Eastern Mediterranean Command)	1918–19	FO 286/699
(visits to British dockyards)	1919	FO 286/717
(purchase of warships)	1920	FO 286/748
(Greek Navy)	1921	FO 286/756
(Constantinople as Greek naval base)	1922	FO 286/812
(naval strength of Turkey)	1923	FO 286/862
(naval intelligence)	1935	FO 286/1125
Guatemala: to and from RN officers	1834–57	FO 252/8, 11, 43, 51, 71 and 75
(naval intelligence)	1940–5	FO 252/732, 739, 751, 755, 760, 768, 773 and 778
Honolulu: to Admiralty and RN officers:	1829–34	FO 331/7
	1839–58	FO 331/28–32
	1844–5	FO 331/47–8
	1872–4	FO 331/17
Ionian Islands (Corfu), to Navy Board and RN officers	1805–7	FO 348/6
Iran/Persia: naval forces in Persian Gulf	1863–93	FO 248/1364
(Bandar Abbas Naval Base)	1969–70	FO 248/1693 and 1695
Iraq: Basra Dockyard	1933	FO 624/1–2
(Persian Navy)	1935	FO 624/4
(Iraqi Navy, training etc.)	1938–43	FO 624/11, 14 and 34
(Naval-Military Mission)	1939	FO 624/17
(movements of HM Ships)	1941–2	FO 624/23 and 29
(naval and Marine discipline)	1942–4	FO 624/29 and 35
Iraq, Consul Basra: warship movements	1891–1901	FO 602/3
(naval defence of Kuwait)	1899–1902	FO 602/19
(lights and buoys in Shatt-al-Arab and Fao)	1903–14	FO 602/24
Italy, Consul Palermo: to and from naval officers	1848–9	FO 651/3
(to Admiralty and RN officers)	1875–95	FO 652/11–12
Japan: intelligence on Russian Fleet at Vladivostok	1920	FO 797/43
(Washington Conference)	1921	FO 262/1548

(Anglo-Japanese Alliance)	1921	FO 262/1514
(naval disarmament)	1931–5	FO 262/1767 and 1893
(attacks on HM Ships in North China)	1937	FO 262/2012
Jedda Agency, blockade of ports during Hejaz War	1924–5	FO 686/142
Korea: to Admiralty and RN officers	1901–5	FO 350/3
(naval graves)	1963	FO 1054/3
Latvia, to Admiralty	1837–47	FO 400/8
Liberia: naval graves	1927	FO 458/96
(1841 Niger expedition memorial)	1929	FO 458/104
Mexico: to and from RN officers:	1824–35	FO 203/16
	1924–9	FO 206/1
(from Admiralty)	1841–5	FO 206/2
(arming of British merchant vessels)	1939	FO 723/293
Morocco: letters from RN officers	1801–69	FO 174/11, 25, 31, 43, 54, 68 and 75
(blockade of Tangier)	1828–9	FO 174/31
(correspondence donated to NMM)	1950	FO 174/347
Netherlands, Consul Flushing, Admiralty reward to Belgian pilot boat	1861	FO 956/77
New Caledonia: correspondence with Australian Navy Office	1915	FO 969/40
(naval correspondence)	1940–7	FO 969/74–5
(from DNI, RAN)	1947	FO 969/85
Norway: letters from Admiralty	1827–79	FO 236/2
(to public offices, including Admiralty)	1832–1907	FO 237/1–26
(to and from Admiralty):	1823–53	FO 330/1
	1912–23	FO 330/13–17
Panama: from Admiralty and RN officers	1829–88	FO 288/2, 21, 26 and 29
(to Admiralty and RN officers)	1875–88	FO 289/20
(defence of Panama Canal)	1934	FO 288/205
(1930 London Naval Treaty)	1937	FO 288/206
Papeete, French Polynesia: to and from RN officers	1900–13	FO 687/11–13
(defences of Tahiti)	1901–8	FO 687/15
(bombardment of Papeete by German cruisers)	1914	FO 687/16
(death of daughter of midshipman of HMS *Bounty*)	1917–23	FO 687/18
(to and from Admiralty)	1940	FO 687/21
Peru: visit of British cruiser squadron	1925	FO 177/479
(proposed British Naval Mission)	1933	FO 177/492
Poland, Polish Navy	1929	FO 688/25/18
Portugal: from Admiralty	1839	FO 556/2
(sale of hovercraft)	1968–9	FO 179/622
Russia: Russian Fleet	1942	FO 181/969/25
(relations with Soviet citizens)	1943	FO 181/981/3
(USSR and German Navy)	1945–6	FO 181/1007/9 and 1013/2

Russia, Consul Archangel, to Admiralty	1833–54	FO 265/5
Spain: letters from RN officers	1810–16	FO 185/22, 27–8, 34–5, 43 and 62
(naval cemetery)	1921	FO 773/2
(complaints against crews of HM Ships)	1936	FO 773/13
Spain, Consul Barcelona, from Admiralty	1901–12	FO 637/42–57
Sweden: to and from Admiralty and RN officers:	1807	FO 334/14
	1807–8	FO 188/2
(to and from Admiralty)	1819–1950	FO 818/1–60
(Anglo-Scandinavian Naval Agreement)	1939	FO 188/315
(Swedish Navy)	1941	FO 188/367
Thailand/Siam: to and from RN officers:	1857	FO 628/1
	1863	FO 628/4
	1867	FO 628/5
	1879–80	FO 628/7–8
	1888	FO 628/12
	1891	FO 628/14
(to C-in-C China Station):	1870	FO 628/5
	1875	FO 628/6
	1880	FO 628/8
	1898	FO 628/19
(mutiny in Siamese Navy)	1934	FO 628/50
Trieste: to Admiralty	1819–1914	FO 590/1–7, 15 and 24
(to and from Admiralty and HM Ships: registers):	1876–1914	FO 591/1–7
	1919–40	FO 593/1–11
	1877	FO 335/140/7
	1881	FO 335/151/6
	1890	FO 335/172/5
(repair of Tunisian cruisers)	1825	FO 335/50/12
(Storekeeper-General's department)	1859	FO 335/110/3
(Hydrographic Office)	1868	FO 335/118/5
(from RN officers):	1813	FO 335/48/5
	1822	FO 335/49/10
	1836–7	FO 335/66/2
	1838	FO 335/67/13–16
	1841	FO 335/74/8–9
	1842	FO 335/78/7
	1843	FO 335/82/14–17
	1844	FO 335/88/1–2
	1845	FO 335/90/2
	1848	FO 335/96/3
	1849	FO 335/97/4
	1865	FO 335/116/5
	1881	FO 335/153/2 and 154/1

	1882	FO 335/155/10
	1883	FO 335/158/2
	1890	FO 335/172/5
	1891	FO 335/175/1
	1899	FO 335/202/3
(from Keith and others)	1800–9	FO 335/46/5
(from Nelson)	1804	FO 335/45/14
(from Collingwood)	1807	FO 335/46/4
(from Hood)	1810	FO 335/46/18
(from Cotton etc.)	1810	FO 335/47/1–2
(from Codrington)	1837	FO 335/66/8
(from Admiral Superintendent Malta Dockyard):	1847–8	FO 335/94/3 and 96/1–3
	1868	FO 335/118/5
	1891	FO 335/175/1
(to Admiralty):	1865	FO 339/96
	1899	FO 335/202/3
(to RN officers)	1856–8	FO 339/67
Tunis, letters from Admiralty	1681–99	FO 335/14/11
Turkey, letters from RN officers:	1831–60	FO 195/104, 198–9, 243, 309, 441, 485, 535 and 599
(Ionian lighthouses)	1861–2	FO 195/701
(visit of German warships)	1914	FO 195/2459
(passage of Dardanelles by Russian warships)	1914	FO 195/2459
(naval liaison)	1940	FO 195/2468
(Turkish Navy)	1940–57	FO 195/2464, 2470, 2487 and 2702–4
(funds for French ships at Alexandria)	1943	FO 195/2479
(visits by HM Ships)	1950	FO 195/2640
Tuscany, Consul Leghorn: recruitment accounts	1744–6	ADM 30/63/1
(distressed seamen etc.)	1790–1832	ADM 17/15–27
Venezuela, to and from Admiralty and RN officers:	1830–60	FO 199/6, 17, 29, 37, 41 and 46–7
	1843–58	FO 201/7 and 12
Uruguay: to and from Admiralty and RN officers	1844–1910	FO 505/14–350
(from Brazilian naval C-in-C)	1826–8	FO 505/2
(Anglo-French blockade)	1848	FO 505/31B
(naval court, HMS *Dwarf*)	1908	FO 508/9
(naval affairs)	1942 and 1950	FO 505/475 and 592
USA: including Admiralty and RN officers	1791–1907	FO 115/1–1468
(naval intelligence):	1912–14	FO 115/1687 and 1804–10
	1915–18	FO 115/1936–50, 2103–8, 2284–8 and 2420

(ventilation in warships)	1913	FO 115/1761
(Admiralty contracts)	1915	FO 115/1843
(blockade)	1915–19	FO 115/1857–65, 2023–4, 2178–82 etc.
(naval attachés, reports):	1917–20	FO 115/2275, 2534–5 and 2617–18
	1918–20	FO 115/2357–8 and 2618
	1921–9	FO 115/2688–3379
(US Navy)	1917	FO 115/2346
(London Naval Conferences)	1930–1 and 1935	FO 115/3393–7, 3405–9, 3412, 3416 and 3420
(USN building programme)	1932	FO 115/3399
(Japanese naval building programme)	1932	FO 115/3401
(British naval building programme)	1936	FO 115/3409
(Coronation naval review)	1937	FO 115/3413
(Anglo-German Naval Agreement)	1937	FO 115/3413
(navies of Brazil and Japan)	1937	FO 115/3414
(Anglo-American Naval Staff conversations)	1938–9	FO 115/3415 and 3417
(naval operations, including Pan-American Patrol)	1939–40	FO 115/3420–1
(British Purchasing Agency, naval stores)	1940	FO 115/3758
(repair of HM Ships)	1941	FO 115/3429
(blockade of occupied Europe)	1943–4	FO 115/3948, 3953, 4057, 4088 and 4094
(disposal of Japanese Fleet)	1945–7	FO 115/4205 and 4329
(US Fleet movements)	1946	FO 115/4268
(US Fleet anchorage Trinidad)	1948	FO 115/4419
(RN pensions and allotments)	1948	FO 700/82
(plates of naval charts)	1948	FO 700/85
(Lease-Lend destroyers, commemoration)	1950	FO 700/110
(naval visits)	1967	FO 1118/1
USA, Consul New York, naval correspondence	1894–9	FO 281/34
Yugoslavia: Yugoslav Navy	1941	FO 536/4
(naval cemeteries, Lissa)	1946–7	FO 988/1

31 Other Ministers and Representatives Abroad

Political Liaison Officer with US forces in Britain and North Africa, French Navy	1942–3	FO 660/4
Minister of State Middle East, French Fleet at Alexandria	1942–3	FO 921/27–8 and 74–9

Minister Resident at Allied Forces HQ North-West Africa
  (Algiers and Paris), naval affairs, including Force X   1943–4   FO 660/90–4
UK representative with French Committee of
  National Liberation at Algiers, French Navy   1944   FO 660/174

32 Treaties

The protocols are the agreed final drafts of treaties, and the ratifications the formal sealed copies exchanged by the parties.

Protocols

Treaties with Algiers	1695–1824	FO 93/7/1
Naval treaties etc. with Russia/USSR:	1801	FO 93/81/4
	1814	FO 93/81/16
	1937–8	FO 93/81/86–7
Naval forces on American lakes	1817	FO 93/8/9C
Sweden, naval instructions	1825	FO 93/101/14
Slave Trade Treaty, naval instructions	1841	FO 93/11/26
Anglo-French joint naval captures:	1854	FO 93/33/55B
	1855	FO 93/87/18
Naval conventions with Turkey:	1855	FO 93/110/8
	1957 and 1967	FO 93/110/140 and 167
Repairs of warships in Egypt	1866	FO 93/32/3
London Naval Conferences:	1908–9	FO 93/1/14 and 39
	1930	FO 93/1/123 and 127
Vessels sunk by Austrian Navy	1919	FO 93/11/75
Washington Naval Conference	1922–3	FO 93/1/63 and 79
Facilities for RN in China	1930	FO 93/23/36
Salvage of torpedoes	1934 and 1938	FO 93/1/170 and 197
Germany, naval armaments	1935–8	FO 93/36/136 and 147–8
Naval Armaments Treaty, UK, USA, France	1936 and 1938	FO 93/1/194 and 201
UK, France, Italy, piracy in Mediterranean	1937	FO 93/1/210
Naval construction	1938	FO 93/1/246
Naval Armament Treaty with Italy	1938	FO 93/48/104 and 106
Naval Armament Treaty with Poland	1938–9	FO 93/129/15–16, 23
US naval bases in British territories	1940–85	FO 93/8/190–472
Aircraft etc. for French Navy	1946	FO 93/33/395
Transfer of naval vessels to China	1948	FO 93/23/65
Blockade of China, detention of British ships	1952–3	FO 965/9 and 12
Training of Nigerian Navy	1969	FO 93/182/2
Terminating 1955 Simonstown Agreement	1975	FO 93/189/9
Salvaging wreck of HMS *Birkenhead*	1989	FO 93/189/12

Ratifications

Anglo-French Convention, joint naval captures	1854	FO 94/454
Arrest of RN officers by Brazilian police	1863	FO 94/556
London Naval Treaty	1930	FO 94/1119–26 and 1139
Facilities for RN in China	1930	FO 94/1145
London Naval Treaties, 1936, 1938	1936–9	FO 94/1301–2, 1309–15, 1338, 1344–5 and 1512

33 Secretary at War and War Office, 1661–1855

These records cover the Marine Regiments of the Army up to their final disbandment in 1749, and thereafter in respect of half-pay and widows' pensions until the death of the last survivors. The War Office also retained some responsibilities for the Corps of Marines (later Royal Marines) established under Admiralty control in 1755.

Commission books	1660–1873	WO 25/1–88
Letters to Admiralty:	1684–90	WO 4/1
	1697–1839	ADM 1/4316–51
	1703–1858	WO 4/2–272
(and naval departments)	1810–16	WO 4/430–455
(Commissariat)	1849–55	WO 58/45 and 60–1
Marine Regiments, establishments:	1715	WO 24/74C
	1739–48	WO 24/187–8, 198, 207, 219, 227, 237, 252, 266 and 276
Army lists	1754–1879	WO 65/1–168
Letters from Admiralty:	1758–63	WO 1/858–62
	1768–75	WO 1/875
	1769–83	WO 1/866–8
	1826	WO 43/257
Letters from various, including naval departments	1759–83	WO 1/863, 865–6, 869–71, 874, 876–7 and 891
Officers' widows pensions (including RM to 1826)	1815–56	WO 23/105
Reports from Transport Accounts Committee and Victualling Board on POWs	1817–22	ADM 98/311–13
GH out-pensions paid by WO	1842–83	WO 22/1–300

Correspondence, Particular Subjects

RM Barracks, Plymouth	1802	WO 40/16
Dockyard men, service in Army of Reserve	1803	WO 40/19
RN Hospital expenses	1807	WO 40/26
RM officers' widows' pensions transferred to Navy Estimates	1824–36	WO 43/569
Paymaster-General combined with Treasurer of Navy	1836	WO 43/650

Army and RN policy on half-pay for the insane	1843–5	WO 43/735
Payment of Greenwich out-pensions transferred to WO	1845	WO 43/850
Claim for wound by midshipman, Naval Brigade	1855–6	WO 43/1054

34 Secretary of State for War and the Colonies, 1794–1855

A third Secretary of State was re-established in 1794 as the Secretary for War, and the colonies were added to his department in 1801. During the Great Wars, 1794–1815, the new department was heavily involved in grand strategy and the conduct of combined operations, although on the coming of peace the colonies came to dominate its work.

African exploration, correspondence:	1794–1843	CO 2/1–25
(entry books)	1825–44	CO 392/1–4
Letters from Admiralty:	1794–1815	WO 1/686–737
	1816	WO 1/675
Letters from departments, including naval boards	1794–1815	WO 1/878–89
Letters to Admiralty:	1794–1816	WO 6/147–55
(secret)	1796	WO 1/405
Letters to Transport Board	1794–1816	WO 6/156–62
Letters to RN officers	1794–1855	WO 6/119–30
Nova Scotia, correspondence	1794–5	WO 1/17
Letters from Transport Board	1795–1817	ADM 108/19–27
Expeditions to South America and the Texel	1796–7	WO 1/178
Letters from C-in-Cs West Indies	1801–5	WO 1/118
C-in-C Mediterranean, correspondence:	1803–4	CO 173/1
	1808	CO 173/2
C-in-Cs, letters to departments, including Admiralty and Navy Board	1806–57	WO 3/192–329
Arctic expeditions, correspondence	1819–40	CO 6/15–18

35 Secretary of State for War and War Office, 1855–1964

These are miscellaneous and unregistered papers of naval relevance from the new, 1855 War Office, which combined the military responsibilities of the former War and Colonial Office, the Secretary at War and the Ordnance Board.

Commissariat, letters to Admiralty	1878–88	WO 58/173–8
Fortifications Branch, plans of Admiralty property	1860–6	WO 396/71–2
Transfer of land at Gosport to Admiralty	1864	WO 396/83
Ex GH in-pensions paid by WO	1868–70	WO 23/24
Letters from Adjutant-General RM	1868–74	ADM 200/1–5

Director of Artillery, coast defence of bases	1892–1948	WO 196/1–37
Spanish and Moroccan coastal fortifications	1938	WO 259/1
Joint Admiralty-WO communiqués	1942	WO 258/27
British Commonwealth POWs, Korean War	1953–4	WO 308/54
RN and RM casualties, Korean War	1953–4	WO 308/54
History of combined operations	1956	WO 277/30

Quartermaster-General

Abyssinia expedition, return from Naval Transport Department	1868	WO 107/8
'China Campaign, 1840–2', by Maj. Rothwell	1881–94	WO 273/1–2
Calais Base, Admiralty limitations	1915	WO 107/29
AA defence of merchant ships	1943	WO 107/236

36 War Office Registered Files

These are examples of War Office registered files of naval interest.

Memorial to RN and Army, Scutari, Crimea	1855–9	WO 32/5999
Awards of Victoria Cross etc. to RN and RM	1855–84	WO 32/7302, 7322, 7345, 7358, 7409 and 7567
Defence of Malta, Admiralty correspondence etc.:	1856	WO 32/7571
	1901–6	WO 32/6375
Naval defence of New Zealand	1858	WO 32/8253
Anglo-French operations against China:	1858	WO 32/8227
	1859–60	WO 32/6343
Chatham Dockyard, transfer of Gunwharf to Admiralty	1860–7	WO 32/18198
Grants of land to RN and Army officers in the colonies:	1860–83	WO 32/6214
(New Zealand)	1861	WO 32/8256
Reports of Committee on RN Cutlasses and Sword-Bayonets	1871–87	WO 32/7070
New ranks in RM	1873–5	WO 32/6698
Reorganisation of Army Medical Department	1876	WO 32/6386
Reports on Naval Brigade in South Africa	1878–81	WO 32/7687, 7708 and 7817
Army Act (1879), discipline of RN forces serving with Army	1881	WO 32/8698
Hayter Committee on RM officers' pay etc.	1883–4	WO 32/6277
Nile expedition, reports of RN Brigade	1884–5	WO 32/6106, 6108 and 6110
RN eligibility for Order of Bath etc.:	1884–5	WO 32/8362–4
	1895	WO 32/8371
	1900	WO 32/8373
	1906–7	WO 32/8478

	1910	WO 32/8521
Army and Navy chaplains:	1888	WO 32/6438
	1906–8	WO 32/5633
Pay of medical officers in RN and Army	1889	WO 32/6293
Admiralty policy on deferred pensions	1890–7	WO 32/6516
Joint Naval and Military Committee on Defence of Ports, memoranda	1890–9	WO 32/6256, 6295, 6355 and 6358
History of Admiralty/WO relations, Army transport etc.	1894–7	WO 32/8770
RN support in Ashanti expedition	1895	WO 32/7645
Committee on Dangerous Buildings, including Admiralty magazines:	1896	WO 32/7128
	1899	WO 32/7130
Skey Committee on Venereal Disease in Army and RN	1896–9	WO 32/6210
Administration of RN Relief Fund etc.:	1897–9	WO 32/8795
	1909–10	WO 32/9124
	1919	WO 32/14925
Inclusion of RM officers in Army List	1897–1954	WO 32/16601
Committee on Soldiers' Rations on Board Ship	1898	WO 32/8777
Seamen and dockyard employees exempted from Militia	1899	WO 32/6488
Alleged violation of Portuguese waters by British ships at Delagoa Bay	1899	WO 32/8015
Reports of naval operations in China	1900	WO 32/6145
Publication of dispatches of Naval Brigade in South Africa	1900	WO 32/7945–6
Naval prize law	1903	WO 32/8344–5
Admiralty representation on the Council of the British Red Cross	1904	WO 32/7150
Transfer of naval buildings at Woolwich to WO	1904–5	WO 32/6480
Military and naval resources of Falkland Islands	1904–12	WO 32/9157–8
Report of Joint Naval and Military Committee on Control of Signalling at Defended Ports Abroad	1905	WO 32/7170
Ruck Committee on Transfer of Submarine Mining to RN	1905–6	WO 32/6364
Sir E Ward's Committee on Naval Pensions	1906–21	WO 32/11204, 11212–17 and 11230
Candidates for Deputy Lieutenants	1908	WO 32/14758
RN and RM medals:	1855–1909	WO 146/1
	1909	WO 32/9046
	1915	WO 32/5416
Supply of shells to Navy	1910	WO 32/9214
Fair wages clause in Admiralty and WO contracts	1910–13	WO 32/9203–5 and 9275
Conference on pay of Admiralty and WO employees	1911	WO 32/7065
Admiralty proposal concerning coastal operations	1911	WO 32/7108
Comparison of Army and Navy pay	1911–12	WO 32/8896

National Insurance Act, relating to seamen	1911–12	WO 32/6486 and 9002
Guards for naval magazines	1911–12	WO 32/7187
Army appointments for RM	1912–14	WO 32/6921
'High Level Bridge' Admiralty-WO Conference	1913–14	WO 32/5294
RN Division, manning, supplying etc.	1914	WO 32/5084
Report on German shelling of Scarborough and Whitby	1915	WO 32/5265
Admiralty contractors	1915	WO 32/5338
Proposed transfer of RN Division to WO	1915–18	WO 32/5074–6
RN and RAF medals:	1916–18	WO 32/4968
	1947–51	WO 32/12520
Income Tax on Army and Navy pay	1917–19	WO 32/10292
Transfer of shipyards from RE to Admiralty	1918	WO 32/5106
Naval, Military and Air Forces (Prolongation of Service) Bill	1918–19	WO 32/9351
Russian Civil War, naval operations	1918–20	WO 32/5671–2, 5684, 5696 and 5710
Navy and Army Canteen Board	1918–24	WO 32/5445–7, 5503, 5506, 5510–11 and 5514
Execution of four men of RN Division for murder	1919–20	WO 141/41
Secret Service, record of meeting at Admiralty	1919	WO 32/21381
Naval History of War by Sir J Corbett, Churchill's objections	1919–21	WO 32/4825–7
Joint Service Committee on Defences of Dardanelles	1919–25	WO 32/5132–3
Peace Treaty with Hungary, naval clauses	1920–1	WO 32/5560
Military, Naval and Air Commissions of Control in Germany	1921–2	WO 32/5794
RN Division war graves, Somme	1921–3	WO 32/5891
Naval memorial, Chatham:	1921–3	WO 32/20465
	1930	WO 32/20663
	1949–60	WO 32/20695
Amalgamation of Works Departments of Navy, Army and RAF	1922	WO 32/4047
Amendments to Naval Discipline Act	1922	WO 32/9355
Washington Naval Treaty and defence of Hong Kong	1922–38	WO 32/5957
RM retired pay	1924–5	WO 32/10474
Explosives Act 1925, Admiralty request for Law Officers' opinion	1925	WO 32/18111
Court martial procedure for RM	1925–36	WO 32/3993–4
British naval and military graves Yokohama	1925–6	WO 32/4147
Cost of Singapore Naval Base	1926–31	WO 32/9611–12
Naval, Military and Air Force Chapels Act 1932	1926–59	WO 32/4033, 12465–6, 12888–90
Alterations to Army List for RM	1928	WO 32/2965

Erection of USN monument in Gibraltar	1928–9	WO 32/3563
Naval aspects of defence of Singapore	1929–30	WO 32/3628
St. Helena, transfer to colonial government of Admiralty buildings	1929–34	WO 32/17522
Admiralty scheme to reduce pay of ratings	1933	WO 32/3022
Cost of military programmes at Singapore Naval Base	1934–9	WO 32/3639
Pensions (Navy, Army, Air Force and Mercantile Marine) Bill 1939	1938–42	WO 32/10298
Naval Reserve Forces	1939–40	WO 32/9978
Thanks for RN evacuation of troops from Norway	1940	WO 32/9631
RN land experimental trench machines:	1940	AVIA 11/2
	1941–56	WO 32/9938
Naval pensioners given commissions	1940–4	WO 32/10586
Amendments to Army Act concerning naval C in-Cs	1941	WO 32/10069
Proposal to transfer Maritime Regiments, Royal Artillery to RM	1942	WO 32/10374
Promotion of RM officers to Army	1942	WO 32/10587
RM Division of Expeditionary Force	1942–3	WO 32/10414
Sinking of SS *Scillin* by HM s/m P212	1942–3	WO 32/18501
Exchange of RN personnel in Italian hands	1943–5	WO 32/10727
Naval land bombardment observed from air	1944–9	WO 32/11038
Combined operations, requirements for ships etc.	1945–6	WO 32/11540
Prizes for service music	1945–6	WO 32/11656
Admiralty reports on recovery of POWs from Far East	1945–6	WO 32/11697
RM Commandos, Amphibian Support Regiments RM	1945–7	WO 32/11539
Amalgamation of common services of Army, Navy, RAF	1946	WO 32/11856
Polish naval forces	1947	WO 32/12255
WRNS and WAAFs enrolled in ATS	1947–9	WO 32/12617
Re-formation of RM Cadets	1947–50	WO 32/12391
Award of DSO to Lt.-Cdr. J S Kerans RN, HMS *Amethyst*	1949	WO 32/18116
Promotion to Admiral of the Fleet, Admiralty correspondence	1949–53	WO 32/21386
Naval Discipline Act	1951–2	WO 32/14534
Merchant Navy memorial, Tower Hill	1951–3	WO 32/15821
Landing ships tank, control and operation in peacetime	1951–63	WO 32/14852
RM guard at Buckingham Palace in Coronation year	1952–3	WO 32/16178
Compensation claim for treatment in RN Hospital	1952–4	WO 32/19598
RN ratings in military prisons	1952–7	WO 32/14980
Purchases of land by Admiralty	1952–7	WO 32/20881, 20883 and 20890
Arrangements for RN review, Spithead	1953	WO 32/17792
Navy, Army and Air Force Reserves Bill	1953–63	WO 32/15200–2
Courts martial on troop transports	1953–4	WO 32/15257

Navy, Army and Air Force Act 1954	1953–69	WO 32/15730
Sale of RNAS Hatston, Kirkwall	1955–70	WO 32/20286–7
Transfer to Admiralty of Fort George, Mauritius	1956–61	WO 32/16682
Joint Services Guided Weapon Establishment, Hebrides	1957–69	WO 32/17467
Use of Sheerness and Southsea saluting stations by Admiralty	1958	WO 32/17346
Replacement landing ship tank, *Sir Lancelot*	1958–69	WO 32/21606
New design LSL:	1959–64	WO 32/21660–1
(trials)	1962–4	WO 32/19975 and 20350
(armament)	1966–9	WO 32/21229
Port facilities, Cyprus	1959–64	WO 32/19164
Title documents to former RN Dockyard Woolwich	1960–6	WO 32/20933
RM mutiny in Russia 1919	1961–3	WO 32/19602
Transfer of Army and Admiralty lands to government of Jamaica	1961–72	WO 32/21787
Command etc. of 3 Commando Brigade, RM	1963–4	WO 32/19531
Landing ship assault trials	1963–4	WO 32/19534
Sale of land by Admiralty	1964–9	WO 32/20867
Disposal of Hong Kong Dockyard	1965–7	WO 32/21281
Naval arms embargo of South Africa	1965–9	WO 32/20753
Sale of RN Careers Office, Hartlepool	1966–9	WO 32/20307
Sale of Admiralty Factory, Alloa	1966–70	WO 32/20285
Biological warfare detection, Naval, General and Air Staff target	1969–73	WO 32/21768

37 War Office Reports and Memoranda

These reports and memoranda were distinct from the correspondence in the War Office registered files, but cover a similar range of subjects.

Black Sea naval operations, sick and wounded	1855–6	WO 33/1–2A
Baltic naval operations	1856	WO 33/2A
Admiralty transport regulations	1858	WO 33/6A
Report of the Committee on Ordnance	1859	WO 33/7
Effect of rockets against shipping	1859	WO 33/7
Defences of Malta	1859	WO 33/7
Order for anchoring ships off Pei-Ho, China	1860	WO 33/9
Proposed Spithead forts	1861	WO 33/10
Transports and store ships for Canada	1862	WO 33/11
Trent affair	1862	WO 33/11
La puissance maritime de la France by Captain Comte de Villeneuve	1862	WO 33/11
Committee on Venereal Disease in the Army and Navy:	1863	WO 33/12

	1866	WO 33/17A
Report on victualling troops on board ship	1863	WO 33/12
Defence of Canada and British naval stations in north Atlantic	1865	WO 33/15
Fortifications for defence of home dockyards:	1866	WO 33/17A
	1874	WO 33/26
Committee on Floating Obstructions and Sub-marine Explosive Machines	1866	WO 33/17A
Defences of Malta and Gibraltar against ironclad ships etc.	1867	WO 33/18
Revised Army and Navy Signal Book	1869–70	WO 33/20 and 21A
Committee on Fitting Troop Ships to Carry Horses	1870	WO 33/21A
US Submarine Mining Establishment and US Naval Torpedo Station	1874	WO 33/26
Joint WO and Admiralty Committee report, HMS *Oberon*	1877	WO 33/30
Method of paying RM	1878	WO 33/32
Army of Ireland, naval reports on suitable places to land troops	1879	WO 35/39–42
Discipline of land forces on board HM Ships	1880	WO 33/35
Report of naval officers attached to the Chilean and Peruvian navies	1881	WO 33/36
RM officers on staff of auxiliary forces	1883	WO 33/40–1
Committee on Pay and Service of RM	1883	WO 33/41
Inter-Departmental Committee on Receipt of Naval or Military Pay with Civil Salary	1885	WO 33/44
Employment of naval and military officers under colonial government	1886	WO 33/46
Promotion in RM	1886	WO 33/46
Inter-Departmental Committee on Transfer of Naval Armaments to Admiralty	1886	WO 33/46
Report of Director of Army and Navy Contracts	1888	WO 33/48
Committee on Pay etc. of Medical Officers in Army and Navy	1889	WO 33/49
Conveyance of reinforcements to colonies in event of war with a maritime power	1889–91	WO 33/49 and 51
Relations between Intelligence Departments of WO, Admiralty and India	1890	WO 33/50
Committee on the Assimilation of Army and Navy Stores	1890	WO 33/50
Claims between WO and Admiralty	1892	WO 33/52
Guide for NCOs and men of the German Army and Navy who are candidates for employment in the Imperial and Prussian Civil Services	1894	WO 33/54
Notes on Navy and Army of USA	1895	WO 33/55
Extension of Hong Kong Dockyard	1896–9	WO 33/1575
Inter-Departmental Committee on Losses of Army and Navy Stores	1897	WO 33/77
Inter-Departmental Committee on Payment of Army and Navy Pensions	1898	WO 33/143

Regulations for commissions in Medical Department of RN	1899	WO 30/114
Dispatches from Naval Brigade in South Africa	1900	WO 105/8
Admiralty-WO Conference on Coast Defence of UK	1900	WO 33/189
Instructions for entry of HM Ships into defended ports in wartime	1901	WO 33/191
Admiralty-WO Conference on Naval and Army Meat Reserves at Gibraltar	1902	WO 33/237
Recommendations for gallantry awards, RN, South Africa	1902	WO 108/156
Land exchanges between WO and Admiralty, Hong Kong	1903–6	WO 33/1605
Committee on Transfer of Mines etc. to RN	1904–5	WO 33/341 and 366–7
Naval and Military Conference on Overseas Expeditions	1905	WO 33/344
Joint Admiralty-WO Committee on Instruction for Royal Garrison Artillery	1905	WO 33/385
Joint Naval-Military Conference on Regulation of Traffic at Defended Ports	1906–8	WO 33/398 and 450
Residence of RN C-in-C East India Station at Kandy	1907	WO 33/438
RN and military staff tour	1907	WO 279/13
Joint RN and military manoeuvres, Malta Command	1908	WO 279/519
Situation of UK in event of war with a European maritime power	1908	WO 33/462
Transfer of land in Malta to Admiralty	1908–13	WO 33/1623
Manual of Combined Naval and Military Operations	1911–13	WO 33/569 and 644
Joint Naval and Military Committee on the Examination Service	1913	WO 33/652
WO-Admiralty Conference on Compensation for Damage done by Gunfire	1913	WO 33/658
Numbers of troops conveyed by sea, including names of ships	1914–18	WO 33/716, 740, 780, 805, 886 and 926
Gallipoli campaign photographs, including warships etc.	1915–16	WO 317/1–14
Admiralty War Staff/General Staff Conference on Possibility of Attack on UK	1916	WO 33/742
Naval co-operation for internal security in India	1932–5	WO 33/1304
Rules on allotment of service wireless call signs	1933	WO 33/1318
Conditions of service of officers in the armed forces	1938	WO 163/608
Anglo-French Joint Service Conference, Singapore	1939	WO 33/2338
List of Service trades in RN, Army and RAF	1939	WO 287/107
Polish Navy attached to RN	1939–50	WO 315/19
Medical report by senior medical officers of RM sub-area, Sicily	1943	WO 222/505
Judge Advocate-General, war crimes: examination of wreck of German liner *Deutschland* by RN divers	1945	WO 309/593
(ill-treatment of RN and RM personnel):	1945	WO 309/1589
	1944–7	WO 311/313 and 330
(scuttling of U-1277):	1946	WO 309/272 and 775
	1946	WO 311/289
Coast artillery and Maritime Royal Artillery	1945–6	WO 33/2411, 2498 and 2545

Medical Services of the armed forces	1946	WO 163/485
RN and RM Reserves Bill and Navy, Army, Air Force Reserves Act	1959	WO 296/48

38   Chief of the Imperial General Staff

The Chief of the General (later Imperial General) Staff was the professional head of the Army.

Papers, including RN	c.1904–13	WO 105/45–8
Correspondence with Admiralty	1938	WO 216/110
Senior Officer Trincomalee	1944–5	WO 216/187
Facilities at Gibraltar for USN	1948	WO 216/692
Visit of US dignitaries	1948–9	WO 216/940
RM Commando Brigade for Korea	1950	WO 216/350
Officers to attend Joint Services Staff College and RN Staff College	1952	WO 216/483
Organisation of RN Mediterranean Command	1952–3	WO 216/544
Role of RM	1956–61	WO 216/927

39   Directorate of Military Operations and Intelligence

Registered files from the Directorate (at some periods, Directorates) which covered the most important functions of the General Staff.

Anglo-Japanese naval talks	1902–12	WO 106/48
Naval operations in China	1906–12	WO 106/25–6
Imperial Conference at Admiralty	1909	WO 106/6293
Preparations (including naval) for Expeditionary Force to France	1910–14	WO 106/49–51
Inter-Departmental Conference on Shipping (Slade Committee)	1914	WO 106/49B/2
Report on the Italian Navy	1914	WO 106/752
Combined operations, naval orders	1915	WO 106/705
Naval co-operation with General Allenby	1917	WO 106/724
Supreme War Council, military, naval and air representatives at Versailles	1919	WO 106/326
Military situation reports, including German naval bases and Navy	1922–41	WO 190/1–893
Singapore Naval Base, policy etc.	1924–36	WO 106/132–3
Instructions to Naval C-in-C and GOC British troops in China	1929–34	WO 106/96
'Certainty of an Anglo-Japanese War' (précis of book by Japanese naval officer)	1933	WO 106/5526

Naval intelligence reports, Hong Kong	1937–9	WO 106/5355–6
Naval intelligence on Dutch East Indies	1937–46	WO 208/1601–2 and 1679
General Staff Shanghai, naval intelligence	1939–41	WO 208/293–6
Combined Services Detailed Interrogation Centre UK, reports of interrogations	1939–45	WO 208/4117–237, 4292–3, 4363–7, 4969 and 5016–18
FAA, including aircraft carriers in British Pacific Fleet	1939–44	WO 193/680
Combined operations	1939–45	WO 193/378–410
Combined operations, Joint Planning Sub-Committee and Inter-Services Planning Staff	1939–45	WO 193/780–825
Intelligence reports passed from Admiralty	1940	WO 106/1663
Mobile naval batteries	1940	WO 193/532
RM and combined operations:	1940	WO 193/404
	1940–1	WO 193/387
Reports on Japanese naval dockyards and establishments	1940	WO 208/881, 886 and 891
Naval Command, Iceland	1940–2	WO 106/3039
Papers for Admiralty liaison officers	1940–2	WO 193/435
Naval and shipping movements, French Indo-China	1940–3	WO 208/640
Mobile naval base defence organisation:	1940–3	WO 193/226
	1944–5	WO 193/225
Naval strategy and general shipping matters	1940–5	WO 193/138
Protection of shipping	1940–5	WO 193/531
Combined operations, plans for Operation CLAYMORE	1941	WO 193/797
Landing craft and ships for assault operations	1941–5	WO 106/4129 and 4144–6
Naval C-in-C, North-West Africa, planning memorandum	1942	WO 106/2701
Report by US NID	1942	WO 208/594
Madagascar, Operation IRONCLAD, Admiralty and Force F	1942	WO 208/1520
South African Dockyard, Salisbury Island, Durban	1942–3	WO 106/4938
Inclusion of RM Division in invasion force	1942–4	WO 106/4199
Naval matters	1942–5	WO 106/4547–50
Translations of enemy publications (including naval)	1942–5	WO 208/2297–817
Chinese Naval Attaché in Australia, dispatches to Chunking government	1942–5	WO 208/394
Allied naval task force to re-occupy Andaman and Nicobar Islands	1942–6	WO 208/63–5
Survey of Solomon Islands, including maps and charts	1943	WO 208/1643–4
US naval intelligence on Japanese landing craft	1943	WO 208/952
NID Handbook on Greek Railways	1943–4	WO 208/700
Chiefs of Staff intelligence reports	1944–5	WO 106/4293–301
Report on German naval gunnery	1944	WO 208/4207
US Joint Army-Navy Intelligence Study of Philippines	1944	WO 208/1719–29
Reports from SBNO Archangel	1944–5	WO 208/1850

Japanese naval respirators and chemical warfare	1944–5	WO 208/2226 and 2236
MI9, awards to RN officers and men for escaping prison camp	1944–6	WO 208/5362–77
Operation DRACULA, naval plans for capture of Rangoon	1945	WO 193/905
Japanese naval suicide attack boats	1945	WO 208/1017
Photographic interpretation report, Bangkok Naval Ordnance Depot	1945	WO 208/1938
MI9 Handbook on Jungle Survival for naval personnel	1945	WO 208/3427
Naval intelligence reports from Hong Kong and SEAC	1945–6	WO 208/750A–B
British Intelligence Objectives Sub-Committee, Japanese naval operations etc.	1945–6	WO 208/3887, 3872, 3877 and 3897–8
Liberated POW interrogation questionnaires, including naval	1945–6	WO 344/360
Mutiny of RIN	1946–7	WO 208/3816

40 Other General Staff Directorates

Registered files from other Directorates of the General Staff.

Geographical Section, later Directorate of Military Survey

Maps and plans (including charts, plans of naval bases etc.)	1627–1953	WO 78/1–6008
Gallipoli campaign naval operations, maps etc.	1915	WO 301/619–27
Meeting of allied naval and military advisers	1920	WO 301/640
Naval operations in the Cameroons, charts	1915	WO 300/155, 159 and 163
Military, naval and RNAS operations, east Africa, charts	1915–16	WO 300/403–6
Charts for FAA	1935	WO 181/77
RAF abridged catalogue of Admiralty charts:	1942	WO 401/73
	1944	WO 401/75
Correspondence with Hydrographic Office	1967–70	WO 181/327

Civil Affairs

Allied Control Commission for Italy, Naval Sub-Commission papers:	1943–5	WO 220/342
(disposition of naval and merchant ships)	1943–7	WO 220/346

Tactical Investigation

Combined operations	1943–5	WO 232/63–4

Air

Correspondence with Admiralty on misuse of Red Cross flag	1943	WO 233/54

Signals
Correspondence with Admiralty on W/T frequencies	1941	WO 244/2

Staff Orders
Operation SIDEWAYS, RN and 51st Division	1940	WO 260/39

Prisoners of War
POW lists, naval forces	1943–5	WO 392/7, 17 and 21

41 War Office, Medal Rolls

These are lists of recipients of campaign medals and decorations.

Medal Rolls (including RN, RN Brigade, RM, RM Artillery, Royal Indian Marine etc.)	1793–1949	WO 100/1–493
Recommendations and awards of Victoria Cross	1856–1975	WO 98/1–11
Register of Distinguished Service Order	1886–1945	WO 390/1–13
RM Labour Corps	1914–18	WO 329/641
RM, RMA, RMLI, RNVR, RN Division, RNAS	1914–18	WO 329/2305, 2956 and 3272
Mombasa Marine Defence Regiment	1914–18	WO 329/2940
Military Medal (awards to RN and RM)	1930–48	WO 326/1
Army awards to RN	1940	WO 373/80/3
Army awards to RM	1942–6	WO 373/88/1

42 Military Headquarters

All military forces in the field came under the command of a Commander-in-Chief or GOC. These reports and files are examples of internal or domestic records from their headquarters.

Den Helder expedition	1799	WO 28/350
Crimea, naval reports	1854–6	WO 28/183–4
Nile Expeditionary Force, Atbara River	1898	WO 28/369
First World War		
Evacuation of Anzac and Suvla	1915	WO 158/585
Naval operations and actions	1915–19	WO 158/663B, 717, 721 and 727
Intelligence circular, naval aircraft	1917	WO 158/993–4
Naval and Military Conference on Water Transport, Dar-es-Salaam	1918	WO 158/904
Enquiry into indiscipline of 6 Battalion RM	1919	WO 158/969
Army of the Black Sea, naval questions	1919	WO 158/745

Joint Service Dardanelles Committee	1919	WO 158/796
Report on situation in Constantinople	1921	WO 158/779
Norway campaign, naval messages	1940	WO 198/3

Home Forces

Anti-invasion measures	1939–45	WO 199/1–3391
Coast defence, including use of naval guns	1939–45	WO 199/2445–52
Defence of Admiralty if moved to Bath	1940	WO 199/1707
RN mobile batteries as anti-tank weapons	1940	WO 199/1694
Operations in connection with French ships	1940	WO 199/2189
RM Brigades, order of battle	1940–1	WO 199/2034
Naval aspects of invasion	1940–2	WO 199/1419
RE liaison with RN on mining of beaches	1940–2	WO 199/2524
Defence of RN air stations	1940–4	WO 199/8–9
Naval co-operation	1940–4	WO 199/431–7
Coast artillery, RM Siege Regiment, naval defence batteries	1940–4	WO 199/519–40
RM directly-controlled static units	1941–2	WO 199/1493
Evacuation of naval ammunition in event of invasion	1941–3	WO 199/2669
Defence of RN bases and Admiralty establishments	1941–4	WO 199/56, 73 and 77
Protection of RN wireless stations	1941–4	WO 199/2538
Naval rocket projectors for beach defence	1942–3	WO 199/1428
Co-operation with RN, defence of Orkney and Shetland	1942–3	WO 199/2723
Transfer of RDF stations to RN	1942–4	WO 199/539
Operation OVERLORD: naval committees	1943–4	WO 199/1243
(RN commitments)	1944	WO 199/3169
(naval movements)	1944	WO 199/2389
Re-organisation of RM	1943–5	WO 199/680
Operation orders, Naval Task Force 127	1944	WO 199/2258
Joint Service postal censorship	1944	WO 199/3082
Infantry training, RM and RM Brigades	1945	WO 199/831, 857

Middle East Forces

Naval situation report	1939	WO 201/2478
Conference on Strategic Situation in HMS *Warspite*	1939	WO 201/2042
RN fuelling base at Suda Bay	1940	WO 201/3
Combined operations, including RN co-operation	1940–4	WO 201/713–805
French Force X	1942–3	WO 201/2262
Joint Service mission to Turkey:	1944	WO 201/1176
(naval subjects)	1944	WO 201/1170

Supreme Headquarters Allied Expeditionary Force

Composition of allied naval forces	1943–4	WO 219/31
Combined Naval Expeditionary Force	1943–5	WO 219/104

PM's minutes to First Lord of Admiralty	1943–5	WO 219/190
Naval defence in southern France	1944–5	WO 219/344
Russian Naval Mission itinerary	1944–5	WO 219/183
Assignment of naval officers to SHAEF	1944–5	WO 229/58/4
Adjutant-general, organisation of Naval Staff, naval plans etc.	c.1943–5	WO 219/388–1229
Naval guns	1944	WO 229/52/28
Awards to naval personnel	1944–5	WO 229/34/5
French Navy	1945	WO 229/29/9
US naval supply	1945	WO 229/43/10
Naval signals:	1943–4	WO 219/4176 and 4381
	1943–5	WO 219/4313 and 4371
	1944	WO 219/5331–5332
Construction of Mulberry harbours:	1943–4	WO 219/377–82 and 947–57
(photographs)	1944	WO 240/1–2
Memoranda on naval gunnery, naval mines	1943–5	WO 219/2024–63
German passive naval defences	1944	WO 219/5121
History of US naval bases in UK	1944	WO 219/3434
Censorship of naval mail	1944–5	WO 219/1705
Naval plans	1944–5	WO 219/2178, 2214, 2378, 2545, 2611, 2619 and 4579–80
Allied Naval Command Expeditionary Force, administration	1944–5	WO 219/4784
Seizure of German naval and merchant vessels	1944–5	WO 219/3383–4
Naval Dispatch Boat Service	1944–5	WO 219/4150 and 4485
Supreme Commander AEF, orders to German Navy	1945	WO 219/5178
SHAEF Mission to France, French Navy	1944–5	WO 202/769
SHAEF and 21 Army Group (microfilms): naval papers	1944–5	WO 229/3/31
(naval supplies)	1944	WO 229/13/16
(naval vessels, operations etc.)	1945	WO 229/88/19

South-East Asia Command

Japanese naval and air strength	1939–4	WO 203/5036
Naval operations	1939–5	WO 203/1189, 2594, 3651, 3654, 4648 and 5384–9
Mountbatten-Cunningham-Ismay correspondence	1943–4	WO 203/5233
Order of battle and staff list of Army, RN, RAF	1943–5	WO 203/5028
Naval strength	1943–6	WO 203/5409
Eastern Fleet, British Pacific Fleet etc.	1943–6	WO 203/4740–54
Naval operations	1944–5	WO 203/4962–6, 5020 and 5035
FAA operations	1944–5	WO 203/220, 521, 530, 3246, 3326, 3611, 3622, 4966, 4983 and 5246
British Pacific Fleet, operational planning	1944–5	WO 203/2948
Naval intelligence	1944–5	WO 203/5420, 5795 and 5804

Naval communiqués	1944–5	WO 203/5086
Combined operations naval plans	1945	WO 203/3494
Interrogation of Japanese naval POWs	1946	WO 203/6311

Allied Forces, Mediterranean Theatre

Plan to use RM Division in Operation TORCH	1942	WO 204/4430
Naval plans and operational orders	1942–4	WO 204/179–208, 245, 4359, 4437, 4439, 4534, 4558–89, 4895, 4960–2, 4242A–B, 4318, 4543–51, 6860, 6913–7607, 8508–10, 8517–20, 8814 and 9077
Minutes of Combined Signal Board, and other Joint Service bodies	1943	WO 204/68–69
De Courten-Cunningham Naval Agreement (Italy)	1943	WO 204/2924
French Navy (including Free French)	1943–5	WO 204/3758, 3819, 3858–9, 4144, 4885, 4890–1 and 5526
Yugoslav Navy	1943–6	WO 204/396–7, 2413, 2416, 5071 and 5527
Italian Navy	1943–7	WO 204/436, 1310, 10551, 2411–12, 2414–15, 2653–4, 2729–31, 2924, 2971–2, 4120, 6072 and 11078
HQ Allied Commission (Italy), Naval Sub-Commission, minutes etc.	1943–7	WO 204/9895–8
Counter Intelligence Corps, reports on naval activities	1944	WO 204/835
G3 Special Operations, special naval operations	1944	WO 204/11597
Naval Agreement with Yugoslavia	1944–5	WO 204/20
Naval correspondence	1944–6	WO 204/369, 380
Naval intelligence reports	1944–6	WO 204/4438, 8382, 8443, 9362, 9365, 9403, 9558, 12794 and 12927
G2 Special Counter-Intelligence, naval sabotage units	1944–6	WO 204/12449–55 and 12944

21 Army Group

Operation OVERLORD, SHAEF Directive	1944	WO 205/75
Naval plans, orders, and reports on naval operations	1944–5	WO 205/253–4, 259, 274, 378, 665, 699, 704, 829, 863–865B and 885
Sixth Airborne Division, 40 Commando RM, organisation and employment	1948	WO 275/11

East Africa Command

Anglo-French staff talks, naval installations etc.	1951–4	WO 276/67
Operational situation report, 41 Commando RM	1964	WO 276/344
British Forces Cyprus, telegrams from Admiralty and C-in-C Mediterranean	1963–4	WO 305/3095

43 War Diaries

British Army practice was for units down to battalion level to maintain war diaries. These are some examples from Royal Marine or naval land units, or from headquarters involved in amphibious operations.

RN Division at Gallipoli	1915–18	WO 95/4290–1
63rd (RN) Division	1916–18	WO 154/73
British Forces Middle East, naval plans	1943	WO 169/24909
Operation HUSKY: naval orders	1943	WO 169/8491–2
(staff afloat)	1943	WO 169/13914–27 etc.
(troop ships)	1943	WO 169/13916
RM AA units	1941	WO 166/3392–3
RM Division	1941–2	WO 166/6544–6
50 Civil Affairs Unit (Marine Section)	1945	WO 166/17837
Carrier-Borne Air Liaison Section	1950–1	WO 281/1200–4

44 Ordnance Bodies, 1855–1950

The abolition of the Ordnance Board and the transfer of its responsibilities to the War Office created a need for specialist bodies to oversee the design and production of guns and ammunition for both services. In 1907 the Naval Ordnance Department was transferred to Admiralty control, but there continued to be many gunnery and ordnance matters requiring liaison between the services. Most of these organisations (including the 'Ordnance Board' created in 1908) were essentially inter-departmental committees with naval representation.

Ordnance Select Committee and Ordnance Committee

Letters from Admiralty	1854–7	ADM 2/1698–701
Correspondence with DGNO	1855–61	WO 46/165
Proceedings:	1855–68	SUPP 6/1–16
	1881–1907	SUPP 6/116–62
	1885–8	SUPP 6/44–7
(abstracts)	1883–97	SUPP 6/79–95
President's annual reports:	1881–1907	SUPP 6/52–67
	1919–38	SUPP 6/194–9
Programmes	1881–1907	SUPP 6/68–77
Reports	1881–97	SUPP 6/96–115

Ordnance Council

Proceedings:	1869–94	SUPP 6/48–51
	1894–1913	SUPP 6/750–2

Ordnance Board

Annual reports:	1908–15	SUPP 6/163–70
	1915–37	SUPP 6/264–86
Minutes:	1908–15	SUPP 6/171–89
	1915–18	SUPP 6/200–63
Reports	1908–12	SUPP 6/190–3
Memoranda	1917–38	SUPP 6/287–360
Naval AA Gunnery Committee, minutes:	1919–21	SUPP 6/609–10
	1919–21	ADM 7/943
Naval Cordite Committee, minutes	1925–7	SUPP 6/611
President's annual reports	1939–49	SUPP 6/361–5
Proceedings	1939–50	SUPP 6/366–504
Report on RN explosives storage in Middle East	1949	SUPP 6/828 and 927
Visit to Canada and USA by Capt. M J Parkes-Buchanan, RN	1949	SUPP 6/895
Application of various studies to naval aviation	1952	SUPP 6/940

Explosives Committee

Reports and proceedings:	1870–1907	SUPP 6/511–26
	1888–91	SUPP 5/794–6

45 Other War Office Establishments

The Royal Hospital is an institution housing former soldiers and NCOs of the Army and Royal Marines, and deriving part of its income from the military share of prize and booty money.

Royal Hospital, Chelsea

Regimental registers of pensioners, including Marine regiments	c.1715–56	WO 120/2
Prize records (Army and RM shares)	1720–1899	WO 164/1–663
Pensioners' service documents	1760–1913	WO 97/1–6383
Register of ships captured by Army	1779–1858	WO 164/4/7
Pensioners' certificates of service	1782–1887	WO 121/1–257
Account of prize monies received and paid	1793–1815	WO 164/642
Register of ships captured by RN and Army	1795–1862	WO 164/531

Signals Experimental, later Research and Development Establishment

Reports, including some naval equipment	1920–43	AVIA 23/1–1089

Military Operational Research Unit

Report on naval radar	1944	WO 291/657
Time and motion study of six-inch naval gun drill	1946	WO 291/954

46 Other Supply Departments

The First World War exposed the War Office's lack of expertise in technical, industrial and contracting matters. To supply what was wanting the new Ministry of Munitions took over the supply of guns, ammunition and aircraft to the Army. It had contacts with the Admiralty departments which supplied the same things to the Navy. In the Second World War the Ministries of Supply and Aircraft Production discharged the same responsibilities (for the Navy as well as the RAF in the case of aircraft), while the Ministry of Production co-ordinated the industrial activities and military contracts of all departments.

Ministry of Munitions, 1915–21

Historical Records Branch	1901–43	MUN 5/1–419
Registered files	1909–37	MUN 4/1–7076
Naval heavy guns, correspondence	1915	MUN 9/16
RN Cordite Factory, experiments etc.	1915–19	MUN 7/235, 238 and 251
Liaison with Admiralty on contracts	1916–18	MUN 7/105A
Department of Aeronautical Supplies including naval aviation equipment	1916–19	MUN 8/39–54
Men suitable for naval artificers	1917	MUN 3/189–94
Admiralty battery containers	1917	BT 66/5
Department of Aircraft Production technical bulletins, including naval aircraft	1918–20	MUN 10/1–51

Ministry of Supply, 1939–59

Naval requirements for propellants, etc.	1917–58	SUPP 14/1–1366
RN Cordite Factory Holton, reports:	1922–37	SUPP 28/358–66
	1927–38	SUPP 5/853–4
(research reports)	1924–35	SUPP 28/360
Admiralty requirements	1939	T 246/41
Naval tracer ammunition for RAF	1939–40	T 246/37
Contract record books	1939–45	SUPP 4/21 and 40
Priority application by Admiralty for 'Hedgehog' ammunition	1942	T 246/76
Disposal of surplus Admiralty shell	1943–4	POWE 5/13
Naval Telecommunications Flying Unit, RAF Defford, reports		SUPP 25
North American supply missions, FAA requirements	1941–2	AVIA 38/580
Inter-service Metallurgical Research Council, minutes and reports, including work of RN Scientific Service, Admiralty Materials Laboratory, etc.	1945–69	SUPP 19/1–1619
ARE polishing process	1955	SUPP 27/53

Ministry of Aircraft Production, 1939–46

Files, including naval aircraft, radar etc.	1939–57	AVIA 15/1–3937

Aircraft data sheets, including naval aircraft	1941–5	SUPP 9/1–2
Private office papers, aircraft for FAA	1942–4	AVIA 9/19 and 42
Coastal Command, A/S warfare	1942–4	AVIA 9/22, 32 and 47

Ministry of Production, 1942–5

Admiralty programme: notes for minister	1941–2	BT 87/57
(acceleration)	1942	BT 28/460
Admiralty inspection of HMS *Jamaica* under construction	1942	BT 28/461
Enquiry into RN Torpedo Factory, Greenock	1942–3	BT 28/425
Admiralty requirements	1942–4	BT 87/10 and 163
Naval stores	1942–6	BT 28/806
Aircraft allocations for FAA	1944	BT 87/161
Admiralty cement	1944–5	BT 28/916

47 Colonial Departments etc.

This list gathers records of various officials and bodies having responsibilities for colonies under the authority of successive Secretaries of State. The Crown Agents were a commercial and purchasing agency acting in Britain on behalf of colonial governments. The Ministry of Overseas Development handled aid, trade and economic relations with former British colonies.

Colonial Governors

Letters to Admiralty	1728–1839	ADM 1/3817–23
Letters from Admiralty (Mediterranean passes)	1730–1815	ADM 2/1319–25

Colonial Office, 1855–1968

Correspondence with Admiralty	1857–68	CO 6/22–43
Correspondence, Dominions:	1907–25	CO 532/1–335
(registers)	1907–26	CO 708/1–37
(registers, out-letters)	1907–26	CO 709/1–12

Crown Agents for the Colonies

African widows' and orphans' pension schemes, naval personnel	1914–56	CAOG 15/265
Explosion of RN ammunition ship at Gibraltar	1951–3	CAOG 10/120
Yarrow Admiralty Research Department training schemes	1968–78	CAOG 16/437

Directorate of Overseas Surveys

RN photography policy	1948	OD 6/605
British Antarctic Survey and HMS *Endurance*	1970–8	OD 6/1519, 1595 and 1683

Ministry of Overseas Development

Singapore Dockyard:	1967	OD 35/189
	1967–9	OD 39/39–41 and 53–60
Malta Dockyard: litigation	1965	OD 20/273
(feasibility survey)	1967–9	OD 38/59–61

48 Dominions Office, later Commonwealth Relations Office, 1925–68

The correspondence and files of the Dominions Office include much relating to naval links between Britain and the Dominions.

Correspondence, Dominions:	1915–71	DO 35/1–10914
(registers)	1927–42	DO 3/1–184
(registers, out-letters)	1927–9	DO 4/1–3

Confidential Print

Imperial conferences:	1887–1925	CO 886/various
	1926–39	DO 114/8–96
Defence	1925–31	DO 114/1, 13, 23 and 32
Territorial claims in Antarctic	1925	DO 114/4

Registered Files

South Africa, Naval Brigade	1899–1901	DO 119/558
Tanganyika Motorboat Expedition, correspondence with Admiralty	1915	DO 119/908
Stores for the Fleet	1926	DO 117/14
Naval Depot, Simonstown	1926	DO 117/52
Dispatches (including Admiralty)	1926ff.	DO 35/6, 27, 52 etc.
Territorial claims in the Antarctic	1926–8	DO 117/2, 7, 13, 17, 42, 83 and 90
Singapore Naval Base:	1926–9	DO 117/38 and 156
	1930–6	DO 35/144/1
	1966	DO 169/479–480
Armed merchant cruisers	1927	DO 117/56
Naval conferences and treaties:	1927–9	DO 117/68 and 173–4
	1930–9	DO 35/88, 95, 101, 134, 528 and 545–6
(consultation with Dominions)	1934	DO 121/3
Naval construction programme	1930–6	DO 35/167/2
Defence:	1937–43	DO 35/543–8
	1947–52	DO 35/2388–485
	1957–65	DO 164/1–136
War, general: Far Eastern strategic situation	1937–43	DO 35/1009–10
(naval forces)	1939–42	DO 35/1007/10–17

Canada, medals for RCN	1938	DO 127/37
Military, naval and air	1939–40	DO 35/527–9
South Africa: control of naval forces	1939	DO 119/1110–13
(naval intelligence)	1940	DO 119/1130
Eire: naval intelligence	1939	DO 130/7
(coastal defence and naval intelligence)	1939–40	DO 35/1008/10–12
(naval co-operation)	1950–1	DO 130/116
(visits of HM Ships)	1953	DO 130/123
War, prize	1939–42	DO 35/1013/1–5
India: Indian ratings serving in HM Ships	1941–8	DO 142/120
(disposal of king's colour of RIN)	1947–9	DO 142/279
(exchange visits by naval officers)	1947–50	DO 142/286–7
Air training, aircrew training in Canada for RN	1942	DO 35/1085/4–5
Prize law, naval prize money	1943–6	DO 35/1212 and 1793–4
Shore facilities in South Africa for FAA	1943–6	DO 35/1670
DNI, photographs of Ocean Island	1945	DO 140/685
Imperial defence etc.	1947–52	DO 35/2264–363
British naval establishments in South Africa	1947–52	DO 35/2364–72
British policy in the Antarctic	1947–52	DO 35/2876A–2884
Courts Martial and Naval Discipline Act	1948–52	DO 35/2178–9
Formation of a Ceylon naval force	1948–52	DO 35/2571
St. John's Naval Base, Newfoundland	1949	DO 127/98
Simonstown Naval Base	1950–5	DO 121/232
Communications Department, Commonwealth Prize Pool	1953–4	DO 35/4842
Defence Department:	1952–60	DO 35/5454–513
	1952–60	DO 35/8250–338
South Atlantic Naval Command System:	1952–6	DO 35/6573–5
	1956–9	DO 35/10555–8
Visits of Lord Mountbatten	1955–6	DO 35/6532–3
Malaya Department, including RN in Malaya	1957–60	DO 35/9839–960
Setting up of Ghana Navy:	1957–60	DO 35/9429–30
	1964–6	DO 221/86–7
Setting up of Nigerian Navy	1958–60	DO 35/10461
Use of Gan Island by USN and USAF	1960–3	DO 196/17
Admiralty land leases in Sierra Leone	1963	DO 166/98
Former naval dockyard, Malta	1963	DO 203/83
Proposal to build a replica of HMB *Endeavour*	1964–6	DO 170/95
West African naval forces	1964–5	DO 195/352
Kenyan and Tanzanian Navies	1964–6	DO 213/49–52
Technical assistance to Ceylon Navy	1965	DO 189/603
Ships and naval training for Pakistan	1965–6	DO 196/546
Bizerta Dockyard and Malta	1965–9	DO 202/58

49 Treasury, Correspondence

The Treasury was concerned with all government activities which involved the spending of public money, the Navy naturally very prominent among them. Until 1920 its correspondence was indexed and registered chronologically, but papers on particular subjects were extracted from the chronological sequence and gathered together. Such papers can be traced from their original (indexed) situation to their final location using the 'skeleton registers'. Early in the nineteenth century the Treasury began experimenting with subject files called 'Long Bundles', and in 1920 it finally adopted a fully registered file system covering the whole range of its concerns, and including many files to do with the Navy and naval activities. Lists 52–7 give examples of such files arranged by Treasury departments.

In-letters:	1685–1920	T 1/2–12626
[Described to 1745 in *Calendar of Treasury Papers, 1556–1728* and *Calendar of Treasury Books and Papers, 1729–1745*.]		
(name registers)	1777–1920	T 2/1–502
(skeleton registers)	1783–1920	T 3/1–110
(subject indexes)	1852–1920	T 108/1–36
Lists of mariners	1691	T 64/298
Secretary's letters to Admiralty:	1698–1839	ADM 1/4283–313
	1704–6	ADM 1/3729
Correspondence with Prize Office	1702	T 64/195–6
Correspondence with Navy Board	1779–81	T 64/200–2
Letters to Navy Board Transport Department	1781–2	ADM 108/4A
Letters to Navy Board	1793–5	T 64/204
Letters to Transport Board	1794–8	ADM 108/4B–7
Navy Office estimates for shipbuilding and repairs	1800	T 38/652
Letters to Admiralty and naval boards	1811–35	T 28/8–37
Letters to Victualling Board Transport Department	1817–29	ADM 108/8–18
'Long Bundles'	c.1820–40	T 1/3411–4404
Slave Trade Adviser: report books	1821–91	HCA 35
(registered papers)	1821–97	HCA 37
(unregistered papers)	1837–76	HCA 36
Letters to Victualling Board	1822–32	ADM 109/53–5
Letters to Admiralty	1849–1920	T 5/1–58
Out-letters relating to ordnance	1855–6	T 28/87
Letters to Paymaster-General etc.	1859–85	T 28/111–13
Out-letters, including naval prizes	1914–20	T 114/1–7
'Long Bundles'		
Prize claims, HMS *Nymph*	after 1781	T 1/3533
Prize claims, Java expedition	after 1812	T 1/4066

Correspondence with Transport Department	c.1816–32	T 1/4320
Arctic expeditions	1819–33	T 1/3415
Stores and fitting of convict ships	c.1820–40	T 1/3418
CG Service	c.1820–40	T 1/3545
Droits of Admiralty	c.1820–40	T 1/3685–6
Accounts of Capt. W F W Owen, Superintendent Fernando Po	c.1820–40	T 1/3741
Salaries etc. in naval departments	c.1820–40	T 1/4030
Abolition of Colonial Naval Officers	c.1820–40	T 1/4031
Prosecutions of pirates in colonial courts	c.1820–40	T 1/4092
Colonial Vice-Admiralty Courts	c.1820–40	T 1/4387–8
Wines etc. for officers of HM Ships	c.1820–40	T 1/4372 and 4376
Expeditions in Africa	1821–31	T 1/3413

Registered Files

Finance Department	1920–48	T 160/1–1418
Supply Divisions	1919–48	T 161/1–1512
Establishments Department	1920–48	T 162/1–1028
General	1920–48	T 163/1–142
Navy Estimates	1920–3	T 163/11/4 and 16/14
Superannuation Division	1920–48	T 164/1–694

50 Treasury, Departmental Accounts

These are accounts from various departments of naval administration, and of other bodies having to do with it.

Treasurer of the Navy	1673–1703 and 1712	T 38/580–613
Abstracts, Army, Navy and Ordnance	1685–1730	T 35/58–9
Navy Estimates	1686–1820	T 38/638–63
Public Accounts Commissioners, report on Lord Orford's Treasurership of the Navy	1689–1704	T 38/614–15
Miscellaneous naval accounts	1699–1717	T 38/664
Prizes	1702–10	T 38/616–37
Sick and Wounded	1705–7	T 38/665–6
Naval debt	1712–14	T 38/667
Declared account, troop transports	1744	AO 1/2310/27
Sale of old stores and ships	1767–86	T 38/669–70
American Loyalists Claims Commissions, supplies furnished to RN:	1780–1835	AO 13/1–10 and 86
	1788–90	AO 12/71–7 and 121
(index)	1788–90	AO 12/77

51   Treasury, Chancellor of the Exchequer's Office

As the office of First Lord of the Treasury came, in the nineteenth century, to take on the duties of Prime Minister, the junior Treasury Minister known as the Chancellor of the Exchequer took over his position as minister for finance. His private office papers, like those of other Cabinet ministers, deal especially with matters of political sensitivity.

Navy Pay Office: organisation	1817	T 172/915
(Establishment book)	1836	T 172/925
Admiralty regulations for Treasurers	1837	T 172/926
Sale of old naval stores	1852	T 172/942
Method of payment in the Navy	1853	T 172/943
Financing of naval and military operations, 1793–1886	1900	T 172/954
Publication of scientific results of Shackleton's expedition	1911	T 172/51
Income Tax on Navy pay	1914–17	T 172/976
Naval and Military War Pensions Committee	1916	T 172/300
Leven Shipyard, work for Admiralty	1917	T 172/568
Navy Estimates: (1919)	1918	T 172/877
(1920)	1919	T 172/1116
(FAA)	1925–6	T 172/1485
Leakage of information from the Admiralty	1923	T 172/1309
Production of Admiralty charts	1925	T 172/1475
London Naval Conference	1929–30	T 172/1693
Reduction in Service pay and pensions	1931	T 172/1742
Admiralty supply and production report	1940	T 172/1931

52   Treasury, Finance Department

These (and the following lists) give examples of the registered files (listed under registry headings) of one of the departments which divided Treasury business under the 1920 scheme.

Departmental functions: list of Treasurers of the Navy	1660–1835	T 160/238
(list of Paymasters-General of the Forces)	1660–1835	T 160/238
(list of Paymasters-General)	1836–1925	T 160/238
Fighting services: requisitioned shipping	1918–34	T 160/145 and 508
(mercantile cruisers)	1919–28	T 160/71
(Turkish ships taken over by RN)	1922–30	T 160/49
Finance: duty free stores for RN	1920–44	T 160/90, 1128 and 1191
(Income Tax on RN pay, Admiralty accounting procedures)	1920–46	T 160/116, 259, 1385 and 1390

(Naval Savings Banks)	1921–34	T 160/506
(RN accounts for Parliament)	1924	T 160/199
(supply of specie for HM Ships)	1926–40	T 160/907
(naval finance)	1931	T 160/398
(local currency for RN at Wei-Hai-Wei)	1935–9	T 160/848
(Polish destroyers serving with RN)	1939–45	T 160/981 and 1332
(London Warships Week, etc.)	1940–3	T 160/1091 and 1138
(disposal of captured currency)	1945–6	T 160/1408
Communications: naval reparations	1920	T 160/16
(naval terms of Versailles Treaty and German naval budget)	1921–2	T 160/102
(Hungarian warships)	1922–3	T 160/135 and 140
(transfer of Admiralty moorings to Irish Free State)	1922–4	T 160/130
(Vichy French shipping and blockade)	1940–5	T 160/1359
Countries: Chile, internment of crew of *Dresden*	1921–5	T 160/94
(Turkey, purchase of warships)	1934–45	T 160/1191–2 and 1351
Insurance, health insurance for RN	1922–6	T 160/145 and 243
Committees: British Naval Commission of Control, Bulgaria	1922–4	T 160/35
(Inter-Allied Naval Commission of Control, Berlin)	1922–4	T 160/144
Compensation, Admiralty claims against Irish Free State	1923–5	T 160/138
Materials, coal, Admiralty claim against German government	1925–6	T 160/220

53 Treasury, Supply Department

Committees, Naval Prize Tribunal	1920–8	T 161/81
Factories: Admiralty Chart Factory, Cricklewood:	1919–29	T 161/1006
	1938–41	T 161/1007
(alternative work for dockyards)	1929–30	T 161/488
Fighting services: RN personnel transferred to RAF	1920–1	T 161/72
(RN Welfare Committee)	1920–4	T 161/46
(naval officers' pay)	1920–5	T 161/19
(arming merchant vessels)	1920–42	T 161/1046
(travel concessions to RN and RM)	1921	T 161/109
(oil depot at Singapore Naval Base)	1921–3	T 161/145
(Singapore Naval Base)	1921–38	T 161/468 and 800
(Basra Dockyard and Tigris-Euphrates Fleet)	1922–31	T 161/610
(future of Sheerness Dockyard)	1923–32	T 161/513
(Geneva Naval Conference)	1925–7	T 161/295
(naval construction programme):	1927–8	T 161/281
	1930	T 161/301
	1937–42	T 161/824 and 1066
	1939–43	T 161/1105

(FAA provision in Estimates)	1927–32	T 161/529
(recruitment of naval aircrews)	1935	T 161/672
(RN, AA re-armament)	1936–40	T 161/989, 851
(motor boats for HM Ships)	1938–9	T 161/921
(FAA policy and bases)	1938–40	T 161/993
Funerals: dockyard workmen	1920	T 161/37
(Mr. R MacDonald's body conveyed by cruiser)	1937	T 161/783
Stationery: Navy List	1920–1	T 161/72
(supply of Admiralty charts)	1926–33	T 161/570
War, compensation to ex-POWs	1920–3	T 161/72
Prize: naval prize disposal	1920–3	T 161/455
(Naval Prize Tribunal, decrees)	1924–8	T 161/8
Materials: oil and coal for RN	1920–31	T 161/455
(meat and flour for RN)	1923–33	T 161/563
Medical, smallpox in RN	1921–6	T 161/112
Contracts: Harland and Wolff, monitors	1921–3	T 161/145
(Admiralty)	1935	T 161/672
Land: Admiralty oil tanks at Port Said	1921–3	T 161/145
(School of Naval Co-operation, Ford)	1936–9	T 161/1395
Purchases and sales, Lord Beatty sold the compass from HMS *Lion*	1922	T 161/172
Finance, Navy Estimates:	1922–3	T 161/206
	1929–46	T 161/534, 621, 754, 905, 1027 and 1231
Communications: transfer of Admiralty Harbour to Dover Harbour Board	1922–44	T 161/1144 and 1243
(loss of HMS *Spider*)	1931	T 161/493
Inventions, torpedo propulsion	1923–31	T 161/470
Countries: Japan, naval programme	1925–35	T 161/648
(Turkey, purchase of guns from Admiralty)	1938–9	T 161/1396
Charities, GH	1932–43	T 161/1108
Defence, Admiralty payment for AA defence	1936–40	T 161/851 and 989
Accommodation: Admiralty HQ and ammunition storage	1937–42	T 161/1073, 1082, 1381, 1396 etc.
Rewards and gifts, to USN servicemen	1938–9	T 161/1396

54 Treasury, Establishments Department

Superannuation Division, registered files: RN pensions, policy and cases	1893–1970	T 164/1–694
(dockyard employees, redundancy and superannuation)	1915–62	T 248/162 and 364

(dockyard employees and RFA)	1930–66	T 248/63, 153, 593 and 648
(Simonstown Naval Base, pensions)	1960–3	T 248/355 and 448
Blue Notes (relating to departmental estimates):		
(Admiralty Building, Whitehall)	c.1897–8	T 165/6, 11 and 13–16
Establishment: Dockyard Schools, teaching staff	1918–39	T 162/54, 298 and 499
(Torpedo Schools, staff)	1921–39	T 162/449
(closure of Rosyth and Pembroke Dockyards)	1925–8	T 162/114
(RN Torpedo Factory, Greenock, wages)	1926–7	T 162/116
(number of RN officers at Admiralty)	1926–7	T 162/118
(Hydrographic Department, allowances)	1926–7	T 162/120
(RRS *Research*, motor landing craft)	1936–41	T 162/598
(HMS *Caledonia*, civilian staff)	1937–47	T 162/920
Establishment Officer's Branch, appointment of Naval Assistant Secretary to CID	1920–39	T 199/9
Entertainment, RN allowances:	1922–7	T 162/129
	1931–43	T 162/681
Fighting services: RM Police, rates of pay	1922–41	T 162/733
(Naval Recruiting Service)	1922–42	T 162/636
(RN Medical Services, rates of pay)	1924–46	T 162/844
(numbers of RN and RM officers required by 1943)	1934–9	T 162/989
(complements of RN medical establishments)	1934–9	T 162/989
Professional, Scientific, Technical and Industrial Staff Division, registered files: pay and conditions of RN civilian employees	1925–62	T 217/1–840
(Malta Dockyard Working Party)	1945–59	T 217/554–5
(burial arrangements for Admiralty staff)	1947–8	T 217/6
(pay of gardeners in RN establishments)	1961	T 217/753
Pensions, RFR and RNR	1936–7	T 162/435
General Division registered files: Naval Reserves, training and mobilisation	1936–60	T 215/983–92
(sex changes by civil servants in naval administration)	1958–9	T 215/550
Manning Division registered files: Capt. D A Watson, RN, career	1949–59	T 216/674
(emergency staffing of Admiralty supply departments)	1954–5	T 216/342
(appeal against Admiralty decision on pay)	1960	T 216/683

55 Treasury, Defence Personnel Division

Registered files	1867–1970	T 213/1–1114
Pay of stewards, HM Yachts	1911–52	T 213/118
Pay and appointments to RN Colleges:	1922–56	T 213/223
	1923–61	T 213/371–97
Pay of dockyard workers:	1923–61	T 213/371–97

	1946–55	T 213/218–19
Naval Staff Historical Section	1923–47	T 213/377
Pay of Hydrographer of the Navy	1925–49	T 213/37
RN pay and allowances:	1925–56	T 213/230–72
	1935–55	T 213/276–7
	1946–8	T 213/17
Staffing of Cape of Good Hope Observatory	1931–60	T 213/414–18
RFA Service	1938–60	T 213/565 and 578–80
Establishment and pay of naval attachés	1943–8	T 213/824–5
Residences for RN captains and FOs in command	1943–55	T 213/221
Pay of Polish naval forces	1946–8	T 213/13
RN promotion	1947	T 213/8
Admiralty Civil Service manpower	1947–59	T 213/840–5
Admiralty accounting systems	1948–52	T 213/36
Admiralty reorganisation of technical classes	1948–54	T 213/163–5
Admiralty departmental grades	1951–4	T 213/162
Directorate of Dockyards, manpower	1952–4	T 213/184–7
RN and RM	1953–6	T 213/203–4
Pensions, HM Dockyard Malta	1956–60	T 213/394–6
Admiralty staff inspections, shore establishments	1959	T 213/634–9
RN officer career structure	1960–3	T 213/934
Navy Estimates:	1960–3	T 213/869–70
	1962	T 213/803
HQ departments	1961–2	T 213/789–91
Increase in strength of RM Commandos	1961–2	T 213/807
Admiralty briefs for Public Accounts Committee	1961–2	T 213/814–15
Reorganisation of RN Engineering Service	1961–7	T 213/892–3
Salary of Director of Naval Works	1962	T 213/788
Manpower to build Polaris submarines	1963	T 213/871
Assisted House Purchase Scheme for RN ratings	1964–5	T 213/1036–7

56 Treasury, Defence Policy and Material Division

Registered files	1911–75	T 225/1–3926
Vessels, RN	1943–55	T 225/63 and 688–90
Estimates, consideration by Cabinet	1945–50	T 225/72–7
Treasury Inter-Services Committee	1948–59	T 225/815–17
Naval Construction Programme	1949–60	T 225/977–83
Defence departments, accounts	1949–50	T 225/80
Admiralty, crop compensation claim	1950	T 225/47
RN Torpedo Factory, Greenock	1935–56	T 225/756
Supply of warships etc. to India and Pakistan	1944–55	T 225/352–7

Losses	1950–4	T 225/48–9
Charter of SS *Gothic* for royal tour	1950–4	T 225/341–7
Ownership of Peterhead Harbour	1950–9	T 225/784
Warship-building contracts, accounting	1950–60	T 225/1277–81
Supply of RNVR units in the colonies	1954–9	T 225/796
Provision of aircraft for FAA	1955–60	T 225/1261–4
Navy Estimates, 1959–60	1958–9	T 225/694–5
Naval Programme, long-term costing, 1962–5	1958–9	T 225/846–8
GH, form of accounts	1959	T 225/785
Facilities in Scotland for US Polaris submarines	1960–4	T 225/2105–14
Development of Malta Dockyard	1960–5	T 225/2242–6

57 Treasury, other Divisions and Departments

Rating of Government Property Department

Valuation of CG properties	1895	T 272/5

Ceremonial Branch

Medals and awards to RN, RM, RNR Merchant Navy etc.:	1909–95	T 333/1–266
	1939–69	T 301/1–33
	1940–65	T 351/1–58
	1943–7	T 300/22
	1946–61	T 300/76–8
	1948–63	T 344/33, 39
	1970–1	T 343/25
(Merchant Navy):	1939–44	T 343/70–1
	1939–47	T 335/1–132
	1943	T 350/4

Civil Service National Whitley Council Official Side

Admiralty Councils, minutes etc.	1919–33	T 275/171–6, 374–5, 379 and 384

Land and Buildings Division

Memorials to Earl Jellicoe and Earl Beatty	1935–50	T 226/92
Admiralty House, accommodation for Minister of Defence	1945–50	T 226/98

Government and Allied Services Division

Official residence of First Lord of Admiralty	1938–58	T 219/472
Admiralty facilities for film companies	1960–1	T 219/918
Transfer of Admiralty staff from Pinner to Earls Court	1960–2	T 219/1002

Organisation and Methods Division
Organisation and methods at the Admiralty	1942–61	T 222/1, 408, 421, 885, 969, 1012, 1256 and 1405

Home Finance Division
Supply of duty-free stores to RN	1944–60	T 233/1930–2
Naval Savings Bank	1934–49	T 233/207–8
Report of Admiralty fact-finding team	c.1950	T 233/256

Trade and Industry Division
Post-war troopship fleet	1947–52	T 228/298

Central Economic Planning Staff
Admiralty sponsored industries	1947–53	T 229/534

Exchange Control Division
Provision of currency for visiting foreign naval personnel	1947–54	T 231/642

Social Services Division
Erection of headstones in naval cemeteries	1948–57	T 227/477
Dispute over N Wilkinson pictures	1949	T 227/38
Sale of Hatston Airfield, Orkney	1960–2	T 227/1809
Naval war pensions	1960–3	T 227/1608–10
Accommodation at Admiralty House	1961–4	T 227/1905
Insurance of ships in custody of Admiralty Marshal	1962–73	T 227/3211
Use of HMS *Belfast* as museum	1968–72	T 227/3621

Imperial and Foreign Division
Compensation for oil stocks taken over by RN	1951–7	T 220/487–8
Proposed closure of colonial dockyards	1957–9	T 220/744
Transfer of Malta Dockyard to private company:	1959	T 220/828 and 940
	1960–2	T 296/102–3, 231–2 and 272–3
	1962–8	T 317/303–6, 506–7, 763–4, 837, 927–9 and 1071–4
GCHQ, Admiralty responsibilities	1958–9	T 220/1419

Accounts Branch
RN Prize Fund	1954–5	T 276/2
MoD(N)	1971–2	T 292/173 and 185

Arts, Science and Lands Division
Admiralty compulsory purchase	1955	T 218/46

Overseas Finance Division

Closure of naval dockyards	1957	T 236/4342
Export credit guarantees for frigates for Argentine Navy	1960–2	T 236/6429 and 6714
Salvage attempt on troopship *Birkenhead*	1958–9	T 231/1217

Home and Overseas Planning Staff

Disposal of Pembroke Dockyard	1958–9	T 234/178–9

Agriculture, Transport and Trade Division

Admiralty explosives jetty, Milford Haven	1962–3	T 224/506
Chatham Dockyard, construction work	1963	T 224/520
Duty-free supplies of groceries by Admiralty to HM Prison Belfast	1964	T 320/196
Scott's Antarctic expedition 1912, gift of film to the nation	1964–5	T 326/1128

Overseas Development Division

Setting up Kenyan Navy	1964–6	T 317/760
Rates of pay in dockyards	1965–6	T 324/34, 47–8 and 60

Environment and Public Purchasing Department

Future of RNAY, Sydenham, Belfast	1971	T 341/178

58 Treasury, Committees

The Naval Expenditure Emergency Standing Committee was set up in August 1914 with representatives of the Admiralty and Treasury, to give quick answers to Admiralty requests not involving major questions of policy. In March 1917 a Shipping Expenditure Emergency Standing Committee was set up to do the same thing for the Ministry of Shipping.

Committee on Trading with the Enemy	1914–17	T 198/1–89
Standing Emergency Committee on Naval Expenditure, minutes:	1914–19	T 204/1–7
	1914 20	T 1/11666–12618
	1915	MT 23/412
	1917–22	T 161/66
Standing Emergency Committee on Shipping Expenditure, minutes:	1917–19	T 203/1
	1917–19	T 1/12066–370
Exchange Requirements Committee, Admiralty requirements	1939–45	T 196/51–5, 80, 95–7, 100 and 122–4
Treasury Inter-Services Committee	1948–59	T 225/815–17
War Works Commission: RNAS Ford	1954–63	T 180/80–1
(Llangennech Naval Stores Depot)	1956–7	T 180/150
(RNAS Brawdy)	1960–2	T 180/106

59 Treasury, Miscellaneous

These miscellaneous Treasury naval documents include papers of William Lowndes, Secretary of the Treasury, 1695–1724.

Lowndes Papers

Appointment of Auditor of RN Stores and Wages	c.1660–79	T 48/29
Victualling the Navy	1671–1710	T 48/89
Administration of the French Navy	1675	T 48/29
Muster Rolls of Marine Regiments	1678–1713	T 48/12
Rates of pay in RN	1678–1713	T 48/12
Valuations of prizes	1678–1713	T 48/12
Solicitor of the Admiralty's accounts	1678–1713	T 48/12
Import of hemp for RN	1678–1713	T 48/12
Passing accounts of Treasurers of Navy (Russell and Falkland)	1678–1713	T 48/12
Charter of hospital ships	1678–1713	T 48/12
Port Mahon Hospital	1678–1713	T 48/12
Tellers' memoranda, Navy	1682–1702	T 48/6
Baltic Squadron	1686–1702	T 48/46
Naval accounts, including Estimates	1688–1701	T 48/90
Abstracts of Naval Estimates	1689–96	T 48/87/186
Payments on Navy bills, wages and victualling	1693	T 48/49
Greenwich Hospital	1695	T 48/21

Miscellanea

Autograph collection	1669–1860	T 64/37
Ordnance for the Navy	1684	T 64/192
Contracts for naval stores:	1684	T 64/193
	1711	T 64/199
Victualling of Mediterranean Squadron	1692–3	T 64/194
Instructions to Paymaster of Marines	1702	T 64/197
Victualling the Navy	1710	T 64/198
Naval expenses	1754–64	T 48/71
Timber and naval stores, imports and exports	1760–82	T 64/276A
Naval timber in the New Forest	1764	T 64/205–6
Parliamentary orders and returns concerning RN	1777–1827	T 64/208A–214
Numbers employed by naval administration and dockyards	1783–1811	T 64/203
Droits of Admiralty on Danish prizes	1807	T 64/326
GH, abstracts of minutes and pensions	1807–20	T 47/20–1
East Florida Claims Commission, correspondence, letters of marque etc.	1763–83	T 77/23–9
Plan for manning the RN	1813	T 48/83

60 Paymaster-General of the Forces

The Paymaster-General of the Forces was the principal Crown accounting officer for Army (that is, Horse and Foot) Regiments. Only those records are listed here which cover Marine Regiments on the Army establishment (that is, up to 1749). Other such records were kept by the Paymaster of Marines.

Officers' half-pay:	1720–33	WO 109/55–84
	1737–1818	PMG 4/1–114
Half-pay cash book	1749–98	PMG 14/86–103
Powers of attorney to collect half-pay etc.	1756–64	PMG 14/142
Officers' widows' pensions	1808–26	PMG 11/1–24
Declared accounts, Marine half-pay:	1827–9	AO 2/4 and 10
	1829–31	AO 2/14 and 18
	1832–4	AO 2/22 and 26
	1834	AO 2/30

61 Paymaster of Marines and Marine Pay Office

The Paymaster of Marines exercised some of the same functions in relation to Marine Regiments as the Paymaster-General of the Forces did for other Army Regiments. These included the payment of half- as well as full-pay, and therefore continued even after the last Marine Regiments had been disbanded in 1749. Other records of the Paymaster-General of the Forces, covering the whole Army, also include Marine Regiments. With the creation of the Marine Corps in 1755 the Paymaster of Marines became a subordinate of the Treasurer of the Navy.

Pay book, Marines at sea	1672	ADM 30/17
Muster Rolls of Marine Regiments	1678–1713	T 48/12
Lists and musters	1688–1837	ADM 96/117–510
In-letters	1690–1810	ADM 96/1–12
Accounts	1695–1831	ADM 96/31–116
Declared accounts:	1701–25	E 351/2569–73
	1701–52	AO 1/1826/518–1827/529
Regimental colonels' agents, attorneys etc.	1702–15	ADM 96/514
Miscellanea:	1702–1831	ADM 96/511–24
(warrants for payments)	1739–52	ADM 96/520–2
(West Indies expedition)	1740–2	ADM 96/512
(prize money)	1780–1810	ADM 96/513
Admiralty orders	1703–18	ADM 2/1250–1
Regimental accounts	1705–45	ADM 96/1–2
Paymaster's warrants etc.	1708–28	ADM 96/112
Loose papers, officers and men DD	1740–64	ADM 96/524

Deputy Paymaster, Chatham Division	1756–69	ADM 1/5116/14
Officers' subsistence money:	1757–1826	ADM 96/482–94
	1796	ADM 96/495
Officers' widows' pensions	1758–76	WO 25/3107
Officers' half-pay:	1763–1827	ADM 96/87–94
	1789–93	ADM 6/410
	1810–20	ADM 96/102
	1824–9	ADM 6/411–13
(reduced officers)	1801	ADM 96/101
(remitted by bill)	1808–27	ADM 96/96–100
Out-letters	1778–1819	ADM 96/13–30
Stoppages from sea pay, NCOs and Marines	1803–8	ADM 96/510
Letters to Portsmouth Division RM	1818–22	ADM 185/113
Loose papers and accounts	1826–7	ADM 96/523

62 Boards of Customs and Excise

These Boards came under the authority of the Treasury, and other letters to the Admiralty were forwarded by the Secretary of the Treasury.

Board of Customs, later Customs and Excise

Letters to Admiralty	1694–1839	ADM 1/3863–77
Letters to Navy Board: register	1808–13	ADM 106/2135–8
(Revenue Cruisers)	1816	ADM 106/3124
Naval stores imported from Russia	1816–23	CUST 91/117
Surveyor for Buildings, register of letters and reports on CG lands and buildings	1828–57	ADM 7/7–39
Victualling of RN with dutiable goods:	1850–1925	CUST 143/1–8
(correspondence)	1840–78	CUST 33/19
Correspondence with Admiralty: flags	1850–1919	CUST 143/11–12
(loan of HMS *Dartmouth*)	1849	CUST 33/367
(Revenue Cruisers)	1856–78	CUST 33/425
(RNR)	1859–76	CUST 33/43
(Confederate Cruiser *Pampero*)	1861	CUST 33/334
(smuggling from HM Ships)	1861–82	CUST 33/134
(Admiralty warrant for arrest of vessels)	1876	CUST 33/349
Victualling accounts of Revenue Cruiser *Vigilant*	1857–1912	CUST 38/59–60
Establishment of RN Volunteers	1859	CUST 141/51
Customs officers serving in RNR: Douglas and Ramsey, IoM	1862–1942	CUST 104/279–81 and 300
(Dover)	1867–1919	CUST 54/370
(Maryport)	1870–1905	CUST 83/129–30

(Arundel)	1891–1941	CUST 57/30
(Scarborough)	1899–1919	CUST 91/110
(Maldon)	1903–31	CUST 101/110
Regulations for Blue Ensign	1865	CUST 141/58
Relations with RN:	1871–97	CUST 46/123–4
	1911	CUST 49/91
	1933–44	CUST 144/20–1, 339 and 397
Instructions to registrars of RNR:	1889–1922	CUST 49/624
	1902–93	CUST 49/1–5948
Recruiting for RNR	1903–16	CUST 49/370
Coal for Russian Fleet	1904–5	CUST 46/332–3 and 339
Warships building at Newcastle upon Tyne	1904–20	CUST 84/419
CG: transfer from Admiralty	1906–9	CUST 46/468–9
(transfer to Admiralty)	1910	CUST 49/30
Naval intelligence from customs officers	1909–21	CUST 49/513
Instructions to staff: Admiralty warrants etc.	1915–35	CUST 144/157–9
(relations with the Navy)	1933–44	CUST 144/20–1, 339 and 397
Victualling yards, dutiable goods	1917–18	CUST 49/413
Blockade of Germany	1919	CUST 49/480
Duty-free supplies for HM Ships:	1925–38	CUST 49/2393
	1933–5	CUST 49/2393
	1933–5	CUST 155/44 and 47
History of customs vessels and Revenue Cruisers	1925	CUST 143/13–14 and 16–20
Admiralty import of quartz crystals from Brazil	1936–42	CUST 106/566
Historical note, RN dutiable stores	1938	CUST 148/67
Contraband control	1939	CUST 106/69
Naval prizes, recovery of light dues	1939	CUST 106/81
Co-operation with Admiralty	1940	CUST 106/205
List of Revenue Cruisers, 1671–1928	1940	CUST 148/73
German naval vessels transferred to British fishing fleet	1947	CUST 49/2825
Private Office papers, duty-free stores for RN	1947–51	CUST 118/501

Board of Excise

Victualling Revenue Cruisers	1825	CUST 142/19
Revenue steamers	1853–6	CUST 121/1020

Collectors of Customs

Letters from Admiralty (Mediterranean passes)	1730–1815	ADM 2/1319–25
Letters to Admiralty (protections)	1756	ADM 1/5116/3–5

63 Board of Stamps and Taxes, later Inland Revenue

Registered files	1804–1997	IR 40/1–19123
Liability to tax of RN officers	1842–75	IR 40/2510
Appointment of Admiralty clerks	1877–80	IR 40/1354, 1450 and 1517
RN officers afloat, tax arrangements	1880	IR 40/1195
Tax on the Naval Department	1880	IR 40/1326
Dispatch of stamps to HM Ships	1880	IR 40/1659
RN officers' appointments stamped free of charge	1901	IR 40/2230
Property of GH	1901–49	IR 40/8294
Bequest to GH	1914	IR 62/619
RAN, relief from estate duty	1917	IR 62/768
Income Tax on prize money:	1919–20	IR 40/2509B
	1924–48	IR 40/9217
Applications for commutation of pension	1933	IR 40/4368
NRS, charitable status	1934	IR 40/4521
Fees for setting and marking naval examination papers	1934–8	IR 40/5473
RN exemption from certain taxes in wartime	1935–45	IR 40/6613
Debt owed to Admiralty	1940	IR 40/6564
Admiral on half-pay, cost of uniform	1940–7	IR 40/13314
Tax on naval medical officers' gratuities	1941	IR 40/7085
Police seconded to Admiralty for Gibraltar	1942	IR 40/7407
Tax on widows' and orphans' annuities	1945	IR 40/8089
Addresses of RN officers	1945–6	IR 40/8368
Deductions for RN officers' expenses	1945–52	IR 40/16036
Tax position of Admiralty	1946	IR 40/8422
House ownership by naval personnel	1953–5	IR 40/11515
Admirals of the Fleet, uniform and entertainment allowances	1955	IR 40/13324
Foreign naval officers training in UK not liable to UK tax	1956	IR 40/12354
Transfer of buildings maintenance staff from Admiralty to Ministry of Public Works	1963–7	IR 82/625
Pensions of merchant seaman killed by enemy action	1968	IR 40/17353

Sample Death Duty Accounts

Boyle, Admiral Sir William, 12th Earl of Cork and Orrery	1967–76	IR 59/1066
Burney, Admiral of the Fleet Sir Cecil	1929–44	IR 59/715
Coppinger, Rear-Admiral Robert Henry	1967–8	IR 59/1136
Fegen, Captain Edward Fogarty, VC	1941	IR 59/806
Ford, Vice-Admiral Sir Denys	1967–9	IR 59/1138
Jackson, Admiral of the Fleet Sir Henry	1930	IR 59/722
Kerr, Admiral of the Fleet Lord Walter	1927–8	IR 59/685
Keyes, Admiral of the Fleet Sir Roger, Baron	1946–8	IR 59/902

McLintock, Admiral Sir Francis Leopold	1907–27	IR 59/280
Moorman, Admiral Richard	1908–37	IR 59/308
Nelson, Vice-Admiral Horatio, Viscount	1805	IR 59/1
Nelson, Admiral Hon. Maurice Horatio	1914–37	IR 59/437
Nares, Vice-Admiral Sir George	1915–37	IR 59/468
Plunkett-Ernle-Erle-Drax, Admiral Sir Reginald	1967–77	IR 59/1075
Stephenson, Admiral Sir Henry	1919–37	IR 59/537
Seymour, Admiral Sir Michael Culme	1921–6	IR 59/608
Sturdee, Admiral Sir Frederick Doveton	1925–41	IR 59/661
Tyrwhitt, Admiral of the Fleet Sir Reginald	1951–3	IR 59/911
Wemyss, Admiral of the Fleet Sir Rosslyn, Baron Wester Wemyss	1933–48	IR 59/845

64 Audit Office

This is a sample of records of the Commissioners of Audit, 1785–1866, the Exchequer and Audit Department, 1867–1984, and the National Audit Office from 1984, which successively inherited from the Exchequer the function of auditing government departments' accounts.

Accounts current:	1801–1906	AO 19/1–123
(Greenwich Hospital)	1829–67	AO 19/109A/3
(droits of Admiralty)	1830–57	AO 19/75/1
(Admiralty, Secret Service)	1835–67	AO 19/75/27
(pensions to Dutch naval officers and widows)	1837–41	AO 19/2/2
(Board of Trade Marine Department)	1850–67	AO 19/109B/29
(naval prize bounty etc.)	1865–7	AO 19/109A/4
Section reference files:	1851–1977	AO 30/1–58
(naval dockyards, local audits)	1937–8	AO 30/21
Declared accounts:	1839–66	AO 20/1–120
(droits of Admiralty)	1845–8 etc.	AO 20 various
(First Lord, Secret Service)	1839–66	AO 20 various
(High Court of Admiralty)	1839–66	AO 20 various
(Greenwich Hospital)	1845–6	AO 20/5/52–3

65 Other Financial Departments

Records of the Paymaster-General for service pensions are in lists 231–4.

Paymaster-General

Army and Navy Branches, arrangement of business	c.1880	PMG 62/1
Dockyard Police pensions	1915–45	PMG 74/78
Admiralty pension/life assurance scheme for RN officers	1936–7	PMG 74/230

National Debt Office

Naval Savings Banks:	1918–49	NDO 900/34
	1928–54	NDO 13/101–2
Pensions Commutation Board, RN commutations	1893–1969	NDO 18/25

National Savings Committee

PO Savings Bank files, including Naval Savings Bank	1866–1948	NSC 9/1–1606
Savings Certificate Office, correspondence including naval savings schemes:	1940–58	NSC 11/1–526
	1948–50	NSC 21/392–3
Files, including Warship Weeks:	1915–78	NSC 7/1–488
	1940–1	NSC 21/315
HM Forces Branch	1916–77	NSC 28/1–24
Posters, including many showing warships etc.:	1893–1973	NSC 25/1–771
	1916–78	NSC 5/1–1068
(RN communications)	1983	NSC 43/6
Publicity scrapbooks, including Warship Weeks	1939–42	NSC 33/1–46
PO Savings Bank accounts, Polish Navy	1940	NSC 21/300
National Savings Stock Register, naval savings	1940–6	NSC 12/176
Correspondence with Admiralty	1945–8	NSC 21/407

War Damage Commission

Damage to RNC	1941–5	IR 37/280
Liaison with Admiralty	1942–4	IR 34/346
Damage by sea mines	1944–8	IR 34/168–9

66 Civil Service Departments

Civil Service Commission

Files, including Admiralty (civil) appointments:	1863–1991	CSC 6/1–102
	1875–1939	CSC 3/1–375
Examination results:	1876–1991	CSC 10/1–5111
	1888–1974	CSC 5/1–1856
Letter books	1859–60	CSC 2/37–8
Case of clerical assistant, HM Dockyard, Devonport	1944	CSC 9/1

Civil Service Department

Manpower Division, including staff complements of RN establishments	1960–75	BA 25/1–379
Pay Group, including RN, RNVR, dockyard workers etc., pay and incentives	1960–78	BA 22/1–627
RNC Dartmouth, civilian teaching staff superannuation scheme	1962–70	BA 27/98

Dockyard employees, compensation for asbestosis	1969–71	BA 27/318
Mallabar Committee recommendations on dockyards	1971–2	BA 17/658
Working Party on Demolition of Admiralty Citadel	1972–3	BA 17/848

Stationery Office

Printing of *Challenger* expedition reports	1876–1900	STAT 12/34/13
Admiralty stationery	1887–88	STAT 12/2/10
Printing of Admiralty charts:	1880	STAT 12/33/7
	1883–1913	STAT 12/12/6
	1911–13	STAT 12/12/4
Song books for Navy	1905–19	STAT 12/41/2
Books etc. for RN Staff College	1905–19	STAT 12/41/4
Printing of Navy List	1915–20	STAT 12/23/6
Correspondence, including Nautical Almanac, Admiralty Manual of Navigation, tide tables, etc.	1871–1996	STAT 14/1–5863
MoD(N), trials of electric v. manual typewriters	1963–70	STAT 14/3026

67 Exchequer, 1660–1871

These records consist mainly of formal accounts 'declared' for audit by various departments of naval administration, or other accountants having dealings with the Navy.

| Naval contractors' bonds | 1842–71 | J 117/33–66 |

Declared Accounts

Prize goods	1544–1715	E 351/2502–47
Woods and forests	1663–1831	LR 4/1–953
HCA: Receiver of Prizes	1664–1825	AO 3/3–18
(Registrar of Prizes):	1806–14	AO 3/17
	1831–2	AO 2/16 and 18
	1832–3	AO 2/24
(Receiver of Droits):	1830–5	AO 2/18, 22, 28 and 30
	1848–54	AO 20/42/1
Treasurer of the Navy:	1544–1715	E 351/2193–352 and 2587–97
	1665–6	AO 1/10/15
	1827–8	AO 2/7/142–8
	1829–30	AO 2/10 and 12
	1831–3	AO 2/16 and 22
	1833–5	AO 2/24 and 30
	1835–6	AO 2/33–4
Transport Board	1690–1719	AO 1/2304/8–2310/26
Victualler of the Navy	1660–1	AO 1/182/550A

Miscellaneous naval	1661–70	AO 1/1830/551
Sick and Hurt Board	1664–1713	AO 1/1820/483–1825/517
Victualling Board	1689	AO 1/484/48
Impressment, Hampshire and IoW	1692	AO 1/1831/552–4
RN salvage	1702–32	AO 1/1828–9
Paymasters of Marines	1702–86	AO 1/1826–7
Navy and Transport Boards, debts	1704–14	AO 1/845/1–3
Sale of Navy and Ordnance debentures	1714–16	AO 1/845/4
Rear-Adm. E Boscawen, C-in-C East Indies	1747–50	AO 1/218/732
American Loyalists Claims Commissions, supplies furnished to RN:	1780–1835	AO 13/1–10 and 86
	1788–90	AO 12/71–7 and 121
(index)	1788–90	AO 12/77
Secret Service: First Lords of Admiralty:	1794–1827	AO 1/2121–30
	1794–1835	AO 3/949
(Lord High Admiral)	1827–8	AO 2/2/163–4
(Lord Melville)	1828–30	AO 2/13/153–4
(Sir J Graham):	1830–3	AO 2/23/79–80
	1833–4	AO 2/27/67–8
(Lords Auckland and Grey)	1834–5	AO 2/31/1–2, 5–6 and 29–30
Compensation for captured ships:	1783	AO 1/458/3
	1794	AO 1/466/47
Sir C Middleton, Commission of Enquiry into Crown Woods	1786–94	AO 1/861/3
F Drake, Minister to Genoa, supplying RN at Toulon	1793	AO 1/578/505
Lord Keith, pay of *Pompée* and *Aréthuse*	1794	AO 1/1831/555
Expenses of Schooners *Hope* and *Cornwallis*	1800–7	AO 1/1831/556
Commission of Naval Enquiry	1805–6	AO 1/861/7
Equipment of Spanish men-of-war at Cadiz	1808	AO 1/1831/557
Acting Commissioner, Upper Canada	1813–14	AO 1/1831/558
Nelson's tomb in St. Paul's Cathedral	1813–14	AO 1/2501/452
British Army Flotilla in Mediterranean	1816–18	AO 1/1831/559
Naval supplies purchased at Sierra Leone	c.1821–5	AO 1/576/497
Paymaster-General, Marine half-pay:	1827–9	AO 2/4 and 10
	1829–31	AO 2/14 and 18
	1832–4	AO 2/22 and 26
	1834	AO 2/30
Treasurer and Paymaster of Ordnance:	1828–31	AO 2/1, 18 and 22
	1832–4	AO 2/24 and 28
	1834–6	AO 2/33–4
Commissioners of GH:	1829–30	AO 2/10 and 16
	1831–2	AO 2/20 and 24
	1833–4	AO 2/30 and 32

68 Surveyors-General, later Commissioners of Woods and Forests, later Crown Estates Commissioners

The administration of Crown lands included much relating to naval property and buildings, and to the supply of timber from the royal forests.

Schedules of deeds of Admiralty and Navy property	1639–1759	LRRO 5/1
Proposed Northfleet Dockyard, deeds	1660–1818	CRES 38/861–3
Declared accounts	1663–1831	LR 4/1–953
Use of Greenwich Palace as hospital for seamen	c.1669	CRES 2/1642
Admiralty Office deeds	1701–13	LR 1/307
Timber for the Navy:	1762–1859	CRES 2/262, 1025–6, 1106, 1596 and 1672
(New Forest)	1742–78	LR 5/2/1 and 11
Site for RN Asylum	1805–20	CRES 2/344
Schedule of deeds of Navy Board	1819	CRES 2/389
Site for RN School, Eltham:	1831–8	CRES 2/361
	1832–8	CRES 2/1642
RNC Greenwich:	1837–9	CRES 2/383
	1905–13	CRES 58/428
	1960–4	CRES 37/1887
(reconstruction of frontage)	1970–97	CRES 64/215
Harwich Naval Yard, leases, deeds etc.:	1743–1863	CRES 38/566
	1812 and 1839	CRES 39/11
	1839–68	CRES 2/294
	1840–2	CRES 2/1725
	1928–61	CRES 58/387 and 389
Letters to Navy Board:	1811–13	ADM 106/3548
(register)	1808–13	ADM 106/2135–8
Woolwich Dockyard, extension	1841–4	CRES 2/402
Holyhead Harbour, Admiralty lease	1846–57	CRES 49/56
Portland, Admiralty land etc.	1851–1958	CRES 35/500, 512, 531–2 etc.
Admiralty report concerning Lincolnshire Estuary Bill	1858–9	CRES 47/13
Dover Harbour Railway	1859	CRES 2/352
Portsmouth Dockyard extensions:	1864–9	CRES 58/558
	1885–1915	CRES 58/564
Deptford Dockyard, sale	1869–75	CRES 34/66
Admiralty Building, Whitehall	1869–1932	CRES 35/2568 and 2624–8
Holy Island CG boathouse	1873–6	CRES 34/136
Portland Naval Base	1875–1904	CRES 38/246
East Cowes, Admiralty lease	1882–1919	CRES 58/627
Dover, naval harbour proposals	1897–9	CRES 58/474 and 481
Portland Bill, Admiralty Signal Station	1898–1904	CRES 63/95–6

Royal Victoria Victualling Yard, Deptford	1898–1930	CRES 35/2648
Landguard, Felixstowe, Admiralty slip	1915–66	CRES 58/1480
Admiralty land purchases and sales	1917–25	CRES 58/205–6
Naval memorial at Plymouth Citadel	1921	CRES 35/477
Channel Islands, transfer of Admiralty land	1921–50	CRES 35/1763
Property managed by Admiralty	1939–51	CRES 36/77
Hartlepool, Admiralty correspondence	1947–50	CRES 58/124
Haslar Jetty, HMS *Hornet* and HMS *Dolphin*	1957–97	CRES 64/56
RM Barracks and RN Gunwharf, Chatham	1958–62	CRES 58/453
Pembroke Dock, Admiralty correspondence	1958–68	CRES 58/1262
Loch Striven, conveyance of seabed to Admiralty	1959–61	CRES 38/2436
Milford Haven, land conveyed to Admiralty	1962–3	CRES 58/1349
Wreck of HMS *Assurance* at the Needles	1969–72	CRES 58/1317
Whale Island, bridge to HMS *Excellent*	1969–74	CRES 58/1311

69 Board of Trade and Plantations, 1696–1782

The papers of this, the first specialist colonial administration created in England, were in the nineteenth century mingled with colonial state papers and reorganised on a geographical basis, making it difficult in many cases to disentangle the originating bodies. Correspondence and papers are included in the *Calendar of State Papers, Colonial ... America and West Indies* (38 vols., 1860–1994, 38) to 1739; Board minutes up to 1703 are calendared in the *Calendar of State Papers, Colonial ... America and West Indies*, and from 1704 to 1782 printed in full in *Journal of the Commissioners for Trade and Plantations* (14 vols., 1920–38).

Correspondence and papers, America and West Indies:	1574–1688	CO 1/1–69
	1606–1822	CO 5/1–1450
Minutes	1675–1782	CO 391/1–120
Letters to Admiralty	1697–1756	ADM 1/3814–16

70 Committee on Trade and Plantations, 1784–6; Board of Trade, 1786–1964

The new Board of Trade lost its colonial responsibilities in 1801 and was thereafter concerned with trade, and later industry.

Correspondence etc.		
Minutes	1784–1952	BT 5/1–158
General in-letters and files:	1791–1863	BT 1/1–569
(registers)	1808–64	BT 4/1–40
(indexes)	1846–95	BT 19/1–21
General out-letters:	1786–1863	BT 3/1–64

	1864–1921	BT 12/1–160
Papers, hemp and flax	1781–1806	BT 6/97–101 and 148
Registers of licences to neutral vessels	1808–22	BT 6/194–213

Various Departments, Registered Files

Scale-beam, Royal Clarence Victualling Yard	1896	BT 101/442
Soldiers' and Sailors' Help Society	1900	BT 58/1610
Admiralty and CID notes for Hague Conference	1905	BT 13/39
Admiralty adoption of BS screw threads	1914	BT 101/801
Meat supplies for the Navy	1914–15	BT 13/59–60
Blockade Advisory Committee	1919	BT 60/1/4
Naval prize money	1920	BT 15/72
Patent Office, including Admiralty patents	1920–49	BT 209/1–1443
Coal Advisory Committee, information from Admiralty	1922	POWE 26/89
Charges for training foreign naval officers	1926	BT 60/11/3
Supply organisation (including naval armaments, allocation of resources etc.)	1928–39	SUPP 3/69–88
Unemployment due to curtailment of naval shipbuilding	1929	BT 56/4
Boots for Army, Navy and Air Force	1929	BT 56/4
Norfolk Flax Ltd., taken over by Admiralty	1929–41	BT 200/1–14
Admiralty action to assist British creosote producers	1930	BT 56/19
Showcases on loan to Admiralty Pattern Rooms	1931–6	BT 61/48/7
War Emergency Legislation Sub-Committee, Admiralty note	1934	POWE 26/284
Import duties on naval stores	1934–9	BT 10/130
Contract, Singapore Naval Base	1938	BT 103/179
Film 'The Navy is Here':	1939–42	BT 103/538
	1940	BT 64/113
Royal Yugoslav Naval and Military Purchasing Commission	1940	BT 103/163
Lease of naval bases to USA	1940–1	BT 11/1667
Shipbuilding and Repair Branch registered files:	1940–71	BT 291/1–199
(Admiralty opinion on dry dock projects)	1958–9	BT 291/117
(naval shipbuilding orders)	1967	BT 291/166–7
Admiralty spare industrial capacity and labour	1941	BT 96/91
Admiralty use of cyphers and codes in wartime	1941–3	BT 61/78/2
RN torpedo factories	1945–8	BT 106/98
Shipbuilding Advisory Committee, minutes	1946–66	BT 199/1–15
Census of Production, Admiralty returns	1947–9	BT 70/177
Compensation for loss of naval uniforms and equipment	1947–54	BT 228/43
Admiralty factory at Crook	1948–63	BT 177/1980
Regulations on weighing and measuring equipment in naval bases	1953–70	BT 290/555
Duty on naval stores, clothing coupons for RN	1954–5	BT 64/4661 and 4676

National Production Advisory Council on Industry, Admiralty reports	1955–9	BT 190/30
Passenger lists of USN ships	1955–60	BT 26/1340–462
Modifications to merchant ships in time of war	1958	BT 193/69
RNC Greenwich, purchase of computer	1962–4	BT 314/15
Building submarines for RAN in dockyards	1963	EW 7/30
Geddes Inquiry into the shipbuilding industry	1964–6	BT 186/1–50
Export licence to South Africa for steel for naval shells	1965	BT 234/81
President of Board to speak to RN Staff College	1965–6	BT 11/6588
MoD, policy on naval orders	1967–8	FV 36/8
Shipbuilding Industry Board, MoD(N) contracts	1967–70	FV 37/63
Employment in dockyard areas	1968–9	EW 7/1181–2
Review of HM dockyards	1969–70	EW 10/12
Future of RN air stations	1970–1	EW 7/986–8
Rolls Royce receivership and naval core production	1971–4	FV 30/28
Reorganisation of naval stores depots	1971–4	BT 177/2757
Shipbuilding grants for submarines for overseas navies	1972–82	FV 36/170

Civil Aviation Department, later Ministry of Civil Aviation

R Series files, including, e.g., Naval Air Traffic Control	1919–60	BT 217/1–2634
Accident Investigation Branch (naval involvement):	1945–59	BT 218/13
	1954	BT 220/82
Belfast, Sydenham, transfer to Admiralty	1946–9	BT 247/97
RAF and RN call signs and codes	1948–54	BT 252/87
RN practice areas	1950–7	BT 247/23

71 Board of Trade Marine Department

This was the first government department to be concerned with merchant shipping. It was subsequently transferred in quick succession to the Ministries of Shipping, Transport and War Transport, with the result that its files are badly scattered. The Ministry of Shipping also took over the former Admiralty Transport Department [109], dealing with the transport of military forces and supplies. It was also concerned with naval control of shipping [214], convoys, shipping losses, shipbuilding and the like. In the Second World War the Ministry of War Transport had very similar responsibilities. At the end of each war these duties, insofar as they were needed in peacetime, reverted to the Board of Trade. This included the Naval Transport Service, renamed Sea Transport Service in 1921. The Coastguard, created in its modern form in 1857 primarily as a naval reserve organisation, was transferred from the Admiralty to the Board of Trade in 1923, although it reverted to naval operational control in wartime.

Out-letters to Admiralty and others:	1851–1939	MT 4/1–1424
(indexes)	1864–1918	MT 5/1–58

Correspondence and papers:	1854–1969	MT 9/1–5974
(registers)	1851–1919	MT 85/1–389
(indexes):	1846–95	BT 19/1–21
	1851–1919	MT 86/1–145
Measures against wreckers in Bahamas	1855–60	BT 210/1–50
Register of awards for gallantry at sea	1856–1981	BT 261/1–17
Correspondence and papers	1864–1920	MT 10/1–2085
Albert Medal register	1866–91	BT 97/1–2
Marine Survey Service, papers	1867–1990	MT 15/1–1590
Subsistence in Naval Hospital Valparaiso	1874	BT 15/10
Thames Traffic Committee, Admiralty involvement	1878	BT 13/9/14
Shipping casualty investigations	1910–88	BT 369/1–400
Sinking of SS *Lusitania*	1915	BT 369/194–9

Ministry of Shipping, 1917–21

Correspondence and papers	1914–28	MT 25/1–88
Sea Transport Service, files	1903–79	MT 40/1–269

Coastguard Service

Correspondence with Admiralty	1906–66	BT 166/1–49
Reorganisation discussions with Admiralty	1922–3	BT 235/34
Abolition of CG Reserve	1925	BT 235/51
Transfer from Admiralty	1927	BT 235/99

Ministry of War Transport, 1941–6

Merchant shipping movement cards	1939–46	BT 389/1–44
Turn round of ships, Admiralty meetings	1941	MT 63/225–6
Oil tankers and oil	1942	MT 62/62
Ministry of War Transport, statistics files (including Admiralty memos)	1939–45	MT 65/various
Merchant Navy mortality and sickness	1940–7	MT 65/107–8
Admiralty Net Defence	1941–4	MT 65/111
Tanker situation, report for First Lord of the Admiralty	1942	MT 65/133
Release of merchant tonnage by the Admiralty	1945–6	MT 65/213
UK share of shipping and shipbuilding, Admiralty report	1953	MT 65/326

72 Admiralty Harbour and Railways Departments, 1848–62, later Board of Trade and Ministry of Transport Harbour and Railways Departments, 1862–1964

These departments originally discharged statutory powers given to the Admiralty to approve railway bridges, harbour works and the like affecting navigable waterways. These departments and their powers subsequently passed to the Board of Trade, and later to the Ministry of Transport.

Railway Department, correspondence and papers:	1840–1966	MT 6/1–3574
(indexes)	1840–1919	MT 7/1–324
(letters to Admiralty)	1918–19	MT 2/451–6
Harbour Department, correspondence and papers:	1842–65	MT 19/1–149
(out-letters):	1848–62	MT 2/1–23
	1850–2	MT 2/457–8
(Crown foreshore)	1841–72	BT 297/1–967
Admiralty reports on Railway and Harbour Acts:	1847–62	RAIL 1149/31–3
(Hartlepool)	1850	RAIL 1069/3–4
(Tees):	1850–1	RAIL 1069/32–3
	1858	RAIL 1021/2/6
(Redcar)	1851	RAIL 1069/24
(Cleveland)	1858	RAIL 1069/1

Maps and Plans

Admiralty survey of Spurn Head	1857	BT 356/9785
Pembroke Dockyard extension	1863	BT 356/5607
Admiralty survey of Dover	1865	BT 356/12789
Spithead, limits of Admiralty jurisdiction	1867	BT 356/171
Bosphorous	1869	BT 356/459
Naval Yard, Nassau, Bahamas	1877	BT 356/610
Deal, Admiralty firing range	1939	BT 356/6237
HMS *Dolphin*, Gosport	1966	BT 356/6617–18
Portland Naval Base, reclamation works	1967	BT 356/7208

73 Registrar-General of Shipping and Seamen

The Registrar of Seamen was established in the Admiralty in 1835 to compile a register of merchant seamen as the basis of a naval reserve. He subsequently acquired a range of statutory duties in relation to merchant ships, their officers and men under the Merchant Shipping Act 1854 and subsequent legislation. The office was transferred to the Board of Trade in 1854.

Precedent books, establishment papers etc.:	1702–1993	BT 167/1–177
(history of the Seamen's Registry)	1702–1905	BT 167/23–4

Registers of Seamen's Sixpences	1800–52	BT 167/38–53
Letters to Admiralty	1835–9	ADM 1/3998
Precedent books, RNR:	1856–1926	BT 167/16–17 and 22
(RNR officers)	1900–45	BT 167/11–12
(RNR forms)	1920–59	BT 167/136
Rolls of Honour, WWI and WWII	1866–1970	BT 339/1–8
Index of WWI medals	1914–25	BT 351/1/1–2
Register of applications for naval armlet	1916–17	BT 167/85
Admiralty fishing agreements, letters L–V	1917–19	BT 167/86
Merchant seamen POW records	1923–52	BT 373/1–3722
Register of certificates of service, including naval service	1929–84	BT 318/1
Log books, crew agreements etc.:	1936–50	BT 380/1–1236
(card index)	1939–50	BT 385
Merchant seamen serving in HM Ships	1939–46	BT 390/1–236
Daily casualty registers and index to ships	1940–5	BT 347/1–8
Merchant seamen in liberation of Europe	1944–5	BT 391/1–120
Award of war medals	1944–58	BT 386/1–10
War medals issued to merchant seamen	1946–2002	BT 395/1

[Database: access via The National Archives' Documents Online (www.nationalarchives.gov.uk/documentsonline/).]

Royal Naval Reserve

Seamen's Savings Bank	1865	BT 15/1
Superannuation of naval officers	1869	BT 13/4/1
RNR estimates for 1875	1874	BT 15/10
RNR pensions	1878	BT 15/14
Royal Naval Reserve	1904	BT 13/37

74 Law Officers of the Crown (Attorney-General and Solicitor-General)

The Law Officers supplied legal advice to all departments of government.

Prize Appeals Commissioners	1665–7	SP 9/240
Opinions for Admiralty:	1680–1839	ADM 1/3665–724
	1733–77	ADM 7/298–9
	1791	ADM 1/5119/1
	1792	ADM 1/5120/1
Opinions for Secretaries of State	1704–82	SP 42/138
Opinions for Sick and Hurt Board	1756–64	ADM 105/43
Opinions, including naval legal questions	1889–1948	LO 3/1–1406
Patents appeal files, including naval apparatus	1919	LO 4/13

75 Treasury Solicitor

The Treasury Solicitor provided legal services to all branches of government. His papers deal with naval inventions, patents and contracts, land, disputes involving the Admiralty or Navy Board and the like. There is a subject index in the series list.

Deeds, leases, contracts etc., including naval property	1539–1947	TS 21/1–2034
Royal warrants for Navy Board salaries	1682–1761	TS 21/12
Sick and Hurt Board, deeds, bonds etc.	1698–1824	TS 21/80–6
Victualling yards, insurance policies	1785–1808	TS 21/84
Warrants for felling New Forest timber for RN	1729 and 1748	TS 21/16–17
Navy Board patent	1731	TS 21/18
£500 advance to John Harrison for timekeeper	1737	TS 21/19
Navy Office, insurance policies	1787 and 1823	TS 21/24
New method of shipbuilding	1795	TS 21/25
Accounts, impeachment of Lord Melville	1805–6	AO 3/699
Port Admiral's house, Portsmouth, deeds and plan	1825 and 1833	TS 21/340–1
Admiralty licence to make patented blocks	1846	TS 21/39
Plymouth Dock, plan of proposed land purchase	1848	TS 21/284
Admiralty electric telegraphs, contracts	1850–65	TS 21/40
Screw propeller patents, Admiralty agreements	1852 and 1859	TS 21/41 and 44
Deptford Victualling Yard, manufacture of mustard	1854	TS 21/42
Brennan Torpedo	1877–87	TS 21/55
Admiralty contracts for coal, optical glass etc.	1924–33	TS 21/101
Admiralty agreements with film companies	1926–34	TS 21/103

Correspondence

Admiralty, Jacobite Rebellion	1746	TS 20/4
From Sick and Hurt Board, Prisoners Department	1746	TS 20/80/11–12
Admiralty:	1840–61	TS 18/356
	1842–55	TS 18/609–21
Admiralty with Doctors' Commons concerning prizes	1844–7 and 1855	TS 18/355

Registered Files

Admiralty	1841–1978	TS 32/1–781
MoD, including Navy	1951–84	TS 54/1–63
MoD, Navy	1964–84	TS 68/1–122

Miscellanea

Admiral Cotes's French prizes	1755–69	TS 18/265
Admiralty cases, reports	1801–58	TS 10/1–3
Case of attempt to rescue a pressed seaman	1802–4	TS 11/1122
Assignment of shares of prize money	1817	TS 11/1135

Appeals in prize cases	1827–78	TS 15/1–8
Naval Knights of Windsor, revision of charter of Travers College:	1838–61	TS 18/255
	1856–86	TS 18/410
Applicability of Marine Mutiny Act to a naval officer	1844	TS 18/50
Admiralty complaint that a new church spire would interfere with semaphore communications	1844–5	TS 18/78
Admiralty and Portsmouth Dockyard Railway	1845–9	TS 18/611
RN captures of slavers, pirates etc.	1849–62	TS 18/39–47
Jail sentence for mutinous conduct	1850	TS 18/614
Two pirates taken by HMS *Plover*	1850	TS 18/615
Search for Franklin expedition	1851–4	TS 18/16 and 413
Admiralty telegraph line to Portsmouth	1851	TS 18/68
Recapture of vessel from Chilean pirates by HMS *Virago*	1852–3	TS 18/616–17
Claim by J O Taylor for his invention for lifting screw propellers	1853	TS 18/54
Re-enlistment of deserters in the Navy	1853	TS 18/59
Costs in prize cases	1854–7	TS 15/7–8
Liberation of slaves by HMS *Alert*	1855	TS 18/60
Chatham Dockyard extension	1859	TS 18/81
Naval prison rules	1862	TS 18/266
Admiralty opposition to railway near Greenwich Observatory	1865	TS 18/63
Officers' Widow and Orphan Permanent Fund and RN Female School, Isleworth	1865–72	TS 18/86
Admiralty order to make Hilsea Bridge navigable	1861–74	TS 18/231
Judge Advocate of the Fleet on treasure trove	1912	TS 18/1396
Loss of HM s/m *Thetis*	1939–46	TS 32/101–27
Review of Naval Discipline Act	1967–9	TS 73/7

76 General Post Office

The General Post Office's responsibilities for foreign mails included the Packet Service, provided under Post Office supervision by chartered vessels built for the purpose. The adoption of the first steam packets led to a transfer of the Packet Service to Admiralty control between 1837 and 1860. Later naval concerns dealt with in Post Office registered files included naval and Admiralty post, the maintenance of submarine cables, Post Office employees in the Naval Reserves and wireless telegraphy. POST series are held by the Post Office Archives.

Letters to Admiralty:	1694–1704	ADM 1/4071
	1776–1839	ADM 1/4072–7
Overseas mail contracts	1722–1936	POST 51/1–114
Payments to packet officers and crews:	1766–1854	POST 6/1–37
	1817–52	POST 5/1–7

Registered files:	1792–1952	POST 30/1–4798
	1921–60	POST 33/1–5590
Admiralty instructions concerning packets	1796	POST 43/120
Packet reports	1807–37	POST 39/1–33
Packet boat actions	1793–1815	POST 43/97–104
Packets, 'daily statements' etc.:	1811–22	ADM 7/978–89
	1815–16	ADM 106/3521
Packet minutes	1811–1920	POST 29/1–1467
Solicitor's Department, prosecution of Rear-Adm. W Bradley	1814	POST 74/235
Falmouth Packet Station, reports to Admiralty	1823–39	ADM 1/4036–52
Packet agents: accounts	1826–50	POST 4/4
(letter books)	1839–1920	POST 48/23–71 and 240–318
(nominations)	1863–70	POST 58/187–94
Passenger lists of steam packets	1830–4	ADM 30/35
Missing letters to RN and military offices	1856	POST 23/45
Postal services to HM Ships	1856	POST 48/178
Survey and cable-laying ships, report of HMS *Bulldog*	c.1860	POST 83/35
Transfer of Packet Service from Admiralty	1860–78	POST 51/36 and 92
Telegrams relating to naval operations in Spanish-American War	1898	POST 56/112
Naval mail and telegrams in wartime	1924–5	POST 56/60
Censorship of naval mail in wartime	1942–68	POST 122/93
PO facilities for naval personnel	1956	POST 122/256 and 362

77 Court of Chancery

The Court of Chancery was an equity court dealing particularly with commercial, inheritance and property disputes. In Chancery procedure all sorts of written evidence (including witnesses' depositions) was submitted to a Chancery Master (that is, judge) who then produced a written report and judgement. Chancery Masters' exhibits are evidences put into court in Chancery suits and not subsequently reclaimed. They include accounts, papers, correspondence and logs to do with merchant shipping and related trades such as broking, shipbuilding, sailmaking and shipchandlery. There are a number to do with privateers, and some navy agents' papers. The list following provides examples of the sorts of material to be found. Chancery Masters' reports, summing up these evidences, are in C 38; depositions in C 24, pleadings in C1–C18.

Depositions: town	1534–1867	C 24/1–2507
(country):	1558–1649	C 21/1–767
	1649–1714	C 22/1–1057
Decrees and orders	1544–1875	C 33/1–1262
Reports and certificates	1544–1875	C 38/1–3330

Chancery Masters' Exhibits

Master Blunt	c.1250–1859	C 103/1–205
Master Tinney	c.1250–1859	C 104/1–289
Master Lynch	1466–1835	C 105/1–58
Master Richards	1216–1853	C 106/1–239
Master Senior	c.1250–1851	C 107/1–224
Master Farrer	c.1220–1845	C 108/1–424
Master Humphreys	c.1180–1857	C 109/1–442
Master Horne	c.1280–1855	C 110/1–189
Master Brougham	c.1250–1848	C 111/1–230
Master Rose	1270–1857	C 112/1–222
Master Kindersley	1234–1860	C 113/1–295
Masters unknown	1557–1852	C 114/1–208
Other documents deposited	c.1700–1918	J 90/1–2100

Robson v. Ekines   1699–1724   C 107/171
  (papers and accounts of Capt. Thomas Ekines, RN and *Ekines Friggott*)
Gray v. East   1700–10   C 109/248
  (correspondence concerning Scottish East India Company)
Unknown   1702–3   C 108/318
  (letters to Capt. P Galloway of *Sarah Galley* privateer from owners)
Unknown   1702–4   C 112/181/17
  (accounts and papers of Richard Povey as Treasurer of Sick and Hurt)
Unknown   1702–4   C 114/188
  (Transport Office Cash Book, troop transports to Spain and Portugal)
Creagh v. Rogers   1708–15   C 104/36–40 and 160–1
  (accounts of *Duke*, *Duchess* and *Marquess* privateers of Bristol)
Unknown   1708–28   C 108/280
  (accounts and correspondence of various ships and ventures)
In *re* Newson   c.1711–50   C 104/77–80
  (logs, correspondence and accounts of Capt. Thomas Newson as volunteer, RN, mate and master of various merchantmen)
Unknown   c.1717–20   C 108/3/6
  (wills, assignments of wages etc. received by Edward Chase, navy agent)
In *re* Hall   c.1730–50   C 103/130–3
  (Swedish and British East India Companies; correspondence, accounts, charter parties, shipbuilding contracts etc.)
Hall v. Hallett   c.1730–50   C 111/95–6
  (accounts and papers of various ships)
Unknown   1742–7   C 112/23
  (correspondence and papers of *Prince of Wales* privateer)
Unknown   1745–50   C 108/286
  (accounts of a shipyard in Gosport)

Unknown   c.1750–70   C 108/23
    (papers of Commander John Veysey)
Locker v. Ward   1757–60   C 103/188
    (accounts of Indiaman *Ilchester*)
Unknown   1772–82   C 106/87–90
    (papers of Robert McCullock, prize agent, merchant, postmaster and naval officer at Charleston, South Carolina, 1772–82)
Burroughs v. Camden   1777–80   C 106/192/2
    (accounts of privateer *Hawke*)
Unknown   1778–9   C 114/36
    (accounts of sale of prizes)
In *re* Johnstone   1782–5   C 103/182
    (accounts and log of brig *Robert* of London in West India trade)
Hayden v. Owen, 1813   1782–1801   C 103/176
    (seamen's probates, administrations and letters of attorney)
Unknown   c.1790–1805   C 108/21
    (papers of Alexander Baxter, Gunner, RN)
Various   1798–1804   C 108/24
    (stock and fowls supplied to ships; underwriter's notebook; sale of ships and gear)
Unknown   1798–1808   C 114/37
    (accounts and correspondence of brig *Venus* to South America and Cape)
Downie v. Chard and Brine   1798–1822   C 114/6–8 and 89–93, 105–11 and 159–63
    (papers of Robert Brine, navy agent; cf. C 38/1259)
Toulmin v. Copland   1800–15   C 106/72–5
    (distribution lists for prize money of sundry HM Ships)
Munnings v. Bridges   1800–22   C 108/56–8, 68, 114 and 282
    (accounts and correspondence, shipping at Cape and in East Indies)
Blackburn v. Blackburn   1801–7   C 108/60–1
    (papers of privateers *Trimmer* and *Lord Nelson*)
Crowder v. Gregg   1802–14   C 110/82 and 157
    (accounts and papers of Indiaman *William Pitt*)
Good v. Blewitt   1803–4   C110/164
    (accounts of *Happy Return* privateer)
Unknown   1806–11   C 114/80
    (accounts of Turnbull and Co., merchants and navy agents at Gibraltar)
Bones v. Fleck   1807   C 109/177
    (proceedings in Prussian Admiralty Court, Memel, loss of *Andalusia*)
Bremridge v. Kingdom   1807   C 108/232
    (accounts of prize money of HMS *Terpsichore*)
Pearce v. Green   1807–8   C 103/180
    (accounts of privateer *Snapdragon*)
Unknown   1808–18   C 103/5
    (papers of Broughton and Co., navy and prize agents)

Unknown   1820–3   C 109/195
   (papers and accounts of *Competitor* in convict and East India trades)

78 Court of Exchequer

The equity side of the Exchequer Court originally dealt with cases in which the Crown had a financial interest, but soon developed into a general equity court. Most suits are to do with land, but they include many on customs duties, port dues, merchant shipping, mines, mills, industry, prize money, privateering, naval victualling etc.; the following list gives some examples. Witnesses' depositions were taken before the Barons of the Exchequer in London, or by commission from witnesses living outside London. H Horwitz, *Exchequer Equity Records and Proceedings, 1649–1841* (2001) is a full guide to these records.

Barons' depositions	1558–1841	E 133
Depositions taken by commission	1559–1841	E 134
Illegal export of ordnance	1603	E 134/45 Eliz I/Hil/19
Spanish prisoners taken 1588	1605	E 134/3 Jas I/Mich/19
Hamburger *Pearl* taken by Sir R Leveson	1607	E 134/5 Jas I/Mich/141
Ownership of privateer *Elizabeth*	1608	E 134/6 Jas I/Mich/16
Office of Sergeant Painter of RN	1609	E 134/6 Jas I/Hil/19
Ships from Dartmouth for Fleet, 1588	1609–10	E/134/7 Jas I/Mich/50, 8 Jas I/Mich/14 and Hil/23
Illegal export of gunpowder to Spain	1610	E 134/8 Jas I/East/9 and Trin/6
Felling timber in New Forest etc.	1610	E 134/8 Jas I/Mich/5
Claim of Peter Pett for payment	1629	E 134/5 Chas I/East/5
Lengthening *John* of Chester	1630	E 134/6 Chas I/East/8
Vice-Admiralty of Devon	c.1630	E 134/600/Misc (1630s)
Prizes of *True Love* of Weymouth	1632	E 134/8 Chas I/Mich/6
Victualling of Fleet on Cadiz expedition	1633	E 134/9 Chas I/Mich/61
Blessing of Burntisland chartered	1635	E 134/11 Chas I/East/42
Bristol privateers and prizes, 1625–35	1636–7	E 134/12 Chas I/Mich/39 and 13 Chas I/East/32
Dover privateers and prizes, 1625–6	1637–8	E 134/13 Chas I/Mich/46 and 14 Chas I/Mich/48
Weymouth, Melcombe and Poole privateers and prizes	1637–8	E 134/13 and 14 Chas I/Hil/13
Victualling squadron in Ireland	1674–8	E 134/26 Chas II/Trin/6 and 30 Chas II/Mich/29
Fraud in supplying slops	1676	E 134/413/Misc
Victualling RN in Ireland	1678	E 134/233/Misc
Victualling RN temp. Charles I	1679	E 134/31 Chas II/Mich/23
Wrecking in Cornwall	1683	E 134/35 Chas II/East/44

HCA and Prize Office charges	1691	E 134/3 Wm and Mary/Mich/38
Boundary of Chatham Dockyard	1694–7	E 134/6 Wm and Mary/Mich/34 and 8 Wm III/East/37
Victualling Falmouth packets	1701	E 134/12 Wm III/Mich/30, 12 and 13 Wm III/Hil/24 and 13 Wm III/East/32
Embezzlement of guns from prizes of *William and Mary Galley*	1701–2	E 134/12 Wm III/Mich/49 and 13 Wm III/Mich/45
Seamen's tickets sold by tapster	1702	E 134/13 Wm III/East/20
Happy Return of Bideford, voyages etc.	1708	E 134/7 Anne/East/10
William and Sheppherd transport; 'Negligence and sottishness' of Master	1708	E 134/7 Anne/Trin/5
Poor quality of beef supplied by grazier	1708–9	E 134/8 Anne/Mich/17, 8 and 9 Anne/Hil/4, 9 Anne/Trin/5
Value of *Mary Juliana* transport	1709	E 134/8 Anne/Mich/18
Supply of slop clothes to RN	1714–28	E 134/13 Anne/Trin/10, 1 Geo I/Hil/22 and 27, 2 Geo I/Mich/27 and 3 Geo I/Hil/10
Sick and Hurt Agent at Jamaica	1714	E 134/1 Geo I/Mich/31
Purveyance of Irish timber for RN	1714	E 134/1 Geo I/Mich/40 and East/15
Method of passing pursers' accounts	1717	E 134/3 Geo I/East/11
Falmouth Packet Agency	1717	E 134/3 and 4 Geo I/Trin/5 and 11, and 4 Geo I/Hil/5
Prize money dispute	1718	E 134/4 Geo I/East/16
Accounts of Mordaunt's Regiment, 1692–8; disputed Marine off-reckonings	1721–7	E 134/8 Geo I/Mich 26, 12 Geo I/East/26 and 12, and 13 Geo I/Trin/11
Passing a surgeon's accounts	1723–4	E 134/10 and 11 Geo I/Trin/6
Accounts of *Prosperous*, seamen's pay	1728	E 134/2 Geo II/Mich/27
Payment for timber supplied to RN	1728–9	E 134/1 Geo II/East/8 and 3 Geo II/Mich/26
Prizes of privateers *Prince Frederick* and *Duke*	1750–7	24 Geo II/Mich/7, 30 George II/Mich/16 and Hil/5
Hope victualling transport	1752	E 134/25 Geo II/Easter/7
Prize money to HMS *Woolwich* for prize *Ascension*	1752–4	E 134/25 Geo II/Trin/1 and 27 Geo II/Trin/2
Embezzlement by officers of HMS *Superb* out of prize *Concordia*	1752	E 134/26 Geo II/Mich/5
Samuel taken while transporting felons	1753	E 134/26 Geo II/Trin/5
Liverpool slaver *Grenada*	1768	E 134/8 Geo III/East/4
Bristol slaver *Juno*	1768	E 134/8 Geo III/East/9
GH claim on booty of Pondicherry	1773	E 134/13 Geo III/East/9
London slaver *Mary*	1774	E 134/14 Geo III/Hil/11
Martha of London recaptured	1780	E 134/20 Geo III/Trin/15

Captain D Parry v. Navy Agent over sale of stock	1782–3	E 134/22 Geo III/East/17, 23 Geo III/Mich/21 and East/10
HMS *Enterprise* and prize *Condé*	1783	E 134/23 Geo III/East/11
Fitting-out of Indiaman *Ganges*, 1779–82	1784	E 134/24 Geo III/Trin/3 and 8
Practices in slave trade	1785	E 134/25 Geo III/Trin/9
Office of Receiver-General of Droits of Admiralty	1785–6	E 134/25 Geo III/Hil/14 and East/4, and 26 Geo III/East/5
Angerstein v. Navy Board (*George III* transport)	1788	E 134/29 Geo III/Mich/11 and E 133/12/71
Independence later *Britannia* privateer	1788–9	E 134/29 Geo III/Mich/22 and 30 Geo III/Mich/18
Supply of timber to RN	1790	E 134/30 Geo III/Mich/18
Lugger privateer *Dolphin*	1804	E 134/44 Geo III/Trin/9
Rex v. Dick (Naval Storekeeper at Jamaica):	1806	E 134/46 Geo III/Trin/5
	1806	E 133/146/30
Encroachments on Portsmouth Harbour	1808	E 134/49 Geo III/Mich/8, 9, 18–19 and E 133/145/15 and 152/38
Schooner *Goodrick* of Guernsey	1809	E 134/49 Geo III/East/5
Seizure of ship under Berlin Decrees	1816	E 134/56 Geo III/Hil/11
Rex v. Lindgren (1795 secret mission to obtain hemp)	1817	E 134/57 Geo III/Mich/4 and E 133/150/56–9

79 Prerogative Court of Canterbury

Before the national registration of wills began in 1837, this church court was the most important probate registry in England, having jurisdiction over those who died at sea, among other categories. The indexes to wills, administrations and exhibits (including many inventories of the testators' property) usually identify the deceased's profession. Much of this can now be searched, and some of it viewed, online (www.nationalarchives.gov.uk/documentsonline/wills.asp).

Wills:	1623–1838	PROB 20/1–2993
	1629–1827	PROB 23/1–85
Exhibits:	1660–c.1720	PROB 4/1–26061
	1643–1836	PROB 5/1–6182
	1653–1721	PROB 36/1–27
	1658–1723	PROB 32/1–71
(including seamen's letters of attorney etc.)	1701–82	PROB 3
Commonplace book, containing details of naval supplies, personnel, etc.	c.1779–95	PROB 49/42
Cause papers, including sea officers etc.	1783–1858	PROB 37/1–218
Martin Frobisher	1594–5	PROB 1/30
Sir John Hawkins	1595–9	PROB 1/31
Samuel Pepys	1701–3	PROB 1/9

Sir Cloudesley Shovell	1701–8	PROB 1/57
John Evelyn	1706	PROB 1/55
Capt. James Cook	1776–80	PROB 1/17
Emma, Lady Hamilton	1811–16	PROB 1/25
Sir John Franklin	1829–55	PROB 1/92
Admiral Sir Thomas Masterman Hardy	1839	PROB 1/87
Capt. Alexander Barclay Branch, RN	1843	PROB 22/12

80 Other Courts

The Court of Requests was an equity court reserved for 'poor men's pleadings', which dealt with many Admiralty suits. The Court of Star Chamber was a summary court of criminal jurisdiction, which occasionally handled Admiralty cases. The Court of King's Bench was the principal criminal court, which handled many cases involving naval affairs or naval men. As in the case of most English court records, it is essential to know the plaintiffs' names to trace a particular suit. There is no easy way to search for cases dealing with any particular subject.

Court of Requests
Proceedings	c.1483–1642	REQ 1–3

Court of Star Chamber
Admiralty and porpoise fishery	1509–47	STAC 2/12
Frobisher v. Parkyns (Cathay Company):	1580–1	STAC 5/F29/8
	1582–3	STAC 5/F23/14
Frobisher v. Miller *et al.* (Cathay Company)	1594–5	STAC 5/F/25/10

Court of King's Bench
Rex v. Naval Officers at Madras	1805–7	KB 33/9/4

Bankruptcy Court
Proceedings under Bankruptcy Acts (including against RN officers, navy agents, etc.)	1832–2000	B 9/1–1745

Companies Court
Winding-up proceedings, Froude-Hurrell Torpedo Co.	1892	J 13/174

Central Criminal Court
Naval spy cases	1915	CRIM 1/153 and 683–5
Contravention of Naval Discipline Act	1967–9	CRIM 1/4676

Courts Martial Appeal Court
Appeal cases (all services):	1952–96	J 135/1–545

(registers)	1952–84	J 152/1–3
Restrictive Practices Court		
RN Barracks, Portsmouth	1971	J 154/487
HMS *Dryad*	1971	J 154/496

81 Admiralty: Warrants and Patents, 1660–1964

These are formal legal instruments appointing persons to public offices.

Warrants to Vice-Admirals of Counties, judges and officials of Admiralty Courts etc.:	1660–1973	HCA 50/3–25
	1663–84	ADM 2/1755
	1673–88	ADM 6/404
	1689–1815	ADM 2/1045–78
Patents appointing Lords Admiral, Admiralty Boards etc.:	1532–1810	ADM 7/723–6
	1707–1964	ADM 4/1–408
	1755–1819	ADM 106/3075–6
	1761–1896	T 64/215–22
	1810	ADM 106/3077
(lists and registers):	1660–1964	ADM 4/409–10
	1673–1727	ADM 7/685
	1819–31	ADM 7/686

82 Lord High Admiral, 1660–73 and 1702–8

This list covers those records which can now be identified from James Duke of York, Prince George of Denmark and the Earl of Pembroke as successive Lords Admiral of England, 1660–73 and 1702–8. Other correspondence conducted in their names is to be found with the Admiralty Board and Office papers.

Orders:	1660–73	ADM 2/1732–6
(to Ordnance Board)	1660–2	WO 55/330
(to Navy Board, abstract)	1660–1700	ADM 106/2066
Orders and instructions:	1660–5	ADM 2/1725
	1665–73	ADM 2/1
Private out-letters	1660–85	ADM 2/1745–6
Notes and precedents	c.1660–76	SP 9/214
Letters from Secretaries of State	1703–8	SP 44/209–11
Orders relating to Marines	1703–8	ADM 2/1247
Orders to Paymaster of Marines	1703–8	ADM 2/1250

Lord Admiral's Council, 1702–8

Out-letters	1702–8	ADM 2/365
Letters from Secretaries of State:	1703–6	SP 44/204
	1703–8	SP 44/209–11

83 Admiralty Board

This list is particularly concerned with the Admiralty Board itself and its members the Lords Commissioners of the Admiralty, including important orders issued and correspondence conducted by them.

Rights and perquisites	1634–1733	ADM 7/668–72
Letters to Navy Board, abstracts:	1666–87	ADM 106/2067–70
	1687–1756	ADM 106/2106–17
	1741–1822	ADM 106/2071–99
Minutes and orders	1673–9	ADM 2/1
Minutes	1673–84	ADM 3/275–8
Orders and instructions:	1674–84	ADM 2/1747–51
	1679–84	ADM 2/1726
	1690–5	ADM 2/1728
(to Navy Board)	1660–1700	ADM 106/2066
Letters to Navy Board, Master-General of the Ordnance and (to 1694) Secretaries of State:	1689–1815	ADM 2/169–332
(pay etc.)	1803–15	ADM 2/333–62
Letters to Secretaries of State:	1689–94	ADM 2/169–74
	1695–1804	ADM 2/363–76
	1700–82	SP 42/6–66
(American Secretary)	1776–82	CO 5/259–60
Letters from Secretaries of State:	1679–84	SP 44/63
	1689–1706	SP 44/204
	1693–6	SP 44/205
	1701–84	SP 44/206–32
'Orders and instructions' to C-in-Cs, officers and subordinate boards	1689–1815	ADM 2/3–167
Minutes:	1689–1802	ADM 3/1–127
	1689–98	ADM 3/279–85
	1761–5	ADM 3/253
(draft):	1741–2	ADM 1/5115/9
	1798–1811	ADM 1/5121/3
(digest)	1763–80	ADM 7/700–2
(appointments)	1787–92	ADM 3/254–5
('rough'):	c.1790–1809	ADM 3/249–52

	1793–1839	ADM 3/128–248
	1794–1811	ADM 1/5121/1–2
	1805–15	ADM 3/256–61
	1858–67	ADM 3/266–72
	1868–81	ADM 3/286
(selected)	1816–24	ADM 3/262
(and memoranda)	1869–1976	ADM 167/1–179
Joint meetings of Lords Justices and Admiralty Board	1692–8	ADM 1/5248
Abstract orders to Victualling Board	1694–1819	NMM: ADM/G/773–98
Memorials and reports to Privy Council	1695–1815	ADM 7/333–47
Letters to Greenwich Hospital	1704–1830	ADM 2/1133–42
Orders relating to Marines:	1708–15	ADM 2/1248–9
	1745–1845	ADM 2/1150–246
Orders to Paymaster of Marines	1708–18	ADM 2/1251
Regulations and Instructions for the Sea Service, original signed copy	1731	ADM 106/3078
Instructions to Sick and Hurt Board:	1741 and 1744	ADM 98/103–4
	1797	ADM 98/102
'Secret orders' for major operations:	1745–1815	ADM 2/1331–82
	1818–55	ADM 2/1692–7
	1855–67	ADM 13/7
Orders to Ticket Office to take off Rs and Qs	1749–53	ADM 49/80
Visitations of the dockyards:	1749	ADM 7/648
	1771–5	ADM 7/659–62
	1802	ADM 7/663–4
	1813–14	ADM 7/593
	1828	ADM 7/665
(Plymouth)	1814	ADM 1/5122/16
Orders to admit Greenwich pensioners:	1763–1815	ADM 2/1143–6
(and discharge)	1821	ADM 65/96
Orders for courts martial	1781–1816	ADM 2/1116–126
Convoy orders:	1793–1800	ADM 2/1097–100
	1795–6 and 1808	ADM 7/67–8
	1801–6	ADM 2/1384
	1807–24	ADM 2/1101–15
Rules for Board business	1796	ADM 1/5122/20
Orders, reorganisation of Navy Office etc.	1796–1801	ADM 2/1393
First Naval Lord, letters to Foreign Secretary	1830	FO 95/9/5
Orders to Accountant-General:	1832–56	ADM 46/1–197
(indexes)	1832–56	ADM 47/1–25
Correspondence on Board reorganisation	1920–1	ADM 225/1

84 First Lord of the Admiralty and Private Office

These documents from the Private Office of the First Lord deal with confidential or politically sensitive information. There are also some equivalent papers of the twentieth-century First Sea Lords.

Ships sold and broken up	1762–4	ADM 7/568
Secret Service, declared accounts:	1794–1827	AO 1/2121–30
	1794–1835	AO 3/949
	1835–67	AO 19/75/27
	1839–66	AO 20 various
(Lord High Admiral)	1827–8	AO 2/2/163–4
(Lord Melville)	1828–30	AO 2/13/153–4
(Sir J Graham):	1830–3	AO 2/23/79–80
	1833–4	AO 2/27/67–8
(Lords Auckland and Grey)	1834–5	AO 2/31/1–2, 5–6 and 29–30
Arctic expeditions, Experimental Squadron, CG etc., papers	1824–45	ADM 3/263
Memoranda by Sir C Wood on manning, shipbuilding, dockyards etc.	1838–9	ADM 3/264
School of Naval Architecture, papers	1841–6	ADM 3/265
Lord Ellenborough's correspondence	1844–6	PRO 30/12/11
Nominations for naval cadet etc.:	1848–52	ADM 11/30
	1869–71	ADM 6/447
	1882–1905	ADM 6/448–51
	1898–1917	ADM 6/464–7
Candidates for flag rank	1893–1944	ADM 196/86–94
Correspondence with Colonial Secretary	1874–8	PRO 30/6/5
Papers of J E Masterton-Smith, Private Secretary	1909–19	CAB 1/31–4
Invergordon Mutiny, correspondence	1932–4	ADM 230/1
First Sea Lord		
Papers	1937–65	ADM 205/1–223

85 Admiralty Secretariat: Reports from Flag Officers, 1693–1839

Commanders-in-Chief and flag officers rendered all their official reports to the Secretary of the Admiralty, who reported them to the Admiralty Board. These official reports usually include those of flag officers and captains under their command, except where they were so far detached from the flag as to make it quicker to report directly to the Admiralty. The boundaries of stations changed from time to time; thus 'Jamaica' included the whole of the Americas until the Leeward Islands and North America were separated in 1745, and reabsorbed the Leeward Islands in 1821.

Unemployed FO, Councils of War etc.	1693–1839	ADM 1/577–607
Portsmouth, Western Squadron etc.	1709–20	ADM 1/897–8
Various Home Commands	1709–21	ADM 1/709
Plymouth and other Home Commands	1709–26	ADM 1/795
Mediterranean	1709–1839	ADM 1/376–466
Sir J Norris, Mediterranean, Channel and Baltic	1711–27	ADM 1/2–3
Index to C-in-Cs' reports:	1711–93	ADM 12/1–4
	1807–14	ADM 12/37
	1813–47	ADM 12/5–14
Jamaica	1713–1839	ADM 1/230–304
Sir G Byng, Baltic and Mediterranean	1715–40 [chiefly 1717–29]	ADM 1/518
Portsmouth	1721–1839	ADM 1/899–1404
Nore:	1722–1839	ADM 1/710–94
	1745–1815	ADM 1/519–76
Plymouth	1734–1839	ADM 1/796–896
Western Squadron and Channel Fleet, including subordinate FO	1743–1815	ADM 1/87–159
East Indies:	1744–1804	ADM 1/160–74
	1805–39	ADM 1/176–220
Downs	1745–1815	ADM 1/648–88
Leeward Islands	1745–1821	ADM 1/305–38
North America	1745–1830	ADM 1/480–517
Newfoundland:	1766–1824	ADM 1/470–9
(survey of fisheries)	1774	ADM 1/5117/4
Dublin	1790–1810	ADM 1/640–7
Channel Islands	1794–1815	ADM 1/221–9
Cork:	1794–1832	ADM 1/612–39
	1821–5	ADM 149/15–16
FO of Russian Squadrons in British waters	1795–1800	ADM 1/3245
Cape and West Africa	1795–1839	ADM 1/55–86
Baltic	1801–14	ADM 1/4–18
Leith	1803–24	ADM 1/689–708
Yarmouth	1803–14	ADM 1/1424–34
Woolwich	1804–39	ADM 1/1405–23
C-in-C Brazils and South America	1807–39	ADM 1/19–53
Lisbon/Gibraltar	1808–39	ADM 1/339–75
Chatham	1812–14	ADM 1/608–11
Detached and Experimental Squadrons	1813–37	ADM 1/3232–41
Sir E Codrington, Mediterranean, to Admiralty, Foreign Office etc.	1826–9	ADM 1/467–9
West Africa	1830–2	ADM 1/1

86 Admiralty Secretariat: Letters from Officers, 1698–1839

These are letters (arranged alphabetically by initial letter of surname) from commissioned officers below flag rank, that is, Lieutenants, Commanders, Captains, some Commodores and equivalent Royal Marine ranks, who were either unemployed, employed ashore or serving in circumstances in which it was not possible or convenient for them to report to their commander-in-chief. Early volumes (to c.1705) of 'Captains and Commanders' also include some dockyard Commissioners, yard officers, Lieutenants-in-command, commanders of privateers and masters of merchantmen. Almost all letters from Lieutenants before 1793 were destroyed in the reorganisation of the Admiralty Record Office in 1808–9. Royal Marine 'promiscuous' correspondence consists mainly of letters about or on behalf of Marine officers.

Captains and Commanders, RN:	1698–1839	ADM 1/1435–2738
(nominal index)	1698–1792	ADM 10/8
(index)	1807–14	ADM 12/37
Regulating captains:	1743–5	ADM 1/3663
	1777–8	ADM 1/5117/9
	1787–90	ADM 1/5118/10
(London)	1815–16	ADM 1/3664
Dutch captains	1744–8	ADM 1/3242–3
Lieutenants, RN	1791–1839	ADM 1/2739–3231
Field officers, RM	1802–39	ADM 1/3317–24
Captains, RM	1802–39	ADM 1/3325–36
Lieutenants, RM	1801–39	ADM 1/3337–46
'RM promiscuous'	1801–28	ADM 1/3347–55
Coast Blockade:	1816–31	ADM 106/3480–90
	1825–8	ADM 7/49
Transport Agents	1832–9	ADM 1/3772
Army officers	1822–39	ADM 1/3811–13

87 Admiralty Secretariat: Letters from other Naval Boards, 1673–1832

This is everyday correspondence to the Secretary of the Admiralty from the equivalent officials of other naval boards, as distinct from formal orders and reports to the Lords of the Admiralty [83]. The following lists [88–92] are the same. Some equivalent correspondence between 1660 and 1673 is among the State Papers [15].

Navy Board:	1673–1738	ADM 1/3545–652
	1738–80	NMM: ADM/B/109–200
	1738–1832	ADM 106/2178–297
	1780–1832	NMM: ADM/BP/1–52D
	1801–9	NMM: ADM/B/201–35

	1832	ADM 1/3653–4
(digest)	1673–88	ADM 12/36D
(harbour and rigging wages)	1688–1721	ADM 7/691
(about Lynch's Island, Jamaica)	1729–31	ADM 106/3544
(shipbuilding and fitting)	1804–9	NMM: ADM/Y/1–10
Navy Board and Transport Board	1689–90	ADM 2/1756
Prize Commissioners	1694–1706	ADM 1/3661–2
Victualling Board:	1704–1809	NMM: ADM/D/1–52
	1765–6	NMM: ADM/DP/101
	1770–80	NMM: ADM/DP/102–12
	1781–1822	NMM: ADM/DP/1–42
	1821	NMM: ADM/DP/201A–201B
	1822–32	ADM 1/3775–801
(surgeons' pay and promotion)	1817–32	ADM 105/1–9
Sick and Hurt Board:	1727–42	ADM 1/3528–9
	1742–1806	NMM: ADM/F/3–37
	1742–1817	ADM 98/1–30
	1756–1806	NMM: ADM/FP/1–49
Medical petitions	1790	ADM 1/5118/21
Transport Board:	1794–1816	ADM 1/3730–69
(POW Department):	1795–1808	ADM 1/3773–4
	1796–1822	ADM 98/107–24
(Medical Department)	1806–17	ADM 98/24–30
Surveyor (R Seppings) on new 'system of shipbuilding'	c.1812	ADM 7/709
Surveyor of the Navy	1813–60	ADM 92/1–21
Transport Accounts Committee	1817–18	ADM 1/3770–1

88 Admiralty Secretariat: Letters from Naval Yards, 1701–1839

Commissioners: Plymouth:	1701–4	ADM 1/3358
	1703–1832	ADM 174/159–95
(Portsmouth and Chatham)	1722–6	ADM 1/3359
(home yards):	1740–8	ADM 1/3360–2
	1796	ADM 1/3363
	1809–33	ADM 1/3372–400
(overseas yards)	1800–8	ADM 1/3364–71
(Deptford)	1807–23	ADM 106/3462
Commissioners, storekeepers etc., overseas naval and victualling yards	1809–39	ADM 1/3441–57
Storekeepers (reporting charts in stock)	1810–17	ADM 1/3524
Admiral Superintendent, Plymouth:	1832–51	ADM 174/196–213
	1834–9	ADM 1/3417–34

	1857–60	ADM 174/313–14
(forwarded by)	1839–56	ADM 174/310
Superintendents, Chatham, Sheerness and Deal:	1834–9	ADM 1/3401–6
(Deptford and Woolwich)	1834–9	ADM 1/3407–12
Superintendent, Pembroke and Storekeeper, Haulbowline:	1834–7	ADM 1/3413–14
	1838	ADM 1/3439
	1839	ADM 1/3416
Admiral Superintendent, Portsmouth:	1834–7	ADM 1/3435–8
	1838	ADM 1/3415
	1839	ADM 1/3440

89 Admiralty Secretariat: Letters from Marine Establishments

Col.-Commandant RM Portsmouth Division:	1787	ADM 1/3290
	1801–39	ADM 1/3291–305
(copies of enclosures)	1803–9	ADM 185/112
CO NSW Detachment	1787–92	ADM 1/3824
Col.-Commandant RM Chatham Division	1801–39	ADM 1/3254–73
Col.-Commandant RM Plymouth Division	1801–39	ADM 1/3274–89
Col.-Commandant in London (to 1825), then Deputy Adjutant-General RM:	1802–3	ADM 1/3317
	1804–31	ADM 1/3246–53
	1826–84	ADM 191/1–59
Col.-Commandant RM Woolwich Division	1805–39	ADM 1/3306–16
Col.-Commandant RMA	1821–31	ADM 1/3356–7

90 Admiralty Secretariat: Letters from other Naval Officials and Establishments

Solicitor of the Admiralty and Law Officers:	1680–1839	ADM 1/3665–724
	1733–1830	ADM 7/298–316
	1778–9	ADM 1/5117/13
	1791	ADM 1/5119/1
	1792	ADM 1/5120/1
Legal correspondence and law papers	1771–1812	ADM 1/3725–8
Register Office and Sixpenny Office	1696–1715	ADM 1/3997
GH, Sixpenny Office etc.	1729–1839	ADM 1/3922–9
Governor of RN Academy:	1772–3	ADM 1/5117/16
	1773–1839	ADM 1/3504–21
Treasurer of the Navy	1793–1829	ADM 1/3655–60
Physicians etc. of RNH Haslar and Stonehouse (officers invalided etc.)	1793–1839	ADM 1/3533–41

Inspector-General of Naval Works	1795–1808	ADM 1/3525–7
Hydrographer of the Navy	1795–1809	ADM 1/3522–3
Surveyor of the Navy:	1813–60	ADM 92/1–21
	1832–9	ADM 222/1–15
Falmouth Packet Station	1823–39	ADM 1/4036–52
Surveyor of Buildings/Civil Architect	1832–9	ADM 1/3501–3
Physician-General	1832–9	ADM 1/3530–2
Controller of Victualling	1833–9	ADM 1/3802–9
Registrar-General of Seamen	1835–9	ADM 1/3998

91 Admiralty Secretariat: Letters from other Officials and Departments

Privy Council:	1673–1839	ADM 1/5138–245
(Irish Committee)	1689–90	ADM 2/1756
Secretaries of State:	1689–1839	ADM 1/4080–277
	1771–81	CO 5/119–32
	1775–82	CO 5/254–5
(covering foreign ambassadors)	1697–1708	ADM 1/4278
(American Department)	1776–82	CO 5/259–60
(operations and intelligence)	1808–9	ADM 1/4279
(index)	1697–1792	ADM 12/17–20
Lord Lieutenant and Lords Justices of Ireland	1691–1806	ADM 1/3988–91
Vice-Admirals and Lords Lieutenant of Counties		
(impressment etc.)	1693–1702	ADM 1/5114/3–6
Board of Customs	1694–1839	ADM 1/3863–77
General Post Office:	1694–1704	ADM 1/4071
	1776–1839	ADM 1/4072–7
Board of Trade	1697–1756	ADM 1/3814–16
Secretary at War	1697–1839	ADM 1/4316–51
Treasury:	1698–1839	ADM 1/4283–313
	1704–6	ADM 1/3729
	1811–35	T 28/8–37
Consuls: Mediterranean passes and intelligence:	1700–25	ADM 1/5114/13
	1719–1839	ADM 1/3825–48
	1738–42	ADM 1/5115/3–8
	1777–8	ADM 1/5117/8
	1786–90	ADM 1/5118/8
	1791	ADM 1/5119/11
	1792	ADM 1/5120/8
(Belgium)	1818–36	FO 606/1–4
(Honolulu)	1829–34	FO 331/7
(Norway):	1823–53	FO 330/1

	1832–1907	FO 237/1–26
(Sweden):	1807	FO 334/14
	1819–36	FO 818/1–2
Board of Green Cloth	1722–89	ADM 1/3921
Colonial Governors etc.	1728–1839	ADM 1/3817–23
Law Officers	1733–77	ADM 7/298–9
High Court of Admiralty	1740–1839	ADM 1/3878–910
Treasury Solicitor (Jacobite Rebellion)	1746	TS 20/4
Collectors of Customs (protections)	1756	ADM 1/5116/3–5
Ordnance Board	1780–1839	ADM 1/3999–4035
Home Office:	1784–1836	HO 29/2–7
	1808–9	ADM 1/4279
	1836–98	HO 34/1–88
Public offices, digest:	1802–7	ADM 12/29–34
(index)	1807–14	ADM 12/37
Commission of Naval Enquiry and Board of Revision	1803–9	ADM 1/4078–9
Foreign Office:	1761–1822	FO 95/355–69
	1777–1805	FO 83/2
	1801 and 1805	FO 95/1/1 and 9/3
	1807–8	FO 95/1/2 and 1/6
	1813 and 1815	FO 95/1/2 and 7/7
	1822–44	FO 91/1–11
King's Private Secretary (petitions)	1830–6	ADM 1/4068–70
Board of Trade Marine Department:	1851–1939	MT 4/1–1424
(indexes)	1864–1918	MT 5/1–58

92 Admiralty Secretariat: other In-letters

Petitions:	1674–88	ADM 7/687
	1793–1839	ADM 1/5138–245
Trinity House:	1702–1807	ADM 6/134
	1808–39	ADM 1/4314–15
East India Company and Board of Control	1710–1839	ADM 1/3911–20
Barber-Surgeons' Company and Royal College of Surgeons	1718–1816	ADM 1/4280–1
Royal Africa and South Sea Companies	1721–92	ADM 1/3810
Foreign consuls	1793–1839	ADM 1/3849–62
Lloyds	1793–1839	ADM 1/3992–6
Concerning convoys	1794–6	ADM 7/60 and 67
Miscellaneous	1801–39	ADM 1/4366–5113
Applications to sail without convoy	1811–15	ADM 7/69–72
British Museum, Royal Society, Royal Astronomical Society etc.	1828–39	ADM 1/4282

93 Admiralty Secretariat: Out-letters

These are for the most part out-letters and orders signed by the Secretary of the Admiralty, not formal Board orders and 'Lords' Letters' [83].

General:		1679–84	ADM 2/1752–4
		1689–1746	ADM 2/377–501
		1708	ADM 2/1744
		1809–15	ADM 2/891–921
	(Marines)	1703–1845	ADM 2/1147–246
	(Marines, index)	1746–54	ADM 12/36A
	(signals and signal stations):	1807–13	ADM 7/589–90
		1814–18	ADM 13/1
	(wages and prize money)	1816–21	ADM 2/1714–18
	(miscellaneous)	1816–21	ADM 2/1719–24
	(officers on half-pay)	1816–46	ADM 2/1446–55
	(officers' appointments)	1816–47	ADM 2/1394–445
	(Home Stations)	1816–59	ADM 2/1473–582
	(Foreign Stations)	1816–59	ADM 2/1583–616
	(civil departments)	1816–59	ADM 2/1617–91
	(circulars)	1819–1914	ADM 7/889–909
	(Packet Service)	1837–55	ADM 2/1282–318
	(engineers)	1840–9	ADM 2/1128–32
	(ports and harbours)	1843–5	ADM 2/1471B
	(Steam Department)	1847–9	ADM 2/1387–91
	(Transport Department):	1847–9	ADM 2/1392
		1854–5	ADM 2/1316–18
Report to Charles II on ships and yards		1684	ADM 106/3566
To Secretaries of State:		1689–1782	SP 42/1–66
		1771–81	CO 5/119–32
		1776–82	CO 5/259–60
To Solicitor of Admiralty		1689–1815	ADM 2/1045–78
To Navy Board:		1660–89	ADM 106/1–69C
		1689–1815	NMM: ADM/A/1/58–3115
		1816–33	ADM 106/70–240
	(Transport Service):	1741–2	NMM: ADM/N/234 and ADM/T/1
		1747–50	NMM: ADM/N/235–6
		1757–81	NMM: ADM/N/237–50
		1783–9	ADM 108/1D
		1793–7	NMM: ADM/RP/1–5
	(abstracts, payments)	1781–1815	ADM 106/2100–5
	(Office of Stores)	1783–8	NMM: ADM/P/3264
	(abstracts, transports)	1790–4	ADM 106/2119

(stores and flags)	1808–21	ADM 106/241
(Revenue Cruisers)	1816	ADM 106/3124
(and Ordnance Board etc.)	1816–18	ADM 2/1709–10
To Agent and Commissioner, Plymouth:	1690–2	ADM 174/317
	1694–6	ADM 174/408
	1711–14	ADM 174/287
To Greenwich Hospital:	1704–1830	ADM 2/1133–42
	1829–69	ADM 65/1–58
(miscellaneous)	1816–21	ADM 2/1711–13
To Sick and Hurt Board:	1702–1806	NMM: ADM/E/1–52
(POW Department)	1743–83	NMM: ADM/M/387–414
To Victualling Board:	1708–1815	NMM: ADM/C/349–748
	1816–32	ADM 109/1–47
(Transport Department)	1817–29	ADM 108/1E–3
(Medical Department)	1817–32	ADM 97/2–18
To Consuls, Governors and Collectors of Customs, Mediterranean passes:	1730–1816	ADM 2/1319–25
(Tunis)	1681–99	FO 335/14/11
To ships going overseas	1737	ADM 7/698
Covering commissions and warrants	1744–1815	ADM 6/33–45
To naval boards and public offices	1746–1815	ADM 2/502–688
'Common Letters' to other correspondents	1746–1808	ADM 2/689–855
To Ticket Office:	1774–1815	NMM: ADM/J/3903–4009
(abstracts and indexes)	1698–1785	NMM: ADM/K/2–17
To Col.-Commandant RM, Portsmouth	1776–1817	ADM 185/82A–104
To Home Office:	1782–93	HO 28/1–13
	1794–1800	HO 28/16–26
To Navy Pay Office	1785–1811	ADM 49/130–1
To C-in-Cs: incomplete	1793–1810	ADM 2/168
(Home Squadrons)	1795–1813	ADM 2/941–68
(Home Commands):	1795	ADM 2/1326
	1795–1815	ADM 2/969–1044
(overseas)	1795–1815	ADM 2/922–40
(standing orders):	1839–44	ADM 2/1330
	1845–78	ADM 13/3–6
To FO unemployed, allied FO, consuls etc.	1795–1815	ADM 2/1090–6
Board circular letters and standing orders:	1795–1815	ADM 2/1079–84
	1809–14	ADM 1/5122/2
	1824–7	ADM 49/171
(to C-in-Cs):	1815–30	ADM 2/1327–9
	1830–8	ADM 13/2
To Inspector-General of Naval Works	1795–1808	NMM: ADM/Q/3320–3
To Transport Board: Prisoners Department	1796–9	NMM: ADM/MT/415–22

(Medical Department):	1807–15	NMM: ADM/ET/53–61
	1816	ADM 97/1
To Sheerness Dockyard	1800–12	ADM 106/3559
Draft secret orders and out-letters	1801–37	ADM 1/4353–65
To Revenue Cruisers etc.	1805–30	ADM 7/226
To officers ashore	1809–15	ADM 2/856–90
To Ordnance Board	1812–55	WO 44/498–502
'Reserved' (i.e., very secret) orders	1813–20	ADM 2/1383
To Surveyor of the Navy	1815–50	ADM 83/1–64
To commissioned officers, miscellaneous	1816–18	ADM 2/1706–7
To Warrant Officers, miscellaneous	1816–18	ADM 2/1708
To Ordnance Board etc.	1816–18	ADM 2/1709–10
Legal Branch:	1816–29	ADM 2/1456–70
	1829	ADM 2/1471A
Concerning Mediterranean passes	1816–50	ADM 7/161–2
To other departments, register	1826–40	ADM 7/360
To Consuls, Norway:	1823–53	FO 330/1
	1827–79	FO 236/2
To Royal Clarence Victualling Yard, Portsmouth:	1834–5	ADM 224/9–10
	1857–8	ADM 224/11–12
To Accountant-General:	1844–50	ADM 2/1472
(index)	1844–50	ADM 12/38
To Foreign Office:	1849–64	FO 83/247
	1873–4	FO 84/1409
(register and index)	1822–90	FO 802/235
To Steam Department	1850–9	ADM 84/1–20
Printed instructions for officers employed in the suppression of the slave trade	c.1873–4	FO 84/1409
To Admiral Superintendent, Portsmouth:	1880–1945	ADM 179/1–50
(index)	1915–47	ADM 179/51

94 Admiralty Secretariat, General Correspondence

From the early twentieth century all internal Admiralty papers took the form of 'jackets' or registered files, circulated as necessary among different branches and divisions, and controlled by a central registry with satellite branch registries in each department. Unfortunately only a few of the registers have survived, and the arrangement of the files has been heavily disrupted, so that twentieth-century Admiralty papers are often difficult to trace. The main collection in ADM 1 is searchable by file title, but different sections of the list are arranged differently, and none of the arrangements is either original or logical. A high proportion of the more important papers were abstracted and bound up into cases [103], or taken by the official historians of the two World Wars and listed separately.

Local Government Board:	1838–92	MH 19/1
	1848–55	MH 13/252
(registers)	1861–1920	MH 20/4
Foreign Office:	1839–83	FO 84/301–1648
(registers)	1808–90	FO 605
Colonial office	1857–68	CO 6/22–43
General series: chronological:	1840–1934	ADM 1/5495–8779
	1873–1938	ADM 1/9191–443
	1885–1937	ADM 1/8869–9190
	c.1952ff.	ADM 1/23059–31037
(used by official historians):	1914–19	ADM 137/1–1798
	1922–68	ADM 199/1–2577
(indexes):	1914–19	ADM 137/3058–9
	1914–19	ADM 137/4837
(alphabetical by subject)	1935–6	ADM 1/8780–868
(numerical by subject):	c.1935–45	ADM 1/9444–19191
	c.1946–51	ADM 1/19192–23058

95 Admiralty Secretariat, Military Branch

These are records identifiable as having been kept by the First Naval Lord's Branch of the Admiralty Secretariat. Much is also to be found among general correspondence [94].

Index to C-in-Cs' reports	1813–47	ADM 12/5–14
Out-letters: to Home Stations:	1816–59	ADM 2/1473–582
	1859–69	ADM 13/8–27
(Nore)	1830–1939	ADM 151/3–92
(Nore, indexes)	1860–1901	ADM 152/1–3
(Plymouth):	1842–65	ADM 131/1–2
	1876–1913	ADM 131/3–55
	1919–25	ADM 131/56–62
(Plymouth, confidential)	1893–1910	ADM 131/63
(Plymouth, indexes)	1876–1912	ADM 143/1–2
(Ireland)	1859–1911	ADM 149/3–14
(Portsmouth)	1885–1947	ADM 179/2–49
(Foreign Stations):	1816–59	ADM 2/1583–616
	1859–69	ADM 13/28–40
('Civil Department'):	1816–59	ADM 2/1617–91
	1859–69	ADM 13/41–63
(index and digest):	1828–56	ADM 12/39–44
	1857–9	ADM 12/46A
(circular letters and memoranda):	1819–1914	ADM 7/889–909

	1880–2	ADM 7/938
(Admiralty Fleet orders etc.):	1909–64	ADM 182/1–293
	1942–68	POST 122/93
	1944–52	NSC 11/424
List books:	1821–53	ADM 8/101–34
	1855–93	ADM 8/135–72
'Board Room Journals' (recording movements and orders of HM Ships)	1842–80	ADM 13/105–79
HM Ships in commission: monthly lists	1846–55	ADM 7/539–48
(register)	1852–80	ADM 7/1004
Arrivals and sailings	1854–6	ADM 7/576
Port and station order books	1858–67	ADM 13/184
Registers of correspondence	1860–8	ADM 13/66–7
Precedent books	1860–1933	ADM 198/1–22
Reports from C-in-Cs, South America	1894–1902	ADM 147/2–10
Branch registers, most secret	1941–52	ADM 12/1736–41

96 Admiralty Secretariat, other Branches

'N' branch, the Second Naval Lord's Department, had particular responsibility for naval personnel.

Naval Branch

Schemes for manning the Navy	1832–46	ADM 7/713–15
Precedent book:	1870–85	ADM 198/23
(*Navy List*)	1875–1902	ADM 198/24
(naval personnel)	1880–1914	ADM 198/57–8
(honours and awards)	1941–71	ADM 198/79–80
Monthly returns of numbers borne in RN	1886–9	ADM 6/452
Mobilisation, schemes of complement	1887–1939	ADM 286/1–197
New training scheme	1902–3	ADM 7/941
Citations for honours and awards	c.1942–60	ADM 1/29358–31004

Contract and Purchase Branch

Papers used for official history	1834–1969	ADM 7/948–52
List of Admiralty contractors	1860–1902	ADM 7/918
Precedent books	1875–1961	ADM 198/59–63
Patent applications	1915–22	ADM 245/5–15
Seniority list	1928	ADM 266/9
Registered files	1950–82	ADM 328/1–42

Legal, later Civil Law Branch

Correspondence with Treasury Solicitor:	1840–61	TS 18/356

	1842–55	TS 18/609–21
Correspondence with Doctors' Commons concerning prizes	1844–7 and 1855	TS 18/355
Courts martial: general	1890–1965	ADM 156/1–317
(indexes and registers):	1803–56	ADM 13/103–4
	1812–55	ADM 12/27F
	1812–1915	ADM 194/42–5
(RM)	1834–1914	ADM 194/1–41
(Nore)	1848–63	ADM 153/1–2
(and boards of enquiry etc.)	1912–51	ADM 178/1–405
Registers of correspondence	1855–63	ADM 13/64–5
Precedent book, sales	1906–39	ADM 198/35

Civil, later Civil Establishment Branch

Dockyard wages and establishments	1848–9	ADM 7/594–6
Precedent books:	1870–85	ADM 198/23
	1873–87	ADM 198/56
	1879–1919	ADM 198/25–7
(pensions)	1873–1923	ADM 23/141–3
Admiralty Staff Conference, minutes	1919	ADM 197/1
Admiralty Whitley Council, minutes	1919–67	ADM 197/2–59 and 103–17
Pay rate books	1924–59	ADM 198/81–6

Political and Secret Branch

Out-letters to public offices	1854–7	ADM 2/1698–701
Out-letters to officers	1854–7	ADM 2/1702–5
Index and digest of out-letters	1854–6	ADM 12/45

Miscellaneous Branch

Registers of correspondence	1858–65	ADM 13/68–9

Commission and Warrant Branch

Precedent and procedure books	1907–35	ADM 198/36–7

Naval Law Division

Registered files	1950–83	ADM 330/1–140

Naval Manpower Department

Circulars allowing changes of complement	1952–69	ADM 299/1–213

97 Admiralty and Navy Board, Admirals' Journals and Ships' Logs

These are official, mainly navigational, records kept by various ship's officers and deposited as evidence of their having fulfilled their duties. Admirals' journals also contain various information about their squadrons. Surgeons' journals were returned to the Physician, later Medical Director-General, of the Navy [110].

Various logs, musters etc.:	1648–1707	ADM 7/778–80
	1669–71	ADM 91/1
Captains' logs	1669–1852	ADM 51/1–4563
Masters' logs:	1672–1840	ADM 52/1–4460
	1808–71	ADM 54/1–337
Admirals' journals:	1702–1916	ADM 50/1–413
(nominal index)	1755–1848	ADM 10/9
(A Keppel conveying Queen of Denmark)	1766	ADM 1/5116/13
(Sir C Hamilton, C-in-C Newfoundland)	1819–24	ADM 80/160–3
(C-in-C Atlantic Fleet)	1905–7	ADM 145/4–5
Lieutenants' logs	c.1720–1815	NMM: ADM/L/A/1–Z/9
Supply armed tender	1791–2	ADM 1/3824
Ships' logs:	1799–1972	ADM 53/1–175013
(voyages of exploration):	1762–95	ADM 51/4520–63
	1766–1904	ADM 55/1–164
Journal of J Macgillivray, naturalist aboard HMS *Herald* in Pacific	1852–5	ADM 7/851–2
Submarine logs	1914–75	ADM 173/1–30705

98 Admiralty Secretariat: Foreign Intelligence and Geographical Information

Much geographical information was preserved by the Hydrographer of the Navy [127], whose records were at the time of writing about to be transferred to The National Archives.

Charts of coast of Brazil	c.1615–50	ADM 7/857
'L'état des officiers de la Marine de France'	1683–1720	ADM 7/829
J Barbot, 'Description des côtes d'Afrique'	1688	ADM 7/830A–B
[Printed in *Barbot on Guinea*, ed. P Hair *et al.* (2 vols., Hakluyt Society, 2nd ser., 175–6, 1992)]		
Reports from Secretaries of State etc.	1697–1748	ADM 1/3930–4
Spanish possessions and trade	1717–81	ADM 7/841
Agents and various informants	1737–1834	ADM 1/3970–6
Description of Mauritius	1738	ADM 7/837
Description of Plymouth Sound	1744	ADM 7/838
Don A de Ulloa's observation in Peru	1746	ADM 7/839
Rotterdam Agency reports	1749–85	ADM 1/3935–69

Foreign agents	c.1740–1810	ADM 1/3977–81
Miscellaneous	c.1750–1809	ADM 1/4352
Descriptions of Bay of Honduras and Mosquito Coast	1765–70	ADM 7/837
Descriptions of the Falkland Islands:	1774	ADM 7/704
	1839–42	ADM 7/705
Reports from agents in France	1778	ADM 1/5117/12
Spanish remarks on Patagonian coast	1786–96	ADM 7/842–3
Nootka Sound and Spanish Fleet	1790	FO 95/7/4
Digest of reports from HM Ships:	1793–1810	ADM 1/6032–6
	1796–1803	ADM 1/3984–6
(indexes):	1794–6	ADM 1/6037
	1803–10	ADM 1/6038–9
Survey of Trinidad	1803	ADM 7/764
Spanish printed Caribbean sailing directions	1810	ADM 80/118
Vocabulary of [Okinawa]	1816	ADM 7/849
Movements of foreign warships	1818–22	ADM 1/3983
Account of an embassy to Cochin	c.1822	ADM 7/850
Reports on USN	1826–52	ADM 7/712
H Raper, 'Latitudes and Longitudes of Maritime Places'	1838	ADM 7/853
Observations at Cape of Good Hope	1841–3	ADM 7/854–5
Foreign navies, intelligence	1845–55	ADM 7/167

99   Admiralty Secretariat etc.: Captured Enemy Documents

A miscellaneous collection of captured documents retained by the Admiralty and other departments, gathered in one list for convenience. Many more such documents are scattered among the prize papers of the High Court of Admiralty [8]. Microfilm of the German Naval Archives, 1860–1945 (formerly GFM 26–9 and 31–2) was returned to the Ministry of Defence.

Log of French warship *Minotaure*	1758–60	SP 9/85
Log of French transport *Marquise de Marboeuf*	1773–5	SP 9/87
Logs of Dutch East Indiamen *Meermin, Duifje, De Geertruy* and *Petronella*	1790–3	ADM 7/844
Correspondence of Vice-Admiral J W De Winter as C-in-C of Dutch Fleet; ship's books of the Dutch warship *Jason*	1795–6	ADM 1/3244
Musters of Dutch warships *Hector* and *Minerva*	1799	ADM 1/4352
Muster etc. of French warship *Duguay-Trouin*	1805	HCA 32/999
Muster etc. of French warship *Formidable*	1805	HCA 32/1026
Muster and log of French warship *Mont Blanc*	1805	HCA 32/1096
Muster etc. of French warship *Scipion*	1805	HCA 32/1171
Austrian naval documents	1900–18	ADM 137/4438–4463

German naval documents:	1860–84	GFM 35/359–63
	1913–16	ADM 137/4156–60
	1914–18	ADM 137/4217–351
	1914–18	ADM 137/4356–437
(Foreign Ministry)	1867–1945	GFM 33/1–4835
(Army)	1916–18	ADM 137/4393–421
Letters of Admiral von Tirpitz	1871–1919	GFM 25/8
Index to German naval charts	1914	ADM 7/997
Memo on Führer Decree to German Naval Staff in Italy	1943	GFM 34/3277

100 Admiralty Office Papers

These are documents concerned with the internal management of the Admiralty Office and its staff.

Admiralty and Navy Office precedents:	1660–1785	ADM 7/633–41
(establishments and pay)	1672–1814	ADM 7/675–84
Navy Estimates:	1708–1905	ADM 181/1–99
	1930–7	ADM 181/110–33
(victualling)	1849–83	ADM 221/1–43
(papers)	1915–30	ADM 181/100–9
(debates, mentions of naval aviation)	1949–57	ADM 1/26669–76
(sketch estimates etc.)	1951–70	ADM 181/142–157 and 160–2
Contingent accounts	1759–1836	ADM 17/7–12
Commission Branch and Record Office, papers	1780–1834	ADM 7/58–9
Admiralty House, building accounts	1786–91	ADM 17/1
Board comments on Committee on Finance:	1792	ADM 1/5123/2
	1799	ADM 1/5120/17
Establishment	1807 and 1810	ADM 7/412
Messengers' expenses	1807–35	ADM 7/297
Administrative reports, reorganisation of Secretariat	1809–39	ADM 1/3158–500
Civil employments created since 1780	1810	ADM 49/69
Record Office papers	1811	ADM 1/5120/21
'Business transacted'	1817–34	ADM 1/5123/6
Seniority of Admiralty and Navy Office clerks	1832	ADM 7/822
Enquiry into Accountant-General's Department	1854	ADM 7/945
Phinn Committee on Secretary's Department	1855	ADM 1/5660
Ad hoc committee reports	1858–1959	ADM 268/1–104
Civil establishment books:	1864–95	ADM 7/919–23
	1885	ADM 7/876
Secretary's Department, Committee	1869	ADM 7/996
'Admiralty re-organisation', papers	1869–80	ADM 7/1001

Admiralty Awards Council	1894–1925	ADM 245/1–3
Admiralty Office memoranda:	1896–1910	ADM 7/1002–3
	1940–66	ADM 211/1–52
Seniority lists, 1st and 2nd division clerks	1905	ADM 266/2
Precedent books, naval finance	1906–59	ADM 198/67–73 and 75–7
Catalogue of pictures, plate etc.	1911	ADM 174/359
Correspondence with Crown Estates Commissioners	1947–50	CRES 58/124
Telephone directory	1956–64	ADM 266/10
Organisation and Methods Department, files	1959–70	ADM 331/1–16

101 Admiralty Secretariat: Miscellanea

These documents are mainly registers, returns and statistics compiled or collected in the Admiralty. They include the formal records of naval courts martial and courts of enquiry. Similar records for the twentieth century are scattered among general correspondence [94], cases [103] and the files of the Naval Law Division [96].

Lists of ships, showing disposition, condition etc.:	1665	SP 109/4
	1693–1748	SP 42/111–16
List books:	1673–1813	ADM 8/1–100
	1696–1714	ADM 7/550A
	1821–53	ADM 8/101–34
Mediterranean passes: registers:	1674–6	ADM 12/28B
	1683–8	ADM 7/75–6
	1729–1843	ADM 7/77–133
	1815–29	ADM 7/154–60
(rules)	1722–1802	ADM 7/631–2
(fees)	1735–7	ADM 7/163
(papers)	1816–18	ADM 7/73–4
(recipients)	1822–45	ADM 7/164
Courts martial minutes:	1680–1839	ADM 1/5253–485
	1677	ADM 106/3538 pt. 1
	1684–1798	ADM 106/3543
	1890–1965	ADM 156/1–317
	1892–1951	ADM 178/1–405
(Lord Torrington)	1690	ADM 7/831
(sentences)	1696–1714	ADM 106/3074
(officers, digest)	1741–1815	ADM 12/27B–E
(Marines, on shore)	1755–1809	ADM 1/5489–94
(J Byng)	1757	ADM 7/946
(A Keppel)	1779	ADM 7/947
(Cape of Good Hope)	1796–7	ADM 1/5487–8

(Nore mutineers)	1797	ADM 1/5486
(Nore Station)	1848–63	ADM 153/1–2
(RM)	1898–1914	ADM 194/33–7
(indexes and registers):	1750–1803	ADM 12/28A
	1803–56	ADM 13/103–4
	1806	ADM 12/35
	1812–55	ADM 194/42
	1812–55	ADM 12/27F
Estimate and establishment of RN	1686	ADM 49/41
Marine Regiments, establishments etc.	1690–1708	ADM 7/832
Printed broadside list of English and Dutch fleets	1692	ADM 7/550B
Precedents, full- and half-pay:	1693–1806	ADM 7/678
	1796–1840	ADM 7/911
(pensions for wounds)	1757–63	ADM 30/63/2
Notes and transcripts from the Pepysian Library	c.1700	ADM 7/770–2
Protections from impressment, registers:	1702–12	ADM 7/363–4
	1740–1815	ADM 7/365–76
	1787–1811	ADM 7/555
(Plymouth Dockyard)	1704–9	ADM 174/279
(statutory)	1740–1828	ADM 7/381–400
(whale fishery)	1793–1811	ADM 7/650
(yards)	1794–1815	ADM 7/377–80
Signals and signal books: convoys	1705	ADM 7/832
(Lord Howe's)	1782	ADM 7/582
(various):	1795–6	ADM 7/808
	1800–45	ADM 7/586–8
(Popham's Telegraphic)	1805–9	ADM 7/975–7
(Lynn's)	1814	ADM 7/583
(Admiralty Semaphore)	1827	ADM 7/584
Registers of foreign passes	1729–1827	ADM 7/134–53
Abstracts of captains' journals	1736–95	ADM 7/569–75
Proclamations on prize money etc.	1740–1846	ADM 7/939
Summary of weekly returns from Home Squadrons:	1741–1804	ADM 7/413–501
	1805–7	ADM 7/652
(guardships)	1764–70	ADM 7/651
(home and foreign)	1830–6	ADM 7/653–4
(Portsmouth)	1833	ADM 7/887
C-in-Cs, contingent accounts	1742–1817	ADM 17/2–6
Convoy lists:	1745–8	ADM 7/61–3
	1793–1815	ADM 7/782–806
	1808–15	ADM 7/64–6
Statistics of men, ships and naval debt	1755–1806	ADM 7/567
Lists of prizes:	1755–62	ADM 7/352

	1793–1827	ADM 7/354–7
Royal Society minutes, transit of Venus	1765–71	ADM 1/5117/2
RN rates of pay	1761–1805	ADM 49/177
Tables of imports and exports	1768–69	ADM 7/592
Timber for shipbuilding, papers	1773–96	ADM 7/840
Letters of marque, registers	1777–1815	ADM 7/317–32 and 649
Vessels seized as smugglers	1783–93	ADM 7/353
Panorama of battle of 1 June	1794	ADM 7/884
Establishment book of HM Ships	1794–1814	ADM 7/556
Secret operational or strategic papers	1795–1826	ADM 1/3542–4
'Board Room Journals' (recording movements and orders of HM Ships)	1796–1829	ADM 7/229–96
'General Abstract State' of RN, giving details of each ship	1800–11	ADM 7/559
Register of ships showing orders sent and reports received:	1802–4	ADM 7/557
	1811–24	ADM 7/560–1
Patents of various naval commissions	1805–45	ADM 5/34–7
'Daily statements' of packet boats	1811–22	ADM 7/978–89
Licences to sail without convoy	1812–15	ADM 7/805
Daily returns of movements of HM Ships	1812–30	ADM 7/502–38
Sussex Coast Blockade, standing orders	1825	ADM 7/225
Punishment returns:	1829–30	ADM 7/886
	1837	ADM 7/888
'Reports of Preparations for Battle' returned by C-in-C on inspection	1835–40	ADM 7/562–4

102 Admiralty Secretariat: Record Office

These are compilations and indexes prepared in the Admiralty Record Office, established in 1807 to control the new system of indexing and digesting correspondence introduced in that year. There are also some specimens of the branch indexes of the twentieth-century Admiralty file system.

Digest of important royal, Admiralty or Navy Board orders	1660–1741	ADM 12/36B
Index to C-in-Cs' reports:	1711–93	ADM 12/1–4
	1807–14	ADM 12/37
	1813–47	ADM 12/5–14
Selective indexes of correspondence and Board minutes	1763–92	ADM 12/52–5
Index and digest of in-letters:	1793–1938	ADM 12/56–1735
	1939–74	ADM 12/1742–892
(compendium)	1830–1963	ADM 12/1893–911
Indexes to in-letters	1807–9	ADM 12/48–51
Record Office papers	1811	ADM 1/5120/21

Index to Parliamentary papers relating to RN	1833–56	ADM 12/46B
Branch indexes, specimens	1870–1918	ADM 900/1–68

103 Admiralty Secretariat: 'Cases' and Particular Subjects

A number of collections on particular subjects have survived from earlier periods, but the Admiralty first began collecting 'subject files' in the 1830s. These files, bound into books, were known in the Record Office as Cases. Later, the records collected by the official historians of both World Wars were kept together and bound as cases, creating two large and important artificial collections of records from various provenances.

Salutes and precedence at sea:	1603–88	ADM 7/729
	1603–1815	ADM 7/666–7
Postillion ketch, proceedings	1693–6	ADM 7/695
Rules for apportioning prize and Head Money	1740	EXT 6/6
Arrest of Rear-Adm. P Mayne	1746	ADM 7/699
Experiments with firing shells	1780–6	ADM 7/940
French corvette *Mutine*, stores etc.	1796	ADM 7/358
Proposals from Capt. J Colnett (attack on South America) and R Fulton (submarine)	1801–4	ADM 1/5121/22
Précis of reports on Scheldt expedition	1805–10	ADM 1/3987 and 6040
Cases:	1809–1871	ADM 7/597–629 and 765–6
	1852–1965	ADM 116/1–6441
(used by official historians):	1914–19	ADM 137/1–1798
	1939–45	ADM 199/1–2577
(indexes):	1914–19	ADM 137/3058–9
	1914–19	ADM 137/4837
Lukin's ventilators	1810–11	ADM 49/105
Capt. F Moresby, narrative of British settlement of Cape Province	1820	ADM 1/5123/7
Smuggling lugger *Banshee*, papers	1822	ADM 7/359
Copper sheathing	1822 54	ADM 49/172
Greenwich Observatory, effects of railway	1835–46	ADM 7/617 and ADM 1/5122/21
Port Essington	1836–49	ADM 7/765–6
Carpenter's screw propeller	1838–45	ADM 7/614
Arthur's spinning machinery	1838–48	ADM 49/172
Niger expedition:	1839–42	ADM 13/180–3
	1840–6	ADM 7/615
Secret and confidential reports	1844–56	ADM 13/185
Arctic expeditions	1845–56	ADM 7/187–200
Officers' retirement	1845–6	ADM 7/610

Relief of Sir J Franklin	1849–57	ADM 7/608 and 611
Slave trade	1850	ADM 7/606
Arctic Committee	1851	ADM 7/612–13
Port Natal	1850–7	ADM 7/717
HMS *Hecla*	1878–9	ADM 7/875
Sir J Fisher, papers entitled 'Naval Necessities'	1904–6	ADM 7/993–5
Naval defence of Canada, 1850–1901	1912	ADM 7/937
Funeral of King George V	1936–8	ADM 7/1005

104 Admiralty, Surveyor, later Controller of the Navy

The office of Surveyor of the Navy, and his duties as the Navy's principal warship designer, were transferred from the Navy Board to the Admiralty in 1832. On the retirement of Sir William Symonds in 1847, however, the Surveyor became responsible for the 'Ships Branch', which included naval architects. The job now rather resembled that of the former Controller, whose title it later adopted. Like the other material departments, the Ships Branch left Somerset House in 1860 and ceased to keep its own records. Later they suffered greatly from 'weeding' at a time when technical matters were not regarded as deserving of the historian's attention. With the expansion of the Admiralty's responsibility in the twentieth century the controller came to be responsible for building merchant ships and aircraft as well as warships.

In-letters, shipbuilding:	1806–60	ADM 87/1–77
(registers)	1832–60	ADM 88/1–16
Letters to Admiralty:	1813–60	ADM 92/1–21
	1832–9	ADM 222/1–15
Letters from Admiralty	1815–50	ADM 83/1–64
Abstract out-letters	1829–60	ADM 91/6–24
Letters from contractors:	1854–9	ADM 89/1–4
(registers)	1854–9	ADM 90/1–2
Letters to Admiral Superintendent, Portsmouth:	1880–1945	ADM 179/1–50
(index)	1915–47	ADM 179/51

Ships Branch

Parliamentary returns on screw steamers etc.	1846–8	ADM 7/1006
Establishment of stores, paddle vessels	1850	ADM 7/578
Boilers	1854–67	ADM 95/1–2
Orders and instructions relating to shipbuilding	1892	ADM 7/957
Turning trials	1895–1927	ADM 95/99–100
Steam Drawing Office, abstract tenders	1896–7	ADM 95/106
Dimensions of masts and yards	1907–15	ADM 95/101
Dockyards, shipbuilding instructions	1909	ADM 95/107
Precedent book	1912–20	ADM 198/51

Register of ships' bells	1920–47	ADM 7/958–63

Directorate of Merchant Shipbuilding
Shipbuilding returns	1946–70	ADM 343

Air Department, later Branch
Inspecting Captain of Aircraft, reports etc.	1913–15	AIR 1/346–60
Registered files:	1914–19	AIR 1/146/15/42–152/15/119, 185/15/226/1–345/15/226/297, 625/17/1–673/17/141/1 etc.
	1914–18	AIR 2/various
	1965–72	ADM 327/1–11
(aircraft carriers)	1915–19	AIR 1/436/15/282–9 etc.
Precedent books	1939–57	ADM 198/52–3
Aircraft Launching Working Party	1950–1	AVIA 54/1123

Director of Aircraft Equipment
Reports	1957	ADM 325

105 Admiralty, Director of Naval Construction

The Chief Constructor, later Director of Naval Construction, was the principal naval architect under the Controller, and himself head of a large department. Ships' books were collections of essential information about ships issued to commanding officers. Ships' covers were folders in which were collected all sorts of working papers relating to the development of particular designs. The Admiralty collection of ships' plans is held by the National Maritime Museum.

Ships' books:	1807–73	ADM 135/1–520
	1854–62	ADM 136/1–50
(HM s/m *Dreadnought*)	1967	ADM 324/6
Photographs of HM Ships	1854–1945	ADM 176/1–1141
Ships' covers	1860–1939	NMM: ADM/138/1–650
Loss of HMS *Victoria*	1893	ADM 229/37
Precedent book	1906–12	ADM 198/39
Reports from technical establishments	1914–79	ADM 281/1–313
Statements of stability	1915–33	ADM 229/96
Reports on American shipbuilding	1917–20	ADM 229/97–9
Effects of underwater explosions	1920–8	ADM 229/38
DNC, correspondence:	1923–41	ADM 229/1–16
(notes and memoranda)	1937–45	ADM 229/17–36
Miscellanea	1926–68	ADM 324/1–7
Damage reports	1939–59	ADM 267/1–145

Admiralty Corrosion Committee	1941–79	ADM 249/1–1667
Correspondence with Defence Research Policy Committee	1945–9	DEFE 9/22
Admiralty Ship Welding Committee	1947–75	ADM 284/1–185
Naval Life-Saving Committee	1948–58	ADM 319/2–37
Working Party on UXW Steel	1953	ADM 229/52–3

106 Controller of Steam Machinery, later Engineer-in-Chief of the Navy, 1837–1964

The office of Controller of Steam Machinery, and his department the Steam Department, were established on the transfer of the Packet Service in 1837, a move which was partly intended to provide the Navy with experience in operating steam vessels. The Engineer-in-Chief subsequently became one of the principal subordinates of the Controller, sharing with the Director of Naval Construction [105] and the Director of Naval Ordnance [107] the responsibility for British warship designs.

Register of steam vessels	1823–47	ADM 95/86
Engineer officers' and ratings' service records:	1837–9	ADM 196/71
	1834–79	ADM 29/105–11
Qualities of steam vessels	1837–45	ADM 95/87–8
Oil fuel	1898–1931	ADM 265/26–38, 41, 43 and 45
Reports and papers	1914–58	ADM 265/39–94
Hydraulic jet propulsion	1915–23	ADM 265/16–17
Miscellanea	1938–45	ADM 265/1–2
Overseas visits and technical missions	1951–6	ADM 265/18–25

Steam Department
Miscellanea	1827–60	ADM 95/97
Steam vessels, repairs and maintenance	1846–50	ADM 95/21–2
Report book	1847–50	ADM 95/20
Letter books:	1847–58	ADM 93/1–17
(index)	1847–54	ADM 94/1
Steam factories, register of correspondence	1849–50	ADM 95/9
Letters from Admiralty:	1850–9	ADM 84/1–20
(registers)	1850–9	ADM 86/1–6
Other in-letters	1850–9	ADM 85/1–58

Packet Service
Packet Service correspondence	1837–9	ADM 1/4053–5
Letters from Packet Stations	1837–9	ADM 1/4056–67
Register of correspondence	1839–40	ADM 7/348
Rates of passage	1840–9	ADM 7/351
Register of passages	1845–53	ADM 7/349–50

Proposals to send mails to Mediterranean by railway 1847 ADM 7/716

Holyhead Packet Station
Out-letters	1836–62	RAIL 837/50–61
Accounts	1837–63	RAIL 837/44–7 and 76
Orders received, register	1837–42	RAIL 837/73
In-letters, register	1837–82	RAIL 837/63–4
Plans	1846–8	RAIL 837/81
Contracts etc.	1847–62	RAIL 837/1–18
Packets, sailing times	1848–9	RAIL 837/77

107 Naval Ordnance Department, later Naval Staff Gunnery Division

The position of Director of Naval Ordnance was established on the abolition of the Ordnance Board in 1855 to represent the naval interest in the design and manufacture of heavy guns. On the creation of the Naval Staff he became head of one of its major divisions. The Naval Gunnery Schools (in particular HMS *Excellent* at Portsmouth and HMS *Cambridge* at Plymouth) and a number of technical and research establishments were under his control.

DNO, correspondence with Ordnance Committee	1855–61	WO 46/165
Register of salaries	1857–1914	ADM 7/917
Mining and Whitehead Torpedo experiments	1882	ADM 179/1
Lists of HM Ships showing armament	1886–1923	ADM 186/838–68
Technical reports and papers	1888–1974	ADM 256/1–159
Directorate of Miscellaneous Weapons Development, reports and papers	1940–5	ADM 277/1–40
Naval Ordnance Inspection Department, reports	1940–69	ADM 257/1–158
Admiralty Gunnery Establishment, reports	1944–61	ADM 263/1–219
Admiralty Experimental Establishment, Welwyn, reports	1947–51	ADM 297/1–24
Naval Guided Weapon Working Party	1958–62	AVIA 65/949
Weapons Department, files	1962–75	ADM 333/1–13

108 Admiralty, Dockyards and Works Departments

On the abolition of the Navy Board the dockyards came under the Controller of the Navy. Their general management became the responsibility of a Director of Dockyards, while civil engineering and architecture came under the Civil Engineer-in-Chief until they were transferred to the Ministry of Public Buildings and Works in 1963 [196–8].

Director of Dockyards
Maps and plans:	1708–1955	ADM 140/1–1448

	c.1906–43	ADM 7/882–3
Register of title deeds	1801–56	ADM 7/878
Numbers of men borne	1805–1901	ADM 49/181
Precedent book	1880–1901	ADM 198/64
Report, 'Armour-Clad Ships of England'	1882	ADM 179/1
Dockyard works programme	1905–13	ADM 181/158–9
Boom defence, photographs	1916–46	ADM 244/1–26
Admiralty Industrial Council, minutes	1919–73	ADM 197/66–80 and 91–100
Shipbuilding Trades Joint Council for Government Departments, minutes	1920–68	ADM 197/60–5, 81–90 and 101–2
Registered files (DM series)	1959–72	ADM 329/1–13
Reports and files		ADM 312
Director-General of Works, records		WORK 81

Surveyor of Buildings/Civil Architect, later Architect-in-Chief and Civil Engineer-in-Chief

Plans and drawings	c.1760–1970	WORK 41/1–671
Dockyard works and buildings, papers	1788–1962	ADM 214/1–45
Letters to Admiralty	1832–9	ADM 1/3501–3
Naval works, photographs:	1857–1961	ADM 195/1–126
(airfields, hangers etc.)	1916–32	AIR 59/1–10
Precedent book	1902–49	ADM 198/38
Oil defence schemes	1940–4	ADM 265/3–15

109 Admiralty Transport Department

The Admiralty Transport Department succeeded to the responsibilities of the former Transport Board [175] and Victualling Board Transport Department [176]. In 1917 it was transferred to the Ministry of Shipping [71].

Pay and pension lists, Deptford and Haulbowline	1829–37	ADM 108/180
Register of movements of HMS and transports, Constantinople	1854–5	ADM 7/576
Transports chartered at Deptford	1854–61	ADM 108/192
Claims, precedent book	1855–68	ADM 108/190
Out-letters: miscellaneous	1857–69	MT 31/1, 5 and 10–13
(to Deptford Victualling Yard)	1861–2	MT 31/2
(to HM Ships)	1861–4	MT 31/3 and 9
(to Admiralty and other departments)	1862–3	MT 31/4 and 8
(to WO)	1862–3	MT 31/6–7
Papers	1866–1917	MT 23/2–820
Transport Service regulations:	1908	ADM 174/377
	1929	ADM 174/357

110 Physician-General, later Medical Director-General of the Navy

The Physician-General, later Medical Director-General, was one of the senior Admiralty officials established in 1832 to inherit the responsibilities of the former naval boards, in his case those successively handled by the Sick and Hurt Board [159], and the medical departments of the Transport Board [160] and the Victualling Board [161].

Reports, naval lunatics	1816–63	ADM 105/28–35
Reports by Sir William Burnett	1822–53	ADM 105/68–73
Surgeons' service records	1825–86	ADM 104/11–29
Letters to Admiralty	1832–9	ADM 1/3530–2
Admiralty orders received	1832–9	ADM 97/19–35
Registered in-letters	1832–62	ADM 97/132–259
Registers of in-letters	1832–62	ADM 132/1–31
Index and digest of in-letters	1832–62	ADM 133/1–31
Surgeons' services:	1838–66	ADM 105/37–9
	1854–1926	ADM 104/45–50
Convention with France on Russian POWs	1854–5	ADM 105/67
Registers of killed and wounded	1854–1929	ADM 104/144–9
Hospital circulars	1855–74	ADM 304/13
Letter from Governor of Yokohama enclosing hospital plans	1871	ADM 105/74
Analysis of deaths by station	1879–1927	ADM 105/78
Precedent book, hospitals and sick quarters	1883–90	ADM 105/77
Registers of deaths not by enemy action	1893–1956	ADM 104/102–21
Registers of deaths by enemy action: ratings and Marines	1900–41	ADM 104/122–6
(RNR)	1914–19	ADM 242/13–15
'Notation books', precedents and memoranda	1911–55	ADM 104/150–3
Notes on admissions to home hospitals	1912–55	ADM 104/153
Nosological returns	1927–37	ADM 104/154
Official History, papers	1937–49	ADM 261/3–12
Registers of deaths from all causes, ratings and Marines	1939–48	ADM 104/127–39
Medical reports from ships lost and list of surgeons lost on active service	1939–45	ADM 261/1
Visits and inspections, reports	1941–2	ADM 261/2
Committee on Human Engineering Research	1971–7	ADM 105/98
Clinical Research Working Party, reports	1972–4	ADM 105/109–12
Registered files	1974–85	ADM 105/97–116

Royal Naval Medical School, later Institute of Naval Medicine

'Gentlemen attending introductory lectures'	1827–40	ADM 305/101
Examination results	1884–1914	ADM 305/71–2
Report on tropical conditions in submarine	1966	ADM 105/95–6
Annual reports:	1967	ADM 105/94

		1972	ADM 105/105
		1974–5	ADM 105/99
Surgeons' Journals			
HM Ships etc.:		1793–1880	ADM 101/80–250
		1854–80	ADM 101/256–93
		1913–63	ADM 101/294–804
Convict ships:		1813–56	ADM 101/1–75
		1850–63	ADM 101/251–5
		1858–67	MT 32/1–12
Emigrant ships		1825–53	ADM 101/76–9
HMS *Belle Isle*		1854–7	ADM 102/850

111 Admiralty, Controller of Victualling

The Controller of Victualling was the Admiralty successor to the former Victualling Board [168].

Miscellanea	1698–1976	ADM 114/1–155
Arctic expeditions	1824–56	ADM 114/16–22
Registered letters:	1832–49	ADM 109/132–232
(indexes)	1832–49	ADM 134/17A–45B
Reports to Admiralty	1833–9	ADM 1/3802–9
Letters to Royal William Yard	1833–68	ADM 174/80–96
Distilling at sea	1834–57	ADM 114/65
Packet Service	1837–51	ADM 114/30
Correspondence on ships' libraries	1839–62	ADM 114/5–9
Niger expedition	1840–1	ADM 114/25
Expedition to China	1840–6	ADM 114/23–4
Famine relief, Ireland and Scotland	1846–50	ADM 114/36–7
Navy Estimates	1849–83	ADM 221/1–43
New scale of purser's necessaries, papers	1851–7	ADM 114/31–2
Somerset House, messengers' duties	1851–62	ADM 49/68
Fresh beef for Baltic Fleet, papers	1854–5	ADM 114/22
Ration scales for troops, passengers and convicts	1865	ADM 174/412–13
Sudan expedition	1885	ADM 174/371
Victualling rate books	1897–1942	ADM 174/392–6
Uniforms etc.	1905–72	ADM 114/144–55
Committee on Canteens and Victualling	1907	ADM 174/404
Victualling Department war organisation	1910–12	ADM 174/419–20
Precedent books	1911–43	ADM 198/40–50
Organisation of Victualling Department	1945	ADM 174/405
Development of clothing and equipment, reports	1947–63	ADM 114/119–43 and 145–6

112 Accountant-General of the Navy

The Accountant-General inherited the former Navy Board Accounts Department [136] in 1832, combined with the Navy Pay Office [157] which had come under the Treasurer of the Navy.

Accounts, miscellaneous	1658–1932	ADM 49/1–182
Pensions Branch precedent book, dockyard men	1809–67	ADM 198/54
Ledgers	1826–60	ADM 21/1–35
Journals	1826–60	ADM 19/1–35
'Demi-official' letter book	1827–49	ADM 49/182
Leith rent account	1831–5	ADM 17/31
In-letters, salaries and pensions	1832–5	ADM 14/9–12
Bill Branch precedent book	1832–42	ADM 198/55
Admiralty orders:	1832–56	ADM 46/1–197
(indexes)	1832–56	ADM 47/1–25
Letters from Secretary	1844–50	ADM 2/1472
Correspondence, medals	1855–1942	ADM 198/74
Precedent books:	1886–1932	ADM 198/28–9
	1922–6	ADM 198/65
	1945–7	ADM 198/66
(Director of Naval Accounts)	1932–53	ADM 198/87
Distribution of staff and business	1905	ADM 266/1
Seniority lists	1913–28	ADM 266/3–8

Naval Pay Branch

Ships' record and establishment books	1857–73	ADM 115/1–1090
History of allotment system	1858	ADM 7/719
Notes on payment of pilotage	1859	ADM 7/856
Ships' ledgers	1872–84	ADM 117/1–1036
Precedent books:	1899–1939	ADM 198/30–1 and 34
(recruiting)	1900–18	ADM 198/32–3

Prize and Wills Department

Prize lists:	1834–1913	ADM 238/11
	1915–27	ADM 238/14–16
Precedent books:	1833–61	ADM 198/78
	1864–1953	ADM 238/19
Draft Orders in Council	1864–5	ADM 238/9
Prize bills, registers	1885–1931	ADM 238/4–5
Prize accounts, index	1889–1945	ADM 238/6
Prize journals	1894–1940	ADM 238/1–3
Prize ledger	1915–21	ADM 238/8
Proclamation, prize shares	1919	ADM 238/18

Salvage of SS *Eskburn*	1930–7	ADM 238/17
Bounty and salvage, index	n.d.	ADM 238/7

113 Solicitor of the Admiralty

The Solicitor of the Admiralty acted both as legal adviser and legal practitioner on the Admiralty's behalf.

Letters to Secretary:	1680–1839	ADM 1/3665–724
	1778–9	ADM 1/5117/13
Letters from Secretary	1689–1815	ADM 2/1045–78
Prize certificates (for Head Money)	1710–1833	ADM 43/1–80
Parliamentary return of expense of Admiralty law suits	1739–49	ADM 49/64
Accounts	1744–1832	ADM 17/108–10
Letters to General Hospital	1774–1865	ADM 65/100–5
Legal opinions	1806–1968	TS 25/1–2091
Letters to Navy Board, register	1808–13	ADM 106/2135–8
Letters to Transport Board POW Department	1808–17	ADM 97/108–13
Reports to Admiralty and Navy Board	1816–68	TS 6/1–15
Journals of proceedings	1828–65	TS 4/1–38
Admiralty causes, including naval prizes	1845–1959	TS 45/1–252
Journals and ledgers	1866–1926	TS 38/1–63

114 Marine Office

The Marine Office was established in 1755 as a consequence of the creation of the Corps of Marines under Admiralty control. In its original form it was purely a civilian secretariat, corresponding with the Marine Divisions whose colonels were the most senior Marine officers. Subsequently a Colonel-Commandant in London was established as the senior officer of the Corps, the forerunner of the modern Adjutant-General.

Prospective officers	1755–6	ADM 1/5116/1
Commissions and warrants	1755–1814	ADM 6/406
Courts martial ashore	1755–1809	ADM 1/5489–94
Correspondence and papers	1761–1972	ADM 201/1–154
Regulations: Marines on shore	1804	ADM 106/3088
(Marines at sea)	1804	ADM 106/3089
(Marine infirmaries)	1820	ADM 106/3090
Letters to Divisions	1806–68	ADM 56/1–107
Commission fee books	1807–21	ADM 96/504–5
Officers' addresses	1816	ADM 96/511

Officers' leave books:	1817–33	ADM 6/414
	1822–6	ADM 96/95
Marines purchasing discharge	1818–24	ADM 6/408
Courts martial	1834–1914	ADM 194/1–41
Accounts Branch standing orders	1886–1902	ADM 193/17
RMLI embarkation and disembarkation returns	1903–6	WO 25/3523–6
Fort record book, Cromarty Garrison	1919	ADM 7/942
War diaries	1939–67	ADM 202/1–603
Unit newsletters	1951–78	ADM 301/1–34
Inspection reports	1960	ADM 276/1–2
Training of Special Boat Service	1967	ADM 185/114

Colonel-Commandant in London, later Adjutant-General

Correspondence and papers	1761–1976	ADM 201/1–154
Letters to Admiralty:	1802–3	ADM 1/3317
	1804–31	ADM 1/3246–53
	1826–84	ADM 191/1–59
Letters to Divisions:	1806–68	ADM 56/1–107
(and WO)	1868–74	ADM 200/1–5
(Woolwich)	1868–9	ADM 57/1–2
(and to Admiralty)	1868–72	ADM 63/27
(Chatham)	1868–84	ADM 58/1–21
(Deal)	1868–84	ADM 62/1–18
(RMA)	1868–84	ADM 59/1–17
(Portsmouth)	1868–84	ADM 60/1–17
(Plymouth)	1868–84	ADM 61/1–17
(Deal Depot)	1868–84	ADM 62/1–18
Out-letters miscellaneous	1834–89	ADM 63/1–30
Confidential reports on RM officers	1862–87	ADM 201/10–12
Standing orders	1888–1976	ADM 64/1–148

115 Royal Marine Divisions

The Corps of Marines as established in 1755 had no regimental structure, but was made up of independent companies distributed among three (later four) divisions, each acting as a home barracks and depot from which detachments were drafted for sea service. In 1804 the Royal Marine Artillery was established to take over the manning of bomb and mortar vessels from the Royal Artillery. The original Marines then became known as the Royal Marine Light Infantry.

Chatham

Letters from Admiralty	1755–1826	ADM 183/121–5
General weekly returns	1755–1869	ADM 183/42–98

Order books:	1755–1941	ADM 183/1A–37
(various)	1879–1919	ADM 183/38–41
Discharge books	1773–1884	ADM 183/101–10
Col.-Commandant, letters to Admiralty	1801–39	ADM 1/3254–73
Embarkation books:	1814–16	ADM 183/111
	1835–61	ADM 183/112
	1874–86	ADM 183/113
	1878–84	ADM 183/99
Letter books	1823–84	ADM 183/126–9
Birth and marriage registers, Marines and NCOs	1865–1913	ADM 183/114–20
Letters from Adjutant-General	1868–84	ADM 58/1–21
Musters	1883	ADM 183/100

Plymouth

Order books:	1760–1881	ADM 184/1–19
	1899–1941	ADM 184/20–3 and 57–93
General weekly returns	1761–1919	ADM 184/24–34
Disposal books	1788–1814	ADM 184/42 and 55–6
Col.-Commandant, letters to Admiralty	1801–39	ADM 1/3274–89
Discharge books	1801–92	ADM 184/38–41
Muster roll	1802	ADM 42/1026
Embarkation books	1803–32	ADM 184/36–7
Letters from Admiralty Marine Office	1806–68	ADM 56/1–107
Baptismal and marriage registers	1862–1920	ADM 184/43–54
Letters from Adjutant-General	1868–84	ADM 61/1–17
Casualty lists	1914–18	ADM 184/35

Portsmouth

Letter books:	1772–1853	ADM 185/71–9
(miscellaneous):	1816–22	ADM 185/80
	1899–1906	ADM 185/81
Col.-Commandant: letters from Admiralty	1776–1817	ADM 185/82A–104
(letters to Admiralty):	1787	ADM 1/3290
	1801–39	ADM 1/3291–305
(copies of enclosures)	1803–9	ADM 185/112
General weekly returns	1797–1820	ADM 185/38–61
Embarkation books	1803–13	ADM 185/62
Letters from Admiralty Marine Office:	1806–68	ADM 56/1–107
(and Marine Pay Office)	1818–22	ADM 185/113
Order books:	1806–1941	ADM 185/1–35 and 105
	1888–1911	ADM 185/36–7
Disposal books	1809–69	ADM 185/106–10
Discharge books	1816–88	ADM 185/63–7 and 111

Letters from Adjutant-General	1868–84	ADM 60/1–17
Marriage register	1869–81	ADM 185/69
Plan of RM Barracks Forton	1878	NMM: ADM/Y/P/151

Woolwich

Embarkation book	1805–14	ADM 81/22
Col.-Commandant, letters to Admiralty	1805–39	ADM 1/3306–16
Discharge books	1806–69	ADM 81/11–21
In- and out-letters	1810–34	ADM 81/1–9
List of foreigners and men on limited service	1814	ADM 6/407
Letters from Admiralty Marine Office	1806–68	ADM 56/1–107
Baptismal and marriage registers	1822–69	ADM 81/23–5
Index to regulations	1826–69	ADM 81/26
Letters from Adjutant-General	1868–9	ADM 57/1–2
General weekly returns	1868–9	ADM 81/10

Royal Marine Artillery

Portsmouth embarkation book	1805–37	ADM 193/7
Letters from Admiralty Marine Office	1806–68	ADM 56/1–107
Portsmouth marriage and baptismal register	1810–53	ADM 193/9
Col.-Commandant, letters to Admiralty	1821–31	ADM 1/3356–7
Portsmouth disposal book	1845–59	ADM 193/8
Letters from Adjutant-General	1868–84	ADM 59/1–17
Portsmouth order books	1890–1918	ADM 193/3–6
Portsmouth orderly books	1917–18	ADM 193/10

Deal Depot

Letters from Adjutant-General	1868–84	ADM 62/1–18
Disposal books	1874–82	ADM 193/1–2

Overseas Units

China Battalion, papers.	1840–65	ADM 201/40 1 and 43
(Canton Brigade)	1858–60	ADM 193/11–12
Operations in Mexico	1861–2	ADM 193/24
Japan Battalion, papers	1862–75	ADM 201/45
Ashanti Battalion, papers	1873–4	ADM 201/39
South African Battalion: correspondence and musters	1879	ADM 193/13–14
(order book)	1879	ADM 183/38
Mediterranean Battalion, quartermaster's diary	1882	ADM 185/70
Esquimalt Battalion, papers	1883–96	ADM 201/44
Suez Battalion, order book	1884–5	ADM 193/15
Suakin Battalion, papers:	1884–5	ADM 201/46–9
(order book)	1885	ADM 193/16

China Battalion, papers	1900–2	ADM 201/42
Special Service Brigade, papers	1916	ADM 201/16
Fifth RM Battalion, correspondence	1918–19	ADM 183/130
Falkland Islands Detachment, reports	1971–2	ADM 201/131

116 Naval Staff and Divisions

In 1912 the Naval Staff was established to provide the Admiralty with professional planning and advice in the conduct of naval operations. It absorbed the existing Naval Intelligence and Naval Ordnance Departments, and subsequently acquired divisions dealing with all aspects of naval operations. Many records of the Naval Staff during the two World Wars are among the records collected by the official historians. The staff also had its own Historical Section, responsible for preparing 'Staff Histories' for internal naval use. Most Naval Staff papers before 1964 are among the general Admiralty files, and only a few divisions preserved their own records.

Naval War Staff papers	1909–14	CAB 1/31–4
Records used by official historians:	1914–19	ADM 137/2523–3057
	1922–68	ADM 199/1–2577
(indexes)	1914–19	ADM 137/3058–9
Admiralty coded telegrams	1916–18	ADM 137/4637–49
Operations Division		
War Room: signals sent reporting movements of ships	1914–15	ADM 137/4483–4
(received reporting enemy movements)	1914–16	ADM 137/4485–7
Q Ship movements	1916–18	ADM 137/4056
Logs of D/F plots	1916–18	ADM 137/4536–61
Weekly D/F Bulletin	1917–18	ADM 137/4672–7
Convoy records	1939–45	ADM 237/1–1619
Mine-laying operations	1939–45	ADM 243/1–18
'Pink Lists' (movements of HM Ships):	1939–45	ADM 187/1–55
	1950–76	ADM 187/56–188
'Blue Lists' (ships building)	1940–6	ADM 209/1–5
'Red Lists' (movements of minor war vessels)	1940–9	ADM 208/1–53
'Green Lists' (movements of landing craft)	1942–6	ADM 210/1–21
Training and Staff Duties Division		
Preparation of manual of combined operations	1921–2	ADM 203/61
Historical Section		
Official History of First World War, drafts:	1929	ADM 137/4827–36
(Jutland)	1919	ADM 137/4825
First World War historical monographs:	1921–39	ADM 275/12–15

(Technical History)	1919–21	ADM 275/19–20
(German Cruiser Warfare)	1940	ADM 275/22
(East Coast Operations)	1940	ADM 275/23
History of the 'Cod War', material	1958–61	ADM 306/1–49

Torpedo and Anti-Submarine Division
Undersurface Warfare Department, files	1964–70	ADM 332/1–9

Department of Operational Research
Reports	1917–73	ADM 219/1–670
Chief Adviser, records		ADM 320

117 Naval Staff, Naval Intelligence Division

The Naval Staff absorbed the former Naval Intelligence Department (originally Committee), first established in 1883. During the First World War NID superintended the cryptographic unit known as 'Room 40', subsequently renamed the Government Code and Cypher School [27] and transferred to Foreign Office control. During the Second World War the Admiralty Operational Intelligence Centre collected information both from NID and GCCS and applied it to the actual conduct of operations. Much naval intelligence, including NID reports, can also be found among the records of the War Office Directorate of Military Operations and Intelligence [39], the Air Staff [206–7] and the Foreign Office [23–5].

Reports:	1914–78	ADM 223/1–882
(German naval operations):	1914–18	ADM 137/3060–2
	1915–18	ADM 137/3964–4046
	1915–19	ADM 137/4123–6
	1917	ADM 137/3839–923
(suspicious merchant ships)	1914–18	ADM 137/4190–216
(German submarines):	1915–18	ADM 137/4098–122
	1915–18	ADM 137/4127 55
	1915–18	ADM 137/4161–7
(miscellaneous):	1908 16	ADM 137/4352 5
	1914–18	ADM 137/4678–821
	1915–19	ADM 137/4172–89
Messages received by NID	1914–18	ADM 137/4057–97
Accommodation in Wallace Collection	1917–18	AR 1/293, 449 and 535
Translations of German documents	1940–8	ADM 203/77
UK beach surveys	1945–92	ADM 326/1–1326

Naval Intelligence Committee, later Department
Reports	1883–1912	ADM 231/1–71

| 'Papers on naval subjects' | 1901–7 | ADM 174/378 and 387–8 |

'Room 40'

British and German codes	1913–19	ADM 137/4650–71
German naval cypher keys and call signs	1914–18	ADM 137/4493–535
Room 40, GCCS Naval Section etc., papers	1914–51	HW 3/1–186
Decrypted German wireless signals:	1915	ADM 137/3956–63
	1915–19	ADM 137/4562–636
(registers of intercepts)	1914–19	ADM 137/4464–82
Wireless signals, various	1918	ADM 137/4488–92
'Wireless News'	1918–21	ADM 233/1–35

Operational Intelligence Centre

| ULTRA digests: | 1941–5 | DEFE 3/1–1018 |
| | 1944–6 | ADM 223/828–9 |

118 Royal Naval Scientific Service

The RN Scientific Service was both a professional body of civilian scientists in Admiralty employ, and the Admiralty organisation responsible for scientific research. It succeeded the Board of Invention and Research, established in 1915 to oversee the work of the Admiralty Experimental Stations. In 1941 the Admiralty undertook on behalf of all the services to co-ordinate research into radio valves.

Reports	1923–48	ADM 283/1–64
Directorate of Research Programmes and Planning, reports	1939–70	ADM 282/1–29
Directorate of Materials Research, files	1941–70	ADM 278/1–6
Admiralty Chemical Advisory Panel:	1944–9	ADM 220/1 and 119–21
	1944–57	ADM 247/1–296
Directorate of Physical Research, reports	1945–75	ADM 285/1–145
Atomic energy to power ships, correspondence with Ministry of Supply	1945–7	AB 1/313B
Naval Weather Service, memoranda	1945–65	ADM 307/1–10
Journal	1945–70	ADM 206/1–144
HQ Departments, report	1946	ADM 206/145
Committee on Admiralty Experimental Establishments:	1946–9	ADM 220/63
	1948	ADM 282/19
Directorate of Aeronautical and Engineering Research, reports	1947–63	ADM 287/1–64
Select Committee on Naval Research, seventh report	1955–6	AVIA 65/1080

Board of Invention and Research

| Minutes, reports and papers: | 1914–19 | ADM 293/1–21 |

	1915–19	ADM 218/8–23
Admiralty Experimental Stations	1915–21	ADM 218/74–91

Co-ordination of Valve Development Department

Reports	1941–78	ADM 272/1–299
Policy and Technical Committees	1943–54	ADM 220/610–19
Inter-Service Technical Valve Committee	1941–56	AVIA 12/47–51
Co-ordination with AEA Metallurgy Division	1962–6	AB 24/9

119 Admiralty Research and Technical Establishments

This list groups the records of a large number of technical establishments belonging to the RN Scientific Service or to divisions of the Naval Staff. There are also some Admiralty factories having laboratories or research departments.

Admiralty Compass Observatory, reports and papers:	1837–1950	NMM: ADM/235
(indexes)	1837–1950	OBS 1/1544
Admiralty Experimental Works, reports	1873–1976	ADM 226/1–1253
A B Wood Collection	1912–64	ADM 218/1–310
Admiralty Experimental Stations	1915–21	ADM 218/74–91
Admiralty Research Laboratory: correspondence and papers	1915–71	ADM 212/1–201
(reports and notes)	1920–73	ADM 204/1–3253
(Fire Control Group, files)	1931–59	ADM 294/1–32
RN Cordite Factory: history	1916–59	ADM 322/1
(experiments on electric cables)	1930	ADM 322/2
Admiralty Engineering Laboratory, memoranda and reports	1920–74	ADM 227/1–2850
Admiralty Centre for Scientific Information and Liaison, reports	1926–56	ADM 213/1–1142
Admiralty Gunnery Establishment, files	1931–59	ADM 294/1–32
Admiralty Experimental Diving Unit, reports	1933–67	ADM 315/1–48
Admiralty Chemical Department, reports	1939–59	ADM 248/1–47
Admiralty Small Craft Experimental Establishment, reports	1941–58	ADM 250/1–86
Central Metallurgical Laboratory, reports	1943–56	ADM 254/1–163
Admiralty Development Establishment, Barrow-in-Furness, reports	1945–58	ADM 251/1–168
Naval Air Fighting Development Unit, reports	1946–55	ADM 314/1–6
Admiralty Materials Laboratory, reports	1947–78	ADM 252/1–672
Admiralty Signal and Radar Establishment, *Radar Reflections for Marine Navigation*	1948	AN 13/2258
Naval Telecommunications Flying Unit, reports	1948–9	ADM 335/69–71
Admiralty Oil Laboratory, reports	1948–74	ADM 289/1–182
Yarrow Admiralty Research Department, project reports	1948–72	ADM 315/1–48

RN Aircraft Yard, Fleetlands, reports	1949–66	ADM 291/1–143
Service Trials Unit, reports	1950–4	ADM 335/72–9
Admiralty Fuels and Lubricants Committee, reports and papers	1951–70	ADM 308/1–70
Amphibious Warfare Experimental Establishment, reports:	1953–4	DEFE 37/1–3
	1954	DEFE 37/21–3
RM Amphibious School:	1955–63	DEFE 37/9–13, 24
	1963–75	DEFE 37/14–20, 25–8
Admiralty Fuel Experimental Station, later Marine Engineering Establishment, reports	1955–70	ADM 309/1–54
Central Dockyard Laboratory, reports and technical memoranda	1957–73	ADM 295/1–35
Joint Services Amphibious Warfare Centre	1958–62	DEFE 37/4–8
Admiralty Marine Technology Establishment, reports	1977–84	ADM 341
Admiralty Research Establishment, reports and files	1984–91	ADM 342

HMS Vernon, Torpedo (later Torpedo and Anti-Submarine) School

Annual reports	1881–1950	ADM 189/1–98
Various reports	1907–51	ADM 189/99–212, 232–4 and 240
Mining School, monthly reports	1921–2	ADM 189/213–31
Mine Design Department and Mining Establishment, reports:	1922–58	ADM 253/1–876
(research and development)	1947	DEFE 9/22
Minutes	1952–8	ADM 189/235–9

Naval Aircraft (later Royal Airship) Works

Correspondence and papers	1911–39	AIR 11/1–255
Airship and engine drawings	1910–31	AIR 12/1–319
Reports, airships and kite balloons	1917–19	AVIA 20/175–250
Drawings, airships and balloons	1917–19	AVIA 24/1–88

Naval Construction Research Establishment

Papers of D E J Offord, Superintendent	1918–53	ADM 311/1–12
Advisory Panel on Underwater Explosion Research: minutes and reports	1942–69	ADM 279/1–139
(minutes)	1942–8	ADM 1/15149
Reports:	1942–77	ADM 280/1–921
	1947–51	ADM 229/39–51

Admiralty Surface Weapons Establishment

Files	1918–74	ADM 220/1–2365
Marine Propulsion Committee	1941–7	ADM 220/22–43

Admiralty Shock in Ships Committee	1941–9	ADM 220/44–7
Admiralty Corrosion Committee	1943–6	ADM 220/2–7
RN Personnel Research Committee	1943–6	ADM 220/60
Admiralty Ship-Welding Committee	1944–50	ADM 220/8–21
Ship Target Trials Committee	1945–9	ADM 220/48–58

Admiralty Underwater Weapons Establishment

Reports:	1929–68	ADM 258/1–345
	1945–9	ADM 292/199–200
	1945–57	ADM 292/205–16
	1945–50	ADM 292/220–1
	1959–76	ADM 302/1–600
(research and development)	1947	DEFE 9/22
Translated German documents:	1930–57	ADM 292/1–198
	1944–6	ADM 292/201–4
	1946–8	ADM 292/217–19
A/S Experimental, later Underwater Detection Establishment, reports:	1930–61	ADM 259/1–695
(research and development)	1947	DEFE 9/22
RN Torpedo Factory and Torpedo Experimental Establishment, reports and technical notes	1930–60	ADM 290/1–655
Underwater Weapons Launching Establishment, reports	1945–59	ADM 260/1–113

120 Greenwich Hospital

This list includes records of the internal management of the Hospital, and of its sources of income, which included light dues and unclaimed prize money. After the closure of the Hospital as an institution accepting resident pensioners in 1865, its funds were inherited by the Greenwich Hospital Foundation, which continued to own the buildings, and to administer a variety of naval pension schemes.

Miscellanea	1639–1957	ADM 80/1–209
Out-letters, lighthouses and light dues	1685–1715	ADM 66/152–7
Subscribers' roll	c.1694	ADM 80/172
Grand Committee, minutes	1695–1700	ADM 67/1
Fabric Committee, minutes:	1696–1702	ADM 67/2
	1699–1702	ADM 76/1
General Court and Directors, minutes:	1703–1829	ADM 67/3–17
(extracts)	1704–6	ADM 67/264
(disciplinary orders)	1704–20	ADM 80/69
(Directors)	1737–1829	ADM 67/18–79
(extracts)	1737–1832	ADM 67/265

(indexes)	1802–52	ADM 67/117–18
Treasurer's ledgers:	1695–1864	ADM 69/1–54
(Greenwich Estate)	1810–1930	ADM 71/1–17
Treasurer's accounts:	1696–1865	ADM 68/1–88
(works):	1696–1829	ADM 68/670–887
	1805–58	ADM 80/113–14
	1806–14	ADM 80/110–12
Officers of the Hospital	1695–1865	ADM 80/169
Contracts	1696–1730	ADM 80/2–3
Warrants for payments:	1704–62	ADM 80/67–8
(French ships)	1724–5	ADM 80/70
Letters from Admiralty:	1704–1830	ADM 2/1133–42
	1829–69	ADM 65/1–58
Directors, out-letters	1704–80	ADM 66/28
Nurses' services	1704–1864	ADM 73/83–5 and 87–8
Council, minutes:	1705–1865	ADM 67/119–236
(digest)	1694–1865	ADM 67/266–7
Household accounts:	1705–1829	ADM 68/344–546
(contingencies)	1714–20	ADM 68/547–9
Treasurer, in-letters:	1717–1829	ADM 65/59–62
(prize money)	1780–1820	ADM 65/63–5
(Deputy Treasurer's)	1809–33	ADM 65/66–75
In-pensioners' wills:	1732–67	ADM 80/108
	1861–9	ADM 80/109
Musters, house labourers	1737–1802	ADM 73/70–7
Prize money, Spanish prizes:	1739–50	ADM 68/317
(unclaimed)	1745–85	ADM 68/318–28
(distributed abroad)	1776–1801	ADM 68/333
(agents' accounts)	1793–1813	ADM 68/314–16
(distribution accounts)	1805–26	ADM 68/305–13
Letters of attorney and prize agents	1747–1802	ADM 68/329–32
Other in-letters	1756–1865	ADM 65/76–112
Governor and Directors, letters to Admiralty	1722–1839	ADM 1/3922–9
Earl of Orford's grant	1747	ADM 76/14
Out-letters, light dues and prize money	1761–93	ADM 66/149
Allegations of Capt. Thomas Baillie	1778–9	ADM 80/92–3
Unclaimed pay of ratings etc. DD	1787–1834	ADM 80/4–12
North and South Foreland lights: papers	1789–1832	ADM 76/14
(plans etc.)	1791–1807	ADM 80/65
(accounts):	1826–8	ADM 80/66
	1827–9	ADM 68/343
Register of Deputy Treasurers	1795–1807	ADM 68/334
Other out-letters	1799–1870	ADM 66/1–67

Secretary, out-letters:	1800–65	ADM 66/32–45
	1824–70	ADM 66/22–7
Register of prizes taken by HM Ships	1800–20	ADM 80/165
Warrants for appointments	1800–65	ADM 73/91–2
Lord Nelson's Trust	1807–11	ADM 76/15
Payments received	1807–12	ADM 68/335–6
Deputy-Treasurer, out-letters	1807–65	ADM 66/46–67
Register of prize appeals cases	1812–18	ADM 68/337
Sale of deserters' effects	1814–31	ADM 68/340–2
Entries of nurses	1817–31	ADM 6/239
Applications to be nurses	1819–42	ADM 6/331
Governor: out-letters	1825–65	ADM 66/9–21
(order book)	1829–65	ADM 80/71–2
(appointments)	1851–64	ADM 73/93
Register of freight charges	1828–1914	ADM 73/453–6
GH Constitution Committee	1829	ADM 67/259
Letters to Victualling Board Medical Department	1829–30	ADM 97/62
Commissioners: declared accounts:	1829–30	AO 2/10 and 16
	1831–2	AO 2/20 and 24
	1833–4	AO 2/30 and 32
(minutes)	1829–65	ADM 67/80–116
(minutes, indexes)	1802–52	ADM 67/117–18
(minutes, extracts):	1845–59	ADM 76/6
	1853–62	ADM 67/268–77
(out-letters)	1830–65	ADM 66/1–8
Staff establishment books	1830–63	ADM 73/78–81
Lieutenant-Adjutant, out-letters	1839–65	ADM 66/148
Burial registers	1844–1981	ADM 73/460–5
Artificers: musters and wage lists	1845–66	ADM 73/132–52
(description book)	1848–62	ADM 73/153
Register of miscellaneous employees	1847–65	ADM 73/86
Register of medal holders	1848–9	ADM 73/94
Post-mortem books	1857–66	ADM 80/208–9
Muster of servants	1865–9	ADM 73/82
Capt. Superintendent, order book	1866–70	ADM 80/106

Greenwich Hospital Foundation

Officers' salaries:	1865–1919	ADM 80/170–1
	1920–57	ADM 80/177–9
Treasurer's ledgers	1865–1937	ADM 69/55–68
Registered files	1870–1978	ADM 169/1–1060
Annual estimates	1924–75	ADM 169/776–872 and 1030–56
Account books	1926–71	ADM 169/985–1029

121 Greenwich Hospital: Pensions Office

These are records of the in- and out-pensioners whom Greenwich Hospital supported.

In-pensioners, admissions:	1704–1846	ADM 73/36–41
('Rough entry books')	1704–1863	ADM 73/51–62
(candidates):	1737–63	ADM 6/223–4
	1781–4	ADM 6/225
	1813–34	ADM 6/267–9
	1815–59	ADM 6/226–66
(entry books)	1764–1865	ADM 73/65–9
(registers)	1779–1869	ADM 73/42–50 and 63–4
Petitions for admission or re-admission	1756–70	ADM 65/81
In-letters, admission of pensioners	1756–1822	ADM 65/81–97
Admiralty Board admission orders	1763–1815	ADM 2/1143–6
Out-pensions:	1781–1801	ADM 73/95–103
	1807–9	ADM 73/131
	1814–46	ADM 22/254–443
	1863–9	ADM 73/63–4
(to officers):	1814	ADM 22/254
	1815–42	ADM 22/47–9
	1846–1921	PMG 71/1–13
	1871–1931	ADM 165/1–6
	1951–61	ADM 165/9
(admissions)	1814–21	ADM 1/5122/19
(paid by WO)	1842–83	WO 22/1–300
(RM applicants)	1862–1908	ADM 201/22–3
Governors' minutes on applications	1789–1859	ADM 6/271–322
Applicants' certificates of service	1790–1865	ADM 73/1–35
Letters from Admiralty, answers to applications	1816–21	ADM 2/1711–13
Admiralty orders for entry and discharge of pensioners	1821	ADM 65/96
Register of cash left by pensioners DD	1863–5	ADM 80/14
Naval officers' pensions	1865–1961	ADM 165/1–9
Chaplains applying for pension	1866–1909	ADM 6/446
Naval and civil officers' pensions	1866–1928	PMG 70/1–30
Ex in-pensions paid by WO	1868–70	WO 23/24
Grants to Warrant Officers' and ratings' orphan girls:	1881–1911	ADM 162/1–2
	1951–9	ADM 162/9
Grants to Warrant Officers' and ratings' orphan boys	1884–1959	ADM 162/3–8
Ratings' widows' pensions:	1882–1917	ADM 166/1–12
(applications)	1892–1933	ADM 166/13–14
Education grants to officers' children:	1883–1922	ADM 163/1–2

	1907–33	ADM 164/1
Allowances to wives of lunatic pensioners	1899–1948	ADM 73/457–9

122 Greenwich Hospital Schools

Five schools belonging to Greenwich Hospital or its Foundation are to be distinguished:
1. Greenwich Hospital School (est. 1716), later Upper School, later Nautical Division, admitting the sons of warrant officers and ratings aged 13 and over.
2. The British National Endeavour (est. 1798), adopted by Parliament, renamed Royal Naval Asylum and merged with Greenwich Hospital 1805, renamed Lower School 1825, admitting naval orphans aged 5–11 (girls to 1841 only).
3. The School for Officers' Sons (1828–61).
4. The Infant School, for children of Hospital in-pensioners and staff.
5. The Royal Hospital School, now at Holbrooke, Suffolk, the successor of No. 1, which admits the children of seafarers of all services.

Miscellanea	1655–1870	ADM 80/98
Accounts:	1727–1829	ADM 68/550–8
(School trustees)	1805–20	ADM 68/559–60
(ledgers)	1805–20	ADM 72/1–9
Applications for GH Schools	1728–1861	ADM 73/154–389
Apprentices' indentures and masters' bonds	1728–1870	ADM 73/390
Discharges from GH Schools	1728–1861	ADM 73/404–6 and 412–17
Board minutes, entry and binding-out of boys:	1752–61	ADM 67/240
	1758–66	ADM 67/245
Governors' nominations for GH Schools:	1767–1824	ADM 73/407–9
	1821–60	ADM 73/400–3
British National Endeavour: register of children and accounts	1800–1	ADM 73/89
(Committee minutes):	1800–5	ADM 67/278
	1801–3	ADM 67/253
RN Asylum: Commissioners' minutes	1801–21	ADM 67/253–4
(Board and Committee)	1805–13	ADM 80/100
(list of subscribers)	1802–5	ADM 80/99
(girl applicants)	1802–41	ADM 73/391–2 and 440–1
(boy applicants)	1803–65	ADM 73/391–7
(staff and boys)	1805–21	ADM 73/449
(boys admitted)	1805–61	ADM 73/410–11
(accounts)	1807–21	ADM 67/255–6
(staff salaries)	1821–29	ADM 73/450
(girls admitted)	1837–40	ADM 73/443
Apprenticeships of GH School boys	1802–70	ADM 73/418–20

Out-letters	1808–81	ADM 66/68–79
Lower School, officers' sons	1828–37	ADM 73/399
Upper School, officers' sons:	1828–61	ADM 73/425
(applicants):	1832–44	ADM 73/415
	1844–61	ADM 73/398
	1861–81	ADM 161/2
(daily musters)	1856–70	ADM 73/451
Fathers of applicants, certificates of service:	1836–54	ADM 29/17, 19, 25, 34, 43 and 50
	1858–61	ADM 29/59
	1864–94	ADM 29/70 and 80–96
Infants' School:	1835–48	ADM 67/257
	1844–68	ADM 73/90
Return of staff in GH Schools	1847	ADM 1/5123/18
Periodic inspections	1883–1904	ADM 203/20
Construction of Royal Hospital School	1928	ADM 80/174–6

123 Royal Observatory and Board of Longitude

The bulk of the records of the Royal Observatory, the Board of Longitude and the Astronomers-Royal are now in Cambridge University Library. Magnetic and meteorological observations from the Royal Observatory, Kew, are among the records of the Meteorological Office [224].

Board of Longitude, 1713–1828

Papers	1605–1830	CUL: RGO 14/1–68
Expenses	1762–1819	ADM 49/65

Royal Observatory

Library catalogue	1827	ADM 190/1
Catalogue of observations etc.	1828	ADM 190/2
History and regulations	1835–1916	ADM 190/8
Catalogue of instruments	1864–1919	ADM 190/13
Visit of King George V	1925	ADM 190/18

Board of Visitors

Letters to Admiralty	1828–39	ADM 1/4282
Minutes	1830–1964	ADM 190/3–6
Letter book	1831–1912	ADM 190/7
Warrants of appointment	1838–1953	ADM 190/9
Elections	1870–1939	ADM 190/14–17

Nautical Almanac Office

Accounts	1832–5	ADM 17/32

Astronomer-Royal

Reports:	1853–70	ADM 190/10–12
	1940–60	ADM 190/19–34

124 Naval Funds and Charities

Charity for Sea Officers' Widows, 1732–1836

Commissioners' minutes	1732–1819	ADM 6/332–4
Accounts and papers	1733–44	ADM 1/5115/1
Pay books	1734–1835	ADM 22/56–237
Court of Assistants, papers	1735–79	ADM 76/15
Paymaster's accounts:	1738–1829	ADM 68/561–668
(drafts)	1732–53	ADM 68/669
Applications	1797–1829	ADM 6/335–84
Marriage certificates of applicants	1801–18	ADM 30/57
Applications referred to Court of Assistants	1808–30	ADM 6/385–402
Applications	1809–28	ADM 22/238

Compassionate Fund and Compassionate List

Applications:	1809–31	ADM 6/323–6
	1832–6	ADM 6/237–8
Out-letters	1809–45	ADM 2/1085–9
Pay books:	1809–51	ADM 22/239–52
	1837–1921	PMG 18/1–38
Registers of pension recipients	1853–1926	ADM 23/42–4, 95–100 and 200–5

Poor Knights of Windsor

Letters Patent	1798	ADM 80/181
Establishment	1803–11	ADM 106/3534
Accounts:	1807–29	ADM 80/194
	1862–92	ADM 80/199 207
Out-letters	1810–80	ADM 80/186–190
Letters Patent	1841	ADM 80/185
In-letters	1841–81	ADM 80/191–2
Travers College, correspondence	1892	ADM 80/193

125 Naval Shore Organisations

Impress Service, 1743–1815

Regulating Captains' reports to Admiralty:	1743–5	ADM 1/3663
	1777–8	ADM 1/5117/9
	1787–90	ADM 1/5118/10
Recruiting expenses, Consul Leghorn	1744–6	ADM 30/63/1
Returns of men raised under Recruitment Acts	1757	ADM 1/5116/6
Rendezvous musters and entries: Hull	1759–60	ADM 36/7158
(Greenock)	1790	ADM 30/63/5
(Falmouth)	c.1792–1800	ADM 30/63/11
(Waterford)	1794–5	ADM 30/63/7
(IoW, Quota Act)	1795	ADM 30/63/8
(Londonderry)	1803	ADM 30/63/10
Officers' expenses:	1793–1800	ADM 30/34
(Edinburgh)	1796–9	ADM 30/63/9
Officers' appointments	1803–15	ADM 11/14–18

Sea Fencibles, 1793–1815

Officers appointed:	1793–1810	ADM 28/145
	1803–15	ADM 11/14–18
Pay lists	1798–1810	ADM 28/1–144
Papers	1798–1810	ADM 28/147
Accounts	1803–10	ADM 17/91–5

Signal Stations, 1803–15

Navy Board correspondence	1803–14	ADM 49/109–17
Accounts	1803–15	ADM 17/96–107
Regulations	c.1803	ADM 7/974

Coast Blockade, 1816–31

In-letters	1816–31	ADM 106/3475–9
Out-letters:	1816–31	ADM 106/3480–90
	1818–31	ADM 106/3496–508
(seizures)	1820–31	ADM 106/3491–5
(to Admiralty)	1825–8	ADM 7/49
Miscellanea	1819–31	ADM 106/3509

126 Naval Colleges

Royal Naval Academy, later College, Portsmouth, 1737–1837
Governor, letters to Admiralty:	1772–3	ADM 1/5117/16
	1773–1839	ADM 1/3504–21
Accounts	1816–20	ADM 17/14

HMS Britannia, later RNC Dartmouth
Examination marks	1877–1902	ADM 6/469–73
Booklets listing 'Officers, masters and cadets'	1931–68	ADM 203/104–98

RNC Greenwich
Applications for appointments	1872–6	ADM 203/17
In letters	1872–1925	ADM 203/1–15
Capt. Superintendent's letter book	1872–6	ADM 203/16
Examination results: lieutenants etc.	1876–1957	ADM 203/21–44
(sub-lieutenants etc.)	1907–57	ADM 203/41–4
Council on Naval Education, papers	1877–1904	ADM 203/18–19
War Course: confidential reports	1904–14	ADM 203/99
(memoranda)	1906–24	ADM 203/100
Board of Studies, minutes	1923–43	ADM 203/45–6
Syllabus, lectures etc.	1923–77	ADM 203/47–60, 63–76 and 78–98
Correspondence on RM Striking Force	1937–8	ADM 203/62
War College, visiting lecturers	1966–77	ADM 203/101–3

RNEC Keyham, later Manadon
Examination results	1897–1909	ADM 7/931

127 Other Admiralty Officials and Departments

At the time of writing the bulk of the records of the Hydrographer were about to be transferred from the Hydrographic Office.

Register Office, 1696–9, and Sixpenny Office, 1699–1836
Commissioners' minutes	1696–9	ADM 105/41
Letters to Admiralty:	1696–1715	ADM 1/3997
	1729–1839	ADM 1/3922–9
Minute book, medical business	1698–1700	ADM 99/1
Miscellanea	1700–10	ADM 76/23
Precedent book	1700–33	ADM 80/164
Collector of Sixpences for London, registers of ships:	1725–1830	ADM 68/194–217
(register of masters' names)	1745–52	ADM 68/219

Receiver of Sixpences, accounts	1732–1830	ADM 68/89–193
Receiver of Sixpences in North America, correspondence	1768–83	ADM 80/131–2
Registers of Seamen's Sixpences	1800–52	BT 167/38–53
Collectors of Sixpences, various outports, registers of ships	1834–6	ADM 68/218

Hydrographer of the Navy

Charts and sailing directions: Scilly Isles etc.	1792–1809	ADM 7/845–6
(coast of Karamania)	1810–12	ADM 7/847
(Africa West Coast sheet 17)	1846	FO 83/1380
(index chart)	1903	ADM 7/998
(Gallipoli campaign)	1915	WO 301/619–21
Letters to Admiralty	1795–1809	ADM 1/3522–3
Accounts	1818–23	ADM 17/28
Correspondence on proposed railways	1846	RAIL 39/24–5, 38 and 211
Tables for the National Grid of Great Britain	1948	OS 3/444
Correspondence with Directorate of Military Survey	1967–70	WO 181/327

Inspector-General of Naval Works

Reports to Admiralty	1795–1808	ADM 1/3525–7
Letters from Admiralty	1795–1808	NMM: ADM/Q/3320–3
Letters from Navy Board	1802–10	ADM 106/2539
Letters to Navy Board	1803–10	ADM 106/3547

Chaplain of the Fleet

Expense of religious books	1812–17	ADM 49/106
Registers of baptisms, marriages and burials	1945–95	ADM 338/1–75

Admiral Commanding Reserves

RNR: statistical returns	1861–1919	ADM 120/215–22
(papers)	1914–39	ADM 120/120–68
(regulations)	1921	ADM 120/224
CG orders and instructions:	1868–1911	ADM 7/774–6
(regulations)	1898–1911	ADM 120/225–7
Reserves general, papers	1875–1920	ADM 120/1–113
RNVR: papers	1914–40	ADM 120/169–206
(regulations)	1923	ADM 120/223
Sea Cadet Corps	1918–24	ADM 120/214
CG Reserve, papers	1919–25	ADM 120/114–19
Shore Signal and Shore Wireless Services	1924–5	ADM 120/213
RN Wireless Auxiliary Reserve	1932–9	ADM 120/207–11
RN Volunteer Wireless Reserve	1937–9	ADM 120/212

Director of Naval Education
Annual reports   1904–13   ADM 7/936

Flag Officer Submarines
Patrol reports   1939–45   ADM 236/1–54

British Admiralty Delegation, Washington
Files   1941–5   AVIA 38/585 and 914
Technical Mission, directory   1941   AVIA 38/124
Newsletters and reports   1943–6   AVIA 22/898

128 Admiralty Publications

The majority of these publications were issued for internal Service use, although some were on sale to the public. The Seniority Lists are incomplete runs. Most twentieth-century publications were issued in the CB ('Confidential Books'), BR ('Books of Reference'), OU ('Office Use') or SP ('Signal Publications') series. As the distinction between these was chiefly the degree of security classification, it was common for books to be transferred from one series to another. The Inter-Service Topographical Unit (formerly NID Geographical Department) issued geographical handbooks. Air Publications include many relating to naval aircraft and air equipment.

Seniority lists: commissioned officers	1717–1846	ADM 118/1–185 and 337–52
(masters):	1780–91	ADM 118/186–90
	1829–41	ADM 118/209–28
	1844–6	ADM 118/183–5
(surgeons):	1780–7	ADM 104/51–6
	1791	ADM 118/191
	1796–1817	ADM 104/57–79
	1813	ADM 118/353
	1820–3	ADM 104/80
	1829–32	ADM 118/209–11
	1834–9	ADM 118/219–25
	1841–2	ADM 118/357
	1844–6	ADM 118/183–5
	1868–86	ADM 104/81–7
(pursers and paymasters):	1810–22	ADM 118/192–207
	1817–20	ADM 118/354–5
	1829–32	ADM 118/209–15
	1832–41	ADM 118/218–28
	1844–6	ADM 118/183–5
(boatswains, gunners and carpenters):	1810–15	ADM 118/192–9
	1816	ADM 118/201 and 354

	1820	ADM 118/205 and 355
	1827	ADM 118/208
	1833	ADM 118/216–17 and 356
	1836	ADM 118/222
	1839	ADM 118/226
	1844	ADM 118/229
(all officers)	1827–1957	ADM 186/1–897
(mates, midshipmen and cadets)	1849	ADM 6/183
Regulations and Instructions for HM Service at Sea:	1731	ADM 106/3078
	1746–7	ADM 7/201–3
	1757	ADM 7/999
	1766 and 1781	ADM 7/204–5
	1798	ADM 106/3079
	1808	ADM 7/206–8 and 971
	1808	ADM 106/3080
	1820	ADM 106/3082
	1824	ADM 7/210 and 1000
	1824	ADM 106/3083
	1825	ADM 7/211 and 990
	1825	ADM 174/367
	1825	ADM 106/3084
(Marine)	1785–1808	ADM 49/58
(supplementary):	1813	ADM 1/5122/13
	1813	ADM 7/209 and 972
	1813	ADM 106/3081
(pursers)	1825	ADM 7/973 and 990
(medical):	1825	ADM 7/221 and 990
	1857	ADM 7/222
(notes and correspondence)	1816–20	ADM 49/63
Signals and Instructions for the Use of HM Fleet	1816	ADM 7/586
Lists of HM Ships showing armament	1886–1923	ADM 186/838–68
Manual of Naval Prize Law	1888	WO 32/8344–5
BR series	1892–1984	ADM 234/1–1187
NID *Papers on Naval Subjects*	1901–7	ADM 174/378 and 387–8
Instructions as to Cash Duties (in dockyards)	1911–31	ADM 49/179–80
Inter-Service Topographical Department (later MOD Joint Intelligence Bureau), surveys, maps and reports	1913–68	WO 252/1–1486
Navy List, confidential edition:	1914–18	ADM 177/1–18
	1939–45	ADM 177/19–61
Air pamphlets	1914–18	AIR 1/2103
Air Publications	1914–19	AIR 1/2321–3
RNAS Training Manual	1915	AIR 10/117
RNAS Bomb Sight Instructions	1915–16	AIR 10/309 and 314

OU series	1915–51	ADM 275/1–31
CB series	1916–85	ADM 239/1–781
RNAS Kite Balloon Training Manual	1917	AIR 10/270
Admiralty monthly intelligence reports	1919–39	ADM 223/807–27
King's Regulations and Admiralty Instructions:	1921	PC 2/450
	1923–4	PC 2/462 and 468
	1926	PC 2/477
	1928–9	PC 2/494 and 498
	1930–1	PC 2/506 and 514
	1933–4	PC 2/534 and 558
	1935–6	PC 2/582 and 585
	1937–8	PC 2/609 and 624
	1939	PC 2/641
First World War historical monographs:	1921–39	ADM 275/12–15
(Technical History)	1919–21	ADM 275/19–20
(German Cruiser Warfare)	1940	ADM 275/22
(East Coast Operations)	1940	ADM 275/23
RM Training Manual	1932	ADM 193/19
Geographical Handbooks, Abyssinia	1938	FO 370/566
'Pink Lists' (movements of HM Ships):	1939–45	ADM 187/1–55
	1950–76	ADM 187/56–188
'Blue Lists' (ships building)	1940–6	ADM 209/1–5
'Red Lists' (movements of minor war vessels)	1940–9	ADM 208/1–53
'Green Lists' (movements of landing craft)	1942–6	ADM 210/1–21
SP series	1940–8	ADM 274/1–4
Air Publications (Naval)	1941–76	ADM 264/1–114
Ship Fire-Fighting Manual	1942–9	HO 187/1543
RN Scientific Service Journal	1945–70	ADM 206/1–144
Defence of Merchant Shipping, Master's Handbook	1948	ADM 324/3
RM Drill Manual	1953	ADM 193/20–3
FAA newsletter	1965–7	ADM 335/81–3
RN official website, weekly copies	2003–4	ZWFB 1/51–99

129 Navy Board, 1546–1642, and Navy Commission, 1642–60

There is no discrete collection of Navy Board records before 1642, but scattered items can be identified among the State Papers.

Quarter books	1562–?	Bodleian Library: Rawlinson MS. A.200–3
Bill books	1642–1826	ADM 18/1–134
Orders from Council of State and General at Sea:	1649–50	SP 18/6

	1650	SP 18/13
	1651–2	SP 18/18
Orders from Admiralty Commission and Generals at Sea:	1653	SP 18/43–4
	1654–6	SP 18/93, 120–1 and 152
	1657–8	SP 18/178 and 199
	1659–60	SP 18/218 and 225
In-letters:	1650–1	SP 18/12 and 17
	1652–3	SP 18/27–30 and 45–62
	1653–7	SP 46/119–21
	1654–5	SP 18/78–92 and 103–18
	1656–7	SP 18/132–50 and 161–76
	1658–9	SP 18/187–97 and 207–17
	1660	SP 18/222–5
Miscellaneous correspondence	1651–7	SP 46/96–9
Petitions etc.	1653	SP 18/64
Pursers' bonds	1655–60	SP 18/119, 151, 177, 198, 218 and 225

130 Navy Board, 1660–1832

These are records other than correspondence [131–2].

Precedents: Navy Office	1616–1734	ADM 7/639
(pay and pensions)	1672–85	ADM 106/3565
(shipbuilding and repair)	1719–63	ADM 95/12
(pursers' accounts etc.)	1752–1800	ADM 30/44
(financial):	1759–1834	ADM 49/83–8
	1784	ADM 49/54
(impressment)	1776–1821	ADM 7/967
Accounts and miscellanea:	1658–1832	ADM 49/1–182
	1681–1832	ADM 106/3542–9
Orders, instructions and precedents:	1660–84	ADM 2/1740
	1660–95	ADM 7/827
	1669–99	ADM 7/732
Minutes etc.:	1660–8	ADM 106/3520
	1667–75	ADM 106/2886–8
	1677 and 1701–7	ADM 106/2888
	1686–7	BL: Additional MS. 9303
	1710–15	ADM 106/2889–91
	1729	ADM 106/2544
	1731–1832	ADM 106/2545–745
	1743–55	ADM 106/2892

	1744–5	ADM 106/2893
	1750–3	ADM 106/2894
(ships, boats, stores)	1757–70	ADM 106/2895
(indexes):	1762–77	ADM 106/2746
	1796–1822	ADM 106/2747–50
(Committee of Accounts)	1796–1820	ADM 106/2751–87
(indexes)	1796–1820	ADM 106/2788–9
Tenders and contracts for naval stores:	1662–73	SP 46/137
	1664	SP 29/108
	1665	SP 29/141
	1666	SP 29/185
	1667	SP 29/229
	1670–88	ADM 49/22–5
(abstracts):	1660–3	ADM 7/828
	1668–1769	ADM 49/26–33
(abstracts, clothing contracts)	1760–98	ADM 49/35
(abstracts, yard contracts)	1762–96	ADM 49/34
(prices)	1660–1800	ADM 49/119–21
Courts martial papers	1672–8	ADM 106/3537 pt. 1
Establishments, guns and stores	1673–1727	ADM 49/123
Navy Estimates:	1673–1830	ADM 7/168–84
	1686	ADM 49/41
	1702–76	ADM 49/42–50
	1708–1905	ADM 179/132–539
	1752–8	ADM 49/41
(correspondence)	1765	ADM 7/703
Survey of necessary repairs to ships and yards	1684	ADM 106/3566
Muster of all ships at all ports 16 September	1688	ADM 106/3541 pt. 1
Reports on harbour and rigging wages	1688–1721	ADM 7/691
Lists of ships, showing disposition, condition etc.	1693–1748	SP 42/111–16
Register of ships refitted and repaired	1698–1705	ADM 49/95
Debt of the Navy, abstracts and estimates	1698–1830	ADM 49/37–40
Particulars of Navy Estimates	1708–1970	ADM 181/1–162
Head Money vouchers	1710–1833	ADM 43/1–80
Enquiry into observance of the regulations	c.1720	ADM 106/3543
Visitation of the dockyards, expenses:	1730–56	ADM 49/171
(minutes)	1810	ADM 106/3552
Regulations and Instructions for HM Service at Sea, original signed copy	1731	ADM 106/3078
Return of Sick and Hurt Board expenditure	1739–49	ADM 7/185
Returns to House of Commons: financial	1740–70	ADM 17/223
(foreign timber)	1771–4	ADM 49/124
Lieutenants' examination, miscellanea	1740–1810	ADM 49/36

Survey of condition of ships of RN	1750–64	ADM 7/551–4
Miscellanea, shipbuilding, timber, hemp etc.:	1743–1807	ADM 49/169
	1759–1801	ADM 49/162
Warships built by contract, lists and accounts:	1755–63	ADM 49/171
	1784–97	ADM 49/94
	1801–17	ADM 49/102
	1805–7	ADM 49/169
Naval expenses in West Indies	1756–66	ADM 49/1
Shipbuilding expenditure	1764	ADM 7/186
Board and Commissioners' patents:	1790–1831	ADM 5/1–23
	1804	ADM 106/3569
Lists of chartered merchantmen	1793–1802	ADM 95/108
Accounts and papers of S G Townsend, Receiver of Fees	1793–1807	ADM 106/3550/1–2
Hired armed ships and vessels: papers	1793–1815	ADM 49/96
(lists and registers):	1792–1813	ADM 49/36
	1803–18	ADM 49/97–9
Chasse-marées, accounts and papers	1795–1802	ADM 49/101
Estimates for shipbuilding and repairs	1800	T 38/652
Contractors' powers of attorney	1805–20	ADM 30/64
Abstract of standing orders, yard officers	1805	ADM 7/407–11
Convoy signals	1805	ADM 49/103
Rates of sea pay	1806 and 1817	ADM 49/81–2
Regulations for pursers:	1807	ADM 106/3085
	1824	ADM 106/3582
	1825	ADM 106/3086
Regulations for naval officers' accounts	1813	ADM 106/3087
Establishment of boatswain's and carpenter's stores	1815	ADM 7/579–81

131 Navy Board: Out-letters and Orders

These out-letters are to the whole range of the Board's correspondents; the orders are to dockyard officers.

Orders to yards:	1658–1817	ADM 49/132–59
	1695–1773	ADM 106/3551
	1714–81	ADM 95/89–96
	1730–65	ADM 49/133
	1734–1817	ADM 49/140–56
(index)	1750–89	ADM 12/47
(Plymouth):	1690–2	ADM 174/317
	1694–6	ADM 174/408
	1695–1822	ADM 174/1–79

	1701–6	ADM 174/409
(stores on standing contracts)	1704–36	ADM 49/122
(Admiralty visitations etc.)	1764–1801	ADM 49/162
(overseas)	1770–1832	ADM 106/2470–506
(Cape of Good Hope)	1797–1814	ADM 123/38–41
Standing orders to yards:	1658–1768	ADM 106/2507
	1658–1786	ADM 49/132–5
	1662–1750	ADM 49/137–8
	1695–1773	ADM 106/3551
	1756–1822	ADM 106/2508–32
(index)	1658–1822	ADM 106/2533–7
(digest)	1658–1765	ADM 106/2538
(abstract)	1662–1750	ADM 49/139
(digest, Portsmouth)	1818	ADM 49/160
Reports to Admiralty:	1673–1738	ADM 1/3545–652
	1689–90	ADM 2/1756
	1738–80	NMM: ADM/B/109–200
	1780–1832	NMM: ADM/BP/1–52D
	1738–1832	ADM 106/2178–297
	1801–9	NMM: ADM/B/201–35
	1832	ADM 1/3653–4
(digest)	1673–88	ADM 12/36D
(about Lynch's Island, Jamaica)	1729–31	ADM 106/3544
(Admiralty visitations)	1749–52	ADM 49/169
(shipbuilding and fitting)	1804–9	NMM: ADM/Y/1–10
Receipts for captains' journals	1674–84	ADM 106/2907
Relating to stores:	1688–1826	ADM 95/13–19
	1752–95	ADM 106/2543
To Secretaries of State	1689–99	SP 42/1–5
To Victualling Board:	1674–99	ADM 106/2349
	1705–13	ADM 49/163–4
	1799–1803	ADM 106/2350–1
	1816–21	ADM 109/1–24
	1822–32	ADM 109/48–52
(Medical Committee)	1822–32	ADM 97/36–8
To Treasurer of the Navy and Ticket Office:	1714–87	ADM 14/176–81
	1811–29	ADM 14/174
To Ticket Office:	1749–53	ADM 49/80
	1774–1822	ADM 14/35–167
	c.1777–1815	ADM 49/171
(abstracts)	1740–1810	ADM 14/168–73
To Treasury	1779–81	T 64/200–2
To Transport Agents:	1784–90	ADM 106/2347

	1829	ADM 106/2348
Abstracts of correspondence	1785–1821	ADM 49/165–8
To Captains	1795–1832	ADM 106/2352–452
To Treasurer of the Navy	1800–15	ADM 14/1–8
To Inspector-General of Naval Works	1802–10	ADM 106/2539
Instructions to yards:	1797	ADM 106/3101–3
	1806–8	ADM 7/223–4
	1814–15	ADM 174/304
	1806	ADM 49/62
	1806	ADM 106/3098
	1833	ADM 106/3099–100
(index)	1806	ADM 7/970
(Timber Masters)	[1801]	ADM 106/3105–6
(engineers and mills)	1814	ADM 106/3104
To Public Boards:	1806–31	ADM 106/2298–340
(transports)	1821–9	ADM 106/2341–6
To Captains and Lieutenants:	1806–32	ADM 106/2453–69
(shore stations)	1830–1	ADM 106/3549 pt. 1
Chief Clerk's correspondence	1807	ADM 49/182
To various (block mills)	1808–19	ADM 106/3519
Letters to dockyards:	1814–33	ADM 95/10–11
(Cape of Good Hope)	1797–1814	ADM 123/38–41
(Sheerness)	1802–3	ADM 106/3560
(Plymouth, breakwater)	1811–31	ADM 106/2540–2
Commissioners Overseas to Victualling Board Medical Committee	1822–32	ADM 97/39

132 Navy Board, In-letters

The Board's in-letters from 1660 to 1673 are included in *Calendar of State Papers, Domestic*.

All correspondents:	1660–73	SP 46/136–7
	1665	SP 29/121–3
	1666	SP 29/153
	1670	SP 29/282–6
	1671	SP 29/296–301
	1672	SP 29/322–31
	1673	SP 29/340–6
	1673–1789	ADM 106/281–1299
	1790–1832	ADM 106/1447–671
	1782–1812	ADM 106/3204
(petitions)	c.1650–1803	ADM 106/3537–46

(transports)	1741–79	ADM 106/274–80
(stores)	1752–95	ADM 106/2543
(abstracts)	1785–1821	ADM 49/165–8
(block mills)	1808–19	ADM 106/3519
(registers)	1808–23	ADM 106/2126–34
(Storekeeper's accounts)	1815–37	ADM 106/3571–2
(index and digest)	1822–32	ADM 106/2153–77
Admiralty:	1660–89	ADM 106/1–69C
(abstracts)	1666–87	ADM 106/2067–70
(abstracts)	1687–1756	ADM 106/2106–17
(abstracts)	1741–1822	ADM 106/2071–99
(abstracts: payments)	1781–1815	ADM 106/2100–5
(abstracts: transports)	1790–4	ADM 106/2119
(stores and flags)	1808–21	ADM 106/241
(shipwright apprentices)	1811–20	ADM 106/3548
(Revenue Cruisers):	1816	ADM 106/3124
	1816–33	ADM 106/70–240
(miscellaneous)	1816–18	ADM 2/1709–10
'Lords' Letters' from Admiralty:	1686–92	ADM 106/3532
	1689–1815	ADM 2/169–332
	1689–1815	NMM: ADM/A/1758–3115
(abstracts)	1660–1700	ADM 106/2066
(pay etc.)	1803–15	ADM 2/333–62
Secretaries of State:	1689–1706	SP 44/204
	1693–6	SP 44/205
	1701–84	SP 44/206–32
Plymouth, Commissioner:	1696–1832	ADM 174/97–158
(forwarded by)	1822–39	ADM 174/308–9
Transport Agents:	1742–89	ADM 106/242–4 and 246–71
	1831–2	ADM 106/245
Dockyards:	1783	ADM 106/3546 pt. 2
	1790–1832	ADM 106/1783–2064
	1814–33	ADM 95/10–11
(Portsmouth)	1780–2	ADM 106/3636
(Antigua)	1797–1825	ADM 241/2–4
(Deptford)	1806–23	ADM 106/3447–61
(Malta)	1813–17	ADM 174/303
(registers)	1808–23	ADM 106/2139–49
(registers, overseas yards)	1808–22	ADM 106/2150–2
(shipwright apprentices)	1813–20	ADM 106/3548
(artificers' petitions)	1816	ADM 106/3008
Sea officers:	1790–1832	ADM 106/1300–446
(registers)	1808–22	ADM 106/2120–5

(Masters)	1808–32	ADM 106/1672–713
Treasury:	1779–81	T 64/200–2
	1793–5	T 64/204
	1811–35	T 28/8–37
Home ports, state and condition of HM Ships	1793–9	ADM 49/100
Sample of waistcloths	1795	EXT 11/128
Navy Office Solicitor:	1801–32	ADM 106/1763–81
(registers)	1808–13	ADM 106/2135–8
Inspector-General of Naval Works	1803–10	ADM 106/3547
Concerning signal stations	1803–14	ADM 49/109–17
Inspectors of Canvas	1803–15	ADM 106/1782
Consuls: Corfu	1805–7	FO 348/6
(Brazil, supply of tallow)	1808–11	FO 129/2
Transport Board Medical Department	1806–17	ADM 98/36–43
Public boards:	1806–32	ADM 106/1714–62
(registers)	1808–13	ADM 106/2135–8
Chief Clerk's correspondence	1807	ADM 49/182
Yard officers applying for superannuation	1809–32	ADM 106/3009–14
Office of Woods and Forests	1811–13	ADM 106/3548
Timber contractors etc.	1813–22	ADM 49/124
Coast Blockade	1820–31	ADM 106/3491–5
Victualling yards	1822–32	ADM 106/2065

133 Navy Board, Particular Subjects

This is a miscellaneous collection of records on particular subjects.

Case of Thomas Beckford, slopseller	1682–83	EXT 6/48
Malt Lottery tickets	1694–7	ADM 49/66–7
Navy Estimates and debt	c.1750–90	PRO 30/8/247
'Mode of Dressing Hemp', by Brulles	1790	ADM 7/968
Acts of Parliament etc. on manning the Navy	1790–6	PRO 30/8/248
Copper sheathing, papers	1792–1854	ADM 49/172
Impress Service, list of officers	1795	PRO 30/8/248
Signal stations: (stores, repairs, land etc.):	1804–14	ADM 106/3135–7
	1807–32	ADM 106/3125–34
(Channel Islands)	1806	ADM 106/3138
(index)	1812–26	ADM 106/3139–43
(register)	1819–32	ADM 106/3144
Arrested Danish merchantmen	1805–9	ADM 49/104
Penang Establishment, papers	1805–13	ADM 49/89
Major J de Warren, mission to buy ex-French masts		

at Königsberg, accounts and correspondence	1814–17	ADM 49/107
Trincomalee Establishment, papers	1815–19	ADM 1/5122/17
Consuls' expenses	1817–24	ADM 49/57
Transport of Cleopatra's Needle	1821	ADM 95/98

134 Controller of the Navy, 1660–1832

The Controller was in effect the Chairman of the Navy Board, and the bulk of his work is reflected in its records. Only a small proportion can be identified as belonging particularly to him.

Logs deposited	1669–71	ADM 91/1
Out-letters	1671–9	ADM 91/1
Shipbuilding estimates:	1689–99	ADM 95/3
	1783–1816	ADM 95/4–8
Ships' pay books	1691–1710	ADM 31/1
Half-pay lists, captains and lieutenants	1704–10	ADM 106/2970–1
In-letters, secret (fraud, sabotage etc.)	1790–1832	ADM 106/3575–6
Seamen and Marines, numbers and wages	1790–2	PRO 30/8/248

135 Surveyor of the Navy, 1660–1832

The Surveyor (later Joint Surveyors) was the Navy's principal warship designer, and his office collected information on the design, building, state and condition of HM Ships. The ships' plans collected by the Surveyor are now deposited in the National Maritime Museum.

Lists and descriptions of HM Ships:	1660–7	ADM 106/3117
(lost, sold or converted):	1688–1730	ADM 106/3120
	1814–18	ADM 106/3522
Contract for building a third-rate	1666	SP 29/169 fo. 78
Ships building and repairing:	1674–80	ADM 106/3118–19
	1771–83	ADM 95/84
Tenders and contracts:	c.1670	ADM 106/3538
	1676–1722	ADM 106/3069–71
	1681–90	ADM 106/3541
(yard work and materials)	1754–6	ADM 106/3624
(shipbuilding)	1755ff.	ADM 106/3072
(timber)	1802–4	ADM 7/969
(abstracts):	1693–1765	ADM 106/3583–607
	1765–9	ADM 49/33
	1770–90	ADM 106/3608–22
	1793	ADM 106/3623

Account of ships coming into cheque	1733–74	ADM 106/3121
Letter from Master Shipwright, Portsmouth	1737	NMM: ADM/Y/P/28
Out-letters:	1688–93	ADM 91/1
	1738–45	ADM 91/2–3
Progress books:	1694–1912	ADM 180/1–18
(index)	1694–1912	ADM 180/26
Dimension books, etc.:	1699–1797	ADM 180/19–25
	1783–4	ADM 7/656
Shipbuilding etc., miscellanea	1727–61	ADM 106/3067
Reports: sailing qualities of ships	1742–1847	ADM 95/23–62
(draught, trim, stowage etc.):	1755–1838	ADM 95/63–76
	1780–1800	ADM 106/3122
(draught and dimensions)	1774–1822	ADM 95/77–82
(complement, trim etc.)	1779–83	ADM 95/83
Sir T Slade, memoranda on stores, fittings etc.:	1750–64	ADM 95/17
	1757–70	ADM 106/2895
	1762–5	ADM 49/32
Home dockyards, tidal observations	1761–2	ADM 106/3523
Prices of naval stores	1762–5	ADM 49/32
Minutes of the Surveyor's Office	1780–96	ADM 106/2790–821
Precedents, mobilisation	1790–6	ADM 106/3036–46
Ships, dimensions and scantlings	1794–1807	ADM 95/85
Shipbuilding at Bombay and Cochin	1802–21	ADM 106/3123
Import of copper from Russia	1805–7	ADM 106/3516
In-letters, shipbuilding	1806–60	ADM 87/1–77
Ships' books	1807–73	ADM 135/1–520
R Seppings to Admiralty, presenting his 'system of shipbuilding'	c.1812	ADM 7/709
Fittings, equipment etc., notes and precedents	1813–14	ADM 7/710–11
Letters to Admiralty	1813–60	ADM 92/1–21
Letters from Admiralty	1815–50	ADM 83/1–64
Letter books	1818–21	ADM 91/4–5
Armaments of HM Ships	1820–8	ADM 7/657
Opinions on plans of temporary rudder	1822	EXT 9/56
Abstract out-letters	1829–60	ADM 91/6–24

136 Navy Board Accounts Department

This department was created in 1796 by amalgamating the Bill and Ticket Offices [140–1]. It was overseen by a committee of the Navy Board.

Accounts, miscellaneous	1658–1932	ADM 49/1–182
Organisation, duties etc.	1796–1832	ADM 49/71

Prize lists	1803–30	ADM 238/12–13
Accounting system, papers	1804–32	ADM 106/3510–13
Establishment book	1805	ADM 7/873
Specimen accounting forms	1807	ADM 106/3633
Tables for valuing labour and stores	1811	ADM 106/3635
Revenue Cruisers, accounts	1816–29	ADM 17/88–9
Journals	1826–31	ADM 19/1–7
Ledgers	1826–60	ADM 21/1–35
Payments to artificers at Fernando Po	1827–35	ADM 49/51
Steam packets, passage monies	1830–6	ADM 49/78–9

137 Controller of Storekeepers' Accounts, 1671–1796; Navy Board Stores Department, 1796–1832

The Controller of Storekeepers' Accounts was originally an auditor or financial controller. The Stores Department was another of the divisions of the Navy Board's business created by the 1796 reorganisation.

Letter book	1752–95	ADM 106/2543
Letters from Admiralty	1783–8	NMM: ADM/P/3264
C Derrick's collection of Navy Board orders, as precedents	1784–1832	ADM 49/76–7
Letters to Sheerness Yard	1786–1806	ADM 106/3564
Minutes	1796–1822	ADM 106/2822–85
Precedents: mobilisation	1790–1815	ADM 106/3036–62
(demobilisation)	1796–1818	ADM 106/3063–6
Tenders for stores	1832	ADM 106/3073

138 Navy Board Transport Service

The Navy Board was responsible for chartering merchant ships to freight naval stores overseas to dockyards and squadrons. From 1717 it also transported troops. All these functions were transferred to the Transport Board [1/5] on its creation in 1796.

Papers, surveys etc.	c.1740–1800	ADM 49/125–7
Letters from Admiralty:	1741–2	NMM: ADM/N/234 and T/1
	1747–50	NMM: ADM/N/235–6
	1757–81	NMM: ADM/N/237–50
	1783–9	ADM 108/1D
	1793–7	NMM: ADM/RP/1–5
Letters from Sick and Hurt Board	1744–63	ADM 106/273
Letters from Ordnance Board	1744–63	ADM 106/273

Letters from Victualling Board:	1744–65	ADM 106/272
	1794	ADM 106/3546 pt. 1
Cost of transports	1754–84	ADM 106/3524–7
Transports chartered in North America	1759–63	ADM 49/171
Lists of transports:	1754–73	ADM 49/126
	1776–82	ADM 7/565
(independent sailings)	1776–80	ADM 7/566
Letters from Plymouth Yard	1773–84	ADM 108/1A
In-letters, promiscuous:	1775–83	ADM 49/2
	1781–2	ADM 108/1B–1C
Survey of transports	1776–83	ADM 106/3528–31
Letters from Treasury	1781–2	ADM 108/4A

139 Navy Office Papers

These are documents to do with the internal management and staff of the Navy Office.

Miscellanea	1748–1828	ADM 49/169
Contingent accounts	1777–1836	ADM 17/33–52
Returns of salaried officials	1783 and 1810	ADM 30/33
Establishment:	1785	ADM 106/2964
	1796	ADM 49/169 and 171
	1796–7	ADM 106/2965–6
	1811 and 1824	ADM 106/2967
Somerset House, land purchases	1794–1809	ADM 49/118
Lists of Navy Office bargemen	1799–1822	ADM 106/2968
Housekeeper's accounts	1803–28	ADM 17/53
Clerks, appointments, services etc.	1807–31	ADM 49/70A–70C
Salary book	1815–21	ADM 7/874
Clerks and messengers	1816–30	ADM 106/3515
Widows' and Orphans' Pension Scheme	1819–20	ADM 106/3515

140 Bill Office

The Bill Office was a financial department of the Navy Board, responsible for the issue of Navy Bills in payment for goods and services.

Bill books:	1642–1826	ADM 18/1–134
(funded into Treasury Stock)	1763–96	ADM 18/144–55
(common bills)	1801–28	ADM 18/138–40
(registers)	1795–1831	ADM 18/141–3

(imprests)	1822–30	ADM 18/135–7
Letters from Storekeeper, New York	1777–82	ADM 49/7
Payments for recaptured prizes	1781–3	ADM 49/93
Expense of transporting Loyalists	1783–6	ADM 49/9
Frauds by William Hunter, clerk	1793–1808	ADM 49/12
Boulogne expedition	1804–5	ADM 49/15
Cancelled and irrecoverable debts	1810–24	ADM 49/18–20
Prize case, US Schooners *Tigres* and *Scorpion*, Lake Huron	1814–20	ADM 49/10
Coast Blockade, financial papers	1822–35	ADM 49/21

141 Ticket Office

The Ticket Office administered the payment of naval wages in conjunction with the Navy Pay Office [157].

Receipts for captains' journals	1674–84	ADM 106/2907
Ships' pay books	1692–1856	ADM 32/1–469
Navy Board minutes as precedents	1693–1713	ADM 14/175
Pembroke, list of tickets issued	1694	EXT 1/40/1
Letters and orders from Navy Board:	1714–87	ADM 14/176–81
	1774–1822	ADM 14/35–167
	1811–29	ADM 14/174
(abstracts)	1740–1810	ADM 14/168–73
Letters and orders from Admiralty:	1774–1815	NMM: ADM/J/3903–4009
	1815–22	ADM 14/13–34
(abstracts)	1698–1785	NMM: ADM/K/2–17

142 Dockyards and other Naval Yards

This is a list of records which deal with all the naval yards. Those relating to individual yards are listed under their names [143–54].

Navy Board orders:	1658–1817	ADM 49/132–59
(overseas yards)	1770–1832	ADM 106/2470–506
Dockyard employees: analysis	1691–1743	ADM 49/157–9
(miscellanea)	c.1748	ADM 49/169
(dismissals)	1784–1811	ADM 106/3006–7
Plate given to master shipwrights	1707–36	ADM 49/161
Maps and plans	1708–1955	ADM 140/1–1448
Lands and works:	1740–1820	ADM 106/3218–21
	1793–1826	ADM 106/3183–203 and 3205–16

(register of title deeds)	1801–56	ADM 7/878
(valuations)	1820	ADM 106/3217
Stores at various yards and stations:	1750–82	ADM 106/3182
	1778–1814	ADM 106/3145–81
Survey of yards	1774	ADM 106/3568
Commissioners and officers to Navy Board:	1783	ADM 106/3546/2
	1793–1822	ADM 106/2053–63
(registers)	1808–23	ADM 106/2139–49
(registers, overseas yards)	1808–22	ADM 106/2150–2
Visitations of the yards, minutes:	1784–85	ADM 106/3222
	1801	ADM 106/3223
	1802	ADM 106/3224
	1810	ADM 106/3225 and 3552
(Portsmouth):	1813	ADM 106/3226–7
	1814	ADM 106/3228
(Plymouth):	1814	ADM 106/3229
	1816–28	ADM 106/3230–9
Visitations of the yards, reports:	1810	ADM 106/3240
	1821	ADM 106/3241–2
	1822	ADM 106/3243
Visitations of the yards, papers etc.:	1764–1801	ADM 49/162
	1801–5	ADM 106/3244
	1810–30	ADM 106/3245–8
Unknown yard, paylists of coopers and labourers	1797–1816	ADM 30/58–61
Plan of proposed Northfleet Dockyard	1804	NMM: ADM/Y/N/1
Yard officers: salaries	1808	ADM 7/824
(superannuation)	1809–32	ADM 106/3009–14
Northfleet Estate, accounts	1811–14	ADM 17/57

143 Chatham Dockyard

Chatham, developed in the mid sixteenth century and closed in 1984, was one of the principal home yards. Being far from the open sea, for most of its history it specialised in shipbuilding and long refits. Like all the yards, its workforce was divided into the Ordinary (established men and ships in reserve) and Extraordinary (unestablished men), according to which division of the Navy Estimates their wages were assigned to. Ships 'under cheque' were not in full commission, but were mustered, victualled and paid by the Clerk of the Cheque of the Dockyard.

Pay books: Ordinary:	1609–10	ADM 17/221
	1660–1836	ADM 42/1–133
(Extra):	1615–17	ADM 17/221
	1660–1829	ADM 42/143–284

(ropeyard)	1660–1814	ADM 42/285–361
Accounts, Ordinary and Extraordinary	1622	SP 14/136
Digest of yard regulations	1660–1790	ADM 12/36C
Commissioner: letters to Navy Board	1673	SP 46/137
(letters to Admiralty):	1722–6	ADM 1/3359
	1740–8	ADM 1/3360–2
	1796	ADM 1/3363
	1809–33	ADM 1/3372–400
Musters, ships under cheque	1690–91	ADM 106/3543
Plans:	1719–1900	NMM: ADM/Y/C/1–71
(fortifications)	1709 and 1755	LRRO 1/272–3
Artificers superannuated	1765–1829	ADM 42/363–9
Description book, artificers	1779	ADM 106/2975
Commissioners and officers, letters to Navy Board	1790–1832	ADM 106/1807–42
Pay lists, inferior officers and Extra men	1831–5	ADM 42/362
Superintendent, letters to Admiralty	1834–9	ADM 1/3401–6
Pay books, yard craft	1836–56	ADM 42/134–42
Registered files	1946–81	ADM 269/1–44

144 Deptford Dockyard

Deptford was one of the two oldest dockyards, and the furthest upriver. In the eighteenth century it was used chiefly as a distribution depot for naval stores and as the headquarters of the Transport Service.

Stores received	1545–6	AO 3/1/1
Pay Books: Ordinary	1660–1843	ADM 42/379–484
(Extra)	1660–1829	ADM 42/485–619
Musters:	1684	ADM 106/3541 pt. 2
(yard craft and ships under cheque)	1667–1798	ADM 39/1–2858
(ships under cheque)	1690–1	ADM 106/3542–3
Letter books:	1690 1831	ADM 106/3289–346
	1702–3	ADM 106/3463
	1702–18	ADM 106/3347–53
	1710–35	ADM 106/3464–70
	1729–1832	ADM 106/3376–400
	1733–62	ADM 106/3354–63
	1750–5	ADM 106/3471
	1764–8	ADM 106/3401
	1772–1822	ADM 106/3402–22
	1781–1819	ADM 106/3472–4
	1785–1824	ADM 106/3364–75

(officers)	1807–23	ADM 106/3423–46
Plans (including victualling yard):	n.d.	NMM: ADM/Y/D/1–5
	1810–78	NMM: ADM/Y/D/6–12
(moorings):	1766	ADM 106/3546 pt. 1
	1766	ADM 49/36 and 169
Salary book	1709–76	ADM 7/858
List of ships under cheque	1733–74	ADM 106/3121
Description books: artificers	1748–1813	ADM 106/2976–8
(artificers and labourers)	1779–1829	ADM 106/2986–3005
Valuations and surveys of prizes	1763–5	ADM 49/90
Pension lists	1766–1829	ADM 42/623–30
Pay lists:	1801–7	ADM 42/620–2
(Transport Department)	1829–37	ADM 108/180
Commissioner: letters to Navy Board	1806–23	ADM 106/3447–61
(letters to Admiralty)	1807–23	ADM 106/3462
Superintendent, letters to Admiralty	1834–9	ADM 1/3407–12

145 Plymouth, later Devonport Dockyard

Plymouth (from 1830 Devonport) Dockyard was established in the 1690s as a base for operations to the westward. From the mid eighteenth century it and Portsmouth were the largest yards, heavily involved with refitting and repairing operational squadrons. Like all the yards, Plymouth also built ships, especially in peacetime.

Pay books: Ordinary:	1681–1843	ADM 42/681–820
	1752–66	ADM 174/417
(Extra)	1691–1829	ADM 42/821–970
(ropeyard)	1697–1815	ADM 42/971–1039
(pay lists)	1830–5	ADM 42/1040
Miscellanea	1690–1938	ADM 174/315–30
Contracts:	1690	ADM 174/316
	1803–9	ADM 174/300
Admiralty and Navy Board orders:	1690–2	ADM 174/317
	1694–6	ADM 174/408
	1701–6	ADM 174/409
	1707–9	ADM 106/3579
	1721–6	ADM 106/3580
	1737–41	ADM 106/3581
Local purchases etc.	1693–1712	ADM 174/278–9
Imprest book	1695–1706	ADM 174/280
Purveyor's proceedings	1695–1708	ADM 174/281
Commissioner: letters from Navy Board	1695–1822	ADM 174/1–79

(letters to Navy Board):		1696–1832	ADM 174/97–158
		1790–1832	ADM 106/1914–65
(letters to Admiralty):		1701–4	ADM 1/3358
		1703–1832	ADM 174/159–95
		1740–8	ADM 1/3360–3362
		1796	ADM 1/3363
		1809–33	ADM 1/3372–400
(out-letters):		1703–5	ADM 106/3578
		1710–11	ADM 174/337
(letters from Admiralty)		1711–14	ADM 174/287
(orders to yard officers):		1745	ADM 174/369
		1803–34	ADM 174/214–60
(orders to Captain of Ordinary)		1816–44	ADM 174/262–73
(minutes)		1822–5	ADM 174/274–7
(letters forwarded to Navy Board)		1822–39	ADM 174/308–9
Precedent book		1697–1807	ADM 174/283
Plans		c.1702–1864	NMM: ADM/Y/PD/1–8
Protections from impressment		1704–9	ADM 174/279
Yard officers' reports to Commissioner		1705–14	ADM 174/284–6
Journal of yard proceedings		1740–54	ADM 174/288–90
Chart of Sound and Hamoaze		1747	MPI 1/253
Bill book		1748–53	ADM 174/368
Leaks and defects in ships in Ordinary		1765–77	ADM 174/299
Pension lists		1765–1830	ADM 42/1041–6
Transport Service, letters to Navy Board		1773–84	ADM 108/1A
General out-letters		1817–34	ADM 174/306–7
Description book, artificers		1779	ADM 106/2979
Yard officers, letters to Navy Board		1790–1832	ADM 106/1914–65
Standing contracts		1803–4	ADM 49/36
Breakwater, accounts etc.		1812–30	ADM 17/58–62
Association for the Labouring Poor, Committee		1816–17	ADM 174/305
Cattewater, register of moorage fees		1817–30	ADM 49/108
Admiral Superintendent: letters to Admiralty:		1832–51	ADM 174/196–213
		1834–9	ADM 1/3417–34
		1857–60	ADM 174/313–14
(letters forwarded by)		1839–56	ADM 174/310
(orders to yard officers)		1850–2	ADM 174/261
(to C-in-C)		1850–6	ADM 174/312
Apprentices, assessments		1838–40	ADM 174/311
Pay lists		1844–56	ADM 42/631–44
Asbestos survey		1965–82	FD 12/386, 389 and 1242

146 Portsmouth Dockyard

Although earlier dates are often given, Portsmouth Dockyard was little more than an anchorage before the seventeenth century, and did not acquire its first dry dock until 1652. It was the eighteenth century and the wars against France which made it the largest of all the British dockyards.

Pay books: Ordinary	1660–1856	ADM 42/1047–214
(Extra)	1660–1828	ADM 42/1215–393
(ropeyard)	1660–1814	ADM 42/1394–468
Musters (ships under cheque)	1690–1	ADM 106/3542–3
Commissioner's journal	1713–14	ADM 106/3567
Commissioner, letters to Admiralty:	1722–6	ADM 1/3359
	1740–8	ADM 1/3360–2
	1796	ADM 1/3363
	1809–33	ADM 1/3372–400
Plans	1723–1884	NMM: ADM/Y/P/1–150
Letter from Master Shipwright to Surveyor of Navy	1737	NMM: ADM/Y/P/28
Valuations and surveys of prizes	1763–5	ADM 49/90
Pension lists	1765–1829	ADM 42/1474–8
Wages and victuals, Ordinary and Extra	1770	ADM 106/3577
Description books, artificers	1779	ADM 106/2980–1
Commissioners and officers, letters to Navy Board:	1780–2	ADM 106/3636
	1790–1832	ADM 106/1866–913
Pay lists:	1803–8	ADM 42/1473
	1812–14	ADM 42/1469–71
	1834–5	ADM 42/1472
(shipwrights)	1800	ADM 30/62
Standing contracts	1802–3	ADM 49/36
Correspondence, block mills	1808–19	ADM 106/3519
Navy Board standing orders, digest	1818	ADM 49/160
Admiral Superintendent: letters to Admiralty:	1834–7	ADM 1/3435–8
	1838	ADM 1/3415
	1839	ADM 1/3440
(letters from Admiralty)	1880–6	ADM 179/1
(correspondence and papers)	1903–24	ADM 179/65–70
Plans	1863–86	LRRO 1/1685–6 and 1693

147 Sheerness Dockyard

For much of its history an out-station of Chatham, Sheerness was excellently situated on the deep-water anchorage of the Nore, where the Thames and Medway meet, but until well into the nineteenth century was cramped, malarial and very short of water.

Pay books: Ordinary	1673–1855	ADM 42/1479–600
(Extra)	1673–1829	ADM 42/1601–714
Plans:	1707–59	NMM: ADM/Y/1–60
	1930	ADM 151/93
Out-letters:	1742–6	ADM 106/3553
	1795–1806	ADM 106/3554–8
(to Navy Board)	1790–1832	ADM 106/1843–65
Pay lists:	1759–1807	ADM 42/1715–18
	1787	ADM 49/36
	1814–18	ADM 42/1719
	1830–5	ADM 42/1720
Pension lists	1765–1829	ADM 42/1721–2
Description books, artificers:	1779–96	ADM 106/2982–3
	1795–1805	ADM 106/3625
	1856–66	ADM 7/914–16
Letters from Surveyor of the Navy	1786–1806	ADM 106/3564
Letters from Admiralty	1800–12	ADM 106/3559
Letters from Navy Board:	1802–3	ADM 106/3560
	1805–9	ADM 106/3561–3
(yard improvements)	1810	ADM 106/2064
Superintendent, letters to Admiralty	1834–9	ADM 1/3401–6
Steam Factory, annual accounts	1856–60	ADM 49/162
Serious medical cases	1867–9	ADM 105/79
Dockyard church	1946–60	ADM 269/35

148 Woolwich Dockyard

Woolwich and Deptford were the oldest of the dockyards, and both were limited by the narrowness and shallowness of the Thames. In the nineteenth century the yard briefly took on a new lease of life as the Navy's first specialised 'Steam Factory'.

Ropeyard, building accounts	1573–6	AO 1/2477/256
Pay books: Ordinary	1660–1856	ADM 42/1723–845
(Extra)	1660–1829	ADM 42/1846–977
(ropeyard)	1660–1814	ADM 42/1978–2056
Stores received	1664–7	SP 46/137

Musters, ships in Extra	1690–1	ADM 106/3542–3
Pay lists:	1803–8	ADM 42/2057
	1831–5	ADM 42/2058
Pension lists	1765–1829	ADM 42/2059–60
Description books, artificers and labourers	1779 and 1802	ADM 106/2984–5
Commissioners and officers to Navy Board	1790–1832	ADM 106/1783–806
Superintendent, letters to Admiralty	1834–9	ADM 1/3407–12
Plans	n.d.	NMM: ADM/Y/W/3–55
New graving dock etc.	1843	RAIL 1057/3517
Steam Factory, annual accounts	1849–59	ADM 49/162

149 Other Home Yards

Most of these establishments were essentially stores depots, although Harwich had a significant role in repairs and building during the Dutch Wars. Pembroke, the only one of these to be a dockyard in the exact sense, was a specialised building yard, opened in 1809 to exploit timber and manpower well away from the established yards. Haulbowline (near Cork) grew in the nineteenth century to be the principal naval establishment in Ireland.

Deal Yard

Letter books:	1696–7	ADM 106/3249
	1703–1823	ADM 106/3250–88
Pay lists	1760–1835	ADM 42/370–8

Falmouth Yard

Letters to Navy Board	1795–1810	ADM 106/1973
Pay lists	1805–14	ADM 42/645

Harwich Yard

Pay books: Ordinary	1660–1713	ADM 42/646
(Extra)	1660–1713	ADM 42/647
Plans	1722–48	NMM: ADM/Y/H/1–9
Pay lists	1775–1827	ADM 42/648–9
Letters to Navy Board	1790–1828	ADM 106/1974–5

Leith Yard

Letters to Navy Board	1793–1828	ADM 106/1978–80
Pay lists	1795–1835	ADM 42/663–5
Pension lists	1826–7	ADM 42/666

Pembroke Dockyard

Commissioner and officers, letters to Navy Board	1810–32	ADM 106/1966–72

Pay lists	1810–35	ADM 42/675–9
Pay books: Extra:	1815–29	ADM 42/667–73
	1843	ADM 42/674
Pension lists	1817–35	ADM 42/680
Superintendent, letters to Admiralty:	1834–7	ADM 1/3413–14
	1838	ADM 1/3439
	1839	ADM 1/3416
Plans	1860–3	NMM: ADM/Y/PE/1–7

Yarmouth Yard

Letters to Navy Board	1798–1830	ADM 106/1976–7
Pay lists	1807–15	ADM 42/2061

Haulbowline Yard

Letters to Navy Board	1812–32	ADM 106/1982–4
Pay lists, Transport Department	1829–37	ADM 108/180
Storekeeper, letters to Admiralty:	1834–7	ADM 1/3413–14
	1838	ADM 1/3439
	1839	ADM 1/3416
Plans:	n.d.	NMM: ADM/Y/Q/1
	1897	ADM 174/398

Kinsale Yard

Pay books: Ordinary:	1694–1700	ADM 42/650
	1702–13	ADM 42/651
	1747–8	ADM 42/651
(Extra):	1695–1700	ADM 42/652
	1702–13	ADM 42/653–4
	1747–8	ADM 42/654
Pay lists	1753–1825	ADM 42/655–62
Letters to Navy Board	1790–1812	ADM 106/1981

150 Mediterranean Yards

Alexandria Yard

Storekeeper's accounts	1801–3	ADM 17/113

Malta Dockyard

Storekeeper's accounts	1800–25	ADM 17/200–19
Letters to Navy Board:	1800–32	ADM 106/2043–52
	1813–17	ADM 174/303
Pay lists	1800–35	ADM 42/2317–34

Entries and discharges	1806–35	ADM 42/2335
Commissioner, out-letters	1817–24	ADM 304/8–9
Pension lists	1822	ADM 42/2220
Proposed extensions	1843	ADM 7/880
Plan	1896	ADM 174/363
Trades unions	1955–68	ADM 121/91–8
Registered files	1956–66	ADM 270/1–7

Minorca Yard (Mahon)

Pay books: Ordinary	1713–21	ADM 42/2343
(Extra)	1714–21	ADM 42/2344–5
Pay lists	1742–1814	ADM 42/2346–54
Entries and discharges	1801–14	ADM 42/2355

Toulon Dockyard

Pay lists	1793–4	ADM 42/2375
Storekeeper's accounts	1793–4	ADM 17/220

151 West Indies Yards

Antigua Yard (English Harbour)

Pay lists	1743–1835	ADM 42/2062–111
Register of artificers	1760–1820	ADM 42/2115
C-in-C and Commissioner, letters to yard officers	1779–85	ADM 241/1
Returns of negroes	1785–1824	ADM 42/2114
Entries and discharges	1785–1835	ADM 42/2113
Letters to Navy Board	1795–1832	ADM 106/1985–9
Yard officers, letters to Navy Board etc.	1797–1825	ADM 241/2–4
Storekeeper's accounts	1800–27	ADM 17/114
Pension lists:	1818–35	ADM 42/2112
	1822	ADM 42/2220
Plans	1855–61	MF 1/5/1 and 1/6

Barbados Yard

Letters to Navy Board	1806	ADM 106/1990
Pay lists	1806–16	ADM 42/2116–20
Entries and discharges	1809–16	ADM 42/2121

Cape Nicola Yard

Pay lists	1798	ADM 42/2218

Jamaica Yard (Port Royal and San Antonio)

Pay lists:	1735–1854	ADM 42/2271–307
(transports)	1797–1805	ADM 108/181
Storekeeper's accounts	1747–1850	ADM 17/174–99
Muster books:	1751–68	ADM 42/2356
	1759–92	ADM 42/2357–71
Entries and discharges	1786–1835	ADM 42/2309
Returns of negroes	1787–1825	ADM 42/2310
Letters to Navy Board	1790–1832	ADM 106/2032–41
Commissioner, letters to Admiralty:	1800–8	ADM 1/3364–71
	1809–39	ADM 1/3441–57
Pension lists:	1822	ADM 42/2220
	1833–5	ADM 42/2308
Plans	n.d.	NMM: ADM/Y/PR/1–2

Martinique Yard

Pay lists	1794–5	ADM 42/2233
Pay lists	1794–1802	ADM 42/2336–9
Entries and discharges	1794	ADM 42/2340

152 Atlantic Yards

Bermuda Dockyard

Pay lists	1795–1857	ADM 42/2122–45
Storekeeper's accounts	1796–1823	ADM 17/115–31
Letters to Navy Board	1796–1832	ADM 106/1991–6
Entries and discharges	1815–35	ADM 42/2146
Pension lists	1822	ADM 42/2220
Lists of Admiralty property	1887–1936	ADM 215/1–2
Correspondence	1889–91	ADM 7/881
Plans (including victualling yard).	1891	ADM 174/397
	1898	NMM: ADM/Y/B/1

Cadiz Yard

List of artificers	1694–6	ADM 106/2974

Fernando Po Depot

Artificers, pay lists etc.	1827–35	ADM 49/51

Gibraltar Yard

Charts and plans	1704–51	NMM: ADM/Y/G/1–29
Title deeds	1719–50	ADM 49/52

Pay lists	1721–1833	ADM 42/2221–54
Letters to Navy Board	1790–1832	ADM 106/2020–6
Entries and discharges	1801–35	ADM 42/2255–6
Pension lists	1822	ADM 42/2220
Proposed extensions	1843	ADM 7/880
Plans of dockyard and naval establishments	1875	NMM: ADM/Y/G/30

Halifax Yard

Storekeeper's accounts	1757–1825	ADM 17/150–73
Entries and discharges	1763–1835	ADM 42/2201–2
Pay lists:	1777–1814	ADM 42/2152–65
	1775–1815	ADM 42/2233
	1814–35	ADM 42/2166 etc.
Letters to Navy Board	1790–1832	ADM 106/2027–30
Commissioner, letters to Admiralty:	1800–8	ADM 1/3364–71
	1809–39	ADM 1/3441–57
Pension lists:	1822	ADM 42/2220
	1823–35	ADM 42/2200
Plan	1859–90	ADM 174/362

Lisbon Yard

Pay lists:	1704–25	ADM 42/2311–13
	1795–9	ADM 42/2314
	1809–14	ADM 42/2315
Letters to Navy Board	1797–1814	ADM 106/2042
Entries and discharges	1809–14	ADM 42/2316

New York Yard

Storekeeper: accounts	1775–83	ADM 17/220
(correspondence with bill office)	1777–82	ADM 49/7
Pay lists	1777–83	ADM 42/2341–2

Rio de Janeiro Yard

Pay lists etc.	1813–15	ADM 42/2373

Quebec Yard

Pay lists	1814–16	ADM 42/2167 and 2170

Sierra Leone Depot

Pay lists	1833–4	ADM 42/2374

Simonstown and Cape Town Yards

Pay lists:	1795–1803	ADM 42/2203–5

	1806–47	ADM 42/2206–16
Letters to Navy Board:	1795–1832	ADM 106/2003–7
(timber)	1811–13	ADM 106/3570
In-letters and orders from Navy Board	1797–1814	ADM 123/38–41
Entries and discharges	1797–1835	ADM 42/2217
Commissioner: letters to Admiralty:	1800–8	ADM 1/3364–71
	1809–39	ADM 1/3441–57
(out-letters)	1811–13	ADM 123/42
Pension lists	1822	ADM 42/2220
Storekeeper, in-letters	1841–2	ADM 123/45
Plan	1860–90	ADM 174/379
Dockyard extension	1898–1903	ADM 123/56

153 Eastern Yards

East Indies Station and Bombay Dockyard

Pay lists	1754–1819	ADM 42/2257–69
Storekeeper's accounts	1771–82	ADM 17/136
Letters to Navy Board:	1795–1821	ADM 106/2008–15
	1822–31	ADM 106/2017
Shipbuilding costs	1806–29	ADM 49/14
Commissioner's correspondence	1808–10	ADM 127/46
Entries and discharges	1813–16	ADM 42/2270
Pension lists	1822	ADM 42/2220
Reorganisation committee	1947	ADM 7/944

Hong Kong Dockyard

Plans:	1863	ADM 174/364
	1880	NMM: ADM/Y/HK/1

Madras Yard

Storekeeper's accounts	1795–1817	ADM 1/137–49
Letters to Navy Board	1813–14	ADM 106/2016
Pension lists	1822	ADM 42/2220

Prince of Wales Island Yard (Penang)

Correspondence and miscellanea	1805–13	ADM 49/89
Pay lists	1811–13	ADM 42/2372

Singapore Dockyard

Registered files	1952–3	ADM 271/1

Sydney Dockyard (Cockatoo Island)
Plan   1896   ADM 174/365

Trincomalee Yard
Pay lists   1813–48   ADM 42/2376–91
Entries and discharges   1820–35   ADM 42/2393
Pension lists: 1822   ADM 42/2220
                                    1826–35   ADM 42/2392
Letters to Navy Board   1822–32   ADM 106/2018–19

154 Other Overseas Yards

Canadian Lakes
Commissioners' declared accounts   1813–14   AO 1/1831/558
Letters to Navy Board   1814–32   ADM 106/1997–2002
Pay lists   1814–35   ADM 42/2166 etc.
Entries and discharges   1815–35   ADM 42/2202
Pay books, Ordinary: (Kingston)   1817–25   ADM 42/2175, 2179 and 2183–4
    (Lake Huron) 1817–21   ADM 42/2176
Pension lists   1822   ADM 42/2220
Storekeeper's accounts   1828–31   ADM 17/132–5

Flushing Yard
Pay lists   1809   ADM 42/2219

Heligoland Yard
Letters to Navy Board   1808–15   ADM 106/2031
Musters, harbourmaster's boat's crew 1808–15   ADM 30/47

Montreal Yard
Pay lists: 1814–20   ADM 42/2166 etc.
                                    1832–5   ADM 42/2197–9
Entries and discharges   1815–35   ADM 42/2202

155 Chatham Chest, later Greenwich Chest

The Chatham Chest, established in 1590, was a charitable fund which paid lump sums or pensions to wounded or disabled warrant officers, ratings and dockyard workmen, or to their widows. In 1803 it was transferred to the management of Greenwich Hospital and in 1814 merged with it.

Abstract accounts	1617–36	SP 16/352 no. 81
Governor's resolutions	1617–1797	ADM 82/128
Accounts:	1637–44	NMM: SOC/15
	1653–7	ADM 82/1–2
	1654–5	NMM: SOC/16
	1681–1743	ADM 82/3–11
	1697–8	NMM: SOC/20
	1712–84	ADM 80/75
	1783–1803	ADM 82/130
Deductions from wages	1639–40	ADM 80/13
Pension pay books	1675–1799	ADM 82/12–119
Smart tickets:	1690–7	ADM 106/3069 and 3543
	1763	ADM 82/126–7
Duties on foreign bottoms, papers	1694–1787	ADM 80/73
Pensions for wounds	1740–82	ADM 82/124–5
Transfer register of tickets	1744–63	ADM 82/120–1
Register of pensioners	1759–84	ADM 82/122–3
Minutes	1803–14	ADM 67/258
Establishment of Greenwich Chest:	1803–13	ADM 80/75
	1814	ADM 76/1
Greenwich Chest pension lists	1831–7	ADM 22/52–5

156 Treasurer of the Navy

The Treasurer's declared accounts represent his formal state of account with the Crown, presented annually to the Exchequer. They are not at all identical to the actual expenditure of the Navy. Note that some commanders-in-chief of overseas expeditions declared their own accounts.

Declared accounts:	1544–1715	E 351/2193–352 and 2587–97
	1558–1642	AO 1/1682/1–1706/89
	1558–60	AO 1/1784/297
	1645–60	AO 1/1706/90–1710/101
	1660–1827	AO 1/1710/102–1783/296
	1665–6	AO 1/10/15

	1827–30	AO 2/7, 10 and 12
	1831–3	AO 2/16 and 22
	1833–5	AO 2/24 and 30
	1835–6	AO 2/33–4
(West Indies expedition)	1585	AO 1/1685/20A
(West Indies expedition)	1595–6	AO 1/1688/30–1
(Cadiz expedition)	1597	AO 1/1830/546
(Navy Debts)	1704–14	AO 1/845/1–3
(summary)	1711–42	ADM 49/128
(sale of Navy debentures)	1714–16	AO 1/845/4
Arrears book (unclaimed wages)	1644–6	SP 46/86/1
Victualling accounts	1655–8	ADM 17/111–12
Ledgers	1660–1836	ADM 20/1–357
Instructions, various	c.1660–1780	ADM 49/54
Payments by Commissioners for Discharging the Navy	1661–3	SP 46/138
Abstracts of payments	1665–6	ADM 106/3117
Papers	1668–73	PRO 30/32/1–4
Navy bills unpresented or assigned	1672–1758	ADM 49/11
Accounts:	1673–1703 and 1712	T 38/580–613
(returns to House of Commons)	1740–82	ADM 17/223–5
(receipts from Exchequer):	1727–38	ADM 17/226
	1742–1823	ADM 17/222
(Navy and naval boards)	1742–94	AO 3/715
(salaries and pensions)	1760–70	AO 3/2/1–6
Navy Board minutes as precedents	1693–1713	ADM 14/175
Letters from Navy Board:	1714–87	ADM 14/176–81
	1800–15	ADM 14/1–8
(register)	1808–13	ADM 106/2135–8
Navy bills funded into Treasury Stock	1763–96	ADM 18/144–55
Victualling Board orders to clear outstanding imprests (from 1747–8) on pursers' accounts	1788	ADM 49/13
Reports to the Admiralty	1793–1829	ADM 1/3655–60
New mode of passing Treasurer's accounts	1810–11	ADM 49/129

157 Navy Pay Office

This was in effect the larger part of the Treasurer of the Navy's Department. Its records of officers' full- and half-pay and ships' pay books constituted the principal official record of officers' and men's services until the nineteenth century. Some of these records were continued by the Admiralty Accountant-General's Department which inherited the Navy Pay Office's functions.

Volunteers' bounty recall list	1672–4	ADM 30/17
Bounty Commissioners' accounts	1672–83	ADM 17/13
Claims for royal bounty for next-of-kin of officers and men killed in action:	1675–93	ADM 106/3023
	1704–11	ADM 106/3024
	1720–2	ADM 106/3025
	1747–52	ADM 106/3026–7
	1798–1821	ADM 106/3021–2
	1805–22	ADM 106/3028–35
(supporting documents)	1675–1822	ADM 106/3023–5
(arrears list, Battle of Malaga)	1704ff.	ADM 106/3015
(arrears list, men lost in the Great Storm)	1715	ADM 106/3016
(pay lists):	1739–87	ADM 106/3018–20
	1795–1832	ADM 30/20
(correspondence with parishes)	1742–82	ADM 106/3017
Arrears of pay:	1689–1710	ADM 30/2–5
(sick quarters)	1739–43	ADM 30/6
Bounty to volunteers:	1691–2	ADM 30/8–9
	1702–8	ADM 30/10–15
	1741–2	ADM 30/16
Officers' half-pay registers:	1697–1836	ADM 25/1–255
	1774–1800	ADM 6/213–19
Officers with pay due on recall	1701	ADM 10/12
Passages for distressed seamen	1729–1826	ADM 30/22–5
Navy Board miscellaneous orders	1743–59	ADM 14/179
Admiralty and Navy Board orders to take off Rs and Qs:	1749–53	ADM 49/80
	1750–61	ADM 14/169
	c.1777–1815	ADM 49/171
Pay lists, sick quarters	1757–8	ADM 30/51–2
Various accounts	1759–1835	ADM 17/221
Letters to East Florida Claims Commission	1763–83	T 77/23–9
Pensions etc. under Order in Council:	1781–1821	ADM 22/1–5 and 17–30
	1818–26	ADM 22/31–6
(paid by remittance)	1828–34	ADM 22/39–46 and 50
Admiralty orders	1785–1811	ADM 49/130–1
Orders to pass officers' accounts	1786–97	ADM 106/2118

Wills of ratings and Marines	1786–1882	ADM 48/1–107
Unclaimed pay of ratings DD	1787–1809	ADM 80/4
Miscellanea	1790–1819	ADM 49/72–3
Certificates of service, applicants to GH:	1790–1865	ADM 73/1–35
(Warrant Officers', for pension)	1802–14	ADM 29/1
(ratings', for pension)	1834–7	ADM 29/9–10 and 12–16
Impress Service expenses	1793–1800	ADM 30/34
Death certificates	1795–1807	HCA 30/455–8
Officers' full-pay registers	1795–1872	ADM 24/1–170
Allotment declaration lists	1795–1852	ADM 27/1–120
Remittance lists:	1795–1839	ADM 26/1–38
(ships paid at Plymouth)	1756–98	ADM 174/291–3
(overseas)	1838–51	ADM 26/39–54
Allotments of pay	1795–1852	ADM 27/1–120
Claims for back pay by ratings' next of kin:	1800–60	ADM 44
(Marines)	1831	ADM 30/27
Precedents etc., pensions to French pilots	1803–9	ADM 30/41
Ratings' certificates of service	1803–16	ADM 29/2
Certificates of service, candidates for lieutenant	1802–48	ADM 107/71–5
Powers of attorney	c.1805–20	ADM 30/64–70
Treasury orders, Orders in Council etc.	1807–18	ADM 49/74
Letters to other departments	1807–30	ADM 49/75
Midshipmen and mates, certificates of service	1814	ADM 6/182
Surgeons' certificates of service	1815–22	ADM 104/30
Expenses of capturing Marine deserters	1817–34	ADM 30/28–30
Certificates of service for pension: cooks	1817–51	ADM 29/5 and 7
(artificers)	1817–45	ADM 29/8
(gunners)	1817–73	ADM 29/3, 24 and 121
(boatswains)	1817–73	ADM 29/4, 23 and 121
(carpenters)	1817–53	ADM 29/5–6
Case of fraud in Navy Pay Office	1821–3	PMG 73/1
Claims for back pay by officers' next of kin	1830–60	ADM 45/1–39
Chaplains' certificates of service	1833–4	ADM 11/41

158 Ships' Muster and Pay Books

The largest surviving collection of these records was deposited in the Navy Pay Office, although other copies went to the Controller [134] and the Ticket Office [141]. The form and use of ships' musters and pay books are fully explained in N A M Rodger, *Naval Records for Genealogists* (Public Record Office handbook, 22, Kew, 1988), pp. 45–66. In 1832 responsibility for these records was transferred to the Accountant-General's Department of the Admiralty [112].

Various musters and logs	1648–1707	ADM 7/777–80
Ships' pay books:	1669–1778	ADM 33/1–703
	1766–85	ADM 34/1–855
	1777–1832	ADM 35/1–4567
(*Quaker* ketch)	1683–96	NMM: ADM/K/101
(various)	1691–1710	ADM 31/1
(*Queen* and *Queenborough*)	1694–7	NMM: ADM/K/101
(ships under cheque)	1690–1	ADM 106/3542–3
(alphabets)	1723–52	ADM 33/41–90
(*Bathurst*)	1821–2	ADM 30/63/18
Musters: series I	1688–1808	ADM 36/1–17471
(*Assistance*)	1701–2	ADM 106/3071
(transports in North America)	1776–9	ADM 49/3
(small vessels in America)	1779–82	ADM 30/45
(series II)	1792–1842	ADM 37/1–10131
(Maltese ratings)	1793–8	ADM 30/63/6
(series III)	1793–1878	ADM 38/1–9376
(hired armed vessels)	1794–1815	ADM 41/1–85
(Dutch ships in British service)	1799–1802	ADM 49/170
(Canadian lakes squadrons)	1813–14	ADM 30/46
(colonial brigs *Kangaroo* and *Emu*)	1813–19	ADM 30/48–50
(Kroomen)	1819–20	ADM 30/26
(CG and Revenue Cruisers)	1824–57	ADM 119/1–141
Pay lists: prison ships at New York	1780	ADM 30/63/3
(volunteers, *Prince William*)	1781	ADM 30/63/4
(fitting out *Bombay*)	1828	ADM 30/63/19
Description book: *Perseus*	1843–9	ADM 6/415
(*Crocodile*)	1850–2	ADM 6/416
Turn-over lists	1844–8	T 172/932

159 Sick and Hurt Board, 1653–1806

This board, initially established in wartime only, was responsible for the care of sick and wounded men ashore (but not afloat) and for prisoners of war of all services. In 1796 it took over much of the seagoing medical service, but handed over prisoners of war to the Transport Board.

Recommendations for widows' pensions	1653–7	SP 18/63, 119, 151 and 177
Declared accounts:	1664–1713	AO 1/1820/483–1825/517
	1671–1711	E 351/2548–73
Accounts and papers of R Povey, Treasurer	1702–4	C 112/181/17
Minutes:	1702–14	ADM 99/2–11
	1740–1806	ADM 99/12–53
Letters from hospitals abroad	1702–54	ADM 97/114
Letters from Admiralty	1702–1806	NMM: ADM/E/1–52
Accounts	1705–7	T 38/665–6
Letters from C-in-C Abroad, colonial governors and surgeon-agents	1709–54	ADM 97/85
Reports to Admiralty:	1727–42	ADM 1/3528–9
	1742–1806	NMM: ADM/F/3–37
	1742–1817	ADM 98/1–30
	1756–1806	NMM: ADM/FP/1–49
Return of expenditure	1739–49	ADM 7/185
Admiralty instructions:	1741 and 1744	ADM 98/103–4
	1797	ADM 98/102
Letters to Navy Board (transports)	1744–63	ADM 106/273
Law Officers' opinions	1756–64	ADM 105/43
Letters from FO and captains	1766–79	ADM 97/86–7
Returns to committees of enquiry	1782–1805	ADM 102/844
Letters to RN officers	1791–1806	ADM 98/67–81
Letters from inspectors of hospitals	1803–17	ADM 105/20–3
Instructions to senior officers	[1804]	ADM 7/219–20
Letters to inspector of hospitals	1804–6	ADM 98/44
Instructions and precedents, collected for Board of Revision	1805	ADM 98/105–6
Regulations for sick quarters	n.d.	ADM 106/3094

160 Transport Board Medical Department, 1806–16

The Transport Board took over the responsibilities of the Sick and Hurt Board on its abolition in 1806.

Letters from inspectors of hospitals	1803–15	ADM 105/20–3
Correspondence of agent in East Indies	1804–13	ADM 102/847
Minutes	1806–16	ADM 99/54–91
Letters to RNH Haslar and Stonehouse	1806–16	ADM 98/50–66
Letters to RN officers	1806–16	ADM 98/82–98
Letters to Admiralty	1806–17	ADM 98/24–30
Letters to other naval boards and government departments	1806–17	ADM 98/36–43
Letters to inspectors of hospitals	1806–17	ADM 98/45–6
Letters from Admiralty:	1807–15	NMM: ADM/ET/53–61
	1816	ADM 97/1
Income Tax charged to salaries	1807–9	ADM 102/841
Register of overseas correspondence	1807–18	ADM 98/99
Letters from physicians afloat	1809–17	ADM 97/88
Abstract accounts of hospitals etc.	1810–22	ADM 100/1–3
Lists of sick men from French prizes	1812–13	ADM 7/848

161 Victualling Board Medical Department, 1817–32

The Victualling Board inherited the responsibility for the Naval Medical Service following the abolition of the Transport Board in 1816.

Reports: experiments and improvements	1816–29	ADM 105/27
(naval lunatics)	1816–63	ADM 105/28–35
Report on GH	1817	ADM 105/24
Letters to RN Hospitals:	1817–19	ADM 98/47
(Haslar and Stonehouse)	1820–2	ADM 98/48
Letters from RN Hospitals at home.	1817–21	ADM 97/42–7
(Stonehouse)	1820–32	ADM 97/72 6
(*Chatham* HS)	1822–8	ADM 97/59
(Deal)	1822–32	ADM 97/61
(Haslar)	1822–32	ADM 97/63–9
Letters from RN Hospitals abroad:	1818–19	ADM 97/47–8
(Bermuda and Cape of Good Hope)	1820–32	ADM 97/60
(Jamaica and Malta)	1820–32	ADM 97/70–1
(Trincomalee)	1822–31	ADM 97/77
Reports to Admiralty, surgeons for promotion	1817–32	ADM 105/1–9
Letters from Admiralty	1817–32	ADM 97/2–18

Letters from commissioners abroad	1820–32	ADM 97/39
Regulations, medical stores	c.1822	ADM 106/3095
Letters from surgeons etc.:	1822–9	ADM 97/90–7
	1830–2	ADM 97/49–58
Letters from Navy Board	1822–32	ADM 97/36–8
Letters from surgeons and storekeepers abroad etc.	1822–32	ADM 97/89
Letters from RM infirmaries	1822–32	ADM 97/78–9
Letters from C-in-Cs	1822–32	ADM 97/40–1
Surgeons' pay and promotion, memoranda	1822–32	ADM 105/10–19
Letters from surgeon-agents	1822–32	ADM 97/80–4
Letters from naval commissioners overseas	1822–32	ADM 97/39
Regulations, medical officers	1825	ADM 106/3093
Letters from GH	1829–30	ADM 97/62

Surgeons' Journals

HM Ships and temporary overseas hospitals	1793–1880	ADM 101/80–250
Convict ships	1813–56	ADM 101/1–75
Emigrant ships	1825–53	ADM 101/76–9

162 Naval Hospitals and Hospital Ships

Responsibility for naval hospitals was transferred to the Transport Board in 1806, and the Victualling Board in 1817, but for convenience their records to 1832 are listed here together. Musters and pay lists of the main naval hospitals are listed by name in Lists 163–5.

Musters and pay lists	1755–1860	ADM 102/1–840 and 853–921
Patients in RNH overseas	1806–29	ADM 102/843
Regulations	1808	ADM 106/3091–2
Death certificates, RNH at home	1809–15	ADM 102/842

163 Royal Naval Hospital, Haslar

The musters include those of various stationary hospital ships in Portsmouth Harbour which acted as 'overflow' accommodation for the Hospital.

List of men DD	1755–64	ADM 102/374
Council minutes	1755–96	ADM 305/1–11
Musters:	1755–1860	ADM 102/271–334, 876–9 and 915
(Marines):	1785–1824	ADM 102/335–47
	1805–9	ADM 102/862

(officers)	1791–1801	ADM 102/348
(*Gladiator* HS)	1793–1802	ADM 102/238–40
(*Le Pegase* HS):	1794–6	ADM 102/478
	1808–9	ADM 102/479
(*Sultan* HS)	1794–6	ADM 102/746
(Russians)	1808–12	ADM 102/349
(soldiers)	1809–16	ADM 102/351–5
(servants)	1814–15	ADM 102/350
(lunatics)	1818–54	ADM 102/356–73
Council out-letters	1756–96	ADM 305/12–16
Inventories of drugs:	1758	ADM 102/399
	1794	ADM 102/400
Pay lists:	1769–1819	ADM 102/375–97
	1820–2	ADM 102/922
	1827–8	ADM 102/398
Prescription books	1787–92	ADM 305/67–70
Ratings discharged unfit for service	1792	ADM 1/5120/19
Physician etc. to Admiralty (reports on officers invalided etc.)	1793–1839	ADM 1/3533–41
Agent's memorandum book	1795–6	ADM 102/846
Governor's out-letters	1795–1807	ADM 305/17–34
Governor and Commissioner, orders and correspondence	1795–1861	ADM 305/35–45
Letters from Transport Board Medical Department	1806–16	ADM 98/59–66
Letters to Victualling Board Medical Department:	1817–21	ADM 97/42–7
	1822–32	ADM 97/63–9
Letters from Victualling Board Medical Department	1817–22	ADM 98/47–9
Medical journals	1825–7	ADM 102/848
Burial registers	1826–1954	ADM 305/103–14
Baptismal register	1829–62	ADM 305/86
Plans:	n.d.	NMM: ADM/Y/P/10
	1877–1906	ADM 305/90–100
Lunatic asylum: journal	1830–42	ADM 305/102
(register)	1861–3	ADM 305/87
Services of medical staff, nurses etc.	1870–90	ADM 305/80
Out-letters:	1871–88	ADM 305/46–66
	1896–8	ADM 305/85
Case books of Thomas Cooper	1869–99	ADM 305/83
Nominal index to muster books	1906	ADM 305/88
Victualling book	1913–15	ADM 305/79
Funerals etc.	1933–57	ADM 305/115–16

164 Other Royal Naval Hospitals at Home

Many small or short-lived hospitals [162] are not listed here by name.

Chatham
Musters and pay lists	1810–59	ADM 102/132–57, 872 and 914
Letters to Victualling Board Medical Department	1822–8	ADM 97/59

Deal
Musters:	1762–3	ADM 102/856
	1789–1833	ADM 102/176–90
	1854–7	ADM 102/873
(officers)	1796–1802	ADM 102/193
(discharges)	1812–15	ADM 102/194–5
(Russians)	1813–14	ADM 102/191–2
Pay lists:	1796–1815	ADM 102/196–202
	1831–3	ADM 102/857
Letters to Victualling Board Medical Department	1822–32	ADM 97/61

Hoxton Lunatic Asylum
Musters and pay lists	1755–1818	ADM 102/415–20

Royal Marine Infirmaries
Regulations	1820	ADM 106/3090
Letters to Victualling Board Medical Department	1822–32	ADM 97/78–9

Stonehouse
Musters and pay lists:	1774–1860	ADM 102/601–701, 894–7 and 919
(*Chatham* HS)	1793–1802	ADM 102/158–61
(*Le Caton* HS)	1794–8	ADM 102/471–4
Physician etc. to Admiralty (reports on officers invalided etc.)	1793–1839	ADM 1/3533–41
Letters from Transport Board Medical Department	1806–16	ADM 98/50–8
Letters to Victualling Board Medical Department:	1817–21	ADM 97/42–7
	1820–32	ADM 97/72–6
(*Chatham* HS)	1822–8	ADM 97/59
Letters from Victualling Board Medical Department	1817–22	ADM 98/47–9
Pay lists	1820–2	ADM 102/921
Establishment book	1829–31	ADM 102/864

Woolwich
Musters and pay lists	1789–1863	ADM 102/800–24, 905–6 and 920

Yarmouth

Musters:	1789–1814	ADM 102/825–35
	1855–6	ADM 102/907
Pay lists	1804–14	ADM 102/836–9
Building	1808–16	ADM 102/840

165 Other Royal Naval Hospitals Overseas

Many minor and temporary hospitals [162] are not listed here by name.

Antigua

Letters to Sick and Hurt Board	1721–54	ADM 97/114/1
Musters and pay lists	1791–1816	ADM 102/5–12

Ascension Island

Musters	1836–59	ADM 102/36–44, 867–8 and 912
Plan	1882	ADM 105/91

Barbados

Letters to Sick and Hurt Board	1702–54	ADM 97/114/4
Musters and pay lists	1795–1816	ADM 102/48–55

Bermuda

History	1794–1878	ADM 104/156
Notes on epidemics	1802–63	ADM 104/155
Musters and pay lists	1812–54	ADM 102/70–91 and 869–70
Letters to Victualling Board Medical Department	1818–32	ADM 97/47–8 and 60
Case books	1832–83	ADM 104/98–101
Works	1842–3	RAIL 1057/3731

Cape of Good Hope

Letters to Victualling Board Medical Department	1818–32	ADM 97/47–8 and 60
Musters and pay lists:	1795–1860	ADM 102/104–31, 871 and 913

Curaçoa

Letters to Sick and Hurt Board	1743–52	ADM 97/114/11
Musters and pay lists	1807–8	ADM 102/173–4

Gibraltar

Plans of proposed hospital	1734–9	NMM: ADM/Y/G/51–6
Musters:	1793–1827	ADM 102/226–36
	1849–51	ADM 102/875

Pay lists	1805–16	ADM 102/237
Medical journal	1813	ADM 105/25
Report on fever outbreak	1828	ADM 105/26

Hong Kong

Musters and pay lists:	1849–60	ADM 102/413–14, 883–6 and 916
(*Alligator* HS)	1847–8	ADM 102/3
Services of medical officers, nurses etc.	1877–1917	ADM 305/81

Jamaica

Pay lists	1742	ADM 102/863
Musters and pay lists	1793–1859	ADM 102/426–62 and 888–9
Letters to Victualling Board Medical Department	1818–32	ADM 97/47–8 and 70
Plans etc.	1848	ADM 105/89

Leghorn

Letters to Sick and Hurt Board	1741–2	ADM 97/114/5
Muster	1800	ADM 102/555

Lisbon

Letters to Sick and Hurt Board	1707	ADM 97/114/6
Musters:	1788–1803	ADM 102/481–2
	1802	ADM 102/555
	1852–60	ADM 102/483–4 and 917
Accounts	1805–9	ADM 102/485
Painting	1851	ADM 105/90

Malta

Musters:	1799–1805	ADM 102/555–6
	1800–51	ADM 102/521–50
	1856–60	ADM 102/890–1 and 918
(Marines)	1817–33	ADM 102/557–9
(Algerine prisoners)	1824	ADM 102/563
In-patients:	1804–40	ADM 304/21–4
	1857–9	ADM 304/33
(fevers)	1870–3	ADM 304/35
Pay lists:	1805–17	ADM 102/560–2
	1829–35	ADM 102/911
Out-letters	1814–65	ADM 304/1–7
Letters to Victualling Board Medical Department	1818–32	ADM 97/47–8 and 71
Cholera returns	1827	ADM 102/564
Construction of Bighi Hospital	1829–32	ADM 304/19–20
Accounts and miscellanea	1829–67	ADM 304/25–32 and 34

Admissions and discharges:	1836–79	ADM 304/14–18
	1852–95	ADM 304/36–41
In-letters	1845–52	ADM 304/10–12
Works	1848–50	RAIL 1057/3731
Admiralty circulars	1855–74	ADM 304/13

Therapia

| Musters and pay lists | 1853–6 | ADM 102/759 and 901 |
| Medical journal | 1853–5 | ADM 102/849 |

Trincomalee

Letters to Victualling Board Medical Department:	1818–19	ADM 97/47–8
	1822–31	ADM 97/77
Musters and pay lists	1819–60	ADM 102/768–74 and 902–3
Report	1820–1	ADM 105/83

Vado

| Letters to Sick and Hurt Board | 1747–9 | ADM 97/114/10 |

166 Sick and Hurt Board Prisoner of War Department, 1653–1796

Accounts, pay books etc.:	1698–1703	AO 3/873
	1793–6	AO 3/874–7
Letters from Secretaries of State:	1702–10	ADM 97/98–101
	1746–50	ADM 97/102
Correspondence with enemy prisoners:	1703–4	ADM 97/114/2
	1742–58	ADM 97/114/2 and 115
	1743–8	ADM 97/116/2–4 and 117
Letters from French authorities, exchange of prisoners:	1707–10	ADM 97/116/1
	1744–68	ADM 97/103–7
	1755–9	ADM 97/117 18
Correspondence concerning British prisoners in Spain	1741–8	ADM 97/114/3 and 7
Letters from Admiralty	1713–83	NMM: ADM/M/387–414
Petitions from enemy prisoners:	1745–8	ADM 97/125
	c.1750–1810	ADM 1/3977–81
	1755–60	ADM 97/119–21
	1779–82	ADM 97/123–4
Letters to Treasury Solicitor	1746	TS 20/80/11–12
French officers, paroles and exchanges	1755–60	ADM 103/502
Prisoners received	1757–8	ADM 103/508
Letters to ship's company of French prize *Galathée*	1757–8	ADM 97/131
Enquiry into servants at Porchester	1762	ADM 105/58

Report on complaints of prisoners at Sissinghurst	1761	ADM 105/42
Lists of British prisoners in France	1779–81	ADM 103/134
Musters of prison ships at New York	1780	ADM 30/63/3
Letters from agents	1780–2	ADM 97/127
Instructions to agents abroad	1793–7	ADM 98/101

167 Transport Board Prisoner of War Department, 1796–1822

Instructions to agents: abroad	1793–7	ADM 98/101
(parole)	1809	ADM 105/93
Lists and registers of British and enemy prisoners	1793–1815	ADM 103/1–648
Accounts:	1793–6	AO 3/874–7
	1808–15	AO 3/751, 755–6 and 774
Cartels and exchanges, papers	1794–1800	ADM 49/171
Out-letters, general	1795–1800	ADM 108/28
Letters to Admiralty:	1795–1808	ADM 1/3773–4
	1796–1822	ADM 98/107–24
Letters from agents	1795–1816	ADM 97/127–8
Correspondence with government departments etc.	1795–1818	ADM 97/129–30
Miscellaneous correspondence	1795–1820	ADM 105/59–66
Title deeds of property, abstract	c.1795–1822	ADM 7/877
Letters from Admiralty	1796–9	NMM: ADM/MT/415–22
Letters to Spanish officials in Britain	1796–1807	ADM 98/303
Visitation reports on prisoner depots etc.	1796–1814	ADM 105/44
Letters to British agents in France, French officials in Britain and French Ministry of Marine, *Bureau des prisonniers*	1796–1833	ADM 98/294–302 and 304
Circulars to agents:	1796–1802	ADM 98/169
	1808–15	ADM 98/170
Correspondence with senior officer prisoners	1796–1808	ADM 97/126/3
Minutes and digest of correspondence:	1796–1816	ADM 99/92–263
(Admiralty business)	1796–1800	ADM 99/266–75
(agents overseas)	1796–9	ADM 99/276–9
(enquiries about British prisoners):	1799–1810	ADM 105/57
	1810–24	ADM 105/47–51
(enquiries about enemy prisoners)	1810–13	ADM 99/281
(notes and precedents)	1810–13	ADM 99/280
Schedule of accounts and papers	1796–1816	ADM 10/14
Letters to public offices	1796–1817	ADM 98/125–37
Letters to agents	1796–1817	ADM 98/171–290
Order book	1796–1817	ADM 98/315–22
Letters to other correspondents	1796–1822	ADM 98/138–68

James Cotes, British Agent in Paris, letters to		
Commission des échanges	1797–1801	ADM 98/323–6
Letters to Dutch naval authorities	1797–1808	ADM 98/293
Returns of deaths of enemy prisoners	1799–1814	ADM 103/639–48
Applications by or for enemy prisoners	1799–1816	ADM 105/52–6
Quarterly returns of staff	1803–15	ADM 104/8–10
Pay lists of British prisoners: Givet	1806	ADM 30/63/12
(Valenciennes)	1806	ADM 30/63/14
(Arras)	1806	ADM 30/63/15
(Verdun)	1806–7	ADM 30/63/13
(Bitche)	1815	ADM 30/63/17
Correspondence with French authorities concerning		
former prisoners	1807–58	ADM 97/126/1–2
Letters to enemy prisoners	1808–15	ADM 98/308–9
Letters to victualling contractors	1808–16	ADM 98/305–7
Letters from Solicitor of Admiralty	1808–17	ADM 97/108–13
Descriptions of escaped prisoners	1810–13	ADM 105/45
Reports on exchanges, pension claims etc.	1810–20	ADM 105/46
Register of in-letters	1811–16	ADM 98/327–35
Letters to Coutts Bank (remittances to British prisoners)	1812–14	ADM 98/310
Letters to US POW Agent	1812–16	ADM 98/291
Letters to British Agent in USA	1812–16	ADM 98/292
Register of decisions on Americans detained	1812–14	ADM 6/417
Agent at Valleyfields, accounts	1817–19	ADM 100/4–5

168 Victuallers of the Navy and Victualling Board, 1543–1832

These are records of the central victualling organisation, the Victualling Board and Victualling Office as it became.

Declared accounts:	1547–1642	E 351/2353–447
	1558–1642	AO 1/1784/298–1802/394
	1660–1	AO 1/182/550A
	1660–98	E 351/2448–70
	1660–98	AO 1/1802/395–1810/436
	1689	AO 1/484/48
(miscellaneous)	1543–97	E 351/2471–500
(Rhé expedition)	1626–31	AO 1/1798/372–3
(Mediterranean Fleet)	1694–5	E 351/2501
Quarter books		BL: Harleian MS. 167
Accounts	1655–8	ADM 17/111–12
Regulations and instructions:	1660–1806	ADM 49/54–62

	1715	ADM 174/370
	1808	ADM 7/216–17
	1808	ADM 174/372
(victualling yards)	1808	ADM 106/3107
(Deptford)	1823	ADM 7/218
Accounts: sea and harbour victuals	1666–95	ADM 112/48–66
(pursers and masters)	1673–1724	ADM 112/70–9
(pursers' extra allowances)	1677–84	ADM 112/80
(provisions returned)	1685–1704	ADM 112/67
(issues and remains)	1689–1702	ADM 112/68–9
(buildings at Woolwich)	1740–7	ADM 112/83
(agent-victuallers overseas)	1776–1831	ADM 112/1–47
(solicitors)	1787–1805	ADM 112/81–2
In-letters: from Navy Board:	1674–99	ADM 106/2349
	1705–13	ADM 49/163–4
	1799–1803	ADM 106/2350–1
	1816–21	ADM 109/1–24
	1822–32	ADM 109/48–52
(from Secretaries of State):	1693–6	SP 44/205
	1701–84	SP 44/206–32
(abstract Admiralty orders)	1694–1819	NMM: ADM/G/773–98
(from Admiralty):	1708–1815	NMM: ADM/C/349–748
	1816–32	ADM 109/1–47
(Army victualling)	1793–1815	ADM 109/102–10
(from Transport Board Medical Department)	1806–17	ADM 98/36–43
(from Malta Yard)	1813–16	ADM 174/407
(various)	1821–32	ADM 109/56–76
(miscellaneous)	1822–32	ADM 109/111–31
(from Treasury)	1822–32	ADM 109/53–5
(from Deptford Yard)	1822–32	ADM 109/76–85
(from other home yards)	1822–32	ADM 109/86–92
(from foreign yards)	1822–32	ADM 109/93–101
(registers)	1823–32	ADM 134/1–16
Out-letters:	1683–9	ADM 110/1
	1702–1822	ADM 110/2–81
(register)	1814–31	ADM 110/82–5
(to Secretaries of State)	1689–99	SP 42/1–5
(to the Admiralty):	1704–1809	NMM: ADM/D/1–52
	1765–6	NMM: ADM/DP/101
	1770–80	NMM: ADM/DP/102–12
	1781–1822	NMM: ADM/DP/1–42
	1821	NMM: ADM/DP/201A–201B
	1822–32	ADM 1/3775–801

(to Navy Board, Transport Service)	1744–65	ADM 106/272
(to Navy Board, general)	1794	ADM 106/3546/1
(to Navy Board, registers)	1808–13	ADM 106/2135–8
(to Agent-Victualler Plymouth):	1762–65	ADM 174/294–7
	1780–91	ADM 174/298
(to Agent-Victualler Portsmouth):	1809–11	ADM 114/68–9
	1831–4	ADM 224/13–14
(on surgeons' pay and promotion)	1817–32	ADM 105/1–9
(enquiries about POWs)	1818–22	ADM 98/314
Correspondence, property at Plymouth	1698–1819	ADM 114/41
Miscellanea	1698–1976	ADM 114/1–155
Minutes:	1701–2	ADM 111/307
	1702–1809	ADM 111/1–191
	1809–32	ADM 111/243–67
	1811–13	NMM: ADM/H/1
(indexes)	1809–31	ADM 111/268–306
(general committee)	1809–22	ADM 111/191–242
Deeds and plans of victualling yards	1701–65	ADM 114/14
Victualling yards: pay and pension lists	1703–1835	ADM 113/1–259
(description books)	1765–1813	ADM 113/273–9
(Army victualling)	1793–1815	ADM 113/261–2
(labourers)	1800–23	ADM 113/265–72
(pensions)	1803–9	ADM 113/263–4
Instructions to agent-victuallers	1704–15	ADM 7/215
Correspondence, Red House and other property at Deptford	1740–1829	ADM 114/40
Royal charter	1752	ADM 224/1
Course of the Exchange:	1768–1831	ADM 114/73–118
	1797–1801	ADM 106/3626–9
(*Prijs-courant der effekten*)	1814	ADM 114/72
Contracts	1776–1828	ADM 112/84–212
Staff and establishment book	c 1784–1810	ADM 7/872
Victualling Office papers	1784–99	PRO 30/8/251–2
Orders to Treasurer of the Navy to clear outstanding imprests (from 1747–8) on pursers' accounts	1788	ADM 49/13
Victualling Office accounts, report	1804–32	ADM 106/3510
Salary books	1805–22	ADM 7/869–71
Warrants appointing yard officers	1809–31	ADM 114/64

169 Deptford, later Royal Victoria Victualling Yard

From the 1740s when the former victualling establishment on Tower Hill was closed, Deptford Victualling Yard became the Board's principal manufacturing site, and the depot from which victuals were distributed to other yards and depots.

Pay and pension lists	1758–1834	ADM 113/58–83
Description books:	1765–73	ADM 113/274–6
	1809–14	ADM 113/277–9
Plans (including dockyard):	n.d.	NMM: ADM/Y/D/1–5
	1810–78	NMM: ADM/Y/D/6–12
	1896	ADM 174/360
	1928	ADM 174/414
Letters to Victualling Board	1822–32	ADM 109/76–85
Instructions:	1823	ADM 7/218
	1823	ADM 174/421
Capt. Superintendent, in-letters	1880–1	ADM 114/67
Correspondence	1886–1904	ADM 7/932–3
Spoilage of pork	1897	ADM 174/418

170 Portsmouth, later Royal Clarence Victualling Yard

Pay and pension lists:	1703–1839	ADM 113/216–46
	1829–35	ADM 113/28–30
(Weevil, labourers)	1712–35	ADM 224/3–4
(Spithead)	1808–14	ADM 113/256
(Weevil)	1814–18	ADM 113/257
Pay books:	1722–1824	ADM 224/56–65
(entries and discharges)	1774–1829	ADM 224/80–3
Letter books:	1740–69	ADM 224/15–16
	1790–1	ADM 224/17–18
	1792–1801	ADM 224/71–2
	1822–35	ADM 224/19–26
	1828–31	ADM 224/73
Contracts	1771–8	ADM 224/6–7
Agent-Victualler, letters from Victualling Board	1809–11	ADM 114/68–9
Monthly issues to hoys and Ordinary	1815–21	ADM 224/91
Letters to Victualling Board	1822–32	ADM 109/89–90
Order book	1829	ADM 224/8
Establishment books	1829–68	ADM 224/85–90
Expenditure on stamps	1830–65	ADM 224/77–8
Letters from Victualling Board	1831–4	ADM 224/13–14

Pay and muster books:	1831–43	ADM 224/66–9
	1891–2	ADM 224/70
(dockyard men)	1897–1903	ADM 224/79
Orders from Admiralty and Controller of Victualling:	1833	ADM 224/48
	1856–63	ADM 224/49–55
Stores issued to and received from hoys	1834–53	ADM 224/76
Circulars received	1834–61	ADM 224/5
Letters from Admiralty:	1834–5	ADM 224/9–10
	1857–8	ADM 224/11–12
Letter books	1834–74	ADM 224/27–47 and 74–5
Plan	1858–91	ADM 174/399
In-letters:	1871–3	ADM 224/2
(register)	1865–7	ADM 224/84

171 Plymouth, later Royal William Victualling Yard

Throughout the eighteenth century the victualling establishment at Plymouth was divided between a number of sites, not united until the construction of the new Royal William Yard in the 1820s.

Pay and pension lists:	1730–1831	ADM 113/180–214
	1829–35	ADM 113/258–60
(Hartshorn)	1722–51	ADM 113/122–3
(South Down)	1809–26	ADM 113/254–5
Pay book	1752–66	ADM 174/417
Letters and orders from Victualling Board:	1762–5	ADM 174/294–7
	1780–91	ADM 174/298
Memoranda books:	1769–1796	ADM 174/400
	1852	ADM 174/401
Out-letters:	1799–1809	ADM 174/411
	1886–1902	ADM 174/336
(Stores Department)	1845–8	ADM 174/406
Establishment books:	1816–31	ADM 174/410
	1824–61	ADM 174/340
	1835–45	ADM 174/416
	1857–63	ADM 174/334
	1864	ADM 174/341
	1865–76	ADM 174/366
	1899–1937	ADM 174/335
	1902	ADM 174/389
Letters to Victualling Board	1822–32	ADM 109/86–7
In-letters from Admiralty etc.	1833–68	ADM 174/80–96

Instructions and regulations:	1852–5	ADM 174/374–6
	1855–1938	ADM 174/342–58
	1890–1912	ADM 174/390–1
	1900–22	ADM 174/380–3
	1910	ADM 174/385
Salary book	1867–1907	ADM 174/373
Confidential letter books	1881–1912	ADM 174/331–3
Plans:	1891	ADM 174/415
	1895	ADM 174/361
(Naval Stores Department buildings)	1940	ADM 174/423
Scantlings for cask and cooperage	1895	ADM 174/386
Notes on wartime victualling	1903–14	ADM 174/402
Superintendent's orders	1906–21	ADM 174/338–9
Naval Stores Department: wartime activities	1939–47	ADM 174/422
(post-war plans)	1941–50	ADM 174/424–6

172 Other Home Victualling Yards and Depots

Yard unknown, Board orders	1723–65	ADM 114/35
Yard unknown, pay list of coopers and labourers	1797–1816	ADM 30/58–61
Register of title deeds	1810	ADM 7/879

Tower Hill

Pay lists	1703–1808	ADM 113/126–75

Chatham

Pay lists	1703–1826	ADM 113/5–27
Description book	1809–13	ADM 113/273
Letters to Victualling Board	1822–32	ADM 109/91

Deal

Pay lists	1728–1857	ADM 113/34–57
Letters to Victualling Board	1822–32	ADM 109/91
Letter books	1823–60	ADM 114/49–54

Dover

Pay lists	1717–1833	ADM 113/84–103
Letters to Victualling Board	1822–32	ADM 109/91

Mylor

Pay lists	1806–35	ADM 113/179

Rotherhithe
Pay lists	1762–93	ADM 113/248

Sheerness
Letters to Victualling Board	1822–32	ADM 109/92
Pay and pension lists	1803–33	ADM 113/249–52

Cork and Haulbowline, later Royal Alexandra
Pay lists	1795–1831	ADM 113/31–3
Letters to Victualling Board	1822–32	ADM 109/92
Plan	1897	ADM 174/398

Kinsale
Pay lists	1771–8	ADM 113/124

173 Other Overseas Victualling Yards and Depots

Antigua
Plans	1855–61	MF 1/5/1 and 1/6

Ascension Island
Letters to Victualling Board	1822–32	ADM 109/93
Letters to Navy Board	1822–32	ADM 106/2065

Bermuda
Letters to Victualling Board	1822–32	ADM 109/94
Plans:	1891	ADM 174/397
	1898	NMM: ADM/Y/B/1

Cape of Good Hope and Simonstown
Pay lists	1796–1835	ADM 113/2–4
Letters to Victualling Board	1822–32	ADM 109/95
In-letters	1832–40	ADM 123/44–5

East Indies
Pay lists	1758–84	ADM 113/124

Fernando Po
Letters to Victualling Board	1822–32	ADM 109/96
Letters to Navy Board	1822–32	ADM 106/2065
Pay lists	1831	ADM 113/104

Gibraltar
Pay lists	1710–1835	ADM 113/105–21
Letters to Victualling Board	1822–32	ADM 109/97
Plan	1875	NMM: ADM/Y/G/30

Halifax
Salaries and allowances	1775–84	ADM 7/858
Letters to Victualling Board	1822–32	ADM 109/98

Jamaica
Letters to Victualling Board	1822–32	ADM 109/98

Leeward Islands
Pay lists	1782–83	ADM 113/124

Lisbon
Pay lists	1806–14	ADM 113/124

Malta
Pay lists	1801–19	ADM 113/176–8
Letters to Victualling Board:	1813–16	ADM 174/407
	1822–32	ADM 109/99
Notes on records	1921	ADM 174/403

Mauritius
Pay list	1812	ADM 113/215

Minorca
Pay lists	1742–7 and 1809–14	ADM 113/215

Montreal
Letters to Navy Board	1822–32	ADM 106/2065

Rio de Janeiro
Pay lists	1808–16	ADM 113/247

St. John's Newfoundland
Letters to Navy Board	1822–32	ADM 106/2065

Sierra Leone
Letters to Victualling Board	1822–32	ADM 109/100
Letters to Navy Board	1822–32	ADM 106/2065
Pay lists	1824–31	ADM 113/253

Trincomalee

Letters to Victualling Board	1822–32	ADM 109/101
Pay lists	1829–32	ADM 113/256

174 Transport Board, 1689–1717

This Transport Board was established initially to support the Army in Ireland, and subsequently in Flanders. It was abolished soon after the end of the War of the Spanish Succession.

Correspondence with Admiralty	1689–90	ADM 2/1756
Letters to Secretaries of State	1689–99	SP 42/1–5
Declared accounts:	1690–1719	AO 1/2304/8–2310/26
(debts)	1704–14	AO 1/845/1–3
Letters from Secretaries of State:	1693–6	SP 44/205
	1701–14	SP 44/206–19
Charter parties, naval stores	1694–1710	ADM 106/3068
Cash book, transports to Spain and Portugal	1702–4	C 114/188
Accounts, salaries and expenses	1704–7	AO 3/1/2
Troops embarked and victualled	1706–18	ADM 106/2973

175 Transport Board, 1796–1816

The second Transport Board, unlike its predecessor, was an amalgamation of all the government sea transport services, both naval and military. When it was abolished in 1816 a Transport Accounts Committee was appointed to wind up its affairs.

Minutes:	1794–1815	ADM 108/31–113
(index)	1800–4	ADM 108/144–7
Letters from Treasury	1794–8	ADM 108/4B–7
Letters to Admiralty	1794–1816	ADM 1/3730–69
Out-letters: general	1795–1800	ADM 108/28
(agents abroad)	1797–1801	ADM 108/29
(Chairman's)	1796–1806	ADM 108/30
(Deal)	1796–1816	ADM 108/184–8
Charter of Hamburg ships	1795–7	ADM 108/169–73
Board patents	1795–1813	ADM 5/24–32
Miscellanea	1795–1816	MT 23/1–2
Letters to Secretaries of State	1795–1817	ADM 108/19–27
Commissioners' and staff salaries	1796	ADM 108/191
Register of transports	1796–9	ADM 108/168
Slop and Transport Office, papers	1796–9	PRO 30/8/252

Salary books	1796–1827	ADM 7/862–8
Ships' ledgers:	1799–1818	ADM 108/148–54
(freight)	1795–1818	ADM 108/158–65
Letters from transport agent, Deal	1796–1816	ADM 108/184–8
Regulations for transport agents	1803	ADM 106/3096
Ships chartered for Ireland, accounts	1803–9	ADM 17/28
Pay books and lists:	1804–17	ADM 108/177–9
(Jamaica)	1797–1805	ADM 108/181
Transports burnt at Aix Roads	1809	ADM 108/174
Rules for transport agents	1814	ADM 108/182

Transport Accounts Committee

Unsettled accounts, abstract	1816	ADM 108/189
Reports to Admiralty	1817–18	ADM 1/3770–1
Reports to WO on POWs	1817–22	ADM 98/311–13

176 Victualling Board Transport Committee, 1816–32

The unified Transport Service passed in 1816 to the Victualling Board.

Correspondence with Treasury	c.1816–32	T 1/4320
Letters from Treasury	1817–29	ADM 108/8–18
Letters from Admiralty	1817–29	ADM 108/1E–3
Letters from naval boards	1817–30	ADM 108/114–43
Accounts: Thames agents	1817	ADM 30/48
(victualling Artillery and Engineers)	1817–29	ADM 108/176
Ships' ledgers:	1817–30	ADM 108/155–7
(freight)	1817–32	ADM 108/166–7
Ledger of agents' accounts	1817–30	ADM 108/175
Index of surveys and tenders	1817–31	ADM 106/3533
Regulations for masters of transports:	1821	ADM 108/183
	1827	ADM 106/3097

177 Board of Revision

The Commission for the Revising and Digesting of the Civil Affairs of the Navy was established in 1805 as an instrument for reforming naval administration according to the ideas of its Chairman, Sir Charles Middleton (soon afterwards created Lord Barham and First Lord of the Admiralty). In its three years of work it collected much evidence and produced an extensive programme of change.

Reports and papers:	1803–11	ADM 106/3111–16
	1804–9	ADM 1/4078–9
	1804–9	ADM 49/92
	1805–9	ADM 7/401–6 and 412
	1805–9	PC 1/13/93
First report	1805–22	ADM 106/2283B
Third–14th reports	1803–11	ADM 106/3108–10
Sick and Hurt Board	1805	ADM 98/105–6
Contingent accounts	1806–8	ADM 17/90
Dockyard instructions:	1805–6	ADM 106/3630–2
	1806–8	ADM 7/223–4
	1806–8	ADM 174/301–2
(out-ports)	1806	ADM 106/3634
Victualling instructions:	1808	ADM 7/216–17
	1808	ADM 106/3107–10
	1808	ADM 114/71
Hospital instructions	1808	ADM 106/3091–2

178 Royal Navy, Records of Home Stations

Records from squadrons and stations during the First World War form a distinct block, but those of the Second World War are scattered among all the other records used by the official historians.

First World War	1914–19	ADM 137/1799–2522
(indexes)	1914–19	ADM 137/3058–9
Second World War	1939–45	ADM 199/1–2577

Channel Fleet, Grand Fleet, Western Squadron etc.

C-in-C's standing orders:	1692	ADM 7/692
	1782	ADM 7/582/1–6
C-in-Cs' letter book	1693	ADM 7/694

Channel, Atlantic and Grand Fleets

Correspondence and papers:	1867–1911	ADM 144/1–34
(index)	1897–1904	ADM 146/2

(letters from Admiralty)	1871–7	ADM 144/2–5
(index)	1871–7	ADM 146/1
Atlantic fleet: correspondence	1902–8	ADM 145/1–3
(C-in-C's journal)	1905–7	ADM 145/4–5
Grand Fleet battle orders	1914–18	ADM 137/4049–55
Grand Fleet gunnery practice	1914–18	ADM 137/4822–3

Channel Islands

C-in-C's correspondence	1794–1801	HO 44/42–4

Downs

Lists of pilots	1812–15	ADM 30/43

Ireland

In-letters, Admiralty and general:	1816–1911	ADM 149/1–14
(index)	1816–1911	ADM 150/1
Out-letters: Admiralty	1821–5	ADM 149/15–16
(general)	1821–5	ADM 149/17–21
Orders and memoranda	1821–5	ADM 148/1–2

Nore

C-in-C, letters from Rear-Adm. Rowley	1805	ADM 151/1
Lists of pilots	1812–15	ADM 30/43
Letters from Admiralty and miscellaneous:	1830–1939	ADM 151/3–92
(indexes)	1860–1901	ADM 152/1–3
Courts martial returns	1848–63	ADM 153/1–2
Confidential and secret memoranda	1910–14	ADM 7/910

Plymouth

State and condition of ships, returns	1793–9	ADM 49/100
Ratings discharged by habeas corpus	1812–15	ADM 6/67
Letters from Admiralty:	1842–65	ADM 131/1–2
	1876–1913	ADM 131/3–55
	1919–25	ADM 131/56–62
(confidential)	1893–1910	ADM 131/63
(indexes)	1876–1912	ADM 143/1–2
C-in-C, letters to Admiral Superintendent	1850–6	ADM 174/312
Orders and memoranda	1859–1928	ADM 130/1–45
Operational records	1914–18	ADM 131/64–124
Search for Aer Lingus airliner	1968	ADM 131/125

Portsmouth

HM Ships lost or disposed of	1860–71	ADM 179/122

C-in-C, letters from Admiralty	1885–1947	ADM 179/2–49
Naval reviews, ceremonials etc.	1887–1924	ADM 179/52–61 and 128–9
Boom defence records	1892–1908	ADM 179/71 and 130
Miscellanea	1904–9	ADM 179/127
Local defences	1905–9	ADM 179/128–9
Collisions etc.	1908–26	ADM 179/64 and 123–6
Portsmouth general orders:	1911–48	ADM 179/72–109
(confidential)	1939–45	ADM 179/110–16
(navigational)	1941–5	ADM 179/117–21
Refitting of HMS *Victory*	1924–31	ADM 179/62
Local defences and operations	1927–48	ADM 179/132–539
RN Barracks, history	1932	ADM 174/384
Navy Weeks	1935–9	ADM 179/63
Toraplane and Doraplane trials	1929–40	ADM 179/137 and 147
WRNS	1939–45	ADM 179/50

Western approaches

War diaries and reports of proceedings	1942–5	ADM 217/1–802

Germany

Papers	1945–9	ADM 228/1–101

179 Royal Navy, Records of Foreign Stations

The domestic or internal records of squadrons and stations were only systematically preserved from the mid nineteenth century. Before that date, however, there are accidental survivals, and individual commanders-in-chief often made collections of their official papers which can be regarded as equivalent to station records.

First World War:	1914–19	ADM 137/1799–2522
(indexes)	1914–19	ADM 137/3058–9
Second World War	1939–45	ADM 199/1–2577

Africa

Correspondence and papers:	1845–1910	ADM 123/1–37 and 46–60
	1867–1930	ADM 123/98–120
(slave trade)	1845–70	ADM 123/170–85
(foreign powers)	1846–70	ADM 123/159–69
(expeditions)	1875–97	ADM 123/121–8
West Africa Division	1857–1932	ADM 123/61–97
Reports of proceedings	1874–1931	ADM 123/129–33
South African War:	1899–1902	ADM 123/134–5

(medical reports and casualty list)	1899–1900	ADM 116/529
First World War	1916–18	ADM 123/136–58
Indexes	1845–1918	ADM 124/1–14

Australia

China Station, Pacific Division	1830–58	ADM 125/131–5
Correspondence and papers	1855–96	ADM 122/1–27

Baltic

Correspondence with Ambassador and Consuls, Sweden:	1807	FO 334/14
	1807–8	FO 188/2
C-in-C, letter book	1854	ADM 7/769

Canadian Lakes

Ships' musters	1813–14	ADM 30/46
Acting Commissioner, declared accounts	1813–14	AO 1/1831/558
C-in-C, imprest account etc.	1815	ADM 49/16

Cape of Good Hope

Courts martial minutes	1796–7	ADM 1/5487–8
Commissioner's out-letter book	1811–13	ADM 123/42
Papers of Commissioner Sir J Brenton	1815–22	ADM 7/2–6
C-in-C, correspondence etc.	1816–24	ADM 7/47–8 and 53–4
Supplies purchased at Sierra Leone, accounts	c.1821–5	AO 1/576/497

China, later Far East

Correspondence: general	1845–1936	ADM 125/1–73
(piracy)	1828–74	ADM 125/144–8
(British trade in China)	1835–1932	ADM 125/92–111
(bases and establishments)	1841–1906	ADM 125/74–91
(monthly returns)	1849	ADM 49/171
(Japan)	1859–77	ADM 125/115–22
(China river gunboats)	1891–1908	ADM 125/123–8
(seal-fishing patrols)	1892–7	ADM 125/129–30
(Sino-Japanese war)	1894–5	ADM 125/112–14
(indexes)	1856–1914	ADM 126/1–6
Letters from Consul, Siam:	1870	FO 628/5
	1875	FO 628/6
	1880	FO 628/8
	1898	FO 628/19
Letters from British Embassy Shanghai	1940	FO 676/431
British POWs	1941–6	ADM 125/149–50
Second-in-Command, Korea, reports		ADM 316

East Indies

Rear-Adm. E Boscawen, C-in-C, declared accounts	1747–50	AO 1/218/732
Papers of Sir E Hughes as C-in-C	1747–85	ADM 7/733–63
Inventories of Dutch East India Company property (including ships) taken in Ceylon	1796	WO 55/1839
C-in-C, correspondence with East India Company Governors	1804–6	ADM 1/175
C-in-C, correspondence with Marquis Wellesley	1801–8	ADM 1/5121/5
Correspondence: general	1838–1930	ADM 127/1–24 and 47
(Persian Gulf):	1825–58	ADM 127/48–71
	1839–1930	ADM 127/25–30
(Red Sea and East Africa)	1877–88	ADM 127/31–45
China Station, East Indies Division	1856–1900	ADM 125/136–43
Royal East African Navy	1951–61	ADM 127/72–5
Commodore Persian Gulf, files		ADM 323

Jamaica

Commissions issued	1757–73	ADM 1/5116/12 and 5117/1
Correspondence, *Sir Edward Hawke* affair	1771	ADM 1/5117/3
C-in-C, letter book	1817–20	ADM 80/156–8

Leeward Islands

Commissions and warrants	1757–73	ADM 1/5116/12 and 5117/1
C-in-C, letters to Antigua Yard	1779–87	ADM 241/1

Mediterranean

Commissions and warrants:	1742	ADM 1/5115/10
	1744–5	ADM 106/2969
Returns of sick men	1742–3	ADM 1/5115/11
C-in-C, letters to Sick and Hurt Board	1743	ADM 97/114/8
Musters of Maltese ratings	1793–8	ADM 30/63/6
Diagram of anchorage off Cadiz	1798	ADM 7/885
Letters to Consul, Tunis:	1800–9	FO 335/46/5
	1804	FO 335/45/14
	1807	FO 335/46/4
	1810	FO 335/46/18 and 47/1–2
	1813	FO 335/48/5
	1822	FO 335/49/10
	1836–7	FO 335/66/2 and 8
	1838	FO 335/67/13–16
Letters to Ambassador and Consuls: Morocco	1801–16	FO 174/11 and 25
(Morocco, blockade of Tangier)	1828–9	FO 174/31
(Greece)	1828–30	FO 286/6

C-in-C, correspondence with Secretary for War:	1803–4	CO 173/1
	1808	CO 173/2
C-in-C, correspondence	1808–12	ADM 7/41–6 and 50–2
Letters from Consul, Corfu	1805–7	FO 348/6
Letters from Ambassador and Consuls, Greece	1828–42	FO 286/12
Correspondence and papers	1843–1968	ADM 121/1–105
SNO Constantinople, correspondence	1860–1914	ADM 137/4175

Newfoundland

'Account of the colony and fishery'	1677	ADM 7/689 and CO 199/16
Governor's patent	1749	ADM 5/33
Governors' orders and proclamations	1749–1811	ADM 80/121–2
Statistical account of French and British fisheries	1774	ADM 1/5117/4
Governor and C-in-C: letter books:	1813–16	ADM 80/151
	1818–24	ADM 80/125–6
(Secretary's letter book)	1813–17	ADM 80/123
(naval order book)	1818–24	ADM 80/127–9
Admiral's journals	1819–24	ADM 80/160–3
SNO, letter book	1822–3	ADM 80/130

North America and West Indies

Repairs to *Georgia* galley, account	1745	AO 3/1/3
Commissions and warrants	1757–70	ADM 1/5116/12
Lists of transports chartered locally	1759–63	ADM 49/171
C-in-C, orders, signals etc.	1778	ADM 106/3544/1
Musters of small vessels	1779–82	ADM 30/45
Note on epidemics at Bermuda	1802–61	ADM 104/155
Correspondence, general:	1810–1913	ADM 128/1–153
(index)	1859–82	ADM 129/1–2
Purchase of local craft in Chesapeake	1814–15	ADM 49/17
Monthly returns	1851	ADM 49/171

Pacific

Letters from Consul, Honolulu	1829–34	FO 331/7
Correspondence and papers:	1843–54	ADM 80/119
	1843–58	ADM 172/1–4
Index	1893–1903	ADM 155/1

St. Lawrence River

Correspondence of Captain Lord Hervey as SNO	1778–91	FO 528/22

South America

Welsh colony of Chubut	1871–1902	ADM 147/1

| Letters to Admiralty and others | 1894–1904 | ADM 147/2–11 |

West Africa
| Musters of Kroomen | 1819–20 | ADM 30/26 |

180 Royal Navy, other Squadrons, Ships and Units

This is a miscellaneous collection of reports of proceedings and the like. Very many more such reports are to be found in the in-letters, and later registered files of the Admiralty [85–6, 94–5 and 103]. Records of individual ships listed here do not include logs, journals, musters and pay books [97 and 158].

RNVR AA Corps	1914–18	ADM 137/4826
RN Division: war diaries and orders	1915–19	ADM 137/3063–88D
(reports and papers)	1915–19	ADM 137/3924–42
RNAS Armoured Car Squadron	1916	AIR 1/147/15/64
Reports of proceedings	1914–19	ADM 137/3089–833
War history cases	1939–45	ADM 199/1–2577
Submarine patrol reports	1939–45	ADM 236/1–54
RN and RM Units at Coronation, orders	1952	ADM 7/992
Officer Commanding Operation MOSAIC	1955–6	ADM 296/1–62

Individual Ships
Captain's letter book, Capt. J Trevor, HMS *Defiance*	1739–40	ADM 7/781
Captain's letter book, Capt. A J Ball, HMS *Alexander*	1796–1800	ADM 7/55
Journal, HMS *Salsette*, Quarantine Service	1831–2	PC 6/12
Captain's letter book, Lt. William Greet, HMS *Perseus*	1847–50	ADM 7/56
Captain's letter book, Cdr. William Greet, HMS *Crocodile*	1850–7	ADM 7/57
Captain's order book, HMS *Peking*	1916–17	ADM 13/252

181 Royal Naval Air Service and Fleet Air Arm

The archival practice of the Royal Air Force, which took over the records of the RNAS in 1918, was such as to scatter them among many other records, so that the following list is only illustrative of the sorts of records which can be found. The Fleet Air Arm was transferred back to naval control in 1939, but it retained many administrative links with the Air Ministry, which continued to collect much information about it.

Royal Naval Air Service
| RN air stations, daily reports: | 1914–18 | AIR 1/186/15/226/3–251/15/226/79 |
| | 1915–20 | AIR 1/433–4 |

	1917–18	AIR 1/310–33
(Great Yarmouth)	1914–19	AIR 1/413–17
RNAS Farnborough, airship log	1914–15	AIR 1/2681
RNAS Experimental Section, experiment book	1914–16	AIR 1/2682
Squadron histories (including RFC)	1914–19	AIR 1/163–84
Photographic Section	1915–16	AIR 20/615 and 702
Squadron record books etc.	1915–19	AIR 1/1440–2020
Airship logs	1910–19	AIR 3/1–66
Aircraft and airship logs	1914–19	AIR 1/2056/204/412/ etc.
Airship stations, monthly reports	1916–18	AIR 1/718/31/1/1–719/31/2/6
Fleet Air Arm		
RAF flying log books:	1918–39	AIR 4/various
	1933–40	ADM 900/69–74
Squadron diaries and record books:	1939–57	ADM 207/1–68
	1941–6	AIR 27/2386–7
(815 Squadron)	1964–5	ADM 335/37
(HMS *Eagle*)	1966–71	ADM 335/38–40
(801 Squadron)	1967–70	ADM 335/42
(various)	1933–71	ADM 335/1–80
Combat reports	1940–5	AIR 50/320–31
RN Flying School, daily logs	1944–5	ADM 207/52–3
Badge of no. 1834 RNVR Squadron	1955	ADM 207/69

182 Ordnance Board, 1546–1660

At this period the activities of the Board were largely concerned with supplying guns and ammunition to the Navy and to forts (which used broadly the same patterns of guns and equipment).

Master of Naval Ordnance: declared accounts:	1546–1589	E 351/2599–607
	1557–60	AO 1/1832/1
(accounts)	1561–3	E 101/64/31
Master and Surveyor, declared accounts:	1546–61	E 351/2614–16
	1561–1604	AO 1/1832/1A–1833/12
	1561–6	E 351/2602
	1563–87	E 351/2617–29
	1588–92	E 351/2609
	1592–1603	E 351/2630–9
	1596–7	E 351/2612
	1625–32	AO 1/1833/13
	1642–51	AO 1/1844/65A

Lieutenant, declared accounts	1561–1640	AO 1/1834/14–1844/65
Sea Service, receipts and issues of guns and stores:	1571–2	WO 55/1625
	1595–1637	WO 55/1626–45
	1625–9	WO 55/1681–5
	1636–7	WO 55/1692
	1646–8	WO 55/1648–9
Treasurer, declared accounts	1587–8	AO 1/1846/68–70
Surveys of naval ordnance:	1588–91	WO 55/1659
	1609	WO 55/1675
	1622	SP 14/133
	1634	WO 55/1691
Storekeeper, declared accounts	1589–92	AO 1/1906/242
Debenture books	1592–1683	WO 49/17–108
Declared accounts, Islands voyage	1596–7	E 351/2611–12
Sir J Hawkins's Squadron, ammunition expenditure	1591	SP 13/D/10
Sea Service, payments and contracts	1627–34	PRO 30/37/1–3
Bill books:	1630–4	WO 51/1
	1654–9	WO 51/2
Returns and papers, including naval	1639	WO 49/110
Sea and Land Service, receipts of guns and stores:	1642–3	WO 55/1660
	1645	WO 55/1665
	1648–53	WO 55/1666
Warrants and orders:	1644–5	WO 47/1
	1645–7	PRO 30/37/4
	1652–9	WO 47/2–4
Contracts	1654–8	PRO 30/37/5

183 Ordnance Board, 1660–1855

These are records of the naval activities of the Ordnance Board, whose military responsibilities (the Artillery, Engineers, fortifications and barracks) grew greatly during this period.

Statutes relating to naval stores	1638–1748	WO 55/1782
Sea Service, issues of guns and stores:	1660–4	PRO 30/37/7
	1666–76	WO 55/1652–4
	1669–73	WO 55/1669
Sea and Land Services, receipts:	1660–5	PRO 30/37/8
	1661–4	WO 55/1667
	1668–73	WO 55/1668–9
Sea Service, surveys and inventories	1662–77	WO 55/1650
Warrants and orders:	1663–6	WO 47/5–8
	1668–76	WO 47/19A–B

	1680–96	WO 47/9–18
	1714–26	WO 47/20A–21A
Sea Service, issues of stores	1673–90	WO 55/1706
Establishment of ordnance stores for HM Ships	1678	WO 55/1650
Sea Service, issues and remains of guns:	1679	WO 55/1715
	1681–3	WO 55/1718
In-letters:	1682–91	WO 44/714–15
(by subject)	1682–1873	WO 44/532–713
(fortifications etc.)	1682–1873	WO 44/1–496
(to Board, registers)	1783–1856	WO 45/1–280
(to Master-General, registers)	1844–54	WO 45/281–4
(from Admiralty):	1812–55	WO 44/498–502
	1854–7	ADM 2/1698–701
Ordnance expenditure on HM Ships	1688–92	WO 55/1793
Establishments and proposed establishments of guns for HM Ships:	1689–92	WO 55/1762–3
	1703	WO 55/1803
	1716–23	WO 55/1739–40
	1743	WO 55/1743
	1765	WO 55/1745
	1818	WO 55/1749
Out-letters: Sea and Land Services	1693–1794	WO 46/3–23
(to Navy Board, transports)	1744–63	ADM 106/273
(to Admiralty)	1780–1839	ADM 1/3999–4035
(to Navy Board, registers)	1808–13	ADM 106/2135–8
List of tenders attached to HM Ships	1694–1706	WO 54/673
Sea Service, inventory of guns	1702	WO 55/1736
HM Ships at Jamaica, gunner's stores	c.1702	WO 55/1782
Ordnance, Admiralty etc. clerks' salaries	1704	WO 55/1796
Board minutes:	1705–8	WO 47/22–5
	1714–20	WO 47/27–33
	1781	WO 47/26
	1786–1856	WO 47/2549–759
	1809–55	WO 47/121–2357
(index):	1691	WO 47/2853
	1737–53	WO 47/2854
	1819–52	WO 47/2855–97
(extracts)	1782–1856	WO 47/2358–759
Coastal defences, reports etc.	1708–1864	WO 55/1548/1–23
Valuation of lands for compulsory purchase for fortification of dockyards:	1709	C 205/18
	1714–1831	C 182/1–12
(Portsmouth)	1815	WO 44/242

Parliamentary votes, Sea and Land Service	1709–39	WO 55/1804
Scheme for reforming Marines	c.1725	WO 55/1810
Gunners' passing certificates	1731–1812	ADM 6/123–9
Gunners' accounts, correspondence:	1754–84	WO 55/1818–19
(register)	1778–98	WO 30/96
Armourers' warrants	1755–62	WO 54/685
Board orders to Surveyor-General	1782–1816	WO 47/2358–548
Registers of ships' guns and stores:	1783–1819	WO 18/214
(A–Z)	1793–1826	WO 55/1830–5
Inventory and valuation of Dutch prizes at Colombo	1796	WO 55/1839
Circular orders	1805–30	ADM 7/227–8
Applications for armourers	1827–38	WO 54/881–2
Reports, naval	1834–58	WO 55/307–9
Registers of transports:	1853–5	WO 55/1933
	1854	WO 44/537

Correspondence, Particular Subjects

Painting guns and carriages of HM Ships	1796–8	WO 44/732
Mess allowances to officers aboard HM Ships	1814	WO 44/732
Salutes from forts and ships, instructions	1838	WO 44/732
Dockyard defences	1844–5	WO 55/1548
Dockyard battalions	1847–73	WO 44/610
Committee on Coast Defence	1852–3	WO 55/1563/7
Inventions	1855	WO 44/620–40
Land purchases, transfers etc. (including Admiralty)	1840–51	WO 44/716–32

184 Ordnance Board Members and Officials

The Ordnance Board, like the Navy Board, transacted much of its business collectively, but some records can be distinguished of individual members and their responsibilities.

Master-General

Lords' Letters from Admiralty:	1660–2	WO 55/330
	1689–1815	ADM 2/169–332
Letters from Navy Board	1682	WO 55/1796
Letters from Secretaries of State:	1693–6	SP 44/205
	1701–84	SP 44/206–32
RN officer on Board of Ordnance	1841	WO 80/4
Coastal defences etc.	1842–5	WO 80/9
Invention to make steamers ball-proof	1843	WO 80/4
Length of waiting list for Marine cadets	1844	WO 80/4

Lieutenant

Declared accounts	1660–70	AO 1/1844/66–1845/67

Surveyor-General

Minutes of proceedings	1749–92	WO 47/34–120
Report books	1753–1858	WO 55/1–230
Board orders	1782–1816	WO 47/2358–548

Treasurer

Debenture books:	1592–1683	WO 49/17–108
	1714–15	WO 49/109
Ledgers	1660–1846	WO 48/1–214
Bill books:	1661–1783	WO 51/3–313
	1783–1859	WO 52/1–782
(Sea Service)	1678–99	WO 50/13–14
(quarterly bills)	1694–1752	WO 50/2–11
Declared accounts:	1670–1827	AO 1/1846/71–1905/239
	1828–31	AO 2/1, 18 and 22
	1832–4	AO 2/24 and 28
	1834–6	AO 2/33–4
(sale of debentures)	1714–16	AO 1/845/4

Inspector of Artillery

Out-letters:	1780–95	SUPP 5/52–3
	1785–94	SUPP 5/107–8
In-letters	1780–1803	SUPP 5/48–51

185 Ordnance Establishments

Woolwich Arsenal was the board's principal home depot and manufacturing centre. Portsmouth and Plymouth Gunwharves served their respective dockyards, while Upnor Castle, originally a defensive battery on the Medway, was converted to become the main powder magazine for Chatham and Sheerness. The Royal Ordnance Factories, listed here for convenience, include establishments originally belonging to the Ordnance Board together with others established later by the Admiralty, the Ministry of Munitions or the Ministry of Supply. Many reports on naval weapons and ammunition from ordnance establishments were inherited by the Royal Armament Research and Development Establishment [221].

Woolwich Arsenal

Royal Carriage Department, correspondence etc.	1811–1904	SUPP 5/13–21
Shell Foundry, correspondence etc.	1888–1906	SUPP 5/32–43

Upnor Castle

Accounts	1736–1855	ADM 160/118–49
Correspondence	1745–1866	ADM 160/1–117
Establishments, returns etc.	1781–1909	ADM 160/150–8
Miscellanea	1801–1905	ADM 160/159

Portsmouth Gunwharf

In-letters	1718–1888	WO 55/1985–2122
Out-letters	1750–7	WO 55/2127–8
Minutes:	1758–1890	WO 55/2137–233
	1808–52	WO 55/2234–48

Plymouth Gunwharf

Building accounts	1722–4	WO 49/229–30

Royal Ordnance Factories etc.

HQ and factory records	1664–1982	SUPP 5/1–1371
Royal Ordnance Factories, accounts etc.	1888–1940	SUPP 2/1–59
Woolwich Dockyard chapel/church, responsibility for repairs	1890–1903	SUPP 5/123 and 127
Royal Gunpowder Factory, Waltham Abbey, accounts	1900–3	SUPP 5/347
Manufacture of cordite	1920	SUPP 5/852
RN Cordite Factory Holton Heath, reports	1927–38	SUPP 5/853–4
Transfer of RN Torpedo Factory to Greenock and Torpedo Range to Loch Long	1908–14	SUPP 5/177 and 182
Martell report on service propellants	1962	SUPP 5/1265
Filling instructions for naval shells	n.d.	SUPP 5/1250

186 The Cabinet, to 1916

With one exception these are records created or retrospectively collected by the Cabinet Office established in 1916. Besides minutes of the Cabinet and its committees, they include numerous memoranda and papers prepared by various departments for the Cabinet's information. Records of eighteenth-century Cabinet and other ministerial meetings in the State Papers are listed in List and Index Society 224.

Minutes and memoranda, 14 February	1760	ADM 1/5123/1
Prime Minister's reports to sovereign	1868–1916	CAB 37/22/36–119/29
Memoranda	1880–1916	CAB 37/1/1–162/33
Navy Estimates and memoranda	1888–1915	CAB 37/22/36–119/29
Anglo-Japanese Treaty	1905	CAB 1/5/27
Supply of Welsh coal for RN	1905	CAB 1/6/1–12
General naval situation	1912	CAB 1/8/13

Enquiry into loss of *Aboukir*, *Cressy* and *Hogue*	1914	CAB 1/10/25
Naval action at Heligoland	1914	CAB 1/10/43
War Council minutes:	1914–15	CAB 22/1
	1914–16	CAB 42/1/1–26/10
Naval affairs at beginning of war	1915	CAB 1/11/2
Submarine threat to British ships	1915	CAB 1/11/31–2
Orders to the Fleet (blockade)	1915	CAB 1/11/57
Naval operations in Dardanelles	1915	CAB 1/12/46
Soldiers' and Sailors' Help Society	1915	CAB 1/13/40
Dardanelles Committee minutes	1915	CAB 22/2
War Committee minutes	1915–16	CAB 22/3–82
Joint War Air Committee minutes	1916	AIR 1/2319
Blockade of Germany by British Fleet	1916	CAB 1/15/1
Munitions of War Act and Admiralty contractors	1916	CAB 1/16/18 and 17/18

187 The War Cabinet, 1916–19

Records created by the new Cabinet Office, dealing with the War Cabinet itself, its committees, and the Inter-Allied Supreme War Council.

Cabinet minutes:	1916–39	CAB 23/1–17
	1917–19	CAB 23/40–4B
Cabinet memoranda	1915–19	CAB 24/1–91
Registered Files		
Registered files	1916–73	CAB 21/1–6078
Russian naval mutiny	1917	CAB 21/96/ii
Guns for merchant ships	1917	CAB 1/22/30
Naval shipbuilding programme	1917	CAB 1/23/16
Note on naval warfare	1917	CAB 1/25/22
Fall of Calais and Boulogne, possible naval situation	1918	CAB 1/26/13
Supreme War Council		
Minutes, including Allied Naval Council	1915–19	CAB 28/1–9
Papers and minutes	1917–19	CAB 25/1–127
Military and naval representatives, minutes	1919	CAB 21/131–3
Committees		
Main series	1915–39	CAB 27/1–663
War Priorities, minutes and papers	1917–18	CAB 15/6/1–3
Post-war Priority and Demobilisation, minutes	1918–19	CAB 33/1–26

188 The Cabinet, 1919–39

The records of the post-war Cabinet resemble those of the War Cabinet except that many defence matters were referred to the Committee of Imperial Defence.

Conclusions:	1919–22	CAB 23/18–39
	1923–39	CAB 23/45–101
Memoranda	1919–39	CAB 24/92–288
Hankey papers, RAN	1932–4	CAB 63/73

Registered Files

Committees, minutes and papers	1915–39	CAB 27/1–663
Registered files	1916–73	CAB 21/1–6078
RN pay and allowances:	1919–20	CAB 27/65
	1925–9	CAB 27/301 and 307–8
	1937–9	CAB 27/636
Naval defence of the empire	1921	CAB 21/187–8
Amalgamation of common services	1922	CAB 27/171–3
Relative ranks of RN, RAF and Army	1922	CAB 27/184
Fighting Services Committee, Naval Estimates	1922	CAB 27/168–70
Naval armament limitation treaties:	1922	CAB 21/238
	1929	CAB 21/321
RN-RAF Co-operation Committee, minutes:	1922–3	CAB 21/225, 227, 258 and 264–7
	1930	CAB 21/333
Naval shipbuilding programme:	1925	CAB 27/273
	1927	CAB 27/355
Limitations on naval armaments	1927	CAB 27/350
Dominions and imperial defence policy	1929–39	CAB 104/17–19
London Naval Conference	1930	CAB 21/339–43
Export of warships	1930–1	CAB 27/445
Anglo-German naval agreements:	1935	CAB 21/404–5
	1935–8	CAB 104/29
Mediterranean Fleet	1936	CAB 27/606
Anglo-French-Belgian Naval Staff contacts	1936–9	CAB 104/59–64

International Conferences, Proceedings

Washington Disarmament Conference	1921–2	CAB 30/1–33
Imperial Conference London	1923	CAB 32/17
London Naval Conferences:	1930	CAB 29/117–35
	1934–6	CAB 29/147–58
Anglo-French Naval Staff conversations	1939	CAB 29/161

189 The War Cabinet, 1939–45

The wartime Cabinet Office included several distinct administrations and a large number of Cabinet committees and sub-committees covering all sorts of inter-departmental activities.

Minutes	1939–45	CAB 65/1/1–57
Memoranda:	1939–41	CAB 67/1–9
	1939–45	CAB 66/1–67
(departmental)	1939–42	CAB 68/1–9
Daily situation reports	1939–45	CAB 100/1–13
International conferences, proceedings	1939–45	CAB 99/1–40
Telegrams	1941–8	CAB 105/1–194
Hankey papers: conduct of the war	1939–41	CAB 63/83–94
(French Fleet)	1940	CAB 63/132
(anti-U-boat campaign)	1940–3	CAB 63/179

Registered Files

Registered files	1916–73	CAB 21/1–6078
Naval AA gunnery	1939	CAB 21/619
Anglo-French naval liaison	1939	CAB 104/152–3
British war casualties	1939–45	CAB 21/909–12
French Navy	1940–3	CAB 21/1448–50
Naval production programme	1940–5	CAB 21/1554
Battle of the Atlantic	1941	CAB 21/1498–9

Other Committees

Lists of Cabinet committees	1939–44	CAB 169/1–4
Military Co-ordination, minutes and papers	1939–40	CAB 83/1–5
Overseas Defence	1939–42	CAB 94/1–4
Home Policy, minutes and papers	1939–45	CAB 75/1–39
Middle East and Africa, minutes	1939–45	CAB 95/1–18
Defence (Operations), minutes	1940–5	CAB 69/1–8
Defence (Supply), minutes	1940–6	CAB 70/1–13
Oil Policy, minutes	1939–46	CAB 77/1–30
Co-ordination of Departmental Action	1940–2	CAB 107/1–10
Far East, minutes	1940–5	CAB 96/1–10
Shipping, minutes	1940–5	CAB 97/1–9
Inter-Service, on chemical warfare	1940–54	CAB 21/3912
Operation AJAX	1941	CAB 98/54
Battle of the Atlantic and Anti-U-boat warfare, minutes and papers	1941–5	CAB 86/1–7
London Munitions Assignment Board, naval construction	1942–3	CAB 109/51–3

Dieppe Raid	1942	CAB 98/22
Naval Construction	1942	CAB 78/4
Service Pay and Allowances	1942–5	CAB 98/24
Psychologists and Psychiatrists in the Services	1942–5	CAB 98/25–9
Supply, Production, Priority and Manpower, Naval Assignment Sub-Committee, minutes and reports	1943–5	CAB 92/123
Joint Technical Warfare	1943–8	CAB 137/1–23
Joint American Secretariat (Lend-Lease)	1944	CAB 110/42
Operation OVERLORD	1944	CAB 98/40
Vulnerable Points Adviser, naval sites	1945	CAB 112/6

Home Defence Executive

Secretary's files	1940–5	CAB 113/1–45
Daily conferences	1940–2	CAB 120/62
Naval matters	1941–5	CAB 114/47 and 52–4

Special Secret Information Centre

Mobile naval base defence organisation	1940–7	CAB 121/177
Enemy naval situation	1941–5	CAB 121/414
Allied Fleet dispositions	1941–6	CAB 121/12–13
Disposal of surrendered enemy fleets	1941–7	CAB 121/415, 551 and 758
Naval equipment	1941–8	CAB 121/266 and 268
Naval policy, including naval air requirements	1941–51	CAB 121/133–4

190 Committee of Imperial Defence

The Committee of Imperial Defence was created in 1888 on the basis of the Colonial Defence Committee, the first permanent inter-departmental organisation of importance. It also inherited the records of the (rather ineffectual) Cabinet Defence Committee, created in 1870. Its function was to co-ordinate defence planning both among Whitehall departments, and between home and colonial governments. The CID Secretariat provided the core of the Cabinet Office in 1916, and at the end of the war it continued in a very close relation with the Cabinet Office, into which it was again absorbed in 1939.

Minutes and memoranda	1888–1914	CAB 38/1–28
Memoranda: home defence (A series)	1888 and 1901–39	CAB 3/1–8
(miscellaneous, B series)	1903–39	CAB 4/1–30
(colonial defence, C series)	1902–39	CAB 5/1–9
(defence of India, D series)	1901–39	CAB 6/1–6
Minutes	1902–39	CAB 2/1–9
Memoranda and miscellanea	1902–19	CAB 17/1–201
Colonial and imperial conferences	1906–11	CAB 17/77–9

Admiralty-WO 'High Level Bridge' Conferences:	1913–14	CAB 18/27
	1913–14	WO 32/5294
Battle of Jutland, dispatches	1916	CAB 16/37/4
Registered files:	1924–39	CAB 64/1–36
(FAA)	1924–39	CAB 64/23–7

Defence, later Naval and Military Defence Committee

Reports and memoranda	1870–89	WO 396/1
Imperial conferences, coaling stations, Channel tunnel etc.	1875–1919	CAB 18/1–99

Colonial Defence, later Overseas Defence Committee

Minutes, reports etc.	1877–1939	CAB 7/1–15
Minutes	1907–39	CAB 10/1–10
Memoranda	1885–1939	CAB 8/1–56
Remarks	1887–1939	CAB 9/1–21
Defence schemes memoranda	1863–1939	CAB 11/1–216

Other Committees

Defence: reports etc.	1891–1903	CAB 18/18 and 20–22B
(minutes):	1895	CAB 1/2/15
	1912	CAB 1/8/14
	1920–3	CAB 2/3
(memoranda, SS series)	1921–2	CAB 34/1
Ad hoc committees	1905–39	CAB 16/1–232
Home Ports Defence, later Home Defence: minutes	1909–39	CAB 12/1–6
(memoranda)	1909–39	CAB 13/1–11
Air: minutes and memoranda	1912–14	CAB 14/1
(annual reports)	1913–14	AIR 1/669/17/122/781
Combined Operations	1916	CAB 21/3
Imperial Communications	1919–39	CAB 35/1–45
Overseas and Home Defence	1920–39	CAB 36/1–23
Co-ordination of Departmental Action on the outbreak of war, inauguration of new Departments Sub-Committee: shipping	1920	CAB 15/7
(insurance of British shipping)	1920–3	CAB 15/9
(trading blockade and enemy shipping)	1920–3	CAB 15/21
Contracts Co-ordinating Committee and Sub-Committees, minutes etc.	1920–63	WO 221/1–44
National Service in a future war:	1921–2	CAB 15/17
	1923–39	CAB 57/1–30
Joint Planning, minutes and memoranda:	1923–39	CAB 55/1–19
(constitution, functions etc.)	1923–39	CAB 104/12–15

Principal Supply Officers:	1924–39	CAB 60/1–73
(armament and equipment)	1932–6	SUPP 3/43–4
Censorship	1924–39	CAB 49/1–20
Oil Board	1925–39	CAB 50/1–19
Committee lists	1927–39	CAB 59/1–6
Industrial Intelligence in Foreign Countries	1928–39	CAB 48/1–10
Questions Concerning the Middle East	1930–9	CAB 51/1–11
FAA	1936–9	CAB 21/423, 523–7 and 905
Vulnerable Places	1936–9	CAB 13/22
Government War Book	1937	CAB 15/38

Minister for the Co-ordination of Defence

Registered files:	1924–39	CAB 64/1–36
(FAA)	1924–39	CAB 64/23–7

191 Chiefs of Staff Committee, 1923–45

The Chiefs of Staff Committee and its sub-committees, originally created under the CID in 1923, united the professional heads of the three Services, and was the main forum for inter-Service co-ordination. In wartime it developed a large staff and administrative apparatus of its own. Post-war records of the Chiefs of Staff Committee are in List 219.

Chiefs of Staff Committee of the Committee of Imperial Defence

Minutes and memoranda	1923–39	CAB 53/1–55
Constitution, functions etc.	1923–39	CAB 104/12–15
Deputy Chiefs of Staff Sub-Committee, minutes and memoranda	1932–9	CAB 54/1–13
Joint Intelligence Sub-Committee: minutes and memoranda	1936–9	CAB 56/1–7
(files)	1939–73	CAB 163/1–211

Chiefs of Staff Committee of the War Cabinet

Minutes	1939–46	CAB 79/1–92
Memoranda	1939–46	CAB 80/1–107

Committees and Sub-Committees

Deputy Chiefs of Staff, minutes and papers	1939–47	CAB 82/1–31
Joint Intelligence:	1939–47	CAB 81/87–141
(minutes)	1942–57	CAB 176/1–63
Other sub-committees, minutes	1939–47	CAB 81/1–86

Joint Planning Committee, later Staff

Minutes and memoranda	1939–47	CAB 84/1–95
Correspondence and papers	1939–48	CAB 119/1–221

Central Office for North American Supplies, minutes and papers 1939–44		CAB 115/1–756
Joint Staff and Joint Services Mission, minutes and memoranda:	1942–52	CAB 138/1–8
(Washington Office)	1940–58	CAB 122/1–1607
Allied Supplies Executive: naval supplies for Russia	1941–5	CAB 111/96, 103–4, 183 and 391–404
(naval supplies for Turkey)	1941–5	CAB 111/247–9

Combined Chiefs of Staff Committee

Minutes and memoranda	1942–9	CAB 88/1–108

192 Committee of Imperial Defence, later Cabinet Office, Historical Section

The official histories of both World Wars were written by a Central Historical Section, not by the individual Services – although the Admiralty insisted that the naval war be treated by its own volumes.

Narratives and papers	1904–57	CAB 45/1–291
Registered files	1906–82	CAB 103/1–709
Official histories, naval, drafts and narratives	1918–22	CAB 44/42–5
London Naval Conference	1930	CAB 101/289
Dispatches and accounts of naval actions	1939–67	CAB 106/1–1225
Naval Research Establishments, histories	1941–72	CAB 102/66–75
Admiralty Delegation (Washington), history	1942–5	CAB 102/110
Admiralty Technical Mission in Canada	1940–5	CAB 102/126
French Fleet and Oran, narrative	1940	CAB 101/95
Disposition of fleets in Mediterranean	1939–40	CAB 101/96
First Lord of Admiralty, ministerial minutes	1939–40	CAB 101/239
Naval operations, narratives:	c.1944–78	CAB 101/166
(East Indies)	1951–8	CAB 101/158
(amphibious etc.)	c.1944–78	CAB 101/234–6
Naval strength	1944	CAB 101/310
Registered files	1906–82	CAB 103/1–709
Historians' correspondence	1940–75	CAB 140/1–162
Enemy Documents Section, Admiralty:	1948–71	CAB 146/187
	1950–71	CAB 146/115–16

193 The Cabinet, 1945–74

Records of the post-war Cabinet, minus the defence responsibilities of the War Cabinet, which passed in 1947 to the new Ministry of Defence [217].

Conclusions	1945–74	CAB 128/1–46
Memoranda	1945–73	CAB 129/1–173
International conferences, proceedings	1944–74	CAB 133/1–400
Registered files		
Registered files	1916–73	CAB 21/1–6078
Nuclear ship propulsion:	1944–54	CAB 126/173–4
	1957–65	CAB 21/4852 and 5536
War books	1948–66	CAB 175/1–4
RNC Greenwich, lectures	1954	CAB 21/3881
AUWE enquiry	1961	CAB 21/6012
Strength of Soviet Navy	1961–4	CAB 21/5547
Training exercises with South African Navy	1966–8	CAB 164/368
Naval training team for Nigeria	1969	CAB 164/610
Naval airborne nuclear weapons	1970	CAB 196/27
Disposal of the Italian Fleet	1947	CAB 134/215
Anglo-French defence collaboration	1970–4	CAB 130/490–5 and 506
Committees		
Defence, minutes	1946–63	CAB 131/1–28
Defence and overseas policy, minutes	1964–76	CAB 148/1–153
Special meeting, Polaris submarines	1966	CAB 130/301
Defence (Transition) Committee, Control of Aliens in War Sub-Committee, correspondence	1950–4	WO 32/19292

194 Prime Minister and Minister of Defence

Although some earlier records were incorporated, these records essentially begin with Churchill's assumption of the joint office of Prime Minister and Minister of Defence in 1940. Files of the Minister of Defence's Secretariat reflect his responsibilities as Minister of Defence. So do the records of the Special Operations Executive and the Combined Operations Headquarters which answered to him. Post-war Prime Ministers continued to be concerned with defence among many other matters.

Prime Minister's Private Office		
Correspondence and papers:	1916–40	PREM 1/1–467
	1945–51	PREM 8/1–1580

	1951–64	PREM 11/1–5219
	1964–70	PREM 13/1–3564
	1970–4	PREM 15/1–2236
	1974–8	PREM 16/1–295
(confidential)	1934–46	PREM 4/1–135
Honours for naval commanders	1918	PREM 2/11
Operations, including naval	1937–46	PREM 3/1–526

Deputy Prime Minister's Private Office

Papers of C Attlee	1938–47	CAB 118/1–91
Correspondence with Admiralty	1940–4	CAB 118/13
Battle of the Atlantic	1941	CAB 118/6
Air policy and the war at sea	1942	CAB 118/2
Enemy blockade running	1942	CAB 118/18

Defence Secretariat

Armed Services (including Navy)	1940–6	CAB 120/209–26
Organisation of the Naval Staff	1940–3	CAB 120/216
Royal Navy:	1940–6	CAB 120/267–90
	1940–6	CAB 120/803
Dutch Merchant Fleet	1940	CAB 120/645
Middle East naval operations	1940–4	CAB 120/632
French Fleet	1940–4	CAB 120/541
German Navy	1940–5	CAB 120/552
Coastal Command and FAA	1940–5	CAB 120/295
Inter-Services Security Board, minutes	1940–5	WO 283/1–14
Japanese Navy	1941–4	CAB 120/611
Naval land equipment cultivator (trench-digging machine)	1941–5	CAB 120/396
Admiral Sir Frederic Dreyer	1942–3	CAB 120/811
German Hospital Ships *Tübingen* and *Gradisca*	1944	CAB 120/560
Director of Scientific Intelligence, reports on U-boat attacks	1943	DEFE 40/4

Special Operations Executive

Support of naval operations: Western Europe	1936–92	HS 6/various
(Far East)	1938–69	HS 3/various
(Balkans)	1938–72	HS 5/various
Histories and war diaries (including naval operations)	1939–88	HS 7/various
HQ records (naval operations)	1940–5	HS 8/766–831
Correspondence between head of SOE and First Lord of Admiralty	1942–5	HS 8/907
Far East registered files, naval	1942–5	HS 1/196 and 330

Combined Operations Headquarters

War diaries, reports etc.	1937–63	DEFE 2/1–2091
Motor Torpedo Boats	1940–2	DEFE 2/799
Letters of Admiral Keyes, Director of Combined Operations	1942	DEFE 2/698
Special Boat Unit (HMS *Rodent*), reports	1942–5	DEFE 2/740–2 and 970
Inter-Service Committee on Raiding Operations	1948–50	DEFE 2/2089–91

195 Central Statistical Office

The Central Statistical Office was created as a unit of the War Cabinet Secretariat, and was initially concerned mainly with measuring aspects of the war effort.

Minutes and papers	1940–87	CAB 108/1–798
Shipbuilding	1940–61	CAB 141/111–25
Balance of payments, Admiralty:	1943–8	CAB 141/71
	1943–6	CAB 139/43
Admiralty civilian non-industrial staff	1943–9	CAB 141/88
RN strength:	1935–47	CAB 141/95
(including allies serving with RN)	1942–5	CAB 141/97
RN contribution to national income	1940–60	CAB 139/282
Shipping losses:	1941–5	CAB 141/105–10
	1941–5	CAB 139/71 and 86–7
	1941–5	CAB 108/1–3 and 25–8
POWs	1941–8	CAB 139/50
Allied casualties	1942–5	CAB 141/98
Absenteeism in shipyards	1942–5	CAB 141/131
Armed forces, strength and casualties	1942–6	CAB 139/56–66
Anglo-American Consolidated Statement, correspondence with Admiralty	1942–6	CAB 139/94
Manpower allocations in armed forces	1943–6	CAB 139/52
Reparation claims on Germany and Japan	1945–7	CAB 139/75–9
Financial history and statistical digest of Second World War	1947–59	CAB 139/428–30
Defence and re-armament	1949–53	CAB 139/331–4
Production of munitions and warlike stores	1952–69	CAB 139/721
Expenditure on defence	1960–70	CAB 139/609

196 Office, later Ministry of Works

The Office of Works represented one of the most ancient of Crown activities, in charge of all sorts of royal building works. Its modern responsibilities covered many public buildings and ancient monuments, as well as the royal parks and buildings in them, such as RNC Greenwich, the Admiralty Arch and Admiralty House. In 1963 it took over all naval works from the Admiralty. Many of its records passed in 1978 to its successor the Property Service Agency [198].

Ancient monuments and historic buildings, registered files	1699–1987	WORK 14/1–2875
Army establishments, including dockyard defences	1713–1963	WORK 43/1–1683
Ceremonial files, RN role in coronations, state funerals etc.	1727–1972	WORK 21/1–276
In- and out-letter books	1730–1881	WORK 1/1–168
Public buildings, England and Wales	1731–1990	WORK 12/1–983
Royal parks and pleasure gardens, registered files	1736–1989	WORK 16/1–2349
Land and buildings for various naval establishments	1794–1990	WORK 17/1–767
Statues and memorials	1810–1985	WORK 20/1–346
Public buildings overseas	1834–1977	WORK 10/1–754
Public buildings, contracts, plans etc.	1844–1951	WORK 13/1–1395
Shanghai Naval Yard	1865–8	WORK 10/432
Yokohama, Naval Hospital and Depot	1879–1960	WORK 10/427–8
Osborne Estate, including RNC Osborne	1902–75	WORK 15/1–182
Responsibility for naval cemeteries	1909–49	WORK 22/307
Maintenance of naval cemeteries	1917–90	CM 4/1–76
Accommodation for service attachés	1922–33, 1954	WORK 10/690–1
Transfer of CG stations to Office of Works	1923–4	WORK 22/176
Old RN School, Greenwich Hospital	1933–8	WORK 17/141
Captain Cook Memorial, Kaarvulu, Hawaii	1938–9	WORK 10/73
Bahrain, naval accommodation	1938–49	WORK 10/64
Accommodation for Admiralty use in war	1939	WORK 28/11/5
Official History of Second World War, 'Building and Civil Engineering Work of the Admiralty'	1939–46	WORK 46/7
Construction of RNAD Ditton Priors	1940–7	WORK 26/14/1
Festival of Britain Office, including use of HMS *Campania*	1948–52	WORK 25/1–293
Deptford Dockyard, drawings	1950–69	WORK 14/1944
Painted Hall, RNC Greenwich	1954–75	HLG 126/296, 318 and 531
DG naval works, Committee on Control of Production Expenditure	1962	WORK 22/704
Merger of Admiralty Works Department with Ministry of Works	1963	WORK 22/423
Imperial War Museum, naval guns at entrance	1965–9	WORK 17/741
New building projects for Navy	1966–7	WORK 59/101

HMS *Belfast* as a floating museum	1968–70	WORK 17/763
RNAY, Wroughton	1985–8	WORK 17/654

197 Ministry of Works, Maps, Plans and Photographs

Admiralty, Whitehall:	1882	WORK 32/699
	1883–1904	WORK 30/476–519
	1885–1914	WORK 30/4153–228
	1890–1922	WORK 30/5821–58
	1921–3	WORK 30/6076–81
	1921–47	WORK 30/6262–5
(Admiralty House)	1862	WORK 30/2885
(Spring Gardens)	1905–15	WORK 30/4229–426
(Admiralty Arch):	1907–8	WORK 30/3266–89
	1919	WORK 36/84–6
(courtyard, with Nelson's Barge)	1923	WORK 30/6081
Somerset House:	1738–1851	WORK 30/259–307
	1842–96	WORK 30/2756–885
	1842–1911	WORK 30/3287–350
	1920–41	WORK 30/6320–6
RNC and Hospital, Greenwich:	1818–1903	WORK 31/326–410
	1844–50	WORK 31/255–61
	1860–95	WORK 31/604–9
	1884–1911	WORK 31/650–70
	1900	WORK 31/411–13
	1911	WORK 31/610
	1914	WORK 31/713
RNC Osborne	1926	WORK 37/213
Sheerness, ordnance and Navy land	1816–24	WORK 43/134–7
Woolwich, RM Barracks	1872	WORK 43/172
Woolwich Dockyard	1849–1955	WORK 43/196 and 1337–8
Woolwich Arsenal, Admiralty land	1872	WORK 43/167/1

Photographs

RNEC Keyham	1898–1902	WORK 55/7, 9
Malta	1901–62	WORK 55/10–15 and 20
Admiralty, Whitehall	1951–66	WORK 65/41
RNEC Manadon, Plymouth	1953–66	WORK 65/21
RNC Dartmouth	1954	WORK 69/21
RN armaments depots, Malta	1959–60	WORK 55/27
HM Naval Base, Portsmouth	1966	WORK 65/45
RNH Plymouth	1968–76	WORK 65/167

198 Property Services Agency

This body inherited in 1978 most of the duties of the former Ministry of Public Buildings and Works, including its responsibilities for naval works and buildings.

Admiralty buildings, protection from lightning	1904	CM 1/511
RNC Greenwich: structural reports	1949–89	CM 8/235, 252
(Applied Mechanics Laboratory)	1961–2	CM 23/181
South-East region, including dockyards and RN establishments	1950–89	CM 18/1–50
Admiralty Building, use for ceremonial occasions	1960–79	CM 8/222
Sierra Leone, Admiralty Oil Fuel Jetty	1961–89	CM 6/91–3
Proposed memorial to Admiral Cunningham	1965–6	CM 23/154
Devonport Dockyard:	1965–81	CM 20/44–92
	1976	CM 1/191
	1981–3	CM 45/9–11
Publicity material, Admiralty breakwaters	1970	CM 36/2
Gibraltar Naval Base:	1971–90	CM 6/86–7
	1985–7	CM 6/102–3
Effluents from royal dockyards	1972	CM 1/440
Portsmouth Dockyard, various reports:	1905–65	CM 1/163–5
	1964–86	CM 1/273–7
	1972–3	CM 23/236
	1974	CM 1/157
Chatham Dockyard:	1976–88	CM 18/41–8
	1981–3	CM 10/72–4 and 170
	1981–3	CM 26/3–5
	1982	CM 1/247
HMS *Osprey*, Portland:	1977	CM 1/431
	1986	CM 1/261
HMS *Cambridge*, architectural competition	1980–1	CM 10/68
Falkland Islands, works	1982–4	CM 6/72–5
Admiralty Compass Observatory, Slough	1982–9	CM 19/6
Portsea Island Naval Requirements Study	1983–5	CM 18/15
RN and RM establishments in Portsmouth area	1984–8	CM 1/281–7 and 525–8
Breakwater Fort, HM Naval Base, Portland	1984–9	CM 19/12
Future of the royal dockyards:	1984–9	CM 52/1–3
	1985–8	CM 10/624–5
	1985–8	CM 24/17–21
Rosyth Dockyard	1986	CM 1/182 and 363
Old Admiralty Citadel, modernisation	1989–90	CM 8/48
Directorate of Defence Services (Navy), registered files	1971–90	CM 26/1–20
Correspondence concerning RNVR	1979–81	CM 41/10
Royal dockyards, manpower planning etc.	1985–6	CM 54/2

199 Board, later Ministry of Agriculture

The Ministry of Agriculture's responsibilities touched the Admiralty's at a number of points, including victualling, fishery protection and land use.

Instructions for fishery protection cruisers	1893–5	MAF 12/10, 17
Fisheries Department: naval protection of fishing vessels	1922–34	MAF 41/701–7
(recruitment of fishermen for naval service)	1937–41	MAF 41/1303
(RNR and RN Patrol Service)	1953–9	MAF 209/75
Sea Fish Commission, Admiralty evidence	1933–6	MAF 29/8
Naval swill	1939–52	MAF 35/528, 726
Food (Defence Plans) Department, fresh food for RN	1939–51	MAF 72/643 and 649
Admiralty correspondence	1939	MAF 74/158
British Food Mission, Washington, Admiralty requirements:	1941–51	MAF 97/915–53 and 1119
(Admiralty delivery instructions)	1944–50	MAF 97/1813–17
Assistance to Admiralty, infestation control	1941–64	MAF 130/16
Admiralty requirements for agricultural land	1942–4	MAF 48/398
Employment of RN personnel on agricultural work	1942–5	MAF 47/116
RN Ships' breweries	1944–51	MAF 84/43–4
Supply of meat and livestock to RN	1941–51	MAF 88/various
Transfer of Admiralty land	1949–57	MAF 142/373
Ministry of Food, ships' stores, supplies for armed services	1954–62	MAF 313/46
Environmental monitoring, including HM Dockyards	1954–81	MAF 336/1–297
Dehydrated foodstuffs for Navy	1955–62	MAF 291/88–91
Royal Commission on Common Land: Admiralty evidence	1956–7	MAF 96/78
(Admiralty comments)	1958–60	MAF 292/8
Minister's papers, Reserves Bill	1958–9	MAF 255/821
Suspected poisoning incident at HMS *Ganges*	1961–3	MAF 284/272

200 Department of the Environment and Predecessors

The various departments representing central government's growing interest in local government had dealings and concerns with many naval establishments at home.

RNC Greenwich, storage of radioactive substances	1959–67	AT 31/17
Institute of Naval Medicine, Alverstoke, storage of radioactive substances	1964–72	AT 31/4
Chatham Dockyard, radioactive effluent from nuclear submarines	1969–71	AT 32/15

Local Government Board

Correspondence with Admiralty:	1838–92	MH 19/1
	1848–55	MH 13/252
(registers)	1861–1920	MH 20/4
School inspections: including naval schools	1871–82	MH 32/110
(nautical approved schools)	1897–1990	BN 62/various
Children's Department, inspection of naval training ships and nautical schools:	1927–51	MH 102/various
(correspondence and papers)	1968	BN 29/2459
Prison Commission, naval prisons and former naval prisons (Lewes, Wormwood Scrubs, Bodmin, Portland etc):	1880–1917	PCOM 7/various
(naval prisoners in civilian prisons)	1938–66	PCOM 9/407, 1431, 1974 and 2216
(Portland Borstal, employment of inmates on war work for Admiralty)	1944	PCOM 9/543
(supply of victuals by Admiralty to prisons)	1953–5	PCOM 9/1865

Ministry of Housing and Local Government

Consultations with Admiralty	1963–4	HLG 131/256
Water supply to RN Base, Portland	1971	HLG 127/1295

Ministry of Town and Country Planning

Merchant Navy War Memorial, Tower Hill	1948	HLG 79/314
Liaison with Admiralty	1949–51	HLG 71/1523
Surplus Admiralty land and buildings	1958	HLG 79/1248

National Parks Commission

Admiralty acquisition of land	1951–3	COU 1/639 and 646
RNAS Kete	1959–65	COU 1/658

201 Board, later Ministry of Education, later Department of Education and Science, 1899–

The Ministry was concerned with naval schools and colleges among others.

Privy Council Committee on Education, annual reports (including Admiralty schools)	1858–62	ED 17/24–7
Secondary education endowment files (including naval endowments)	1868–1944	ED 27/1–9922
RN and RM children's homes (endowments)	1902–28 and 1940	ED 49/2802 and 11822
Watts Naval Training Institute School:	1904–39	ED 30/76, 134 and 177
	1913–44	ED 98/118 and 254

(inspection report)	1935	ED 114/692
Parkstone Sea Training School, Dr. Barnardo's homes (formerly Russell Cotes Nautical School and Watts Naval Training School)	1948–67	ED 162/827
Admiralty Committee on the Training of Naval Cadets	1905–6	ED 24/170A
RN Scholarship Fund, Eltham:	1906–12	ED 35/1134–7
	1911–13	ED 43/373
Royal School for RN and RM Officers' Daughters:	1906–18	ED 35/1866
	1918–21	ED 35/5524
(endowments):	1868–1944	ED 27/various
	1912–15	ED 43/734
(inspection reports):	1917–37	ED 109/4380–3
	1956–7	ED 172/254/3
Navy League in secondary schools	1912	ED 24/1653
RNC Osborne and Dartmouth:	1912–25	ED 12/305
(inspection reports)	1912–38	ED 109/820–4
Admiralty examinations for boys	1912–41	ED 12/244 and 475
Admiralty Committee on Education of Seamen	1913	ED 24/1888
HMS *Conway* Cadet School:	1915–41	ED 35/181 and 6809–10
	1961–9	ED 216/43
	1966–7	ED 207/50
TS *Mercury*, Hamble:	1909–35	ED 27 and ED 37/456–8
	1920–42	ED 98/30–1, 200
(inspection reports):	1914	ED 114/247
	1938	ED 114/248
	1946–52	ED 109/8813
School accommodation at Rosyth	1919	ED 24/1632
Salaries of naval schoolmasters	1919–22	ED 24/1782
RN and RM Orphan Home School	1924–33	ED 21/29713
Recruitment of boys for RN	1926–44	ED 12/245 and 477
HMS *Worcester* (Thames Nautical Training College, Greenhithe)	1931–42	ED 35/4679 80
Nautical training, reports etc.	1936–44	ED 46/193
Financial assistance to naval cadets	1936–45	ED 12/486 7
Training of naval schoolmasters	1936–45	ED 86/84
Recruitment to RNC Dartmouth	1940–2	ED 12/496
Admiralty grants to Sea Scouts, Sea Cadets and Girls' Naval Training Corps	1942–4	ED 124/54, 63 and 102
Dockyard technical colleges	1948–59	ED 46/383 and 891
RN School of Music, inspection reports:	1948–55	ED 109/9042
	1949–52	ED 109/8862
HMS *Ganges*, Suffolk	1951–61	ED 74/103
HMS *St. Vincent*, Gosport:	1952–66	ED 74/53

(inspection report)	n.d.	ED 114/1246
RN educational establishments, inspection reports	1953–4	ED 23/833
RN Schools Malta, Gibraltar, Singapore and Mauritius:	1960–2	ED 121/907 etc.
(inspection reports)	1966–74	ED 193/7 etc.
Technical and Dockyard School, RN Vocational Training Centre, Portsmouth, (inspection reports)	1965	ED 193/4 and 19

Pensions Branch

RN Education Service (commissioned officers)	1946–55	ED 131/156
Teachers' superannuation (RNC)	1951–5	ED 131/180
Service in RN schools overseas	1949–66	ED 131/232

202 Ministry of Labour, later Department of Employment, 1916–

This Ministry was originally set up to handle wartime conscription and allocation of labour. Its files also include many dealing with Naval Reserves, civilian employees of the Admiralty and Navy and the like.

Unemployment Assistance Board, RNVR proficiency bonus	1935	AST 7/111
Correspondence:	1886–1955	LAB 2/1–1191
(index, including HM Navy)	1913–18	LAB 7/154
(index, naval demobilisation)	1918–19	LAB 7/24
(index, HM forces recruiting)	1918–29	LAB 7/46
(index, training ex-servicemen)	1919–24	LAB 7/278
Industrial disputes (including Admiralty)	1895–1980	LAB 10/1–3929
Trade dispute over new pattern sea boot	1912	LAB 2/25/IC4059/1912
Admiralty, pay of carpenters	1916–17	LAB 2/38/IC3189/1917
Admiralty Shipyard Labour Department	1917	LAB 2/92/IC5407/1917
Whitehead Torpedo Works, pay dispute	1918	LAB 2/97/IC3494/1918
Admiralty, recruitment of women	1918	LAB 2/237/ED29159/2/1918
Naval demobilisation:	1918	LAB 2/1519/DRA299/2/1918
	1919	LAB 2/484/DF9966/2/1919
Admiralty industrial councils, etc.:	1918–22	LAB 2/638–9, 664, 709, 794–6, 866, 872–3, 879–80 and 1148
	1918–54	LAB 10/6, 165, 312, 449, 1181, 1664, 1359 and 3267
	1919–73	ADM 197/66–80 and 91–100
Trade union membership in naval establishments:	1918–46	LAB 41/143
	1919–64	LAB 69/82, 92
	1922–73	LAB 83/3922–6
Training of disabled officers and men	1919	LAB 16/631

Statistics Department, statistics on RN, Army and RAF	1919–46	LAB 98/26
Civil servants in RNR and RNVR	1921	LAB 2/1817/OE/W582/1948/I–VI
Admiralty, concerning Trade Boards	1922	LAB 2/18/TBM164/1922
Intelligence and Statistics Department	1924	LAB 2/1562/I&S783/1924
Admiralty civil servant standing for Parliament	1924	LAB 2/1774/CEB136/1924
Admiralty timber inspectors, salaries	1927	LAB 2/2122/IR824/1927
Recruitment to RN	1929	LAB 2/177/EDJ936/1929
Award for improved form of loose leaf binder	1929	LAB 2/1864/S&E1033/1930
Admiralty contracts for flax and hemp	1930	LAB 2/1696/OTB/FH1456/1930
Visit by Royal Swedish Navy Band	1931	LAB 2/2080/ETAR681/1931
Arbitration tribunals, including dockyard workers etc.	1937–56	LAB 3/44–1146
Employment policy, including dockyards etc.	1937–59	LAB 8/263–2443
Naval recruitment	1937–76	LAB 6/1–742
War emergency measures, employment of women by Admiralty	1935–6	LAB 25/78
Manpower requirements of Navy	1937	LAB 25/101
Admiralty labour requirements, naval personnel	1937–40	LAB 25/69, 74
Admiralty memorandum on engineering industry	1940	LAB 25/12
Admiralty inspection of Devonport Dockyard	1945	LAB 8/1114
Discussions with Admiralty on occupational advice	1945	LAB 12/332
Resettlement in civilian employment, RN, RM, WRNS:	1940–63	LAB 32/22
	1945, 1954	LAB 29/249–50 and 535
Naval Emergency Reserve	1948	LAB 80/19
Admiralty and emergency mobilisation of civil servants	1948–51	LAB 12/802
Training courses for naval instructors	1953–7	LAB 18/718
Management training for RN officers	1953–7	LAB 18/718
Careers information booklets, *The Royal Navy*:	c.1953	LAB 44/187
	1965	LAB 44/61
Enquiry into shortage of recruits to RN	1955	LAB 19/535
Plan for reduction in size of RN	1957	LAB 43/286
Reduction of labour force in dockyards	1963–4	LAB 43/408
Disabled naval personnel at Netley Hospital	1962–4	LAB 20/1147
MoD(N), evidence to Royal Commission on Trade Unions:	1965	LAB 10/2600
	1965–8	LAB 28/6, 211
RFA and British Shipping Federation	1967–74	LAB 10/3147

203 Ministry of Pensions, later Pensions and National Insurance, 1917–66

Selected war pensions award files, service prior to 1914	1854–1979	PIN 71/1–3869
Selected First World War pensions award files	1871–1950	PIN 26/1–22801
War pensions, registered files	1901–97	PIN 15/1–5011
Selected Second World War pensions award files	1907–90	PIN 80/1–45
First World War widows' pensions forms	1910–32	PIN 82/1–183
Second World War pensions award files (Far East POWs)	1915–89	PIN 91/1–170
Transfer of Roehampton Artificial Limb Factory	1917–19	PIN 38/411
War pensions, RNH Yarmouth	1917–59	PIN 67/71
War pensions, policy	1920–95	PIN 59/1–429
HM Dockyard, Bermuda, contributions	1940–50	PIN 4/156
Orders in Council (Navy and Marines)	1947–75	PIN 14/39
Industrial injury cases	1959–60	PIN 62/821
Naval, Military and Air Forces (Disablement and Death) Service Pensions Order, 1978	1977–9	PIN 31/236–9

204 Air Ministry, 1918–64

On the establishment of the Royal Air Force in 1918 the Air Ministry inherited all responsibility for naval air operations. In 1939 the Fleet Air Arm (that is, naval aircraft afloat) reverted to Admiralty control, but the Air Ministry continued to be responsible for land-based naval aircraft (Coastal Command) and for many Joint-Service air matters including aircraft design and production, flying training and the like.

Registered files:	1897–1930	AIR 2/1–381
	1919–59	AIR 5/1–1438
	1930–9	AIR 2/382–1525
	1930–83	AIR 20/1–12760
	1936–53	AIR 2/1526–13508
	1953–77	AIR 2/13509–19134
Air publications: (including naval aircraft)	1913–79	AIR 10/1–9374
(*Coastal Air Pilot*)	1943	AIR 20/2104
Inventions, including naval aircraft etc.	1915–60	AVIA 8/1–536
Submission papers to sovereign (for appointments etc.)	1918–72	AIR 30/1–303
Admiralty claim for Naval Air Force	1919–20	AIR 20/609
Spotting naval gunfire by kite balloon	1919	AIR 1/725/101/2
Flying-boat development flight	1922	AIR 20/597
Amphibians and shipboard aircraft, performance	1922–31	AIR 20/415–17
Torpedo bomber design and development:	1925–38	AIR 20/3
(Vickers Vildebeeste)	1931–5	AIR 20/177
Aircraft and equipment for FAA	1925–45	AVIA 8/132, 191–2, 196 and 442

Combined operations exercises:	1929	AIR 20/157
(Singapore)	1937	AIR 20/183
Night torpedo attacks	1930	AIR 20/487
Electrical fittings for FAA flying boats	1932–44	AVIA 13/453
FAA personnel	1934–47	AIR 20/10
Future of FAA	1935–6	AIR 20/30
Torpedoes and torpedo bombers	1935–43	AIR 20/422–3, 887, 1795 and 3028
FAA scheme of formation flying lights	1937–50	AVIA 13/521–2
Inter-Service Recognition Committee	1938–40	AIR 20/226
Reconnaissance and torpedo bomber requirements	1938–40	AIR 20/229
A/S operations:	1938–43	AIR 20/236 and 6155
	1942–6	AIR 20/801, 805, 841 and 848
(Admiralty co-operation)	1942–4	AIR 20/846–7
Establishment of RNVR Air Branch	1939	AVIA 2/1564
Defence of home naval bases	1939	AIR 20/237
Use of air mail service by Mediterranean Fleet	1939–40	AVIA 2/1636
Operations against German Fleet:	1939–40	AIR 20/225, 274 and 303
	1939–43	AIR 20/235
Port Defence Committee	1939–42	AIR 20/299
Bombing of submarine bases	1940	AIR 20/419
Balloon Command, shipborne balloons	1940–5	AIR 13/70–5
Combined operations, history	1940–5	AIR 20/9503
Radar for fighter director ships	1941–4	AIR 20/6025
Accident reports (including naval aircraft)	1941–52	AVIA 5/19–45
Break out of *Scharnhorst* and *Gneisenau*	1942	AIR 20/11351
Torpedoes and glider bombs	1942–3	AIR 20/383–4
Carrier fighters	1942–5	AIR 20/845
Conduct of joint sea/air operations	1942–9	AIR 20/7182–3
Naval aircraft designs	1943	AVIA 10/366
Qualities of Mitsubishi Type 0	1943	AVIA 10/415
Jet-engined fleet reconnaissance fighter	1943	AVIA 28/3109
Radar for FAA aircraft	1943–5	AVIA 7/2223–30
Surface and underwater explosions, reports	1943–5	AIR 20/6218
A/S warfare, mines	1943–5	AIR 20/11505
British Bombing Survey Unit, U-boat shelters	1945–6	AIR 20/7294
Assessment of U-boat casualties	1939–45	AIR 20/6907
Coastal Command war statistics	1939–45	AIR 20/6826
Enemy shipping losses in Mediterranean	1940–45	AIR 20/9598
Report on A/S warfare	1946	AIR 52/155
History of the RAF and FAA, 1903–45	1946	AIR 20/6349
The RAF in Maritime War, 1939–46	1946	AIR 41/19, 45, 47–8, 54 and 73–9
RN pilots, basic flying training	1946–7	AIR 20/7322
Joint RAF/RN exercises	1946–51	AIR 20/6834 and 7422

Balance of post-war sea, land and air forces	1946–51	AIR 20/6566
Shore-based maritime aircraft	1946–54	AIR 20/8857
Air and sea troop transport policy	1947–52	AIR 20/7370
Regulations for prevention of collisions at sea	1947–53	AIR 20/6801
Joint war production staff papers	1947–58	AIR 20/7471
Operation SEAWARD	1948	AIR 20/6802
Coastal Command aircraft for Berlin airlift	1948–9	AIR 55/211
Use of naval carriers	1948–9	AIR 20/7209
Operation DOUBLE QUICK, sea communications	1948–9	AIR 20/8194
Certificate of airworthiness, Supermarine Sea Otter	1948–9	AVIA 4/12 and 63–5
Joint A/S School	1948–55	AIR 20/6831–3 and 7415
Joint RAF/RN requirement for A/S torpedo	1948–61	AIR 20/6809 and 9775
RAF assistance to HMS *Amethyst* (Yangtse Incident)	1949	AIR 20/7076
Naval assistance in support of foreign and colonial policy	1949–50	AIR 20/7084
Amphibious Warfare Handbook	1950	AIR 20/6691
Exercise PORCUPINE	1950	AIR 20/6391
Review of RAF and RN airfield requirements	1950–2	AIR 20/7366
Proposal to base USN aircraft at Malta	1950–2	AIR 20/7366
Control of maritime air forces	1950–5	AIR 20/11365
Costs of shore-based versus carrier-based aircraft	1951	AIR 77/100 and 104
Sea Fury, powered elevator	1952	AVIA 10/466
Committees etc.	1953–69	AIR 20/10072–2333
Coastal Command aircraft, operations etc.:	1954–69	AIR 20/10221–2322
	1956	AIR 20/12322
	1967	AIR 20/11913–15
FAA aircraft, operations etc.	1954–71	AIR 20/10247–2318
RNAS Gosport, closing ceremony	1955–8	AIR 20/10248
Combined operations, progress reports	1955–60	AIR 20/9401
Co-ordination of inter-Service exercises	1956–7	AIR 20/10324
RN and Coastal Command, relationship	1958–60	AIR 20/10538–40
Ships and shipping	1958–68	AIR 20/10119–1666
Royal Navy	1958–71	AIR 20/10141–2319
RAF co-operation with RN on aircraft requirements	1960–2	AIR 20/10567
Joint Admiralty/Air Ministry study, future aircraft carriers	1961–5	AIR 20/11423–5 and 11506
Maritime Shackleton, modernisation:	1961–4	AIR 20/11928
(provision of Mk 44 Torpedo)	1962–3	AIR 20/11342
Organisation of Coastal Command	1963	AIR 33/83
Shackleton aircraft replacement	1964	AIR 20/11509
Transfer of powers from Admiralty on formation of MoD	1964	AIR 30/296
RN and RAF requirements, aircrew	1964–8	AIR 20/11478

Aircraft Carrier Study Group	1965	AIR 20/11973–8
Global strategy, aircraft carriers and RAF bases	1965	AIR 20/12130
Phasing out of aircraft carriers	1969–70	AIR 20/12223
P1127 (Harrier) naval version	1965–8	AIR 20/11927
18 Maritime Group	1967–71	AIR 20/12316–19
Harrier GR Mk 1, trial of integrated naval attack system	1972	AIR 38/457

205 Secretary of State for Air, Private Office

These are registered files from the Secretary of State's Private Office.

RAF-RN relations	1922–30	AIR 19/96–105
Colwyn Committee	1925	AIR 19/120–2
Admiralty air requirements	1926	AIR 19/125
Deck landing trials	1927	AIR 19/132
FAA organisation and carriers	1929	AIR 19/136
Inskip Inquiry	1936–7	AIR 19/23
FAA personnel	1937–9	AIR 19/32
Mediterranean Fleet, air reconnaissance	1940	AIR 19/191
Coastal Command:	1940–57	AIR 19/183 and 554
	1960–4	AIR 19/893
Battle of the Atlantic	1941	AIR 19/263 and 508–15
Air attacks on shipping	1941	AIR 19/271
Escape of enemy warships from Brest	1941–6	AIR 19/270
Defence of shipping	1941–7	AIR 19/243–5
A/S warfare	1942–6	AIR 19/358–9
Correspondence with Admiralty	1944	AIR 19/563
Amalgamation of common services	1945–60	AIR 19/444 and 551
Requirements for maritime aircraft	1950–3	AIR 19/820
Maritime shadowing operations	1953–80	AIR 19/974, 1104 and 1158
RN and RAF requirements	1956–61	AIR 19/862 and 869
Miscellaneous naval	1958–61	AIR 19/875
RN carrier force	1961–5	AIR 19/997 and 1049
Involvement with RN	1962–6	AIR 19/1067

206 Air Staff

These are registered files of naval interest which can be linked to the Air Staff and its members. Many others dealing with the work of the Air Staff are among the main series of Air Ministry registered files.

Chief of the Air Staff
Registered files	1918–82	AIR 8/1–2744
Chiefs of Staff (Maritime Air) Committee	1950–3	AIR 20/11372

Vice-Chief
Rules for naval and air bombardment	1939	AIR 20/6127
Battle of the Atlantic	1940–2	AIR 20/2895–6
Naval-air co-operation, Middle East	1941–2	AIR 20/2992
Coastal Command: operational control:	1941–50	AIR 20/2889–92
	1945–7	AIR 20/933
(Admiralty requirements)	1941–3	AIR 20/3045
(organisation)	1944–5	AIR 20/810
Escape of *Scharnhorst* and *Gneisenau*	1942	AIR 20/3061
Operation TORCH: A/S patrols	1942–3	AIR 20/2522
(French Fleet)	1943–5	AIR 20/2528
Attacks on *Tirpitz*	1942–5	AIR 20/2682, 5321 and 6187
Air Defence of Shipping and Sea-Air Warfare Committee	1942–50	AIR 20/2569–76
Combined training for post-war RAF	1945	AIR 20/3202
Proposed transfer of Coastal Command to RN	1958–60	AIR 20/10141–4
Discussions with Vice-Chief Naval Staff	1968–9	AIR 20/12070

Deputy Chief
Air-Sea Interception Committee	1941–3	AIR 20/3449–55
Operation BOWLER (attack on Venice)	1943–5	AIR 20/3216
A/S operations	1943–5	AIR 20/3241–3 and 4214
Amphibious operations	1943–5	AIR 20/3244
Mediterranean Allied Coastal Air Force operations	1944	AIR 20/6184
A/S warfare research	1957–63	AIR 20/10306

Assistant Chief (Technical Requirements)
A/S and anti-ship bombs	1941–5	AIR 20/1747–51
Air-sea warfare, research and development	1942–5	AIR 20/1791
Maritime aircraft	1944	AIR 20/1776

Assistant Chief (Policy)
Defence of Indian Ocean area	1941–5	AIR 20/3832–7

Operation TERMINAL, shipping requirements	1941–6	AIR 20/5078–93
Combined operations	1941–50	AIR 20/5011–23
Coastal Command, expansion	1942–3	AIR 20/4562
Discussions with RN (Coastal Command etc.)	1942–3	AIR 20/4568
Formation of torpedo squadrons	1942–3	AIR 20/6170
Habbakuk floating airfields	1942–6	AIR 20/4546 and 5102–4
Coastal Command, policy and requirements	1942–7	AIR 20/3810–15
Operation HUSKY, naval planning	1943	AIR 20/4541
British Pacific Fleet, RAF liaison	1945	AIR 20/3824
RAF use of torpedoes	1945–6	AIR 20/4566

Assistant Chief (General)

Merchant shipping attacks on aircraft	1940	AIR 20/4288
Offensive against *Scharnhorst, Gneisenau* and *Prinz Eugen*	1940–2	AIR 20/4377 and 6018
Hispano guns for RN	1941	AIR 20/4278
Air raid damage to ports and shipping	1941	AIR 20/4279
CAM Ships, operations:	1941–3	AIR 20/4294 and 5187
	1942	AIR 20/2315
RAF co-operation with RN and Army	1941–5	AIR 20/4312
RAF pigeons	1942–3	AIR 20/4305
Coastal Command, publicity	1942–5	AIR 20/4188
Air cover for Russian convoys	1943	AIR 20/5625
Naval matters	1944–5	AIR 20/4185

War Room

Anti-shipping operations:	1941–5	AIR 20/3546–56
	1943	AIR 20/2305
	1943–4	AIR 20/843 and 849

Central Statistical Unit

RN, Army and RAF casualties	1939–43	AIR 20/1938
Coastal Command: aircraft wastage	1940–4	AIR 20/1883
(bombs dropped)	1941–?	AIR 20/1921
(operations etc.)	1940–5	AIR 22/163–5, 221–3, 251, 305–6 and 357–62

207 Air Staff Directorates

Examples of registered files from various Air Staff Directorates which deal with naval warfare.

Operations and Intelligence
Registered files	1918–49	AIR 9/1–494
Intelligence reports and papers	1926–84	AIR 40/1–3126
Attacks on ships	1939–45	AIR 40/305–6, 1537–8, 1542–3 and 2187
Torpedo dropping tactics	1941–5	AIR 40/289–91, 297 and 300
Merchant Ship Fighter Unit report of attack on convoy	1942	AIR 40/297
Anti-U-boat warfare	1945	AIR 40/292–3

Operations (Maritime)
Files:	1942–6	AIR 20/1091–333
	1940–5	AIR 20/5601–18
Allied warships lost or damaged in Mediterranean	1940–5	AIR 20/7883
Summaries of attacks on shipping	1944–5	AIR 20/7882
Naval prize money and prize bounty for RAF	1945–6	AIR 20/5612

Operations (Home)
Atlantic shipping, fighter defence	1940	AIR 20/2078

Operations (Overseas)
Anti-U-boat Warfare Committee	1942–4	AIR 20/5455

Plans
Registered files	1918–49	AIR 9/1–494
Target-towing aircraft for Admiralty	1941–3	AIR 20/5551
British Admiralty Pacific Mission to Australia	1941–4	AIR 20/5561–5

Fighter Operations
Firing by merchant ships	1941	AIR 20/2289
Operations against French Fleet	1940	AIR 20/5295
Operations against German Fleet	1940–3	AIR 20/5294

Bomber Operations
German shipping and shipbuilding	1941–5	AIR 20/4781
Bomber Command sea mining operations	1941–7	AIR 20/5837
Air Torpedo Attack Committee	1942–3	AIR 20/5838

Air Tactics

US Pacific Fleet operations	1941–5	AIR 20/6049–53
Torpedo Liaison Committee	1942	AIR 20/3618
Torpedo Attack Committee:	1942–3	AIR 20/2368 and 3687
	1942–3	AIR 20/3613–17
Attacks on U-boats	1943	AIR 20/2186–98
Aircraft Anti-U-boat Committee	1943–5	AIR 20/3633–9
Aircraft Anti-Ship Committee	1943–6	AIR 20/3622–32, 3640 and 3647

Naval Co-operation

Files:	1940–4	AIR 20/1027–90
	1936–45	AIR 20/4440–54
Operations record book	1939–42	AIR 20/6260

War Organisation

Composition of convoys	1942–3	AIR 20/6136

Signals

Amphibious operations in Mediterranean	1943	AIR 20/6146

208 Air Ministry Research Establishments etc.

Royal Aircraft Factory, later Establishment

Reports, including development of naval aircraft, equipment and missiles:	1914–91	AVIA 13/1–1429
	1919–91	AVIA 6/1–25477
Aircraft plans	1914–19	AVIA 14
Liaison with Admiralty Mining Establishment	1940–8	AVIA 15/809–10
Naval Air Department	1957–62	AVIA 6/17229–37 and 17378

Telecommunications Research, later Royal Radar, later Signals and Radar Establishment

Files, including naval radar and equipment	1923–63	AVIA 7/1–3783
Reports, including naval radar	1921–91	AVIA 26/1–2158
Quarterly reports	1944–52	AVIA 36/1–31

Marine Aircraft Experimental Establishment

Reports	1924–56	AVIA 19/1–1298
Facilities	1941–5	AVIA 15/1536 and 2952
Monographs	1946–8	AVIA 44/531–3

Aeroplane and Armament Experimental Establishment

Reports, including naval aircraft and equipment	1930–74	AVIA 18/1–4560

Central Photographic Interpretation Unit

U-boat shelters, *Tirpitz*, E-boat bases, Heligoland etc.	1938–45	AIR 34/656–86 and 853
Shipping at sea	1940–5	AIR 34/142–7
Mediterranean Allied Photo-Reconnaissance Command	1942–5	AIR 34/389–404
Naval interpretation reports	1943–4	AIR 34/95
Interpretation reports, attacks on *Tirpitz*	1943–4	AIR 34/141

National Gas Turbine Establishment

Reports, including ships and naval aircraft	1939–77	AVIA 28/1–3926
Naval Marine Wing	1951–67	AVIA 28/2200–34
Naval Auxiliary Machinery Department	1977	AVIA 28/3896–915

Aircraft Torpedo Development Unit

Reports:	1937–76	AVIA 16/1–376
	1941–5	AIR 29/770B
	1942–3	AIR 20/3612
	1951–5	AIR 29/2358–9
(files)	1932–61	AVIA 32/1–64

Coastal Command, later Air-Sea Warfare Development Unit

Reports	1942–70	AIR 65/1–489
Joint A/S School, use of helicopters	1954	AIR 20/10246–7

209 Royal Air Force Commands

Coastal Command operated land-based aircraft on maritime operations. Training Command was responsible for FAA as well as RAF aircrew. Bomber Command sometimes flew mine-laying and other naval missions. Ferry and Transport Commands delivered aircraft to both Services.

Home Commands

Coastal Command: registered files	1930–74	AIR 15/1–957
(combat reports)	1939–44	AIR 50/302–19
(operations record books)	1951–5	AIR 24/2192–209
Bomber Command, registered files	1936–68	AIR 14/1–4590
Training Commands, registered files etc.:	1939–76	AIR 32/1–501
(combined operations)	1942	AIR 32/8
Ferry and Transport Commands, support of Pacific Fleet	1944–5	AIR 38/261 and 268

Overseas Commands

Mediterranean Coastal Air Force	1939–44	AIR 51/23–38
RAF Middle East, 201 (Naval Co-operation) Group	1941–4	AIR 23/6792–808
HQ Mediterranean Allied Coastal Air Forces	1942–5	AIR 23/7141–313

US Pacific Fleet, carriers etc.	1942–5	AIR 23/4703–9, 4731–5 and 4742
USN Hydrographic Office	1943–4	AIR 23/4749, 4750 and 4755–7
US Pacific Fleet, Intelligence Division	1943–4	AIR 23/4736–41
AOC-in-C Middle East (attacks on shipping etc.)	1943–4	AIR 23/7314–64
Air Component North-West Expeditionary Force (Norway):		
aircraft from HM Ships *Glorious* and *Furious*	1940	AIR 36/16–17
(RN and Army co-operation orders)	1940	AIR 36/18
Mediterranean Allied Air Forces, naval situation reports	1943–4	AIR 51/269

Supreme Headquarters Allied Expeditionary Force

Operational Research Section report on Coastal Command	1941–4	AIR 37/483
Operation OVERLORD, air defence of warships	1943–4	AIR 37/753
Aircraft mines	1943–4	AIR 37/799
Spotting for naval bombardment	1944	AIR 37/821
Employment of FAA personnel	1944	AIR 37/135
Operation NEPTUNE, naval administration orders	1944	AIR 51/461
Directives, plans and orders of battle	1944–5	AIR 37/1005–6

210 Royal Air Force, Operations Record Books

This is a list limited to Naval Air Units, or RAF Units engaged primarily in maritime operations. It does not include those many other RAF Units (for example of Bomber Command) which undertook naval operations from time to time.

School of Naval Co-operation	1917–39	AIR 29/438
HMS *Leander*, no. 720 (catapult) flight	1937–9	AIR 29/887
Coastal patrol flights	1939–40	AIR 29/891
No. 31 Coastal Squadron SAAF	1939–44	AIR 54/113 and 118–20
200 Coastal Command Group	1939–41	AIR 25/793–4
201 (General Reconnaissance/Naval Co-operation) Group	1939–44	AIR 25/795–800
Coastal Defence and AA Units	1939–45	AIR 29/438–40
Coast Artillery Co-operation Unit (no. 1)	1939–45	AIR 29/439
Coastal Command:	1939–50	AIR 24/364–439
	1951–5	AIR 24/2192–209
	1956	AIR 24/2422–5
	1956–9	AIR 24/2487–91
	1956–60	AIR 24/2379–82
	1959	AIR 24/2567
	1960	AIR 24/2612–13
	1961	AIR 24/2647–8

	1963	AIR 24/2734–5
	1964–5	AIR 24/2785–8
	1966–9	AIR 24/2860–70
Flying Boat Training Squadron	1940–3	AIR 29/609
Coastal Command Development Unit HQ	1940–4	AIR 29/771–2
Coastal Operational Training Units/Detachments	1940–7	AIR 29/609–10, 636–7 and 705–7
Coastal Flight no. 35 SAAF	1941–3	AIR 29/862
Merchant Ship Fighter Units:	1941–3	AIR 29/437
(combat reports)	1939–43	AIR 50/472
30 (Coastal) Wing (Iceland Command)	1941–5	AIR 24/764–93
Aircraft Torpedo Development Unit, Gosport:	1941–5	AIR 29/770B
	1951–5	AIR 29/2358–9
FAA Squadrons	1941–6	AIR 27/2386
Coast Defence Wing, India	1942	AIR 26/578
Coastal Defence Flight (no. 6) (India)	1942	AIR 29/889
Naval Liaison Section, Bombay	1942–3	AIR 29/434
Advanced Ship Recognition Flight (no. 1476)	1942–4	AIR 29/870
Catalina Flight (Aden)	1942–4	AIR 29/891
Advanced flying boat bases	1942–5	AIR 29/34
RNorN Air Service Flight (no. 1477)	1943	AIR 29/870
Coastal Command Unit, Portreath	1943–4	AIR 29/33
105 (Combined Operations) Wing	1943–4	AIR 26/156–7
Torpedo Depot, Ceylon	1943–4	AIR 29/799
247 Coastal Command Group	1943–6	AIR 25/1044–63
Torpedo Refresher School and Torpedo Training Units	1943–7	AIR 29/702
Air-Sea Warfare Development Unit:	1944–5	AIR 29/913–16
	1951–5	AIR 29/2361–3
Coastal Command Flying Instructors' School	1944–5	AIR 29/631
HMS *Largs*, Air Section	1944–5	AIR 29/434
Joint Flying Control Centre, Karachi	1944–5	AIR 29/458
Ship Recognition School, Colombo	1944–5	AIR 29/1165
USN Field Signals Unit, Dunkeswell	1944–5	AIR 29/1197
Coastal Command Anti-U-boat Devices School	1945	AIR 29/1134
Ship Unit HQ	1945–6	AIR 29/1186
Far East Flying Boat Wing	1950–4	AIR 26/599
Joint Air Reconnaissance Centre	1951–60	AIR 29/2418–20 and 2989
Joint A/S School, Londonderry	1951–60	AIR 29/2302–7 and 2577
Coastal Command Categorisation Board, St. Mawgan	1953–5	AIR 29/2427
Flying Boat Training Squadron	1953–6	AIR 27/2886
Coastal Command Modification Centre	1954–5	AIR 29/2428
Coastal Command Gunnery School	1955	AIR 29/2374
Joint Services Trials Unit	1955–60	AIR 29/2400, 2576, 2703–5, 2740 and 2775–6

Joint Services Port Unit, Famagusta	1964–5	AIR 29/3612
18 HQ (Maritime) Group	1969–70	AIR 25/1754–7

211 Ministry of Health, 1919–

Registered files (including naval health matters)	1936–62	MH 55/1–2791
National Service Medical Board examinations	1939–52	MH 114/1–5456
Welsh Board of Health, registered files (including seamen with TB, sanitary inspections of RN establishments etc.)	1915–44	MH 96/1–2352
Billeting of dockyard and Admiralty staff	1942–8	HLG 7/1–1057
Government Lymph Establishment (supplies to Services)	1907–9	MH 78/111
Health of Mercantile Marine and Navy, Joint Advisory Committee	1922–35	MH 55/350–8
Tropical diseases, liaison with RN Medical Service	1923–4	MH 58/255 and 258
Housing of dockyard workers	1925–7	HLG 52/879
RN requisition of PLA launch	1944	MH 79/556
Amendment of Naval Enlistment Act	1946–52	MH 137/377–8
Admiralty Sub-Committee on Housing for RN Personnel and Civilian Workers	1946–56	HLG 101/143, 147–8
National Blood Transfusion Service, supply to RN	1948–61	MH 123/489
Superannuation of Admiralty staff serving in unhealthy climates	1952–7	MH 108/524
Official History of the Second World War, RN Medical Services	1952–70	MH 76/624–7
Admiralty correspondence, Mental Health Act	1959–60	MH 140/2
Admiralty liaison, radiation hazards	1963–4	MH 58/718
Inter-Departmental Committee on Medical Certificates, Admiralty evidence	1948–9	MH 135/738
RNH Yarmouth Transfer Bill 1957	1950–7	MH 80/70
RN Scientific Service, Bragg Laboratory, discharge of radioactive waste	1960–1	HLG 120/302
RNH Haslar, operating theatre	1967–77	HLG 156/103
TS *Formidable*, Portishead, annual inspections	1975–81	MH 152/276

212 Medical Research Council

Reports by RN surgeons	1910–82	FD 1/various
Cerebro-spinal meningitis in RN	1918	FD 4/17
RN Medical Consultative Board	1923–5	FD 5/151
Colour vision requirements in RN	1933	FD 4/185
Vaccine trials in RN	1938–52	FD 1/1115, 1814 etc.
Applied Psychology Unit, Cambridge, work for RN	1938–53	FD 1/4147–51 etc.
Prophylactic Vitamin C trials in RN	1939–40	FD 1/4391

Malaria prophylaxis in RN and Merchant Navy	1940–3	FD 1/6239–40
Naval intelligence tests	1941	FD 1/5500
Nutrition of workers in heavy naval work	1941–2	FD 1/5521
Proposed Medical Research Institute for RN	1941–52	FD 1/6061–6
RN Personnel Research Committee, reports and correspondence:	1941–70	FD 1/6067–92, 7027, 8008, 9145–7 etc.
	1942–67	ADM 298/1–485
	1943–4	ADM 1/15579 and 18069
	1961–3	FD 23/597
	1982–9	FD 7/3434–87
(evidence on occupational deafness)	1960	PIN 20/189
RN Statistical Committee	1943–6	FD 1/6968
Asbestos diseases in dockyards	1965–82	FD 12/386, 389, 1242
Visit to RN Physiological Laboratory	1969	FD 7/1613
Tropical Medicine Research Board, 'The Role of the Royal Navy in Tropical Medicine Studies'	1973	FD 9/1221
Alcohol consumption in the RN	1974	FD 23/2176
RN Dockyards Asbestos Research Project Advisory Committee and Scientific Advisory Sub-Committee	1975–7	FD 7/3274

213 Ministry of Transport, 1919–

Dockyards, proposed commercial use	1919–20	MT 48/1
Retention of barges purchased for war purposes	1920	MT 49/112
Severn Barrage, Admiralty correspondence	1924–30	POWE 13/25, 35 and 44
Admiralty and Dover Harbour Board	1926	MT 47/108
Navy Estimates debate	1941	MT 45/262
Admiralty liaison	1942–5	MT 47/308
Admiralty disputes with port authorities	1942–62	MT 56/180, 469 and 471
Trinity House and special Admiralty operations	1944	MT 101/20
Admiralty responsibility for merchant shipbuilding and repair	1945–7	MT 73/13
Ferries Committee, Admiralty correspondence	1946–7	MT 41/36
Admiralty-Ministry of Transport Joint Committee on Shipbuilding and Ship Repairs, minutes etc.	1947–50	MT 73/78–9, 96 and 178
Admiralty Dry Dock Committee, reports	1948–53	MT 73/102–3 and 203
Admiralty-Ministry of Transport Committee on Applications for Ship Repairs Abroad	1949–50	MT 73/117
Admiralty Working Party on Shipbuilding and Repair, reports	1949–52	MT 73/155–6, 189
Specifications for RFA tankers	1950–1	MT 73/200
Admiralty request for tonnage figures (1941–5)	1950–5	MT 73/201
NATO exercises in Clyde, arrangements at Faslane Naval Base	1951–64	MT 82/51, 80 and 93
Yarrow ARE, report on nuclear power for ships	1957–9	MT 73/278

Admiralty interest in Milford Haven	1958–60	MT 81/365
Future of Sheerness Dockyard	1960	MT 81/369
Transfer of ex-RN vessels to foreign powers	1960–8	MT 73/404
Transfer of Faslane Port to Admiralty	1963–4	MT 132/94
MoD representation on Harbour Authorities	1965–73	MT 81/746

Marine Departments

Radio navigation aid development by ASWE:	1947–64	BT 243/217
	1960–78	BT 243/393
RNR and Blue Ensign	1951–65	BT 238/137
Merchant Navy War Memorial, Tower Hill	1951–60	BT 238/17–18 and 99–101
RN and RFA service for certificates of competency	1951–81	BT 238/146
Admiralty meetings, search and rescue at sea	1953–61	BT 243/439–40 and 443
Salvage awards to naval personnel	1955–68	BT 243/153
Admiralty and Peterhead Harbour Trustees	1956–60	BT 243/4
Admiralty correspondence, tides	1957–82	BT 243/245
Ministry of Civil Aviation, transfer of Admiralty functions	1959	MT 45/597
Transfer of control of shipbuilding and repair from Admiralty	1959–60	BT 239/48
Ex-RN personnel, able seaman certificates	1960–75	BT 238/153
Communications between merchant ships and HM Ships	1961–72	BT 243/28
Marine (Safety) Division: registered files, including correspondence, plans etc. of naval vessels	1921–2000	MT 146/1–1444

British Transport Commission

| RN Minewatching Organisation | 1951–3 | AN 13/2577 |

British Railways Board

Woolwich Dockyard	1953–9	AN 157/146, 150
Training of RN officers	1957	AN 174/1192
Collision between MV *Brading* and Admiralty Launch	1960	AN 157/184

214 Ministry of War Transport, Ministry of Transport, Board of Trade etc., Control of Shipping Departments

This list is of the organisation concerned with wartime naval operational control of merchant shipping movements, which belonged to the Ministry of War Transport 1941–6, the Ministry of Transport 1946–65, the Board of Trade 1965–70, the Department of Trade and Industry 1970–4, and the Department of Trade 1974–84.

Shipping control and operation, correspondence and papers	1930–83	MT 59/1–3516
Construction of US naval bases in UK	1941	MT 59/518
Convoys, list of vessels, Admiralty instructions etc.	1940–5	MT 59/540

Operation TORCH	1942–4	MT 59/588
Damage to merchant ships fuelling or servicing naval craft	1941–5	MT 59/714
Narvik Convoys, Admiralty reports	1939–40	MT 59/799
Coasters movements and casualties, Admiralty telegrams	1939–41	MT 59/1250–1
British Pacific routes	1940–1	MT 59/1383
Irish ships forbidden to call at British ports	1942–5	MT 59/1464
French ships and seamen in Free French ports	1940–2	MT 59/1699, 1728 and 1797
Children's overseas reception scheme	1940	MT 59/1860
Oil tankers and oil, Admiralty requirements	1939–43	MT 59/1889–2202
US War Shipping Administrator	1941–5	MT 59/2209 and 2218
Draft Naval Prize Manual	1954–5	MT 59/2966
Naval counter-piracy operations in North Borneo	1962–4	MT 59/3230
British China Sea trade in event of war	1940	MT 59/1384

215 Ministry, later Central Office of Information, 1939–

Film production documents	1931–97	INF 6
Original art work	1939–46	INF 3/1–1861
Posters and publications, naval	1939–76	INF 13/122 and 271–4
Guard books, publicity material on RN etc.	1939–78	INF 2/1–211
Photographs, naval:	1939–79	INF 14/14–18
(Board of Admiralty)	1951–60	INF 14/426
(Last Tot of Rum)	1970	INF 14/427/2
(First Sea Harrier)	1979	INF 14/427/1
Censorship arrangements with Admiralty	1940–4	INF 1/529
Recruiting and publicity leaflets for RN etc.	1950–76	EXT 1/14–39 and 41–7
Admiralty, general policy	1950–2	INF 12/246–9
Naval recruitment	1962–3	INF 12/973
Music score from film 'Five Steps Towards a Commission in the Royal Navy'	1967	INF 15/22

216 Ministry of Fuel and Power, later Department of Energy, 1942–

Petroleum Division, including oil supplies for RN	1901–71	POWE 33/1–2653
Monthly imports of fuel oil for Navy	1932–48	POWE 33/212–14
Tanker Tonnage Committee	1935–40	POWE 34/39–41
Atomic Energy Authority, RN submarine reactor	1958	POWE 14/1157
Correspondence with Admiralty	1962–3	POWE 33/2530 and 2572
Inspectorate of Nuclear Installations, reports on reactor at RNC Greenwich	1961–72	POWE 74/66–8, 83 and 381

Nuclear warships, safety considerations	1964	POWE 14/2335
Hydrographic Office and offshore oilfield development:	1964–5	POWE 62/14
	1974–5	POWE 63/1187
Public Safety Scheme, HM Dockyard Rosyth	1966	POWE 74/139
Port of Hull Safety Scheme for visits of nuclear warships	1967–72	POWE 74/332
Sizewell B Inquiry, RN submarine propulsion	1982	EG 2/2459
Hinkley Point C Inquiry, RN	1988–90	EG 4/2578

National Coal Board

Photograph of HMS *St. George* coaling off Salonika	c.1915	COAL 13/82
Admiralty pulverised coal requirements	1941	COAL 14/854

217 Ministry of Defence, 1947–

These are records of the Ministry of Defence as created in 1947 to co-ordinate the three Armed Services, some of which were inherited from its predecessors the War Cabinet [189] and the Committee of Imperial Defence [190]. Later records were created by the new unified Ministry of Defence of 1964.

Joint Naval and Military W/T Committee etc., minutes and papers	1917–73	DEFE 59/1–30
Scientific Advisory Council, reports and papers	1939–69	WO 195/1–16894
Committees and working parties	1942–77	DEFE 10/1–987
Defence Research Policy Committee:	1945–52	DEFE 9/1–38
(undersea warfare)	1945–9	DEFE 9/22
(trials of Hook's Hydrofoil)	1947–51	DEFE 9/20, 22
Admiralty/Air Ministry Joint Sea/Air Warfare Committee, papers	1946–55	AIR 20/6381–90, 6698, 6842–3, 7082, 7389, 7635, 9209–11 and 9831–4
Australian Royal Commission into UK Nuclear Weapons Testing in Australia, proceedings and evidence:	1947–85	DEFE 16/1–975
(Radiac instruments for RN)	1950 and 1956	DEFE 16/871 and 879
(Admiralty records of nuclear test)	1951–3	DEFE 16/395–7 and 433–5
(provisioning RN ships at Fremantle)	1952	DEFE 16/838
(decontamination of ships)	1952–4	DEFE 16/737
(Admiralty Materials Laboratory reports)	1954–7	DEFE 16/47
Infra-Red Committee, reports issued by Admiralty:	1948	WO 195/9701
(MoD and Admiralty contracts)	1951	WO 195/11629
Maritime Air Defence Committee reports	1950–3	AIR 20/6567, 7939
Defence Signals Staff, registered files	1954–82	DEFE 26/1–22

Defence Board, 1958–64/Defence Council, 1964–, minutes and memoranda	1958–64	DEFE 30/1–4
Operational Evaluation Group, and Submarine Tactics and Weapons Group, reports	1964–76	DEFE 67
Defence Operational Analysis Establishment, naval reports	1965–95	DEFE 48/1–957
Central Tactics and Trials Organisation, reports	1967–77	DEFE 56/1–136
Phantom tactics for air defence of warships	1970–2	DEFE 56/44 and 62
Nimrod maritime reconnaissance aircraft	1973–5	DEFE 56/92 and 130–4
Reconstitution of the Defence Council	1978	DEFE 17/4
Defence Evaluation and Research Agency, reports and files	1991–2001	DEFE 75/1–51

Minister of Defence, Private Office

US naval bases in UK	1950–64	DEFE 13/11, 274 and 1006–7
RN co-operation with South African Navy	1954–5	DEFE 13/36
Nuclear submarine programme	1957–63	DEFE 13/606 etc.
Naval construction programme	1957–65	DEFE 13/186–8 and 436
Various naval matters	1960–4	DEFE 13/85
Replacement of Shackleton aircraft:	1960–4	DEFE 13/206
	1964	DEFE 24/66–7
Defence review, shape of future Fleet	1966–7	DEFE 13/540
Harrier and Sea Harrier aircraft development	1975	DEFE 13/1066
Cod War with Iceland	1975–6	DEFE 13/1033–5 and 1072–5

218 Ministry of Defence, Registered Files

These are registered files from both the 1947 and 1964 Ministries of Defence.

General series	1942–76	DEFE 7/1–2401
Permanent Under-Secretary	1956–84	DEFE 23/1–136
Defence Secretariat Branches	1956–83	DEFE 24/1–891
Unrest in the Navy	1931	DEFE 24/242
Cod War with Iceland	1959–76	DEFE 24/915–44
Signals and reports from HM Ships	1973–6	DEFE 24/939–44
Fleet Requirements Committee, minutes:	1961–3	DEFE 24/8
	1975	DEFE 24/687
Provision of Napalm to RN	1962–3	DEFE 24/73
RN construction and conversion programme	1963–4	DEFE 24/1
Replacement of Shackleton aircraft	1964	DEFE 24/66–7
British surveillance of Russian Fleet	1964–5	DEFE 24/20
Naval intelligence requirements	1966	DEFE 24/299–300

Prof. Arthur Marder, access to Admiralty records	1966–7	DEFE 24/96
Future Fleet Working Party	1966–8	DEFE 24/128, 149–50, 194, 234–5 and 238–9
RN Hydrographic Service	1967–73	DEFE 24/521
Russian naval presence in Orkneys	1968–9	DEFE 24/14
FAA Working Party, reports	1968–9	DEFE 24/363–5
Use of Diego Garcia by USN	1970–3	DEFE 24/599
RN catering frauds, Committee of Enquiry	1972–3	DEFE 24/282
Royal dockyards	1973–7	DEFE 23/134
Lt.-Cdr. Swabey, appeal against dismissal	1975–6	DEFE 47/13
Naval service of HRH Prince of Wales	1973–6	DEFE 24/642 and 912–13
Admiralty Board meetings, briefs etc.	1976	DEFE 24/910

219 Ministry of Defence, Committees, Departments and Directorates

Chiefs of Staff Committee

Minutes	1947–73	DEFE 4/1–279
Registered files	1946–77	DEFE 11/1–793
Secretary's standard (i.e., sensitive) files	1946–83	DEFE 32/1–21
Memoranda	1947–73	DEFE 5/1–197
Joint Planning Staff and Defence Planning Staff, reports	1947–68	DEFE 6/1–106
Committees and sub-committees, minutes	1947–64	DEFE 8/1–78
Air, Coast and Seaward Defences Committee	1947–59	DEFE 8/1–15, 24–6, 33–7, 42–4, 50, 64–7 and 71
Maritime Air Defence Committee:	1950–4	DEFE 8/23, 30 and 40
	1955–7	DEFE 10/267

Joint Intelligence Committee

Files (including naval intelligence)	1939–73	CAB 163/1–211
Minutes	1947–68	CAB 159/1–50
Memoranda	1947–68	CAB 158/1–71
Fragmentary records	1947–74	CAB 191/1–17
Weekly reviews and surveys	1956–63	CAB 179/1–11
Sub-committees, minutes and memoranda	1957–76	CAB 182/1–92
Minutes and memoranda	1966–74	CAB 185–90

Defence Intelligence Staff

Intelligence assessments, reports etc.:	1944–91	DEFE 44/1–298
	1946–85	DEFE 63/1–65
	1965–78	DEFE 64/1–27
Registered files	1957–79	DEFE 31/1–162
Correspondence with Naval Attaché, Moscow	1964–71	DEFE 31/100–6 and 162

Minutes	1970–1	DEFE 27/1–5
CANUKUS Naval Intelligence Conference	1971	DEFE 31/116
Soviet A/S warfare	1971–4	DEFE 31/139

Directorate of Forward Plans, Registered Files

History of deception in Second World War	1939–45	DEFE 28/47–9
HABBAKUK	1946–8	DEFE 28/188
Forward planning instructions, Admiralty	1951–2	DEFE 28/72
General naval deception	1953–61	DEFE 28/141

Central Staffs, Registered Files

Collision between HMS *Fittleton* and *Mermaid*	1976–7	DEFE 68/6
Hodges's paintings of New Zealand	1961–7	DEFE 68/16
Submarine-launched anti-ship weapons	1968	DEFE 68/82
US Marine Corps, Harrier programme	1972–4	DEFE 68/207–8
Management Review Team, interviews Navy Department	1975	DEFE 68/181
Expenditure on RN equipment	1976–8	DEFE 68/115
Navy Department use of real estate	1976–8	DEFE 68/167
Defence Services Secretariat, recommendations for honours and awards	1993–	DEFE 74

Central Defence Scientific Service

Organisation of naval research and development	1950–1	DEFE 19/22
Naval air defence	1960–1	DEFE 19/43
Enquiry into carrier task forces	1962–5	DEFE 19/20
Naval Panel study on A/S warfare	1963–6	DEFE 19/53
Underwater warfare	1964	DEFE 19/95

Defence Lands Service, Registered Files

RNAD Charlesfield, Roxburgh	1948–64	DEFE 51/76–9
RN Torpedo Establishment, Greenock	1956–8	DEFE 51/73
Sale of HM Dockyard Sheerness	1958–63	DEFE 51/30–2
HMS *Ganges*, Shotley, Suffolk	1964–8	DEFE 51/35–7
Royal Greenwich Observatory, Herstmonceaux	1964–8	DEFE 51/95
Chatham Dockyard, listed buildings	1968–70	DEFE 51/102
Defence Lands Review Committee, Navy	1971–3	DEFE 57/12 and 16

Navy Department, 1969–87, Registered Files

Main series	1969–87	DEFE 69/1–604
Naval Personnel Division:	1959–81	DEFE 49/1–97
(family planning for WRNS)	1968–9	DEFE 49/19
(abolition of rum ration)	1966–71	DEFE 49/57–64
(RNR Review Committee, report)	1975–6	DEFE 49/95

Finance Division:	1956–71	DEFE 50/1–33
(Tamar Bridge and Torpoint Ferry tolls)	1956–64	DEFE 50/3
(modernisation of Haslar Hospital)	1963–9	DEFE 50/20
(Navy Estimates)	1964–5	DEFE 50/1
(warship sales to Iran and Saudi Arabia)	1964–71	DEFE 50/26–8
(Gift of harmonium to St. Nicholas church, Trincomalee)	1965	DEFE 50/15
(transporting Prime Minister to Scilly Isles)	1965–7	DEFE 50/16
(UK bids to build warships for USN)	1965–7	DEFE 50/29–31
(purchase of Phantom aircraft)	1965–8	DEFE 50/7–11
(Antigua Harbour)	1966–9	DEFE 50/6
(HMY *Britannia*, running costs)	1971	DEFE 50/2

Admiralty, War Office, Air Ministry and Press Committee, 1919–93

This 'D-Notice Committee' was responsible for liaising with the press to restrict publication of sensitive information.

Unregistered papers	1912–71	DEFE 53/1–20

Defence Publications

Defence Council instructions, RN:	1964–70	DEFE 45/1–54
	1978	DEFE 17/1
Joint Service Command, various publications	1962–74	DEFE 73/1–21

220 Chief of Defence Staff, Registered Files

Under the 1964 Defence Organisation, a Chief of the Defence Staff presided over the former Chiefs of Staff Committee, and over a Joint-Service Central Staff.

Naval papers:	1961–8	DEFE 25/148–55
	1962–5	DEFE 25/213–18
	1962–7	DEFE 25/167–84
Central Organisation for Defence, policy	1962–4	DEFE 25/9, 68–71
Long-term 'island strategy'	1962–3	DEFE 25/39–40
Future of aircraft carriers	1962–7	DEFE 25/144–7 and 173
Defence and Overseas Policy Committee	1963–5	DEFE 25/269
Buccaneer aircraft	1963–5	DEFE 25/112
Nuclear propulsion for surface ships	1963–5	DEFE 25/45
Nuclear submarine programme:	1964–5	DEFE 25/46
(Polaris):	1967–8	DEFE 25/108
	1973, 1978–9	DEFE 25/334–5
Defence review:	1964–5	DEFE 25/151–3 and 202–7

	1974	DEFE 25/221–4, 275–9 and 331–3
Indonesian threat to Malaysia	1964–5	DEFE 25/156–66 and 210–12
Concepts of naval operations	1966–7	DEFE 25/111
Defence of the Falkland Islands	1969–74	DEFE 25/316
Service pay review	1977	DEFE 25/328

221 Ministry of Defence Research Establishments

These absorbed or inherited records from many Ordnance Board and other establishments. RARDE reports and memoranda (many of them having to do with naval weapons) include those from the Explosives Research and Development Establishment, 1948–74; the Royal Gunpowder (later Royal Ordnance) Factory, Waltham Abbey, 1783–1945; the Chemical Research and Development Department, 1945–8; and the Propellants, Explosives and Rocket Motor Establishment, 1977–84.

Royal Armament Research and Development Establishment

Technical reports and memoranda	1808–1991	DEFE 15/1–2331
Reports	1888–1971	SUPP 28/72–94
Wood used in naval construction	1880	DEFE 15/100
History of RN Ordnance Depot, Priddy's Hard	1893	DEFE 15/73
Visit by students on RN gunnery long course	1929	DEFE 15/6
Naval gun requirements	1948	DEFE 15/269–80

Atomic Weapons Research Establishment

Collaboration with Admiralty and RN Scientific Service	1944–86	ES 1/1–1658
Anti-radiation materials for RN	1953–69	ES 5
Operation MOSAIC, naval plan	1956	ES 12/523
Feasibility study of warhead for RN	1962	ES 7/4
Decontamination studies, metals for HM Ships	1965–70	ES 12/308–14
Specifications for naval equipment; report on RN nuclear weapons	1971–3	ES 4

Chemical and Biological Defence, later Microbiological Research Establishment, Porton Down

Trials of naval respirators etc.:	1916–95	WO 188/1–1567
	1935–95	WO 189/1–1111
Reports and technical papers	1940–79	DEFE 55/1–417
Admiralty site for biological warfare trials	1953	DEFE 55/250
Biological weapons agents tested over the sea	1955	DEFE 55/261
Survival of micro-organisms in warships	1967–77	DEFE 55/83–6, 89, 99, 102 and 380

222 Ministry of Aviation, 1959–66

The Ministry of Aviation was the former Ministry of Supply with the addition of the civil aviation responsibilities transferred from the Ministry of Transport. It supplied aircraft, missiles and related equipment to all three Services, until these functions passed to the new Ministry of Defence in 1964. In 1966 its civil aviation functions passed to the Board of Trade, and the residue was inherited by the Ministry of Technology.

Naval Research Establishments, histories	1832–1945	AVIA 46/220–6
Registered files:	1933–62	AVIA 22/1–3298
(research)	1945–65	AVIA 54/1–2326
(contracts)	1946–62	AVIA 53/1–641
(aircraft development)	1946–75	AVIA 65/1–2429
Naval aircraft type biographies	1936–44	AVIA 46/136–44
Machine tools and naval production	1936–45	AVIA 46/317–18
Burney torpedoes	1939–42	AVIA 53/202
'Naval land equipment' (trench diggers):	1940	AVIA 11/2
	1940–1	AVIA 22/1019–21
Type 271 radar	1940–2	AVIA 12/185–7
British Central Scientific Office: naval radar	1940–2	AVIA 42/42–3
(seawater distillation)	1941–5	AVIA 42/89
Aircraft data sheets and photographs	1941–5	SUPP 9/1–236
Radio Equipment Department and Admiralty Signal Establishment	1943–7	AVIA 46/36–8
Application for award: torpedo bomber	1946–9	AVIA 53/225
(Mulberry harbour)	1949–51	AVIA 53/317
Tropical Testing Establishment, reports	1946–59	AVIA 45/1–816
Naval research, financial arrangements	1946–59	AVIA 65/524
Admiralty Research Establishments	1947–50	AVIA 46/29
Aircraft Modification Committee	1947–50	AVIA 55/41
Naval Air Material Policy Committee	1948–51	AVIA 54/1073
Naval requirements	1949–52	AVIA 46/10
Joint Service Mission Washington	1950–3	AVIA 46/536
Naval gas weapons	1951	AVIA 44/157
Sea Hawk	1952–3	AVIA 55/12
Fairey Gannet	1952–65	AVIA 53/474
Admiralty relations, naval aircraft	1953	AVIA 46/531
Naval strike aircraft	1954–9	AVIA 53/494
Aircraft Costs Committee, naval aircraft	1958–60	AVIA 65/1274
Naval Guided Weapon Working Party	1958–62	AVIA 65/949
Hovercraft development	1960–77	AVIA 98/1–238
Meetings with Admiralty	1963–5	AVIA 65/1955

223 Atomic Energy Agency

Atomic energy to power ships, correspondence with Admiralty	1945–7	AB 1/313B
Atomic Energy Research Establishment: papers	1946–81	AB 6/1–2677
(reports, submarine reactors)	1952–4	AB 15/805, 2043, 2324 and 3535
Northern Groups: reports (including submarines)	1946–90	AB 7/1–27176
(papers)	1946–71	AB 8/1–1171
(papers)	1946–92	AB 38/1–2181
(Hinton papers)	1957	AB 19/48
(nuclear surface ships)	1966	AB 64/379
(nuclear submarine safety)	1964–70	AB 62/532–9 and 543–4
Nuclear submarine project	1955–9	AB 16/1763–4
Submarine reactors	1955–65	AB 16/various
Land-based naval reactor:	1956–70	AB 60/5
(services and charges)	1960–9	AB 61/67
(reports)	1966–7	AB 65/340
Nuclear Ships Committee	1958–84	AB 62/306–10 and 385
Health and safety	1959–90	AB 62/1–961
Submarine reactor fuel storage	1962	AB 9/1113
Contracts etc. with Admiralty:	1961–70	AB 65/10–11, 197 and 238
	1962–5	AB 48/302
	1963–5	AB 65/169
Admiralty, co-ordination of valve development	1962–6	AB 24/9
Scientific and Technical Administration	1962–8	AB 48/various

224 Other Ministers and Departments

Lord Lieutenant and Lords Justices of Ireland

Letters to Admiralty	1691–1806	ADM 1/3988–91

India Board of Control, 1784–1858

Letters to Admiralty	1784–1839	ADM 1/3914–20
Expenses of 1840 China expedition	1839–47	AO 3/23–33

Royal Mint

Medals, including naval medals	1805–1948	MINT 16/1–123
Registered files, including naval medals	1901–86	MINT 20/1–4509
Naval medals: correspondence	1912–19	MINT 28/10
(designs)	1926–47	MINT 24/1–393

Forestry Commission

New Forest: returns of naval timber	1809–87	F 24/76
(maps):	1810–1904	F 17/188–91, 200, 336–9 and 364
	1849	F 25/6
Forest of Dean, timber for RN	1833–59	F 16/36
Surplus RN periscopes for fire spotting	1959–71	F 31/34

Meteorological Office

Kew Observatory	1821–1968	BJ 1/1–439
Observations from HMS *Nassau*	1851–2	BJ 1/96
Registers of instruments, including Admiralty instruments	1854–c.1915	BJ 10/1–6
Magnetic observations from HMS *Plover*	1857	BJ 1/169
Committee of Inquiry into Meteorological Office	1865–6	BT 13/1/1–3
Meteorological Committee and Council, minutes and reports	1867–1937	BJ 8/1–8
RRS *Research*, specifications:	1935–9	BJ 1/412–14
	1936–41	T 162/598
	1937	ADM 1/9090
Reorganisation of Marine and Naval Division	1935–46	BJ 5/29
Future of Deutsche Seewarte (German Naval Meteorological Research Observatory)	1945–6	BJ 5/214
Relations with Naval Meteorological Branch, Admiralty; co-operation with Naval Weather Service	1946–53	BJ 5/224, 249

Ordnance Survey

Admiralty survey of Thames estuary	1860–4	OS 2/654
Special surveys for Admiralty	1958–70	OS 1/1481

Lord Chancellor's Department

Naval Prize Bill	1901–6	LCO 2/146
Warrants and patents, Admiralty	1924–51	LCO 6/28–33, 38 and 1680
RAF, FAA and RN personnel, powers of command	1935–8	LCO 53/2
Naval court martial procedure, Naval Discipline Act etc.	1949–64	LCO 53/126, 160 and 183
Silver Oar of the Admiralty	1951–67	LCO 2/5879 and 6694
Admiralty evidence to Franks Committee	1955–6	LCO 15/8

Charity Commission

Registered files, Admiralty	1915–37	CHAR 3/34
Services charities	1961–70	CHAR 11/140

Ministry of Reconstruction

Naval demobilisation, including correspondence with Admiralty etc.	1915–20	RECO 1/1–964

Department of Scientific and Industrial Research

Fuel Research Station, reports:	1919–59	AY 6/1–179
(to Admiralty)	1942–9	AY 7/4–6

Tate Gallery

Loan of works to RN Establishments	1927–51	TG 4/9

Lord President of the Council

Correspondence with Lord Chatfield (Minister for Co-ordination of Defence)	1939–40	CAB 123/261
Admiralty research	1943	CAB 123/164
Admiralty comments on shipbuilding industry	1944–5	CAB 124/207
Release of *Queen Elizabeth* and *Queen Mary* from service as troopships	1946	CAB 124/624
Proposals for preservation of HMS *Implacable*	1948–9	CAB 124/1103
Committee on Safety of Nuclear Ships	1959–64	CAB 124/2562–6

Lands Tribunal

Claims, including claims against the Admiralty	1939–58	LT 6/1–74
Compulsory purchase orders, including those involving Admiralty	1950–72	LT 13/3155

Imperial War Museum

Transfer of HMS *Belfast*	1968–76	ED 245/14 and 86

225 Quasi-Official and other Bodies

Royal Household

Lord Chamberlain, records of special events (including state funerals of naval officers, Spithead reviews, etc.)	1500–1911	LC 2/1–150
Board of Green Cloth, letters to Admiralty	1722–89	ADM 1/3921
HM Private Secretary to Admiralty (petitions)	1830–6	ADM 1/4068–70

Trinity House

Ordnance certificates	1628–38	SP 16/16–17
Masters' passing certificates:	1660–73	SP 46/136–7
	1665–6	SP 29/141 ff. 306–7
	1660–1830	ADM 106/2908–50
	1703–55	ADM 106/3544
Letters to the Admiralty:	1702–1807	ADM 6/134
	1808–39	ADM 1/4314–15
Pilots' passing certificates	1759–70	ADM 30/36

Vice-Admirals and Lords Lieutenant of Counties

Declared account, impressment, Hampshire and IoW	1692	AO 1/1831/552–4
Letters to Admiralty (impressment etc.)	1693–1702	ADM 1/5114/3–6
Returns of men raised for RN under Quota Acts: (IoW)	1795	ADM 30/63/8
(London)	1795	ADM 7/361
(Edinburgh)	1796–9	ADM 30/63/9
(Essex)	1797	ADM 7/362

Trustees of Ramsgate Harbour

Accounts	1761–87	ADM 17/63–87
Accounts and minutes	1792–1863	MT 22/1–53

Royal Patriotic Fund

Records	1854–1972	PIN 96/1–34

Royal Fine Arts Commission

Papers, including RN and Merchant Navy war memorials	1924–98	BP 2/1–301
HMS *Victory*	1971	BP 2/242
RNC Greenwich: Painted Hall	1937–50	BP 2/101–2
(mess staff uniforms)	1938	BP 2/104
RN Establishments, Portsmouth, new buildings	1944–58	BP 2/113–14

226 Chartered and other Companies

Many of these companies exercised quasi-governmental functions within the areas of their charters. The East India Company's Chinese records (which are calendared) include much relating to the Navy, such as the Amherst Embassy, convoying, operations against pirates, relations with the Chinese authorities and Chinese orders to Portuguese (as well as British) warships. They are mainly in the form of orders from the Chinese authorities and petitions from RN officers to the Chinese Viceroy. The Secretary of Lloyd's acted as a clearing-house of naval and maritime intelligence which was passed to the Admiralty. The Stationers' Company registration forms include some early photographs of warships.

Cathay Company

Accounts and papers	1576–8	E 164/35–6
Frobisher v. Parkyns:	1580–1	STAC 5/F29/8
	1582–3	STAC 5/F23/14
Frobisher v. Miller *et al.*	1594–5	STAC 5/F/25/10

East India Company

Letters to Admiralty	1710–1839	ADM 1/3911–20
Letters to Navy Board, register	1808–13	ADM 106/2135–8

Chinese Secretary's Office, Chinese-language correspondence and papers	1793–1834	FO 1048/1–35/29

Royal Africa Company
Letters to Admiralty	1721–92	ADM 1/3810
Register of in-letters, including from Admiralty and Navy Board	1799–1811	T 70/1202–4

South Sea Company
Letters to Admiralty	1721–92	ADM 1/3810

Lloyd's Coffee House
Letters to Admiralty	1793–1839	ADM 1/3992–6

Hudson's Bay Company
RN Arctic expeditions	1824–66	BH 1/1798–801
Sales to RN	1891–1903	BH 1/2221
Agreement with Admiralty	1894	BH 1/2214
Navy League of Canada	1918	BH 1/2215
Correspondence with Admiralty	1922–9	BH 1/2714

Stationers' Company
Copyright Office registration forms	1837–1912	COPY 1/1–1235

Various
Contracts: shipbuilding and stores	c.1670	ADM 106/3538
(ship repair, stores etc.)	1681–90	ADM 106/3541
(abstracts):	1693–1765	ADM 106/3583–607
	1765–9	ADM 49/33
	1770–90	ADM 106/3608–22
	1793	ADM 106/3623
(dockyard work and materials)	1754–6	ADM 106/3624
(shipbuilding)	1755ff.	ADM 106/3072
Contracts and tenders, various	1676–1722	ADM 106/3069–71
Charter parties for transporting stores	1694–1710	ADM 106/3068
Tenders for timber and stores	1832	ADM 106/3073

227 Railway Companies

The records of private railway companies passed into the hands of the Crown as a result of the nationalisation of 1947. They include correspondence with the Admiralty Harbour and Railway Departments, 1842–62 [72] over engineering works affecting navigable waterways. There is also much to do with ports and harbours, railway shipping, and the carriage of coal, explosives and naval passengers by rail.

Description	Date	Reference
Birkenhead Railway, Admiralty survey of Birkenhead Docks	1848	RAIL 35/42
Birmingham and Oxford Railway, Admiralty correspondence	1846	RAIL 39/24-5, 38 and 211
Channel tunnel companies, including Admiralty objections	1869–1930	RAIL 779/1–229
Cockermouth, Keswick and Penrith Railway, carriage of explosives	1904	RAIL 123/50
Dover Harbour Board records	1897–1933	RAIL 821/1–6
Easton and Church Hope Railway, Admiralty line	1898–1945	RAIL 188/11–17, 43 and 79–80
Great Central Railway, carriage of explosives	1903–5	RAIL 226/446 and 466
Great Western Dock Company, plans of Plymouth Docks	1849	RAIL 857/17
Great Western Railway: papers including Admiralty contracts	1834–1981	RAIL 252/1–2425
(Admiralty correspondence)	1874–1904	RAIL 258/235
(RN preference for railborne coal)	1888	RAIL 257/11
(Admiralty coal trains)	1913–16	RAIL 253/777
(RN facilities at Fishguard)	1936	RAIL 788/378
Hartlepool Dock and Railway, Admiralty correspondence	1853	RAIL 294/20
London Midland and Scottish Railway, contracts etc. including Admiralty	1896–1971	RAIL 420/1–423
London and North-Eastern Railway: claim against the Admiralty	1923	RAIL 390/368
(Spithead review)	1937	RAIL 390/1097
London and South-Western Railway: including Admiralty telegraph and telephone cables	1838–67	RAIL 411/1–1133
(Spithead naval reviews)	1902	RAIL 981/291
Maryport and Carlisle Railway, carriage of explosives	1904	RAIL 472/127
Metropolitan railway, naval and military special traffic arrangements	1915	RAIL 1135/373
South Devon Railway, including dealings with Admiralty	1844–51	RAIL 631/1–484
South-Eastern and Chatham Railway, lines serving Woolwich Dockyard	1915	RAIL 633/527
South Wales Mineral Railway, Admiralty report	1861	RAIL 639/34
South Wales Railway, including Admiralty agreements	1843–65	RAIL 640/1–616
Southern Railway: correspondence including Admiralty	1923–72	RAIL 1188/1–377
(Spithead reviews)	1935–7	RAIL 648/52
(agreement with Admiralty)	1944	RAIL 647/55

Taff Vale Railway, including naval colliery line	1823–1962	RAIL 684/1–346
Railway Clearing House, RN reserves mobilisation, timetables:	1897	RAIL 981/551
	1897	ZLIB 10/31
(regulations for RN passenger traffic)	1939–52	RAIL 1093/23–5
Railways Staff Conference: RNR, RNVR and RFR	1936–48	RAIL 1172/1814
(boilermakers required by Admiralty)	1941	RAIL 1172/2127
Miscellaneous, refreshments for naval ratings	1903–32	AN 109/739
Harwich Naval Crane, built 1666	n.d.	RAIL 1005/444

228 Learned Societies, Professional Bodies etc.

Barber-Surgeons' Company, later Royal College of Surgeons

Surgeons' passing certificates	c.1700–96	ADM 106/2952–63
Letters to Admiralty	1718–1816	ADM 1/4280–1

Royal Society

Minutes: transit of Venus	1765–71	ADM 1/5117/2
Letters to Admiralty	1828–39	ADM 1/4282

Christ's Hospital

Boys apprenticed to the sea	1766	T 64/311
Navy Board nominations	1781–1822	ADM 106/3514

British Museum

Letters to Admiralty	1828–39	ADM 1/4282

Royal Astronomical Society

Letters to Admiralty	1828–39	ADM 1/4282

229 International and Inter-Governmental Bodies

Supreme War Council, 1917–19

Minutes, including Allied Naval Council	1915–19	CAB 28/1–9
Papers and minutes	1917–19	CAB 25/1–127
Military representatives, minutes	1917–19	AIR 1/2299–300
Military and naval representatives, minutes	1919	CAB 21/131–3

Central Mine Clearance Board, 1946–51

Reports	1946–51	ADM 232/1–113

US Strategic Bombing Survey
Submarine plant reports   1945   AIR 48/170-4

United Nations Command Korea
Operations reports   1950-7   DEFE 12/1-43

230 Miscellanea

HMS *Vanguard*, midship section   1840   RAIL 1057/3492-3
HMS *Dido* and *Sampson*, midship sections; HMS
  Penelope, engine and boilers   1841-2   RAIL 1057/3495
Reports from naval and other establishments on
  development of hovercraft   1957-80   BT 268/1-1002

Extracted Maps
Including Admiralty charts, maps and plans of naval
  establishments, bases, dockyards, naval air stations,
  inventions etc.:   1565-1962   MFQ 1/1-1411
                                                    1587-1966   MF 1/1-70
                                                    c.1542-1955 MFC 1/1-208
                                                    c.1660-1944 MPHH 1/335
                                                    1661-1945   MPH 1/1-1216
                                                    1612-1949   MPG 1/1-1251

Extracted Photographs
From ADM series   1856-1956   CN 1/1-42
From CO series (Antigua Dockyard)   1950   CN 3/49
From AIR series (airships, warships etc)   1916-62   CN 5/1-32
From DEFE series (including HMS *Campbeltown*)   1942-5   CN 10/1-3

Private Publications
H Raper, 'Latitudes and Longitudes of Maritime Places' 1838   ADM 7/853
Course of the Exchange   1768-1831   ADM 114/73-118
                                                    1797-1801   ADM 106/3626-9
Prijs-courant der effekten   1814   ADM 114/72
Jones's Woolwich Journal and Army and Navy Gazette 1846-50   WO 62/48

231 Appendix I: Officers' Service Records

Appendices I–IV are an artificial grouping of documents in the nature of service records, whose archival provenance is obscure or complicated, and which it is convenient to treat as a whole. All but the most recent transfers are listed in much greater detail in two other National Archives handbooks, *Naval Records for Genealogists* and *Tracing your Naval Ancestors*. The arrangement of this appendix is a simplified version of the classification adopted in *Naval Records for Genealogists*. Many other records giving information about named individuals which are covered by one or both of these handbooks are listed elsewhere in this guide under the names of the originating departments.

All officers' service records were the responsibility of the Admiralty from 1832, and it is convenient to list them together, although some of these undoubtedly originate from the subordinate Boards which were responsible for issuing many warrants until 1832. After 1832 these records were kept mainly by the Military, Civil, Commission or Commission and Warrant Branches according to the rank or branch of the officer. Some registers of pay and pensions were kept by or subsequently transferred to the Paymaster-General's Department. Other records of officers of their branches were kept by the Medical Director-General [110] (who also compiled casualty lists) and the Engineer-in-Chief of the Navy [106]. Accounts of Marine officers' 'subsistence money' (that is, shore pay) were kept by the Marine Office. Notes of candidates for nomination as naval cadets, and for promotion to flag rank, were kept in the First Lord's Private Office [84]. Certificates of service, half- and full-pay registers and other financial records were compiled by the Navy Pay Office [157]. Pensions to widows were also paid by the Charity for Sea Officers' Widows [124] until 1836, and those to orphans by the Compassionate Fund, later Compassionate List [124]. Records of RNR officers were kept by the Registrar-General of Shipping and Seamen [73]. Examination records were also held by the various Royal Naval Colleges [126]. Printed seniority lists are also to be found among Admiralty publications [128].

Analyses of Services

Lieutenants on half-pay	1791	ADM 1/5119/3
Surgeons	c.1808	ADM 11/40
Masters' Assistants and Clerks	1835	ADM 1/5123/15
Boatswains, gunners and carpenters	1836	ADM 1/5123/16
Military commissioned officers	1844	ADM 11/64
Lieutenants	1847	ADM 6/174
Masters on half-pay	1847	ADM 11/6
Military commissioned officers:	1848	ADM 11/10
	1893–1900	ADM 11/80

Applications for Promotion, Employment etc.

Commissioned and Warrant Officers	1673–89	ADM 6/428
Warrant Officers and chaplains	1770–95	ADM 6/187–9
Lieutenants	1799–1818	ADM 6/170–2

To be superseded	1801–3	ADM 6/212
For Poor Knights of Windsor	1812–21	ADM 106/3535
Warrant Officers	1818–20	ADM 6/190
Masters	1823–31	ADM 106/3518
Surgeons, for appointment to convict ships	1829–33	ADM 6/186
All officers:	c.1841–61	ADM 11/1
	1842–58	ADM 6/1–2
Lieutenants	1845–53	ADM 6/181

Appointments

Commissioned officers, impress service	1793–1800	ADM 30/34
Commissioned officers, Sea Fencibles	1793–1810	ADM 28/145
Lieutenants, to cutters, Sea Fencibles, signal stations, tenders etc.	1803–7	ADM 6/55
Commissioned officers, to Sea Fencibles, Impress Service, signal stations etc.	1803–15	ADM 11/14–18
Sub-lieutenants	1805–10	ADM 11/19
Lieutenants and midshipmen, to signal stations etc.	1810–14	ADM 7/591
Midshipmen, to signal stations etc.	1810–16	ADM 30/53–4
Midshipmen etc.	1815–54	ADM 2/1252–81
Lieutenants, masters and boatswains, to Revenue Cruisers:	1816–31	ADM 6/56
	1822–32	ADM 2/1127
Foreign junior officers under training	1830–58	ADM 11/27–30 and 81

Black Books

Commissioned officers	1741–1815	ADM 12/27B–27D
Warrant Officers	1741–1814	ADM 11/39
Digest of courts martial	1755–1806	ADM 12/21–6
Commissioned officers, court martial convictions	1810–16	ADM 12/27A
Mates, midshipmen etc.	1826–48	ADM 11/27–9
Captains and Engineers	1835–42	ADM 11/49
Military commissioned officers	1846–72	ADM 6/445
Casualties, dismissals and resignations	1903–33	ADM 10/16

Commissions

Commission and warrant books	1695–1815	ADM 6/3–32
Marine officers	1703–13	ADM 6/405
Commissions and warrants: dispatched:	1744–98	ADM 6/33–8
	1802–27	ADM 6/46–7
	1832–49	ADM 6/48–9
(overseas):	1742–68	
	(chiefly 1756–63)	ADM 6/61–3

	1787–1805	ADM 6/64–5
	1807–15	ADM 7/558
	1824–46	ADM 6/68–72
(tabular summary)	1804–6	ADM 6/53
Commissions, fees payable:	1730–1818	ADM 10/13
	1802–27	ADM 6/46–7
	1832–9	ADM 6/48–9
From half-pay	1795–1815	ADM 6/54
Original lieutenant's commission	1800	ADM 7/767
Commanders-in-chief etc.	1860–70	ADM 7/919
Mates/sub-lieutenants	1829–81	ADM 11/22 and 89
Original lieutenant's commission	1846	ADM 7/768
RM officers	1849–58	ADM 201/8

Candidates for Promotion, Employment etc., and Confidential Reports

For RN College Portsmouth:	1811–36	ADM 11/53
	1813–25	ADM 7/1
Midshipmen and mates	1814–16	ADM 6/176–80
Nominations for CG officers	1819–66	ADM 175/74–81 and 99–100
Masters	1820–31	ADM 106/3517–18
Warrant Officers	1828	ADM 11/38
Surgeons:	1817–32	ADM 105/1–9
	1822–32	ADM 105/10–19
	1829–94	ADM 104/31–42
Mates:	1830	ADM 6/198
	1845–53	ADM 6/181
Master's Assistants	1839–49	ADM 11/21
Military commissioned officers	c.1841–61	ADM 11/1
Lieutenants, masters and pursers	1847–54	ADM 11/88
Paymasters etc.:	1856	ADM 11/45–6
	1884–1920	ADM 196/173–4
	1903–39	ADM 196/176
Lieutenants	1861	ADM 196/69–70
RM officers	1862–87	ADM 201/10–12
For surgeon, physical examination	1870–1902	ADM 6/468
Commanders:	c.1879–95	ADM 7/929–30
	1908–31	ADM 196/125–9
Gunners, from HMS *Excellent*:	1881–1900	ADM 6/462
	1900–12	ADM 196/166
For naval cadet etc.	1882–1905	ADM 6/448–51
Lieutenants and sub-lieutenants:	1885–1928	ADM 196/140–51
(indexes)	1885–1928	ADM 196/138–9
Nursing sisters	1890–1908	ADM 104/95

For flag rank	1893–1944	ADM 196/86–94
Officers attending War Course	1904–22	ADM 203/99
Mates and lieutenants promoted from mate	1914–30	ADM 196/154–5

Certificates of Service for Promotion or Pension

Mates and midshipmen:	1744–1819	ADM 6/86–118
	1802–48	ADM 107/71–5
	1814	ADM 6/182
Masters	c.1800–50	ADM 6/135–68
Warrant Officers	1802–14	ADM 29/1
Candidates for purser, boatswain, gunner and carpenter	1803–4	ADM 6/121
Gunners	1803–5	ADM 6/128
Surgeons	1815–22	ADM 104/30
Gunners	1817–73	ADM 29/3, 24 and 121
Carpenters:	1817–53	ADM 29/5–6
	1870–3	ADM 29/121
Chaplains	1833–4	ADM 11/41
Boatswains and gunners	1840–70	ADM 29/23–4
Candidates for lieutenant, master and purser	1847–54	ADM 11/88
Boatswains, gunners and carpenters	1870–3	ADM 29/121
Engineers	1870–3	ADM 29/112

Disposition Lists

Captains, commanders and lieutenants	1673–1813	ADM 8/1–100
Pilots, Nore and Downs	1812–15	ADM 30/43
Mates, midshipmen and cadets	1849	ADM 6/183
Gunners	1893–1924	ADM 6/463
Temporary surgeons	1914–16	ADM 104/44
RNAS	1914–18	AIR 1/2108–11
WRNS	1917–19	ADM 321/1–2

Examinations

Lieutenants	1795–1832	ADM 107/64–70
Midshipmen, mates etc., in navigation	1816–18	ADM 6/119
Mates and sub-lieutenants	1829–81	ADM 11/22 and 89
Commissioned officers' gunnery qualifications	1841–2	ADM 6/60
RN Medical School	1884–1914	ADM 305/71–2
Candidates for government employment, including RN, RM and Admiralty Civil Service	1886–1991	CSC 10/1–5111

Honours and Awards

Commissioned officers	1793–1807	ADM 7/706

Medal Rolls	1793–1952	ADM 171/1–77
All officers	1833–46	ADM 11/51–2
All officers and ratings	1852–1898	ADM 7/912
Recommendations	1914–19	ADM 171/78–88
Medal Rolls	1914–72	ADM 171/89–166
Foreign decorations	1916–21	ADM 171/172
RNR officers, awards and casualties	1939–45	BT 164/23

Leave Books

Captains and lieutenants	1762–77	ADM 106/2972
Commissioned officers	1783–1847	ADM 6/207–11
Warrant, Marine and yard officers	1804–46	ADM 6/200–6

Marriage Certificates

All officers:	1801–18	ADM 30/57
	1806–1902	ADM 13/70–1 and 186–92

Oaths of Allegiance, Tests etc.

Sea and yard officers	1660	C 215/6
C-in-C and FO	1673–1837	C 214/1–21
Sea and naval officers	1696	C 213/382–92
Sea officers	1726–1817	ADM 7/696–7

Pensions to Widows and Orphans

Sick and Hurt Board recommendations	1653–7	SP 18/63, 119, 151 and 177
'Admiralty', paid by Order in Council:	1673–1781	ADM 18/53–118
	1689–1785	ADM 7/809–14
	1707–1818	ADM 181/1–27
	1781–1821	ADM 22/1–5 and 17–30
	1819–29	ADM 6/330
	1832–5	ADM 6/222
	1807–9	ADM 22/51
	1818–28	ADM 22/31–6
	1830–7	ADM 23/22 and 29
	1832–5	ADM 22/50
	1836–70	PMG 16/2–5 and 7–14
	1857–76	ADM 23/76–7
	1866–1915	ADM 23/30–1, 84–8 and 161–4
	1870–1911	PMG 20/1–4, 6, 8, 10, 12, 17–20
	1911–19	PMG 20/22–3
	1916–20	PMG 44/8–9
	1916–32	ADM 23/168–9
(Coastguard):	1857–84	ADM 23/17–21

	1857–1935	PMG 23/1–49
(outports)	1828–32	ADM 22/39–46 and 253
(supplementary)	1916–20	PMG 43/1
Ex-Charity for Officers' Widows:	1836–1929	PMG 19/1–94
	1836–9	ADM 23/45–6
	1836–78	ADM 23/55 and 106–7
	1867–1932	ADM 23/47–52, 108–23 and 145–60
(Coastguard):	1857–1929	PMG 19/15–94
	1857–1926	ADM 23/17–21, 71–5 and 194–9
(RM)	1866–85	ADM 23/53–4 and 124
Deaths on active service:	1836–70	PMG 16/2–14
	1866–80	ADM 23/30–2
	1870–1919	PMG 20/1–23
	1880–1932	ADM 23/84–8, 161–4, 168–9
RM, Naval Ordnance Department, RFA, QARNNS	1878–1932	ADM 23/83–8, 161–7 and 172

Pensions for Wounds and Good Service

Wounds:	1673–1781	ADM 18/53–119
	1689–1785	ADM 7/809–14
	1708–1818	ADM 181/1–27
	1781–1821	ADM 22/1–5 and 17–30
	1830–6	ADM 23/22–3
	1832–5	ADM 6/222
	1836–1920	PMG 16/1–31
	1857–76	ADM 23/76–7
	1866–1900	ADM 23/32 and 89–94
	1870–80	ADM 23/24
	1916–28	ADM 23/206–7
	1917–19	PMG 42/13–15
	1928–31	ADM 23/144
Good service:	1837	ADM 23/23
	1839–1920	PMG 16/3–31
	1857–76	ADM 23/76–7
	1916–28	ADM 23/206–7
	1928–31	ADM 23/144

Passing Certificates

Masters:	1660–73	SP 46/137
	1660–1830	ADM 106/2908–50
	1665–6	SP 29/141 ff.306–7
	c.1830–50	ADM 6/135–68

Lieutenants:		1851–63	ADM 13/72–4
		1691–1832	ADM 107/1–63
		1744–1819	ADM 6/86–116
		1779–81	ADM 106/3544/1
		1854–67	ADM 13/88–101
		1868–1902	ADM 13/207–36
	(failing certificates)	1801–10	ADM 30/31
	(registers):	1795–1832	ADM 107/64–70
		1829–80	ADM 11/22 and 89
	(passing abroad):	1788–1818	ADM 6/117–18
		1794–1803	ADM 1/5123/3
	(in navigation and gunnery)	1869–82	ADM 13/237–8
	(from acting sub-lieutenant)	1895–7	ADM 13/251

[See *Royal Navy Lieutenants' Passing Certificates, 1691–1902*, ed. B Pappalardo (2 vols., List and Index Society, 289–90, 2001).]

Surgeons	c.1700–96	ADM 106/2952–63
Gunners:	1731–1812	ADM 6/123–9
	1856–87	ADM 13/86–7 and 249–50
Pilots	1759–70	ADM 30/36
Boatswains:	1810–13	ADM 6/122
	1851–87	ADM 13/83, 85 and 193–4
Pursers:	1813–20	ADM 6/120
	1851–89	ADM 13/79–82 and 247–8
Carpenters	1851–87	ADM 13/83–4 and 195
Clerks and assistant paymasters	1852–99	ADM 13/75–8 and 196–9
Naval Instructors	1853–73	ADM 13/246
Midshipmen	1857–99	ADM 13/102 and 240–5
Engineers	1863–1902	ADM 13/200–5

Full-Pay

Arrears	1661–3	SP 46/138
Officers with pay due on recall	1701	ADM 10/12
Annual lists	1747	ADM 30/32
Commissioned officers, masters, surgeons and chaplains	1795–1872	ADM 24/1–170
Warrant Officers' allotments	1795–1852	ADM 27
Engineers:	1847–73	ADM 22/444–57
	1871–3	ADM 29/113
Warrant Officers	1853–74	ADM 22/458–74

Half-Pay

All officers entitled:	1697–1836	ADM 25/1–255
	1774–1800	ADM 6/213–19

	1778–80	ADM 104/4–5
	1834–45	ADM 6/220–1
	1836–1920	PMG 15/1–182
	1846–86	ADM 25/256–60
	1867–81	ADM 23/33–41
	1881–1900	ADM 23/125–40
	1900–24	ADM 23/264–76
Marine regimental officers (serving to 1749)	1737–1818	PMG 4/1–114
Captains and lieutenants	1704–10	ADM 106/2970–1
Surgeons (decisions and precedents)	1817–32	ADM 105/1–19
Masters	1819–22	ADM 11/5
Remittances via customs officers	1837–41	PMG 22/1–5
RM officers	1867–71	ADM 23/35

Other Pay

Surgeons' Twopences and Chaplains' Groats	1681–1743	ADM 82/3–11
Surgeons' 'free gifts'	1789–1803	ADM 102/851–2
Masters' pay and conditions	1782–1815	ADM 6/130–1
Pilots' claims for pilotage	1793–1807	ADM 30/37–9
French pilots	1802	ADM 1/5121/10
Chaplains' bounty	1805–22	ADM 30/7
Claims for back pay by next of kin	1830–60	ADM 45/1–39
Casual payments and arrears	1904–5	ADM 24/171

Superannuation and Retirement Pensions

'Admiralty', paid by Order in Council:	1673–1781	ADM 18/53–118
	1689–1785	ADM 7/809–14
	1707–1818	ADM 18/1–27
	1781–1821	ADM 22/1–5 and 17–30
	1807–9	ADM 22/51
	1818–28	ADM 22/31–6
	1832–5	ADM 22/50
(Warrant Officers):	1830–6	ADM 23/22–3
	1832–5	ADM 6/222
(outports)	1828–32	ADM 22/39–46 and 253
French pilots	1802–9	ADM 30/40
Commissioned officers:	1836–1920	PMG 15/1–174
	1867–81	ADM 23/33–4 and 36–41
	1881–1934	ADM 22/488–522
Commissioned and Warrant Officers:	1836–9	ADM 23/45–6
	1867–32	ADM 23/47–52, 108–23 and 145–60
Warrant Officers:	1836–1874	PMG 16/1–17

	1867–1931	ADM 23/33–41, 101–5 and 173–9
	1874–1924	PMG 69/1–29
Pilots and VCs:	1836–70	PMG 16/2–5 and 7–14
	1870–1919	PMG 20/1–12, 17–20 and 22–3
Surgeons	c.1840	ADM 104/66
Coastguard:	1857–1926	ADM 23/17–21, 71–5 and 194–9
	1857–1935	PMG 23/1–49
RM officers	1871–1932	ADM 22/475–87
Disabled, naval ordnance, nursing sisters	1878–1932	ADM 23/83–8, 161–7 and 172

Service Registers

Commissioned officers	1660–88	ADM 10/10 and 15
Masters:	c.1800–50	ADM 6/135–68
	c.1840	ADM 11/1
Assistant surgeons	1806–22	ADM 104/33
Surgeons:	c.1808–13	ADM 11/40
	1840–95	ADM 196/8–10
(with confidential reports)	1829–94	ADM 104/31–42
Chaplains:	1812–80	ADM 6/440–1
	1837–60	ADM 196/68
Commissioned officers	c.1814	ADM 6/50–2
Gunners (qualifying at HMS *Excellent*)	1838–98	ADM 196/167–70
Military commissioned (later executive) officers:	c.1840	ADM 11/1
	1843–6	ADM 11/11–13
	c.1843–75	ADM 196/1–6
	1846–1907	ADM 196/36–56
	1860–78	ADM 196/13–20
	1912–17	ADM 196/117–24
(transfers from RNR etc.)	1906–16	ADM 196/96
(transfers to RAF)	1918–19	AIR 76/1–567
Lieutenants:	1846	ADM 11/11
	1895–8	ADM 196/137
Masters, surgeons and paymasters:	c.1843–75	ADM 196/1
	1848–92	ADM 196/74–82
RM officers	1845–1915	ADM 196/58–65 and 83
Warrant Officers and chaplains	1848–55	ADM 196/74–6
Carpenters	1848–1912	ADM 29/114–15
Paymasters:	1852–84	ADM 196/11–12
	1886–1910	ADM 196/171–2
	1916–22	ADM 196/85
	1904–37	ADM 196/175
Foreign officers under training	1852–98	ADM 7/912
Masters and navigating officers:	1853–72	ADM 196/21–2

	1856–82	ADM 196/77–81
	1864–74	ADM 196/73
Warrant Officers:	1855–90	ADM 196/29–32
	1903–31	ADM 196/156–63
	1903–46	ADM 196/34–5
(boatswains)	1860–1912	ADM 29/16–119
(gunners)	1901–18	ADM 196/164–5
Engineer officers:	1856–86	ADM 196/23–5
	1893–1918	ADM 196/130–3
Staff and Fleet Surgeons	1859–86	ADM 104/29
Inspectors of Hospitals	1861–94	ADM 105/75–6
Lieutenants and sub-lieutenants RNR	1862–1901	ADM 240/3–12
Honorary officers RNR	1862–1960	ADM 240/34–6
Midshipmen and Engineers RNR	1865–1907	ADM 240/20–33
All officers, record cards	c.1880–1960	ADM 340/1–456
CG officers	1886–1947	ADM 175/103–10
RNR executive officers	1887–1964	ADM 240/51–69
Paymasters, chaplains and naval instructors:	1891–1916	ADM 6/443–4
	1916–22	ADM 196/85
RNR Engineer officers	1892–1964	ADM 240/70–3
Commissioned Gunners	1903–12	ADM 196/84
RNR supply officers	1904–64	ADM 240/74–81
Acting artificer engineers	1911–28	ADM 196/134–6
Lieutenants and sub-lieutenants	1913–14	ADM 196/152
RNAS officers	1914–18	ADM 273/1–31
Temporary surgeons	1914–19	ADM 104/170
RNR officers:	1913–22	ADM 240/82–3
	1914–20	ADM 240/37–50
(indexes)	1914–20	ADM 240/84–8
WRNS officers	1917–19	ADM 318/1–556
Lieutenants from warrant rank	1918–31	ADM 196/153
Schoolmasters	1919–26	ADM 196/177

Succession Books

Commissioned and Warrant Officers	1673–88	ADM 6/425–6
Captains and commanders	1688–1725	ADM 7/655
Midshipmen ordinary, chaplains, masters-at-arms, schoolmasters and scholars of RNA:	1699–1756	ADM 6/427
	1757–1824	ADM 6/185
Masters, surgeons and sailmakers:	1733–55	ADM 106/2896–7
	1770–1807	ADM 106/2899–901
Commanders-in-chief:	1742–1808	ADM 12/15
	1755–1848	ADM 10/8

Pursers, boatswains, gunners, carpenters and yard officers:	1764–1831	ADM 106/2898 and 2902–6
	1780–1848	ADM 11/65–72
	1800–12	ADM 6/192
	1812–39	ADM 11/31–3
Commissioned officers:	1780–1847	ADM 11/65–72
	1795–1804	ADM 6/57–9
	1797–1801	ADM 11/56–7
Military commissioned officers	1806–1903	ADM 11/58–63 and 73–9
Surgeons:	1789–1807	ADM 102/851–2
(and mates)	1790–1822	ADM 104/6–7
(hospital staff)	1809–17	ADM 104/1–2
Caulkers and ropemakers	1790–1807	ADM 106/2900–1
Mates, sub-lieutenants, midshipmen and cadets:	1802–3	ADM 6/175
	1815–88	ADM 11/23–30 and 81–7
Sub-lieutenants	1805–10	ADM 11/19
Coastguard	1816–1918	ADM 175/1–73
Clerks	1821–49	ADM 11/25–9 and 47
Master's assistants etc.:	1824–9	ADM 6/169
	1829–49	ADM 11/20–1
Masters, surgeons, chaplains and cooks	1832–48	ADM 11/71
Engineers	1835–49	ADM 11/48–9
Engineers, boatswains, gunners and carpenters	1854–1861	ADM 29/122
Surgeons	1870–1924	ADM 104/88–94
Navigating Branch, surgeons, paymasters, chaplains and CG	1870–84	ADM 7/925–7
Warrant Officers	1872–96	ADM 29/125–30
Commissioned and Warrant Officers	1903–9	ADM 8/173–4
FOs and staff	1913–19	ADM 6/461
QARNNS and wardmasters	1921–39	ADM 104/96

Surveys of Officers' Ages and Services

Boatswains, gunners and carpenters	1816–18	ADM 11/35–7
Commissioned officers:	1817	ADM 9/2–17
(indexes)	1817	ADM 10/2–5
(loose papers)	1817 and 1828	ADM 6/66
(ages)	1822	ADM 6/73–83
RM officers, ages	1822	ADM 6/409
Masters, ages	1822	ADM 106/3517
FOs:	1828	ADM 9/1
(index)	1828	ADM 10/1
Commanders and lieutenants, ages	1831	ADM 6/84–5
Masters	1833–5	ADM 11/2–3

Pursers	1834	ADM 6/193–6
Military commissioned officers:	1846	ADM 9/18–61
(indexes)	1846	ADM 10/6–7
Mates and masters, ages	1847	ADM 11/10
Masters:	1851	ADM 11/7–8
(indexes):	1851	ADM 10/6–7
	1855 and 1861	ADM 11/9
Paymasters:	1852	ADM 11/42–3
	1859	ADM 11/44

Seniority Lists

Captains and commanders:	1652–1737	ADM 7/549
	1673–1754	ADM 6/424
	1688–1746	ADM 10/10
(alphabetical):	1660–85	ADM 10/15
	1660–88	ADM 10/10
	1688–1737	ADM 7/549
Commissioned officers:	1717–1846	ADM 118/1–185 and 337–52
	1814	ADM 6/50–2
RNA and RNC scholars:	1733–56	ADM 6/427
	1757–1824	ADM 6/185
	1809–39	ADM 1/3506–21
	1817–32	ADM 30/21
Marine officers:	1760–1886	ADM 192/1–44
(*Army List*)	1879–1900	WO 66/1–86
Masters:	1780–4	ADM 118/186–9
	1791	ADM 118/190
	1809	ADM 6/132
Surgeons:	1780–7	ADM 104/51–6
	1791	ADM 118/191
	1796–1823	ADM 104/57–80
	1813	ADM 118/353
Pursers	1810–22	ADM 118/192–201 and 354–5
Masters, surgeons and pursers:	1829–36	ADM 118/209–21
	1839–42	ADM 118/223–8 and 357–8
	1844–6	ADM 118/183–5
Boatswains, gunners and carpenters:	1810–17	ADM 118/192–201 and 354
	1820	ADM 118/205 and 355
	1827	ADM 118/208
	1833	ADM 118/216–17 and 356
	1836	ADM 118/222
	1839	ADM 118/226
	1844	ADM 118/229

Chaplains	1844–6	ADM 118/183–5
Sub-lieutenants RNR	1862–1906	ADM 240/13–17
Surgeons:	1868 and 1878	ADM 104/81–5
	1886	ADM 104/86–7
	1891–1926	ADM 104/166–9
Lieutenants RNR	1902–7	ADM 240/7
Commanders RNR	1904–7	ADM 240/1

Other Lists and Registers

Death certificates	1795–1807	HCA 30/455–8
Lieutenants unfit for service, prisoners etc.	1804–11	ADM 6/173
Officers' addresses	1837	PMG 73/2
Officers' obituaries:	1833–46	ADM 11/51–2
	1846–72	ADM 6/445
Casualties, dismissals and resignations	1903–33	ADM 10/16
Sample medical records:	1912–21	MH 106/1–2389
(Sub-Lt. A J Palmer, RNVR)	1916–17	WO 339/73853
Deaths on active service	1914–20	ADM 242/1–6
Register of places of burial	1914–20	ADM 242/7–10
Medical officers killed on service	1939–45	ADM 261/1
Japanese index cards of allied POWs (including RN)	c.1941–5	WO 345/1–58

Warrants

Commission and warrant books	1695–1815	ADM 6/3–32
Chaplains and masters-at-arms:	1699–1756	ADM 6/427
	1757–1824	ADM 6/185
Commissions and warrants dispatched:	1802–27	ADM 6/46–7
(fees payable):	1744–98	ADM 6/33–8
	1832–49	ADM 6/48–9
Commissions and warrants, overseas:	1742–68	
	(chiefly 1756–63)	ADM 6/61–3
	1787–1805	ADM 6/64–5
	1807–15	ADM 7/558
	1824–46	ADM 6/68–72
Warrant book	1800–15	ADM 6/191
Artificers	1798–1831	ADM 6/197
Surgeons, pursers, boatswains, gunners and carpenters	1800–15	ADM 6/191
Yard officers	1803–17	ADM 11/14–18
Pursers, boatswains, gunners, chaplains and masters-at-arms	1804–6	ADM 6/53
Pursers	1810–14	ADM 11/50
Second masters	1816–33	ADM 6/133

Mates:	1829–60	ADM 11/22
	1840–5	ADM 6/184
Gunners, overseas	1842–68	ADM 6/61
Tabular summary, commissions and warrants	1804–6	ADM 6/53

232 Appendix II: Ratings' Service Records

Arrears of pay:	1661–3	SP 46/138
	1689–1710	ADM 30/2–5
(sick quarters)	1739–43	ADM 30/6
Bounty recall list	1672–4	ADM 30/17
Bounty to volunteers:	1691–2	ADM 30/8–9
	1702–8	ADM 30/10–15
	1741–2	ADM 30/16
Pay lists, sick quarters	1757–8	ADM 30/51–2
Discharges, unfit for service	1781–3	ADM 1/5118/5
Wills of ratings and Marines:	1786–1882	ADM 48/1–107
(registers)	1786–1882	ADM 142/1–19
Medal Rolls	1793–1952	ADM 171/1–77
Bounty to relatives of slain	1795–1832	ADM 30/20
Death certificates	1795–1807	HCA 30/455–8
Remittances of pay	1795–1851	ADM 26/1–54
Allotments of pay	1795–1852	ADM 27/1–120
Sea Fencibles	1798–1810	ADM 28/1–144
Claims for back pay by next of kin	1800–60	ADM 44
Registers of ratings and Marines killed in service:	1802–61	ADM 141/1–9
	1859–78	ADM 154/1–9
Certificates of intestacy	1805–7	HCA 30/455–8
Midshipmen and ratings appointed to signal stations etc.:	1810–14	ADM 7/591
	1810–16	ADM 30/53–4
Sale of deserters' effects	1814–31	ADM 68/340–2
CG succession books	1816–1918	ADM 175/1–73
Cooks' certificates of service for pension	1817–51	ADM 29/5 and 7
Artificers' certificates of service	1817–45	ADM 29/8
Nominations for CG men:	1819–66	ADM 175/74–81 and 99–101
	1831–50	ADM 6/199
Impressed smugglers	1824	ADM 1/5123/25
Applications for armourers	1827–38	WO 54/881–2
Appointments of CG boatmen	1831–50	ADM 6/199
Certificates of service for pension:	1834–45	ADM 29/9–10, 12–18, 20–2 and 26–32

	1845–94	ADM 29/35–42, 44–9 and 51–96
Entries of stokers	1834–46	ADM 29/107
Certificates of fathers' service, applicants to GH Schools:	1836–61	ADM 29/17, 19, 25, 34, 43, 50 and 59
	1864–94	ADM 29/70 and 80–96
Entries of Engineers' boys	1839–53	ADM 29/106
Honours and awards	1852–1898	ADM 7/912
RN coast volunteers	1853	ADM 7/718
Seamen Schoolmasters' passing certificates	1853–66	ADM 13/246
Continuous service records:	1853–5	ADM 188/1–4
	1853–72	ADM 139/1–1027
	1873–1923	ADM 188/5–1177
(transfers to RAF)	1918–28	AIR 79/1–2807
CG retirement pensions:	1857–1926	ADM 23/17–21, 71–5 and 194–9
	1857–1935	PMG 23/1–49
CG discharges:	1858–68	ADM 175/102
	1919	ADM 175/91–6
RNR ratings:	1860–1908	BT 164/1–23
	1908–55	BT 377/1–27
Widows' pensions, accidental deaths	1863–5	ADM 80/107
ERAs, service records	1868–88	ADM 29/123–4
ERAs, passing certificates	1877–86	ADM 13/206
RNVR service registers	1894–1922	ADM 337/1–128
CG ratings' services	1900–23	ADM 175/82A–90
RNVR divisional record books (specimens)	1904–39	ADM 900/75–86
Sample medical records	1912–21	MH 106/1–2389
RN Division	1914–19	ADM 339/1–3
Register of places of burial	1914–20	ADM 242/7–10
Medal Rolls	1914–72	ADM 171/89–166
RNAS Russian Armoured Car Squadron:	1915–18	ADM 11/1717
	1915–18	ADM 137/3943B
WRNS service registers:	1918–19	ADM 336/1–29
(transfers to WAAF)	1914–18	AIR 80/1–268
CG ratings discharged	1919	ADM 175/91–6
Widows' pensions:	1921–6	PMG 72/1–2
(RNR and T124)	1922–6	ADM 23/170–1
CG Shore Signal Service	1921–9	ADM 175/111
RNR widows' pensions	1922–5	ADM 23/170

233 Appendix III: Civilian Employees' Service Records

Admiralty and Navy Commissioners, Admiralty and Navy Office staff etc., salaries:	1689–1832	ADM 7/809–21 and 823
	1793–1819	ADM 22/6–16
Yard officers' salaries:	1689–1708	ADM 7/809–10
(foreign and minor yards)	1708–1832	ADM 7/810–21
(home yards)	1808–32	ADM 7/859 and 861
Yard officers' superannuation	1809–32	ADM 106/3009–14
Salaries of foremen, quartermen, clerks etc. of home yards	1813–33	ADM 7/860
Officers' and widows' pensions:	1834–6	ADM 23/25
	1836–1918	PMG 24/1–64
	1866–1910	ADM 23/26–8, 78–82, 192–3
	1910–26	ADM 23/196–9
(merchant seamen killed in action)	1914–28	PMG 56/1–9
Employees' and widows' pensions:	1830–7	ADM 23/1–2
	1847–1926	ADM 23/3–16, 56–70 and 108–91
Employees' retirement pensions:	1830–7	ADM 23/1–2
	1836–1928	PMG 25/1–101
	1847–1926	ADM 23/3–16, 56–70 and 108–91
(nursing sisters)	1878–1932	ADM 23/83–8, 161–7 and 172
Hospital pharmacists' services	1845–1957	ADM 104/159–60
Admiralty second division clerks, services	1876–1913	ADM 7/924
Nursing sisters' services:	1884–1909	ADM 104/43
	1894–1959	ADM 104/161
(QARNNS Reserve)	1914–19	ADM 104/162–5
Massage sisters	1917–25	ADM 104/171
Selected civilian personnel files		ADM 310

234 Appendix IV: Royal Marine Service Records

Seniority lists of officers	1757–1850	ADM 118/230–336
Lists of officers	1760–1886	ADM 192/1–44
Discharge certificates	1761–1843	ADM 193/18
Attestation papers:	1790–1925	ADM 157/1–3625
(indexes)	1834–1925	ADM 313/1–26
Description books	1790–1940	ADM 158/1–299
Registers of service:	1842–1936	ADM 159/1–213
	1879–1966	ADM 196/97–116
(indexes):	1843–1925	ADM 313/27–30
	1842–1925	ADM 313/79–84

	1914–18	ADM 313/109
(RMA)	1798–1870	ADM 196/66
(indexes, RMA):	1859–1923	ADM 313/52–4
	1904–23	ADM 196/110

235 Appendix V: Committees and Commissions

This is an incomplete chronological list of the records of all sorts of non-permanent naval committees, commissions, boards of enquiry and the like, particularly those whose records are in unlikely places; it does not include those in series consisting wholly of *ad hoc* committee records, such as ADM 268, CAB 16 or DEFE 10.

Commission of Naval Enquiry	1608	SP 14/41 and ADM 7/825
Commission of Naval Enquiry:	1618	SP 14/100–1 and ADM 7/826
[Large extracts of these two are printed by A P McGowan, *The Jacobean Commissions of Enquiry* (NRS, 116, 1971).]		
(declared accounts)	1618	AO 1/1830/546–8
Commission of Naval Enquiry:	1626–8	SP 16/45
(declared accounts):	1626–8	E 351/1274
	1626–8	AO 1/861/1
Northumberland Enquiry	1636	SP 16/336–8
Enquiries under special commission	1636	C 205/14/14 and 17–19
Commissioners for Discharging the Navy, payments	1661–3	SP 46/138
Bounty Commissioners, accounts	1673–4	ADM 17/13
Public Accounts Commissioners, report on Lord Orford's Treasurership of the Navy	1689–1704	T 38/614–15
Committee on Navy and Army Debts:	1713–14	ADM 114/13, ADM 17/223–5, ADM 49/37–40, 169 and 173
East Florida Claims Commission, correspondence from Navy Pay Office	1763–83	T 77/23–9
Commission on Fees in Public Offices: clerks' fees	1785–6	ADM 49/36
(Sick and Hurt and Victualling)	1787	ADM 49/172
(seventh report)	1788	ADM 7/412
Commissioners of Woods and Forests:	1787–93	CRES 28/1–8
(declared accounts)	1786–94	AO 1/861/3
Select Committee on Public Finance: (reorganisation of Navy Office etc.)	1796–1801	ADM 2/1393
(Sick and Hurt Board and RNH)	1797	ADM 102/844
French Refugees Relief Committee, naval papers	1797	T 93/55
Commission of Naval Enquiry:	1802–5	ADM 1/4078–9
	1805	ADM 106/2064
(Sick and Hurt Board and RNH)	1798–1805	ADM 102/844

(papers)	1803–11	ADM 106/3111–16
(declared accounts)	1805–6	AO 1/861/7
Prize Agency Commission, accounts	1803–4	AO 1/861/6
Committee on Ships' Store Establishments, Rigging Warrants etc.:	1814	ADM 106/3574
	1814–16	ADM 106/3549/2
	1829–30	ADM 106/3549/1
Committee on Navy Office Clerks	1817	ADM 106/3515
Transport Accounts Committee reports to Admiralty	1817–18	ADM 1/3770–1
Committee on Slop Clothing	1820	ADM 106/3510
Committee on Warrant Officers' Accounts	1823	ADM 106/3573
Commission on Book-Keeping, Victualling Department and Navy Pay Office	1827–30	T 92/153B–155
GH Committee	1829	ADM 67/259
Report on prevention of dry rot	1837	RAIL 1124/14
Nelson Memorial Committee	1838–44	WORK 6/119
Lightning Committee	1839	ADM 1/607
Committee on Naval Architecture, letters	1842–4	ADM 7/577
Committee on Communication between London and Dublin, Admiralty correspondence	1842–63	MT 27/38 and 126
Committee on Accounts and Audit sixth report, Naval Ordnance Department	1845	T 172/933
La Beche-Playfair Report on Coal for the Navy	1848	RAIL 1059/2
Committee on Coast Defence, reports	1852–3	WO 55/1563/7
Special Commission into Ships Building for Russia	1854	C 205/3/14
Phinn Committee on Admiralty Secretariat	1855	ADM 1/5660
Committee on Naval Contracts	1857	ADM 114/12
Royal Commission on Harbours of Refuge	1858–9	ADM 7/720–1
Committee on Ordnance	1859	WO 33/7
Admiralty Committee on Dockyard Economy	1859	ADM 49/178
Royal Commission on GH	1859–65	ADM 76/5
Committee on Venereal Disease in the Army and Navy:	1863	WO 33/12
	1866	WO 33/17A
GH Joint Committee	1864–71	ADM 67/279, ADM 80/167 and 173
Committee on Floating Obstructions and Submarine Explosive Machines	1866	WO 33/17A
Admiralty Secretary's Department Committee	1869	ADM 7/996
Committee on Fitting Troop Ships to Carry Horses	1870	WO 33/21A
Slave Trade Instructions Commission	1881–2	FO 317/3
Channel Tunnel Defence Committee	1882	ADM 1/8370/57
Hayter Committee on RM Officers' Pay etc.:	1883–4	WO 32/6277
	1883	WO 33/41

Select Committee on Admiralty Expenditure and Liabilities	1885	ADM 7/952
Inter-Departmental Committee on Receipt of Naval or Military Pay with Civil Salary	1885	WO 33/44
Committee on Admiralty Financial Arrangements	1885	ADM 7/952
Boat Armament Committee	1885	ADM 179/1
Ratings' Widows' Pensions Committee	1886	ADM 76/15
Northcote Inter-Departmental Committee on Transfer of Naval Armaments to Admiralty:	1886	WO 33/46
	1886–7	WO 32/7030
Royal Commission on Naval and Military Administration:	1888–90	HO 73/35/1–36/5
	1892	HO 45/9791/B4267
Committee on Pay etc. of Medical Officers in Army and Navy	1889	WO 33/49
Committee on the Assimilation of Army and Navy Stores	1890	WO 33/50
Committee on Purchase, Custody and Accounts of Naval Stores	1890–5	WO 32/7031
Select Committee on GH Pensions	1892	ADM 76/16/1
Committee on Naval Magazine Accommodation	1895	ADM 179/127
Skey Committee on Venereal Disease in Army and RN	1896–9	WO 32/6210
Inter-Departmental Committee on Losses of Army and Navy Stores	1897	WO 33/77
Inter-Departmental Committee on Payment of Army and Navy Pensions	1898	WO 33/143
Admiralty-WO Conference on Coast Defence of UK	1900	WO 33/189
Naval Prize Law Committee:	1900–4	FO 83/1880 and 1978
	1900–4	PC 10/17–20
Admiralty-WO Conference on Naval and Army Meat Reserves at Gibraltar	1902	WO 33/237
Antarctic Relief Committee	1903	ADM 7/934–5
Naval and Military Conference on Overseas Expeditions	1905	WO 33/344
Committee on Armaments of Home Ports	1905	SUPP 6/645
Joint Admiralty-WO Committee on Instruction for Royal Garrison Artillery	1905	WO 33/385
Joint Naval and Military Committee on Control of Signalling at Defended Ports Abroad	1905	WO 32/7170
Committee on the Training of Naval Cadets	1905–6	ED 24/170A
Ruck Committee on Transfer of Submarine Mining to RN:	1904–5	WO 33/341 and 366–7
	1905–6	WO 32/6364
Naval Ordnance Committee	1905–12	SUPP 5/161 and 163

Hydrographic Department Committee	1906	ADM 268/1
Joint Naval-Military Conference on Regulation of Traffic at Defended Ports	1906–8	WO 33/398 and 450
Ward Committee on Naval Pensions	1906–21	WO 32/11204, 11212–17 and 11230
Committee on Armament of Defended Ports Abroad	1907	SUPP 6/645
Committee on Canteens and Victualling	1907	ADM 174/404
Magazine Committee	c.1907	ADM 179/127
(Beresford) Naval Policy Inquiry	1909	CAB 16/9A–9B
Conference on Pay of Admiralty and WO Employees	1911	WO 32/7065
Admiralty Committee on Aeronautics	1912	AIR 1/656/17/122/541
Admiralty Oil Committee	1912–13	ADM 265/29–30
Joint Naval and Military Committee on the Examination Service	1913	WO 33/652
WO-Admiralty Conference on Compensation for Damage done by Gunfire	1913	WO 33/658
Royal Commission on Fuel and Engines	1913	ADM 265/32–5
'High Level Bridge' Admiralty-WO Conference:	1913–14	WO 32/5294
	1913–14	CAB 18/27
Court of Enquiry, Morbeke Affair	1914	ADM 137/4824
Committee on Dazzle Painting of Ships	1915–20	ADM 245/4
Admiralty Air Constructional Equipment Committee	1916	AIR 1/146/15/51
Cabinet Committee on Naval and Military Pensions	1916	PIN 4/111
Admiralty War Staff/General Staff Conference on Possibility of Attack on UK	1916	WO 33/742
Committee on Projectiles	1916–17	ADM 137/3834–8
Dardanelles Commission	1916–19	CAB 19/1 and 28–33
Allied Naval and Shipping Conference	1917	CAB 21/9
Admiralty Reconstruction Committee	1917–19	ADM 137/3943A–3955
Admiralty Dardanelles Committee	1919	AIR 1/2323/223/41/1550–1
Joint Service Dardanelles Committee:	1919	WO 158/796
	1919–25	WO 32/5132–3
Royal Commission on Awards to Inventors: (Tomlin Commission)	1919–37	T 173/1–830
(Morris Committee)	1927–40	T 288/1–17
(Cohen Commission)	1939–55	T 166/10, 12 and 79
Blockade Advisory Committee	1919	BT 60/1/4
Colwyn Committee on Admiralty Labour Problems	1919	BT 65/2
International Danube Commission, Troubridge Mission	1920	BT 65/5
Capital Ship Committee	1920–1	CAB 16/37/1–3
Reparation Commission, British Delegation: pensions to naval etc. victims of the war	1920	T 194/45
(SS *Rio Pardo* sunk by German Navy)	1921	T 194/205

(compensation for ships scuttled at Scapa Flow)	1922	T 194/234
Weir Committee on Admiralty, WO and Air Ministry Establishments	1920–3	T 163/11/4 and 16/14
Balfour Committee on RN-RAF Relations:	1923	CAB 16/48
	1923–4	AIR 8/66
RNC Greenwich Committee on Overhead Charges and Accommodation	1924	ADM 203/16
Colwyn Committee on RN, Army and RAF Expenditure	1925	AIR 19/120–2
Singapore Naval Base Committee	1925–8	CAB 16/63
Inter-Departmental Committee on Research, Design etc. of Guns and Ammunition	1925–9	T 162/120
Admiralty Transport Arbitration Board	1927	T 80/10
Conference on Supply of Duty-Free Stores to RN	1933–5	CUST 155/44, 47 and 49/2393
Royal Commission on Arms Manufacture (Bankes Commission), Admiralty memoranda	1935	T 181/11
Committee on Vulnerability of Capital Ships to Air Attack	1936	CAB 21/425
Inter-Departmental Committee on Admiralty and RAF Flying Danger Areas	1937–9	AVIA 2/1230
Development of Alexandria Harbour Committee	1938	CAB 16/192
Anglo-French Joint Service Conference, Singapore	1939	WO 33/2338
Toraplane and Doraplane Development Committee:	1939–40	ADM 179/137 and 147
	1939–42	AVIA 53/202
Wodehouse Committee on Life-Saving	1940–1	ADM 1/11127
Air-Sea Interception Committee:	1941–2	AVIA 10/56
	1941–3	AVIA 15/1470
Committee on the Care of Shipwrecked Personnel	1942	ADM 1/12193
Operation OVERLORD, Joint Planning Committee minutes	1943–4	HO 186/1699 and 1702
Evershed Report on Internal Organisation of Naval Aviation	1944–5	HMC 3/14–17
Talbot Committee on Naval Life-Saving Equipment	1945–6	ADM 319/1 and ADM 1/19235
Bombay Dockyard Re-organisation Committee	1947	ADM 7/944
Committee on Admiralty Experimental Establishments:	1946–9	ADM 220/63
	1948	ADM 282/19
Naval Air Tactical Conference	1948	AIR 65/312
US Naval Technical Mission to Japan	1948	HO 228/2
Leech-Porter Committee on RM Band Service	1949	ADM 201/121
Working Party on Submarine Propulsion	1951	ADM 265/52–5
Strang Report on Wartime Control of Radiation, Admiralty evidence	1954	CAB 125/167
Defence Review Committee, naval aircraft	1954–5	AVIA 65/70
Wilson Committee on Noise, Admiralty evidence	1961	MH 146/180

Fleet Requirements Committee	1961–3	DEFE 24/8
Martell Report on Service Propellants	1962	SUPP 5/1265
Logistic Ship Staff Requirement Committee, trials of LSL	1962–4	WO 32/20350
National Incomes Commission, Admiralty evidence on dockyard pay	1963	NICO 1/6–7
Third Naval Air Conference	1964	ADM 335/55
Future Fleet Working Party	1966–8	DEFE 24/128, 149–50, 194, 234–5 and 238–9
Committee of Inquiry into Trawler Safety, RN evidence	1968	BT 149/30 and 69
FAA Working Party, reports	1968–9	DEFE 24/363–5
Malabar Committee on Government Industrial Establishments:	1969–71	BA 2/1–9
	1970–1	BA 26/20
	1970–1	T 316/140
Defence Lands Review Committee, Navy	1971–3	DEFE 57/12 and 16
Committee on Human Engineering Research	1971–7	ADM 105/98
RN catering frauds, Committee of Enquiry	1972–3	DEFE 24/282
Fleet Requirements Committee	1975	DEFE 24/687
RNR Review Committee	1975–6	DEFE 49/95

236 Appendix VI: Personal Collections

This is a list of collections of documents, naval or bearing on naval matters, made by or pertaining to named individuals. Some of them are private papers, but the majority are either personal collections of official correspondence, or official papers relating to business with a single individual.

ABBOT, Charles, 1st Baron COLCHESTER, Chief Secretary for Ireland, 1801–2:		
Intelligence of planned Franco-Spanish invasion	1801	PRO 30/9/132
Irish naval affairs, including *Temeraire* Mutiny	1801–2	PRO 30/9/105–73
ABBOT, Captain Charles, 2nd Baron COLCHESTER, journals, correspondence etc.	1812–44	PRO 30/9/3–8, 20–2 and 49–52
ACLAND, Captain W A D, HMS *Australia*, papers concerning visits to Lisbon and Brest	1895–7	ADM 179/19B
ALEXANDER, General Harold, 1st Earl Alexander of Tunis, Supreme Allied Commander Mediterranean, 1944–5, including naval matters, North African, Sicilian and Italian campaigns	1942–51	WO 214/1–71
AMHERST, General Jeffrey, 1st Baron, correspondence, including some naval	1712–86	WO 34/1–260
ANDERSON, Sir Alan, Controller of the Navy, 1917–18:		
Correspondence with Director of Naval Transports	1916	PRO 30/68/2

Papers as Controller	1917–18	PRO 30/68/21
ARDAGH, Major-General Sir John, correspondence with Admiral Lord Charles Beresford	1883–99	PRO 30/40/2–3 and 10
ARNOLD, Dr. James, of the HCA, notes on prize appeals	1786–1829	HCA 30/468–74
ASHLEY COOPER, Anthony, 1st Earl of SHAFTESBURY, as Vice-Admiral of Dorset:		
List of HM Ships	1631	PRO 30/24/7
Lists of seamen in Dorset, including pressed:	1664–5	PRO 30/24/7
	1673	PRO 30/24/7
BAILLIE, Captain Thomas, allegations against GH investigated	1778–9	ADM 80/92–3
BALL, Captain Alexander, HMS *Alexander*, letter book	1796–1800	ADM 7/55
BANKS, Sir Joseph, President of the Royal Society, correspondence including with Admiralty and RN officers	1764–1820	RM 3/1–21
BAXTER, Alexander, Gunner RN, papers	c.1790–1805	C 108/21
BEAVERBROOK, William Aitken, Lord, Minister for Aircraft Production, note on FAA requirements	1941	CAB 127/252
BENTHAM, George, botanist, correspondence including with Admiralty, RN officers etc.	1799–1897	RM 4/1–64
BRENTON, Captain Sir Jahleel, Commissioner, Cape of Good Hope Station, reports:	1811–13	ADM 123/42
	1815–22	ADM 7/2–6
BRIDGES, Sir Edward, Secretary of the Cabinet, later Permanent Secretary of the Treasury, appointment of Senior Admiralty Staff	1945–56	T 273/73
BRINE, Robert, Navy Agent, papers	1798–1822	C 114/6–8, 89–93, 105–11 and 159–63
BUCHAN, Captain David, Senior Officer Newfoundland, letter book	1822–3	ADM 80/130
BURNETT, Sir William, Physician-General of the Navy, medical reports	1822–53	ADM 105/68–73
BYNG, Admiral George, Viscount TORRINGTON, C-in-C Baltic and Mediterranean, reports	1715–40 (chiefly 1717–29)	ADM 1/518
CANNING, Stratford, 1st Viscount STRATFORD de REDCLIFFE, diplomat, correspondence, including British, French and Russian officers and naval authorities	1810–58	FO 352/1–46
CHAMBERLAIN, Sir Austen, Foreign Secretary, papers on naval disarmament conferences etc.	1924–9	FO 800/256–63
COCHRANE, Hon. Basil, Agent-Victualler East Indies, dispute with Victualling Board:	1790–1820	ADM 7/40 and 991
	1813–16	ADM 114/3–4
	1818–22	T 64/207

CODRINGTON, Vice-Admiral Sir Edward, C-in-C Mediterranean:		
Correspondence with Admiralty, Foreign Office etc.	1826–9	ADM 1/467–9
Letter to I K Brunel	1828	RAIL 1008/79
COLLINGWOOD, Admiral Cuthbert, Lord, correspondence as C-in-C Mediterranean with Secretary for War	1808	CO 173/2
COLLINS, Grenville, Master RN, journal	1676–9	ADM 7/688
CORBETT, Thomas, Secretary of the Admiralty, digest of important orders and precedents	1660–1741	ADM 12/36B
CORNWALLIS, Charles, 1st Marquis, correspondence including naval and combined operations	c.1777–99	PRO 30/11/1–292
CORNWALLIS, Admiral Hon. William, letters to his brother Marquis Cornwallis	1781–97	PRO 30/11/275
COTTON, Admiral Sir Charles, C-in-C Mediterranean, correspondence	1808–12	ADM 7/41–6 and 50–2
CUNNINGHAM, John, Navy Agent, correspondence	1758–65	E 140/15/5
DALE, Sir Henry, member of the Cabinet Scientific Advisory Committee, notes on naval research and development	1944–5	CAB 127/232
D'AUVERGNE, Rear-Admiral Philip, styled Prince de Bouillon, C-in-C Channel Isles, correspondence:	1793–1815	FO 95/602–33
	1794–1801	HO 44/42–4
(with Audit Office)	1798	WO 1/878
(letters from Secretary for War)	1798	WO 6/214
(letters to Admiralty):	1799–1801	FO 95/612
	1811–12	FO 95/625
(letters to RN officers)	1800–1	FO 95/616
(letters from Admiralty)	1808–12	FO 95/622, 624
(intelligence etc.):	1786–1809	PC 1/115–22
	1788	FO 95/2/3
	1793	FO 95/3/2
	c.1793–9	PC 1/134–5
	1793–1802	HO 69/1–32
	1794–1814	PC 1/4490–516
	1794–1815	WO 1/917–26
	1794–1815	ADM 1/221–9
	1799–1806	FO 95/615, 618 and 629
(French emigrés):	1794–1809	HO 69/33–9
	1799–1806	T 64/354
DELAVALL, Admiral Sir Ralph, Joint C-in-C Allied Main Fleet, letter book	1693	ADM 7/694
DE WINTER, Vice-Admiral Jan Willem, correspondence as C-in-C of Dutch Fleet	1795–6	ADM 1/3244

DILL, Field Marshal Sir John, correspondence with Admiralty, Air Ministry etc.	1936	WO 282/4
DOUGLAS, Andrew Snape, British Chargé d'Affaires in Palermo and Naples, 1811–22, correspondence with and concerning RN and Neapolitan officers, naval authorities etc.	1811–22	PRO 30/7/1-2
DRAKE, Sir Francis: tax records	1585	E 179/146/269
(will)	1595–6	PROB 1/2
DUNDAS, Admiral Sir James W, probate file	1863	J 121/709
EKINES, Captain Thomas, accounts and papers	1699–1724	C 107/171
EYRES-MONSELL, Sir Bolton, First Lord of the Admiralty, correspondence with Sir R Keyes on Invergordon Mutiny	1932–4	ADM 230/1
FENNING, William, underwriter's notebook	1799	C 108/24
FINCH, Daniel, of the Navy Pay Office, private and semi-official in-letters	1728–9	SP 46/161/9
FITZROY, Captain Robert:		
Correspondence and papers	1843–81	BJ 7/1-1070
Dispatches as Governor of New Zealand	1845	CO 209/36
FLINDERS, Commander Matthew, narrative of imprisonment	1806	ADM 7/707-8
FROBISHER, Captain Martin, tax records	1588	E 179/396/4 m. 4
GALLOWAY, Captain Patrick, of *Sarah Galley* privateer, letters from owners	1702–3	C 108/318
GEORGE, Captain Sir Rupert, Chairman of Transport Board, out-letter book	1796–1806	ADM 108/30
GILLESPIE, Dr. Leonard, private diary	1785–1803	ADM 101/102/1-12
GOODALL, Stanley, Naval Constructor, reports on US shipbuilding	1917–20	ADM 229/97-9
GORREQUER, Lieutenant-Colonel Gideon, records of conversations with RN and Army officers	1807–41	J 76/5/4 and 8/2
GREET, Commander William, commanding HM Ships *Perseus* and *Crocodile*, Captain's letter books	1847–57	ADM 7/56-7
GREY, Sir Edward, Foreign Secretary, Admiralty correspondence	1905–16	FO 800/87-8
HAMILTON, Vice-Admiral Sir Charles, Governor and C-in-C of Newfoundland:		
Letter and order books	1818–24	ADM 80/125-9
Admiral's journals	1819–24	ADM 80/160-3
HANKEY, Maurice, Lord, Secretary of the Cabinet, 1916–38, papers	1908–44	CAB 63/1-193
HARMSWORTH, Cecil, Under-Secretary of State, Foreign Office, 'The Blockade'	1919	FO 800/250
HERBERT, Henry, 4th Earl of CARNARVON, Colonial Secretary, 1866–7 and 1874–8:		
Admiralty memoranda for Cabinet	1874–7	PRO 30/6/115
Correspondence with First Lord of the Admiralty	1874–8	PRO 30/6/5

Map showing RN stations etc.	1879–80	PRO 30/6/131
HERVEY, Captain John Augustus, Lord:		
Correspondence as SNO St. Lawrence	1778–91	FO 528/22
Correspondence as British Minister to Tuscany, relating to occupation of Toulon	1792–4	FO 528/13–17
HOOKER, Sir William, Director of the Royal Botanical Gardens, correspondence including with Admiralty, RN officers etc.:	1805–1980	RM 6/1–40
	c.1825–c.1925	RM 5/1–155
HOPE, Captain Herbert, of Room 40, diary and papers	1914–17	ADM 137/4168–71
HOSTE, Captain Sir William, grant of baronetcy	1814	ADM 106/3536
HOWE, Admiral Richard, Earl:		
As C-in-C North America, orders, signals, line of battle, etc.	1778	ADM 106/3544/1
As C-in-C Channel, standing orders	1782	ADM 7/582/1–6
HUGHES, Vice-Admiral Sir Edward, order and letter books, logs and journals	1747–85	ADM 7/733–63
HULTON, H, Receiver of Sixpences in North America, correspondence	1768–83	ADM 80/131–2
HULTON-SAMS, G H:		
Midshipman's journals in HMS *Aurora*	1899–1902	ADM 7/954–5
Lieutenant's journal in HMS *Algerine*	1908–10	ADM 7/956
HUNTER, William, Navy Office Clerk, frauds	1793–1808	ADM 49/12
ISMAY, General Sir Hastings, Secretary of Chiefs of Staff Committee, etc.:		
Letter regarding 1914 RN mobilisation	1935	T 273/386
Correspondence with Vice-Admiral R L Ghormley, USN	1941	CAB 127/16
JACKSON, F J:		
Correspondence with Hood and Hotham as C-in-C Mediterranean	1792–5	FO 353/72
Naval affairs in Baltic	c.1806–8	FO 353/80
JAMES, Duke of York, Lord Admiral of England and Scotland, private out-letters	1660–85	ADM 2/1745–6
JOHNSTONE, Commodore George, reports from Cape expedition	1781	ADM 1/54
JOHNSTONE, Dr. James, Sick and Hurt Agent at Portsmouth, 'memorandum book'	1795–6	ADM 102/846
JONES, Flight-Lieutenant H A, RAF, photographs and papers on carrier flying	1934	AIR 1/719/35/11–12 and 720/35/19
KEATS, Vice-Admiral Sir Richard, letter books:	1789–1809	ADM 80/133–50
	1804	ADM 80/141
	1815–16	ADM 80/151

KEITH, Vice-Admiral George Keith Elphinstone, Viscount:		
Order book	1800–3	ADM 80/152
Letters from Rear-Admiral B S Rowley	1805	ADM 151/1
KEPPEL, Captain Hon. Augustus, reports from West Africa expedition	1758	ADM 1/54
KEPPEL, Captain George, orders received	1778	ADM 106/3544/1
KERGUELEN DE TREMAREC, Captain Yves-Joseph, Comte de, correspondence and papers	c.1750–81	SP 46/146–8
KEYES, Admiral Sir Roger:		
Correspondence with Sir B Eyres-Monsell on Invergordon Mutiny	1932–4	ADM 230/1
Correspondence as Director of Combined Operations	1942	DEFE 2/698
KILLIGREW, Admiral Henry, Joint C-in-C Allied Main Fleet, letter book	1693	ADM 7/694
KING, Captain Richard, reports from Cape	1783	ADM 1/54
KITCHENER, General Horatio Herbert, Lord:		
Dardanelles campaign papers	1915	PRO 30/57/59–66
Correspondence with Churchill, Fisher, Beresford, Jellicoe, Battenberg	1914–15	PRO 20/57/72 and 80
LAW, Edward, 1st Earl of ELLENBOROUGH, First Lord of the Admiralty 1846:		
Correspondence	1844–6	PRO 30/12/4–6, 11 and 34
Patronage books	1846	PRO 30/12/5
LINDEMANN, Professor F A, papers including Coastal Command, FAA etc.	1940	AIR 8/470
LORAINE, Sir Percy, diplomat, correspondence with Lord Herschell of NID	1917–18	FO 1011/278
LUARD, Commander W B, Naval Operations Liaison Officer Coastal Command, papers	1940–53	ADM 333/1–13
McCULLOCK, Robert, navy agent, merchant, postmaster and naval officer at Charleston SC, papers	1772–82	C 106/87–90
MACDONALD, James Ramsay, Prime Minister 1924 and 1929–35, papers:		
Pamphlets on naval defence etc.	1896–1935	PRO 30/69/1833
Map of Spithead review, June	1911	MPI 1/469
Naval policy	1924	PRO 30/69/47–9
Anglo-American Conference, warship orders etc.	1927	PRO 30/69/1437
London Naval Conference, photographs:	1930	PRO 30/69/1671/10 and 13
	1930	PRO 30/69/1668/282
MacGILLIVRAY, John, naturalist aboard HMS *Herald* in Pacific, journal	1852–5	ADM 7/851–2

MACKENZIE, Flight-Commander C R, RNAS, papers	1915–18	AIR 1/686/21/13/2249
MALCOLM, Sir Ian, British Government Director of Suez Canal Company, 1919–39: letters from Admiralty etc.	1919–38	T 206/1–23
MASTER, Sir H, estate	1720–5	ADM 80/115
MASTERTON-SMITH, J E, First Lord's Private Secretary, papers	1909–19	CAB 1/31–4
MILLER, D G, Assistant Surgeon RN, remarks on West Coast of Africa	1830–1	ADM 105/92
MORESBY, Captain Fairfax, narrative of early British settlement in Cape Province	1820	ADM 1/5123/7
MOSTYN, Sir Roger, Paymaster of Marines, regimental accounts etc.	1705–45	ADM 96/1–2 and 112
NAPIER, Vice-Admiral Sir Charles, C-in-C Baltic:		
Letter book	1854	ADM 7/769
Correspondence, maps and plans	c.1854–8	PRO 30/16/1–23
NARBROUGH, Captain John, HM Ships *Prince* and *St. Michael*, journals	1672–3	ADM 7/731
NELSON, Vice-Admiral Horatio Viscount:		
Chart of St. John's Harbour	1784	MPI 1/95
Letter to Directors of East India Company	1786 (5 May)	PRO 30/70/1/5
Pension	1797 (11 October)	PC 1/40/129
Dispatches as C-in-C Mediterranean	1803–4	CO 173/1
Diary and will	1803–6	PROB 1/22
Organisation of his funeral	1805–6	WORK 6/362/2 and 184/10
Annuity to his descendants:	1806–16	TS 11/317–35
	1890–1956	T 248/135–8
NEWSON, Captain Thomas, Master Mariner, papers	c.1720–40	C 104/77–80
NICHOL, Sir John, Judge of the HCA, case notes	1781–1817	HCA 30/464–7
NICHOLAS, Sir Edward, Secretary of the Admiralty, 1625–38, out-letters	1624–60	SP 14/215
NICHOLSON, Robert, Master RN, correspondence	1758–65	E 140/15/5
NORRIS, Sir John, reports as C-in-C Mediterranean, Channel and Baltic	1711–27	ADM 1/2–3
NOURSE, Commodore Joseph, C-in-C Cape of Good Hope, correspondence etc.	1816–24	ADM 7/47–8 and 53–4
O'CONNOR, Midshipman J J, log in HMS *Royal Sovereign*	1807–9	ADM 305/82
OFFORD, D E J, Superintendent of Admiralty Underwater Explosion Research Establishment, papers	1918–53	ADM 311/1–12
OSBORNE, Sir Thomas, Treasurer of the Navy, papers	1668–73	PRO 30/32/1–4
PALMER, Sub-Lieutenant A J, RNVR, medical records	1916–17	WO 339/73853
PALMER, Lieutenant George, examination papers	1779	ADM 49/171

PENN, Vice-Admiral Sir William, papers	c.1619–71	ADM 7/729
PETRIE, James, logs etc. aboard HM Ships	1788–98	PRO 30/17/5–6
PETT, Peter, Purveyor of Navy, 1607–18, enquiry into timber purchases	1636	C 205/14/14
PICKMORE, Vice-Admiral Francis, letter book	1816–23	ADM 80/153–5
PITT, John, 2nd Earl of Chatham, First Lord of the Admiralty, 1788–94:		
Naval papers	c.1790–1815	PRO 30/8/246–59 and 364–9
Walcheren correspondence	1809	PRO 30/8/260–3
PITT, William, 1st Earl of Chatham, naval papers	c.1750–95	PRO 30/8/246–59
POPHAM, Rear-Admiral Sir Home:		
Copy of Spanish printed Caribbean sailing directions	1810	ADM 80/118
Letter book as C-in-C Jamaica	1817–20	ADM 80/156–8
POTTINGER, Sir Henry, Governor of Hong Kong, correspondence with C-in-C China:	1841–4	FO 705/60, 63, 69 and 73
(index)	1841–3	FO 705/45
POVEY, Richard, Treasurer of Sick and Hurt Board, accounts and papers	1702–4	C 112/181/17
RAINIER, Admiral Peter, C-in-C East Indies, correspondence:		
(with Marquis Wellesley)	1801–8	ADM 1/5121/5
(with East India Company Governors)	1804–6	ADM 1/175
RODNEY, Admiral George Brydges, Lord:		
Journals and correspondence	1742–92	PRO 30/20/1–26
Letters to Admiralty	1782	PRO 30/97/3
Biographical notes by G B Mundy	1828–30	PRO 30/97/1–4
ROGERS, Captain Woodes, accounts of *Duke*, *Duchess* and *Marquess* privateers of Bristol	1708–15	C 104/36–40 and 160–1
ROOKE, Admiral Sir George, Secretary's journal	1700–2	ADM 10/11
ROSS, Captain Sir James Clark, correspondence and papers	1833–75	BJ 2/1–14
ROWLEY, Rear-Admiral B S, letters to Lord Keith	1805	ADM 151/1
RUSSELL, Admiral Hon Edward:		
Order book as C-in-C Allied Main Fleet	1692	ADM 7/692
Public Accounts Commissioners, report on his Treasurership of the Navy	1689–1704	T 38/614–15
as Earl of ORFORD, bequest to GH	1747	ADM 76/14
RUSSELL, Odo, 1st Baron AMPTHILL, correspondence with First Lord of the Admiralty etc.	1871–83	FO 918/18, 34, 36, 58, 61, 63 and 78
SABINE, Sir Edward, scientist and explorer, correspondence and papers	1818–77	BJ 3/1–84

SAMSON, Wing Captain C R, RNAS, later Air Commodore RAF, reminiscences	1911–23	AIR 1/724/76/1–6
SCOTT, William, Lord STOWELL, notebooks on Admiralty cases	c.1780–1820	HCA 30/1041–2
SEPPINGS, Robert, Surveyor of the Navy, describing his 'system of shipbuilding'	c.1812	ADM 7/709
SEYMOUR, Rear-Admiral Sir George, C-in-C Pacific, correspondence and papers	1843–58	ADM 172/1–4
SHAFTESBURY, 1st Earl of, see ASHLEY COOPER, Anthony, Vice-Admiral of Dorset		
SHOVELL, Rear-Admiral Sir Cloudesley, Joint C-in-C Allied Main Fleet, letter book	1693	ADM 7/694
SIMON, Sir John, Foreign Secretary, papers on naval disarmament conferences etc.	1931–5	FO 800/285–91
SLADE, Sir Thomas, Surveyor of the Navy, memoranda on fittings, stores, etc.:	1750–64	ADM 95/17
	1757–70	ADM 106/2895
	1762–5	ADM 49/32
SLESSOR, Air Marshal Sir John, AOC Coastal Command, papers:		
Seaplanes and the RAF	1914–45	AIR 75/129
RAF/Navy controversies	1941–52	AIR 75/17
Maritime Air-RAF relations	1942–61	AIR 75/12–20
FAA carrier policy	1952–3	AIR 75/16
NATO and western union	1963–5	AIR 75/80
Draft article 'The Case against Carriers'	1964	AIR 75/89
SMITH, George, Chief Clerk, Navy Office, correspondence	1807	ADM 49/169 and 182
SMITH, W H, First Lord of the Admiralty, papers on reorganisation of Army and RN	1883–8	WO 110/8
STOPFORD, Admiral Sir Robert, Governor of GH, letter book	1841–6	ADM 80/159
SUETER, Commodore Sir Murray, Inspecting Captain of Aeronautics, 1912, Superintendent of Aircraft Production, 1915–17, papers	1908–17	AIR 1/7 and 2435–662
SWABEY, H M, Deputy Registrar of HCA, papers	1750–1835	HCA 30/1001
THOMPSON, Robert, Master of HMS *Gloucester*, journal	1698–1700	ADM 7/833
TIRPITZ, Admiral Alfred von, letters	1871–1919	GFM 25/8
TIZARD, Sir Henry, papers on anti-shipping weapons	1941–3	AIR 20/2343 and 2350–1
TOWNSEND, Spencer George, Receiver of Fees of the Navy Office, accounts and papers	1793–1807	ADM 106/3550/1–2
TREVOR, Captain John, HMS *Defiance*, letter book	1739–40	ADM 7/781
VEYSEY, Commander John, papers	c.1750–70	C 108/23

WAGER, Admiral Sir Charles, First Lord of the Admiralty, official and semi-official correspondence	1726–43	SP 42/81–4
WARNEFORD, Flight-Sub-Lieutenant R A J, VC, RNAS, newspaper cuttings relating to his service	1915–17	PRO 30/71/7
WARREN, Major Joseph de, accounts and correspondence concerning his mission to buy ex-French masts in Königsberg	1814–17	ADM 49/107
WATSON-WATT, Sir Robert, radar for FAA and Coastal Command	1942–3	AVIA 10/64 and 69
WELLESLEY, Henry, 1st Baron COWLEY, British Ambassador to France, papers on the French Navy	1839–46	FO 519/70
WELLESLEY, Henry, 2nd Baron and 1st Earl COWLEY, British Ambassador to France, correspondence from Admiralty etc.	1852–69	FO 519/208
WENTWORTH, John, expenses surveying timber in Nova Scotia	1783–93	ADM 49/8
WHITE, Lieutenant Charles of HMS *Vestal*, charts, log etc.	1788	PRO 30/8/258
WHITE, Captain Thomas, deposition	1816	ADM 7/773
WHITMARSH, Dr. John, private medical journal of fever outbreak at Gibraltar	1813	ADM 105/25
WILLIAM HENRY, Captain Prince, HMS *Andromeda*, letter book	1788–9	ADM 80/120
WISHART, Admiral Sir James, correspondence as Naval Envoy to the Netherlands	1711–12	SP 84/237
WOLSELEY, Field Marshal Sir Garnet, Viscount:		
Admiralty papers on Nile expedition	1884–5	WO 147/43
NID reports	1886–9	WO 147/50
WOOD, Dr. A B, scientific reports and papers	1912–64	ADM 218/1–310
WYNDHAM, Charles, 2nd Earl of EGREMONT, Secretary of State, 1761–3:		
Papers concerning Havana and Manila expeditions	1762–3	PRO 30/47/18/5 and 20/3
Naval papers	1761–3	PRO 30/47/23/1–5

Index

This index is predominantly in natural word order, but many subject entries have been grouped under the headings of Admiralty and Royal Navy. Principal references are in bold type. Ships' names refer to HM Ships unless otherwise indicated, with the date of launch or mention for identification. Officers are of the Royal Navy unless otherwise indicated; ranks are distinguished from employments by initial capitals. The index was prepared by Moira Bracknall. REFERENCES ARE TO LIST NUMBERS, NOT PAGES.

Abbot, Captain Charles, 2nd Baron Colchester, 236; Charles, 1st Baron Colchester, Chief Secretary for Ireland, 236
Aboukir (1900), 186
absenteeism in shipyards, 195
Abyssinia, 23, 35, 128; *see also* Ethiopian Navy
Accident Investigation Branch, 70
accident reports, 204; naval aircraft, 204
accommodation, 196, 201; for Admiralty, 196; for RN in Bahrain, 196; for school at Rosyth, 201; for service attachés, 196; in Wallace Collection, 117
Accountant-General of the Navy, 83, 100, **112**, 157, 158; accounts 112; Bill Branch, 112; correspondence, 112; Enquiry (1854), 100; orders from Admiralty Board, 83, 112; Pensions Branch, 112; precedent books, 112; seniority lists (1913–28), 112
accounts, Admiralty, 64; American Loyalists Claims Commissions, 67; Board of Trade, 64; Chamber, **2**–3; Clerks of the King's Ships, **2**, 3; Commission of Naval Enquiry, 67; dockyards, 64; droits of Admiralty, 8, 64; expedition to France (1492), 3; expeditions (1585–1626), 6; First Lords of the Admiralty, 64, 67; Greenwich Hospital, 56, 64, 67; High Court of Admiralty, 8, 64, 67; impressment, 67; Lords Admiral, **2**; Navy agents, 8; Navy Board, 67; Ordnance and Ordnance Board, 3, 6, 50, 67; Paymaster of Marines, 61, 67; Paymaster-General, 67; Paymaster-General of the Forces, 60; prizes, 6, 8, **10**, 50, 67; pursers, 78; purveyors, **2**; roperies, 6; salvage, 67; Sick and Hurt Board, 67; Transport Board, 67; transports, 6; Treasurer of the Navy, 6, 50, 59, 67; troopships, 50; 'Various', 3; victualling, 6, 67; Victualling Board, 67; Wardrobe, **2**–3; Woods and Forests, 67; works, 2
Acland, Captain W A D, 236
act books, High Court of Admiralty, 8; Prize Appeals Commissioners, 14

Acting Artificer Engineers, 231
Acting Sub-Lieutenants, 231
Acts of Parliament, 133; *see also* under their names
Ad Hoc Committees (of Committee of Imperial Defence, 1905–39), 190
Aden, Catalina Flight (1942–4), 210; Naval Task Force, 25
Adjutant-General, 42
Adjutant-General Royal Marines, 115; correspondence with RM Depots and Divisions, 115; correspondence with Secretary for War, 35; *see also* Colonel-Commandant in London
Admiral Commanding Reserves, 127
Admiral Superintendent, Chatham, 88; Malta, 30; Plymouth, 88, 145, 178; Portsmouth, 88, 104, 146; *see also* Captains Superintendent
admirals, 97, 179, 236; journals, 97, 179, 236; *see also* flag officers, flag rank
Admirals of the Fleet, 36, 63
Admiralty, 81, 195, 199, 200, 201, 202, 204, 205, 236; accounting methods, 55–6, 235; accounts, 64; and balance of payments, 195; and creosote production, 70; and film companies, 57, 70, 215; and Fleet Air Arm, 204; 'Black Books', 231; cement, 46; chocolate, 17; claims against, 56; codes and cyphers, 70; contracts, 17, 30, 36, 46, 53, 56, 70, 75, 96, 217, 223, 226, 235; committees, 235; couriers, 24; deeds, 108, 142; evidence to Royal Commission on Common Land, 199; evidence to Sea Fish Commission, 199; examinations for boys, 201; explosives, 17; factories, 17, 19, 36, 57, 70; grants to Sea Scouts, Sea Cadets and Girls' Naval Training Corps, 201; land, 36–7, 68, 75, 200, 224; land requirements, 199; liaison officers, 39; magazines, 36; publications, 17, 24, 231; publicity, 215; research establishments, 222, 235; screw threads, 70; secret service accounts, 64; shipyards, 36; Silver Oar, 224; supply departments, 54, 70

331

— employees, 36, 54–5, 57, 59, 198, 231, 233; billeting of, 211; housing of, 211; sex changes by, 54; superannuation of, 211; wages of, 36, 55, 57, 66, 235
Admiralty Air Constructional Equipment Committee (1916), 235
Admiralty and Cinque Ports Committee (of Parliament, 1647), 11
Admiralty Arch, 196, 197
Admiralty Awards Council, 100
Admiralty Board, **5**, **7**, 81, 82, **83**, 85, 97, 102, 110, 112, 121, 131, 132, 141, 145, 157, 159, 168, 170, 184, 185, 194; air requirements, 205; 'Board Room Journals', 95, 101; co-operation with Air Ministry, 204; memoranda for Cabinet, 236; memorandum on engineering industry (1940), 202; meetings with Lords Justices 83; memorials to Privy Council, 13, 83; minutes, 7, 12, 83, 218; orders, 7, 15; patents, 81, 224; petitions, 92; photographs, 215; precedents, 101; proclamations, 101; punishment returns, 101; rights and perquisites, 83; rules for Board business (1796), 83; study on future aircraft carriers (1961–5), 204; suppression of slave trade, 23; transfer of powers to Ministry of Defence (1964), 204; visitations of dockyards, 83, 131; warrants, 81, 224

— correspondence, 7, **85–93**; about convoys, 101; about Mediterranean Passes, 93; circulars, 93, 95; general, 92, 93; indexes, 91, 102; on Board reorganisation (1920–1), 83; registers, 96; with Admirals Superintendent, 88, 143, 144, 146, 147, 149; with Admiralty Transport Department, 109; with agents in France, 98; with Army officers, 86; with Atomic Energy Agency, 223; with Barber-Surgeons' Company, 92; with Board of Customs and Excise, 62, 91; with Board of Green Cloth, 91, 225; with Board of Revision, 91; with Board of Trade, 71–2, 91; with Board of Trade and Plantations, 69; with British ambassadors, 30; with British consuls, 30, 91, 93; with British Museum, 92, 228; with Captains RN, 86; with Central Statistical Office, 195; with Chief of the Imperial General Staff, 38; with Christ's Hospital, 228; with Civil Architect, 90, 108; with Coast Blockade, 86, 125; with Collectors of Customs, 62, 91, 93; with Colonels Commandant RM, 89, 114, 115; with Colonial governors, 47, 91, 93; with Colonial Office, 47; with Commanders-in-Chief, 85, 95, 178, 179, 236; with commanders of privateers, 86; with Commanders RN, 86; with Commission of Naval Enquiry, 91; with Commissioners of home dockyards, 86, 88, 93, 143–6; with Commissioners of overseas yards, 88, 151, 152; with Commodores, 86; with Controller of Storekeepers' Accounts, 137; with Controller of the Navy, 104, 135; with Controller of Victualling, 90, 111; with Deputy Adjutant-General RM, 89; with Deputy Prime Minister, 194; with dockyards, 147 (see also Commissioners, yard officers); with Field Marshall Sir J Dill, 236; with Doctors' Commons, 75, 96; with Dominions Office, 48; with Dutch Captains (1744–8), 86; with East India Company, 92, 226; with Falmouth Packet Station, 90; with Flag Officers, 85; with foreign Consuls, 92; with Foreign Office, 20–4, 91; with Foreign Secretaries, 26; with General Post Office, 76, 91; with General Staff directorates, 40; with Greenwich Hospital, 83, 90, 93, 120; with High Court of Admiralty, 8, 91; with Home Office, 91; with Hudson's Bay Company, 226; with Hydrographer of the Navy, 90, 127; with India Board of Control, 92, 224; with Inspector-General of Naval Works, 90, 127; with King's Private Secretary, 91; with Law Officers, 36, 74, 90, 91; with Lieutenants RN, 86; with Lloyd's Coffee House, 92, 226; with Local Government Board, 200; with Lords Lieutenant of Counties, 91; with Lords Lieutenant and Lords Justices of Ireland, 91, 224; with Master-General of the Ordnance, 83, 184; with masters of merchantmen, 86; with Ministry of Agriculture, 199; with Ministry of Fuel, 216; with Ministry of Health, 211; with Ministry of Housing, 200; with Ministry of Labour, 202; with Ministry of Reconstruction, 224; with Ministry of Town and Country Planning, 200; with Ministry of Transport, 213; with National Savings Committee, 65; with Navy Board, 83, 87, 93, 130–2, 138; with Ordnance Board, 91, 93, 183; with Ordnance Select Committee, 44; with Paymaster of Marines, 61; with Pensions Office, 121; with Physician-General of the Navy, 90, 110; with Physicians of naval hospitals, 90, 163, 164; with Privy Council, 13, 91; with Prize Commissioners, 87; with railway companies, 227; with Registrar of Seamen, 73, 90; with Regulating Captains, 86, 125; with Rotterdam Agency, 98; with Royal Africa Company, 92, 226; with Royal Astronomical Society, 92, 228; with Royal Marine Divisions, 115 (see also Colonels-Commandant); with Royal Marine Officers, 86; with Royal Naval Academy, 90, 126; with Royal Society, 92, 228; with Secretaries of State, 15, 83, 91, 93, 98; with Secretary at War, 91; with Secretary for War (1794–1855), 34; with Secretary of State for Air, 205; with Sick and Hurt Board, 87, 93, 159, 166; with Sixpenny Office, 90, 127; with Solicitor of the Admiralty, 90, 93, 113; with South Sea Company, 92, 226; with Stationery Office, 66; with Steam Department 93, 106; with Storekeepers, 88, 149; with Suez Canal Company,

Index (references are to list numbers, not pages)

236; with Surgeons' Hall, 92, 228; with Surveyor of Buildings, 90, 108; with Surveyor of the Navy, 87, 90, 104, 135, 236; with Transport Accounts Committee, 87, 175; with Transport Agents, 86; with Ticket Office, 141; with Transport Board (1689–1717), 87, 174; with Transport Board (1796–1816), 87, 175; with Transport Board Medical Department (1806–16), 87, 160; with Transport Board Prisoners of War Department, 87, 167; with Treasurer of the Navy, 90, 156; with Treasury, 49, 91; with Treasury Solicitor, 75, 91, 96; with Trinity House, 92, 225; with Vice-Admirals of Counties, 91, 225; with Vice-Admiralty Courts, 9; with Victualling Board, 87, 93, 168; with Victualling Board Medical Department, 87, 93, 161; with Victualling Board Transport Department, 93, 176; with Victualling Yards, 93, 170, 171; with War Office (1661–1855), 33; with War Office (1855–1964), 36–7; with yard officers, 86

— orders and instructions, about convoys, 83, 92; about Greenwich pensioners 83, 121; about Marines, 83; about Navy Office 83; for courts martial, 83; important, 102; *Regulations and Instructions* (1731), 83; secret, 83; to Accountant-General, 83; to Coast Blockade, 101; to Commanders-in-Chief, 83; to consuls, 23; to Navy Board, 83, 132; to Navy Pay Office, 157; to officers, 83; to Paymaster of Marines, 83; to Physician-General, 110; to Plymouth Dockyard, 145; to Royal Clarence Victualling Yard, 170; to Sick and Hurt Board, 83, 159; to subordinate boards, 83; to Ticket Office, 83, 141; to Victualling Board, 83, 168

Admiralty Building, 24, 54, 68, 197, 198; plans, 197
Admiralty Centre for Scientific Information and Liaison, 119
Admiralty Chart Factory, Cricklewood, 53
Admiralty Charts, 13, 40, 51, 53, 66, 230; index, 127; of Bahamas, 72; of Bosphorous, 72; of Deal, 72; of Dover, 72; of Guernsey, 13; of Herm, 13; of Karamania, 127; of Portland, 72; of Spithead, 72; of Spurn Head, 72; of Sark, 13; of Thames, 224, of West Africa, 127; *see also* charts
Admiralty Chemical Advisory Panel, 118
Admiralty Chemical Department, 119
Admiralty Citadel, 66, 198
Admiralty Commission (1645–60), **7**, 129
Admiralty Commissioners, 233; *see also* Admiralty Board
Admiralty Committee (of Council of State, 1649–53), 11
Admiralty Committee on Aeronautics (1912), 235
Admiralty Committee on the Education of Seamen (1913), 201

Admiralty Committee on the Training of Naval Cadets (1905–6), 201, 235
Admiralty Compass Observatory, Slough, 54, 119, 198
Admiralty Corrosion Committee, 105, 119
Admiralty Court, *see* High Court of Admiralty
Admiralty Dardanelles Committee (1919), 235; *see also* Dardanelles Committee, Joint-Service Dardanelles Committee
Admiralty Delegation (Washington), 192
Admiralty Development Establishment, Barrow-in-Furness, 119
Admiralty Dry Dock Committee (1948–53), 213
Admiralty Enemy Documents Section, 192
Admiralty Engineering Laboratory, 119
Admiralty Experimental Diving Unit, 119
Admiralty Experimental Establishment, Welwyn, 107
Admiralty Experimental Establishments, *see* Committee on Admiralty Experimental Establishments
Admiralty Experimental Stations, 118, **119**
Admiralty Experimental Works, 119
Admiralty Explosives Jetty, Milford Haven, 57
Admiralty Factory, Alloa, 36; Crook, 70
Admiralty, First Lord of, *see* First Lord of the Admiralty
Admiralty fishing agreements (1917–19), 73; *see also* fishing boats and vessels
Admiralty Fleet Orders, 95
Admiralty Fuel Experimental Station, 19, 119; *see also* Fuel Research Station
Admiralty Fuels and Lubricants Committee, 119
Admiralty Gunnery Establishment, 107, 119
Admiralty Harbour Department, 68, **72**, 227
Admiralty House, Whitehall, 57, 100, 196; plans, 197
Admiralty Industrial Council, 108, 202
Admiralty Manual of Navigation, 66
Admiralty Marine Engineering Establishment, 119
Admiralty Marine Technology Establishment, 119
Admiralty Materials Laboratory, 46, 119, 217
Admiralty Mining Establishment, 208
Admiralty Net Defence, 71
Admiralty Office, 68, 82, **100**; Air Department, later Branch, 104; aliens forbidden in, 17; Branch indexes, 102; Branch registers, 95; 'Cases', 103; Civil Branch, 96, 231; Civil Establishment Branch, 96, 100; Civil Law Branch, 96; civilian staff, 63, 66, 100, 195, 202, 233; Commission Branch, 100, 231; Commission and Warrant Branch, 96, 231; contingent accounts, 100; Contract and Purchase Branch, 96; convoy lists, 101; courts martial minutes, 96, 101; enemy documents, 99; establishment of, 13, 100; establishment of, in Bath, 42; Intelligence Department, *see* Naval

Intelligence Department; intelligence received, 15, 20, 22, 27, 30, 39, 98; Legal Branch, 96; list books, 101; lists of HM Ships, 15, 95; Marine Office, 113–15, 231; messengers, 100; Military Branch, 95, 231; Miscellaneous Branch, 96; movements of foreign ships, 98; movements of HM Ships, 95, 101; Naval Branch, 96; Naval Law Division, 96; Naval Manpower Department, 96; naval officers in, 54; Organisation and Methods in, 57, 100; pictures and plate, 100; Political and Secret Branch, 96; precedents, 96, 100; registered files, 96; secretariat, 100, 235; senior staff, 236; security, 51; speaking of Welsh in, 17; stationery, 66; statistics, 101; telephone directory, 100; weekly returns, 101; Whitley Councils, 57, 96
Admiralty Oil Committee (1912–13), 235
Admiralty Oil Fuel Jetty, Sierra Leone, 198
Admiralty Oil Laboratory, 119
Admiralty Operational Intelligence Centre, 117; ULTRA digests, 117; *see also* Naval Staff
Admiralty Pattern Rooms (1931–6), 70
Admiralty Principal Officers, *see* Accountant-General, Controller of the Navy, Physician-General, Storekeeper-General
Admiralty Railways Department, 68, **72**, 227
Admiralty Reconstruction Committee (1917–19), 235
Admiralty Record Office, 86, 100, **102**
Admiralty Research Establishment, 46, 119
Admiralty Research Laboratory, 119; Fire Control Group, 119
Admiralty Secretary's Department, 7, 100, 235; *see also* Admiralty Office
Admiralty Secretary's Department Committee (1869), 100, 235
Admiralty Semaphore, 75, 101
Admiralty Ship Welding Committee, 105, 119
Admiralty Shipyard Labour Department, 202
Admiralty Shock in Ships Committee, 119
Admiralty Signal and Radar Establishment, 119
Admiralty Signal Establishment, 222
Admiralty Signal Stations, 68, 93, 125, 132, 133; officers, 231; ratings, 232
Admiralty Small Craft Experimental Establishment, 119
Admiralty Solicitor, *see* Solicitor of the Admiralty
Admiralty Staff, *see* Admiralty War Staff, Naval Staff
Admiralty Staff Conference (1919), 96
Admiralty Surface Weapons Establishment, 119, 213
Admiralty Technical Mission in Canada, 192
Admiralty telegraphs, 75, 227; *see also* signals and signalling
Admiralty Transport Arbitration Board (1927), 235
Admiralty Transport Department, 35, 36, 37, 71, 93, **109**, 144, 149; *see also* Naval Transport Service, Sea Transport Service
Admiralty Underwater Explosion Research Establishment, 236
Admiralty Underwater Weapons Establishment, **119**, 193
Admiralty, War Office, Air Ministry and Press Committee (1919–93), 219
Admiralty War Staff, 116; and invasion of Britain (1916), 37, 235
Admiralty Water Works, Llanegryn, 17
Admiralty Whitley Council, 57, 96
Admiralty Works Department, 36, 196; *see also* Director of Naval Works
Admiralty-Air Ministry Joint Sea/Air Warfare Committee, 217
Advanced Flying Boat Bases (1942–5), 210
Advanced Ship Recognition Flight No. 1476 (1942–4), 210
Advisory Panel on Underwater Explosion Research, 119
Aer Lingus, 178
Aeronautical and Engineering Research, *see* Directorate of Aeronautical and Engineering Research
Aeroplane and Armament Experimental Establishment, 208
Africa, exploration of, 34, 43; *see also* North and East Africa, South Africa, West and Central Africa
Africa Station, 127, **179**, 236; *see also* West Africa
Agents for Hospitals, *see* Hospital Agents
Agents for Prisoners, *see* Prisoner of War Agents
Agents for Transports, *see* Transport Agents
Agents, *see* intelligence, Hospital Agents, Navy agents, Prisoner of War Agents, prize agents, Transport Agents, Victualling Agents
Agent-Victuallers, 168, 170, 236
agriculture, 199
air attacks, on capital ships, 235; on French Navy, 207; on German Navy, 207; on ports, 206; on shipping, 206, 207, 209; on submarines, 207
Air, Coast and Seaward Defences Committee (1947–59), 219
Air Commission of Control, Germany (1921–2), 36
Air Committee (of Committee of Imperial Defence), 190
air defence of British ships, 207, 209, 217, 219; *see also* merchant shipping, Royal Navy, ships and vessels
Air Ministry, 181, **204**, 206, 235, 236
Air pamphlets (1914–18), 128
Air Publications, 128, 204
Air Staff, 117, **206**; Directorates, **207**

Index (references are to list numbers, not pages)

Air Stations, *see* Royal Naval Air Stations
Air Torpedo Attack Committee (of Air Staff, 1942–3), 207
Airborne Divisions, 42
aircraft, 181, 204, 205, 206, 207; accident reports, 204; British naval, 32, 46, 204–7, 209, 222, 235; catapult, 210; data sheets, 222; development, 208; foreign naval, 42; logs, 181; plans, 208; requirements, 222, 235; target-towing, 207; type biographies, 222; *see also* bombers, fighters, helicopters, seaplanes, torpedo-bombers
Aircraft Anti-Ship Committee (1943–6), 207
Aircraft Anti-U-boat Committee (1943–5), 207
Aircraft Carrier Study Group, 204
aircraft carriers, 104, 204, 205, 219, 220, 236; in British Pacific Fleet, 39; in US Pacific Fleet, 209
Aircraft Costs Committee (1958–60), 222
Aircraft Launching Working Party (1950–1), 104
Aircraft Modification Committee (1947–50), 222
Aircraft Production, *see* Ministry of Aircraft Production
Aircraft Torpedo Development Unit, **208**, 210
aircrew, naval, recruitment (1935), 53; requirement, 204; training, 48, 204
airfields, 108, 204, 206
air-raids, effect of, 19; shelters, 19; *see also* air attacks
Air-Sea Interception Committee (1941–3), 206, 235
air-sea warfare, 206
Air-Sea Warfare Development Unit, **208**, 210
airships, 119, 181
Aix Roads, action (1809), 175
Ajax, *see* Operation AJAX
Alarm (1758), 13
Albert Medal, 71
Alert (1855), 75
Alexander (1778), 180, 236
Alexander, General Harold, 1st Earl Alexander of Tunis, 236
Alexandria, Egypt, French fleet at (1942–3), 30
Alexandria Harbour Committee (1938), 235
Alexandria Naval Yard, 150
Algiers, 31, 32, 165
aliens, 16
Aliens Office, *see* Home Office
allegations, High Court of Admiralty, 8
Allenby, General Sir Edmund, 39
Allied Control Authority (1945–6), Naval Directorate, 28
Allied Control Commission for Italy, Naval Sub-Commission, 40, 42
Allied Expeditionary Force (1943–5), 42, Naval C-in-C, 28; *see also* Supreme Headquarters Allied Expeditionary Force

Allied Forces Head Quarters North Africa, 31
Allied Forces Mediterranean, **42**
Allied Naval and Shipping Conference (1917), 235
Allied Naval Council (1915–19), 187, 229
Allied Supplies Executive, 191
Alligator (1821), 165
Allotment Declaration Lists (1795–1852), 157
Altmark, German naval auxiliary (1940), 24
ambassadors, British, 30, 179, 236; foreign, 15, 91
America and Latin America, Foreign Office correspondence, 25
America and West Indies, State Papers, 15, 69
American Civil War, 21, 26
American Department, *see* Colonial Secretary (1768–82)
American Loyalists Claims Commissions, 50, 67
American Secretary, *see* Colonial Secretary (1768–82)
Amethyst (1943), 36, 203
Amherst, General Jeffrey, 1st Baron, 236; William Pitt, 2nd Baron, 226
ammunition, naval, 53, 182; *see also* magazines, shells
Amphibian Support Regiments, 36
amphibious operations, 192, 207; *see also* combined operations
Amphibious Warfare Experimental Establishment, 119
Amphibious Warfare Handbook (1950), 204
Ampthill, 1st Baron, *see* Russell, Odo
Ancient Correspondence, 1
Ancient monuments and historic buildings, 196
Ancient Petitions, 1
Andalusia, merchantman (1807), 77
Andaman Islands (1942–5), 39
Anderson, Sir Alan, Controller of the Navy, 1917–18, 236
Andromeda (1780), 236
Angerstein, John Julius, shipowner, 78
Anglesey, 13
Anglo-American Consolidated Statement, 195
Anglo-American Naval Staff conversations (1938–9), 30
Anglo-Belgian-French Naval Staff contacts, 188
Anglo-French Defence Collaboration, 193
Anglo-French Joint Service Conference, Singapore (1939), 37, 235
Anglo-French Naval Commission, New Hebrides (1886–8), 23
Anglo-German Naval Agreements (1935–8), 30, 32, 188
Anglo-Japanese Alliance (1901–22), 30, 186
Anglo-Japanese naval talks (1902–12), 38
Anglo-Scandinavian Naval Agreement (1939), 24, 30
annuities, 203; to Nelson family, 236
Antarctic, 48, 51, 57; *see also* British Antarctic Survey
Antarctic Relief Committee (1903), 235

Antigua Naval Hospital, 165
Antigua Naval Yard, English Harbour, 132, 151, 179, 219, 230
Antigua Victualling Yard, 173
Anti-Submarine Experimental Establishment, 119
Anti-submarine warfare, 189, 204–7, 219; air, 204, 207; Soviet, 219
Anti-U-boat Warfare Committee (of Air Staff, 1942–4), 189, 207
Anzac Cove, Gallipoli, 42
Applied Psychology Unit, Cambridge, 212
appointments, of Admiralty clerks, 63, 66; of Board of Visitors of Greenwich Observatory, 123; of commanders-in-chief, 1; of Deputy Lieutenants, 36; of naval attachés, 24; of naval officers, 63, 231; of Navy Office clerks, 139; of Royal Marine officers, 36–7; of Vice-Admiralty Courts, 9; to Impress Service, 125, 231; to public offices, 1; to Sea Fencibles, 125, 231
apprentices, 122, 132, 145, 228
Arabia and Middle East, Foreign Office correspondence, 25
Arbitration Tribunals (1937–56), 202
Archangel, Russia, 30, 39
Arctic Committee (1851), 103
Arctic expeditions (1824–5), 84, 111; (1845–56), 103, 111; correspondence with Foreign Office, 21; with Hudson's Bay Company, 226; with Treasury, 49; with War Office, 34; *see also* Franklin, Sir John
Ardagh, Major-General Sir John, 236
Aréthuse (1793), 67
Argentina, 30
Argentine Naval Commission (1938), 24
Argentine Navy, frigates for, 57
Ark Royal (1937), 25
Ark Royal (1950), 25
armaments, naval, 107, 128, 135, 188; transfer to RN (1886), 37, 235; *see also* guns, Ordnance
armed merchant cruisers, 48, 52
Armed Services, British, 194, 195, 199, 204
armed ships and vessels, *see* hired armed ships and vessels
armed tenders, 97
Armourers, 183, 232
Army, British, 188; casualties (1939–43), 206; co-operation with RAF, 206; establishments, 196; pay, 36; reserves, 36–7; reorganisation (1883–8), 236; relative rank (1922), 188; statistics, 202; ships and vessels, 67; trades in, 37; victualling, 168; *see also* War Office
Army Act (1879), 36
Army and Navy Signal Book (1869–70), 37

Army List, 33, 36
Army Medical Department, 36
Army of Reserve (1803), 33
Army officers, 36, 37, 86
Arnold, Dr. James, of the High Court of Admiralty, 236
Arras, France, 167
Arrears lists, 156, 157
Arthur's Spinning Machinery, 103
artificers, 120; dockyard, 132, 136, 143–8, 151, 152; naval, 46; services, 157, 231–2
Arundel, Sussex, 62
asbestos and asbestosis, 17, 66, 145, 212
Ascension, prize (1752–4), 78
Ascension Island, 25
Ascension Island Naval Hospital, 165
Ascension Island Victualling Yard, 173
Ashanti expedition (1896), 36, 115
Ashley Cooper, Anthony, 1st Earl of Shaftesbury, Vice-Admiral of Dorset, 236
Asia, *see also* South-East Asia,
assignation books, High Court of Admiralty, 8; Prize Appeals Commissioners, 14
Assistance (1699), 158
Assistant Chiefs of Air Staff, 206
Assistant Paymasters, 231
Assistant Surgeons, 231
Association for the Labouring Poor, 145
Assurance (1747), 68
Astronomer-Royal, 123
asylum, diplomatic, 25
Atbara River, 42
Atlantic, air operations, 207; Battle of, *see* Battle of the Atlantic
Atlantic Fleet, 97, 178; *see also* Channel Fleet, Grand Fleet
atomic bomb, *see* nuclear weapons
Atomic Energy Agency, **223**; Metallurgy Division, 118
Atomic Energy Authority, 216
Atomic Energy Research Establishment, **223**
Atomic Weapons Research Establishment, **221**
attachés, *see* naval attachés
Attlee, Clement, Deputy Prime Minister (1940–7), 194
Auckland, George Eden, 1st Earl of, First Lord of the Admiralty, 67, 84
Audit Office, **64**, 236
Aurora (1887), 236
Australia, 39, 179, 207
Australia (1886), 236
Australian Navy Office, 30; *see also* Royal Australian Navy

Index (references are to list numbers, not pages)

Australian Royal Commission into UK Nuclear Weapons Testing in Australia, 217
Austria, British administration (1945–9)
Austrian Navy (1914–18), 32, 99
Aviation, Ministry of, *see* Ministry of Aviation
awards, 42, 39, 96, 219, 231, 232; British, to foreigners, 24; British Army, to RM and RN, 41; citations, 96; foreign, to British personnel, 24, 231; naval gallantry, 37, 57, 71; salvage, 213; to inventors, 100, 222, 235; *see also* Albert Medal, honours, medals, Victoria Cross
Azores, expedition to (1596–7), 6

Bahamas, Naval Yard, *see* Nassau; US bases in, 24; wreckers in, 71
Bahia, Brazil, British consul, 30
Bahrain, 196
Baikie, William, explorer, 21
bail bonds (Navy agents), 8
Baillie, Captain Thomas, 120, 236
Balfour Committee on RN-RAF Relations (1923), 235
Balkans, Special Operations Executive in, 194
Ball, Captain Alexander J, 180
Balloon Command, 204
balloons, 119, 204; *see also* kite balloons
Baltic, naval operations (1856), 37
Baltic Fleet, Squadron and Station, 59, 85, 111, **179**, 236
Bandar Abbas Naval Base, Iran, 30
Bangkok, Thailand, 39
Bankes Commission (1935), 235
Bankruptcy Court, **80**
Banks, Sir Joseph, President of the Royal Society, 236
Banshee, smuggling lugger (1822), 103
Baptismal Registers, 115, 127, 163
Barbados Naval Hospital, 165
Barbados Naval Yard, 151
Barber-Surgeons' Company, 92, 228
Barbot, Jean, 'Description des côtes d'Afrique' (1688–98), 98
Barcelona, British consul (1902–12), 30
Barham, Lord, *see* Middleton, Rear-Admiral Sir Charles
barracks, *see* Royal Marine Barracks, Royal Naval Barracks
Barrow-in-Furness, Lancs., 24, 119
Basra, British consul, 30
Basra Dockyard, 30, 53
Bath, Soms., 42
Bathurst (1821), 158
Battle of Jutland (1916), 116, 190
Battle of the Atlantic, 189, 194, 205, 206
Battle of the Atlantic Committee, 189

Baxter, Alexander, gunner, 77, 236
beach surveys (1945–92), 117
Beatty, Admiral of the Fleet David, Earl, 53, 57
Beaverbrook, William Aitken, Lord, Minister for Aircraft Production, 236
Beckford, Thomas, slopseller, 133
Bedford, Francis Russell, 6th Earl of, 6
beef, for RN, 78, 111; *see also* meat
Beira Patrol, 25
Beirut, British consul, 30
Belfast, HM Prison, 57
Belfast (1938), 57, 196, 224
Belgium, 30, 91, 188
Belle Isle (1819), 110
'Benevolence' (1614–17), 6
Bentham, George, botanist, 236
Beresford, Admiral Lord Charles, 235, 236
Berlin, Germany, 25, 52, 204
Berlin Decrees, 78
Bermuda Dockyard, **152**, 203
Bermuda Hospital, *see* Royal Naval Hospital Bermuda
Bermuda, US base in, 25
Bermuda Victualling Yard, 173
Bighi Hospital, *see* Royal Naval Hospital Malta
bill books, Navy, 129, 140; Ordnance Board, 182, 184; Plymouth Dockyard, 145; Prize Appeals Commissioners, 14
Bill Branch (of Accountant-General's Department), 112
Bill Office, 136, **140**
billeting of Admiralty employees, 211; of RN personnel, 16
biological warfare, 36, 221
Birkenhead, troopship (1845), 32, 57
Birkenhead Docks, 227
Birkenhead Railway, 227
Birmingham and Oxford Railway, 227
births, registration of, 18, 115
Bitche, British prisoners at, 167
Bizerta Dockyard, Tunisia, 48
Black Book of the Admiralty, 8
Black Sea, naval operations (1855–6), 37; (1919), 42
Blessing, of Burntisland (1633), 78
Bletchley Park, Bucks., 27
Blockade Advisory Committee (1919), 70, 235
Blockade Committee (1939–45), 29
blockades, 22; of Axis Powers (1939–45), 24, 26, 28–30, 194; of China (1952–3), 32; of Confederate States, 23; of Danzig (1849–55), 30; of France (1940–4), 52; of Germany (1914–18), 26, 30, 62, 70, 186, 191, 235; of Greece (1886), 23; of Tangier (1828), 20, 30; of Uruguay (1848), 30; *see also* Ministry of Blockade (1916–19), Ministry of Economic Warfare (1939–45)

blocks, 75; block mills, 131, 132, 146
'Blue Lists' (of ships under construction, 1940–6), 116, 128
Bône, Algeria, 24
Board of Admiralty, *see* Admiralty Board
Board of Agriculture, *see* Ministry of Agriculture
Board of Control, *see* East India Company, India Board of Control
Board of Customs, 62, 91; Private Office, 62
Board of Education, **201**; *see also* Ministry of Education
Board of Excise, **62**
Board of Green Cloth, 91, 225
Board of Invention and Research, 118; *see also* Royal Naval Scientific Service
Board of Longitude, 13, 123
Board of Revision, 13, 91, 177
Board of Stamps and Taxes, **63**; *see also* Inland Revenue
Board of Trade, **70**, 91, 222; accounts, 64; Civil Aviation Department, 70 (*see also* Ministry of Civil Aviation); correspondence, 70; Harbour Department, **72**; Marine Department, **71**, 91, 214; minutes, 70; President, 70; Railway Department, **72**; Shipbuilding and Repair Branch, 70
Board of Trade and Plantations (1696–1782), **69**
'Board Room Journals', 95, 101
Boards of Enquiry, 96
Boat Armament Committee (1885), 235
boats, 130, 154; *see also* Royal Navy, ships and vessels
Boatswains, services, 128, 157, 231; stores, 130
Bodmin, HM Prison, 200
boilers, 104; boilermakers, 227
Bomb Census (1941–4), 19
bomb sights, 128
bomb vessels, 115
Bombay (1828), 158
Bombay Dockyard, 135, **153**; *see also* East Indies Station
Bombay Dockyard Reorganisation Committee (1947), 235
Bomber Command, 207; registered files, 209
bombers, attacks on German shipping, 207; on U-boat shelters, 204; minelaying, 207; torpedo, 222; *see also* British Bombing Survey Unit, United States Strategic Bombing Survey
bombing decoy sites, 19
bombs, anti-submarine, 206; glider, 204
Book for Sea Causes (1559) 5
Boom Defence, 108, 178
boots, for RN, 70
Boscawen, Rear-Admiral Hon. Edward, 67
Bosphorous, chart, 72

Bouillon, Prince de, *see* D'Auvergne
Boulogne, France, 140, 187
bounties, for next-of-kin, 232; for volunteers, 13, 157, 232; prize, *see* Naval Prize Bounty
Bounty, armed transport (1787), 30
Bounty Commissioners (1673–4), 157, 235
Bowler, *see* Operation BOWLER
Boyle, Admiral Sir William, 12th Earl of Cork and Orrery, 63
boys, in RN, 16; *see also* apprentices, Royal Navy, manning and personnel
Brading, MV (1960), 213
Bradley, Rear-Admiral William, 76
Branch, Captain Alexander Barclay, 79
Brazil, British consuls in, 30; British embassy in, 24; charts of, 98; quartz crystals from, 62; revolution (1894), 21; tallow from, 132; treaty with, 32
Brazilian Navy (1937), 30
Brazils Squadron and Station, 30, 85
Brennan Torpedo, 75
Brenton, Sir Jahleel, Commissioner, Cape of Good Hope, 179, 236
Brest, France, 205, 236
Bridgend, Glamorgan, 17
Bridges, Sir Edward, Secretary of the Cabinet, later of the Treasury, 236
Brigandine, Robert, Clerk of the King's Ships, 3
Brine, Robert, Navy agent, 77, 236
Bristol, privateers and prizes of, 78, 238
Britannia (1953), 219
Britannia, privateer (1788–9), 78
Britannia, training ship, 126; *see also* Royal Naval College Dartmouth
British Admiralty Delegation, Washington, 127
British Admiralty Pacific Mission to Australia (1941–4), 207
British Antarctic Survey (1970–8), 47
British Bombing Survey Unit, 204
British Central Scientific Office, 222
British Expeditionary Force (1914–18), 39
British Food Mission, Washington, 199
British Forces Cyprus (1963–4), 42
British Forces Middle East, 43
British Honduras, 21
British Intelligence Objectives Sub-Committee (1945–6), 39
British Legion Royal Naval Club, 17
British Museum, 92, 228
British National Endeavour, 122; *see also* Greenwich Hospital Schools, Royal Naval Asylum
British Naval Commission of Control, Bulgaria (1922–4), 52

British Naval Mission to Greece (1928–9), 30
British Pacific Fleet, *see* Pacific Fleet
British Purchasing Agency in USA (1940), 30
British Railways Board, 213
British Red Cross, 36; *see also* Red Cross
British Shipping Federation, 202
British Transport Commission, 213
Broughton & Co., Navy and Prize Agents, 77
Brown, George, Foreign Secretary, 26
Brunel, Isambard Kingdom, 236
Buccaneer aircraft, 220
Buchan, Captain David, Senior Officer Newfoundland, 236
Buckingham Palace, 36
buildings, *see* Admiralty Building, Royal Navy, establishments
Bulgaria, British Naval Commission of Control (1922–4), 52
Bulgarian Navy (1944–5), 27
Bulldog (1845), 76
buoys, in Thames, 13
burial registers, 120, **127**, 163
Burma, 30
Burmese Navy (1948), 30
Burnett, Sir William, Physician-General of the Navy, 110, 236
Burney, Admiral of the Fleet Sir Cecil, 63
Burney torpedoes (1939–42), 222
Butler, R A, Foreign Secretary, 26
Byng, Admiral George, *see* Torrington, Viscount; Admiral Hon. John, 101

Cabinet (to 1916), **186**, 236; Dardanelles Committee, 186; Joint War Air Committee, 186; Naval and Military Pensions Committee, 235; War Committee, 186; War Council, 186; *see also* War Cabinet
Cabinet (1919–39), 188, 236; Fighting Services Committee, 188; RN-RAF Co-operation Committee, 188
Cabinet (1945–74), **193**; Defence Committee, 193; Defence and Overseas Policy Committee, 193
Cabinet Office, 186, 187, 190; Historical Section, *see* Committee of Imperial Defence
Cabinet Scientific Advisory Committee, 236
cables, electric, 119; submarine, 23; cable ships, 76
cadets, *see* Royal Marine Cadets, Naval Cadets
Cadiz, 179; expedition to (1597), 6, 156; expedition to (1625), 78; Naval Yard (1694–6), 152
Caerwent, Monmouthshire, 17
Cairo, Egypt, 30
Calais, France, 1, 35, 187
Caledonia, shore establishment at Rosyth, civilian staff (1937–47), 54

call signs, *see* radio, wireless
Cambeltown (1940), 230
Cambridge, Gunnery School, 107, 198
Cambridge University Library, 123
Cameroons, naval operations (1915), 40
Camouflage Committee (of Ministry of Home Security), 19
Campania (1943), 196
Canada, defence of, 37, 103; expedition to (1713), 15; naval visits to, 25; proposed expedition to (1746–8), 15; transport to (1862), 37; *see also* Royal Canadian Navy, Upper Canada
Canadian Lakes Naval Yards, **154**; Station, 158, **179**; *see also* Great Lakes
Canning, Stratford, 1st Viscount Stratford de Redcliffe, diplomat, 236
canteens, naval, 235
Canterbury, Archbishop of, Prerogative Court, *see* Prerogative Court of Canterbury
Canton, China, British operations at (1856), 21, 23, 30, 115
CANUKUS naval intelligence conference (1971), 219
Cape Nicola Naval Yard, 151
Cape of Good Hope, 98, 236; Observatory (1931–60), 55
Cape of Good Hope Station, 85, 101, 131, **179**, 236
Cape Province, South Africa, 103, 236
Cape Town, shipping to, 77; Slave Trade Mixed Commission, **9**
Cape Town and Simonstown Victualling Yard, **173**
Cape Town Hospital, *see* Royal Naval Hospital Cape Town
Cape Town Naval Yard, *see* Simonstown
Capital Ship Committee (1920–1), 235; *see also* Committee on Vulnerability of Capital Ships (1936)
Captain Superintendent, of Deptford Dockyard, 88, 144; of Deptford Victualling Yard, 169; of Greenwich Hospital, 120; of RNC Greenwich, 126; *see also* Admirals Superintendent
Captains RM, 86
Captains RN, half-pay, 134; logs, 97; journals, 101, 131, 141, 236; petitions by, 13; orders to, 7; reports by, 30; reports on slave trade by, 22–3; services, 231
— correspondence, with Admiralty, 86; with commanders-in-chief, 85; with Navy Board, 131; with Sick and Hurt Board, 159
Caribbean, 98; *see also* West Indies
Carnarvon, Henry Herbert, 4th Earl of, Colonial Secretary, 236
Carpenter's screw propeller, 103
Carpenters, pay, 13, 202; services, 128, 157, 231; stores, 130

Carrier Borne Air Liaison Section (1950–1), 43
Cartagena de Indias, expedition to (1741–2), 15, 61; *see also* West Indies
cartels, 167; *see also* prisoners of war, exchanges
Casablanca, Morocco, 25
case books, medical, 163, 165; Prize Appeals Commissioners, 14
casualties and casualty lists (1695–1860), 157, 163; (1899–1902), 179; (1914–18), 115, 231; (1939–45), 189, 195, 206, 231; (1952–4), 35
Catapult Aircraft Merchantmen (CAM Ships), 206
Catapult Flights, 210
Catering Frauds, Committee of Enquiry (1972–3), 235
Cathay Company (1580–95), 80, 226
Cattewater, Plymouth, 145
caulkers, services, 231
cemeteries and war graves, British naval, 21, 24–5, 30, 36, 57, 196
censorship, 42, 76, 215; Committee, 190; *see also* Naval Censor
Census of Production (1947–9), 70
censuses, 18
Central Criminal Court, **80**
Central Defence Scientific Service, **219**
Central Dockyard Laboratory, 119
Central Economic Planning Staff, 57
Central Metallurgical Laboratory, 119
Central Mine Clearance Board (1946–51), 229
Central Office for North American Supplies, 191
Central Office of Information, **215**
Central Photographic Interpretation Unit, **208**
Central Statistical Unit (of Air Staff), 206
Central Statistical Office, **195**
Central Tactics and Trials Organisation, 217
Centre for Scientific Information and Liaison, *see* Admiralty Centre for Scientific Information and Liaison
Ceylon, 48, 179, 210
Challenger (1858), expedition, 66
Chamber accounts, **2–3**
Chamberlain, Sir Austen, Foreign Secretary, 26, 236
Chancellor of the Exchequer, Private Office, **51**
Chancellor's Rolls, **2**
Chancery, **1**; Court of, *see* Court of Chancery
Chancery Masters, 77; exhibits, 77
Channel Fleet (1692–1782), 85, 178, 236; *see also* Grand Fleet, Western Squadron
Channel Fleet (1867–1911), 178, *see also* Atlantic Fleet, Grand Fleet
Channel Islands, administration, 1; Admiralty land, 68; commanders-in-chief, 85, 178, 236; signal stations, 133; *see also* Guernsey, Herm, Sark
Channel tunnel, 190; Companies, 227

Channel Tunnel Defence Committee (1882), 235
chapels, naval, 36
Chaplain of the Fleet, 127
chaplains, 36, 231; Bounty, 231; groats, 231; pensions, 121; services, 157
Charity Commission, 225
Charity for Sea Officers' Widows, **124**, 231
Charles I, King of England, 5
Charles II, King of England, 93
Charleston, South Carolina, 77
charter parties, 174
charts, 13, 230, 236; for Fleet Air Arm (1935), 40; German, 99; of Brazil, 98; of Cameroons, 40; of East Africa, 40; of Gallipoli, 127; of Ireland, 17; of Plymouth Sound, 145; of St. John's Antigua, 236; of Scilly Isles, 127; of Solomon Islands, 39; *see also* Admiralty charts
Chase, Edward, navy agent, 77
chasse-marées, 130
Chatfield, Admiral of the Fleet Sir Ernle, Lord, 224
Chatham, 1st Earl of, *see* Pitt, William; 2nd Earl of, *see* Pitt, John
Chatham, Commander-in-Chief, 85
Chatham, hospital ship, 161, 164
Chatham, Kent, 185; naval war memorial, 36; RM Barracks, 68
Chatham Chest, **155**
Chatham Division, Royal Marines, 61, 89, 114, **115**
Chatham Dockyard, **143**; Admiral Superintendent, 88, 143; boundary (1694–7), 78; Commissioner, 88, 143; construction work (1963), 57; extension (1859), 75; Extraordinary, 143; listed buildings, 219; Master Shipwright, 13; Ordinary, 143; plans, 143; radiation in, 17, 200; Ropeyard, 143
Chatham Gunwharf, 36, 68
Chatham Hospital, *see* Royal Naval Hospital Chatham
Chatham Victualling Yard, **172**
Cheadle Wireless Station, 27
Chemical Advisory Panel, *see* Admiralty Chemical Advisory Panel
Chemical and Biological Defence Establishment, 221
Chemical Research and Development Department (1945–8), 221
Chemical Warfare Committee (of the War Cabinet), 189
Chesapeake Bay, 179
Chester, 78
Chief Constructor, *see* Director of Naval Construction
Chief of the Air Staff, **206**
Chief of the Defence Staff, **220**
Chief of the Imperial General Staff, **38**

Index (references are to list numbers, not pages)

Chiefs of Staff Committee (1923–45), **191**, 236
Chiefs of Staff Committee (1947–73), **219**, 220; Maritime Air Committee, 206
Chiefs of Staff, intelligence reports (1944–5), 39
Children's Overseas Reception Scheme (1940), 214
Chile, British ambassador to, 30; British naval war graves in, 30; independence celebrations, 25; internment of German personnel, 52; pirates, 75
Chilean Navy, reports on (1881), 37; sales to, 30
China, 226; blockade of (1952–3), 32; expedition to (1900), 30, 36; government in Chungking (1942–5), 39; Naval Academy (1948), 30; naval attachés, 39; naval operations in (1906–12), 39; treaties with, 32; visas for British officers, 24
— hostilities with, (1840–2), 30, 35, 111, 224; (1856), 21, 23, 30; (1858–60), 36
China Sea, 214
China Squadron and Station, 30, 39, **179**, 236; East Indies Division, 179; Pacific Division, 179; *see also* East Indies, Far East
Chinese Navy, 21, 30; transfer of ships to, 32
cholera, 165
Christ's Hospital, 228
chronometers, 75
Chubut, Patagonia, 179
Churchill, Sir Winston, 36
Cinque Ports, 2
Civil Affairs Units, 43
Civil Architect of the Admiralty, 90
Civil Aviation, Ministry of, *see* Ministry of Aviation, Ministry of Civil Aviation
Civil Engineer-in-Chief, *see* Surveyor of Buildings
Civil Establishment, *see* Admiralty Office
Civil Law Branch, *see* Admiralty Office
Civil Service Commission, **66**
Civil Service Department, **66**
Civil Service National Whitley Council Official Side, 57
Claymore, *see* Operation CLAYMORE
Cleopatra's Needle, 133
Clerks, Admiralty, 63, 100, 183; Navy Board, 13, 100, 139, 140, 236; Ordnance, 183
Clerks of the Cheque, 143
Clerks of the King's Ships, **2**, **3**
Clerks RN, 231
Cleveland, Yorks., 72
Clinical Research Working Party, 110
Close Rolls, **1**
clothing, 111, 130; *see also* slops
Clyde, River and estuary, 213
coal, 52; carried by train, 227; for RN, 53, 75, 186, 216, 227, 235; for belligerent warships, 23, 62

Coal Advisory Committee (of Board of Trade), 70
coaling stations, 190
Coast Artillery Co-operation Unit (1939–45), 210
Coast Blockade (1816–31), 86, 101, **125**, 132, 140
Coast Defence Wing, India (1942), 210
coast defences, 37, 42, 183, 184, 235
Coastal Air Pilot (1943), 204
Coastal Command, 194, 204, 205, 206, **209**, 236; anti-submarine warfare, 46; Anti U-boat Devices School (1945), 210; Categorisation Board, St. Mawgan (1953–5), 210; combat reports, 209; Development Unit, **208**, 210; Flying Instructors' School (1944–5), 210; Groups, 210; Gunnery School (1955), 210; Modification Centre (1954–5), 210; operations record books, 209–10; registered files, 209
Coastal Command Unit, Portreath (1943–4), 210
Coastal Defence Flight No. 6 (India), 210
Coastal Operational Training Units/Detachments (1940–7), 210
coastal operations, proposed (1911), 36
Coastal Patrol Flights (1939–40), 210
coasters, 214
Coastguard Reserve, 71, 127
Coastguard Service, 49, 62, 71, 84, 127, 158, 196; boatmen, 232; land and buildings, 57, 62, 68; officers, 231; ratings, 232
Cochin, India, 98, 135
Cochrane, Admiral Thomas, Lord, later 10th Earl of Dundonald, 24; Hon. Basil, Agent-Victualler East Indies, 236
Cock, Peter, pilot extra, 13
Cockatoo Island, *see* Sydney Dockyard
Cockburn Sound, Australia, 25
Cockermouth, Keswick and Penrith Railway, 227
'Cod War', *see* Iceland
codes, *see* cyphers
Codrington, Vice-Admiral Sir Edward, C-in-C Mediterranean, 85, 236
Cohen Commission on Awards to Inventors, 235
Colchester, 1st Baron, *see* Abbot, Charles; 2nd Baron, *see* Abbot, Charles
Collectors of Customs, correspondence with Admiralty, 62, 91, 93
Collectors of Sixpences, 127, *see also* Register Office
Collingwood, Vice-Admiral Cuthbert, Lord, 30, 236
Collins, Grenville, Master RN, 236
collisions, 23, 178, 204
Colnett, Captain J, 103
Colombian Navy, 24
Colombo, Ceylon, 183
Colonel-Commandant in London, later Adjutant-General RM, 89, 114

Colonels-Commandant RM, 89, 115
colonial defence, 23, 37, 190; *see also* imperial defence
Colonial Defence Committee, 190
Colonial governors, 47, 91, 93, 159, 179
Colonial Office (1855–1968), **47**; *see also* Colonial Secretary
colonial policy, 204
Colonial Secretary (1768–82), correspondence with Admiralty, 15, 83, 91; *see also* Secretaries of State
Colonial Secretary (1855–1968), 84, 236; *see also* Colonial Office
colonies, defence of, *see* colonial defence
Colwyn Committee on Admiralty Labour Problems (1919), 235
Colwyn Committee on Service Expenditure (1925), 205, 235
Combined Chiefs of Staff Committee, **191**
Combined [Intelligence] Bureau Middle East (1940), 27
Combined Operations, 40, 42, 206; exercises (1924 and 1937), 204; exercises, in East Indies (1944–5), 42; staff history, 35, 204; Inter-Service Planning Staff (1939–45), 39; Manual (1911–13), 37; orders (1915), 39; requirements (1945–6), 36; staff history, 35; *see also* amphibious operations
Combined Operations Committee (1916), 190
Combined Operations Headquarters (1941–5), 39, 194
Combined Services Detailed Interrogation Centre, reports, **39**
Combined Signal Board (1943)
Commander-in-Chief, Baltic, 236; Cape of Good Hope, 179; Channel Isles, 178; China, 30, 39, 236; East Indies, 37, 67, 179, 236; Leeward Islands, 179; Mediterranean, 34, 179, 236; Nore, 178; North America, 179, 236; North-West Africa (1942), 39; Pacific, 236; Plymouth, 178; Portsmouth, 178; West Indies (1801–5), 34;
commanders, of privateers, 86
Commanders, services, 231
commanders-in-chief, accommodation, 37, 55; accounts, 67, 101, 179; appointments, 1; correspondence with Secretaries of State, 15; correspondence with Secretaries for War, 34; journals, 97, 178; military, 42; services, 231
Commando Brigades, Royal Marines, 36; *see also* Royal Marine Commandos
Commissariat, correspondence with War Office (1661–1855), 33; *see also* War Office (1855–1964)
Commission and Warrant Branch, *see* Admiralty Office
Commission des échanges, 167
Commission for Naval Information (1945), 28
Commission for Revising and Digesting the Civil Affairs of the Navy, *see* Board of Revision

Commission of Enquiry into Crown Woods (1786–94), 67
Commission of Naval Enquiry (1608), 5, 235; (1618), 5–6, 235; (1626–8), 5–6, 235; (1636), 5, 235; (1805–6), 67, 91
Commission on Book-Keeping (1827–30), 235
Commission on Fees in Public Offices (1785–8), 235
Commissioned gunners, 231
commissioned officers, *see* naval officers, sea officers
Commissioners, for Discharging the Navy (1661–3), 156, 235; of Audit, *see* Audit Office; of Crown Estates, 68; of Dockyards, 88, 132, 143, 144, 161; of Greenwich Hospital, 67, 120; of RN Hospitals, 163; of the Navy, 75, 232 (*see also* Navy Board); of Public Accounts, 50; of Sick and Hurt, 13 (*see also* Sick and Hurt Board); of Transports, 175 (*see also* Transport Board); of Woods and Forests, 68
commissions, RM and RN, 101, 114, 179, 231
Committee of Accounts (of Navy Board), 130
Committee of Imperial Defence, 70, 188, **190**, 191, 217; committees, 190; Historical Section, **192** (*see also* official histories); Naval Assistant Secretary, 54
Committee of Inquiry into Trawler Safety (1968), 235
Committee on Accounts and Audit (1845), 235
Committee on Admiralty Experimental Establishments (1946–9), 118, 235
Committee on Admiralty Financial Arrangements (1885), 235
Committee on Armament of Defended Ports Abroad (1907), 235
Committee on Armaments of Home Ports (1905), 235
Committee on Army and Navy Stores (1890), 235
Committee on Canteens and Victualling (1907), 111, 235
Committee on Coast Defence (1852–3), 183, 235
Committee on Communication between London and Dublin (1842–63), 235
Committee on Control of Production Expenditure (1962), 196
Committee on Dangerous Buildings (1896), 36
Committee on Dazzle Painting of Ships (1915–20), 235
Committee on Dockyard Economy (1859), 235
Committee on Finance, 100
Committee on Fitting Troop Ships to Carry Horses (1870), 235
Committee on Floating Obstructions (1866), 37, 235
Committee on Human Engineering Research (1971–7), 110, 235
Committee on Naval Architecture (1842–4), 235
Committee on Naval Contracts (1857), 235
Committee on Naval Magazines (1895), 235
Committee on Naval Prize Law (1900–4), 13

Committee on Navy and Army Debts (1713–14), 235
Committee on Navy Office Clerks (1817), 235
Committee on Ordnance (1859), 37, 235
Committee on Pay of Medical Officers (1889), 235
Committee on Projectiles (1916–17), 235
Committee on Purchase, Custody and Accounts of Naval Stores (1890–5), 235
Committee on Safety of Nuclear Ships (1959–64), 224
Committee on Ships' Store Establishments (1814–30), 235
Committee on Slop Clothing (1820), 235
Committee on the Care of Shipwrecked Personnel (1942), 235
Committee on the Training of Naval Cadets (1905–6), 201, 235
Committee on Trade and Plantations (of Privy Council), 12, 70
Committee on Trading with the Enemy (1914–17), 58
Committee on Venereal Disease in the Army and Navy (1863–6), 235
Committee on Vulnerability of Capital Ships to Air Attack (1936), 235; see also Capital Ship Committee (1920–1)
Committee on Warrant Officers' Accounts (1823), 235
Commodore Persian Gulf, 179
Commodores, 86, 179; prize money, 13
Commonwealth Prize Pool (1953–4), 48
Commonwealth Relations Office, **48**
Companies Court, **80**
Compassionate Fund, 36, 124, 231
Compassionate List, 124, 231
compensation, for gunfire damage, 37, 235
Competitor, convict ship (1820–3), 77
Concordia, prize (1752), 78
Condé, prize (1783), 78
condemnations of prizes, High Court of Admiralty, 8
Confederate States of America, 23; Navy, 23
Conference on Pay of Admiralty and War Office employees (1911), 235
Conference on Supply of Duty-Free Stores (1933–5), 235
Conferences, Admiralty-War Office (1900–16), 37, 190, 235; Geneva (1927), 23, 53, 236; Hague (1904–5), 22, 70; hydrographic (1899–1905), 22; Imperial, 39, 48, 190; Lausanne (1922–3), 24; London (1906–9), 23, 32; London (1930), 26, 30, 32, 51, 188, 192, 236; London (1935–6), 30, 32, 188; naval (1924–39), 26, 32, 48, 236; naval intelligence (1971), 219; Nyon (1937), 32; Potsdam (1945), 24; Singapore Anglo-French (1939), 37, 235; Versailles (1919), 24; Washington (1870–1), 21; Washington (1921–3), 23, 30, 32, 36, 188

Confidential Print, Dominions Office, 48; Foreign Office, 23
Congo Brazzaville, 30
Constantinople, 30, 42, 109, 179
consuls, British, expenses, 125, 133; consuls, foreign, 92
— correspondence with Admiralty, 23, 30, 93; with commanders-in-chief, 179; with Navy Board, 132;
Continuous Service, 232
Contract and Purchase Branch, *see* Admiralty Office
contractors, 67, 96, 104, 130, 132, 186; *see also* Admiralty, Navy Board
contracts, buildings, 196; clothing, 130; dockyard, 130, 135, 145, 146; hemp, 202; naval stores, 130, 131; Ordnance, 182; prices, 130; shipbuilding, 130, 135; timber, 135; victualling, 170
Contracts Co-ordinating Committee, 190
Control Commission for Germany, **28**; Naval Division, 28
Control of Aliens in War Sub-Committee, 193
Controller of Steam Machinery, **106**; *see also* Steam Department, Packet Service
Controller of Storekeepers' Accounts (1671–1796), 137; *see also* Navy Board Stores Department
Controller of the Navy (1545–1832), 108, **134**, 158, 236
Controller of the Navy (1832–), **104**, 105; correspondence, 87, 90, 104; *see also* Surveyor of the Navy
Controller of Victualling, 90, 111, 170; *see also* Victualling Board, Victualling Department
convict ships, stores and fitting, 49; Surgeons' journals 110, 161; victualling, 111
convoys, 116; Admiralty orders, 83; air defence of, 206, 207; composition, 207; correspondence, 92; licences to sail without, 92, 101; lists of, 101, 214; signals, 101, 130; to Narvik (1940), 214
Conway, boys' training ship, 17, 201
Cook, Captain James, 79, 196
Cooks, 157, 232
Cooper, Thomas, Greenwich Pensioner, 163
coopers, 13, 142, 172
Co-ordination of Departmental Action Committee (of the War Cabinet), 189
Co-ordination of Valve Development Department, 118, 223
copper sheathing, coppering, 103, 133
Coppinger, Rear-Admiral Robert Henry, 63
Corbett, Sir Julian, 36
Corbett, Thomas, Secretary of the Admiralty, 236
cordite, 16, 44, 146, 185
Corfu Island, 24, 132, 179; *see also* Ionian Islands
Cork, Ireland, 85 (*see also* Haulbowline); Victualling Yard, *see* Royal Alexandra Victualling Yard

corn, scarcity of (1795), 13
Cornwall, wrecking in, 78
Cornwallis, Charles, 1st Marquis, 236; Admiral Hon. William, 236
Cornwallis, schooner (1800–7), 67
Coronation Naval Review (1937), 30, 227; *see also* Naval Reviews
coronations, 180, 196
Corps of Marines, 114, 115; *see also* Marines, Royal Marines
Corsica, expedition to (1793–4), 16
Cotes, James, British Agent in Paris, 167; Rear-Admiral Thomas, 75
Cotton, Admiral Sir Charles, C-in-C Mediterranean, 30, 236
Council, of Greenwich Hospital, 120; of Haslar Hospital, 163; on Naval Education, 126; *see also* Privy Council
Council of State (1649–60), **11**, 129; Admiralty Committee, 11
Councils of War, 85
Course of the Exchange, 168, 230
Court of Assistants (of Sea Officers' Widows' Charity), 124
Court of Chancery, **77**
Court of Exchequer, **78**; depositions, 78
Court of King's Bench, **80**
Court of Requests, **80**
Court of Star Chamber, **80**
courts martial, 48, 83, 96, 101, 130, 178, 179, 224, 231; in troopships, 36; Royal Marine, 36, 96, 101, 114
Courts Martial Appeal Court, **80**
Coutts Bank, 167
Cowley, 1st Baron, *see* Wellesley, Henry; 2nd Baron and 1st Earl, *see* Wellesley, Henry
creosote, 70
Cressy (1899), 186
Crimean War, *see* Russian War
crimping, in US ports, 21
Croatian Navy (1944–5), 27
Crocodile (1825), 158, 180, 236
Cromarty, 114
Cromwell, Major-General Oliver, 'Lord Protector of England', 11
Crown Agents for the Colonies, **47**
Crown Estates Commissioners, **68**, 100
Cuba, Soviet activities in (1970–1), 26
Cuban Navy, 25
Cunningham, Admiral Sir Andrew, 30, 198; correspondence, 42
Cunningham, John, Navy agent, 236
Curaçoa Hospital, 165

Customs, Board of, *see* Board of Customs
Customs and Excise, Board of, *see* Board of Customs and Excise
customs duties, on candles, 13; on foreign bottoms, 155; on stores of HM Ships, 13
Customs officers, 62, 231; naval intelligence, 62; *see also* Collectors of Customs
cutlasses, 36
Cuxhaven, Germany, 28
cyphers and cryptography, 27; British, 27, 117; German, 27, 117; Japanese, 27; Russian, 27
Cyprus, ports, 36

'D Notice' Committee (1919–93), 219
Daily Situation Reports (1939–45), 189
Dale, Sir Henry, of the Cabinet Scientific Advisory Committee, 236
Danish Navy, blockade of Danzig (1849–55), 30
Danzig, Danish blockade (1849–55), 30
Dardanelles, 23, 30, 186, 236; defences of, 36
Dardanelles Commission (1916–19), 235
Dardanelles Committee (1915), 186
Dardanelles Committee (1919), 42, 235; *see also* Admiralty Dardanelles Committee, Joint-Service Dardanelles Committee
Dar-es-Salaam, East Africa, 42
Dartmouth, Devon, ships of (1588), 78
Dartmouth (1813), 62
D'Auvergne, Rear Admiral Philip, styled Prince de Bouillon, C-in-C Channel Isles, 236
De Courten-Cunningham Naval Agreement with Italy (1943), 42
De Geertruy, Dutch East Indiaman, 99
De Winter, Vice-Admiral Jan Willem, C-in-C of Dutch Fleet, 99, 236
Deal, Kent, Admiralty firing range, 72; Hospital, *see* Royal Naval Hospital Deal; Naval and Victualling Depot, 88, 149, 172, 175; Royal Marine Depot and Division, 114, 115
deaths, by enemy action, 18, 110; certificates, 157, 162; lists and analyses, 110; of enemy prisoners of war, 167; registration of, 18; *see also* casualties and casualty lists
debentures and debenture books, 156, 182, 184
deception, 219
declared accounts, *see* accounts
decorations, *see* awards, medals, Victoria Cross
decrees, High Court of Admiralty, 8
deeds of conveyance, 1, 68, 75, 168
Defence and Overseas Policy Committee, 193, 220
Defence Board (1958–64), minutes, 217
Defence Committee (of Cabinet, 1870–88), 190

Index (references are to list numbers, not pages)

Defence Council (1964–), minutes, 217
Defence Council Instructions, **219**
Defence Evaluation and Research Agency, 217
Defence Intelligence Staff (1957–79), **219**
Defence Lands Review Committee, Navy (1971–3), 219, 235
Defence Lands Service, 219
Defence Ministry, *see* Ministry of Defence
Defence of Merchant Shipping, Master's Handbook (1948), 128
Defence Operational Analysis Establishment, 217
Defence (Operations) Committee (of the War Cabinet, 1939–45), 189
Defence Planning Staff (1947–68), 219
Defence Publications, 219
Defence Research Policy Committee, 105, 217
Defence Review (1964–7), 217, 220; (1974), 220
Defence Review Committee (1954–5), 235
Defence Schemes Memoranda, 190
Defence Secretariat, 194
Defence Services Secretariat, 219
Defence Signals Staff, 217
Defence Staff, *see* Chief of the Defence Staff
Defence (Supply) Committee (of the War Cabinet, 1940–6), 189
Defence (Transition) Committee (of Cabinet, 1950–4), 193
defended ports, 36; entry in wartime, 37, 235; regulations, 37; signalling at, 36, 235
Defiance (1675), 13; (1695), 180, 236
Delagoa Bay, East Africa, 36
Delavall, Admiral Sir Ralph, Joint C-in-C Allied Main Fleet, 236
demobilisation, 137, 187, 202
Den Helder expedition (1799), 42
denizations, 1
Denmark, British ambassador to, 30; merchant shipping, 133; Prince George of, Lord High Admiral, 82; Queen Charlotte of (1766), 97; visits by RN, 30
Department of Aeronautical Supplies (of Ministry of Munitions, 1916–19), 46
Department of Aircraft Production (of Ministry of Munitions, 1918–20), technical bulletins, 46
Department of Energy, **216**
Department of Scientific and Industrial Research, 224
Department of the Environment, 200; *see also* Local Government Board, Ministry of Housing and Local Government, Ministry of Town and Country Planning, National Parks Commission
Department of Trade, 214; *see also* Board of Trade
Department of Trade and Industry, 214

Deptford Dockyard, **144**; Captain Superintendent, 88, 144; Commissioner, 88, 132, 144; plans, 196; sale (1869–75), 68; transport service, 109
Deptford Victualling Yard, 75, 109, 168, **169**; Captain Superintendent, 169; *see also* Royal Victoria Victualling Yard
Deputy Chief of the Air Staff, 206
Deputy Chiefs of Staff Committee, 191
Deputy Lieutenants (of counties), 36
Deputy Paymaster of Marines, Chatham, 61
Deputy Prime Minister's Private Office, 194
Deputy Treasurer (of Greenwich Hospital), 120
Derrick, Charles, Navy Office clerk, 137
description books, 169; Chatham Dockyard, 143; Chatham Victualling Yard, 172; *Crocodile* (1850–2), 158; Deptford Dockyard, 144; Deptford Victualling Yard, 169; *Perseus* (1843–9), 158; Plymouth Dockyard, 145; Portsmouth Dockyard, 146; Sheerness Dockyard, 147; Woolwich Dockyard, 148
deserters, 120, 157
Deutsche Seewarte (1945–6), 224
Deutschland, German liner (1945), 37
Devon, Vice-Admiralty, 78
Devonport Dockyard, 66, 75, **145**, 202; Admiral Superintendent, 88, 145, 178; asbestos, 17, 82; *see also* Plymouth Dockyard
diaries, 115, 236
Dick, John, Storekeeper at Jamaica, 78
Dido (1836), 230
Diego Garcia Island, US base, 25, 218
Diego Suarez, Madagascar, French naval base, 25
Dieppe Raid Committee (1942), 189
Dill, Field Marshall Sir John, 236
dimension books, 135
direction finding (D/F), 116
Director of Aircraft Equipment, 104
Director of Army and Navy Contracts (1888), 37
Director of Combined Operations, 194, 236
Director of Dockyards, 55, **108**
Director of Naval Accounts, 112
Director of Naval Construction, **105**, 106
Director of Naval Education, 127
Director of Naval Intelligence, *see* Naval Intelligence Division
Director of Naval Ordnance, *see* Director-General of Naval Ordnance
Director of Naval Transports, 236
Director of Naval Works, *see* Admiralty Works Department, Director-General of Naval Works
Director of Scientific Intelligence, 194
Directorate of Aeronautical and Engineering Research, 118

Directorate of Air (of Imperial General Staff), 40
Directorate of Civil Affairs (of Imperial General Staff), 40
Directorate of Defence Services (Navy), 198
Directorate of Forward Plans, 219
Directorate of Materials Research, 118
Directorate of Merchant Shipbuilding, 104
Directorate of Military Intelligence (of Imperial General Staff), **39**
Directorate of Military Operations (of Imperial General Staff), **39**
Directorate of Military Survey (of Imperial General Staff), **40**, 127
Directorate of Miscellaneous Weapons Development, 107
Directorate of Overseas Surveys, **47**
Directorate of Physical Research, 118
Directorate of Prisoners of War (of Imperial General Staff), 40
Directorate of Research Programmes and Planning, 118
Directorate of Signals (of Imperial General Staff), **40**
Directorate of Staff Orders (of Imperial General Staff), **40**
Directorate of Tactical Investigation (of Imperial General Staff), **40**
Director-General of Naval Ordnance, 44, 107
Director-General of Naval Works, 55, 108, 196
Directors, of East India Company, 236; of Greenwich Hospital, 120
discharges, by habeas corpus, 178; from dockyards, 151–4; from RN Hospitals, 164, 165; from RM, 115; from victualling yards, 170
dispatches and reports of proceedings (1939–45), 192
disposal books, RM, 115
Distinguished Service Order (1886–1945), 41
docks, damage to, 19; see also dry docks
Dockyard Battalions, 183
Dockyard Commissioners, 86, 88, 93, 132, 142–54, 161
Dockyard Police, **17**, 63, 65
dockyards, British, 70, 84, 135, 142, 198, 218; accounts, 64, 128, 142; Admiralty visitations of, 83, 131; alternative work for (1919–30), 53, 213; and Board of Revision, 177; and Navy Board, 131, 132, 142; and ship repairs, 13; colonial, 57; defences, 16, 37, 183, 196; Director of, *see* Director of Dockyards; economy in, 235; environmental effects, 198, 199; extensions, 152; land, 142; Malabar Committee on, 66; maps and plans, 142, 152; Master Shipwrights, 142; mills, 131, 132; Navy Board visitations of, 130, 142; officers, 142–9, 231, 233; orders and instructions, 104, 131, 142; schools, 54; stores, 142; Technical Colleges, 201; visits to, 23; workmen, 33, 53–5, 66, 96, 112, 142, 170, 198, 202, 211, 233 (*see also* Admiralty employees); works and buildings, 108; *see also* Basra, Bermuda, Bombay, Chatham, Deptford, Devonport, Durban, Gibraltar, Harwich, Haulbowline, Hong Kong, Malta, naval yards, Northfleet, Pembroke, Plymouth, Portsmouth, Rosyth, Sheerness, Simonstown, Singapore, Sydney, Toulon, Trincomalee, Woolwich
Dockyards Departments, *see* Director of Dockyards
Doctors' Commons, 75, 96; *see also* High Court of Admiralty
Doenitz, Grand Admiral Karl, 27–8
Dolphin, lugger privateer (1804), 78
Dolphin, shore establishment at Haslar, Hants., 68, 72
Dominions Office, **48**; Confidential Print, 48
Doraplane, *see* Toraplane
Dorset, 236
Double Quick, *see* Operation DOUBLE QUICK
Douglas, Andrew Snape, British chargé d'affaires in Palermo and Naples, 236
Douglas, Isle of Man, 62
Douglas-Home, Sir Alec, 26
Dover, Kent, Customs officers, 62; privateers and prizes of (1625–6), 78; survey, 72
Dover Harbour Board, 53, 213, **227**; railway, 68
Dover Victualling Depot, 172
Downs anchorage, pilots, 231
Downs Station, 85, 178
Dracula, *see* Operation DRACULA
Drake, Francis, British minister at Genoa, 67
Drake, Sir Francis, 236
Dreadnought (1960), 105
Dresden, German cruiser (1907), 52
Dreyer, Admiral Sir Frederic, 194
Droits of Admiralty, 49, 59; accounts, 64
dry docks, 70, 149, 213
dry rot, 235
Dryad, shore establishment (1971), 80
Dublin, Ireland, 85, 235
Duchess, Bristol privateer (1708–15), 77, 236
Duguay-Trouin, French warship, 99
Duifje, Dutch East Indiaman, 99
Duke, Bristol privateer (1708–15), 77, 236
Duke, privateer (1750–7), 78
Dundas, Henry, 1st Viscount Melville, *see* Melville; Admiral Sir James W, 236; Robert, 2nd Viscount Melville, *see* Melville
Durban Dockyard, 39
Dutch East India Company, 179, 183
Dutch East Indies, naval intelligence of, 39

Index (references are to list numbers, not pages)

Dutch Navy, 99, 101, 158, 167, 236; co-operation with, 25, 86
Dwarf (1898), 30

Eagle (1804), 13
Earl's Court, London, 57
East Africa, 179; operations (1915–16), 40
East Africa Command, **42**
East Cowes, Isle of Wight, 68
East Florida Claims Commission (1763–83), 59, 157, 235
East India Company, 16, 77, 92, 179, **226**, 236; Chinese Secretary, 226; *see also* Scottish East India Company, Swedish East India Company
East Indies Station, 37, 67, 192; commanders-in-chief, 85, 179, 236
East Indies Victualling Establishment, 173
Eastern Europe, Foreign Office correspondence, 25
Eastern Fleet (1943–6), 42
Eastern Mediterranean Command (1918–19), 30
Easton and Church Hope Railway, 227
Eckernforde, Germany, *Torpedoversuchsanstalt* (1946–50), 28
Economic Warfare, Ministry of, *see* Ministry of Economic Warfare
Ecuador, 30
Eden, Sir Anthony, Foreign Secretary, 26
Edinburgh, 125, 225; HRH Prince Philip, Duke of, 24
Edward VI, King of England, 5
Egremont, Charles Wyndham, 2nd Earl of, Secretary of State, 236
Egypt, British ambassador, 25, 30, 32
Egyptian Navy, 30
Eire, 48; *see also* Ireland
Ekins, Captain Thomas, 77, 236
Ekins Friggott (1699–1724), 77
electoral registration, 18
Elizabeth, privateer (1608), 78
Elizabeth I, Queen of England, 5
Ellenborough, Edward Law, 1st Earl of, First Lord of the Admiralty, 84, 236
embargoes, on arms exports, 36; on merchant shipping, 8, 13
embarkation books, RM, 115
Emes, Captain Fleetwood, 13
emigrant ships, 110, 161
Emma, Lady Hamilton, 79
Empire Windrush, troopship (1954), 30
Emu, colonial brig (1813–19), 158
Endeavour (1768), replica of, 48
Endurance (1967), 47
Energy, Department of, *see* Department of Energy
Engine Room Artificers, services, 232

Engineer's Boys, 232
Engineer-in-Chief of the Navy, 106, 231
engineers, *see* naval officers
English Harbour, *see* Antigua Naval Yard
ENIGMA cypher machine, 27
Ennerdale, RFA, 25
enrolled accounts, *see* accounts
ensigns, of British ships, 13, 62, 93, 132, 213
Enterprise (1783), 78
Enterprize (1774), 13
epidemics, 165, 179
Eskburn, SS, 112
espionage, 80
Esquimalt, British Columbia, 115
Essex, quotas, 225
Essex, Robert Devereux, 2nd Earl of, 6
establishment books, Greenwich Hospital, 120; HM Ships, 101; Navy Board Accounts Department, 136; RN Hospital Stonehouse, 164; Royal William Victualling Yard, 171; Victualling Board, 168
establishments, 100; of Admiralty staff, 13, 100; of Air Ministry staff, 235; of Greenwich Chest, 155; of guns, 13, 130, 183; of men, 13, 101; of Navy Office, 139; of Navy Pay Office, 13; of Ordnance stores, 183; of Poor Knights of Windsor, 124; of Royal Clarence Victualling Yard, 170; of ships' stores, 104, 130, 235; of Upnor Castle, 184
estate duty, 63
Ethiopian Navy, 25
Europe, *see* Eastern Europe, Southern Europe, Western Europe
Evelyn, John, Commissioner of Sick and Hurt, 79
Evershed Report on Naval Aviation (1944–5), 235
Examination Service (1913), 37, 235
examinations, 66, 126, 130, 201, 231, 236; fees, 63; physical, 231
examinations and answers, High Court of Admiralty, 8
Excellent, shore establishment at Portsmouth, 68, 107, 231
Exchange Requirements Committee (1939–45), 58
Exchequer, 1, **2**, **67**, 156; audits 3, 64; Barons of, 78, books, 3; Chancellor of, *see* Chancellor of the Exchequer; Court, *see* Court of Exchequer; declared accounts, **6**, **67**; foreign accounts, 2; Tellers of, 59; warrants, 5; warrants for issues, 2
Exchequer and Audit Office, *see* Audit Office
Excise Board, *see* Board of Excise
exemplars, High Court of Admiralty, 8
Exercise Porcupine (1950), 204
exercises, inter-Service, 204
Exeter (1929), 30
Experimental Section (of Royal Naval Air Service), 181

Experimental Squadron (1824–5), 84, 85
Experimental Stations, *see* Admiralty Experimental Stations
explosions, 105, 204
explosives, 16, 227
Explosives Act, 1925, 36
Explosives Committee (1870–91), 44
Explosives Inspectorate, 17
Explosives Research and Development Establishment (1948–74), 221
Export credit guarantees, 57
exports, 101
Extraordinary (of dockyards), 143–50
Eyres-Monsell, Sir Bolton, First Lord of the Admiralty, 236

Fabric Committee (of Greenwich Hospital), 120
Factory Inspectorate, **17**
Falkland, Anthony Cary, 5th Viscount, Treasurer of the Navy, 59
Falkland Islands, 36, 98, 198; defence of, 200; naval base (1934), 30; RM detachment, 115
Falmouth, Cornwall, rendezvous, 125; *see also* Mylor
Falmouth Naval Yard, 149
Falmouth Packet Station, 76, 78, 90
famine relief (1846–50), 111
Far East and Pacific, Foreign Office correspondence, 25
Far East Command, 25, 194
Far East Committee (of the War Cabinet), 189
Far East Flying Boat Wing (1950–4), 210
Faroe Islands, British consul, 30
Farouk, King of Egypt (1945), 30
Faslane Naval Base, 213
fees, High Court of Admiralty, 8
Fegen, Captain Edward Fogarty, VC, 63
Fenning, William, underwriter, 236
Fernando Po Naval Depot, 49, 136, 152; Victualling Depot, 173
Ferries Committee (1946–7), 213
Ferry Command, 209
Festival of Britain Office, 196
fevers, 165, 236
Field Officers RM, 86
Fighter Direction Ships, 204
fighters, for protection of shipping, 207
Fighting Services Committee (of Cabinet, 1922), 188
Finch, Daniel, of the Navy Pay Office, 236
Fine Rolls, **1**
Finland, 30
Finnish Navy, 30
Fire Brigades, 17

Fire Control Group, 119
fire-fighting, 17, 128
First Lord of the Admiralty, 71; correspondence, 194, 236; minutes, 192; oath, 13; Private Office, **84**, 231, 236; Private Secretary, 236; residence, 57 (*see also* Admiralty House, Whitehall); secret minute, 26, 42; secret service accounts, 64, 67
First Naval Lord, 94, **95**; correspondence with Foreign Office, 20, 83; *see also* First Sea Lord
First of June, Battle of, 101
First Sea Lord, 84
First World War, official history, 116; RN records, 178, 179; staff histories, 116, 128
Fisher, Admiral Sir John, First Sea Lord, 103
fisheries, Newfoundland, 85, 179; porpoise, 80; seal, 179; whale, 101
Fisheries Department, *see* Ministry of Agriculture
Fishguard, Pembrokes., 227
fishing agreements, *see* Admiralty fishing agreements
fishing boats and vessels, British, attacked by Iceland, 25; British, attacked by Russia, 23; protection of, 199
Fittleton (1954), 219
Fitzroy, Captain Robert, Governor of New Zealand, 236
Flag Officer, Gibraltar, 85; submarines, 127
Flag Officers, candidates, 84; correspondence 30, 85, 159; orders to, 7; services, 231; uniforms, 63; *see also* Admirals, commanders-in-chief
flags, *see* ensigns, Red Cross
Flanders, 174
flax, 202
Fleet Air Arm, aircraft, 32, 56, 204, 236; carriers, 236; charts, 40; combat reports, 181; Estimates, 51, 53; Evershed Report (1944), 235; flying log books, 181; in East Indies (1944–5), 42; in South Africa (1943–6), 48; Operation OVERLORD (1944), 209; operations (1954–71), 204; operations record books, 181, 210; organisation and status (1929–36), 204, 205; personnel, 204, 205; policy (1938–40), 53; radar, 204, 236; registered files, 190, 191; requirements (1941–2), 46, 236; squadrons, 181; staff history, 204; *see also* aircrew
Fleet Air Arm Sub-Committee (of Committee of Imperial Defence), 190
Fleet Air Arm Working Party (1968–9), 218, 235
Fleet Requirements Committee, 218, 235
Fleet Surgeons, 231
flour, for RN, 53
Flushing, British consul (1861), 30; Naval Yard (1809), 154
Flying Boat Training Squadron, 210
flying log books, 181

Index (references are to list numbers, not pages)

Food (Defence Plans) Department (of Ministry of Agriculture), 199
Force F (1942), 39
Force X (French, 1942–3), 42
Ford, Vice-Admiral Sir Denys, 63
Foreign Affairs Committee (of Privy Council), 12
Foreign Office, **20**, 117; Chief Clerk's Department, 20; Claims Department, 24; Political Intelligence Department, 24; Political Warfare Executive (1941–4), 24; War Department (1914–20), 24
— correspondence, **21–3**; Confidential Print, 23; Ottoman Empire, 20; slave trade, 20; with Admiralty, **20–1**, 91; with Flag Officers, 20, 85, 236
— registered files, **24–5**
Foreign Secretary, **20**, 83, 236; Private Office, **26**
Foreign Trade Department (1916–19), *see* Ministry of Blockade
Forest of Dean, Glos., 224
Forestry Commission, **224**
Formidable, French warship (1805), 99
Formidable, training ship, Portishead, 211
Formosa, 24; *see also* Taiwan
Fort George, Mauritius, 36
fort record books, 114
fortifications of dockyards, 143, 183
Four Power Naval Commission (1946–7), 28
France, agents in, 98; British ambassadors to, 236; Committee of National Liberation, Algiers (1944), 31; defences (1944), 42; émigrés from, 236; expedition to (1492), 3; naval relations with, 188, 189; treaties with, 32
France, Ministry of Marine, Bureau des Prisonniers, 167
Franklin, Captain Sir John, 75, 79, 103
Franks Committee (1955–6), 224
frauds, 78, 134, 140, 157, 236
freight, freight money, 120, 175, 176
Fremantle, Western Australia, 217
French Indo-China, reports (1940–3), 39; (1950), 30
French Navy, 42; (1839–46), 236; (1940–3), 189; administration (1675), 59; attacks on (1940), 189, 192, 207; at Alexandria (1942–3), 30, 31; at Oran (1940), 192; co-operation with (1973), 25; 'Free French', 25, 42; in Indian Ocean (1971), 25; in Indo-China (1940–3), 39; Operation TORCH, 206; prizes from, 99, 120; reports on (1811), 23; (1862–99), 23; transfer of aircraft to, 32; visits by, 25
frigates, Argentine, 57
Frobisher, Sir Martin, 79, 80, 226, 236
Froude-Hurrell Torpedo Company (1892), 80
Führer Decrees, 99
Fuel, Ministry of, *see* Ministry of Fuel and Power
Fuel Research Station, 224; *see also* Admiralty Fuel Experimental Station
Fugitive Slaves Commission, 22
Fulton, Robert, 103
funerals, 163; of dockyard workmen, 53–4; of Lord Nelson, 236; of prime ministers, 53; state, 196
Furious (1916), 209
Future Fleet Working Party (1966–8), 218, 235

Galathée, French prize (1757), 166
Gallipoli Campaign (1915–16), charts and maps, 40, 127; photographs, 37; reports, 42
Galloway, Captain Patrick, 77, 236
Gan Island, USN bases on, 48
Ganges, Indiaman (1779–82), 78
Ganges, shore establishment, Shotley, 199, 201, 219
Gannet aircraft, 222
gas turbines, for RN, 25
Gascon Rolls, **1**
Gascony, 1
Geddes Inquiry into the Shipbuilding Industry (1964–6), 70
General and Generals at Sea, orders from, 11, 129
General Court and Directors (of Greenwich Hospital), 120
General Post Office, **76**, 91; mail contracts, 76
General Register Office, **18**
General Staff, *see* Imperial General Staff
Geneva Arbitration (1871–2), 21
Geneva Naval Conference (1927), 23, 53
Genoa, Italy, British minister (1793), 30, 67
George III, transport (1788), 78
George V, King of Great Britain, 103, 123
George of Denmark, Prince, *see* Denmark
Georgia, galley (1745), 179
German Army, reports on (1922–41), 39
German civil service (1894), 37
German Navy, air attacks on (1939–45), 207–8; and Soviet Union (1945–6), 30; captured documents, 99, 117, 119; cruiser warfare (1914–18), 116; cyphers, 27, 117; deserters from, 16; dockyards (1945–8), 28; E-boats, 208; establishments (1945–8), 28; future of (1945), 24; gunnery (1944), 39; hospital ships, 194; in China (1898), 30; in Turkey (1914), 30; limitations on (1967–71), 25; meteorological observatory (1945–6), 224; operations against, 204, 207; operations of, 117; orders to (1945), 42; personnel (1894), 37; (1945–8), 28; prize regulations (1915–18), 26; R-boats, 28; records (1947–8), 28; reports on (1922–41), 39; ships scuttled (1919), 235; ships transferred to Britain (1947), 62; submarines, 28, 117; in Mediterranean (1917–18), 30; U-boat shelters, 208; wireless signals, 117

Germany, Admiralty claim against (1925–6), 52; Allied blockade of (1914–18), 26, 30, 62, 186; British administration (1945–9), 28; Führer Decrees, 99; Inter-Allied Naval Commission of Control (1922–4), 52; reparations (1945–7), 195; RN Command, 178; shipping and shipbuilding, 207; treaties with, 32, 188

Ghanaian Navy, establishment of, 48

Ghormley, Vice-Admiral Robert L, USN, 236

Gibraltar, defence of, 25, 37; explosion of ammunition ship at (1951), 47; Flag Officer, 85; foreign naval visits to, 25; meat reserves (1902), 37, 235; Naval Hospital, *see* Royal Naval Hospital; USN at, 36, 38

Gibraltar and South Atlantic, Foreign Office correspondence, 25

Gibraltar Dockyard, 25, 63, **152**, 198

Gibraltar Victualling Yard, 173

Gibson, Lieutenant John, 13

Gilbert Islands, 23

Gillespie, Dr Leonard, 236

Girls' Naval Training Corps, 201

Givet, France, British prisoners in (1806), 167

Gladiator, hospital ship (1793–1802), 163

Glasgow (1976), 17

Glorious (1916), 209

Gloucester (1695), 236

Gneisenau, German battleship, 204, 206

Goodall, Stanley, naval constructor, 236

Goodrick, schooner of Guernsey (1809), 78

Gorrequer, Lieutenant-Colonel Gideon, 236

Gosport, Hants., 35; shipyard in, 77

Gothic, SS (1950–4), 56

Government Code and Cypher School, **27**, 117; Naval Section, 27

Government Communications Head Quarters, 57

Government Lymph Establishment (1907–9), 211

Government War Book Sub-Committee (1937), 190

Governor, of Greenwich Hospital, 120, 121, 122, 236; of Haslar Hospital, 163; of Newfoundland, 179; of RN Academy, 90, 126; *see also* colonial governors

Gradisca, German hospital ship (1944), 194

Graham, Sir James, First Lord of the Admiralty, 67, 84

Grand Committee (of Greenwich Hospital), 120

Grand Fleet, 178; *see also* Channel Fleet

graving docks, *see* dry docks

Great Central Railway, 227

Great Lakes of North America, warships on, 23, 32; *see also* Lake Huron

Great Seal of England, 1

Great Western Dock Company, 227

Great Western Railway, 227

Great Yarmouth RN Air Station, 181; *see also* Yarmouth

Greece, blockade of (1886), 23; British ambassadors and consuls, 179; British Naval Missions to (1912–29), 30; railways, 39

Greek Navy (1917–35), 30; officers of, 24

Green Cloth, Board of, *see* Board of Green Cloth

'Green Lists' (of landing craft, 1942–6), 116, 128

Greenock, Renfrews., 25, 125, 185

Greenwich Chest, see Chatham Chest

Greenwich Hospital, 59, 63, 68, **120**, 161; accounts, 56, 64, 67, 120; Board, 13; booty money, 78; burial registers, 120; Captain Superintendent, 120; Commissioners, 120; contracts, 120; correspondence, 83, 90, 93, 120, 161; Council, 120; estates, 120; Deputy Treasurer, 120; Directors, 120; Fabric Committee, 120; Foundation, 53, 120; General Court, 120; Governor, 120; Grand Committee, 120; in-pensions, 35, 83, 120, 121, 157; Lieutenant-Adjutant, 120; light dues, 120; Lord Nelson's Trust, 120; nurses, 120; Orford grant, 120, 236; out-pensions, 33, 83, 121, 157, 235; Pensions Office, 83, **121**, 157; plans, 197; Royal Commission, 235; schools, **122**, 232; Secretary, 120; subscribers, 120; Treasurer's ledgers, 120; wills, 120; *see also* Royal Naval College

Greenwich Hospital Committee (1829), 120, 235

Greenwich Hospital Joint Committee (1864–71), 235

Greenwich Observatory, *see* Royal Observatory

Greet, Commander William, 180, 236

Grenada, slaver of Liverpool (1768), 78

Grey, Sir Edward, Foreign Secretary, 26, 236

Grey, Thomas Philip, 2nd Earl de, First Lord of the Admiralty, 67, 84

guardships, 101

Guatemala, reports from, 30

Guernsey, charts of, 13

gun boats, 13, 179

Gunners, pensions, 13, 157; services, 128, 157, 183, 231

gunnery, naval, 42; anti-aircraft, 189; drill, 45; Grand Fleet, 178; long course, 221; qualifications, 231; schools, *see Cambridge, Excellent*

gunpowder, export of, 78

guns, British naval, 46, 59, 130, 182, 183, 187, 196, 206, 221, 235; carriages, 183; export of, 78; foreign naval, 23; *see also* Ordnance

Habbakuk, 219

habeas corpus, 178

Hague Conferences (1904–5), 22, 70

half-pay, 93, 101, 134, 157; *see also* naval officers, sea officers

Halifax, Edward Wood, 3rd Viscount, Foreign Secretary, 26

Index (references are to list numbers, not pages)

Halifax Naval Yard, 152
Halifax Victualling Yard, 173
Hamburg, Germany, 78, 175
Hamilton, Vice-Admiral Sir Charles, Governor and C-in-C of Newfoundland, 97, 236
Hamoaze, 145; *see also* Plymouth Dockyard
Hampshire, 67, 225
Hankey, Maurice, Lord, Secretary of the Cabinet, 188, 189, 236
Happy Return, of Bideford (1708), 78
Happy Return, privateer (1803–4), 77
harbour and rigging wages, 87, 130
harbours, 93; damage to, 19; of refuge, 235; *see also* ports
Hardy, Admiral Sir Thomas Masterman, 79
Harland & Wolff, Belfast, 53
Harmsworth, Hon. Cecil, 26, 236
Harrier aircraft, 204, 217, 219
Harrison, John, clockmaker, 75
Hartlepool, co. Durham, 36, 68, 72
Hartlepool Dock and Railway, 227
Hartshorn, *see* Plymouth Victualling Yard
Harwich Dockyard, 68, **149**; crane, 227
Haslar, Hants., Hospital, *see* Royal Naval Hospital Haslar; Jetty, 68
Hatston, Orkney, 36, 57
Haulbowline Dockyard, 88, 109, **149**; *see also* Cork
Havana, expedition to (1762), 236; Slave Trade Mixed Commission, **9**
Hawaii Island, 196
Hawke, privateer (1777–80), 77
Hawkins, Sir John, Treasurer of the Navy, 5, 79, 182
Hayter Committee on Royal Marine Officers' Pay (1883–4), 36, 235
Head Money, 103, 113, 130
Health, Ministry of, *see* Ministry of Health
Health and Safety Executive, **17**
Health of Mercantile Marine and Navy Advisory Committee (1922–35), 211
Hector, Dutch warship, 99
Hedgehog (anti-submarine weapon), 46
Hejaz, naval operations against (1924–32), 30
Helder, *see* Den Helder
helicopters, against submarines, 208
Heligoland Island, 208; Battle of (1914), 208; Naval Depot, 154
Hellenic Navy, *see* Greek Navy
hemp, and flax, 70, 133; for RN, 59, 78, 130, 202
Henry VIII, King of England, 5
Henry Grace à Dieu (1514), 3
Herald (1852–5), 97, 236
Herbert, Arthur, *see* Torrington, Earl of; Henry, *see* Carnarvon, Earl of

Herm, charts of, 13
Herschell, Richard, 2nd Baron, 236
Hervey, Captain John Augustus, Lord, 179, 236
High Court of Admiralty, 7, **8**; accounts, 8, 64, 67; assignation books, 8; act books, 8; allegations, 8; appeals from, 14; appeals to, 8; case papers, 8; condemnations, 8; correspondence, 8, 91; decrees, 8; Deputy Registrar, 236; examinations and answers, 8; exemplars, 8; fees, 8, 78; instance jurisdiction, **8**; interlocutaries, 8; interrogatories, 8; Judge of, 7–8, 81, 236; law reports, 75; letter books, 8; letters of attorney, 8; libels, 8; Marshal of, 8, 57; minutes of acts, 8; monitions, 8; prisoners, 8, 16–17; Prize Court, **8**; prize distributions, 8; proctors, 8; receipt books, 8; Receiver of Droits, 8, 67; Receiver of Prizes, 8, 67; Registrar of Prizes, 8; sentences, 8; warrants, 8, 81
High Level Bridge (1913–14), 36, 190, 235
Hilsea Bridge, Hants., 75
Hinkley Point C Inquiry, 216
Hinton Papers, 223
hired armed ships and vessels, 130, 158
histories, *see* official histories, staff histories
Hodges, William, painter, 219
Hogue (1900), 186
Holland, Sub-Lieutenant T (1949), 24
Holton Heath, *see* Royal Naval Cordite Factory
Holy Island, Northumberland, 68
Holyhead, Anglesey, 68; Packet Station, 106
home commands, 85, 93, 178; *see also* commanders-in-chief
Home Defence Committee, 190
Home Defence Executive, 190
Home Office, **16**; Aliens Office, 17; Fire Brigades Division, 17; Fire Services Department, 17
Home Policy Committee (of the War Cabinet), 189
Home Ports Defence Committee, 190
Home Secretary, **16**; Admiralty warrants, 16; correspondence, 16, 91; prize appeals, 16
Home Security, Ministry of, *see* Ministry of Home Security
home stations, *see* home commands
Honduras, 98
Hong Kong, 36, 39, 236
Hong Kong Dockyard, 36, 37, 153
Hong Kong Hospital, *see* Royal Naval Hospital Hong Kong
Honolulu, British consul (1829–74), 30, 91, 179
Honourable East India Company, *see* East India Company
honours, 96, 194, 219, 231; *see also* awards
Hood, Admiral Samuel, 1st Viscount, 13, 236; Rear-Admiral Sir Samuel, 30

351

Hook's hydrofoil, 217
Hooker, Sir William, Director of the Royal Botanical Gardens, 236
Hope, Captain Herbert, 236
Hope, schooner (1800–7), 67
Hope, victualling transport (1752), 78
Hopton, John, Clerk of the King's Ships, 3
Hornet, shore establishment at Haslar, Hants., 68
horses, transport of by sea, 37
Hospital Agents, East Indies, 160; Haslar, 163
Hospital Pharmacists, 233
hospital ships, 22, 59, 161, **162**, 163–5
hospitals, 110, 159, 160, 161, 177; *see also* medical establishments, Royal Naval Hospitals
Hoste, Captain Sir William, 236
Hotham, Vice-Admiral William, 236
House of Commons, 130, 156
House of Lords Record Office, 4
Housekeeper (of Navy Office), 139
hovercraft, 30, 222, 230
Howard, Sir Edward, Lord Admiral of England, 2
Howard of Effingham, Charles, Lord, Lord Admiral of England, 7
Howe, Admiral Richard, Earl, 101, 236
Hoxton, RN Lunatic Asylum, 164
hoys, 13, 170
Hudson's Bay Company, 226
Hughes, Vice-Admiral Sir Edward, 179, 236
Hull, Yorks., 125, 216
Hulton, H, Receiver of Sixpences in North America, 236
Hulton-Sams, Lieutenant G H, 236
Hungarian Navy, 52
Hungary, peace treaty with (1920–1), 36, 52
Hunter, William, Navy Office clerk, 140, 236
Husky, *see* Operation HUSKY
hydraulic jet propulsion, 106
hydrofoils, 217
Hydrographer of the Navy, 24, 55, 90, 98, **127**
hydrographers, 13
Hydrographic Conferences (1899–1905), 22
Hydrographic Department, Hydrographic Office, 30, 54, 216; Committee on (1906), 235; correspondence with Directorate of Military Survey, 40; *see also* Hydrographer of the Navy
Hydrographic Service (1967–73), 218

Iceland, fishery dispute with, 25, 116, 217, 218
Iceland Command (1940–2), 39; No. 30 (Coastal) Wing, 210
Ilchester, Indiaman (1757–60), 77
Île de Ré expedition (1626), 6, 168

Imperial Communications Committee, 190
Imperial Conferences, 48; (1909), 39
imperial defence, 188; Committee of, *see* Committee of Imperial Defence; *see also* colonial defence
Imperial General Staff, and invasion of Britain (1916), 37; Chief of, **38**; Directorates, **39**, **40**; Geographical Section, **40**; MI9, 39
Imperial War Museum, 196, 224
Implacable (1805), 225
imports, 101
Impress Service, expenses, 125, 157; officers, 125, 133, 231; reports, 125
impressment, 75, 91, 130, 225; declared accounts, 67, 225; of smugglers, 232; warrants for, 13; *see also* seamen, protections, watermen
imprests, 140, 145, 156, 168, 179
Income Tax, 36, 51–2, 160
Indefatigable, boys' training ship, 17
indentures, apprentices', 122; of retinue, 3
Independence, later *Britannia*, privateer (1788–9), 78
India, 190; Coastal Defence Wing, 210; internal security, 37
India Board of Control (1784–1858), 224
India Office Intelligence Department (1890), 37
Indiamen, 77–8
Indian Navy, ships for, 56
Indian Ocean, 25, 206
Indonesia, threat to Malaysia, 220
industrial disputes, 202
Industrial Intelligence Sub-Committee, 190
Infant School, 122; *see also* Greenwich Hospital Schools
infestation control, 199
Information, Central Office of, Ministry of; *see* Central Office of Information, Ministry of Information
Infra-Red Committee, 217
Inland Revenue, **63**
Inquisitions Miscellaneous, **1**
Inskip Inquiry (1936–7), 205
Inspecting Captain of Aeronautics, of Aircraft, 104, 236
Inspector of Artillery, 184
Inspectorate of Nuclear Installations, 216
Inspectorate of Schools, 17
Inspector-General of Naval Works, 90, 127, 131, 132
Inspectors of Canvas, 132
Inspectors of Hospitals, correspondence, 159, 160; services, 231
Institute of Naval Medicine, Alverstoke, 110, 200
insurance, *see* marine insurance
Integrated Naval Attack System (for Harrier Aircraft), 204

Index (references are to list numbers, not pages)

Intelligence and Statistics Department, *see* Ministry of Labour
Inter-Allied Naval Commission of Control, Berlin (1922–4), 52
Inter-Departmental Committee on Admiralty and RAF Flying Danger Areas (1937–9), 235
Inter-Departmental Committee on Army and Navy Pensions (1898), 235
Inter-Departmental Committee on Army and Navy Stores (1897), 235
Inter-Departmental Committee on Guns and Ammunition (1925–9), 235
Inter-Departmental Committee on Medical Certificates, 211
Inter-Departmental Committee on Naval or Military Pay with Civil Salary (1885), 235
interlocutaries, High Court of Admiralty, 8; Prize Appeals Commissioners, 14
International Danube Commission (1920), 235
interrogation of enemy prisoners, 39, 42
interrogatories, High Court of Admiralty, 8
Inter-Service Committee on Chemical Warfare (1940–54), 189
Inter-Service Committee on Raiding Operations, 194
Inter-Service Metallurgical Research Council, 46
Inter-Service Recognition Committee (1938–40), 204
Inter-Service Technical Valve Committee, *see* Co-ordination of Valve Development Department
Inter-Service Topographical Department, 128
Inter-Services Security Board, 194
invasion, measures against (1797), 13; (1916), 235; (1940–2), 42
inventions, 183; aircraft, 204; armour, 184; awards for, 222, 235; torpedoes, 53
Invergordon Mutiny (1931), 84, 236
Ionian Islands, 30
Iranian Navy, base at Bandar Abbas, 30; sales to, 25, 219
Iraq, and RN, 30
Iraqi Navy, 30
Ireland, charts, 17; famine relief (1846–50), 111; Lord Lieutenant, 224; Lords Justices, 224; operations (1921), 16; potential landing operations (1879), 37; squadron (1674–8), 78; State Papers, 5; timber, 78; *see also* Eire, Irish Free State, Northern Ireland
Ireland Station, 95, 174, 175, 178, 236; *see also* commanders-in-chief
Irish Committee (of Privy Council), 13
Irish Free State, 17, 52; *see also* Eire
Irish Office, **17**
Ironclad, *see* Operation IRONCLAD

ironclads, 37, 108; Confederate, 23; French, 23
Islands Voyage (1596–7), 182
Isle of Wight, impressment in, 67, 225; quotas, 125, 225
Ismay, General Sir Hastings, 42, 236
Israeli Navy, 25
Issue Rolls, **2**
Italian Navy, reports on (1888), 23; (1914), 39; (1935), 30; (1943–7), 42; disposal of (1947), 193
Italy, 32, 36, 236

Jackson, F J, 236; Admiral of the Fleet Sir Henry, 63
Jacobite Rebellion (1745–6), 75, 91
Jamaica, Admiralty lands, 36; Sick and Hurt Agent, 78; Slave Trade Mixed Commission, **9**; Storekeeper, 78
Jamaica (1940), 46
Jamaica Hospital, *see* Royal Naval Hospital Jamaica
Jamaica Naval Yards (Port Royal and San Antonio), 151
Jamaica Station, 85, 175, 179, 183; *see also* Leeward Islands, North America, West Indies
Jamaica Victualling Yard, 173
James, Duke of York, *see* York
James I, King of England, 5
Japan, 39, 115, 179, 195
Japanese Navy (1904–5), 21; (1921–37), 30; Air Force (1941–5), 27; building programme (1925–35), 53; chemical warfare, 39; cyphers, 27; dockyards, 39; prisoners, 42; reports on (1940–5), 39, 42, 194; suicide boats, 39
Jason, Dutch warship, 99
Java, expedition to (1812), 49
Jedda Agency (1924–5), 30
Jellicoe, Admiral of the Fleet John, 1st Earl, 57
John, of Chester (1630), 78
Johnstone, Commodore George, 236; Dr. James, Sick and Hurt Agent at Portsmouth, 236
Joint Admiralty-War Office Committee on Royal Garrison Artillery (1905), 235
Joint Air Reconnaissance Centre (1951–60), 210
Joint American Secretariat (Lend-Lease) (1944), 190
Joint Anti-Submarine School, Londonderry, 204, 208, 210
Joint Committee on Shipbuilding and Ship Repairs (1947–50), 213
Joint Flying Control Centre, Karachi (1944–5), 210
Joint Intelligence Bureau, 128
Joint Intelligence Committee (1939–73), **219**
Joint Intelligence Sub-Committee, 191
Joint Naval and Military Committee on Signalling at Defended Ports Abroad (1905), 235

Joint Naval and Military Committee on the Examination Service (1913), 235
Joint Naval and Military Wireless Committee, 217
Joint Naval-Military Conference on Defended Ports (1906–8), 235
Joint Planning Committee, 190, 191
Joint Planning Staff (1947–68), 219
Joint Service Command, publications, 219
Joint Service Dardanelles Committee (1919–25), 235; *see also* Admiralty Dardanelles Committee, Dardanelles Committee
Joint Service Mission Washington (1950–3), 222
Joint Services Amphibious Warfare Centre, 119
Joint Services Guided Weapon Establishment, Hebrides (1957–69), 36
Joint Services Port Unit, Famagusta (1964–5), 210
Joint Services Staff College (1952), 38
Joint Services Trials Unit (1955–60), 210
Joint Staff and Joint Services Mission, 191
Joint Technical Warfare Committee (of the War Cabinet), 189
Joint War Air Committee (1916), 186
Joint War Production Staff, 204
Jones, Flight Lieutenant H A, RAF, 236
Jones's Woolwich Journal and Army and Navy Gazette, 230
Journal of the Royal Naval Scientific Service, 118, 128
journals, 146, 236; Admirals', **97**, 178, 179, 236; Captains', 101, 131, 141, 180, 236; Lieutenants', 236; Midshipmen's, 236; Masters', 236; Secretaries', 236; Surgeons', 101, 161, 163, 165; *see also* logs
— financial, Accountant-General, 112; Accounts Department (of Navy Board), 136; High Court of Admiralty, 8; Prize Commissioners, 10; Solicitor of the Admiralty, 113
Judge Advocate-General, 37
Judge of the Admiralty, 7–8; *see also* High Court of Admiralty
Judges' reports, 16
Juno, slaver of Bristol (1768), 78
Jutland, Battle of, *see* Battle of Jutland

Kandy, Ceylon, 37
Kangaroo, colonial brig (1813–19), 158
Karamania, Turkey, 127
Keats, Vice-Admiral Sir Richard, 236
Keeper of Ports and Galleys, 2
Keith, Admiral George Keith Elphinstone, 1st Viscount, 30, 67, 236
Kenyan Navy, 25, 48, 57
Keppel, Admiral Hon. Augustus, 1st Viscount, 97, 101, 236; Captain George, 236
Kerans, Lieutenant Commander J S, 36

Kerguelen de Tremarec, Captain Yves-Joseph, comte de, 236
Kerr, Admiral of the Fleet Lord Walter, 63
Kew Observatory, 224
Key Points Intelligence Directorate, 19
Keyes, Admiral of the Fleet Sir Roger, 1st Baron, 63, 194, 236
Kiangnan Dockyard, China (1916–17), 30
Kiel Dockyard (1946), 28
killed and wounded, 110; *see also* casualties
Killigrew, Admiral Henry, 236
King, Captain Richard, 236
King's Bench, *see* Court of King's Bench
King's Messengers, 24
King's Private Secretary, 91
King's Regulations and Admiralty Instructions, 128; *see also* Regulations and Instructions
King's Remembrancer's Memoranda Rolls, **2**
Kingston, Ontario, 154; *see also* Canadian Lakes Naval Yards
Kinsale Naval Yard, 149
Kinsale Victualling Depot, 172
Kitchener, General Horatio Herbert, Lord, 236
kite balloons, 128, 204
Königsberg, East Prussia, 133
Korea, naval war graves in, 30
Korean War, 35, 38, 179, 229
Kroomen, 158, 179
Kuwait, naval defence (1899–1902), 30

La Beche-Playfair Report on Coal for the Navy (1848), 235
La Rochelle, France, 30
laboratories, *see* Royal Navy, establishments
labour, 136, 202
labourers, 142, 144, 148, 168, 170, 172; *see also* Admiralty, employees, Dockyards, workmen
Lake Huron, 8, 140, 154; *see also* Canadian Lakes Naval Yards
land, Admiralty, 183, 196, 199, 200; agricultural, 199
Land Service, *see* Army
Landguard Fort, Felixstowe, Suff., 68
Landing craft, British, movements, 116, 128; requirement (1941–5), 39; Japanese, 39
Landing Ship Assault, 36
Landing Ship Logistics, 36, 235
Landing ships, requirement (1941–5), 39
Landing Ships Tank, 36
Lands Tribunal, 224
Largs (1938), Air Section, 210
Latitudes and Longitudes of Maritime Places, H Raper (1838), 98

Index (references are to list numbers, not pages)

Latvia, 30
Lausanne Peace Conference (1922–3), 24
Law, Edward, *see* Ellenborough, Earl of
Law Officers, **74**, 90, 91; opinions, 14–15, 36, 74, 159; *see also* Attorney-General, Solicitor-General
Law Reports, 23
Le Caton, hospital ship (1794–8), 164
Le Pegasse, hospital ship (1794–6), 163
Leander (1931), 210
leave books, 114, 231
Leech-Porter Committee on Royal Marine Band Service (1949), 235
Leeward Islands Station, 85, 179; *see also* Jamaica, North America, West Indies
Leeward Islands Victualling Yard, Antigua, 173
Legal Branch, *see* Admiralty Office
Leghorn, British consul (1744–6), 30, 125; Hospital, 165
Leith, Midlothian, 85, 112; Naval Yard, 149
letter books, 236; Accountant-General, 112; Civil Service Commission, 66; C-in-C Baltic, 179; C-in-C Jamaica, 179; C-in-C Main Fleet, 178; C-in-C Newfoundland, 179; Commissioner, Cape of Good Hope, 179; Controller of Storekeepers' Accounts, 137; Deal Naval Depot, 149; Deal Victualling Depot, 172; Deptford Dockyard, 144; Dockyard Police, 17; High Court of Admiralty, 8; Office of Works, 196; Packet Agents, 76; Plymouth Victualling Yard, 171; Portsmouth Victualling Yard, 170; Prize Appeals Commissioners, 14; RM Divisions, 115; Royal Observatory Board of Visitors, 123; Steam Department, 106
'L'état des officiers de la Marine de France' (1683–1720), 98
letters close, 1
letters of attorney, 8, 120
letters of marque, 8, 23, 59; bonds and bails for, 8; registers, 101; warrants for, 8
letters of reprisal, 5
letters patent, 1, 7, 124; *see also* patents
Leven Shipyard (1917), 51
Leveson, Sir Richard, 78
Lewes, HM Prison, 200
libels (High Court of Admiralty), 8
Liberate Rolls, Chancery, **1**; Exchequer, **2**
Liberia, naval graves, 30
libraries, 111
Libyan Navy, 25
Lieutenant of Ordnance, **6**, 182, 184
Lieutenant-Adjutant of Greenwich Hospital, 120
Lieutenants RM, 86
Lieutenants RN, correspondence, 86, 131; examinations, 126, 130; half-pay, 134; logs and journals, 97, 236; services, 157, 231

Lieutenants-in-Command, 86
life-saving, 235
light dues, 62, 120
lightning, 198
Lightning Committee (1839), 235
lights and lighthouses, in Ionian Islands (1861–2), 30; in Thames (1797), 13; North and South Foreland, 120
lignum vitae, 13
Lincolnshire Estuary Bill (1868–9), 68
Lindemann, Professor F A, 236
Lion (1910), 53
Lisbon Command, 85, 236
Lisbon Hospital, 165
Lisbon Naval Yard, 152
Lisbon Victualling Yard, 173
Lissa Island, British naval cemetery, 30
list books, 95, 101
Liverpool, Lancs., 13
livestock, 77
Llanegryn, Cardigan, 17
Lloyd's Coffee House, 92, 226; naval intelligence reports, 226
Local Government Board, 200
Loch Long, Admiralty Torpedo Range, 185
Loch Striven, Argyll, 68
Logistic Ship Staff Requirement Committee (1962–4), 235
logs, aircraft, 181; Admirals', 236; airships, 181; Captains', 97, 134, Lieutenants', 97, 236; Masters', 97; Midshipmen's, 236; of enemy ships, 99; ships', 97; submarine, 97; *see also* journals
London, 135; Prize Commission (1672–4), 10; quotas, 225; Regulating Captains, 86; St. Paul's Cathedral, 67; shipping of (1629), 5; Ship Money (1599), 6; Warship Weeks (1940–3), 52
London and North-Eastern Railway, 227
London and South-Western Railway, 227
London Midland and Scottish Railway, 227
London Munitions Assignment Board, 189
London Naval Conference (1906–9), 23, 32; (1930), 26, 30, 32, 51; (1935–6), 30, 32
Londonderry, 125; *see also* Joint Anti-Submarine School
Longitude, Board of, *see* Board of Longitude
Loraine, Sir Percy, diplomat, 236
Lord Admiral of England, 7; correspondence, 82, 236; enrolled accounts, 2; instructions for, 13; orders, 7, 82; patents, 7, 81; powers, 5; secret service accounts, 67, 84; standing orders, 7
Lord Admiral's Council (1702–8), 82
Lord Chamberlain, 225
Lord Chancellor's Department, 224

Lord High Admiral, *see* Lord Admiral
Lord Lieutenant of Ireland, 91
Lord Nelson, privateer (1801–7), 77
Lord Nelson's Trust (1807–11), 120
Lord President of the Council, 224
Lord Protector of England, 11
Lord Treasurer's Remembrancer's Memoranda Rolls, **2**
Lords Commissioners of the Admiralty, 83; *see also* Admiralty Board
Lords Justices (1692–8), minutes, 12, 83; of Ireland, 91
Lords Lieutenant of Counties, 91, 225
'Lords' Letters' from Admiralty, 83, 132
Lower School (of Greenwich Hospital), 122
Lowndes, William, Secretary of the Treasury, 59
Loyalists, American, 140
Luard, Commander W B, 236
luggers, hire of, 13
Lukin's Ventilators (1810–11), 103
lunatics, 110, 121, 161, 163; asylums, *see* Hoxton, Royal Naval Hospital Haslar
Lusitania, SS (1915), 71
Lynch's Island, Jamaica, 87, 131
Lynn's signals, 101

McCullock, Robert, prize agent etc. of Charleston, South Carolina (1772–82), 77
MacDonald, James Ramsay, Prime Minister, 53, 236
MacGillivray, John, naturalist, 97, 236
Mackenzie, Flight Commander C R, RNAS, 236
Madagascar, naval visits to, 25; Operation IRONCLAD, 39
Madras, India, 80
Madras Naval Yard, 153
Magazine Committee (1907), 235
magazines, naval, 36, 44, 53, 235
Mahon, *see* Minorca Yard
mail packets and steamers, 23
mails, 106, 204
Malabar Committee on the Dockyards (1971–2), 66
Malabar Committee on Government Industrial Establishments (1969–71), 235
Malaga, Battle of (1704), 157
malaria, 212
Malaya, 48
Malaysia, 220
Malaysian Navy, 25
Malcolm, Sir Ian, Director of Suez Canal Company, 236
Maldon, Essex, 62
Malkin, Sir William, 26
Mallow (1915), 30
Malt Lottery (1694–7), 133

Malta, 24, 197, 204; Admiralty land, 37; defence of (1856–1906), 36–7; RN Armaments Depot, 197
Malta Dockyard, 25, 47–8, 55–7, 132, 150; Admiral Superintendent, 30; Commissioner, 150; Storekeeper, 150; Working Party (1945–59), 54
Malta Hospital, *see* Royal Naval Hospital Malta
Malta School, *see* Royal Naval Schools
Malta Victualling Yard, 168, 173
Maltese ratings, 24, 158, 179
Management Review Team (1975), 219
Manila, expedition to (1762), 15, 236
manning, *see* Royal Navy
Manual of Combined Operations, 116
Manual of Naval Prize Law (1888), 128
maps, 128, 142, 236; *see also* Admiralty charts, charts
Marder, Professor Arthur, 218
Marine, Marines, *see* Royal Marine, Royal Marines
Marine Aircraft Experimental Establishment, **208**
Marine Barracks, 13; *see also* Royal Marine Barracks
marine insurance, 77, 191; *see also* underwriters
Marine Mutiny Act, 75
Marine Office, 113–15, 231
Marine officers, half-pay, 60–1, 231; pay, 60–1; services, 114, 234; subsistence money, 61, 231; widows' pensions, 33, 60–1; *see also* Royal Marine officers
Marine Pay Office, 115; *see also* Paymaster of Marines
Marine Propulsion Committee, 119
Marine Regiments (1665–1749), **33**, 45, 60, **61**, 101; colonels, 61; Muster Rolls, 59, 61; off-reckonings, 78
Marine Society, 13
Marine Survey Service (of Board of Trade), 71
mariners, *see* seamen
Marines, Corps of (1755–1801), 33, 61; *see also* Royal Marines
Marines, pay, 61; services, 157, 234
Maritime Air Defence Committee, 217, 219
Maritime Air Forces, 204, 236
Maritime Regiment Royal Artillery, 36–7
marque, letters of, *see* letters of marque
Marquess, Bristol privateer (1708–15), 77, 236
Marquise de Marboeuf, French transport, 99
marriages, registration of, 18, 115, 124, 127
Marshal of the Admiralty, *see* High Court of Admiralty, Marshal of
Marshalsea, HM prison, 16, **17**
Martell Report on Service Propellants (1962), 185, 235
Martha, of London (1780), 78
Martinique Naval Yard, 151
Mary, slaver of London (1774), 78
Mary I, Queen of England, 5
Mary Juliana, transport (1709), 78
Maryport, Cumb., 62

Maryport and Carlisle Railway, 227
Massage Sisters, 233
Master, Sir H, 236
Master of Naval Ordnance, **6**, 182
Master of Ordnance, **6**, 182; *see also* Master-General of the Ordnance
Master Shipwrights, 13, 135, 142, 146
Master's Assistants, 231
Master-General of the Ordnance, 83, 183, 184
Masters, at RN College Dartmouth, 126; of apprentices, 122; of merchantmen, 86, 127, 128; of transports, 176
Masters RN, accounts, 168; correspondence, 132, 236; logs and journals, 97, 236; passing certificates, 225; services, 128, 231
Masters-at-Arms, 231
Masterton-Smith, J E, First Lord's Private Secretary, 84, 236
masts, 104
Materials Research Directorate, *see* Directorate of Materials Research
Mates, 128, 157, 231
Mauritius, 25, 98; Fort George, 36; School, *see* Royal Naval Schools
Mauritius Victualling Yard 173
Mayne, Rear-Admiral Perry, 103
meat, for RN, 53, 70; reserves at Gibraltar (1902), 37, 235; *see also* beef, victualling
Medal Rolls, **41**, 231, 232
medals, naval and Marine, 36, 41, 48, 112, 120, 73, 224, 231, 232; RAF, 36; *see also* awards
medical, reports, 110, 179; stores, 161
Medical Department, *see* Transport Board (1806–16), Victualling Board (1817–32)
Medical Director-General of the Navy, 90, **110**, 231
medical establishments, 54; *see also* Royal Naval Hospitals
medical officers, 161; commissions, 37; gratuities, 63; journals, 163, 165, 236; of hospitals, 163; pay, 37, 54, 235; services, 165; *see also* Surgeons
Medical Research Council, **212**
Mediterranean, air operations (1940–4), 209; amphibious operations (1943), 207; Foreign Office Correspondence, 25; piracy, 32
Mediterranean Allied Air Forces (1943–4), 209
Mediterranean Allied Coastal Air Forces (1942–5), 209
Mediterranean Allied Photo-Reconnaissance Command (1942–5), 208
Mediterranean Coastal Air Force (1939–4), 206, 209
Mediterranean Fleet and Squadron (1692–5), 59, 168; (1719–45), 85, 179, 236; (1798–1813), 34, 179, 236; (1822–1913), 23, 85, 115, 179; (1935), 30; (1939–47), 42, 204, 205, 207; (1952–3), 38; (1967–72), 25
Mediterranean passes, 13, 30, 47, 62, 93, 101

Medway River, 185
Meermin, Dutch East Indiaman, 99
Melcombe Regis, Dors., 78
Melville, Henry Dundas, 1st Viscount, First Lord of the Admiralty, 75; Robert Saunders Dundas, 2nd Viscount, First Lord of the Admiralty, 67, 84
Memoranda Rolls, **2**
memorials, to Captain J Cook, 196; to Sir A Cunningham, 198; *see also* war memorials
men, *see* ratings, Royal Navy, manning and personnel, seamen
meningitis, 212
Mental Health Act (1959–60), 211
Merchant Navy, health of, 211; medals and awards, 56; memorial, 36, 213, 225; rates of sickness and death (1940–7), 71
Merchant Ship Fighter Units, 207, 210
Merchant Shipping Act (1854), 73
Merchant ships and shipping, 77, 78, 86, 128, 206, 235; air defence of, 206, 207; anti-aircraft defence of (1943), 35; armament of (1917–42), 53, 187; attacks on (1941–5), 205, 206; chartered (1793–1802), 130 (*see also* hired armed ships and vessels); damage to (1941–5), 214; Danish (1805–9), 133; Dutch, 179, 194; enemy (1940–5), 204, 206, 207; French (1940–5), 52, 214; German (1941–5), 207; insurance of, *see* marine insurance; Irish, 214; losses (1941–5), 195; masters of, 86, 127, 128; neutral (1808–22), 70; of London (1629), 5; requirements, 206; survey of (1582), 5; suspicious (1914–18), 117; wartime (1939–46), 71; *see also* Ministry of Shipping; Ministry of War Transport, Naval Control of Shipping, Registrar-General of Shipping and Seamen
merchants, litigation by, 8
Mercury, training ship, 201
Mermaid (1972), 219
mess allowances, 183
messengers, 100, 111, 139
Meteorological Committee and Council (1867–1937), 224
Meteorological Office, 123, 224; Committee of Inquiry (1865–6), 224
Metropolitan Police, 17
Metropolitan Railway, 227
Mexican Navy, 25
Mexico, 21, 30, 115
Microbiological Research Establishment, **221**
Middle East and Africa Committee (of the War Cabinet), 189
Middle East Command (RAF, 1943–4), 209
Middle East Forces (British Army command, 1939–44), 42

Middle East, naval operations (1940–4), 194, 206; naval situation (1918), 30; Sub-Committee, 190
Middleton, Rear-Admiral Sir Charles, later 1st Lord Barham, 67, 177
Midshipmen, 33; services, 128, 157, 231; journals, 236
Milford Haven, Pembrokes., 57, 68, 213
Military Commission of Control, Germany (1921–2), 36
military commissioned officers, *see* naval officers
Military Co-ordination Committee (of the War Cabinet), 189
Military Intelligence, *see* Imperial General Staff, Secret Intelligence Service, Security Service, War Office
Military Medal, 41
Military Operational Research Unit, 45
Military Representatives (on Supreme War Council), 187
Military Training Act (1939), 18
Militia (1899), 36
Miller, D G, Assistant Surgeon, 236
Mine Design Department, *see* HMS *Vernon*
Minerva, Dutch warship, 99
mines and minelaying, 42, 65; anti-submarine, 204; by aircraft, 207, 209; experiments (1882), 107; of beaches (1940–2), 42; operations (1939–45), 116; 'sub-marine explosive machines' (1866), 37, 235; transfer to RN (1905–6), 36–7, 235
Mining Establishment, *see Vernon*
Mining School, *see Vernon*
Minister for Aircraft Production, 236
Minister for Co-ordination of Defence, **191**, 224
Minister of Defence, 194; accommodation, 57; Private Office, **217**
Minister of State Middle East (1942–3), 31
Ministry of Agriculture, **199**
Ministry of Aircraft Production (1939–46), **46**; Private Office Papers, 46
Ministry of Aviation, **222**; Radio Equipment Department, 222; *see also* Ministry of Civil Aviation
Ministry of Blockade (1916–19), **29**
Ministry of Civil Aviation, **70**, 213; *see also* Ministry of Aviation
Ministry of Defence (1947–64), **217–18**
Ministry of Defence (1964–), 204, **218–21**, 222; Defence Secretariat, 218; contracts, 70; Permanent Under-Secretary, 218; registered files, **218**; publications, 219; typewriters, 66
Ministry of Defence Navy Department (1969–87), 57, 75, **219**; Finance Division, 219; land, 219, 235; Naval Personnel Division, 219
Ministry of Economic Warfare (1939–45), **29**
Ministry of Food, 199
Ministry of Fuel and Power, **216**

Ministry of Health, **211**
Ministry of Home Security (1939–46), **19**; Camouflage Committee, 19; Research and Experiments Department, 19
Ministry of Housing and Local Government, 200
Ministry of Information, **215**
Ministry of Labour, **202**
Ministry of Munitions (1915–21), **46**, 185
Ministry of National Service (1916–20), **17**
Ministry of Overseas Development, **47**
Ministry of Pensions (1917–66), **203**
Ministry of Production (1942–5), **46**
Ministry of Public Buildings and Works, 63, 108, 196–8
Ministry of Reconstruction, 224
Ministry of Shipping (1917–21), **71**, 109
Ministry of Supply (1939–59), **46**, 118, 185, 222; contract record books, 46
Ministry of Technology, 222
Ministry of Town and Country Planning, 200
Ministry of Transport, 71, **213**, 222; Marine Departments, 213–14
Ministry of War Transport (1941–6), **71**, 214
Ministry of Works, *see* Ministry of Public Buildings and Works
Minorca, 13; Hospital, 59
Minorca Naval Yard (Mahon), 150
Minorca Victualling Yard, 173
Minotaure, French warship, 99
Minutes, Admiralty Board, 7, 12, 83, 102; Admiralty Commission 7; Admiralty Whitley Councils, 57, 96; Board of Invention and Research, 118; Board of Trade (1696–1782), 69; Board of Trade (1785–1954), 70; British National Endeavour, 122; Cabinet and Committees, 186–93; Charity for Sea Officers' Widows, 124; Chatham Chest, 155; Chiefs of Staff, 191, 219; Committee of Imperial Defence, 190; Council of State Admiralty Committee, 11; Defence Board and Council, 217; Greenwich Hospital, 120, 122; London Prize Commission, 10; Lords Justices, 12; Meteorological Council, 224; Navy and Customs Committee, 11; Navy Board, 130, 135, 137, 141, 142, 156; Ordnance Board (1545–1855), 183; Ordnance Board (1908–), 44; Privy Council, 12; Prize Appeals Commissioners, 14; Register Office, 127; RN Asylum, 122; RN Hospital Haslar Council, 163; Royal Observatory Board of Visitors, 123; Sick and Hurt Board, 159; Supreme War Council, 229; Transport Board, 175; Medical Department, 160; Prisoner of War Department, 167; Victualling Board, 168
minutes of acts (High Court of Admiralty), 8

Index (references are to list numbers, not pages)

Miscellaneous Branch, see Admiralty Office
Mobile Naval Base Defence Organisation (1940–5), 39, 189
Mombasa, Kenya, 23
Mombasa Marine Defence Regiment (1914–18), 41
monitions, High Court of Admiralty, 8
Mont Blanc, French warship, 99
Montreal Naval Yard, 154
Montreal Victualling Yard, 173
Moorman, Admiral Richard, 63
Morbeke affair (1914), 235
Mordaunt's Regiment (1692–8), 78
Moresby, Captain Fairfax, 103, 236
Morocco, 30, 35, 179
Morris Committee on Awards to Inventors, 235
mortar vessels, 115
Mosaic, see Operation MOSAIC
Mosquito Coast, Nicaragua, 98
Mostyn, Sir Roger, Paymaster of Marines, 236
Motor Torpedo Boats, 194
Mountbatten, Admiral of the Fleet, Earl, 30, 42, 48
Mulberry harbours, 42, 222
Mundy, Major-General G B, 236
Munitions, Ministry of, see Ministry of Munitions
Munitions of War Act, 186
murder, aboard *Quebec*, 13; by Dutch seamen, 13
music, prizes for, 36
mustard, for RN, 75
musters and muster books, of dockyards, 151, 170; of Greenwich Hospital employees, 120; of Kroomen, 158, 179; of prizes, 99; of prisoners of war, 166; of recruits, 125; of RM units, 115; of RN Hospitals and Hospital Ships, 162–5; of Victualling Yards, 170; of yard craft, 144; see also ship's musters
Mutevellian's invention (1938–9), 30
Mutine, French corvette (1796), 103
mutiny and mutineers, see Royal Indian Navy, Royal Marines, Royal Navy, manning and personnel
Mylor Victualling Depot, 172

napalm, for RN, 218
Napier, Vice-Admiral Sir Charles, C-in-C Baltic, 236
Naples, Italy, 236
Narborough, Captain John, 236
Nares, Vice-Admiral Sir George, 63
Narvik, Norway, 214
Nassau (1851), 224
Nassau Naval Yard, Bahamas, 72
National Audit Office, see Audit Office
National Blood Transfusion Service, 211
National Coal Board, 216
National Debt Office, 65

National Fire Service, 17
National Gas Turbine Establishment, 208; Naval Auxiliary Machinery Department, 208; Naval Marine Wing, 208
National Grid, 127
National Incomes Commission, 235
National Insurance Act, 36
National Maritime Museum, 136
National Parks Commission, 200
National Production Advisory Council on Industry (1955–9), 70
National Savings Banks, 65
National Savings Committee, **65**
National Service, see Ministry of National Service
National Service in a Future War Committee, 190
National Service Medical Board (1939–52), 211
Nautical Almanac, 66, 173
Nautical Almanac Office, 123
Nautical Division, see Greenwich Hospital Schools
Naval and Marine Pay and Pensions Act (1865), 13
Naval and Military War Pensions Committee (1916), 51
Naval Air Conference (1964), 235
Naval Air Fighting Development Unit, 119
Naval Air Material Policy Committee (1948–51), 222
Naval Air Tactical Conference (1948), 235
Naval Air Traffic Control, 70
Naval Aircraft Works, 119
Naval and Military Committee on Defence of Ports (1890–9), 36
Naval and Military Conference on Overseas Expeditions (1905), 37, 235
Naval and Military Defence Committee (of Cabinet, 1870–88), 190
Naval Anti-Aircraft Gunnery Committee (1919–21), 44
naval architecture, 104, 235
Naval Armament Limitation Treaties (1922 and 1929), 188; see also London Naval Conference, Washington Naval Conference
Naval Assignment Sub-Committee, 189
naval attachés, Chinese, in Australia, 39; pay of, 55
— British, accommodation for, 24, 196; appointment of, 24; in France, 30; in Soviet Union, 219; in USA, 30; instructions to, 22;
Naval Branch, see Admiralty Office, Naval Branch
Naval Brigades, 41; Crimea (1854–6), 33, 42; Nile (1884–5), 36; South Africa (1878–81), 36; (1899–1902), 36–7, 48
Naval Cadets, 84, 126, 128, 201, 231; training, 96, 235
Naval Censor (1914–19), 16; see also censorship
Naval Commission of Control, Germany (1921–2), 36

Naval Construction Committee (of the War Cabinet), 189
Naval Construction Research Establishment, 119
Naval Control of Shipping, 25, 71, **214**
Naval Cordite Committee (1925–7), 44
Naval Courts, 30
naval debt, 50
naval depots, *see* Deal, Fernando Po, Heligoland, Sierra Leone; *see also* dockyards, naval yards
Naval Discipline Act (1922), 36; (1948–52), 36, 48, 224; (1967–9), 75, 80
Naval Dispatch Boat Service (1944–5), 42
Naval Emergency Reserve (1948), 202
Naval Enlistment Act, 211
Naval Expenditure Emergency Standing Committee (1914–20), 58
naval finance, 51–2, 58, 100, 101, 235; *see also* Navy Estimates
Naval Forces Germany (1944–7), 28
Naval Guided Weapon Working Party (1958–62), 107, 222
naval hospitals and hospital ships, 22, 33, 36, 59, 71, 110, **159–65**, 194, 196, 219; *see also* Royal Naval Hospitals
Naval Instructors, 201, 202, 231
Naval Intelligence Committee, 117, 128, 236,
Naval Intelligence Department, 37, 117, 128, 236
Naval Intelligence Division, **117**; and signals intelligence, 27; enemy documents, 99; Geographical Department, 39, 128; Monthly Intelligence Reports (1919–39), 128; organisation in South America, 30; *see also* Naval Staff
naval intelligence reports, 15, 20, 22, 27, 30, 37, 39, 42, 48, 91, 98, 128, 207, 219, 226, 236; requirements, 218
Naval Knights of Windsor, 16, 75, **124**, 231
'Naval Land Equipment' (1940–2), 194, 222
Naval Law Division, *see* Admiralty Office, Naval Law Division
Naval Liaison Section, Bombay (1942–3), 210
Naval Life-Saving Committee, 105
Naval Manpower Department, *see* Admiralty Office, Naval Manpower Department
Naval Marriages Acts, 18
Naval Medical Research Institute (1941–52), 212
Naval Meteorological Branch, 224
Naval Military and Air Forces Bill (1918–19), 36
Naval Military and Air Force Chapels Act (1932), 36
naval officers, accounts, 130, 157, 235; addresses, 63, 231; appointments, 3, 125; career structure, 55; casualties, 231; certificates of service, 231; children, 121; compensation for loss of effects, 70; correspondence, 96; death certificates, 231; Dutch, 64; duty-free stores for, 52, 57, 62, 235; eligibility for civil salaries (1885), 37, 235; embezzlement by, 78; employed by colonial governments, 37; Engineers, 231; entertainment allowances, 54; expenses, 63; foreign under training, 63, 70, 231; grants of land, 36; half-pay, 33, 63, 231; insane, 33; leave for, 231; legal assistance for, 17; liability for income tax, 63; marriage certificates, 231; marriage allowances, 18; numbers required (1943), 54; obituaries, 231; passing certificates, 231; passports and visas, 24; pay, 36, 51, 53, 55, 220, 231; pensions, 65, 121, 231; promotion, 55, 231; remittances, 231; seniority lists, 231; services, 231; superannuation, 73, 103, 231; training, 202; uniform, 70, 111; wine, 49; *see also* Captains, Commanders, Commodores, Flag Officers, Lieutenants, sea officers
Naval Officers [i.e., Navigation Act officials], 49
Naval Ordnance Committee (1905–12), 235
Naval Ordnance Department, 107, 116, 231, 235
Naval Ordnance Inspection Department, 107
Naval Pay Branch, 112; *see also* Navy Pay Office
Naval Policy Inquiry (1909), 235
Naval Prison Rules, 75
Naval Prize Bill (1901–6), 224
Naval Prize Bounty, 64, 112, 207
Naval Prize Fund (1954–5), 57
Naval Prize Law Committee (1900–4), 235
Naval Prize Manual (1904–9), 23, 36; (1954–5), 214
Naval Prize Tribunal (1918–21), 8; (1920–8), 53
Naval Representatives (on Supreme War Council), 187
Naval Reviews, 178, 225; (1902), 227; (1911), 236; (1935), 227; (1937), 30, 227; (1953), 36; (1968–9), 25
Naval Savings Banks, 52, 57
Naval Staff, 107, **116**, 119, 188, 194; Gunnery Division, 107, 116; Historical Section, 55, 116; Intelligence Division, *see* Naval Intelligence Division; Operational Research Department, 116; Operations Division, 116; targets, 36; Torpedo and Anti-Submarine Division, 116; Training and Staff Duties Division, 116; *see also* Admiralty War Staff, Naval Intelligence Division
naval stores, 37, 48, 93, 130–2, 142, 199, 235, 236; contracts, 59, 130, 137, 226; establishments, 104, 130; for signal stations, 133; imports, 62, 70; prices, 135, 136; received, 144, 148; sale of, 13, 50, 51; transport of, 174
Naval Stores Department, 171
Naval Task Force 127 (1944), 42
Naval Telecommunications Flying Unit, 46, 119
Naval Transport Service, **71**; *see also* Admiralty Transport Service, Sea Transport Service
Naval Weather Service, 118, 224

Index (references are to list numbers, not pages)

Naval Yards, 88, 142; *see also* Alexandria, Antigua, Barbados, Cadiz, Canadian Lakes, Cape Nicola, Cape Town, dockyards, Falmouth, Flushing, Halifax, Jamaica, Kinsale, Leith, Lisbon, Madras, Martinique, Minorca, Montreal, Nassau, naval depots, New York, Prince of Wales Island, Quebec, Yarmouth
Navigating Officers, 231
Navy agents, 77, 236; accounts, 8; bail bonds, 8
Navy and Army Canteen Board, 36
Navy and Customs Committee (1642–57), 11
Navy, Army and Air Force Acts, 36, 37
Navy Bills, 59, 67, 140, 156
Navy Board, 5, **130–3**; accounts and estimates, 67, 130, 133; Auditor of Stores and Wages, 59; Chief Clerk, 131, 132; contracts, 226; Committee of Accounts, 130; deeds, 68, 108, 142, 152; Head Money vouchers, 130; in-letters, 132; minutes, 130, 135, 137, 141, 142, 156; nominations to Christ's Hospital, 228; officers' stores, 130; patents, 75, 130; petitions, 132; Receiver of Fees, 130; regulations, 130; reports, 13; salaries, 75; Transport Department and Service, 6, 49, 93, 131, 132, **138**, 144, 145, 168, 179, 183; *see also* Commissioners of the Navy, Navy Office
— correspondence, about block mills, 131; about naval stores, 131; of Chief Clerk, 131, 132; with Admiralty, 87, 93, 131, 132; with Board of Customs and Excise, 62; with consuls, 132; with contractors, 132; with dockyards, 131, 132, 142–9, 151–4; with East India Company, 226; with Inspector-General of Naval Works, 127, 131, 132; with Navy Office Solicitor, 132; with Ordnance Board, 183, 184; with sea and naval officers, 131, 132; with Secretaries of State, 131, 132; with Signal Stations, 125; with Solicitor of the Admiralty, 113; with Ticket Office, 131, 141; with Transport Agents, 131, 132; with Transport Board, 132; with Transport Service, 145; with Treasurer of the Navy, 131, 156; with Treasury, 49, 131, 132; with Victualling Board, 131, 161, 168; with Victualling Yards and Depots, 132, 173; with Woods and Forests, 68, 132
— orders, from Admiralty, 82, 102; to Navy Pay Office, 157; to Ticket Office, 141; to yards, 102, 130, 131, 137, 142, 145, 146, 152;
Navy Board Accounts Department, 112, 136
Navy Board Transport Service, 138, 159, 168; *see also* Transport Board
Navy Commission (1642–60), 7, 11, 129
Navy Commissioners, *see* Navy Board
Navy Estimates, 13, 33, 56, 100, 101, 111, **130**, 133, 186, 188, 213, 219; foreign, 23; Treasury papers, 49, 51, 53, 55, 59; *see also* naval finance
Navy League, 201; of Canada, 226
Navy List, 53, 66, 96, 128

Navy Office, **139**; accounts, 139, 236; bargemen, 139; clerks, 13, 139, 233, 235; establishment, 139; frauds, 236; insurance, 75; lists of HM ships, 15, 130; pensions, 139; precedents, 100, 130; quarter books, 129; reorganisation, 130; Solicitor, 132; Somerset House, 139; *see also* Navy Board
Navy Pay Office, 112, 141, **157**, 158, 231, 235, 236; establishment of, 13, 51; organisation (1817), 51
Navy Records Society, 63
Navy Royal, survey of (1588), 5; *see also* Royal Navy
Navy Weeks (1935–9), 178
Needles Rocks, Isle of Wight, 68
negroes, 151; *see also* slaves
Nelson, Vice-Admiral Horatio, Viscount, 30, 63, 197, 236; tomb, 67; Admiral Hon. Maurice Horatio, 63
Nelson Memorial Committee (1838–44), 235
Nemo, British schooner (1888), 22
Neptune, *see* Operation NEPTUNE
Netherlands, relations with, 15, 25, 236; *see also* Dutch Navy
Netley Hospital, 202
New Caledonia, 30
New Forest, Hants., 13, 59, 68, 75, 78, 224
New Hebrides, 23
New York, 30, 158, 166
New York Naval Yard, 140, 152
New Zealand, 36, 236
Newcastle upon Tyne, 62
Newfoundland, 96, 97; commanders-in-chief, 85, 97, 179, 136, 236; fisheries, 85, 179; Governors, 97, 179, 236
Newgate Prison, 16
Newson, Captain Thomas, 77, 236
Nichol, Sir John, Judge of the High Court of Admiralty, 236
Nicholas, Sir Edward, Secretary of the Admiralty (1625–38), 236
Nicholson, Robert, Master RN, 236
Nicobar Islands (1942–5), 39
Niger River, expeditions to, 21, 23, 30, 103, 111
Nigeria, 25
Nigerian Navy, establishment of, 48; sales to, 25; training of, 32, 193
Nile River, expedition (1884–5), 36, 236; (1896–9), 21, 42
Nimrod aircraft, 217
Nootka Sound, Vancouver Island, 20, 98
Nore Command, 85, 95, 96, 178; mutiny (1797), 13, 101; pilots, 178, 231
Norfolk Flax Ltd, 70
Norman Rolls, **1**
Normandy, 1
Norris, Admiral Sir John, 85, 236

North and East Africa, Foreign Office correspondence, 25
North America, 127, 138, 158
North America Station, 85, 179, 236
North American Supply Missions (1941–2), 46
North Atlantic, naval bases in, 37
North Atlantic Treaty Organisation, 25, 213, 236
North Borneo, 214
North Foreland Light, 120
North West Expeditionary Force (1940), Air Component, 209; *see also* Norwegian Campaign
Northcote Committee on Transfer of Naval Armaments to Admiralty (1886–7), 235
Northern Ireland, RN and USN visits to, 17
Northern Squadron (1627–9), 6
Northfleet, proposed dockyard, 68, 142
Northumberland, Algernon Percy, 10th Earl of, 5, 235
North-West Africa Command (1942), 39
Norway, British ambassadors and consuls, 30, 91
Norwegian campaign (1940), 36, 42, 209
'Notation Books', 110
Nourse, Commodore Joseph, C-in-C Cape of Good Hope, 236
Nova Scotia, 34, 236
nuclear propulsion, 193, 216, 223
Nuclear Ships Committee (1958–84), 223
nuclear weapons, 193, 221; tests (1947–56), 16, 217, 221
Nuremberg War Crimes Trials, 28
nurses, 120
Nursing Sisters, services, 163, 165, 231, 233; *see also* Queen Alexandra's Royal Naval Nursing Service
Nymphe (1780), 49

O'Connor, Midshipman J J, 236
Oberon Report (1877), 37
Ocean Island, 48
Office of Stores, 93
Office of Woods and Forests, *see* Woods and Forests
Office of Works, **196**; *see also* Ministry of Works
officers, *see* naval officers, sea officers
Officers' Widow and Orphan Permanent Fund (1865–72), 75
official histories, 24, 27, 96, 110, 115, **192**; naval, of First World War, 36, 116; RN medical, of Second World War, 211; *see also* staff histories
Official Press Bureau (1914–19), 16
Offord, D E J, Superintendent of Admiralty Underwater Explosion Research Establishment, 236
oil, fuel for RN, 30, 53, 57, 71, 106, 214, 216, 235; tankers, 71, 214, 216
Oil Board, 190
Oil Defence Schemes, 108

Oil Policy Committee (of the War Cabinet), 189
oilfields, offshore, 216
Okinawa Island, 98
Operation AJAX (1941), 189
Operation BOWLER (1943–5), 206
Operation CLAYMORE (1941), 39
Operation DOUBLE QUICK (1948–9), 204
Operation DRACULA (1945), 39
Operation HUSKY (1943), 43, 206
Operation IRONCLAD (1942), 39
Operation MOSAIC (1955–6), 180, 221
Operation NEPTUNE (1944), 209
Operation OVERLORD (1944), 190; air operations, 209; intelligence organisation, 27; Joint Planning Committee, minutes, 19, 235; naval organisation, 42
Operation SEAWARD (1948), 204
Operation SIDEWAYS (1940), 40
Operation TERMINAL (1941–6), 206
Operation TORCH, 206, 214; Royal Marine Division, 42
Operational Evaluation Group, 217
Operational Research Department, *see* Naval Staff Operational Research Department
Operational Research Section, 209
Operations Division, *see* Naval Staff Operations Division
operations record books, **210**; of Air Staff Directorates, 207; of RAF commands, 209–10
optical glass, for RN, 75
Oran, Algeria, 192
Order of the Bath, 36
orders, by Admiralty Board, 7, 39, 61, 83, 102, 110, 121, 141, 145, 157, 168, 170, 186; by Admiralty Commission, 129; by Board of Trade, 70; by Controller of the Navy, 104; by Controller of Steam Machinery, 106; by Council of State, 11, 129; by Court of Chancery, 77; by flag officers, 127, 178, 179, 236; by Generals at Sea, 11, 129; by King, 1; by Lords Admiral, 7, 82; by Navy and Customs Committee, 11; by Navy Board, 102, 130, 131, 137, 141, 142, 145, 146, 152, 157; by Ordnance Board, 182–4; by Parliament, 59; by Privy Council, 12; by Secretaries of State, 15; by SHAEF, 42; by Treasury, 157; by Victualling Board, 156, 168, 171, 172; for convoys, 83; for courts martial, 83; to Accountant-General, 83; to Admiralty, 15; to Captains, 7; to dockyards, 130, 131, 142, 145, 152; to flag officers, 7, 37, 83, 93; to German Navy, 42; to Greenwich Hospital, 83, 121; to HM Ships, 93; to Navy Commission, 7, 11, 129; to Navy Pay Office, 157; to Ordnance Board, 82; to Packet Stations, 106; to Paymaster of Marines, 61, 82, 83; to Physician-

Index (references are to list numbers, not pages)

General, 110; to Ticket Office, 83, 141; to Treasurer of the Navy, 156, 168; to Victualling Board, 83, 168; to Victualling Yards, 170–2
Orders in Council, **12**, 15, 112, 157, 204, 231
Ordinary (dockyard), 143–50, 154, 170
Ordnance, accounts, 3, 50; certificates, 5; indentures 3; Master-General, *see* Master-General of the Ordnance
Ordnance Board (1545–1855), 5, 35, 44, 82, 107, **182, 183**, 185; bill books, 182; contracts, 182; debentures, 67, 182; declared accounts, 6, 182; establishments of guns and stores, 183; issues and remains, 182, 183; minutes, 183; orders, 183, 184; surveys, 182; warrants, 182, 183
— correspondence, 183; with Admiralty, 91, 93, 183; with Home Secretary, 16; with Lord Admiral, 82; with Navy Board, 138, 183
Ordnance Board (1908–), **44**
Ordnance Committee, **44**, 49, 107
Ordnance Council, **44**
Ordnance Select Committee, **44**
Ordnance stores, 182, 183, 195
Ordnance Survey, 224
Orford, 1st Earl of, *see* Russell, Edward
Organisation and Methods Department, *see* Admiralty Office
Orkney Islands, 42, 218
Osborne, Sir Thomas, Treasurer of the Navy, 236
Osborne Estate, Isle of Wight, 196; *see also* RN College Osborne
Osprey, shore establishment at Portland, 198
Ottoman Empire, 20; *see also* Turkey
Overlord, *see* Operation OVERLORD
Overseas and Home Defence Committee, 190
Overseas Defence Committee (of the War Cabinet), 189
Overseas Development, Ministry of, *see* Ministry of Overseas Development
overseas expeditions (1905), 235
overseas yards, *see* Dockyards, Naval Yards, Victualling Yards
Owen, Captain W F W, 49

P212, HM submarine, 36
Pacific Fleet (1944–5), 39, 42, 206; aircraft for, 209
Pacific Ocean, 97; *see also* Far East and Pacific
Pacific Station, **179**, 236
packet agents, 76
Packet Service, **76**, 93, 106, 111; Packet Stations, *see* Falmouth, Holyhead
packets, steam packets, 76, 101, 136; victualling, 78, 111; *see also* mail packets and steamers

paddle vessels, 104
Pakistani Navy, 48; ships for, 56
Palermo, Italy, 30, 236
Palmer, Sub-Lieutenant A J, RNVR, 231, 236; Lieutenant George, 236
Panama, 30; Canal, 30
Pan-American Patrol (1939–40), 30
Papeete, French Polynesia, 30
Papers on Naval Subjects (1901–7), 128
Paris, Declaration of (1856), 23
Parker, Richard, mutineer, 13
Parkstone Sea Training School, 201
Parliament, 183, 202; Acts of, *see* under their names; committees of, **11**, 159, 235 (*see also* under individual names); elections to, 18; papers for, 15, 59, 102; petitions to, 1, 4; statutes **4**, 183
Parliament Rolls, **4**
parole of prisoners of war, 166, 167
Parry, Captain D, 78
Passing Certificates, 231, 232; Gunners', 183; Masters', 225; pilots', 225; Surgeons', 228
Patagonia, 98
Patent Office, 70
Patent Rolls, **1**
patents of invention, 1, 13, 74; *see also* letters patent
patents of office, 81, 96, 101, 130, 175; *see also* letters patent
patronage books, 236
pay, 83, 87, 100, 101, 130, 188; Admiralty Office, 100, 183; Admiralty employees, 202; allotments, 157; arrears, 157; Carpenters', 202; claimed by next of kin, 60, 157, dockyards, 142, 144; Greenwich Hospital, 120, 122; income tax, 160; Naval Ordnance Department, 107; Navy Office, 139; Ordnance Office, 183; recalls, 157; Schoolmasters', 201; Surgeons', 87, 161, 168; Transport Board, 174, 175; unclaimed, 120, 157; Victualling Yards, 171, 173; *see also* naval officers, ratings, Royal Navy, manning and personnel, sea officers
pay books, 124, 134, 143–50, 154, 158, 166, 170, 171, 175; Charity for Sea Officers' Widows, 124; Compassionate Fund, 124; Dockyards, 143–9, Naval Yards, 149, 150, 154; pensions, 155; ships, 134, 158; Sick and Hurt Board Prisoner of War Department, 166; Transport Board, 175; Victualling Yards, 170, 171; yard craft, 143
Pay lists, 125, 142–54, 157, 158, 162–5, 167–73, 175; Admiralty Transport Department, 144; coopers and labourers, 142; Dockyards, 109, 143–50, 152, 153; Hospitals, 162–5; Naval Yards, 149–54; prisoners of war, 167; prison ships, 158; Royal Bounty, 157; Sea Fencibles, 125; Sick Quarters, 157; Transport Board, 175; Victualling Yards, 168–73

pay rate books, 96
Paymaster of Marines, 59, 60, **61**, 82, 83; accounts, 61, 67, 236; *see also* Marine Pay Office
Paymaster of Ordnance, 67
Paymaster-General, 33, 52, **65**, 231; correspondence with Treasury, 49; Marine half-pay, 67
Paymaster-General of the Forces (1660–1835), 52, **60**, 61; declared accounts, 60
Paymasters, 128; *see also* Pursers
Pearl, of Hamburg (1607), 78
Pei-Ho River, China, 37
Peking (1916), 180
Pembroke, Thomas Herbert, 8th Earl of, First Lord of the Admiralty and Lord Admiral, 82
Pembroke (1694), 141
Pembroke Dockyard, 17, 68, 88, **149**; closure and disposal, 54, 57; plans, 72
Penang, 133; *see also* Prince of Wales Island
Penelope (1843), 230
Penn, Vice-Admiral Sir William, 236
pension pay books, 155
pensions and pensioners, 13, 36–7; Army, 37, 45; Chatham Chest, 155; Chelsea, 45; committee on (1905–21), 36; commuted, 63; deferred, 36; for good service, 231; for wounds, 33, 101, 155, 231; Greenwich Hospital, 121; military, 235; naval, 36, 54, 57, 121, 231–2, 235; naval reserve, 54, 73, 231–2; payable by War Office, 121; payable in USA, 30; war (1914–18), 51
— remitted, 157; to Admiralty civilian employees, 66, 233; to African widows and orphans, 47; to Chaplains, 121; to civil officers, 121; to dockyard officers, 132; to dockyard police, 65; to dockyard workers, 54–5, 109, 143–54, 233; to Dutch officers and widows, 64; to Gunners, 13; to Marine officers' widows, 33, 60–1; to Master Shipwrights, 13; to merchant seamen, 63, 233; to Naval Instructors, 201; to naval officers, 65, 231; to nursing sisters, 231, 233; to officers' children, 13; to orphans, 63, 124, 139, 231; to schoolmasters of RN College Dartmouth, 201; to victualling yard workers, 168–72; to widows, 63, 121, 139, 159, 231, 233, 235
Pensions Branch, *see* Accountant-General of the Navy
Pensions Commutation Board, 65
Pensions (Navy etc.) Bill (1939), 36
Pepys, Samuel, Secretary of the Admiralty, 79
Pepysian Library, Cambridge, 101
Permanent Committee on Naval Demilitarisation (1945), 28
Pernambuco, Brazil, 30
Perseus (1812), 158, 180, 236
Persia, 21; *see also* Iran
Persian Gulf, Squadron, 30, 179; RN bases in (1900–5), 21; (1935), 30

Peru, 30, 98
Peruvian Navy, reports on (1881), 37
Peterhead Harbour, 56; Trustees, 213
petitions, Ancient, 1; by Captains, 13; by Lieutenants, 13; by prisoners of war, 166; by Pursers, 13; by seamen, 13; by sea officers, 13; for admission to Greenwich Hospital, 121; for prize money, 13; to Admiralty Board, 91, 92; to Admiralty Commission, 7; to Navy Board, 132; to Navy Commission, 129; to Parliament, 1, 4; to Privy Council, 13
Petrie, James, 236
Petronella, Dutch East Indiaman, 99
Pett, Peter, 78, 236
Phantom aircraft, 219
Philippines, 39
Phinn Committee on Admiralty Secretariat (1855), 100, 235
photographic interpretation reports, 39, 208
Photographic Section, *see* Royal Naval Air Service
photographs, 105; of Boom Defence, 108; of HM Ships, 105; of naval works, 108; of London Naval Conference, 236; on carrier flying, 236
Physical Research Directorate, *see* Directorate of Physical Research
Physician-General of the Navy, 90, **110**
Physicians, 90, 160, 163, 164
Pickmore, Vice-Admiral Francis, 236
pigeons, 206
pilots, 13, 112, 157, 178; French, 231; passing certificates, 225; of aircraft, *see* aircrew
'Pink Lists', 116, 128
Pinner, Middx., 57
Pipe Rolls, **2**
piracy, pirates, 16, 32, 49, 75, 179, 214
Pitt, John, 2nd Earl of Chatham, 1st Lord of the Admiralty, 236; William, 1st Earl of Chatham, 236
plans, 142; Admiralty Building and House, 197; dockyards, 142–7, 149, 150, 152, 153, 169, 197; hospitals, 163, 165; naval land, 197; Naval Stores Department buildings, 171; naval yards, 149, 151, 152; Ordnance land, 197; public buildings, 196; RM Barracks, 197; RN Colleges, 197; Somerset House, 197; victualling yards, 144, 152, 168–73; Woolwich Arsenal, 197
Plate, River, Battle of (1939), 24; proposed expedition to (1790), 22; survey of (1871), 30
Plover (1842), 75
Plover (1855), 224
Plunkett-Ernle-Erle-Drax, Admiral Sir Reginald, 63
Plymouth, Commander-in-Chief, 85, 95, **178**
Plymouth, Devon, Breakwater, 131; Citadel, 68; Millbay Docks, 227; RM Barracks, 13, 33
Plymouth Division RM, 89, 114

Index (references are to list numbers, not pages)

Plymouth Dockyard, 13, 101, 131, 138, **145**, 198; Commissioner, 88, 93, 145; *see also* Devonport Dockyard
Plymouth Gunwharf, 185
Plymouth Sound, 98, 145
Plymouth Victualling Yard, 171; *see also* Royal William Victualling Yard
Poland, 32
Polish Navy, reports on (1929), 30; attached to RN, 37, 52, 55, 65
Political and Secret Branch, *see* Admiralty Office, Political and Secret Branch
Political Liaison Officer in North Africa (1942–3), 31
Political Warfare Executive, *see* Foreign Office
Pompée (1793), 67
Pondicherry, India, 78
Poole, Dors., 78
Poor Knights of Windsor, *see* Naval Knights of Windsor
Popham, Rear-Admiral Sir Home, 236
pork, 169; *see also* meat
Port Defence Committee (1939–42), 204
Port Essington, British Columbia, 103
Port Mahon, *see* Minorca
Port Natal, 103
Port of London Authority, 211
Port Royal, *see* Jamaica Yard
Port Said, Egypt, 53
Portchester Castle, Hants., 166
Portland, Dorset, HM Prison, 200
Portland Bill, 68; Admiralty Signal Station, 68
Portland Harbour and Naval Base, 68, 72, 198, 200
Portobello, expedition to (1739–40), 15
ports, 93, 206; *see also* defended ports, harbours
Portsea Island, Hants., 198
Portsmouth, Hants., harbour, 78; Parliamentary elections, 18; RN Barracks, 80
Portsmouth Command, 85, 88, 95, 101, **178**, 197
Portsmouth Division, Royal Marines, 61, 89, 114, **115**
Portsmouth Dockyard, 13, 17, **146**; Admiral Superintendent, 88, 146, Commissioner, 88, 146; extension (1864–1915), 68; fortifications, 183; Port Admiral, 75; railway, 75
Portsmouth Gunwharf, 185
Portsmouth Victualling Yard, **170**; *see also* Royal Clarence Victualling Yard
Portugal, 174, 226; British Minister (1839), 30; naval relations with, 24; sale of hovercraft to (1968–9), 30; territorial waters, 36
Post Office Savings Bank, 65
Post War Priority and Demobilization Committee, 187

Postillion, ketch (1693), 103
post-mortem books, 120
Potsdam Conference (1945), 24
Pottinger, Sir Henry, Governor of Hong Kong, 236
Povey, Richard, Treasurer of Sick and Hurt Board, 77, 159, 236
powers of attorney, 8, 60, 77, 79, 120, 130, 157
precedents, Admiralty, 95, 96, 100, 101, 104, 105, 108–12, 236; dockyards, 145; hospitals, 110; impressment, 13; Lord Admiral, 82; Navy Board, 100, 130, 137, 141; Navy Pay Office, 157; pay, 101; pensions, 112, 157; prisoners of war, 13, 167; Register Office, 127; Registrar-General of Shipping and Seamen, 73; Royal Naval Reserve, 73; sea officers, 13; Sick and Hurt Board, 13, 159; Surgeons, 231; Transport Board, 167; Treasurer of the Navy, 156; victualling, 111
Prerogative Court of Canterbury, **79**
prescription books, 163
Prijs-courant der effekten, 168, 230
Prime Minister, 42, 51, 186, 194, 219; Private Office, **194**
Prince (1670), 236
Prince Frederick, privateer (1750–7), 78
Prince of Wales, privateer (1742–7), 77
Prince of Wales Island Naval Yard, Penang, 153
Prince William (1780), 158
Principal Supply Officers Committee, 190
Prinz Eugen, German cruiser, 206
Prison Commission, 200
prison ships, 13, 158
Prisoner of War Agents, 166, 167
Prisoner of War Department, *see* Sick and Hurt Board, Transport Board (1796–1816)
prisoners of war
— British, compensation (1920–3), 53; escapes, 39; exchanges, 13, 36, 166, 167; in Far East (1941–5), 36, 39, 179, 203, 231; in Germany (1939–45), 37; in Italy (1943–5), 36; Korean War, 35; liberated (1944–6), 39; lists of (1941–5), 40, 195, 231; merchant seamen, 73; naval, 166, 167
— enemy, 167, 175; Algerine, 165; depots, 167; escapes, 167; French, 166, 167; on parole, 166, 167; Russian, 110; senior officers, 167
privateers, 8, 23, 77, 78, 86, 236
Privy Council, **12**, 83, 91; Committee on Education, 201; Committee on Trade and Plantations, 12, 70; correspondence 13; Foreign Affairs Committee, 12; Irish Committee 13, 91; Lord President, 225; minutes, 12; Orders in Council, **12**, 15, 112, 157, 204, 231; papers, 13; petitions to, 13; registers, 12
Privy Seal, 1
Prize Agency Commission (1803–4), 235

365

prize agents, 120; *see also* Navy agents
Prize and Wills Department (of Accountant-General), 112
Prize Appeals Commissioners, **14**, **74**, 120, 236;
Prize Commissions, **10**, 16, 87; *see also* Prize Office
Prize Courts, *see* High Court of Admiralty, Vice-Admiralty Courts
prize droits, 8; *see also* Droits of Admiralty
prize goods, declared accounts, 6, **10**, **67**
prize money, 13, 48, 70, 75, 78, 93, 101, 112, 120; claimed, 49; income tax on, 63; of Army, 45; of commodores, 13; of Marines, 45, 61; of RAF, 207; petitions for, 13; shares, 103, 112; unclaimed, 120
Prize Office, 10; accounts, 50; correspondence with Treasury, 49; fees, 78; *see also* Prize Commissions
prize tenths, 10
prizes, 48, 53, 75, 77; adjudication, 8; American, 10, 140; captured by British Army, 45; case papers, 8; compensation for, 67; Danish, 10, 59; Dutch, 10; French, 10, 75, 160; Head Money, 113; light dues owed by, 62; lists, 8, 45, 101, 112, 120, 136; Portuguese, 10; recaptured, 140; regulations, 23; ships' papers, 8; Spanish, 120; valuations, 144, 146
proclamations, 1
proctors, High Court of Admiralty, 8
Production, Ministry of, *see* Ministry of Production
progress books, 135
propellants, 185
Propellants, Explosives and Rocket Motor Establishment (1977–84), 221
Property Services Agency, 196, 198; *see also* Ministry of Public Buildings and Works
Prosperous, merchantman (1728), 78
protections from impressment, 62, 91, 101, 145
Protocols, *see* treaties
Prussian Admiralty Court, Memel, 77
Prussian civil service (1894), 37
Prusso-Danish War (1864), 22
Psychologists and Psychiatrists in the Services Committee (1942–5), 189
Public Accounts Commissioners (1689–1704), 50, 235, 236
Public Accounts Committee (1961–2), 55
public buildings, 196
Public Works, *see* Ministry of Public Works
pubs, billeting in, 16
punishment returns, 101
Pursers, accounts, 78, 130, 156, 168; allowances, 168; bonds, 129; necessaries, 111; regulations, 128, 130; services, 128, 231
Purveyor of the Navy, 236
Purveyors, 145

Q Ships, 116
Quaker, ketch (1671), 158
quarantine, 13, 180
quarter books, Navy Board, 129; Victualling Board, 168
Quartermaster-General, *see* War Office (1855–1964)
Quartermasters RM, 115
quartz crystals, 62
Quebec (1760), 13
Quebec Naval Yard, 152
Queen Alexandra's Royal Naval Nursing Service, 231, 233; Reserve, 233
Queen (1673), 158
Queen Elizabeth, SS, 224
Queen Mary, SS, 224
Queenborough (1671), 158
Questions Concerning the Middle East Sub-Committee, 190
Quota Acts (1795–6), 125, 225

radar, airborne, 204, 236; naval, 45, 204, 207; stations, 42; Type 271, 222
Radar Reflections for Marine Navigation (1948), 119
radiation, 17, 211, 221, 235
radio, call signs, 70; valves, 118 (*and see* Co-ordination of Valve Development Department); *see also* wireless
Radio Direction-Finding, *see* radar
Raeder, Grand Admiral Erich, 28
Railway Clearing House, 227
railways, 106, 127; *see also* railway companies by name
Railways Staff Conference, 227
Rainier, Admiral Peter, C-in-C East Indies, 236
Ramsey, Isle of Man, 62
Ramsgate Harbour Trustees, 225
Rangoon, Burma (1945), 39
ranks, relative, 188
Raper, Henry, 230
Ratifications, *see* treaties
ratings, allotments, 157, 232; deaths, 110, 232; discharges, 163, 178, 232; house purchase scheme, 55, 63; in military prisons, 36; Indian, 48; Maltese, 158, 159; next of kin, 157; orphans, 121; pay, 36, 51, 101, 120, 156–7, 220, 232; remittances, 232; services, 157, 232; uniform, 70, 111; widows' pensions, 121, 235; wills, 157, 232; *see also* seamen
Ratings' Widows' Pensions Committee (1886), 235
Ré, *see* Île de Ré
receipt books, High Court of Admiralty, 8
Receiver of Droits of Admiralty, 78; declared accounts, 8, 67; *see also* Droits of Admiralty, High Court of Admiralty
Receiver of Fees (of Navy Office), 130, 236

Index (references are to list numbers, not pages)

Receiver of Prizes, declared accounts, 8, 67; *see also* High Court of Admiralty
Receiver of Sixpences, 127; in North America, 127, 236
Reconstruction, *see* Ministry of Reconstruction
record and establishment books (1857–73), 112
recruitment, 112, 125, 202; *see also* impressment
Recruitment Acts, 125
Red Cross flag, 40
'Red Lists' (1940–9), 116
Red Sea, 179
Redcar, Yorks., 72
refits, 130, 178; *see also* dockyards, repairs
Register Office (1696–9), 90, 127; *see also* Sixpenny Office
Registrar of Prizes, declared accounts, 8; *see also* prizes
Registrar of Seamen, **73**, 90
Registrar-General of Shipping and Seamen, **73**, 231
Registrars of Vice-Admiralty Courts, 9
registration, electoral, 18; for military service, 18; of births, deaths and marriages, 18
Regulating Captains, 86, 125
Regulations and Instructions for HM Service at Sea, 83, 128, 130; *see also* King's Regulations
remittance lists, 157
rendezvous, 125; *see also* impressment
repairs, 130, 135; *see also* dockyards, refits
Reparation Commission, British Delegation (1920–2), 235
reparations, German (1920–2), 52; German and Japanese (1945–7), 195; Hungarian (1922–3), 52
report books, 184
reports, by Admiralty, 13; by Board of Revision, 13; by Captains, 22–3, 30; by Chiefs of Staff, 39; by HM Ships (1973–6), 218; by Navy Board, 13; by Prize Commission, 10; by Signals Experimental Establishment, 45; by Transport Accounts Committee, 33; by US Army, 39; by US Naval Intelligence, 39; by Victualling Board, 33; by War Office, 37; damage, 19; interrogation of prisoners of war, 39; Judges', 16; law, 23; naval intelligence, 15, 20, 22, 27, 30, 37, 39, 42, 48, 98, 219, 226; on Chilean Navy, 37; on French Indo-China, 30, 39; on French Navy, 23; on Gallipoli Campaign, 42; on German Army, 39; on German Navy, 39; on Guatemala, 30; on Italian Navy, 23, 30, 39, 42; on Japanese Navy, 39, 42; on New Caledonia, 30; on Peruvian Navy, 37; on Philippines, 39; on Polish Navy, 30; on slave trade, 22–3; on Soviet Navy, 30, 218; on Spain, 30; on Spanish Navy, 20, 23, 27; on Turkish Navy, 30; on US Army, 37; on US Navy, 30, 37; on Yugoslav Navy, 30, 42; photographic interpretation, 39, 208; 'Preparations for Battle', 101; to Privy Council, 13

reprisal and reprisals, 10; letters of, 5
Requests, *see* Court of Requests
Research, RRS, 54, 224
Research and Experiments Department (of Ministry of Home Security), 19
Research Programmes and Planning Directorate, *see* Directorate of Research Programmes and Planning
Reserves, *see* Admiral Commanding Reserves, Royal Naval Reserve, Royal Naval Volunteer Reserve
Reserves Bill, 199
Restriction of Enemy Supplies Department (1916–19), *see* Ministry of Blockade
Restrictive Practices Court, **80**
revenue cruisers, 62, 93, 132; accounts, 136; musters, 158; officers, 231
Rhé, *see* Île de Ré
Rio de Janeiro, Brazil, 24, 30; Naval Yard, 152; Victualling Yard, 173
Rio Pardo, SS, 235
Robert, brig of London (1782–5), 77
Rockall Island, 16
rockets, 37; for coast defence (1942–3), 42
Rodent, Special Boat Unit shore base, 194
Rodney, Admiral George Brydges, Lord, 236
Roehampton artificial limb factory, 203
Rogers, Captain Woodes, 77, 236; Thomas, Clerk of the King's Ships, 3
Rolls Royce Ltd., 70
Rooke, Admiral Sir George, 236
'Room 40', 27, 117; *see also* Government Code and Cypher School, Naval Intelligence Division
ropemakers, 231
roperies, ropeyards, 6, 143, 145, 146, 148
Rosen, Count Alexander von, 22
Ross, Captain Sir James Clark, 236
Rosyth, Fife, schools, 201
Rosyth Dockyard, 54, 198, 216
Rotherhithe Victualling Depot, 172
Rotterdam Agency, 98
Romania, naval relations with (1972), 25
Rowley, Rear-Admiral B S, 178, 236
Royal Africa Company, 92, 226
Royal Air Force, 202; airfields, 204; call signs, 70; casualties, 206; charts, 40; commands, 209; common services, 188; history, 204; medals, 36; No. 18 (Maritime) Group, 210; personnel transferred from RN, 53, 231; pigeons, 206; prize money, 207; relations with RN, 188, 204–6, 235, 236; relative ranks, 188; requirements, 204, 205; reserves, 36–7; strategy, 204; trades, 37; training, 206; weapons, 204, 206; Yangtse Incident (1949), 204; *see also* Air Staff

Royal Air Force Defford, 46; Ford, 53, 210; St. Mawgan, 210
Royal Air Force in Maritime War 1939–46 (1946), 204
Royal Air Force Middle East, 201 (Naval Co-operation) Group (1941–4), 209
Royal Aircraft Establishment, **208**; Naval Air Department, 208
Royal Aircraft Factory, **208**
Royal Airship Works, 119
Royal Alexandra Victualling Yard, Haulbowline, 172
Royal Armament Research and Development Establishment, 185, **221**
Royal Artillery, 115; Maritime Regiments, 36–7
Royal Astronomical Society, 92, 228
Royal Australian Navy, 63, 188; Cockburn Sound base, 25; Director of Naval Intelligence, 30; submarines, 70; *see also* Australian Navy Office
Royal Botanical Gardens, 236
Royal Bounty (to next of kin of men killed in action), 157
Royal Canadian Navy, medals for, 48
Royal Carriage Department, 185
Royal Clarence Victualling Yard, Portsmouth, 70, **170**; *see also* Portsmouth Victualling Yard
Royal College of Surgeons, 92, 228
Royal Commission on Arms Manufacture (1935), 235
Royal Commission on Awards to Inventors, 235
Royal Commission on Common Land, 199
Royal Commission on Fuel and Engines (1913), 235
Royal Commission on Greenwich Hospital (1859–65), 236
Royal Commission on Harbours of Refuge (1858–9), 235
Royal Commission on Naval and Military Administration (1888–90), 235
Royal Commission on Population (1944–9), 18
Royal Commission on Trade Unions, 202
Royal East African Navy, 179
Royal Engineers, 36, 42
Royal Fine Arts Commission, 225
Royal Fleet Auxiliary Service, 54–5, 202; officers, 231; tankers, 213
Royal Fleet Reserve, 227; pensions, 54; training, 17
Royal Garrison Artillery, 37, 235
Royal Greenwich Observatory, Herstmonceaux, 219
Royal Gunpowder Factory, Waltham Abbey (1783–1945), 185, 221
Royal Hospital, Chelsea, **45**
Royal Hospital School, 122; *see also* Greenwich Hospital Schools
Royal Indian Marine, 41
Royal Indian Navy, 48; mutiny (1946–7), 39

Royal Marine, Royal Marines, 82, 83, 86, 89, 93, 96, 101, 110, 114; and combined operations (1940–1), 39; awards to, 57; courts martial, 96, 101, 114; deaths, 110; deserters, 157; discharges, 114; drill, 128; in hospital, 163, 165; mutiny (1919), 36, 42; newsletters, 114; organisation (1943–4), 42; pay of, 37, 157; pensions, 121; promotion of, 37; ranks in, 36; regulations, 114; role (1956–61), 38; services, 121, 234; training, 42, 128; wills, 157; *see also* Marine, Marines, Royal Marine officers
Royal Marine Amphibian Support Regiments, 36
Royal Marine Amphibious School, 119
Royal Marine Anti-Aircraft Units (1941), 43
Royal Marine Artillery, 41, 89, 114, 115, 234
Royal Marine Band Service, 235
Royal Marine Barracks, 197; Chatham, 68; Forton, 115; Plymouth, 13, 33; Portsmouth, 80
Royal Marine Cadets, 36, 184
Royal Marine Commandos (1945–8), 36, 42; (1961–2), 55; Commando Brigades, 36, 38, 42
Royal Marine Division (1942–3), 36, 43
Royal Marine Divisions, **89**, 114, 115; *see also* Chatham, Deal, Plymouth, Portsmouth, Woolwich
Royal Marine Infirmaries, 114, 161, 164
Royal Marine Labour Corps (1914–18), 41
Royal Marine Light Infantry, 41, 114, 115
Royal Marine officers, 114; Army appointments, 36; Colonels Commandant, 89; commissions, 114; correspondence, 86, 89; Deputy Adjutant-General, 89; half-pay, 67; in *Army List*, 36; in auxiliary forces, 37; leave, 231; numbers required (1943), 54; orders to, 82, 83; passports, 24; pay, 36–7, 235; pensions, 231; promotion, 37; retired pay, 36; services, 114, 231, 234; *see also* Marine officers
Royal Marine Police, 54
Royal Marine Striking Force 126
Royal Marine Sub-Area, Sicily (1943), 37
Royal Marine Units overseas, 115
Royal Mint, 224
Royal Naval Academy, Portsmouth, 13, 90, 126, 231
Royal Naval Air Service, 41, 128, 181; Armoured Car Squadron, 180, 232; Experimental Section, 181; officers' services, 231; operations, 40, 181; Photographic Section, 181; Training Manual (1915), 128
Royal Naval Air Stations, 42, 70; Brawdy, 17, 58; Farnborough, 181; Ford, 58; Gosport, 204; Great Yarmouth, 181; Hatston, 36, 57; Kete, 200
Royal Naval Aircraft Yard, Fleetlands, 119; Sydenham, Belfast, 57, 70; Wroughton, 196
Royal Naval and Royal Marine Children's Homes, 201
Royal Naval and Royal Marine Orphan Home School, 201

Index (references are to list numbers, not pages)

Royal Naval Armaments Depot, Bridgend, 17; Charlesfield, 219; Ditton Priors, 196; Malta, 197; Milford Haven, 17
Royal Naval Artillery Volunteers, 62
Royal Naval Association, 13
Royal Naval Asylum, 68, 122; *see also* Greenwich Hospital Schools
Royal Naval Barracks, Portsmouth, 80, 178
Royal Naval Benevolent Fund, 13
Royal Naval Careers Offices, 36
Royal Naval Coast Volunteers, 232
Royal Naval College Dartmouth, 66, 197, 201
Royal Naval College Greenwich, 68, **126**, 198; applied mechanics laboratory, 198; Board of Studies, 126; Committee on Overhead Charges (1924), 235; computer, 70; damage to, 65; foreign officers in, 24; lectures, 126, 193; nuclear reactor, 200, 216; Painted Hall, 196, 225; plans, 197; War College, 126; War Course, 126, 231
Royal Naval College Osborne, 196, 201; *see also* Osborne Estate
Royal Naval College Portsmouth, 90, 126, 231
Royal Naval Cordite Factory, Holton Heath, 16, 46, 119, 185, 197
Royal Naval Diving School, 17
Royal Naval Division, 36, 41, 43, **180**, 232
Royal Naval Dockyards Asbestos Research Project, 212
Royal Naval Engineering College, Keyham, 126; Manadon, 197
Royal Naval Female School, Isleworth (1865–72), 75
Royal Naval Flying School, 181
Royal Naval Hospital, Bermuda, 161, 165; Cape Town, 161, 165; Chatham, 164; Deal, 161, 164; Gibraltar, 162, 236; Haslar, 90, 60, **163**, 211, 219; Hong Kong, 165; Jamaica, 161, 165; Malta, 161, 165; Stonehouse, 90, 160, 161, 164, 197; Trincomalee, 161, 165; Yarmouth, 164, 203, 211; *see also* Antigua, Ascension Island, Barbados, Curaçoa, Hoxton, Leghorn, Lisbon, Minorca, Therapia, Vado, Woolwich
Royal Naval Hospitals, 33, 36, 161–5, 235; pharmacists, 233; *see also* medical establishments
Royal Naval Medical Consultative Board (1923–5), 212
Royal Naval Medical School, 110, 231
Royal Naval Medical Service, 211
Royal Naval Minewatching Service, 213
Royal Naval Ordnance Depot, Priddy's Hard, 221
Royal Naval Personnel Research Committee, 119, 212
Royal Naval Physiological Laboratory, 212
Royal Naval Propellant Factory, Caerwent, 17
Royal Naval Relief Fund, 36
Royal Naval Reserve, 22, 62, 73, 110, **127**, 213, 227; members of, 13, 202; officers' services, 231; pay of, 26; pensions, 54; Review Committee (1975–6), 219, 235
Royal Naval School, Eltham, 68, 201
Royal Naval School of Music, 201
Royal Naval Schools, 201
Royal Naval Scientific Service, 46, 118, 119, 221; Bragg Laboratory, 211
Royal Naval Staff College (1952), 38, 70; books for, 66
Royal Naval Statistical Committee, 212
Royal Naval Stores Depots, 70; Llangennech, 58
Royal Naval Sub-Depot, Dale Castle, 17
Royal Naval Torpedo Factories, 70, 185; Greenock, 46, 56, 119, 219
Royal Naval Torpedo Range, Loch Long, 185
Royal Naval Vocational Training Centre, Portsmouth, 201
Royal Naval Volunteer Reserve, 41, 127, 198, 202, 227; Air Branch, 204; Anti-Aircraft Corps, 180; colonial units, 56; Northern Ireland Division, 17; service records, 232
Royal Naval Volunteer Wireless Reserve, 127
Royal Naval Welfare Committees, 53
Royal Naval Wireless Auxiliary Reserve, 127
Royal Navy, establishments, 196, 198, 200, 225; air-raid shelters for, 19; bomb damage to, 19; gardeners, 54; laboratories, 17; official website, 128; protection of (1940–4), 42; sanitary inspections, 211; staff of, 66; visits to, 22; wireless stations, 17, 42; *see also* Admiralty factories, Admiralty research establishments, dockyards
— Fleets and Squadrons, *see* Aden Task Force, Baltic Squadron, Brazils Squadron, China Squadron, Eastern Fleet, Eastern Mediterranean Command, East Indies Station, Iceland Command, Ireland, Mediterranean Fleet, Naval Forces Germany, Northern Squadron, North-West Africa Command, Pacific Fleet, South Atlantic Command, Summer Fleet, West Indies Squadron
— manning and personnel, 5, 13, 59, 84, 96, 133, 195, 202, 215; allies (1942–5), 195; and alcohol, 212; casualties, 35, 110, 115, 157, 163, 179, 189, 195, 206; colour vision, 212; Commonwealth citizens, 16; complaints against, 30; demobilisation (1918–20), 224; deserters, 21, 75; disabled, 202; education, 201; Engineering service, 55; establishments of men, 13; health, 179, 211–12; health insurance, 52; Indian, 48; Maltese, 24, 158, 179; medals, 30, 36, 57; mobilisation, 96, 133, 135, 137, 202, 227, 236; mutinous conduct, 75; mutiny (1797), 13, 101; mutiny (1801), 236; numbers borne, 96, 101, 108, 195, 202; punishments, 24; rail travel, 227; reserves, 36–7; song books, 66; trades, 37; training, 96; transferred

to RAF, 53; travel concessions, 53; vaccine trials, 212; *see also* aircrew, boys, ratings, pensions, seamen, watermen
— ships and vessels, 56; air defence of, 207, 209, 217; anti-aircraft armament (1936–40), 53; armament, 13, 101, 107, 128, 135, 183; attacks on (1939–45), 207; availability, 25; bells, 104; boats, 17, 53; breweries, 199; broken up, 84; building, 116, 135; collisions, 23, 178; complement, 96, 101, 135; condition, 15, 101, 130, 132, 178; construction programme, 48, 49, 53, 56, 70, 95, 217, 218; damage to, 19; dazzle painting, 235; design, 106; dimensions, 135; disposition, 15, 101, 130; exercises, 204; fitting-out, 87, 131, 158; fittings, 135, 236; gold for, 52; guns, 206; in dockyard hands, 135, 143, 144, 146, 158; in Ordinary, 145; lists of, 23, 95, 101, 107, 128, 130, 135, 236; logs, 97; losses, 110, 135, 178, 207; marriages aboard, 18; movements, 95, 101, 109, 116, 128; nuclear-powered, 25, 118, 193, 213, 216, 220, 223, 224; oil fuel for, 30 (*see also* oil); photographs of, 105; repair of, 49, 130, 135; repair of, in USA, 30; reports from, 98, 218; sailing qualities, 135; sales of, 25, 30, 50, 84, 135, 178, 188, 213, 219; stability, 105; steam, 104, 106; stores, 183, 199; tenders, 183; torpedoes, 204; trials, 104, 205; visits to foreign ports by, 25, 30; *see also* Admiralty, Fleet Air Arm, Naval Brigades, Navy Royal

Royal Navy, careers information booklets (1953, 1965), 202

Royal Navy Catering Frauds, Committee of Enquiry (1972–3), 218

Royal Navy-Royal Air Force Co-operation Committee, 188

Royal Norwegian Naval Air Service, 210

Royal Observatory, Greenwich, 75, 103, 123; Board of Visitors, 123; Kew, 123; *see also* Royal Greenwich Observatory

Royal Ordnance Factories, 185; Waltham Abbey (1783–1945), 185, 221

Royal Parks and Pleasure Grounds, 196

Royal Patriotic Fund, 225

Royal Radar Establishment, **208**

Royal School for RN and RM Officers' Daughters, 201

Royal Society of London, 92, 101, 228, 236

Royal Sovereign (1786), 236

Royal Swedish Navy Band, 202

Royal Victoria Victualling Yard, Deptford, 68, 75, 109, **169**

Royal William Victualling Yard, Plymouth, **171**

Ruck Committee on Mines (1905–6), 36, 235

Rules of Engagement, naval, 25

rum ration, 215, 219

Russell, Admiral Hon. Edward, 1st Earl of Orford, 50, 59, 235, 236; Odo, 1st Baron Ampthill, 236

Russell Cotes Nautical School, 201

Russia, British detainees in, 24; convoys to, 191, 206; copper from, 135; intelligence co-operation with (1931–45), 27; naval stores from, 62; treaties with, 23, 32; *see also* Soviet Union

Russian Civil War, naval operations, 36

Russian Naval Mission (1944–5), 42

Russian Navy (1795–1800) 85; (1808–14), 163, 164; (1904–5), 21, 23, 62; (1919), 24; Baltic Fleet, 21, 23; mutiny (1917), 187; ships building for (1854), 235; *see also* Soviet Navy

Russian War (1853–5), Baltic naval operations, 37; Black Sea naval operations, 37; Naval Brigade, 42; prize cases, 8

Russo-Japanese War, 21

Sabine, Sir Edward, scientist and explorer 236

sabotage, 42, 134

safe conducts, 15

Sailing Directions, 127, 236

Sailmakers, services, 231

St. George (1892), 216

St. Helena, Admiralty buildings, 36; Vice-Admiralty Court, 9

St. John's Antigua, 236

St. John's Newfoundland, 48; Victualling Yard, 173

St. Lawrence River, 179, 236

St. Michael (1669), 236

St. Paul's Cathedral, London, 67

St. Vincent, shore establishment at Gosport, 201

salaries, *see* pay

Salisbury Island, *see* Durban, South Africa

Salonika, Thessalonika, Greece, 216

Salsette (1807), 180

salutes, between warships, 22, 103; in foreign ports, 30, 183

salvage, 112, 213

Sampson (1844), 230

Samson, Wing Captain C R, RNAS, later Air Commodore RAF, 236

Samuel, merchantman (1753), 78

San Antonio, *see* Jamaica Naval Yard

São Paolo, Brazil, 30

Sarah Galley, privateer (1702–3), 77, 236

Sark, charts of, 13

Saudi Arabian Navy, sales to, 219

scantlings, of casks, 171; of ships, 135

Scapa Flow, Orkneys, 235

Scarborough, Yorks., 36, 62

Scharnhorst, German battleship (1942), 204, 206

Index (references are to list numbers, not pages)

Scheldt expedition (1809), 103, 236
Schniewind, Admiral Otto, 28
School for Officers' Sons (1828–61); *see* Greenwich Hospital Schools
School of Naval Architecture, 84
School of Naval Co-operation, RAF Ford (1917–39), 53, 210
Schoolmasters, 201, 231
schools, 200, 201; *see also* Royal Naval Schools
Scientific Advisory Council, 217
Scientific and Industrial Research, Department of, *see* Department of Scientific and Industrial Research
Scillin, SS, 36
Scilly Isles, 127, 219
Scipion, French warship, 99
Scorpion, US schooner (1814), 8, 140
Scotland, English wars with, 1; famine relief (1846–50), 111; State Papers, 5
Scots Rolls, 1
Scott, Captain R F, 57; William, Lord Stowell, 236
Scottish East India Company, 77
screw propellers, 75; steamers, 104
Scutari, Crimea, 36
Sea-Air Warfare Committee, 206
Sea Cadet Corps, 127
Sea Fencibles, **125**, 231, 232
Sea Fish Commission, 199
Sea Fury aircraft, 204
Sea Harrier aircraft, 215, 217
Sea Hawk aircraft, 222
sea officers, children of, 13; correspondence, 132, 133, 159, 160; courts martial, 101; dismissed from RN, 13; half-pay, 13, 93, 157; ill, 163, 164; invalided, 90, 163, 164; next of kin, 157; orders, 83; pay, 13, 36, 101, 157; pensions, 121; petitions by, 13; promotion, 231; tests and oaths, 231; wills, 79; wives of, 13; *see also* naval officers
Sea Otter aircraft, 204
Sea Scouts, 201
Sea Service, 182 4; *see also* Royal Navy
Sea Transport Service, **71**; *see also* Admiralty Transport Service, Naval Transport Service
seal-fishing, 179
seamen, British, 134, 236; bounties for, 13; casualties, 73; Certificates of Competency, 213; Certificates of Service, 73; distressed, 30; impressment of, 13, 236; killed in action, 63; lists, 49; litigation by, 8; marriage allowances, 18; on T124 articles, 232; pay, 13, 59, 156–7, 101; petitions by, 13; prisoners of war, 73; shipwrecked, 235; tickets, 78; tuberculous, 211; widows of, 13; wills, 77, 79; wives of, 13; *see also* ratings, Royal Navy, manning and personnel

— foreign, Dutch, 13; German, 16; Norwegian, 17; Russian, 16, 163, 164; Spanish, 6; Yugoslav, 17
Seamen Schoolmasters, 232
Seamen's Savings Bank, 73
Seamen's Sixpences, 73, 127
seaplanes, 236
searchlights, 19
Seaward, *see* Operation SEAWARD
seawater distillation, 222
Second Masters, 231
Second Naval Lord, 96
Second World War, 178, 179, 195
Secondary Education Endowment Files, 201
Secret Intelligence Service, Secret Service (MI6), 36
Secretaries of State, **5, 15**; American, 15; Colonial (1768–82), 15; Foreign, *see* Foreign Secretary; for War and Colonies, *see* Secretary for War and Colonies; Home, *see* Home Secretary; intelligence, 15; Northern, 15; orders, to Admiralty, 15; passes to export tobacco, 15; prize decisions, 15; safe-conducts, 15; Southern, 15; warrants, 15
— correspondence, concerning expeditions, 15; with Admiralty, 15, 83, 91, 93, 98; with captains, 15; with C-in-Cs, 15; with Law Officers, 74; with Lord Admiral, 82; with Master-General of the Ordnance, 184; with naval boards, 15; with Navy Board, 131, 132; with Sick and Hurt Board, 166; with Transport Board, 174; with Victualling Board, 168
Secretary at War (1661–1855), **33**, 91
Secretary for War (1855–1964), **35**
Secretary for War and Colonies (1794–1855), 16, **34**, 179, 236
Secretary of Greenwich Hospital, 120
Secretary of State for Air, Private Office 205
Secretary of State for Foreign Affairs (1782ff.), *see* Foreign Secretary
Secretary of State for the Colonies (1768–82), *see* American Secretary
Secretary of State for the Colonies (1855–1968), *see* Colonial Secretary
Secretary of the Admiralty, *see* Admiralty Secretary
Secretary of the Cabinet, 236
Secretary's Department, *see* Admiralty Secretary's Department
Security Service (MI5), **17**
Select Committee on Admiralty Expenditure (1885), 235
Select Committee on Greenwich Hospital Pensions (1892), 235
Select Committee on Naval Research, 118
semaphore, *see* Admiralty Semaphore
seniority lists, 96, 112, 128, 231

sentences, High Court of Admiralty, 8; Prize Appeals Commissioners, 14
Seppings, Robert, Surveyor of the Navy, 87, 135, 236
Sergeant Painter of the Royal Navy (1609), 78
servants, Greenwich Hospital (1865–9), 120; Haslar Hospital (1814–15), 163; Portchester Castle (1762), 166
Service Pay and Allowances Committee (of the War Cabinet), 189
Service Records, **231–4**; Engineers', 106; Surgeons', 110
Service Trials Unit, 119
Severn Barrage, 213
Seymour, Rear-Admiral Sir George, C-in-C Pacific, 236; Admiral Sir Michael Culme, 63
Shackleton, Sir Ernest, 51
Shackleton aircraft, 217, 218
Shaftesbury, 1st Earl of, *see* Ashley Cooper, Anthony
Shanghai, China, 39, 179
Shatt-al-Arab, navigation marks, 30
Sheerness, Kent, 36, 197
Sheerness Dockyard, 53, 88, 131, 137, **147**, 213, 219
Sheerness Victualling Yard, 172
Shell Foundry (of Woolwich Arsenal), 184
shells, 36, 46, 103, 185, 235; *see also* ammunition
Shere, Sir Henry, Commissioner of Tangier, 13
sheriffs, 2, 13
Shetland Islands, defence of (1942–3), 42
Ship Damage Reports, 19
Ship Fire-Fighting Manual (1942–9), 128
Ship Money (1599), 6
Ship Recognition School, Colombo (1944–5), 210
shipbuilding, 84, 87, 104, 130, 131, 135, 213, 224, 226; American, 105, 236; at Bombay and Cochin, 135, 153; contracts, 135; estimates, 130, 134; Geddes Enquiry, 70; German, 207; instructions, 104; methods, 75, 87, 135, 236; naval, 187, 188; statistics, 104, 135, 195; timber, 101; *see also* shipyards
Shipbuilding Advisory Committee (of Board of Trade, 1946–66), 70
Shipbuilding Industry Board (1967–70), 70
Shipbuilding Trades Joint Council for Government Departments, 108
shipowners, litigation by, 8, 77–8
shipping, *see* merchant shipping
Shipping, Ministry of, *see* Ministry of Shipping
Shipping Committee (of the War Cabinet), 189
Shipping Expenditure Emergency Standing Committee (1917–19), 58
ships and vessels (not Royal Navy), air defence of, 207; crew lists, 73; lights, 23; logs, 8, 73; musters, 5; navigation requisitioned for RN, 52; wartime modification, 70; *see also* Indiamen, luggers, mail packets, merchant shipping, prizes, slavers, warships; for HM Ships, *see* Royal Navy, ships and vessels
ships' books, 99, 105, 135
Ships Branch (of Controller of the Navy's Department), 104
ships' covers, 105
ships' ledgers, 112, 176
ships' libraries, 111
ships' logs, *see* logs
ships' musters, **158**, 179
ships' pay books, 134, 141, **158**
ships' plans, 105, 136
Ship Target Trials Committee, 119
shipwrights, 146; apprentices, 132
shipyards, 19, 36, 195; *see also* shipbuilding
shore bombardment, 36; air spotting for, 209
Shore Signal Service, 127, 232
Shore Wireless Service, 127
Shovell, Admiral Sir Cloudesley, 79, 236
Siam, 179; *see also* Thailand
Siamese Navy, 30
Sick and Hurt Board, **159**, 177, 235; accounts, 67, 130, 159, 236; Agents, 78, 236; Commissioners, 13; deeds, 75; minutes, 159; orders, 83, 159; precedents, 13; recommendations for pension, 231; Treasurer, 77, 236
— correspondence, with Admiralty, 87, 93, 159; with commanders-in-chief, 159, 179; with hospitals, 159, 165; with Law Officers, 74, 159; with Navy Board, 138, 159; with RN officers, 159;
Sick and Hurt Board Prisoner of War Department (1653–1796), 75, **166**; *see also* Portchester Castle, Sissinghurst
Sick and Wounded, *see* Sick and Hurt
sick quarters, 110, 157, 232
Sideways, *see* Operation SIDEWAYS
Sierra Leone, 48, 67, 179; Slave Trade Mixed Commission, 9
Sierra Leone Naval Depot, 152
Sierra Leone Victualling Depot, 173
Signal Stations, *see* Admiralty Signal Stations
Signals and Instructions for the Use of HM Fleet (1816), 128
Signals and Radar Establishment, **208**
signals and signalling, Army and Navy, 37, 42; at defended ports, 36, 235; convoy, 101, 130; naval, 42, 93, 101, 179, 236; RAF and RN, 207; semaphore, 101; telegraph, 101; wireless, 116
Signals Experimental Establishment, reports, 45
signals intelligence, 27
Signals Intelligence Centre Far East (1940–5), 27

Index (references are to list numbers, not pages)

Signals Research and Development Establishment, reports, 45
Signet, 1
Simon, Sir John, Foreign Secretary, 26, 236
Simonstown Agreement (1955), 25, 32
Simonstown Dockyard and Cape Town Naval Yard, 48, 54, **152**
Singapore, Anglo-French Conference (1939), 37, 235; Combined Operations Exercise (1937), 204; defence of, 36, 39; School, *see* Royal Naval Schools
Singapore, Dockyard and Naval Base, 25, 36, 47–8, 70, 152, 153; oil depot, 53
Singapore Naval Base Committee (1925–8), 235
Sino-Japanese War, 179
Sir Edward Hawke, schooner (1771), 179
Sir Lancelot, RFA, 36
Sissinghurst, HM Prison, 166
Sixpenny Office (1699–1836), 90, 127
Sizewell B Inquiry, 216
Skey Committee on Venereal Disease (1896–9), 36, 235
Slade, Sir Thomas, Surveyor of the Navy, 135, 236
Slade Committee on Shipping (1914), 39
slave trade, 78, 103, 179; Foreign Office correspondence, 20, 22–3; treaties, 32
Slave Trade Adviser (of Treasury), 49
Slave Trade Instructions Commission (1881–2), 235
Slave Trade Mixed Commissions, **9**
slavers, 9, 75, 78
slaves, liberated, 75
Slessor, Air Marshall Sir John, AOC Coastal Command, 236
Slop and Transport Office, 175; *see also* Transport Board
slops, for RN, 78, 133, 235
smallpox in RN, 53
Smart Tickets, 155
Smith, George, Chief Clerk, Navy Office, 236; W H, First Lord of the Admiralty, 236
smugglers and smuggling, 62, 101, 103, 232
Snapdragon, privateer (1807–8), 77
soldiers, 36, 37, 163
Soldiers' and Sailors' Help Society (1900), 70, 186
Solicitor of the Admiralty, 59, 90, 93, **113**
Solomon Islands, charts of (1943), 39
Somerset House, 104, 111, 139, 197
Somme Campaign (1916), 36
South Africa, export of steel (1965), 70; Foreign Office correspondence, 25; naval arms embargo, 36; Naval Brigade (1878–81), 36; Naval Brigade (1899–1901), 36–7, 48; naval intelligence, 48; naval relations with, 25, 32, 48, 193, 217; RM battalion, 115

South African Air Force, No. 31 Coastal Squadron (1939–44), 210; Coastal Flight No. 35, 210
South African Navy, 193, 217
South African War (1899–1902), 179
South America, expedition to (1796), 34, 103
South America Station, 85, 95, 179
South Atlantic Command (1952–9), 48
South Devon Railway, 227
South Down, *see* Plymouth Victualling Yard
South-East Asia, Foreign Office correspondence, 25
South-East Asia Command (1939–45), **42**; naval intelligence, 39, 42
South-Eastern and Chatham Railway, 227
South Foreland Light, 120
South Sea Company, 92, 226
South Wales Mineral Railway, 227
South Wales Railway, 227
Southern Europe, Foreign Office correspondence, 25
Southern Railway, 227
Southsea, Hants., 36
Soviet Navy, activities in Cuba (1970–1), 26; anti-submarine warfare, 219; decrypted signals of, 27; in Indian Ocean, 25; in Orkneys, 218; incidents with (1968–72), 25; reports on (1942–6), 30 (1960–5), 193, 218; visits to foreign ports, 25; *see also* Russian Navy
Soviet Union, Foreign Office correspondence, 25; naval treaties with, 32
Spain, coastal fortifications (1938), 35; gunpowder exported to (1610), 78; hostilities with (1569–1603), 5, 6; naval cemetery in, 30; relations with, 167; reports on (1810–16), 30
Spanish Navy, prisoners (1588), 78; intelligence of (1790), 20, 98; intelligence of (1884), 23; intelligence of (1936–45), 27; sales to (1967–8), 25; ships of (1808), 67
Spanish Succession War (1702–13), 174
Spanish-American War (1898), 76
Special Boat Service, 114
Special Boat Unit (HMS *Rodent*), 194
special operations, in Mediterranean (1944), 42
Special Operations Executive, **194**
Special Secret Information Centre, 190
Special Service Brigade, RM, 115
Spider (1931), 53
Spithead, charts, 72, 170; Forts, 37; *see also* Naval Reviews
Spring Gardens, *see* Admiralty Building
Spurn Head, Yorks., 72
Squadron Diaries (Fleet Air Arm), 181
Squadron Histories (Royal Naval Air Service), 181
Squadron Record Books, 181

Sri Lanka, *see* Ceylon

staff histories, 'Cod War', 116; combined operations, 35, 204; First World War, 116, 128; Fleet Air Arm, 204; German cruiser warfare (1914–18), 116; naval transport service, 36; RN Barracks Portsmouth, 208; Second World War, 192, 195, 196; Special Operations Executive, 194; *see also* Admiralty, publications

Staff Surgeons, 231

Stamps and Taxes, Board of, *see* Board of Stamps and Taxes

Star Chamber, *see* Court of Star Chamber

State Papers, **5**, 7; America and West Indies, 15, 69; Domestic, **5**, 7, **11**; Foreign, **5**; Ireland, 5; Scotland, 5

Stationers' Company, 226

Stationery Office, HM, **66**

statistics, 101, **195**, 202, 204

statues, 196

Statute Rolls, **4**

statutes, *see* Parliament

Steam Department, 93, **106**; *see also* Controller of Steam Machinery

Steam Drawing Office, 104

Steam Factories, 106, 148, 149; *see also* Dockyards

Stephenson, Admiral Sir Henry, 63

stewards, 55

stokers, services, 232

Stonehouse Hospital, *see* Royal Naval Hospital Stonehouse

Stopford, Admiral Sir Robert, Governor of Greenwich Hospital, 236

Storekeeper of Ordnance, declared accounts, **6**, 182

Storekeeper-General (of the Admiralty), 30

Storekeepers, 88; accounts, 150–4; correspondence, 88, 132, 140, 149, 152, 161

stores, *see* Boatswain's stores, naval stores, Ordnance stores, Victualling stores

Stores Department, 171

Stowell, Lord, *see* Scott, William

Strang Report on Wartime Control of Radiation (1954), 235

strategy, British naval, 101; (1940–5), 39; in Far East (1937–43), 48; 'Island' (1962–3), 220

Sturdee, Admiral Sir Frederick Doveton, 63

Suakin, RM battalion, 115

Sub-Lieutenants (1805–10), 231; (1860–), services, 231

Submarine Propulsion Working Party (1951), 235

Submarine Tactics and Weapons Group, 217

submarines, 97; for export, 70; German, 28, 117, 186, 208; logs, 97; nuclear-powered, 200, 216, 217, 220, 223; patrol reports (1939–45), 127, 180; periscopes, 224; Polaris, 55, 193, 220; proposed by R Fulton, 103; weapons, 219

Subscribers' Roll, Greenwich Hospital (*c.*1694), 120

Subsidy Rolls, 6

Suda Bay, Crete, 42

Sudan, expedition (1885), 111; naval operations (1924), 30

Sueter, Commodore Sir Murray, Inspecting Captain of Aeronautics (1912), Superintendent of Aircraft Production (1915–17), 236

Suez, Egypt, 30; RM battalion, 115

Suez Canal Company, 236

Sultan, hospital ship (1794), 163

Summer Fleet (1637), 5

superannuation, *see* pensions

Superb (1736), 78

Superintendent of Aircraft Production, 236

Superintendents, *see* Admirals Superintendent, Captains Superintendent

Supply, armed tender (1791–2), 97

Supply, Ministry of, *see* Ministry of Supply

Supply, Production, Priority and Manpower Committee (of the War Cabinet), 189

Supreme Headquarters Allied Expeditionary Force, **42**, **209**; *see also* Allied Expeditionary Force

Supreme War Council (1917–19), 39, **187**, **229**

Surgeon-Agents, 161

Surgeon's Mates, 13

Surgeons, accounts, 78; correspondence, 161; 'free gifts', 231; journals, 97, 110, 161; losses, 110; passing certificates, 228; pay, 36, 87, 161, 168; services, 110, 128, 157, 161, 231; twopences, 231

survey ships, 76

Surveyor of Buildings, Admiralty, 90, 108; Board of Customs, 62

Surveyor of Ordnance, Surveyor-General of Ordnance, **6**, 182–4

Surveyor of the Navy, **135**; contracts, 135; correspondence, 87, 90, 104, 135, 146, 147, 236; dimension books, 135; progress books, 135; ships' books, 135; *see also* Controller of the Navy

Sussex Coast Blockade, *see* Coast Blockade

Surveyors-General of Woods and Forests, *see* Woods and Forests

Suvla, Gallipoli, 42

Swabey, Lieutenant Commander C C, 218; H M, Deputy Registrar of High Court of Admiralty, 236

Sweden, 30, 32, 91, 179

Swedish East India Company, 77

Swedish Navy, 30; *see also* Royal Swedish Navy

sword-bayonets, 36

Sydney Dockyard (Cockatoo Island), 153

Symonds, Sir William, Surveyor of the Navy, 104

Index (references are to list numbers, not pages)

Taff Vale Railway, 227
Tahiti, French Polynesia, 30
Talbot Committee on Naval Life-Saving Equipment (1945–6), 235
tallow, 132
Tamar Bridge, 219
Tanganyika Motorboat Expedition (1915), 48
Tangier, Morocco, 13, 20, 30, 179
Tanker Tonnage Committee (1935–40), 216
Tanzanian Navy, 48
Tartar (1702), 13
Tate Gallery, 224
Taylor, J O, inventor, 75
Technical and Dockyard School, Portsmouth, 201
Technology, Ministry of, *see* Ministry of Technology
Tees, River, 72
Telecommunications Research Establishment, **208**
telegrams, 115
Tellers of the Exchequer, 59
Tellers' Rolls, **2**
Temeraire (1798), 236
Templeton-Cotill, Rear-Admiral J A, 25
Terminal, *see* Operation TERMINAL
Terpsichore (1785), 77
territorial waters, 36
Texel, expedition to (1797), 34
Thailand, British ministers and consuls, 30
Thames (1758), 13
Thames, Estuary, 224; River, 13
Thames Nautical Training College, Greenhithe, *see* HMS *Worcester*
Thames Traffic Committee (1878), 71
'The Navy is Here' film (1939–42), 70
Therapia Hospital, 165
Thetis (1939), 75
Thompson, Robert, Master RN, 236
Ticket Office 83, 131, 136, 158; correspondence, 83, 131, 141; pay books, 141
tickets, 141, 155
tidal observations, 135
Tigress, US schooner (1814), 8, 140
Tigris-Euphrates Fleet (1922–31), 53
Tilbury, Essex, 13
timber, for RN, 59, 68, 75, 78, 101, 130, 152, 221, 224, 226, 236; contracts and contractors, 132, 135; inspectors, 202; Irish, 78
Timber Masters, 131
Tirpitz, Admiral Alfred von, 99, 236
Tirpitz, German battleship, 206, 208
Tizard, Sir Henry, 236
tobacco, 15
Tomlin Commission on Awards to Inventors, 235

Toraplane and Doraplane Development Committee (1939–42), 235; trials, 178
Torch, *see* Operation TORCH
Torpedo and Anti-Submarine Division, *see* Naval Staff Torpedo and Anti-Submarine Division
Torpedo Attack Committee, *see* Air Torpedo Attack Committee
torpedo bombers, 204, 206
Torpedo Depot, Ceylon (1943–4), 210
Torpedo (later Torpedo and Anti-Submarine) School, 119
Torpedo Liaison Committee (1942), 207
Torpedo Refresher School, 210
Torpedo Schools, 54
Torpedo Training Units (1943–7), 210
torpedoes, 53, 107; air-dropped, 204, 206, 207; treaties concerning, 32; *see also* Brennan, Burney, Whitehead
Torpoint Ferry, 219
Torrington, Admiral Arthur Herbert, Earl of, 101; Admiral George Byng, Viscount, 85, 236
Tostedt, German torpedo depot (1949–50), 28
Toulon, France, expedition to (1793), 16, 30, 67, 236
Toulon Dockyard, 150
Tower Hill victualling establishment, 169
Townsend, Spencer George, Receiver of Fees of the Navy Office, 130, 236
tracer ammunition, 46
Trade, Trade and Plantations, *see* Board of Trade, Board of Trade and Plantations, Committee on Trade and Plantations, Department of Trade
Trade Boards, 202
Trade Unions, 150, 202, 206
Training and Staff Duties Division, *see* Naval Staff Training and Staff Duties Division
Training Command, registered files, 209
training ships, 200, 201
Transport, Ministry of, *see* Ministry of War Transport
Transport Accounts Committee, 87, 235; reports on prisoners of war, 33, 175
Transport Agents, 86, 131, 132, 175, 176
Transport Board (1689–1717), 77, 87, **174**
Transport Board (1794–1816), 151, **175**; accounts, 67, 175; correspondence, 34, 49, 87, 175, 236; deeds, 167
Transport Board Medical Department (1806–16), 87, 110, **160**; correspondence, 87, 132, 160, 163, 164, 168
Transport Board Prisoner of War Department (1796–1822), 87, 137, **167**; *see also* Valleyfields Depot
Transport Command, and Pacific Fleet (1944–5), 209
Transport Department (1816–32), *see* Victualling Board Transport Department
Transport Department (1832–1917), *see* Admiralty Transport Department

375

Transport Service (1546–1796), *see* Navy Board; (1796–1816), *see* Transport Board; (1816–32), *see* Victualling Board; (1832–1917), *see* Admiralty Transport Department; (1917–21), *see* Naval Transport Service; (1921–), *see* Sea Transport Service
Trappenkamp Naval Depot, Germany (1946–7), 28
Travers College, 75, 124; *see also* Naval Knights of Windsor
trawlers, 235; *see also* fishing boats and vessels
Treasurer of Greenwich Hospital, 120
Treasurer of Ordnance, declared accounts, **6**, 67
Treasurer of the Navy, 33, 52, 61, 112, **156**, 157; accounts, 6, 50, 59, 67, 156; correspondence, 90, 156
Treasurer of the Ordnance Board, 182, 184
Treasury, **49–57**; Defence Personnel Division, **55**; Defence Policy and Material Division, **56**; departmental accounts, **50**; Establishments Department, 49, **54**; Finance Department, 49, **52**; First Lord of, 51; Long Bundles, 49; Professional, Scientific, Technical and Industrial Staff Division, 54; Secretary of, 49 (*see also* Lowndes, William); stock, 140, 156; Superannuation Division, 49; Supply Department, 49, **53**
— correspondence, with Admiralty, 49, 91; with Prize Office, 49; with Navy Board, 49, 131, 132, 138; with Navy Pay Office, 157; with Paymaster-General, 49; with Transport Board, 49, 175; with Victualling Board, 49, 168, 176
Treasury Inter-Services Committee (1948–59), 56, 58
Treasury Solicitor, **75**, 91, 96, 166
Treaties, **32**, 166
Treaty Rolls, **1**
trench machines, naval, 36
Trent affair (1862), 37
Trevor, Captain John, 180, 236
Trieste, British consul, 30
Trimmer, privateer (1801–7), 77
Trincomalee, Ceylon, 38, 133; Hospital, *see* RN Hospital Trincomalee; St. Nicholas Church, 219
Trincomalee Dockyard, 153
Trincomalee Victualling Yard, 173
Trinidad, 30, 98
Trinity House, 92, 213, **225**; ordnance certificates, 5, 225
Tripartite Naval Commission (1945–7), 28
troopships (1706–18), 174; (1914–18), 37; (1947–52), 57, 204; accounts (1744), 50; as horse transports, 37, 235; courts martial aboard, 36; military discipline aboard, 37; rations and victualling, 36, 37, 111
Tropical Medicine Research Board, 212
Tropical Testing Establishment (1946–59), 222
Troubridge Mission (1920), 235
True Love, privateer of Weymouth (1632), 78

tuberculosis, 211
Tübingen, German hospital ship (1944), 194
Tunis, 30, 179
Tunisian Navy (1825), 30
Turkey, British ambassadors and consuls, 30; British joint-service mission to (1944), 42; foreign naval visits, 30; RN cemeteries in, 21; treaties with, 32; *see also* Ottoman Empire
Turkish Navy, purchase of naval guns by, 53; purchase of warships by, 52; reports on (1923, 1940–57), 30; supplies for (1941–5), 191; warships taken over by RN, 52
Turnbull & Co., merchants and Navy agents at Gibraltar, 77
Tuscany, 236
Tuttel, Thomas, hydrographer, 13
typewriters, 66
Tyrwhitt, Admiral of the Fleet Sir Reginald, 63

U-1277 German submarine, 37
U-boats, 189, 194; *see also* submarines, German
Ulloa, Captain Don Antonio de, 98
ULTRA intelligence digests, 117
Undersurface Warfare Department, 116
Underwater Detection Establishment, 119
underwater warfare, 217, 219
Underwater Weapons Launching Establishment, 119
underwriters, 236; *see also* marine insurance
unemployment, 70
Unemployment Assistance Board, *see* Ministry of Labour
uniform, *see* naval officers, ratings
Union of Soviet Socialist Republics, *see* Soviet Union
United Nations, Foreign Office correspondence, 25
United Nations Command Korea, 229
United States Army, 37, 39
United States Marine Corps, 219
United States Naval Academy, 25
United States Naval Intelligence Division, 39
United States Naval Submarine Mining Establishment (1874), 37
United States Naval Technical Mission to Japan (1948), 16, 235
United States Naval Torpedo Station (1874), 37
United States Navy, 42, 70; destroyers transferred to RN (1942), 30; memorial at Gibraltar, 36; OMEGA navigation system, 25; operations in Atlantic (1939–40), 30; passenger lists (1955–60), 70; Polaris submarines, 56; prizes taken from, 140; reports on, 30, 37, 98; rewards to (1938–9), 53; ships for, 219; use of Gibraltar, 36, 38; visits to Britain, 30

Index (references are to list numbers, not pages)

— bases, in Bahamas, 24; in Bermuda, 25; in UK, 214, 217; on Ascension Island, 25; on Diego Garcia, 25, 218; on Gan Island, 48;
United States Navy Department, 19; Prisoner of War Agent, 167
United States Navy Field Signals Unit, Dunkeswell (1944–5), 210
United States Navy Hydrographic Office, 209
United States of America, Admiralty contracts, 30; Foreign Office correspondence, 21; naval visits to, 25; treaties with, 32
United States Pacific Fleet, air operations, 207; Intelligence Division, 209
United States Strategic Bombing Survey, 229
United States War Shipping Administrator (1941–5), 214
Upnor Castle, Kent, 185
Upper Canada, Acting Commissioner, 67
Upper School (of Greenwich Hospital), 122
Uruguay, 30
Uruguayan Navy (1942–50), 30
UXW steel, 105

Vado Hospital, 165
Valenciennes Prison, 167
Valleyfields Prisoner of War Depot, 167
Valparaiso, Chile, Naval Hospital, 71
Vancouver, Captain George, 16
Vanguard (1835), 230
venereal disease, report (1865), 13, 37, 235; report (1896–9), 36, 235
Venezuela, 30
Venezuelan Naval Mission (1952), 24
Venice, Italy, 206
Venona project, 27
Venus, brig (1797–1808), 77
Venus, transit of, 101, 228
Verdun Prison, 167
Vernon, Torpedo School, 119
Versailles Peace Conference and Treaty (1919), 24, 39, 52
Vestal (1779), 236
Veysey, Commander John, 77, 236
Vice-Admiral of Dorset, *see* Ashley Cooper, Anthony, 1st Earl of Shaftesbury
Vice-Admirals of Counties, 91, **225**; warrants to, 7, 81
Vice-Admiralty Courts, 7, **9**; appeals from, 8–9; colonial, 9, 49; patents of, 9; Registrars of, 9
Vice-Chief of the Air Staff, **206**
Vice-Chief of the Naval Staff, 206
Victoria (1887), 105
Victoria Cross, 36, 41; pensions, 231; *see also* awards

Victory (1759), 178, 225
Victuallers of the Navy, declared accounts, 67; enrolled accounts, 6; *see also* Victualling Board
Victualling Agents, imprests, 13
victualling and victuals, 171, 177, 200; accounts, 156; dried food, 199; estimates, 100; fresh food, 199; of Army, 168, 199; of RN, 13, 59, 62, 78, 235; of troopships, 36, 37, 111
Victualling Board, **168**, 235; accounts, 168; contracts, 167, 168; declared accounts, 67; deeds, 168, 172; hoys, 13; minutes, 168; plans, 168; regulations, 168; reports on prisoners of war, 33
— correspondence, 168; with Admiralty, 87, 93, 168; with Agent-Victuallers, 168, 170; with Navy Board, 131, 138, 168; with Secretaries of State, 168; with Transport Board, 168; with Treasury, 49, 168; with victualling yards, 168–73
— orders, from Admiralty, 83, 168; to Agent-Victuallers, 168, 171, 172; to Treasurer of the Navy, 156, 168
Victualling Board Medical Committee, 131
Victualling Board Medical Department **93**, 110; correspondence, 93, 161, 163, 164, 165
Victualling Board Transport Committee (1816–32), 176
Victualling Board Transport Department, 49, 93, 109, 131, 132, 144, **176**
Victualling Controller, *see* Controller of Victualling
Victualling Department (of Admiralty), 111
Victualling Office, 168, 235; *see also* Victualling Board
victualling rate books (1897–1942), 111
victualling stores, 170
Victualling Yards and Depots, 88; and dutiable goods, 62; correspondence, 88, 132, 168; deeds, 168, 172; insurance, 75; pay lists, 168, 172; plans, 144, 152; *see also* Antigua, Ascension Island, Bermuda, Cape Town, Chatham, Deal, Deptford, Dover, Fernando Po, Kinsale, Mylor, Plymouth, Portsmouth, Rotherhithe, Royal Alexandra, Royal Clarence, Royal Victoria, Royal William, Sierra Leone, Simonstown
Vidal (1951), 16
Vigilant, revenue cruiser, 62
Vildebeeste aircraft, 204
Villeneuve, comte de (1862), 37
Virago (1842), 75
Visitations of the Dockyards, Admiralty, 83, 131, 142; Navy Board, 130, 142
Vitamin C, trials (1939–40), 212
volunteers, 157, 158
Vulnerable Places Sub-Committee, 189
Vulnerable Points Adviser, 189

Wager, Admiral Sir Charles, First Lord of the Admiralty, 236
wages, *see* pay
waistcloths, 132
Walcheren expedition (1809), 103, 236; *see also* Scheldt expedition
Wales, 1; HRH Charles, Prince of, 25, 218; naval establishments in, 17
Wallace Collection, 117
War Cabinet (1916–19), **187**
War Cabinet (1939–46), **189**, 195, 217; Committees, 189
War College, *see* RN College Greenwich
War Committee (1915–16), 186
War Council (1914–16), 186
War Course, *see* RN College Greenwich
war crimes (1945–8), 28, 37
War Crimes Executive (1945–6), 28
War Damage Commission, **65**
war diaries, 43, 114, 178, 180, 194
War Emergency Legislation Sub-Committee (1934), 70
War Emergency Measures, 202
war graves, *see* cemeteries
War History Cases (1939–45), 103, 180
war memorials, 225; Chatham, 36; Merchant Navy, 36, 200, 225; Plymouth, 68; USN at Gibraltar, 36
War Office (1661–1855), **33**
War Office (1855–1964), **35**, 121; aliens forbidden in, 17; Commissariat, 35; committees, 235; contracts, 36, 46; correspondence with Adjutant-General RM, 114; with Admiralty, 36–7, 109, 190; with Transport Accounts Committee, 175; Director of Artillery, 35; employees, 36; employees, wages of, 36, 235; Fortifications Branch, 35; Intelligence Department (1890), 37; land, 37; Quartermaster-General, 35; registered files, **36**; reports, **37**; vessels belonging to, 17; *see also* Imperial General Staff
War Priorities Committee, 187
War Room (of Admiralty), 116, 206
War Transport, Ministry of, *see* Ministry of War Transport
War Works Commission, 58
Ward Committee on Naval Pensions, 36, 235
Wardmasters, services, 231
Wardrobe accounts, **2–3**
Warneford, Flight-Sub-Lieutenant R A J, VC, RNAS, 236
warrant officers, *see* naval officers, sea officers
warrants, Greenwich Hospital, 120; High Court of Admiralty, 8, 81; Ordnance Board, 182, 183; Royal Marines, 114; Royal Navy, 179, 231; Royal Observatory, 123; yard officers, 168

Warrants for issue (Exchequer), 2
Warren, Major Joseph de, 133, 236
Warship Weeks, 52, 65
warships, allied, lost or damaged (1940–5), 207; foreign, lists of, 23; *see also* aircraft carriers, armed merchant cruisers, capital ships, frigates, hired armed ships, ironclads, mortar vessels, paddle vessels, Q ships, submarines
Warspite (1913), 42
Washington Conference (1870–1), 21;
Washington Naval Conference (1921–3), 23, 30, 32, 36
Waterford, Ireland, 125
watermen, impressment of, 13; *see also* Royal Navy, manning and personnel
Waters, Captain Joseph, 13
Watson, Captain D A, 54
Watson-Watt, Sir Robert, 236
Watts Naval Training Institute School, 201
Weapons Department, 107
Weevil, *see* Portsmouth Victualling Yard
Wei-Hai-Wei, China, 21, 30, 52
Weir Committee on Admiralty, War Office and Air Ministry Establishments (1920–3), 235
Wellesley, Henry, 1st Baron Cowley, British ambassador to France, 236; Henry, 2nd Baron and 1st Earl Cowley, British ambassador to France, 236; Richard, 1st Marquis, 179
Welsh Board of Health, **211**
Welsh Office, **17**; correspondence with Admiralty, 17; Planning Division, 17
Welsh Rolls, 1
Welsh War (1294–5), 3
Wemyss, Admiral of the Fleet Sir Rosslyn, Baron Wester Wemyss, 63
Wentworth, John, 236
West Africa, expedition to (1758), 236; naval forces, 48
West Africa Division, 179
West Africa Station, 85, 179
West and Central Africa, Foreign Office correspondence, 25
West Indies, expedition to (1585), 6, 156; expedition to (1595–6), 6, 156; expedition to (1740–2), 61; Foreign Office correspondence, 25; operations in (1756–66), 130; operations in (1803), 24; *see also* North America and West Indies
West Indies Squadron (1801–5), 34
Western Approaches Command, 178
Western Europe, Foreign Office correspondence, 25
Western Squadron, 85; *see also* Channel Fleet
Western Union, 236
Weymouth, Dors., 78
whale fishery, 101

Index (references are to list numbers, not pages)

Whale Island, Hants., 68
Whitby, Yorks., 13, 36
White, Lieutenant Charles, 236; Captain Thomas, 236
Whitehead Torpedo, 107, 202
Whitmarsh, Dr. John, 236
Wilhelmshaven Dockyard (1945–8), 28
Wilkinson, John, ironfounder, 13; Norman, artist, 57
William and Mary Galley, privateer (1701–2), 78
William and Sheppherd, transport (1708), 78
William Henry, Captain Prince, 236
William Pitt, Indiaman (1802–14), 77
wills, 77, 79, 120, 157, 236
Wilson Committee on Noise (1961), 235
Winter, Vice-Admiral Jan Willem, *see* De Winter
wireless, call signs, 37, 70, 117; frequencies, 40; intelligence, 27, 117; *see also* radio
'Wireless News' (1918–21), 27, 117
Wishart, Admiral Sir James, 15, 236
Wodehouse Committee on Life-Saving (1940–1), 235
Wolseley, Field Marshall Sir Garnet, Viscount, 236
women, employment by Admiralty, 202
Women's Auxiliary Air Force, 232
Women's Royal Naval Service, 178; family planning, 219; officers' services, 231; ratings' services, 232
Women's Royal Naval Service Benevolent Trust, 13
Wood, Dr. Albert B, physicist, 119, 236; Sir Charles, First Lord of the Admiralty (1855–8), 84
Woods and Forests, Commissioners and Surveyors-General, **68**, 132; declared accounts, 67
Woolwich, Kent, naval buildings, 36; RM Barracks, 197
Woolwich (1749), 78
Woolwich Arsenal, 185, 197

Woolwich Division RM, 89, 114, **115**
Woolwich Dockyard, 36, 68, 85, **148**, 197, 213; Chapel, 185; railway, 227
Woolwich Hospital, 164
Worcester, HMS (Thames Nautical Training College), 201
Works, accounts, 2; *see also* Ministry of Public Works
Works Department (Admiralty), 108; *see also* Surveyor of Buildings
World War I, *see* First World War
World War II, *see* Second World War
Wormwood Scrubs, HM Prison, 200
wounds, pensions for, 101, 155
wrecking, in Bahamas, 71; in Cornwall, 78
writs, Chancery, 1, 2
Wrotham, William of, Keeper of Ports and Galleys, 2
Wyndham, Charles, *see* Egremont, Earl of

Yachts, Royal, 54; *see also Britannia*
Yangtse Incident (1949), 204
yard craft, 143, 144; *see also* hoys
yard officers, *see* dockyards
yards, *see* dockyards, naval yards, victualling yards
Yarmouth, Norf., 2, 85
Yarmouth Hospital, *see* Royal Naval Hospital Yarmouth
Yarmouth Naval Yard, 149
Yarrow Admiralty Research Department, 47, 119, 213
Yokohama, Japan, 36, 110, 196
York, James Duke of, Lord Admiral of England and Scotland, 82, 236
Yugoslav Navy, purchases (1940), 70; reports (1941), 30; (1943–6), 42
Yugoslavia, British naval cemetery, 30; naval agreement with (1944–5), 42